Office 2008 *for* Macintosh

THE MISSING MANUAL

*The book that
should have been
in the box*®

Office 2008 *for* Macintosh
Fourth Edition

Jim Elferdink

POGUE PRESS™

O'REILLY®

Beijing · Cambridge · Farnham · Köln · Paris · Sebastopol · Taipei · Tokyo

Office 2008 for Macintosh: The Missing Manual
by Jim Elferdink

Copyright © 2008 Jim Elferdink. All rights reserved.
Printed in the United States of America.

Published by O'Reilly Media, Inc., 1005 Gravenstein Highway North, Sebastopol, CA 95472.

O'Reilly books may be purchased for educational, business, or sales promotional use. Online editions are also available for most titles (*safari.oreilly.com*). For more information, contact our corporate/institutional sales department: (800) 998-9938 or *corporate@oreilly.com*.

Printing History:

March 2008:   Fourth Edition.

ISBN: 978-0-596-51431-0
[M]   [5/08]

Table of Contents

Chapter 7: Editing Long Documents..209

Part Two: Entourage

Part Three: Excel

Part Five: Office As a Whole

Chapter 18: Saving Time with the Project Gallery and Toolbox......... 719

Chapter 19: Making the Most of Graphics..733

The Missing Credits

About the Author

 Jim Elferdink's first book, *AppleWorks 6: The Missing Manual*, was one of the original three Missing Manuals. He went on to write *iWork '05: The Missing Manual* and with this volume completes a hat trick of books about productivity suites for the Macintosh. In former lifetimes a commercial photographer, carpenter, and cabinetmaker; currently, he runs Macs for the Masses, a Macintosh consulting company in the redwoods of far Northern California. He balances writing, Mac consulting, and training with gourmet cooking, digital photography, and racing sports cars. Humboldt State University introduced him to the original Macintosh and to comely professor Joy Hardin. He bought one and married the other. They share a home in coastal Humboldt County with a staff of imaginary servants and a backlog of very real chores.

Jim welcomes courteous commentary on this book by email: *elferdinkoffice@gmail.com*.

About the Creative Team

Nan Barber (editor) has worked with the Missing Manual series since its inception. She lives in Massachusetts with her husband and G4 Macintosh. Email: *nanbarber@oreilly.com*.

Dawn Frausto (editor) is assistant editor for the Missing Manual series. When not working, she rock climbs, plays soccer, and causes trouble. Email: *dawn@oreilly.com*.

Nellie McKesson (production editor) is a graduate of St. John's College in Santa Fe, New Mexico. She currently lives in Cambridge, Mass., where her favorite places to eat are Tacos Lupita and Punjabi Dhaba. Email: *nellie@oreilly.com*.

Alison O'Byrne (copy editor) is a freelance editor from Dublin, Ireland. Alison has provided editorial services for corporate and government clients at home and internationally for over six years. Email: *alison@alhaus.com*. Web: *www.alhaus.com*.

John McGimpsey (technical reviewer) is a Microsoft MVP (Most Valuable Professional) specializing in Office for the Macintosh. Web: *www.mcgimpsey.com*.

Matt Silver (technical reviewer) is the Apple System Administrator for O'Reilly Media in Sebastopol, California. In his spare time, he plays the drums in a hard rock band and maintains a "mild" obsession with World of Warcraft.

William **Smith** (technical reviewer) works as a technical analyst in St. Paul, Minn., where he supports integrating Macs into a Windows world for online and print publishing. William has been a Microsoft Most Valued Professional (MVP) for five years and is also an avid technology enthusiast. He is a regular contributor to the Entourage Help Blog *http://blog.entourage.mvps.org*. Email: *bill@blog.entourage.mvps.org*.

Tina **Spargo** (technical reviewer), her husband (and professional musician) Ed, their toddler Max, their two silly Spaniels, Parker (Clumber), and Piper (Sussex), all share time and space in their suburban Boston home. Tina is currently an at-home mom busy promoting and marketing her husband's musical projects as well as freelancing as a Virtual Assistant. Tina has over 15 years' experience supporting many top level Executives from a variety of industries. Web: *www.tinaspargo.com*.

Acknowledgments

I'd like to thank my editor, Nan Barber; and Dawn Frausto, Nellie McKesson, Peter Meyers, and the rest of the fabulous O'Reilly crew for doing such a first-rate job on this and the rest of the Missing Manuals. Thanks also to the crack tech-editing team of John McGimpsey, Tina Spargo, William Smith, and Matt Silver; copy editor Alison O'Byrne; indexer Ron Strauss—and David Pogue for getting me into this racket in the first place.

I'm full of gratitude for Karin Lubin's insightful guidance and love always; Kate McClain's garden veggies and help picking up the slack in my life over the last few months; and Edda Butler's tireless reading, eagle eye, and perceptive comments.

Mostly I'd like to thank my wife, Joy, who has been a relentless editor and thoughtful critic throughout this endeavor—and the most understanding, supportive, loving, and amusing partner, always.

—Jim Elferdink

The Missing Manual Series

Missing Manuals are witty, superbly written guides to computer products that don't come with printed manuals (which is just about all of them). Each book features a handcrafted index and cross-references to specific pages (not just chapters).

Recent and upcoming titles include:

Access 2007: The Missing Manual by Matthew MacDonald

AppleScript: The Missing Manual by Adam Goldstein

AppleWorks 6: The Missing Manual by Jim Elferdink and David Reynolds

CSS: The Missing Manual by David Sawyer McFarland

Creating Web Sites: The Missing Manual by Matthew MacDonald

Digital Photography: The Missing Manual by Chris Grover and Barbara Brundage

Dreamweaver 8: The Missing Manual by David Sawyer McFarland

Dreamweaver CS3: The Missing Manual by David Sawyer McFarland

eBay: The Missing Manual by Nancy Conner

Excel 2003: The Missing Manual by Matthew MacDonald

Excel 2007: The Missing Manual by Matthew MacDonald

Facebook: The Missing Manual by E.A. Vander Veer

FileMaker Pro 8: The Missing Manual by Geoff Coffey and Susan Prosser

FileMaker Pro 9: The Missing Manual by Geoff Coffey and Susan Prosser

Flash 8: The Missing Manual by E.A. Vander Veer

Flash CS3: The Missing Manual by E.A. Vander Veer and Chris Grover

FrontPage 2003: The Missing Manual by Jessica Mantaro

GarageBand 2: The Missing Manual by David Pogue

Google: The Missing Manual, Second Edition by Sarah Milstein, J.D. Biersdorfer, and Matthew MacDonald

The Internet: The Missing Manual by David Pogue and J.D. Biersdorfer

iMovie 6 & iDVD: The Missing Manual by David Pogue

iMovie '08 & iDVD: The Missing Manual by David Pogue

iPhone: The Missing Manual by David Pogue

iPhoto 6: The Missing Manual by David Pogue

iPhoto '08: The Missing Manual by David Pogue

iPod: The Missing Manual, Sixth Edition by J.D. Biersdorfer

JavaScript: The Missing Manual by David Sawyer McFarland

Mac OS X: The Missing Manual, Tiger Edition by David Pogue

Mac OS X: The Missing Manual, Leopard Edition by David Pogue

Microsoft Project 2007: The Missing Manual by Bonnie Biafore

Office 2004 for Macintosh: The Missing Manual by Mark H. Walker and Franklin Tessler

Office 2007: The Missing Manual by Chris Grover, Matthew MacDonald, and E.A. Vander Veer

PCs: The Missing Manual by Andy Rathbone

Photoshop Elements 6: The Missing Manual by Barbara Brundage

Photoshop Elements 6 for Mac: The Missing Manual by Barbara Brundage

PowerPoint 2007: The Missing Manual by E.A. Vander Veer

QuickBase: The Missing Manual by Nancy Conner

QuickBooks 2008: The Missing Manual by Bonnie Biafore

Quicken 2008: The Missing Manual by Bonnie Biafore

Switching to the Mac: The Missing Manual, Tiger Edition by David Pogue and Adam Goldstein

Switching to the Mac: The Missing Manual, Leopard Edition by David Pogue

Wikipedia: The Missing Manual by John Broughton

Windows 2000 Pro: The Missing Manual by Sharon Crawford

Windows XP Home Edition: The Missing Manual, Second Edition by David Pogue

Windows XP Pro: The Missing Manual, Second Edition by David Pogue, Craig Zacker, and Linda Zacker

Windows Vista: The Missing Manual by David Pogue

Word 2007: The Missing Manual by Chris Grover

The "For Starters" books contain only the most essential information from their larger counterparts—in larger type, with a more spacious layout, and none of the more advanced sidebars. Recent titles include:

Access 2003 for Starters: The Missing Manual by Kate Chase and Scott Palmer

Access 2007 for Starters: The Missing Manual by Matthew MacDonald

Excel 2003 for Starters: The Missing Manual by Matthew MacDonald

Excel 2007 for Starters: The Missing Manual by Matthew MacDonald

PowerPoint 2007 for Starters: The Missing Manual by E.A. Vander Veer

Quicken 2006 for Starters: The Missing Manual by Bonnie Biafore

Windows Vista for Starters: The Missing Manual by David Pogue

Windows XP for Starters: The Missing Manual by David Pogue

Word 2007 for Starters: The Missing Manual by Chris Grover

Introduction

Wherever you go, there you are—and wherever you are you're probably not far from a computer running Microsoft Office. Installed on Macs and Windows PCs, no other program is so enmeshed in the world of business and academia. In most corporations, anyone *not* using Word, Excel, and PowerPoint is considered an oddball. But Office isn't just for the office—many home computers are also running Microsoft's ubiquitous productivity software.

Office has been on the Mac in one form or another since 1985, but it gained greater acceptance with the release of Office 2001, when Entourage debuted—the all-in-one email-cum-personal-information-manager program. Then before the year 2001 was even torn off the calendar, Office X exploded onto the scene with some of the first—and best—productivity programs available for the Mac's new operating system, Mac OS X. With each new version, Microsoft has not only given Office greater speed and more new features, but has designed the programs to work better together. This continued evolution led to the subject of this book: Office 2008.

Keeping Up with the Macs

The first time you launch Office 2008 you'll think that it's experienced an Extreme Mac-over. The windows, toolbars, and icons have been modernized and de-cluttered, helping Office blend in better with your other Mac programs—instead of sticking out like the "I'm a PC" guy at a Mac user group meeting.

To go along with its updated look, Office 2008 features a host of brand new features, including the Elements Gallery (Figure I-1), offering quick access to document templates and graphics; Word's Publishing Layout View, a complete page layout program replete with templates for newsletters, flyers, brochures, and so on; a gallery of Excel spreadsheet templates called Ledger Sheets; completely revamped Excel charting capabilities; and My Day, a desktop portal to Entourage showing your current appointments and to dos.

Other improvements are less obvious, but no less important: the new XML file format, Automator support, font ligatures, and the ability to put your PowerPoint presentation on an iPod.

Figure I-1:
Top: The new Elements Gallery appears in Word, PowerPoint, and Excel, and gives you a quick way to insert pre-designed document elements like cover pages, tables, charts, and SmartArt graphics.

Bottom: MyDay functions as a portal into your Entourage calendar and to-do list. This way you can keep an eye on your day's essentials—without falling into the black hole of your email.

More Integrated Than Ever

Although Microsoft originally designed Word, Excel, and PowerPoint as individual, disparate programs, over the years it's designed the programs to look and work more alike—sharing elements and working much more like a cohesive whole. This trend continues with Office 2008, letting you work more effectively within Office *and* with other programs. For example:

- The Office Toolbox has absorbed the Formatting Palette to become headquarters for all things adjustable or insertable, giving you access to the new Object Palette, Clip Art, and your iPhoto library.

- The Office Art graphics engine makes the most of the Mac's Quartz graphics, providing effects like 3-D, reflections, and shadows to enhance objects and charts.

- Excel's new charting templates—thanks to Office Art graphics—let you easily create modern looking charts that can include 3-D, transparency, and shadows. You can insert charts directly in Word and PowerPoint using the Elements Gallery.

- SmartArt graphics offers a collection of dozens of carefully designed graphic elements that can help you visually represent lists, hierarchies, and processes in Word, PowerPoint, and Excel.

- My Day gives you a simplified view of your appointments and to-do items without even opening Entourage—and without the danger of getting sucked into your email.

- Word's new Publishing Layout View is a true page-layout program, complete with dozens of professionally designed templates that make it incredibly easy to produce complex document like newsletters, brochures, or posters.

- Excel's new Formula Builder helps even non-mathematicians create formulas quickly and accurately, search for functions, and easily learn more about any function.

- Ledger sheets bring preformatted layouts to Excel to perform common tasks such as checkbook registers, invoices, budgets, expense reports, and so on. These templates open with all the appropriate columns and formulas built in.

- PowerPoint gets the template treatment also with an array of slide themes that help you get a visually attractive presentation underway in no time.

Rather than marketing the programs individually, Microsoft pushes the Office suite for the same reason that there's one Missing Manual covering all four programs: If you use only one of the Office programs without the others, you miss out on a lot of timesaving shortcuts.

What's New in Office 2008

Microsoft gave Office 2008 significant improvements over its predecessor, Office 2004. You can't miss the new Toolbox, Elements Gallery, SmartArt graphics, or My Day—but there's also an array of less obvious enhancements. Here's a list of the most interesting new features.

Office's Three Delicious Flavors

Office 2008 comes in different versions for different needs—three to be exact. This book is based on the standard edition, which is now just called Office 2008 for Mac. It contains the four Office programs—Word, Excel, Entourage, and Power-Point—as well as support for Microsoft Exchange Server for big corporations, and Automator Actions to help speed up repetitive tasks. This version retails for $400. (If you decide your office needs just one of the programs instead of all three, you can buy any one for $230.)

The Special Media Edition includes all of the above plus Microsoft Expression Media, a professional digital asset management program to catalog and organize digital photo and video files. This version goes for $500—a bargain considering Expression Media alone sells for $300.

What used to be known as the Student and Teacher Edition is now called the Mac Home and Student Edition. Now you don't have to feel guilty about buying this low-priced edition even though you're not a student or teacher. This version contains Word, Excel, PowerPoint, and Entourage but lacks Microsoft Exchange Server support and the Automator Actions. This edition contains three licenses so you can install it on three Macs—and retails at $150.

If you own Office 98 or later, you can upgrade to Office 2008 and save yourself $160 for Office 2008 ($200 for the Special Media Edition). Consult *www.microsoft.com/mac* for additional information.

Word

- **Publishing Layout view.** This new view, or working environment, is really more like a complete page-layout program within Word. By starting with one of dozens of professionally designed templates for brochures, newsletters, and so on, you can quickly create a complex document, replacing placeholder text and photos with your own.

- **Document Elements.** A variety of Word templates that help automate some common document-creation tasks. You can add Document Elements to any Word document to provide cover pages, tables of contents, headers, footers, and bibliographies.

- **Ligatures.** Ligatures are groupings of usually two letters that share common components when printed next to each other in order to improve the appearance and readability of the text. For example, there's a common three-character ligature (ffi) in the word Office.

Excel

- **Ledger sheets.** No longer does every Excel spreadsheet have to begin with the daunting empty worksheet. Preformatted ledger sheets, available from the Elements Gallery, are ready to handle a variety of common Excel tasks—from simple shopping, address, or inventory lists, to checkbook registers, budgets, and stock tracking reports.

- **Formula Builder.** Finding your way through Excel's forest of functions has never been an exercise for the faint of heart. The new Formula Builder helps you create formulas without having to memorize functions or syntax. You can also use it to search for functions and get detailed help on each function's use.

- **Formula AutoComplete.** Now, when you type a formula in a cell, Excel lets you choose from a pop-up list of valid functions, see the proper syntax, and link to a help window to see detailed information on the chosen function.

- **Improved charting.** Excel's all-new charting system has been updated with new templates and tools including special effects like transparency, shadows, reflections, and 3-D. Best of all, once you create a chart in Excel you can use it in the other Office programs, and you can always edit its data later.

PowerPoint

- **Slide themes.** PowerPoint comes packed with dozens of professionally designed slide themes—presentation templates with coordinated fonts, backgrounds, and effects—that you can use to assemble your presentation quickly, yet with elegant results. Slide themes are at your fingertips in the new Elements Gallery.

- **Custom layouts.** Customize slide layouts to precisely fit your own needs, and then save them in the Elements Gallery where they'll be available along with the stock PowerPoint layouts. Custom layouts can contain text and image placeholders, static text and images, and background designs.

- **Export to iPhoto—and iPod.** Keep your presentations always available on your iPod—no laptop required! Now you can give presentations directly from a video iPod thanks to PowerPoint's ability to export presentations to iPhoto. Then transfer the resulting photo album to your iPod, which you can then connect to a video projector, for example.

- **Apple remote control enabled.** If you're giving your presentation on a MacBook, iMac, or other Mac that came with a remote control, put it to use controlling your presentation without being anywhere near your computer.

Entourage

- **My Day.** This standalone program lets you keep tabs on your appointments and to-do list items—even when Entourage isn't open. And by removing the temptation to check your email, you may even get some of those 22 items done.

- **Spotlight search.** Find what you're looking for quickly with Spotlight—which now can search even in message attachments.

- **Enhanced junk filter.** Entourage now does an even better job filtering out junk e-mail—and can even warn you when it detects phishing messages.

Office as a Whole

- **Elements Gallery.** Quickly find templates, charts, tables, SmartArt graphics, and so on in the Elements Gallery—located below the toolbar in Word, Excel, and PowerPoint.

- **SmartArt graphics.** Quickly create designer-quality diagrams and charts using SmartArt graphics. Use these highly customizable graphic elements to illustrate processes, hierarchies, and so on.

- **The Toolbox.** No more tool palette confusion! The Formatting Palette, Object Palette, Compatibility Report, Scrapbook, Reference Tools, and Project Palette now all appear under the umbrella of the redesigned Toolbox, giving you one-stop access to tools, clip art, photos, and so on.

- **Improved Help.** Alas, Max—the hyperactive Mac Plus help icon—is no more. In his place is a revamped Help system that can connect to the online version of Help, delivering to your desktop up-to-date new topics, troubleshooting information, links to Office discussion forums, and so on.

- **XML file format.** Office 2007 for Windows introduced the new XML file formats—which create smaller files and can make it easier to recover damaged file information. Office 2008 for Mac uses this new standard format for Word, PowerPoint, and Excel documents—though you can still open and save documents in the Office 97-2004 format.

- **Universal binary.** Microsoft completely rewrote Office 2008 as a universal binary program so it can take full advantage of both Intel- and PowerPC-based Macs.

The Very Basics

You'll find very little jargon or nerd terminology in this book. You will, however, encounter a few terms and concepts that you'll see frequently in your Macintosh life. They include:

- **Clicking.** This book gives you three kinds of instructions that require you to use the mouse or trackpad attached to your Mac. To *click* means to point the arrow cursor at something onscreen and then—without moving the cursor at all—to press and release the clicker button on the mouse (or laptop trackpad). To *double-click*, of course, means to *click* twice in rapid succession, again without moving the cursor at all. And to *drag* means to move the cursor while keeping the button continuously pressed.

  When you're told to ⌘-click something, you click while pressing the ⌘ key (next to the Space bar). Such related procedures as *Shift-clicking, Option-clicking,* and *Control-clicking* work the same way—just click while pressing the corresponding key in the lower corner of your keyboard.

- **Menus.** The menus are the words in the lightly shaded bar at the top of your screen. The menu titles are slightly different in each of the Office programs. You can either click one of these words to open a pull-down menu of commands (and then click again on a command), or click and *hold* the button as you drag down the menu to the desired command (and release the button to activate the command). Either method works fine.

- **Keyboard shortcuts.** Every time you take your hand off the keyboard to move the mouse, you lose time and potentially disrupt your creative flow. That's why many experienced Mac fans use keystroke combinations instead of menu commands wherever possible. ⌘-B, for example, is a universal keyboard shortcut for boldface type throughout Office 2008 (as well as in most other Mac programs). ⌘-P opens the Print dialog box, ⌘-S saves whatever document you're currently working in, and ⌘-M minimizes the current window to the Dock.

  When you see a shortcut like ⌘-W (which closes the current window), it's telling you to hold down the ⌘ key, and, while it's down, type the letter W, and then release both keys.

- **Pop-up buttons.** The tiny arrows beside many of Office 2008's buttons are easy to overlook—but don't. Each one reveals a pop-up menu of useful commands. For instance, the arrow button next to the Undo button on the Standard toolbar lets you choose any number of actions to undo. Meanwhile, the arrow next to the New button in Entourage lets you specify what *kind* of item you want to create—an appointment for the calendar, an address book entry, and so on.

- **Choice is good.** Microsoft wouldn't be Microsoft if it didn't give you several ways to trigger a particular command. Sure enough, nearly everything you could ever wish to do in Office 2008 is accessible by a menu command *or* by clicking a toolbar button *or* by pressing a key combination. Some people prefer the speed of keyboard shortcuts; others like the satisfaction of a visual command array available in menus or toolbars.

One thing's for sure, however: You're not expected to memorize all of these features. In fact, Microsoft's own studies indicate that most people don't even *know* about 80 percent of its programs' features, let alone use them all. And that's OK. Great novels, Pulitzer Prize–winning articles, and successful business ventures have all been launched by people who never got past Open and Save.

On the other hand, as you skim this book, be aware that the way you've been doing things in Word or Excel since 1998 may no longer be the fastest or easiest. Every new keystroke or toolbar you add to your repertoire may afford you more free time to teach ancient Greek to three-year-olds or start your own hang-gliding club.

As for the programmers in Redmond, let them obsess about how many different ways they can think of to do the same thing. You're under no obligation to try them all.

About This Book

Office 2008 comes in a shiny, attractive package adorned with a distinctive stylized "O" logo. What you won't find inside, however, is a printed manual. To learn this vast set of software programs, you're expected to rely on sample documents in the Project Gallery, a PDF guide, and built-in help screens.

Although Office Help is detailed and concise, you need to know what you're looking for before you can find it. You can't mark your place (you lose your trail in the Help program every time you close an Office program), you can't underline or make marginal notes, and, even with a laptop, reading in bed or by firelight just isn't the same.

The purpose of this book, then, is to serve as the manual that should have accompanied Office 2008. Although you may still turn to online help for the answer to a quick question, this book provides step-by-step instructions for all major (and most minor) Office features, including those that have always lurked in Office but you've never quite understood. This printed guide provides an overview of the ways this comprehensive software package can make you act like a one-person, all-purpose office.

About the Outline

This book is divided into five parts, each containing several chapters.

- Parts 1 through 4, **Word, Entourage, Excel,** and **PowerPoint**, cover in detail each of the primary Office programs. Each part begins with an introductory chapter that covers the basics. Additional chapters delve into the more advanced and less-frequently used features.

- Part 5, **Office as a Whole,** shows how the programs work together for even more productivity and creativity. For example, it covers the Project Gallery and Toolbox, the graphics features that work in all Office programs, how to customize Office's menus and keystrokes, and more.

- Three appendixes await you at the end of the book: Appendix A offers guidance on installing, updating, and troubleshooting the software; Appendix B explains the Office online help system; and Appendix C, "Office 2008: Menu by Menu" describes the function of each menu command in each of the four major programs, with cross-references to the pages where these features are discussed more completely.

About → These → Arrows

Throughout this book, and throughout the Missing Manual series, you'll find sentences like this one: "Open the System → Libraries → Fonts folder." That's shorthand for a much longer instruction that directs you to open three nested folders in sequence. That instruction might read: "On your hard drive, you'll find a folder called System. Open that. Inside the System folder window is a folder called Libraries. Open that. Inside *that* folder is yet another one called Fonts. Double-click to open it."

Similarly, this kind of arrow shorthand helps to simplify the business of choosing commands in menus, as shown in Figure I-2.

Office Up to Date

Writing complex software is never easy—and few companies write more complex software than Microsoft. It's also no wonder that few companies issue more "Service Packs" and updates than Microsoft—with the possible exception of Apple. You'll do yourself a big favor by making sure that you have the most updated versions of both Office 2008 and Mac OS X.

To get the latest Office update, go to *www.microsoft.com/ mac* and look under "Downloads" at the top of the page. When you reach the download page, follow the onscreen instructions.

Of course, you can avoid all that hassle if you wish. When you install Office 2008, it automatically installs Microsoft's AutoUpdate for Mac. After that, your Mac will periodically check Microsoft's Web site and prompt you to download the latest updates to your Office suite. You can determine how often you want to "Check for Updates"—daily, weekly, or monthly—by choosing Help → "Check for Updates" from any of the Office programs. Or turn on the "Manually" radio button in the AutoUpdate window. That way, AutoUpdate will run only when you choose Help → "Check for Updates".

With the help of AutoUpdate, you'll always have every update and fix that Microsoft makes to Office 2008.

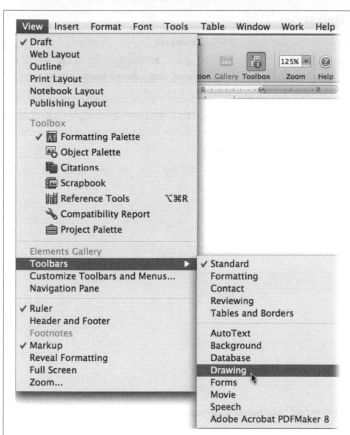

Figure I-2:
When you read "Choose View → Toolbars → Drawing" in a Missing Manual, that means: "Click the View menu to open it; click Toolbars in that menu; choose Drawing in the resulting submenu." (If you read "Choose Edit → Preferences → Mail tab," that means you should click the tab called Mail in the dialog box that appears.)

About MissingManuals.com

At the *missingmanuals.com* Web site, you'll find news, articles, and updates to the books in this series.

But if you click the name of this book and then the Errata link, you'll find a unique resource: a list of corrections and updates that have been made in successive printings of this book. You can mark important corrections right into your own copy of the book, if you like.

In fact, the same Errata page offers an invitation for you to submit such corrections and updates yourself. In an effort to keep the book as up to date and accurate as possible, each time we print more copies of this book, we'll make any confirmed corrections you've suggested. Thanks in advance for reporting any glitches you find!

In the meantime, we'd love to hear your own suggestions for new books in the Missing Manual line. There's a place for that on the Web site, too, as well as a place to sign up for free email notification of new titles in the series.

Safari® Books Online

 When you see a Safari® Books Online icon on the cover of your favorite technology book, that means the book is available online through the O'Reilly Network Safari Bookshelf.

Safari offers a solution that's better than e-Books. It's a virtual library that lets you easily search thousands of top tech books, cut and paste code samples, download chapters, and find quick answers when you need the most accurate, current information. Try it free at *http://safari.oreilly.com*.

Part One: Word

1

Basic Word Processing

Go ahead and skip these next few chapters. You don't need them. After all, everyone knows how to use Word to type a letter to Mom, tap out a report on the Komodo dragon, or clack out a recipe. But you can also use it to chart the Sweet Sixteen as they struggle through March Madness, snap off a To Do list that's as attractive as it is helpful, or put together a company newsletter that gets you noticed. Word offers the basic features of a desktop publisher, graphics utility, Dictaphone, and about a hundred other programs rolled into one convenient—if somewhat large—package.

The next few chapters teach you how to unwrap that package and put it to good use. From typing your first word to formatting complex layouts and creating templates for mass-producing your own favorite documents, these chapters will teach you everything that you've ever wanted to know about Word...and perhaps more. So, on second thought, you better not skip these chapters after all.

Creating and Opening Documents

There are at least four ways to create a new document from scratch. They are as follows:

- Choose File → Project Gallery and click the Word Document icon, as described on the next page.

- Choose File → New Blank Document.

- Press ⌘-N.

- Click the New Blank Document button (the very first icon) on the Standard toolbar that appears just beneath your menu bar.

However you do it, the result is a pristine, empty document, willing and able to become your next note to self, pithy sermon, or environmental impact report.

Tip: In fact, this new document isn't really empty at all. Behind the scenes, it's already loaded up with such settings as an automatic font, margin settings, style sheets, and so on. It inherits these starter settings from a special document called the Normal template.

You can read much more about Templates on page 230. For now, though, it's enough to know that you can modify the Normal template so that each new document you open automatically has your own favorite settings.

The Project Gallery

The first thing you see when you launch Word is the Project Gallery (see Figure 1-1), where you choose the kind of document you'd like to create.

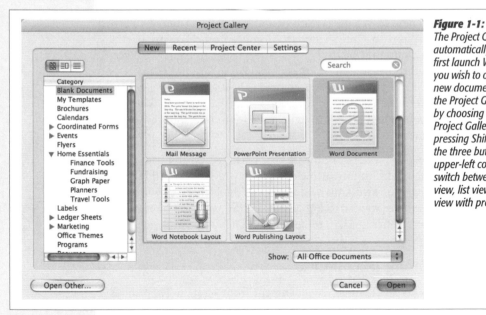

Figure 1-1:
The Project Gallery opens automatically when you first launch Word. When you wish to open another new document, just open the Project Gallery again by choosing File → Project Gallery or pressing Shift-⌘-P. Use the three buttons in the upper-left corner to switch between icon view, list view, and list view with preview.

The Project Gallery is your entry point to the many types of documents Office 2008 (not just Word) is equipped to handle. Your choices include brochures, spreadsheets, and even email messages. (For more detail, see Chapter 18.)

When the Project Gallery opens, the Word Document icon is highlighted, as shown in Figure 1-1. If you click Open (or press Return or Enter) now, a new blank Word document opens, just as if you'd chosen File → New Blank Document (or pressed ⌘-N).

Opening any kind of document in the Project Gallery works the same way: Click the list items in the Category list on the left until you see the desired template or document type on the right. Then double-click the document icon to open it.

Opening Documents with the Open Command

If you're entering the world of Word for the purposes of editing an existing document, just double-click the document in the Finder (or click it in the Dock, if that's where you stashed it). If you're already in Word, though, simply choose the fastest of the following options:

- Choose File → Open Recent and select a recently used file from the list.

- Click the Recent tab in the Project Gallery and double-click a recently used file in the list.

- Choose File → Open.

- Press ⌘-O.

- Click the second (arrow-from-folder) icon on the Standard toolbar.

No matter which method you use, Mac OS X's standard Open box appears (Figure 1-2). It has a column view, just like the Mac OS X Finder, and a pop-up menu to make it easier to access the document you seek. (See *Mac OS X: The Missing Manual* for a complete list of Save and Open dialog box features.) Once you've located the document you want in this dialog box, double-click to open it.

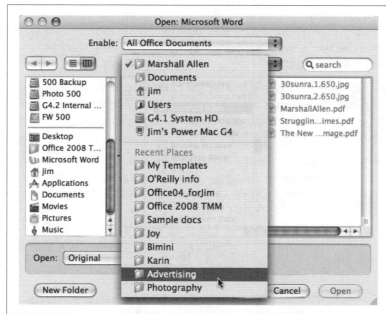

Figure 1-2:
The fastest way to use Mac OS X's Open dialog box is to take advantage of the folder selection menu. It lists the folders you've been using recently as well as a quick way to hop to the desktop or your Home folder. Because Word 2008 can open so many different document formats, leave the Enable pop-up menu set to All Documents so you can take, say, a plain text document and open it in Word—and take advantage of all Word's powerful features.

Tip: When you choose File → Open, Word shows you the contents of the folder you last opened. But if you keep all your Word files in one folder, you might rather see *that* list of files when you use the Open command.

To make it so, choose Word → Preferences. Click the File Locations button (in the bottom row), then Documents, and then Modify. Navigate to and highlight the folder you use most often, and then click Choose. From now on, choosing File → Open automatically uses your favorite starting folder.

In addition, Microsoft has added the following special features of its own to the Open dialog box:

- **Enable.** Use this pop-up menu (at the top of the Open dialog box) to choose which kinds of documents you want to see. The setting "All Readable Documents" lets the Open dialog box display any possible document on your Mac that you can open in Word—not just Microsoft Office documents, but text files, JPEG graphics, HTML Web page documents, and so on. If you know that the document you're seeking is of a certain type, you might save time by telling Word to show *only* those choices (other kinds of documents are "grayed out.") No need to waste time browsing through, say, HTML files when you're looking for an RTF document.

Tip: Don't miss the "Recover text from any file" option listed in this pop-up menu; it's a spectacular tool. It lets you extract recognizable text from any *file* and place it into a new window. It was intended to rescue usable prose from a corrupted Word document, of course, but it means what it says: *any file.*

- **Folder Selection Menu.** The pop-up menu underneath the Enable pop-up menu lets you quickly select a folder. You may then browse its contents in the center panel. This list includes the folders that you've recently visited—handy stuff for accessing commonly used folders.

- **Open.** This pop-up menu lets you choose one of the three different ways Word can open the same document. **Original** opens the document itself; **Copy** opens a copy, leaving the original untouched; and **Read-Only** opens the document but doesn't let you make changes to it.

  Most of the time, you'll open the original and get to work. But opening a *copy* is a convenient way of leaving an electronic paper trail of your work. No matter how many changes you make or how badly you mess up a document, you still have an unsullied copy saved on your Mac. To save changes you've made to a Read-Only document, you have to save it under a different title by choosing File → Save As (or just attempt to save your changes and Word will guide you to the Save As dialog box).

- **View Buttons.** The two List View and Column View buttons at the top left of the Open dialogue box switch the view from the list to the vertical dividers, as shown in Figure 1-3. Clicking the list icon displays the folders and documents in the selected location. Click the flippy triangle to view a folder's contents, which

In Search of Files

The Open dialog box offers a streamlined means of travel-ing directly to the document you want to open—assuming you remember where you stored it. Until Word 2004, the Open dialog box offered a powerful but somewhat clunky Find File feature that searched your Mac for Word files con-taining certain properties or even keywords. Microsoft has consigned Find File to the feature graveyard, probably because there's a much more elegant search system built right into Mac OS X—Spotlight.

Click the little magnifying-glass icon at the right end of your menu bar (or press ⌘-Space bar) to open the Spotlight search box. Type a portion of the file name you're searching for. As you do, the menu expands below, showing all the results Spotlight can find that match what you've typed so far. The more you type, the more refined your search becomes. Spotlight actually searches not only file *names*, but the file *contents*—the words within those files.

The Spotlight results menu lists items by category—docu-ments, folders, images, and so on—and highlights one Top Hit at the top of the list that is its best guess at what you're looking for. If you see the object of your search, click it to open it. If Spotlight's Top Hit is indeed what you're search-ing for, instead of reaching for the mouse, press ⌘-Return to open that file. If you don't see your longed-for file, click Show All to open Spotlight's detailed results window. Here you can group and sort those results by various criteria, choose which timeframe to look at, and determine which drive to search through if you have multiple hard drives.

The Spotlight menu isn't the only way to find files on your Mac. Click the Finder icon on the Dock and then choose File → Find or press ⌘-F. Doing so opens the Search dialog box, prepared to search anywhere on your computer for any kind of file created at any date. To find a file, type the portion of the file name you remember into the text entry box at the top.

As you type, the Mac searches (it's actually Spotlight at work behind the scenes) and displays a list of all files that match your search term, in a neatly categorized list.

If, instead of searching your whole computer, you want to target your search, you can use the buttons at the top of the Search window—Servers, Computer, Home, Others—to restrict Spotlight's sleuthing to certain areas. Likewise, you can use the next rows of criteria buttons to instruct Spotlight what to search for. The buttons for Kind and Last Opened which appear the first time you use the Search window, are just the tip of a very large iceberg of more than 125 diverse search criteria—everything from email recipients to file extensions to the exposure setting of the camera used to take a photograph. Add or remove criteria by using the + or - buttons in each row.

The foregoing serves as a *very* brief introduction to the wonders of Spotlight. For the full story, check out an entire chapter about Spotlight in *Mac OS X: The Missing Manual* by David Pogue.

will be displayed below and indented from the folder (just like the list view in Finder windows). Clicking on the three-pane column icon displays the files in multiple panels. In this view (just like the Column view in Finder windows), clicking on a folder in the one panel displays its contents in a panel to the right. Column view is better for diving through swarms of nested folders, while list view lets you see more information about each file.

- **New Folder.** You guessed it—creates a new folder in the selected location. For example, you know you want to save your document into a folder called Resumes08 in your Job Search folder…but you don't have a folder called Resumes08. No problem. Navigate to the Job Search folder and click the New Folder button. Type the new folder's name in the little dialog box that appears, and click Create to forge the folder.

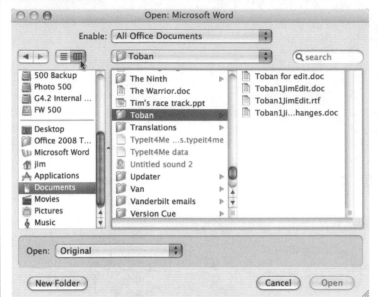

Figure 1-3:
You can change the way you navigate the Open dialog box by clicking the List View and Column View buttons. The list view displays the contents of folders below the selected folders, while column view has two or more panels. When you click a folder in one column, its contents are displayed in the column to the right.

Returning to Favorite Documents

Like most people, you probably work with the same documents and templates over and over again. Word knows that and offers three shortcuts to retrieving files you've used recently or you intend to use frequently.

The Recent files list

You'll find a list of recently opened Word documents when you choose File → Open Recent. Just choose a file name to open the corresponding document, wherever it may be on your machine. (That is, unless it's no longer *on* your machine, or you've moved it from the location where you last saved it, in which case you get only a cheerful error message.)

Tip: You control how many documents are listed here by choosing Word → Preferences → General. Set the "Recently used file list" number to 0 if you don't want Word to track your files at all, or 99 for maximum tracking.

The Project Gallery

Choose File → Project Gallery and click the Recent tab to see a long list of recently used Office files. You can narrow your choices to only Word documents by using the Show pop-up menu near the bottom. The Project Gallery's memory for recently used files can be long indeed; it can recall the last 999 Office files you've worked on. Click the Settings tab and adjust the number in the box marked "Show this number of recently opened files."

Purging the Recent List

I'm not so sure I want my boss (boyfriend, children) seeing which files I've been working on recently. Is there any way to delete the document names listed in the File menu?

You should have thought of that before you created those documents! However, Word is certainly willing to help you with your covert ops. Open any Word document. Choose Word → Preferences → General. Turn off the checkbox for "Track recently opened documents" and press Return. The list of names in the File → Open Recent menu disappears, and Word stops remembering them.

Removing just the current collection of recent files is much easier: choose File → Open Recent → Clear Recent. Word expunges all references to your recently used files. It starts remembering again from this point on—but that last embarrassing batch remains obliterated.

Of course, you can avoid the whole messy issue by living your computer life as if you have nothing to hide.

The Work menu

Word's Work menu is a vestigial appendage left over from when it was difficult to file frequently used documents for easy retrieval—before the Mac OS X Dock, Sidebar, and Desktop icons made it simple. You can use this menu to store your current project files, book outlines, invoice templates, and so on for easy access, but the Work menu isn't even in the same organizational ballpark as Office 2008's Project Center, which automatically compiles a folder of *all* Office files related to a specific project—not just Word documents. (For more information on the Project Center, see Chapter 11.)

The Work menu still works and it's easy to add items to it. The problem is, it's difficult and confusing to remove items from the menu. To add a Word document to the Work menu, save it, and then choose Work → Add to Work Menu. Now click the Work menu; the name of your document appears, ready for opening just by choosing its name.

You can only remove a document from the Work menu the way you'd remove any Word menu command—see page 769 for instructions.

Word Processing Basics

Once a document is onscreen, your administrative efforts are complete, and the creative phase can begin. While odds are good that you've processed words before, Chapter 2 covers the nuts and bolts of editing in detail.

As a reminder, here are the very, very basics of word processing:

- **Don't hit Return at the end of a line.** Word automatically wraps the text to the next line when you reach the edge of the window.

- **Don't type hyphens to break end-of-line words, either.** To divide words at the end of lines, use Word's hyphenation feature, as described on page 139.

- **Press Return at the end of a paragraph.** To create a blank line between paragraphs, don't press Return twice; that can cause awkward problems, such as an extra space at the top of a page. Instead, change the paragraph's *style* to leave more space after each paragraph, as described on page 127. Using this more advanced and graceful method also lets you edit, add, and subtract paragraphs at will. As you do so, the spacing between the paragraphs remains consistent.

- **For similar reasons, don't press Tab to indent the first line of a paragraph.** If, instead, you set a *first line indent* using the Formatting Palette, as described on page 109, Word automatically creates the indents each time you start a paragraph. Indents created this way remain consistent as you edit the document. In addition, the amount of indentation you choose isn't dependent upon the positions of your tab stops.

- **Don't press Return at the end of a page.** Word automatically wraps the text to the next page. If you want your next thought to start at the top of a new page, choose Insert → Break → Page Break instead. Now, no matter how much you edit before or after the section break, your new section always starts at the top of a new page.

- **Press the Space bar only once—not twice—after punctuation such as periods, colons, and semicolons.** Double-spacing after punctuation is a holdover from the days of the typewriter, when you had to manually add extra space after punctuation for an attractive, readable result. Word automatically places the correct amount of space after each period or other punctuation mark. Adding an extra space is superfluous, clutters your file with extra characters, and cramps your thumbs.

- **Save early, save often.** Choose File → Save (or press ⌘-S) after every paragraph or so.

A Window into Word

The tools you use most often—those for navigating your document and for basic formatting—are clustered around the main text window, as shown in Figure 1-4.

Title Bar

Word 2008's title bar does all the usual Mac things—sends the window to the Dock when double-clicked, moves it when dragged, and so on—but it has a few unheralded powers, too. It also performs like a Mac OS X *folder* window in two key respects:

- To find out which folder your document is nested in, ⌘-click the document's title. As shown in Figure 1-5, a shortcut menu appears, identifying your document's location on the hard drive. Click any folder or drive on the list to open it in a new Finder window.

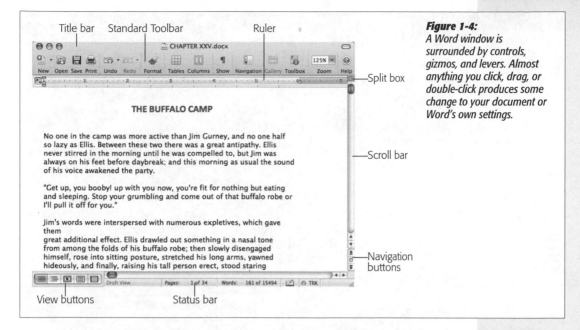

Figure 1-4:
A Word window is surrounded by controls, gizmos, and levers. Almost anything you click, drag, or double-click produces some change to your document or Word's own settings.

- See the small Word icon next to the document's name in the title bar? That's your *document proxy icon,* which works just like the *folder* proxy icon in every Finder window title bar. As shown at right in Figure 1-5, you can drag that icon just as you would any icon in the Finder. You might do so to move the current document to a different folder, to copy it to a different disk, or even to drag it directly to the Trash. In true Mac OS X fashion, you see a translucent ghost of the icon as you move it. (You have to hold the cursor down on this icon for about one second, making it turn dark, before you can drag it in this way. If you drag it too quickly, Word thinks you're simply trying to move the window on the screen.)

Note: The document proxy icon appears faded out (turned off) whenever you've edited your document without saving the changes—and you can't drag it to move, copy, or trash your document when you haven't saved changes. (Need another clue that your document has unsaved changes? Glance at the red *close* button in the upper-left corner of any document window. If there's a black dot in the center of the red button, you need to save.) Only when you choose File → Save (⌘-S) does the proxy icon spring to life, ready for dragging.

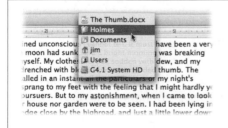

Figure 1-5:
Left: When you ⌘-click the document name, you can choose and open, in a Finder window, any folder or disk in the list.

Right: After holding for a second, you can drag the tiny icon anywhere on your desktop.

Document Protection

Word makes it easy to open documents; almost too easy, if you're trying to keep certain documents private or unmodified. Never fear: Word offers three levels of document-protection features designed to keep spies and busybodies out of your files.

- **Suggest Read-Only.** When someone tries to open a document protected in this manner, a dialog box politely suggests that he use the read-only option. That person can make changes, but can only save the file under a new name. The original, read-only file remains intact. To save a file this way, choose File → Save As; click Options, click the Show All button, and then click the Security button. On the Security panel, turn on "Read-only recommended," and press Return. Click Save or press Return again to complete the process.

- **Password to Modify.** This trick makes Word ask for a password at the moment the document is opened. People you give the password to can edit the document and save the changes just as you can; for everyone else, the document opens as read-only. To protect a document this way, choose File → Save As; click Options, click the Show All button, and then

click the Security button. In the Security dialog box, type a password in the Password to Modify box. Click OK or press Return. Word asks the forgetful among us to retype the password. Do it.

- **Password to Open.** This highest level of document protection requires readers to enter a password before they can even open the document. In the Save As dialog box, click Options, click the Show All button, and then click the Security button. On the Security panel, type a password in the "Password to open" box and press Return (or the mouse-happy can click OK). Re-enter the password when Word asks for it, click OK, and your document is protected.

If you use one of the password methods, write the password down and keep it somewhere safe. If you lose the password, don't bother calling Microsoft. They can't help you open the protected document, and even Recover Text From Any File doesn't work on *these* files. (You could probably find a few thousand Internet hackers that could handle it for you, but that's a different book. Anyway, writing down your password is easier.)

The Ruler

The ruler across the top of the page displays the current settings for margins, tabs, and indents. See page 109 for details on how to use these settings.

Scroll Bar and Navigator Buttons

Figure 1-4 shows the *Navigator buttons*—double arrows flanking a little round button at the lower-right of the Word window. When you first open a document, these Navigator buttons act as Page Up/Page Down buttons. But once you've used the "Find and Replace" command (see page 55), or in some other way changed the *browse object*, the double arrows act differently.

For instance, after you've used "Find and Replace", clicking the Navigator buttons takes you from each occurrence of the word you're trying to find to the next. For more detail on the Browse Object feature and Navigator buttons, see page 53.

Split Box

Figure 1-4 also shows the small blue *Split box* at the upper-right of the window. When you point to it, the cursor changes to a double-pointing arrow. Dragging that arrow divides the window into two panes, each with its own, independent, vertical scroll bar. (Choosing Window → Split, or pressing Option-⌘-S, does the same thing.)

This arrangement is handy when you're working at the end of a long document and need to refer to material earlier in the document. You can use the upper window to scroll through the entire document, while meanwhile back at the lower window, you can continue typing without losing your place.

Tip: It's often faster to simply *double-click* the Split box. Doing so gives you two evenly split panes of the window. To adjust their relative proportions, just drag the *resize bar* (the gray dividing line between the panes) up or down.

Double-click this dividing line a second time to restore the window to its single-pane status. (The *bottom* half of the window disappears, even if it contained the insertion point–a potentially alarming behavior.)

Once you've split the window, you can drag the light gray bar between the two panes up or down to adjust their relative sizes. Like the scroll bars, the Page Up, Page Down, and arrow keys work as usual *within* each pane, meaning you can't use them to travel from one pane to the next. To switch *between* panes, you can use the mouse, or just press F6, which acts as a toggle key to the other pane and back again.

To restore a split window back to a single one, drag the resize bar all the way to the top of the window, double-click the resize bar, or press Option-⌘-S again.

Window Menu

You can't split a window into more than two panes—nor create *vertical* panes— using the Split box described above. However, you can get these effects using the Window menu (see Figure 1-6).

Choosing Window → New Window creates a clone of your document window, which you can scroll, position, or zoom independently. Each can be in a different Word *view* too (one in Outline view, one in Draft, and so on). The new windows are different peepholes into the same document —you haven't created a new document. Therefore, any change you make in one window appears in both windows simultaneously. When you use File → Save, you save *all* the windows.

There's almost no limit to the number of windows you can create in this way. You can place two windows side by side and work on the first and last pages of your document at the same time, or you can create five windows, each scrolled to a different region of your manuscript. The title bar identifies the windows as "Introduction:1," "Introduction:2," and so on. To reconstitute your document, just close the extra windows.

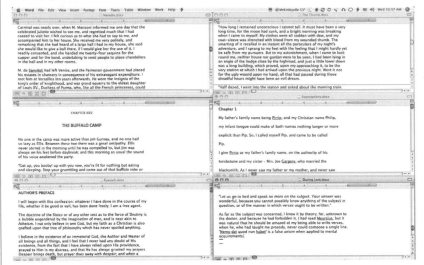

Figure 1-6:
If your screen is cluttered with Word documents and duplicate windows, the Window → Arrange All command fills the screen with a patchwork of all your open windows. If you just need to find one of your document Windows instead of keeping them all open simultaneously, use Mac OS X's Exposé feature instead. Press F10 to show all your Word document windows, and then click the one you want to see in the foreground.

Status Bar

The light gray bar running across the bottom of the window (see Figure 1-4) is called the *status bar*. Divided into segments by etched vertical lines, the status bar presents a variety of statistics about your current location within the document.

- **View buttons.** The status bar begins at the left with a group of buttons for changing your document view—the same as choosing one of the items at the top of the View menu. As you mouse over the buttons, the neighboring cell displays the view name, and when your mouse isn't hovering over those buttons, it displays the currently selected view. Click one of the buttons to change the view.

- **Pages: 4 of 10.** The third section shows the page number containing the insertion point (not necessarily the page you're viewing) followed by the total pages. For instance, if you're at the end of a three-page letter, this readout says 3 of 3.

Tip: Click anywhere in the Pages segment of the status bar to open the Go To tab of the "Find and Replace" dialog box, described on page 55. The idea, of course, is to provide you with a quick way to jump to a different page of your document without scrolling.

- **Words: 244 of 3654.** The second number shows the total number of words in your document, and the first indicates which word has your insertion point, as counted from the first word of the document. If you highlight some text in your document, the first number tells you how many words are in the selected passage.

  If this part of the status bar is blank, it's probably because your word count feature is turned off. To turn it on, choose Word → Preferences; in the Preferences dialog box, click the View button. Turn on Live Word Count (in the Window section) and click OK. Now, when you start typing, the word count number is revised after every few words you type; hence the name Live Word Count. With long documents, this feature can slow Word down considerably. In that case, leave it turned off in Preferences and check the word count as described in the following Tip.

Tip: Click the word-count segment to summon the Word Count dialog box, which provides the number of pages, paragraphs, lines, and other countable items, as well as the word count. (It's the same box that appears when you choose Tools → Word Count.)

- **The little book.** This icon is the spelling and grammar–checking status indicator. As you type, a little pencil moves across the pages, indicating that Word is checking for spelling and grammar errors. Most of the time, when you're at rest, a red X appears on the book icon, meaning that Word has found an error somewhere in your document. (That is, an error according to Word's sense of spelling and grammar.) When you've just completed a spelling and grammar check and made no new errors, the icon shows a checkmark instead of an X.

  To review Word's spelling and grammar flags starting from the insertion point, click the book icon. At each error, a shortcut menu offers alternative spelling and punctuation choices and commands that lead you to relevant spelling and grammar dialog boxes (see page 62).

Note: If you don't see the little book icon, it may be because you've turned off "as you type" spelling and grammar checking (Word → Preferences → Spelling & Grammar panel).

- **TRK** corresponds to the Track Changes command (see page 171). Click this segment of the status bar to turn track changes on, and illuminate the blue TRK indicator. Now your own edits show up in a different color, so that your colleagues can see exactly which changes you've made.

Tip: Clicking the TRK indicator turns on revision tracking (or, if it's on, turns it off). That's a *huge* time-saver if you're used to turning on tracking in the usual way (Tools → Track Changes → Highlight Changes; turn on "Track changes while editing"; click OK).

If you don't find any of these status indicators particularly helpful—and you'd rather dedicate the screen space to your writing—just hide them. Choose Word → Preferences, click the View button, and turn off the "Status bar" checkbox near the bottom of the dialog box. Then click OK.

Standard Toolbar

Word 2008 can slip in and out of many guises—a picture or movie editor, a database manager, or a Web browser, to name just a few. Each primary function comes complete with its own *toolbar* filled with icons relevant to that task.

If all these icons were available all the time, your screen would be filled with toolbars. As a result, you'd have to do all your typing in a leftover space the size of a

---

Triscuit. Fortunately, Word 2008 is very considerate of your screen real estate. You can open, close, resize, reshape, or relocate toolbars at will, like so:

- To open a toolbar, choose View → Toolbars and choose a toolbar from the submenu. Alternatively, carefully Control-click one of the dotted dividing lines on any open toolbar, choose Toolbar from the shortcut menu, and select a toolbar from the submenu.

  Word comes with 12 toolbars, including the Standard toolbar; you can also design new toolbars of your own (see Chapter 20). There's no limit to the number you can have open at once. To close a floating toolbar, click the tiny close button in the upper-left corner, just like any other Mac window, or choose its name a second time from the View → Toolbars command.

- Each toolbar has a place where it likes to appear. The Drawing toolbar, for example, opens vertically at the far left of the screen the first time you use it. The standard toolbar only appears docked inside your document window. The other four toolbars in the top part of the menu — Formatting, Contact, Reviewing, and "Tables and Borders" (and Outlining when you're in Outline View)— appear docked inside your document window the first time you use them. To turn them into floating toolbars, Control-click one of the dotted dividing lines in the toolbar, or the gray area to the right of the buttons, and choose "Dock Toolbar in Window" to remove the checkmark from this menu item and remove the toolbar from your document window. Repeat the process to park it back inside the document window.

- You can move floating toolbars anywhere you like. To move a toolbar around onscreen, drag the shaded bar at the top (or left side), just as though it's a shrunken version of a standard Mac title bar. As you drag a toolbar near one of the screen edges, or near another toolbar, it jumps neatly into place.

- To resize a toolbar, drag the tiny, striped, lower-right corner. You can change most toolbars from a long, narrow bar (either horizontal or vertical), into a squarish palette.

- If you forget the name of a *button,* just point to it without clicking and wait one second; a yellow screen tip appears.

The Standard toolbar (Figure 1-7) is the only one that opens automatically when you create a new Word document; it has icons for printing, saving, and other tasks you perform frequently. Each button on it instantly does something that would normally take two or more mouse clicks: opening a new blank document, opening an existing file, saving the document, and so on.

From left to right, the buttons on the Standard toolbar are:

- **New, Open, Save.** These buttons correspond to the equivalent commands in the File menu.

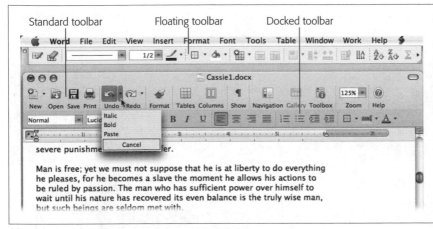

Standard toolbar   Floating toolbar   Docked toolbar

Figure 1-7:
*The Standard toolbar is
the only one that always
appears inside the
document window. Some
of its commands, like the
Undo command, are
pop-up buttons. Other
toolbars can be either
docked in the window, or
free floating.*

- **Print.** This button isn't the same thing as the File → Print command; it's a much more streamlined function. It prints the current document—all pages, one copy—on the currently selected printer. For more control over what Word prints (number of copies, which pages, which printer), use the File → Print command (⌘-P), which opens the Print dialog box (see page 23).

- **Undo.** Clicking this curved arrow undoes your last bit of typing, pasting, or whatever. The tiny triangle next to it, however, is where the power of Undo is truly unleashed. Clicking the Undo triangle pulls down a list that displays, in reverse order, the last several steps you took in Word—from major style changes to single deletions. You can retrace your steps pages and pages into the past. As you drag down this pop-up menu, the button at the bottom of the list (see Figure 1-7) tells you how many things you're about to undo. Letting go of the mouse button triggers Undo. If you change your mind, be sure to move the cursor off the Undo list until the button says Cancel before letting go. (*Keyboard shortcut:* ⌘-Z or F1, either of which only undoes one action at a time.)

- **Redo.** This button and triangle let you *redo* whatever you've just undone. If you just undid your last 10 moves, for example, you can drag the Redo list as far as "Redo 10 Actions." As with the Undo list, you can scroll up and down in this list to redo as much or as little as you like. (*Keyboard shortcut:* ⌘-Y or Option-Return, either of which only redoes one action at a time.)

- **Format Painter.** Just as you can pour color onto a selected area in a painting program, you can also "pour" a set of formatting choices onto any number of words or an entire paragraph. See page 111 for details.

- **Insert Table.** Another quick way to create a table is to click this button, whose pop-up menu is a small expanse of white squares. Drag over the squares to select the table size you want: 2×2 (two rows by two columns), 3×3, and so on. When you release the mouse button, a table of the size you selected appears in your document at the insertion point. See page 150 for more on the Table tool.

Tip: Don't feel cramped by the 4×5 shape of the pop-up menu itself. If you drag beyond the boundaries of the proposed 4×5 grid, the pop-up menu itself expands until it's enormous.

POWER USERS' CLINIC

Secrets of the Re-branching Undo Tree

Having a multiple-level Undo is great; there's no debating that a program with one is much better than a program without one.

But the multi-Undo can also be frustrating on one occasion. Imagine something like this: You decide that you really wanted paragraph 13 the way you originally wrote it. Trouble is, you've since rewritten it and made hundreds of other changes to the manuscript. How can you recapture the glory of paragraph 13 the way it was two hours ago?

Unfortunately, you can't use a thousand Undos to recreate it. Remember, you've done a lot of great work in the meantime, in other paragraphs that you want to keep. If you were to Undo all the way back to paragraph 13, just for the purpose of restoring it, you'll also lose all the other paragraphs you've written or edited in the meantime.

The sneaky solution is this: Undo all the way back to the point where paragraph 13 was originally by pressing ⌘-Z over and over again—all the while coolly watching all your editing work disappear. When you finally see paragraph 13 return to its original version, highlight the paragraph and copy it (⌘-C).

Now redo all the changes, using ⌘-Y repeatedly until Word beeps, indicating that you've restored the document to its latest condition.

Finally, highlight paragraph 13 (which is back to its unsatisfactory version) and paste over it (⌘-V), replacing it with the good, earlier version. Fortunately, all those Redos don't affect what you copied to the clipboard.

- **Columns.** This button's pop-up menu lets you create columns; drag down and across to choose the number of columns you want. (You can drag beyond the borders of the pop-up menu if four columns across aren't enough, you crazed designer, you.) When you release the mouse button, you find yourself in Print Layout view, with your entire document divided equally into the number of columns you chose. For details on using columns, see page 136.

- **Show/Hide ¶.** Clicking this button exposes paragraph markers (¶) and other nonprinting characters. This display is useful when, for example, you're copying a paragraph and want to make sure you're copying *all* the formatting. (Word stores formatting for each paragraph in the invisible ¶ mark that follows it.) Click this button a second time to render the characters invisible once again. (*Keyboard shortcut:* ⌘-8.)

- **Navigation Pane.** Clicking this button displays or hides the Navigation Pane to the left side of your document. The pane is a big help when working with long documents. It lets you go to a page by quickly scrolling to it in the left pane, and then clicking it to view in the main pane. Select the view you want from the pop-up menu at the top of the pane. Thumbnail (small page pictures) or the old standby Document Map (outline of the document) are the choices.

- **Gallery.** Clicking this button with your document in Print Layout view, Web Layout view, or Publishing Layout view, displays or hides the Elements Gallery thumbnails in the document window between the toolbar and your document—the same effect as choosing View menu → Elements Gallery or clicking one of the Elements Gallery tabs (see Figure 1-8).

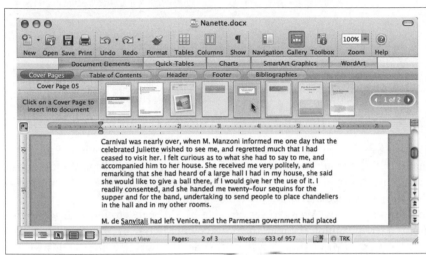

Figure 1-8:
The new Elements Gallery lets you quickly insert preconfigured title pages, headers, tables, and so on by clicking one of the Gallery thumbnails. This feature is available only in Word's Print Layout view, Publishing Layout view, or Web Layout view.

- **Toolbox.** Making its first appearance in Office 2004, the toolbox for 2008 absorbed the Formatting Palette—helping to reduce palette clutter, and making it the one-stop headquarters for some of the most powerful tools in Office. Click this button to reveal or conceal this multipurpose palette of tools. Here you can format text, tables, and document margins; manage your bibliography citations; access your Scrapbook text, clipart, and photos; and insert shapes and symbols (page 291). It's also where you conduct compatibility reports (page 731) that troubleshoot documents from earlier versions of Word or on computers from the PC side. The Toolbox also provides a gateway into the world of the Office 2008 Project Center, which is covered in more detail in Chapter 10, and a window into Word 2008 reference tools, which presents itself in greater detail in Chapter 18.

- **Zoom.** There are two ways to zoom (enlarge or shrink your document's representation on the screen) from the toolbar. First, you can enter a number in the box and press Return. (100% is roughly life-size; 125% is a more comfortable size on high-resolution monitors.)

  Second, you can select a magnification from the pop-up menu. Page Width magnifies or reduces your view so that it fills the document window, no matter how wide or narrow you've made it. Even if you make the window bigger or smaller, Word automatically adjusts the text so that it always neatly fills the window, with nothing chopped off and no extra space.

In Page Layout view and Publishing Layout View, you get a Whole Page command in this pop-up menu, too. It does the same thing as Page Width, but in both dimensions; in other words, Word scales the picture of your document so that the entire page fits within the window. Similarly, the Two Pages command (only in Page Layout View) forces two side-by-side pages to fit inside your window—a terrific option if you're the proud owner of one of Apple's gigantic flat-panel screens. (Make your window as wide as possible before choosing this option; otherwise, the font may become too small to read.) These and more zoom options are also available by choosing View → Zoom.

Note: Zooming never changes the actual printed size of your document. It only makes the type larger or smaller on screen, as though you're moving closer to the page or farther from it.

- **Help.** Max, the hyperkinetic Mac Plus Help mascot really wanted to be helpful, though to many he came off as just plain annoying. No matter how you feel about Max, in Office 2008 the little fellow is no more, replaced by a new and improved—and completely without character—Help system. Also accessible via the Help key on your keyboard or the Help menu, Word Help now optionally links via the Internet (assuming you have an active Internet connection) back to Redmond to get you the most up-to-date help files from Microsoft.

Note: Not all of the buttons on the toolbar have keyboard shortcuts. In fact, two of them don't even have menu equivalents: Format Painter and Show/Hide ¶. (Of course, you can always *add* these commands to your menus, as described in Chapter 20.)

The Views

Word can display your document in any of five different views, including the just-introduced Publishing Layout view. Each offers different features for editing, reading, and scrolling through your work. Some people spend their entire lives—or at least their Mac lives—in only one of these views, while power users may switch regularly back and forth between them.

In any case, using the views feature doesn't change your actual document in any way unless you change to Notebook view or Publishing Layout View. If you're using Draft or Print Layout View, the document *prints* exactly the same way. Views are mostly for your benefit while preparing the document onscreen.

Here are the five Word views, as they appear in the View menu.

Tip: You can also switch views by clicking one of the four icons at the very lower-left corner of your document window. (Except Web Layout view, which you can only get to via the View menu.)

Draft View

Formerly known as Normal View, Draft view presents the Standard toolbar, the Ruler, and all the window accessories described in the previous section (see Figure 1-4). In Draft view, your entire document scrolls by in a never-ending window, with only a thin blue line to indicate where one page ends and the next begins. Draft view is where you can focus on *writing* your document. Many page-layout elements, including headers and footers, drawing objects, and multiple columns, don't appear at all in Draft view. As a result, Draft view offers the fewest distractions and the fastest scrolling.

Web Layout View

This view shows what your document will look like if you convert it to a Web page, as described in Chapter 9. (And if you'd never in a million years dream of using Microsoft Word as a Web-design program, then this is only the first of many discussions you can safely skip in this book.)

For example, in Web Layout view, you don't see any page breaks, even if a particular page requires 47 consecutive feet of scrolling. After all, unlike a printed document when a Web page is long, you don't turn pages, you just keep scrolling. The Ruler goes away, too, because Web pages don't offer true indents or tabs. (Your existing tabs and margins still work, but you can only change them by using the various commands in the Format menu.) Any backgrounds, drawings, and images you've added to your document are visible, and look as they would when your document is viewed in a Web browser.

Outline View

In Outline view, Word automatically formats your paragraphs into outline form, saving you from remembering whether your next point should be labeled I., a., i., or whatever. Outline view lets you move your topics and supporting facts up and down, and in and out of the hierarchy, using the mouse or keyboard—and remembers everything on the fly. Chapter 6 has a full tutorial on using Word's outliner.

Print Layout View

This view gives you a second ruler along the *left* side of the page—a vertical ruler. (The parts of the ruler that are your page margins are blocked out with blue shading.) In Page Layout view, you can see—and manipulate—everything. You can adjust margins by dragging them as described in Figure 1-9. You can edit headers and footers by double-clicking where the cursor changes (see page 209). You can create drawing objects using the tools found in the Drawing toolbar, summoned by clicking View → Toolbars → Drawing (see Chapter 18 for more detail on drawings), and move them around by dragging. To see more of your page at once while in Page Layout view, simply change the Zoom box setting in the Standard toolbar.

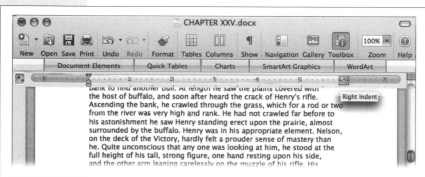

Figure 1-9:
When pointing to the ruler located at the margin boundary, the cursor turns into a double-sided arrow. You can now drag the arrow to reset the margin.

Notebook Layout View

You may want to use this layout for your personal or scholastic note-taking needs, or as an information organization tool. This view lets you draw images directly on the Notebook using the Scribble tool, and reorganize notes or even entire sections with a simple drag and drop. Choosing this view converts your document to a notebook complete with lined pages, and places the Notebook Layout tools on the toolbar. See Chapter 6 for more details on the Notebook Layout view.

Note: Notebook Layout view offers many of the features of a full-fledged note-taking program, such as Circus Ponies' Notebook or Microsoft's OneNote. You can use it to take notes and rapidly rearrange them, organize graphics and photos, sketch out ideas, and even record notes to yourself or lectures using the Audio Notes feature. Unless you require specialized features like keywords or notebook sharing, you can organize your life without investing 50 bucks in a separate notebook program.

Publishing Layout View

New to Office 2008, the Publishing Layout view brings a complete page-layout program to Word. Like the other document views, you can switch to this view to see or convert your document to a publishing layout document. Usually, however, page-layout documents begin life in this view—often by choosing one of the Publication Templates from the Elements Gallery. Here you'll find dozens of brochures, flyers, menus, and so on, which you can choose as a basis for your page-layout project. Of course—if you have more time and more creativity—you can also start with a completely blank page. See Chapter 8 for an in-depth look at this new view.

Every Conceivable Variation on Saving

The first thing to do with a completed document—or even a document you've just started—is to save it onto your hard drive, preserving it in case of an unforeseen system crash or accidental surge-suppressor power-switch toe-press. However, if you're still not in the habit of pressing ⌘-S every few sentences, paragraphs, or minutes, Word's AutoRecovery feature may save your hide.

Tip: If you have more than one Word document open at a time, press the Shift key as you choose File → Save. The Save command becomes Save All, which saves the changes to all open documents one by one. When you press Shift, you'll also notice that Close becomes Close All.

AutoRecovery

At preset intervals, Word saves the current document into a separate AutoRecover file. If your Mac freezes, crashes, or blacks out in a power failure, the AutoRecover file opens automatically. Once *you've* recovered, if you're satisfied that the Recovered file is the most recent and the one you want to keep, save it under a new name and continue working. (The file under the old name is the document as it was when you last carried out a real Save.)

Although AutoRecover runs in the background as you work, it produces a momentary and detectable slowdown. In other words, you want Word to save often, but not *too* often. To set the AutoRecover interval, choose Word → Preferences, and then click the Save button. Under "Save options," turn on the Save AutoRecover checkbox and enter a preferred number of minutes in the adjoining box.

Save As Options

The first time you save a document, or anytime you choose File → Save As, you open the Save dialog box (see Figure 1-10). The first thing to do is choose a folder for storing your newly created document. Next, click in the Save As box (or press Tab so that it's highlighted) and then name your document. (You certainly can do better than *Document1*.) Use the Format pop-up menu below to save your document into a different word processing file format, if you like.

Tip: If you frequently save documents in the same format, you can change the preferred format setting so that you don't have to choose your document format every time the Save As box appears. Click the Options button in the Save As dialog box, which is a shortcut to the Word → Preferences → Save panel. There you'll find a pop-up menu called "Save Word files as," which lets you specify the format you prefer.

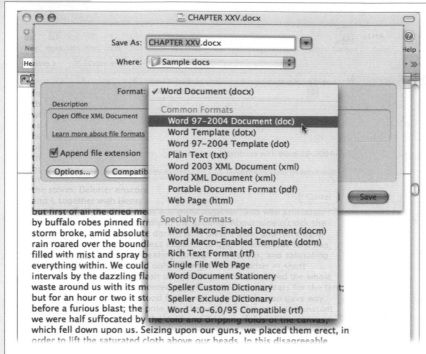

Figure 1-10:
Word can convert your document into many formats. If you save it as a "Word document (docx)" (the proposed choice), then only the most recent versions of Microsoft Word—specifically Word 2008 (on the Mac), or Word 2007 (Windows)—can open it without any conversion or translation. If you're exchanging documents with others, and you're not certain they have the latest version of Word, Word 97-2004 Document (doc) is the most likely to be readable in any version of Word on any computer.

Finally, you'll generally want to leave the "Append file extension" checkbox turned on. It tacks a three-or four-letter extension (*.docx* for standard Word files, *.doc* for Word 97-2004 files, and so on) onto your file names. Although *you* don't need to see these odd letters, they help computers identify the files. You can hide these suffixes, if you like, either globally in Mac OS X (choose Finder → Preferences) or on a file-by-file basis (highlight the file, choose File → Show Info, and choose Name & Extension from the pop-up menu). The appropriate extension-hiding controls appear before you.

Tip: It's a good idea to run a compatibility report if you're sending the document to people using a different version of Word. Do so by clicking the Compatibility Report button at the bottom of the Save As dialog box. Word runs a compatibility test and serves notice if it finds any issues. (You can do the same thing from the Compatibility tab of the Toolbox. For details, see Chapter 18.)

Backing Up

No discussion of saving would be complete without a word about backing up your work. Saving preserves your document in its current condition; backing up creates an additional, *extra* copy of the same file. For an extra measure of security, you can place this extra copy on a USB flash drive, an external hard drive, or even your electronic iDisk (see *Mac OS X: The Missing Manual*) in case something goes wrong with the copy on your Mac's hard drive.

Word can create backup copies automatically. Here's the process:

1. **Choose File → Save As and click Options.**

   You can also access this tab of Save options by choosing Word → Preferences → Save button.

2. **Turn on the "Always create backup copy" checkbox and click OK. Click Save.**

   Word saves both the current document and an identical backup copy in the same folder; the duplicate has "Backup of" in front of its file name.

From now on, Word will automatically update the backup whenever you save the original document, providing a useful "last saved" version.

GEM IN THE ROUGH

Slick Saving Tricks

Renaming or moving the Finder icon of an open document used to be a no-no. But these days you can be rather cavalier. With a Word document open on the screen, try switching back to the Finder and renaming it. When you return to the Word document and next use the Save command, the Word document instantly takes on the new name you gave it in the Finder!

Now try switching to the Finder and moving the icon into a different folder. When you return to Word, ⌘-click the title

of your Word window, you'll see that the program somehow knows about the icon's new location without missing a beat.

Another gem in the rough: When you close a document without first saving changes, Word displays the usual "Do you want to save the changes?" dialog box. Your choices—Don't Save, Cancel, and Save—can all be triggered from the keyboard. Just press D, C, or S, respectively.

Printing

Even with so many people relying on email and the Web for communicating information, you can't use Word for very long without printing something on paper. As with so much else in Word, printing can be as simple or as complicated as you care to make it.

The Print Button

Printing doesn't get any simpler. Click the printer icon on the Standard toolbar to print one copy of your document to the currently selected printer. No dialog box, no page ranges, no flexibility.

File → Print

This method is still simple, but lets you be more specific. Choose File → Print (or press ⌘-P) to open the Print dialog box, where you can tell Word how many copies of which pages of your document to print (and which printer you want to use, if you have several).

The Print dialog box is comprised of a series of *panels* that you expose by choosing from the pop-up menu in the middle of the box. This remodeling was much more than cosmetic, however, as you can now do things from the Print window (such as add a border or create an Adobe Acrobat [PDF] document), which used to require opening a separate dialog box—or a separate program!

The features in the Print box vary depending upon which printer you choose, but here are a few of the classics.

Copies and Pages

This panel is the preselected pop-up menu choice when the Print dialog box opens. Often, these are the only settings you need.

- **Copies.** Enter the number of copies you need. Hit Return to print, or Tab to move on to more settings.

- **Collated.** Turning on this checkbox prints out each copy of your document in page order. For instance, if you print multiple copies of a three-page letter with collating turned off, you'll get all your copies of page one, followed by all page twos, and so on. With collating turned *on,* you'll get page one, page two, page three, followed by another complete set of pages one, two, and three, and so on.

- **Pages.** The All button is initially selected, but you can also hit Tab and enter page numbers for a page range. For more control over which pages to print, read on.

Tip: If you don't see "Print odd/even pages only" or other common printing options, choose Microsoft Word from the pop-up menu, as described in Figure 1-11.

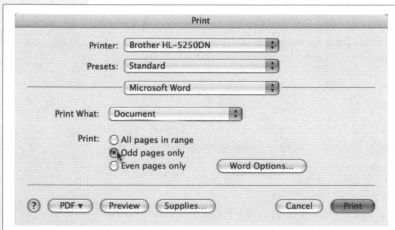

Figure 1-11:
The ability to choose odd or even pages is hidden behind the easily overlooked Microsoft Word pop-up menu choice. You can print double-sided pages—even if your printer doesn't have duplex capabilities—if you print the odd pages first, then turn them over, reinsert them into the printer, and then print the even sides. (Experiment with just a couple of pages first until you figure out how to get them right side up on both sides.)

- **Range.** Clicking this button activates a text box where you can be more specific about which pages you want Word to print. Actually, you can be very specific. To print an individual page, type its number in this box (*12*, for example). Separate additional single pages by commas. (Typing *12, 20*, for example, prints page 12 and page 20.) You can add ranges to your print batch as well, by using hyphens, like this: *12, 20, 25-30, 100-102*. These combinations prints page 12, page 20, pages 25 through 30, and 100 through 102.

Layout

This menu choice offers a shortcut to a feature formerly available only in the Page Setup dialog box: the ability to print more than one Word page on each sheet of paper—a great paper-saving tool for printing rough drafts.

The Layout panel also features a surprise: the Border menu. You can choose one of four simple page border options (single hairline, double hairline, and so on). The beauty and power of this menu is that you can apply the border to only one print job, or only one *page*, without actually changing your document in the "Borders and Shading" dialog box. (When you choose a border type from the menu, the preview box at the left presents an idea of what the border will look like.)

Print settings

The options in this panel (and even the name of the panel itself) depend on the kind of printer you've selected. Here's where you can choose from a list of paper types (plain, glossy, and so on), and whether you want to use black and white or color. Choosing the print option that matches the type of paper you're using effectively changes settings in the printer (amount of ink released, printing speed, and so on) to achieve the best results on that paper. If you're using photo paper to print documents containing digital photographs, for example, it's especially important to specify that here.

It's also where you can adjust print *quality*—high for good looks, low to save ink when printing out rough drafts or file copies.

Advanced settings

This panel, too, appears only for certain printers. It may provide finer control over quality, such as letting you specify the exact dpi (number of dots per inch) that the printer uses. For a professional-looking invitation or newsletter, for example, use at least 300 dpi.

Microsoft Word

This panel lets you restrict your printout to odd or even pages, as described in Figure 1-11. It also offers the **Print what** pop-up menu, which is usually set to Document. However, this menu lets you print out some fascinating behind-the-scenes Word information sheets. They include:

- **Document Properties** provides a page of statistics for the pathologically curious. In addition to the usual number of pages, the title, and the author, you can see how many minutes you've spent on the document.

- If you have tracked changes or comments visible in Word's reviewing feature (see page 171), choose **List of Markup** to print out lists of the comments, additions and deletions that appear in the document. (They print on separate pages, not the way you see them on screen.)

- If you do a lot of work with **Styles** (if you're charged with keeping them consistent in all your company documents, for example, or if you're just a total control freak), this choice lets you print a list of all styles the current document uses, complete with a full description of each. (Much more on Styles in Chapter 3.)

- Similarly, if you've created a lot of **Auto Text entries** in your copy of Word 2008 and you're getting confused, this option prints out a list of them. You can get the same information by choosing Tools → AutoCorrect → AutoText tab and scrolling through the list.

  If you're one of those power users who uses more than one *global template* (see page 226), this command is the way to create a separate AutoText cheat sheet for each template. It's also a quick way to print a list of all your address-book contacts, since they're considered AutoText entries; that way, you can review the list and decide which ones you want to add or delete.

- **Key Assignments** produces a handy cheat sheet to remind you of the keyboard-shortcut keystrokes you've created, as described at the end of Chapter 20.

This panel also shows the **Word Options** button, which opens the Print tab of the Preferences dialog box.

Summary

This command calls up a box showing all current print settings: number of copies, page range, layout options, and so on. It's a quick way to review all your choices with one stroke of the pop-up menu. You can't print this information, and probably won't need to. Use the Custom option (described below) to save your favorite settings.

Saving custom settings

You've gone through every choice on the pop-up menu and gotten everything just the way you want it. For instance, you know you'll always print two copies, always want them collated, and almost always want to print with black ink (saving the more expensive color ink for photographs). To save this combination of settings for repeated use, choose "Save As" from the Presets pop-up menu *after* you've set all the other panels to your liking. Fill in a name for your presets, and you're good to go.

From then on, all you have to do is press ⌘-P and choose the name from the Presets menu in the Print dialog box. Then press Return to print, or you can go on to adjust any of the settings if you need to deviate from your usual custom set (print three copies instead of your usual two, for example).

PDF

This button is the key to one of Mac OS X's best features: its ability to turn any printable document—including Word documents, of course—into a PDF (Acrobat) file.

Because all Macs and PCs can view Adobe Acrobat documents, you can attach a PDF file to an email and know that your recipient, no matter what kind of computer she has, will be able to open and read it, with all your fonts and layout intact. That makes PDF an ideal format for resumes, flyers or brochures, booklets, and other documents that need to look good for their intended audiences.

To "print" your Word document as an Acrobat file, simply click the PDF button at the bottom of the Window and choose Save as PDF from the pop-up menu. But, as one peek into this pop-up menu shows, Mac OS X is willing to do a lot more with your PDF than just save it. Here's what else you might consider doing:

- **Save PDF as PostScript.** This file format is intended for use by graphic designers or print shops. It has the most accurate printing instructions for their PostScript laser printers.

- **Fax PDF.** Instead of printing your file, this option sends it to Mac OS X's built-in fax system. If your computer has a modem and a telephone line connection, you can enter a phone number and send your document to any fax machine.

- **Compress PDF** creates a smaller PDF file—at the expense of quality. This is a good choice for e-mailing or viewing on screen, but not for printing.

- **Encrypt PDF** creates a password-protected PDF document. It can only be opened by someone who knows the password you assign to it.

- **Mail PDF** opens Apple Mail and attaches the PDF to a new outgoing message. This only works with Apple Mail—even if you've designated Entourage, for example, as your regular email program.

- **Save as PDF-X.** This option saves a streamlined style of PDF favored in the printing industry.

- **Save as PDF to iPhoto** creates your PDF and automatically deposits it in your iPhoto library—which is a great place to keep all kinds of graphic files, not just photographs.

- **Save PDF to Web Receipts Folder** is intended as a way to save copies of receipts for the things you buy online, without actually printing them out. This way, the records from your online buying sprees end up in your Home → Documents → Web Receipts folder.

- **Edit menu** lets you tidy up this PDF menu, removing those commands you never use.

Preview

The Preview button is your gateway to the magnificent built-in Mac OS X print preview function. Click the button to get a picture of what your page will look like when printed. Mac OS X actually creates a PDF file of your document on the fly, and pops it open in your Mac's Preview program. Accordingly, you get to use all of Preview's bells and whistles—things Word's built-in Print Preview never dreamed of. You can flip forward and backward through your recently viewed pages, type in a page number to jump to it, page through your document a page at a time, zoom in and out, and even choose a page to view from a drawer containing each page in the document. And, oh yeah, after giving it the once over, you can also print the document if you so desire (click the Print button).

The Preview toolbar includes the following buttons:

- **Drawer.** Clicking this button slides out the drawer that displays the pages of the current document. Simply click a page to go to it—a convenient way to preview long documents.

- **Previous/Next.** Pages up and down through the pages displayed in the drawer.

- **Page Window.** Type a number to go directly to that page.

- **Back/Forward.** Click the arrows to flip through the document pages you've viewed.

- **Zoom In/Out.** Clicking the + magnifying glass zooms in the document. That's good for studying images within the document, or when you left your glasses in the bedroom. Clicking the – magnifying glass zooms out.

- **Tool Mode.** The Tool Mode offers three modes. The left button (a cross) activates the hand tool, which lets you move and scroll through the document. Clicking the A button to activate the text tool to select text within the document. The dotted square button lets you select a section of a page (to zoom in on, for example). The last button is the Annotate Tool—click and hold this button to choose between Text Annotation and Oval Annotation. Text annotation lets you draw a box on your document into which you can type a comment. Oval annotation, on the other hand, lets you circle portions of the document requiring your readers' attention.

Tip: Yes, you can also turn your Word files into PDF documents using the Print dialog box as described on page 27—but this way, you get to review it before committing.

Supplies

Clicking this button takes you on a side trip from printing to the online Apple Store, which offers to sell you ink and toner for your selected printer. When you're done ordering (or not), you'll find the print dialog boxes patiently waiting for you when you return.

Cancel

Click here if you've reconsidered the whole printing thing. Pressing Esc also dismisses the Print dialog box.

Print

When you're ready to print your document, after making any adjustments in the print dialog box, clicking this button will get the job done. And, since this button is pulsing blue, so will a press of the Return key.

File → Page Setup

Some of the settings that appear when you choose Page Setup are a function of your printer's software, not of Word. As in the Print dialog box, choose your printer from the pop-up menu at the top to see exactly what's available. Generally you'll find options like these:

- **Paper Size.** Make sure the page size here matches what you've got in your printer. You can choose envelopes as well as paper, but if you use Word's envelope feature (see page 277), this setting is taken care of automatically.

- **Orientation.** You can change thedirection that Word prints the page on the paper (vertical *portrait* versus horizontal *landscape* mode).

- **Scaling.** Most of the time, you print at 100%, but in some cases this might not be your best option. For instance, if your document is just two lines too long to fit on one page, try printing at 90%. (You'll know if you've adjusted the document correctly by checking the File → Print Preview before committing the document to paper.)

You can set custom page sizes by clicking Custom Paper Size, as shown in Figure 1-12. Turn on "Use custom page size," and then enter the dimensions of your paper. Remember that width is the measurement of the edge that you feed into the printer. After setting up your page, click OK (or press Return) to save your page settings. Click Reset to return all settings to their original configuration.

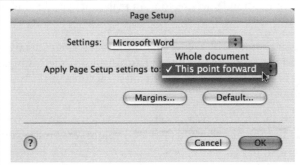

Figure 1-12:
Choose Microsoft Word from the Settings menu if you need to change the printer settings for just part of the document. Then choose "This point forward" from the "Apply Page Setup settings to" pop-up menu. This feature comes in handy if you have letters and envelopes together in the same document, for example.

For more advanced settings, choose Microsoft Word from the Settings menu. If you need to adjust the document's margins before printing, clicking the Margins button is a quick way to open the Format → Document → Margins tab, as described on page 593). Finally, if you find yourself frequently changing from the default settings to your own configuration (2 Up, 99% reduction, and so on), click the Default button to make that your *new* default page setup. Word asks if you want to change the default settings for all new documents based on the Normal template (in other words, all new, blank Word documents that you open).

Note: Clicking Default in the Page Setup dialog box changes the defaults only for the settings *in the Page Setup dialog box.* If you took a side trip to the Margins dialog box, those settings won't be affected. To change the default margins, click Default in the Format → Document → Margins tab itself.

Print Preview

Word's Print Preview feature was created in the old days, before Apple added a system-wide Preview function to Mac OS X itself. Like the Mac OS X version, the built-in Word view lets you see an onscreen representation of how your document will look on paper—a terrific way to avoid wasting paper on printouts that get chopped at the margin or have straggling one-line orphans on the last page. To see for yourself, choose File → Print Preview. (*Keyboard shortcut:* ⌘-F2.) A special preview window opens, displaying a full view of one page of your document.

Because most windows are smaller than 8.5"×11", the image is probably reduced. You can see the percentage of reduction in the Print Preview toolbar, as shown in Figure 1-13. (Unlike most toolbars, you can't choose this one from the View menu; you have to open the Print Preview window to see it.)

The Print Preview window opens in magnification mode. For a closer look at a certain word or a particular portion of your document, click the page with the magnifying-glass icon (Figure 1-13). You can also change the view size by typing a percentage in the Zoom box (also shown in Figure 1-13). Remember, 100% isn't necessarily life-size; it's the size that lets you see one full printed sheet at a time.

If your close inspection turns up an error, turn off the magnifying glass by clicking its toolbar icon, putting you in Edit mode, where you can make changes directly to your document.

If your document is going to be bound with facing pages, you can see how the two-page spread will look by clicking (and holding the cursor down on) the Multiple Pages pop-up button. Drag to highlight two or more panes, and then click; Word simultaneously displays that number of pages.

The most powerful button on the Print Preview toolbar is the "Shrink to Fit" button. When the last page of a document has just a few lines, you may want to avoid wasting that whole extra piece of paper. Or suppose you've been given a five-page limit, and you're just a couple of paragraphs too long. If you have neither the time nor the inclination to edit down your document, you can click the "Shrink to Fit"

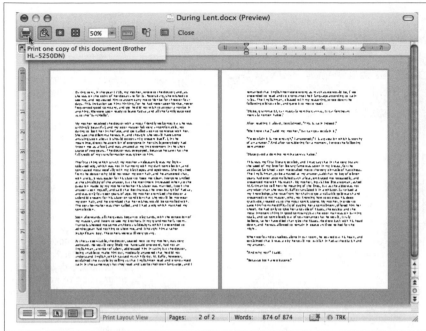

Figure 1-13:
Word's Print Preview window displays an overview of how your document will look on the page. When you're ready to print, click the printer icon on this toolbar to immediately print one copy without visiting the Print dialog box. You can dismiss the Print Preview window by clicking the close box, pressing Esc, or clicking back in any other document window.

button. Word adjusts the type sizes, across the entire document, just enough to eliminate that last fraction of a page.

Tip: If you don't like the effect of "Shrink to Fit", you can choose Edit → "Undo Shrink to Fit", press F1, or press ⌘-Z. But once you save and close the file, you can't restore the original font sizes with the Undo command. You have to do so manually.

Pointing to the other buttons on the Print Preview toolbar, without clicking, prompts their identifying screen tip labels. These other buttons include:

- **View Ruler.** Click to make both horizontal and vertical rulers appear. As shown in Figure 1-14, you can use these rulers to adjust the margins of your document quickly and easily.

- **Full screen.** Because of the reduced view, Microsoft gives you this one-click way to maximize the available screen space. Clicking here collapses your tool palettes, enlarges the window to the edges of your monitor, and hides Word's usual assortment of status bars around the window edges.

- **Close button.** Click to return to whatever view you were using before opening the print preview.

Print Preferences

Believe it or not, Word 2008 offers yet another swath of printing settings—none of which even appear in the usual Print and Page Setup dialog boxes.

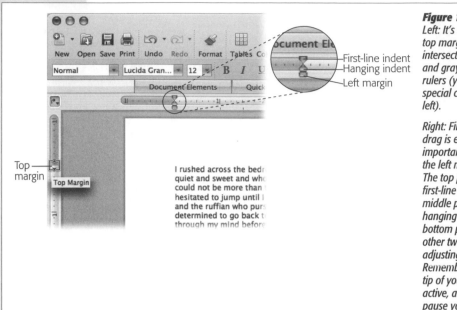

Figure 1-14:
Left: It's easy to adjust the top margin. Just drag the intersection of the white and gray regions on the rulers (you can see the special cursor shape at left).

Right: Finding the spot to drag is extremely important when adjusting the left margin markers. The top part controls the first-line indent, the middle part controls the hanging indents, and the bottom part moves the other two in concert, adjusting the left margin. Remember, only the very tip of your arrow cursor is active, and when you pause your cursor for a moment over the margin markers, a screen tip appears.

Specifically, the controls that govern the printing of fields, hyperlinks, drawings, and other advanced features are tucked away in the Word → Preferences → Print dialog box, as shown in Figure 1-15.

- When **Update fields** is turned on, Word checks all the *fields* in your document (page 235) and verifies they contain the most recent information. The date is updated, for example, and captions are renumbered.

- Turning on **Update links** tells Word to check all hyperlinks (page 46) in the document and fix any whose destination document *on your hard drive* has moved. (Word can't update *Web* links this way, alas. Instead, you have to update Web links manually, as explained on page 336.)

- **Reverse print order** tells Word to print starting with the last page first. If your printer puts out sheets right side up, with each new sheet on top of the previous one, this option saves you from shuffling the pages into their proper order.

- Turning on **Document properties** prints the information from the General, Summary, and Statistics tabs of the File → Properties dialog box onto a separate sheet at the end of the document.

- When **Field codes** is turned on, Word prints the field codes (see page 235) instead of the *results* of those codes. For instance, a Date field would print as { DATE \@ "M/d/yy" * MERGEFORMAT } instead of 10/31/08.

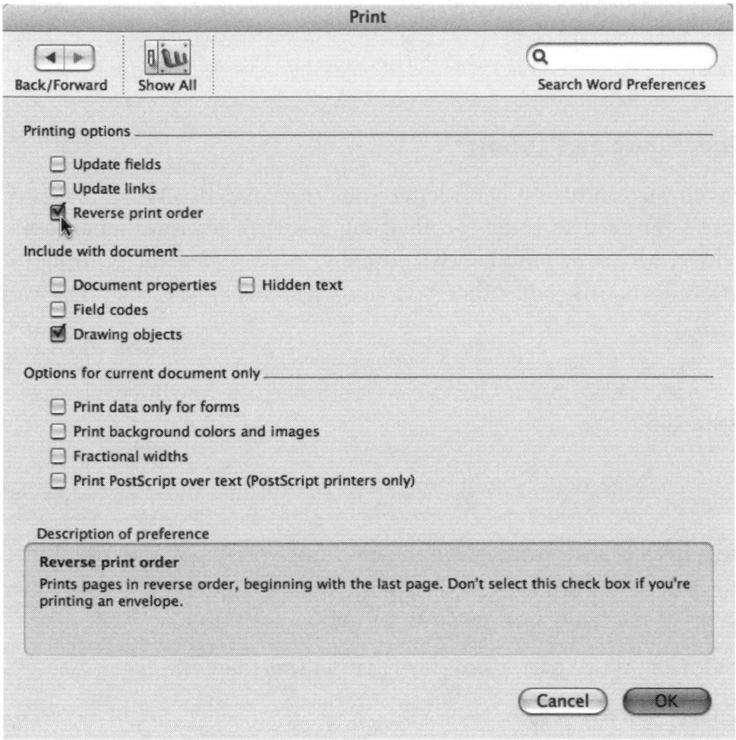

Figure 1-15:
The three checkboxes under "Options for current document only" need to be turned on each time you use them. For example, if you really do want to use up your expensive ink and make your document harder to read, you'll have to turn on "Print background colors and images." You can also access this dialog box by clicking the Word Options button in the Microsoft Word panel of the Print dialog box.

- Turning on **Drawing objects** prints all images, including drawings, paintings, Clip Art, and WordArt. Turning it off suppresses images and prints text only.

- When **Hidden text** is turned on, any hidden text (page 100) in your document prints, along with all the other text.

- **Print data only for forms** suppresses the main text of the form document and prints only information that has been entered into form fields, as described on page 262.

- The precision that the Mac can use to place characters onscreen is limited to the screen's resolution of 1/72 of an inch. But with **Fractional widths** turned on, the printer possesses much greater precision and flexibility to place each character in its typographically correct position on the page. For the best-looking printouts, turn on Fractional widths just before printing.

Note, however, that when Fractional widths is turned on, Word's approximation of the printed appearance can result in overlapping, awkward-looking spacing on the screen. (Interestingly, when you switch to Page Layout view, Word *automatically* turns on Fractional widths, because Page Layout view is intended to show you how the page will look when printed.)

Note: If you're not connected to a PostScript printer and haven't used any <print> fields (page 235) in your document, the "Print PostScript over text" box is grayed out. If you have—you desktop publishing professional, you—turning on this box prints watermarks and other PostScript-generated figures *on top of* the text.

Printing Envelopes and Labels

There's a big temptation to just hand-letter your envelope, but Word makes it so easy that there's no need to settle for anything less than a professional-looking, printed envelope. Moreover, the Labels command is equipped for printing business cards, Rolodex cards, and other odd-shaped items. These are tools worth learning.

Note: You can also print a whole mass of labels or envelopes at once, based on addresses in your Office Address Book; see page 36.

Printing envelopes

Before starting, inspect your printer and the envelope you're going to use. Practice fitting the envelope into the feed slot. Check the printer's manual to see if you need to flip any levers or mash any buttons to accommodate envelopes.

Now it's time for the Word part of envelope printing, as follows:

1. **Choose Tools → Envelopes.**

   The Envelope dialog box opens, as shown in Figure 1-16.

2. **Fill in the Delivery address and Return address boxes.**

   To change the return address, turn off the "Use my address" box. (Word automatically fills in your name and address as you entered them in the Word → Preferences → User Information panel.)

   Alternatively, click the address-card icon located next to the address box to select a name and address from the Office Address Book.

   Click the Font button to choose any of Word's fonts, type styles, and font sizes, as described on page 92.

3. **Click one of the Position buttons; use the arrow buttons in the Address Position dialog box to adjust the addresses on the envelope, if you wish.**

   The Preview pane displays the results of your repositioning actions. Click OK when done.

4. **Click Page Setup or Custom in the Printing Options pane.**

   If your printer has an envelope slot, and you're using a standard envelope size (as opposed to an oddly shaped greeting card envelope, for example), you're in luck. Click Page Setup and choose the envelope size in the Print dialog box (#10 is a standard business envelope). Click OK to return to the Envelope dialog box.

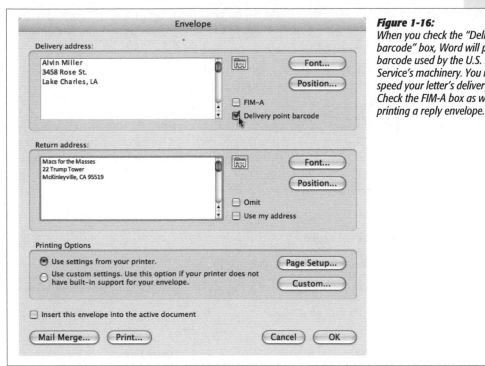

Figure 1-16:
When you check the "Delivery point barcode" box, Word will print the barcode used by the U.S. Postal Service's machinery. You may actually speed your letter's delivery as a result. Check the FIM-A box as well if you're printing a reply envelope.

Click Custom if your printer doesn't have an envelope feed or doesn't accommodate your size envelope. In the Custom Page Options dialog box (Figure 1-17), choose the "Envelope size" menu, and then click the preview window that most closely resembles how you plan to insert that envelope into your printer's feed. Click OK when done.

You're almost ready to print. When you do, Word will create a new document to hold the envelope text. To store the envelope in the same document that you've been working in, check "Insert this envelope into the active document."

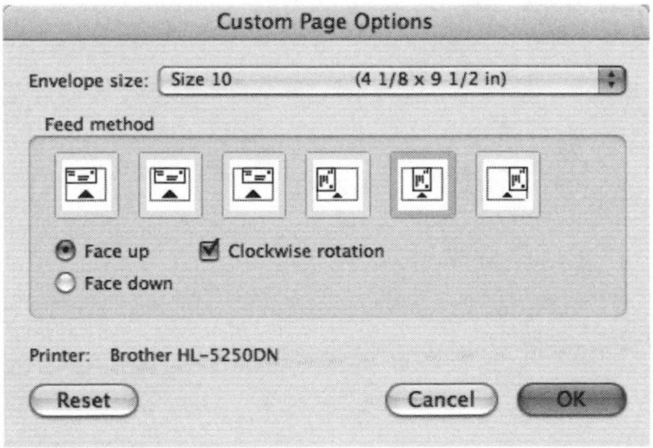

Figure 1-17:
When you turn the "Clockwise rotation" box on and off, and click the "Face up" and "Face down" radio buttons, the small preview windows show you the differences in how you'll be feeding the envelope into your printer.

5. If you'd like to use the envelope you've just set up in a *mail merge* (see page 262), click Mail Merge to open the Mail Merge Manager and use the envelope with a list of addresses.

Otherwise, click Print or OK to print the envelope with the current address.

Printing labels

As mentioned above, Word's label function can print more than plain white address labels. You can make name tags, Rolodex or index cards, postcards, and so on. When you buy blank labels or cards for printing, they usually come on a convenient 8.5" × 11" sheet that fits nicely into your printer's feed. You can then detach the individual labels after printing.

To print labels in Word, proceed as follows:

1. **Choose Tools → Labels.**

    The Labels dialog box opens, as shown in Figure 1-18.

2. **Type an address—or other label information—into the Address window.**

    See Figure 1-18 for full details.

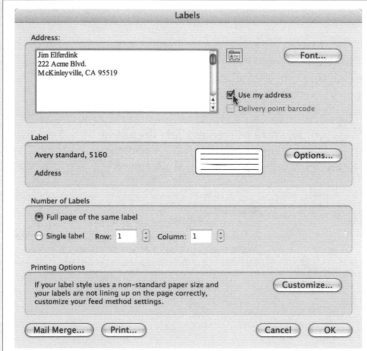

Figure 1-18:
When typing in the Address window, click Font to use any of Word's fonts or text formatting. Check the "Use my address" box to have Word insert your name and address from the Word → Preferences → User information tab (which is also reflected in the Entourage Address Book entry you created for yourself). Click the contact icon to choose a name and address from the Entourage address book.

3. **Click Options in the Label pane to tell Word what kind of label or card you're using, as shown in Figure 1-19.**

   The choices may seem overwhelming, but Word can help. Once you've chosen a manufacturer and item number, click Details to see a preview (with measurements) of the label itself.

   If you have an odd-sized or unidentified label, click New Label. Word opens a dialog box where you can enter your custom dimensions. (You'll need a ruler to measure the label itself in this case; however, Word has enough built-in labels that you'll rarely need to get this creative.) Click OK.

   If your odd-sized labels come on odd-sized sheets (something other than 8.5"×11"), click Customize in the Printing Options pane. Here you set the page size and feeding method, as described earlier and shown in Figure 1-20.

4. **If you're printing only one label, click the "Single label" radio button and choose a row and column to tell Word where to print the label.**

   This way, if you have a sheet with some blank labels left over, you can have Word print on one of those remaining labels. No waste!

   If you're printing more than one label, on the other hand, click Mail Merge and use the Mail Merge Manager (see page 263) to give Word a list of addresses to use.

5. **Click Print or OK when done.**

   To avoid wasting labels, print on a blank piece of paper first. Hold the printed sheet over a label sheet (preferably against a window or light) to see if the labels are going to line up. If they don't align correctly, choose Tools → Labels, click Options, and click Details to adjust the print area and spacing of each label.

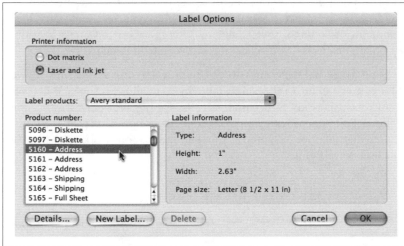

Figure 1-19:
Choose the name of the manufacturer from the "Label products" menu before choosing from the "Product number" list. Look on the label package for this information.

Sending It Electronically

These days, it's rare that a document is sent into the world on paper or disk. Instead, it's usually transmitted electronically. Word's File → Send To command gives you two ways of transmitting your work electronically: via email and as a PowerPoint presentation.

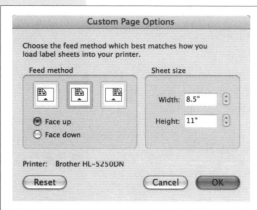

Figure 1-20:
Practice on a blank sheet of paper to determine whether your printer feeds face up or face down, and which corner the labels start to print from. Then, if necessary, use the buttons in this dialog box to match Word with what your printer is doing. If you're using one of the standard label types, you probably won't have to bother with these settings.

- **File → Send To → Mail Recipient (as HTML).** This alternative offers a prettier, though riskier, way of emailing a Word document. It converts the Word text into HTML and plunks it directly into the body of an email message. Why riskier? Because your recipient won't be able to see it if her email program's HTML options are turned off or nonexistent.

- **File → Send To → Mail Recipient (as Attachment).** This long-winded command launches Entourage and opens a new email message. The document you were just working on in Word is automatically attached to the message, and your address book is open—ready and waiting for you to choose a recipient from your list of contacts. (See Chapter 10 for more on Entourage's Address Book.) Congratulations—you've just saved several tedious steps.

- **File → Send To → PowerPoint.** You can import a Word outline into Power-Point for conversion into a slideshow, but why go to all the trouble? When your Word document is ready to become part of your big show, choose this command. PowerPoint opens with your Word document now displayed as a Power-Point presentation. See Chapter 16 for full details on working with your document in PowerPoint.

Editing in Word

Despite all the whiz-bang, 21st-century innovations in Word 2008, some things haven't changed, including…well, typing and clicking. The basics of adding, deleting, and moving text around work essentially the same way as they did in Word 1.0, which fit on a single floppy disk and had to be started up with a hand crank.

Most of the editing and formatting techniques in Word and the other Office programs require a two-step procedure: select, then do. That is, first select the thing (character, word, paragraph, sentence) that you intend to act upon, then use keystrokes or menu commands to tell the Mac *what* to do to it.

The Many Ways to Select Text

Dragging with the mouse is the way most people first learned to select text. In this time-honored method, you click at the start of where you want to select text, and while holding down the mouse button, drag until the text in question is highlighted.

Note: Don't forget Word's multi-selection feature, which has been around since Word X. You can select bits of text far apart from each other simultaneously and then cut, copy, and paste them all at once. You can grab a single sentence from the first paragraph of a document and a couple sentences from the second—and scrap everything else (see page 42).

Assuming you mastered dragging a long time ago, here are some more streamlined ways to select text. (Some of these moves are second nature to power users.)

- **Shift-arrow.** If you undershoot or overshoot the mark when dragging manually, don't start over—just remember the Shift–arrow key trick. After you release the mouse button, don't click again or do anything else. Hold down the Shift key and then press the arrow keys to expand or shrink the size of the selection—one character or line at a time. Add the Option key to expand or shrink the selection one *word* at a time.

- **Dragging with the mouse and Option key.** When dragging with the mouse, you'll notice that Word highlights text in one-word chunks, under the assumption that you'll very rarely want to edit only the first syllable of a word. Even if you begin dragging in the center of a word, the program instantly highlights all the way from the beginning to the end of that word, including the space after it. Usually, this behavior is what you want, and lets you drag somewhat sloppily.

Tip: If you dislike the way Word automatically selects in one-word increments, you can turn it off by choosing Word → Preferences and clicking the Edit tab. The checkbox called "When selecting, automatically select entire word" is the on/off switch for this feature.

Every now and then, however, you *do* want to edit only the first syllable of a word—perhaps to correct a typo. In those situations, Word's tendency to highlight the entire word can induce madness. On those occasions, press the Option key as you drag. Word responds by respecting the precise movements of your mouse.

Tip: Option-dragging *vertically* is a sneaky trick that lets you highlight only a tall, skinny block—a useful way to shave off the garbage characters at the beginnings of the lines of text you've pasted in from an email message, for example.

- **Clicking with the mouse.** Using the mouse and *not* dragging can save you time. Double-click a word to select that one word as a whole. Triple-click to select an entire paragraph.

  With one paragraph selected in this way, hold down Shift and click the mouse elsewhere, even pages away, to select more text in one-paragraph increments.

- **Using the Shift key and the mouse.** By using the Shift key, you can enjoy all the convenience of using the mouse without the wrist-wearying effort of holding down the mouse button. Just click at where you want to start selecting, hold down the Shift key, then click the mouse a second time where you want the selection to end (even if you have to scroll the document between clicks). Word highlights everything between the two clicks. If you overshoot the mark, you can back up in one-unit (letter, word, paragraph, whatever) increments by holding down Shift and clicking back into the selection. (Unfortunately, you can't change the *beginning* of the selection using this method.)

- **Using Shift with other keys.** If you do a lot of word processing, you may find it faster to keep your hands at the keyboard as much as possible, without stopping to grasp the mouse. In fact, it's possible to select text without using the mouse at all. Just use the arrow keys to get to where you want to begin selecting. Hold down the Shift key and use the arrow keys to adjust the size of the selection—line by line for the up and down arrow keys, and one character at a time for the right and left arrow keys.

If you hold down Option and Shift, the right and left arrow keys select in one-*word* increments, and the up and down arrow keys select in one-*paragraph* increments. (Your original selection is preserved, however, even if it was only part of a paragraph.)

You can use the Shift key with the Home, End, and Page Up/ Page Down keys as well. **Shift-Home** or **Shift-End** selects from the insertion point to the beginning or end of the line.

Shift-Page Up/Page Down selects one "screenful" (about half a page, depending on your monitor size) up or one down from the insertion point.

- **Using ⌘ with the mouse.** Here's a great command to memorize: ⌘-click anywhere within a sentence to select exactly that sentence, neatly and quickly, period and all. Release the ⌘ key and click to deselect the sentence, then ⌘-click again to select a different sentence.

- **Using the selection strip.** To the left of your text, just inside the left window edge, is a thin margin—an empty white space about a quarter of an inch wide. It's an invisible but extremely useful tool called the selection strip. (In Page Layout view, the selection strip is beefier—about as wide as the visible margin.)

When your cursor ventures into this area, the arrow pointer points to the *right* instead of left as usual. Now you can click once to highlight a single line of text, twice to select a paragraph, or three times to select the whole document.

Tip: ⌘-clicking in the selection strip also highlights the entire document—unless some text is already selected. If that's the case, ⌘-clicking selects an additional *line* instead. As for the peculiar highlighting that appears when you Option-⌘-click in the selection strip: Well, you tell *us* what Word's doing.

You can also drag vertically through the selection strip to highlight a vertical chunk of text—one of this strip's most frequent uses. (As always, you can click there once, then Shift-click elsewhere in your document to highlight all lines of text between the two clicks.)

- **Using Extend mode.** Pressing F8 activates Extend mode, the most powerful (if disorienting) way to select text. Position the insertion point where you want to begin selecting, activate Extend mode, then use the arrow and Page Up or Down keys to select text automatically. (Microsoft has removed the Extend mode EXT button from the Status bar in Word 2008—so you can only tell it's active by the odd selection behavior.) To cancel Extend mode, press ⌘-period to turn it off.

Exactly as when you're *not* in Extend mode, pressing the Option key with the arrows forces Word to select in one-word (right and left arrow) or one-paragraph (up and down arrow) increments.

Note: Early versions of Word let you use the numeric keypad as cursor keys. By pressing Shift-Clear, you brought out the pad's second personality as a navigation keyboard, where the keys surrounding the 5 key acted as cursor keys, the 0 key acted as Insert, and so on. But Microsoft evidently fielded one too many desperate tech-support calls from customers who'd entered this mode accidentally, and couldn't figure out why they could no longer type numbers with the numeric keypad. Ever since Word 2001, the number keypad has done just one thing—type numbers.

Multi-Selection

To use Word's multiple-selection feature, highlight a piece of text using any of the methods described above involving the mouse. Then press ⌘ as you use the mouse to select more text. Bingo: You've highlighted two separate chunks of text.

For instance, drag to select part of a sentence. Then scroll down a couple of pages and, while pressing ⌘, triple-click to select another entire paragraph. Finally, you can ⌘-double-click a single word to add it to the batch selection.

Note: Selecting text using the Shift key and keyboard, then pressing ⌘ and using the mouse to select additional areas creates (or adds to) a multi-selection. Multi-selections have to be in the same document (you can't select text simultaneously in different windows).

When you're done selecting bits of text here and there, you can operate on them en masse. For example:

- You can make them all bold or italic with one fell swoop.
- When you cut, copy, or paste (as described in the next section), the command acts upon all your multi-selections at once.
- You can drag any *one* of the highlighted portions to a new area, confident that the other chunks will come along for the ride. All of the selected areas will wind up consolidated in their new location.

Tip: This feature has special ramifications for the Find command described on page 55. The Find dialog box has a "Highlight all items found" checkbox. It makes the *software* perform your work for you, simultaneously highlighting every occurrence of a certain word or phrase within the entire file.

Moving Text Around

Three commands—Cut, Copy, and Paste—appear in every word processing program known to humankind, Word included. But Office 2008 has more powerful ways of manipulating text once you've selected it.

Copy (or Cut) and Paste

To copy text, highlight it as described above. Then choose Edit → Copy (or click the corresponding Standard toolbar button), click the mouse or use the arrow keys to transport the insertion point to your new location, and choose Edit → Paste. A copy of the original text appears in the new locale. To move text instead of copying it, use Edit → Cut and Edit → Paste; the selected text moves from one place to another, leaving no trace behind.

Alternatively, after selecting the text, you can also Control-click the selection (or click the right mouse button if you have one), and choose Copy or Cut from the shortcut menu. Similarly, when you arrive at the place where you want to paste, you can Control-click, then select Paste.

If this procedure sounds like a lot of work, you're right—especially if you're trying to choose these menu commands using a laptop trackpad. Cut/Copy and Paste is the sequence you'll probably use extremely often. By learning the keystroke equivalents, the time you save avoiding the mouse really adds up. For example:

Table 2-1. *Copy, Cut, and Paste commands*

Function	Command	Keystrokes
Copy	Edit → Copy	⌘-C or F3
Cut	Edit → Cut	⌘-X or F2
Paste	Edit → Paste	⌘-V or F4

Note: Long, long ago, when keyboard commands were first handed out, Print got in line ahead of Paste and received the coveted ⌘-P keystroke assignment. But using ⌘-V for paste makes sense since V's right next to the C key, so all the editing keys—undo, Cut, Copy, and Paste—line up in a neat row on your keyboard. The V also looks like the caret mark proofreaders use to mean "insert." Or just think of V as standing for *voilà, there it is!*

The Paste Options smart button

No matter which Cut/Copy and Paste method you use, you'll notice a small, square button hovering over the surface of your document just by where you pasted. This is Word 2008's Paste Options smart button, shown in Figure 2-1.

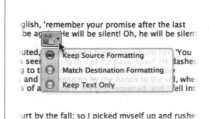

Figure 2-1:
Appearing immediately after you paste, the Paste Options smart button lets you choose exactly how you want imported text to look with a simple click of the mouse. Instant gratification!

Clicking this button provides three options: Keep Source Formatting, Match Destination Formatting, and Keep Text Only. If you choose Keep Source Formatting, the text looks just like it did when you lifted it from its previous residence. Go this route if you like the way the original text looked, and want to import that styling into your current document. For instance, if you spent a lot of time getting the formatting of your newsletter heading just right, and now want to use it again in next month's issue, use Keep Source Formatting to preserve your hard work.

Conversely, if you choose Match Destination Formatting, your text takes on the formatting of its new surroundings. This selection is a popular choice because it lets you import text from disparate locations without that imported-from-disparate-locations look.

The final option, Keep Text Only, does just that—keeps the text only, eliminating any additional formatting, such as bold, italics, and so on. You may need to click Keep Text Only *after* you choose to retain source destination formatting. Although those options format text as described above, they don't remove bold, italics, underlining, and so on. For example, if you imported text that was 14 point Verdana bold and pasted it into the middle of your 10 point Times font, selecting Match Destination Formatting would convert the text to 10 point Times, but you would then need to select Text Only to clear the bold.

Paste Special

The Edit → Paste Special command dictates—as described below—how your text looks and acts once it reaches its final destination. The options include pasting the information as either a linked object or embedded object, and various types of text formatting. Your first choice is to decide whether to paste your text directly into the document or paste it as a link. To choose, click the appropriate radio button in the Paste Special dialog box. Here's what the choices mean:

- **Paste.** Creates an *embedded* object. When you click an object you've pasted this way, the *source* (original) program opens in a separate window, where you can edit the object without actually leaving Word. When you make changes in that window, you're also making those changes in the source file (if there is one). Think of it as the opposite of a linked object, described below.

- **Paste Link.** Creates a *linked* object that refers back to the source file. In other words, an inserted Excel object is merely a *link* to the original Excel file, and you can't click to edit it in Word. Instead, Word opens the source (original) file where you can make changes to the file itself. See "Object Linking and Embedding" on page 753 for more detail.

- **Display as Icon.** If you choose Paste Link, you may also want to turn on the Display as Icon box. Doing so displays your pasted object as an icon representing the program from which it was drawn. Essentially, your Word document is the "launching pad" for the linked document. Double-click the icon to open it.

After choosing Paste or Paste Link, you have to choose from the following options in the right panel of the Paste Special dialog box.

- **Microsoft Word Document Object.** This command nests one self-sufficient Word document inside another, as an embedded object. See page 753 for more detail.

- **Word Hyperlink.** Inserts a hyperlink as discussed in the next section.

- **Formatted Text (RTF).** RTF stands for Rich Text Format, a file format that Microsoft devised to simplify the transfer of formatted text documents between incompatible programs. An RTF file is a lot like a text file, except that most common formatting specifications—bold, italic, font selections, line breaks, style sheets, and so on—survive the conversion to RTF and back again. Every modern word processor, for Mac or Windows, can open and export RTF documents. You'll rarely need it for transferring text between programs, thanks to the Styled Text feature offered by most Mac programs (more on that in a moment).

Note: Once upon a time Rich Text Format (RTF) was a big deal. The computing world was full of different word processing programs, and different operating systems to run them on. RTF was the common file that most programs could read. But now that most word processing programs can open and read .doc files (that is, Word 97/2004 format), you'll rarely use RTF, if at all.

- **Unformatted Text.** Paste this way when you want to paste the text without any formatting (font, bold or italic, Word styles, and so on). Text pasted as unformatted picks up the current font, style, and formatting at the insertion point wherever you paste it. (Unformatted text does carry its own paragraph breaks.)

- **Picture.** When you paste text *as a picture,* from that moment on, Word treats it just like a picture (and switches you into Page Layout view). Text pasted in this way plays with your head a little bit, since you don't get an insertion point for editing when you click inside the text. Instead, the Formatting Palette's image tools (like Image, Size, Rotation, and Ordering) come into view (see page 744).

  What you can never do again is *edit* the text—check spelling, delete words, and so on. But once you have the text just the way you want it, Paste Special → As Picture is a great way to create a poster, letterhead, watermark, or any document that you *don't* want anyone to edit later.

Note: The Office Clipboard, which debuted in Office 2001, is with us no longer. It has been replaced by the Office Scrapbook, which works about the same, but better. Get the whole Scrapbook story on page 727.

Mac OS X also has its own Clipboard, by the way. Unfortunately, it only remembers the last item pasted to it. To view the Mac OS X Clipboard, in the Finder, select Show Clipboard from the Edit menu.

- **Styled Text.** This option preserves all font and paragraph styles in the pasted text. This Macintosh-only feature explains why you can copy some text from, say, a Web page or email: When you paste it into Word, the font sizes, bold-face, and other formatting arrives intact.

Most modern Mac programs, including word processors and page-layout programs, automatically copy styled text to the Scrapbook whenever you copy.

• **HTML Format.** Use this option when you're creating a Web page (see Chapter 9) and pasting in text from another type of document. Word adds HTML formatting commands to the text you're moving.

Paste as Hyperlink

This command lets a Word document become a living table of contents—a launcher—for the chapters in your book project, pages on the World Wide Web, people in your email address book, or even programs on your hard drive.

Text that's pasted as a hyperlink remembers where it came from, wherever that may be. Here are the kinds of hyperlinks possible in Word:

• **Within the same document.** Select some text, choose Edit → Copy, then use Edit → "Paste as Hyperlink". Text that you've pasted as a hyperlink becomes a blue, underlined link to its point of origin.

For example, using "Paste as Hyperlink", you can paste text from the last chapter of your book into the introduction. From then on, you can click the link to jump directly to the last chapter. You can also use this command to construct a "live" table of contents, as shown in Figure 2-2.

When you position the cursor over a hyperlink without clicking, a yellow screen tip balloon identifies the name and location of the file it's connected to.

Etherlords II is mixes the best of role-playing, strategy, and card-based titles into an enthralling game. Players will build the power of their hero as they travel through the troubled lands in search of the evil that plagues their people.

Table of Contents

Figure 2-2:
To create this linked table of contents, the headings from each section of the training manual were copied (Edit → Copy) and pasted as hyperlinks (Edit → "Paste as Hyperlink"). When you move the cursor over one of these links, it turns into a pointing hand. When you click it, you jump to that heading in the document.

• **Between two different Word documents.** You can use the same technique to create a link between two different Word documents, even if they're on different disks. When you click the hyperlink, Word opens the document.

Note: If you click a link to a file on a removable disk (such as a CD or external hard drive) that isn't currently in the drive or plugged in, or a LAN station (a drive or folder on a computer on your home or office network) that you're not currently connected to, an error message appears.

Editing a link can be tricky, since you can't exactly click it to plant the insertion point or drag it to highlight some text. If you try, you'll simply trigger the link itself. The secret is to Control-click (or right-click) the link and choose Hyperlink → Edit Hyperlink from the shortcut menu. A dialog box appears letting you easily edit the link's text.

Drag-and-Drop

Drag-and-drop is the easiest way to move text from one place to another, especially if both the starting and ending locations are onscreen simultaneously. Because it lets you grab chunks of text and drag them directly around the paragraph or sentence before you, drag-and-drop is an extremely direct and satisfying way to rearrange your prose. As a bonus, drag-and-drop doesn't involve the Scrapbook; whatever you've most recently copied or cut remains there, ready for pasting, no matter how many times you drag-and-drop in the meantime.

After highlighting some text, position the cursor anywhere within the highlighted area. Press the mouse button and drag carefully. A dotted outline of the original text block moves as you drag, along with a non-blinking insertion point at your arrow-cursor tip. Move the mouse until the insertion point is where you want the relocated text to *start*. When you release the mouse button, the text jumps immediately into its new location. (If it didn't wind up exactly where you intended, choose Edit → Undo move, or press ⌘-Z or F1, to return everything to the way it was.)

FREQUENTLY ASKED QUESTION

Linking Word to the Web

When I copy a link from a Web site to paste into a Word document, the Paste as Hyperlink command is grayed out. So how can I create a hyperlink?

Don't make things hard for yourself! You can create a link to the Web in any Word document simply by dragging the link from Safari into your document. Click the favicon (the icon to the left of the address) and drag the actual address out of the browser's address bar.

When you click the resulting link in Word, your browser opens and takes you to the Web page specified by the link. (If you connect with a modem and you're not already online, the Mac may or may not dial up the Internet in the process, depending on your settings in System Preferences → Network → Modem → PPP → PPP Options.)

Note: Within a Word document, drag-and-drop acts like a Cut and Paste operation—your text *moves* from one place to another. When you drag while pressing the Option key, however, or whenever you drag-and-drop between Office programs (see below), drag-and-drop acts like *Copy* and Paste—the original text remains where it was. (Drag-and-drop also acts like Copy and Paste when you drag between different open Word documents.)

Drag-and-drop between programs

In addition to working within Word, drag-and-drop also lets you drag text or graphic elements *between* Office programs. Position the two windows side by side, select your text or graphic, and then drag the highlighted block toward the destination window.

Note: Ever want to drag text to a window that's buried beneath several others? With Mac OS X's Exposé feature you can, as shown in Figure 2-3.

Watch what happens before you let go of the mouse button:

- If you're dragging to an Excel spreadsheet, a dotted outline appears around the destination cell.

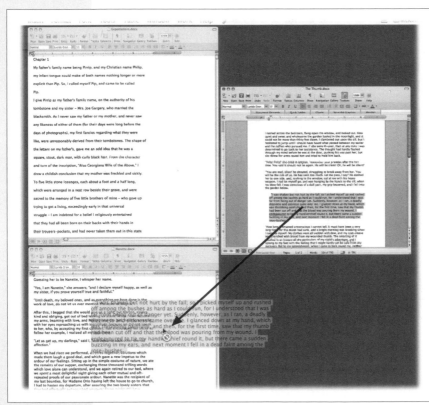

Figure 2-3:
Take advantage of Mac OS X's Exposé to drag selected text to a buried window. First select the text, then click and start to drag. As you do, press the F9 key. Exposé displays all your open windows in miniature form. Move the cursor to the destination window and press F9 again…the window under your cursor moves to the front. Wait until you get the green + sign before depositing your text at the insertion point.

- If you're dragging to an Entourage email message, a highlight line appears around the message or address text boxes, or the insertion point starts flashing in the subject box. You can drop text into any of these locations.

- If you're dragging into a PowerPoint presentation, you can drop your text into a slide, notes area, or list. A colored outline indicates where the dragged material will appear when you let go of the mouse.

When your desired destination is correctly highlighted, let go of the mouse button; your text appears in its new home.

Tip: Don't feel limited to dragging and dropping within Microsoft programs. Almost every modern Macintosh program can accept drag-and-drops. For example, you can drag from Word into AppleWorks, a Gmail email message in your Web browser, TextEdit, or Stickies. Conversely, Office 2008 programs can also accept drag-and-drops from other drag-and-drop–savvy programs.

GEM IN THE ROUGH

Cut Out to Be Smart

Have you noticed that when you cut and paste in Word, your pasted text is always perfectly spaced? In other words, when you paste a word with a space after it in front of a period, the extra space magically disappears and the period comes right smack after the word, where it belongs. And when you paste one word after another, a space appears between the two words, even if you forgot to put one there yourself.

That's Word's Smart Cut and Paste feature. You turn it on and off by the checkbox on the Word → Preferences → Edit panel—but turning it off is probably a bad idea. The golden rule of computing: Whenever your software offers to take over boring, microscopic, annoying work for you, let it.

Dragging and dropping to the desktop

When you drag and drop a chunk of selected text outside the boundaries of your document and onto the desktop, Word creates a *clipping file* (see Figure 2-4). Clipping files are pieces of text-in-waiting that you can later drag and drop.

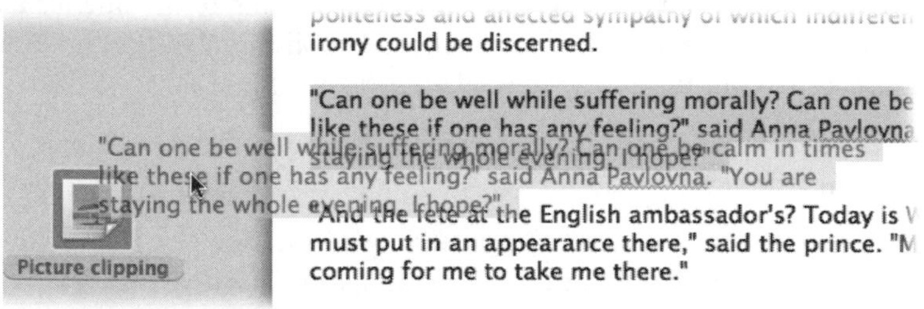

politeness and affected sympathy of which indifferent irony could be discerned.

"Can one be well while suffering morally? Can one be like these if one has any feeling?" said Anna Pavlovna staying the whole evening, I hope.

"And the fete at the English ambassador's? Today is V must put in an appearance there," said the prince. "N coming for me to take me there."

Picture clipping

Figure 2-4:
As a bonus, when you drag and drop to the desktop, Word copies the text to the clipping file. It doesn't cut it, so you can store a clipping for safekeeping before you edit the original.

Later, when you drag a clipping file back into a document, Word pastes a copy of the clipping text; the clipping file remains on the desktop, where you can use it again and again. In effect, you can use your desktop like a giant pasteboard to store

---

boilerplate paragraphs that you use frequently. Dragging the clippings to a folder in the Dock keeps them handy, but still out of the way. You can also create clipping files from Word pictures or drawing objects. Just select the object and drag it to the desktop. (Mac OS X names it a *picture clipping*, as shown in Figure 2-4.)

Note: In Mac OS X, the Finder names every clipping "Picture clipping," even if it includes text. Be sure to rename your clippings quickly and carefully so that you can remember what's in them. (You can rename a clipping file as you would any Finder icon: For example, click its name once, then press Return to make the "renaming rectangle" appear.)

Navigating Your Documents

Word 2008 gives you a bunch of ways to navigate your document, some of which aren't as immediately obvious as the scroll bar.

Tip: Using the scroll bar has its own reward: As you drag the blue "elevator" scroll-box handle up and down, a pop-out screen tip balloon identifies the major headings in your document as you scroll by. By scanning this readout, you'll know exactly where you'll be when you stop scrolling.

What the Keys Do

It's by far one of the most frequently asked questions among new (and even some veteran) Mac fans: What on earth are all of those extra keys for on the standard Mac keyboard?

In many cases, the answer is "nothing." In most Mac programs (games excluded), such keys as the F-keys on the top row and the Num Lock key don't do anything at all. In Office, however, there's scarcely a single key that doesn't have a function. For example:

- **Esc.** Short for "Escape," this key provides a quick way of dismissing a dialog box without having to click the Close or Cancel button. It also closes a menu you've pulled down, once you decide not to use it.

- **Home.** This key moves the insertion point to the beginning of the line it's currently in. (You were expecting it to take your insertion point to the top of the document, weren't you? It's a trick; to do that, press ⌘-Home.)

- **End.** The End key, if you have one, takes you to the end of the current line. The ⌘-End combination takes you to the very end of the document.

- **Ins.** The Ins key (short for Insert), if you have one, is a very quick shortcut to the Paste command—even quicker than ⌘-V, and more intuitive than F4.

- **Delete.** The Delete key acts as a backspace key. It backs over and erases the last character you typed. In fact, ⌘-Delete comes set to delete the entire *word* before the cursor, which is often far more useful than deleting just one character— especially when you're in the middle of a writing frenzy.

- **Forward Delete.** This key deletes the character to the *right* of the insertion point—not a use most Mac fans are familiar with, but an extremely useful one once you know it. For example, when trying to correct a typo, you sometimes place the insertion point on the wrong side of the letter you want, especially when you're working with italics. In such cases, one tap on this key does just the trick.

- **Clear.** This key acts as a forward delete key, too. On some keyboards, it shares a space with the Num Lock key.

- **Help.** Pushing the Help button opens the Word Help window. If the dog ate your Help key, ⌘-/ does the same thing.

- **Page Up and Page Down.** These keys move you up and down in the document, one screen at a time. (If you actually do want to jump from the top of one page to the top of the next, use the Navigator buttons instead, as described on page 53.)

Tip: Remember that you can combine some of these keystrokes—Home, End, Page Up, Page Down—with the Shift key to *select* text instead of simply scrolling.

Keystrokes: The Missing Manual

Microsoft apparently employs seething crowds of programmers who do nothing but dream up keyboard shortcuts for every conceivable Word function. With the Shift, Option, and ⌘ keys in various combinations, for example, the top-row function keys described in this chapter have second, third, fourth, and fifth functions— far more keyboard shortcuts than any human being could possibly remember (or fit in an 800-page book).

To print out a list of all Word shortcut keys for future reference, choose Tools → Macros. Click ListCommands in the macro list, then click Run. In the dialog box that appears, click "Current menu and keyboard settings," then click OK. When the dialog box goes away and the shortcut key list appears in a new Word document, press ⌘-P or click the Print button in the Standard toolbar.

The list is several pages long and has commands you may never use. But when you find yourself using the same menu commands over and over, it's worth taking a look to see if a keyboard shortcut exists.

The Go To Command

The scroll bar and arrow keys can get you pretty close to where you want to go in a long document, but now you can get there with much greater precision by telling Word. Double-clicking the Go To (Pages) button in the Status bar (see page 12), pressing ⌘-G (or F5), or choosing Edit → Go To opens the Go To tab of the "Find and Replace" dialog box, as shown in Figure 2-5.

POWER USERS' CLINIC

The F-keys

On some Macs, they're tiny; on others, they're full-sized. On some Macs, you have 12 of them; on others, 15. They're the function keys (or F-keys) stretched along the topmost row of your keyboard.

Once you're familiar with the many benefits of the F-keys, you may become addicted. The following is how the function keys come defined in a new copy of Word 2008—but remember that it's easy enough to change their functions (see Chapter 20).

F1 means Undo (the same as ⌘-Z). (There's no predefined F-key for Redo, although ⌘-Y or Edit → Redo are on hand if you change your mind again.)

F2, F3, and F4 correspond to the Cut, Copy, and Paste commands described earlier in this chapter (⌘-X, ⌘-C, and ⌘-V).

You're entitled to wonder, by the way, why you might use the F-keys for simple functions like copying and pasting when you're already in the habit of using the ⌘-key combinations.

The answer is on your keyboard: Many Mac laptops have only one ⌘ key—on the left side. If you have one of these, you'll probably find the single F-key to be more convenient than a two-key combination.

F5 (Go To Same, also ⌘-G) calls up the Go To tab of the "Find and Replace" dialog box (page 53).

F6 (Other Pane) moves the insertion point to the other pane of a split window. You can use Shift-F6 to return to the original pane, but why? Hitting F6 a second time performs the same function.

F7 (Proofing, also Option-⌘-L or Tools → "Spelling and Grammar") takes you to the first instance of a misspelling or instance of questionable grammar (as defined by Microsoft), and calls up the "Spelling and Grammar" dialog box.

F8 (Extend Selection) puts you in Extended selection mode, as described on page 41.

F9 now belongs to Mac OS X's Exposé feature—it reveals all your open windows in miniaturized form (see Figure 2-3). It's part of some keyboard shortcuts for Word's fields feature (see page 235).

F10, along with F9 and F11, is part of Exposé. It reveals all the windows for the current program—extremely helpful when you have a batch of Word documents open.

F11, like F9, works in Exposé when alone (it reveals the Desktop), or for working with fields, in combination with other keys (page 235).

F12 (Save As) opens the Save As dialog box. (Note: There's no F-key shortcut for the Save function.)

The Go To tab looks simple, but there's quite a lot you can do with it:

- Enter a page number. If you know what page you want to access, just enter the number in the "Enter page number" box and hit Return (or click Go To if you're a mouser).

- Jump a certain number of pages forward or back, as described in Figure 2-5.

- Step through your document page by page. Just keep pressing Return (or Enter) without doing anything else in between—after entering 1, for example, in the "Enter page number" box. (Microsoft calls this *browsing*.) Of course, a less dialog box–intensive method of jumping from one page to the next is to use the Navigator buttons described below.

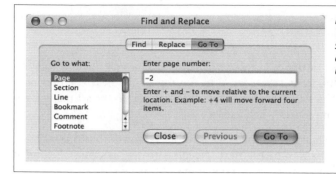

Figure 2-5:
Typing -2 in the "Enter page number" box will scroll the document back exactly two pages. It also moves the insertion point back. Choose your unit of measure (pages in this example) in the "Go to what" box.

- Choose a specific item type to go to in the "Go to what" box at the left. It can be as much as a section (see page 122) or as little as a line. You can check all your comments (see page 170) or footnotes at once by hitting Return repeatedly after selecting your unit of choice. (Jumping from one Heading, Graphic, Table, Comment, or Footnote to the next can be particularly useful in complex documents.) Or if you've placed Bookmarks in the document (Insert → Bookmark), you can jump to a previously placed bookmark (page 240).

The Navigator Buttons

All these nifty browsing features are also available by mouse, at the lower-right corner of every Word window, as shown in Figure 2-6. It also shows the double-headed arrows called Navigator buttons. By choosing an item in the "Go to what" box (see Figure 2-6), you can click the Navigator buttons to move forward and backward from one to the next.

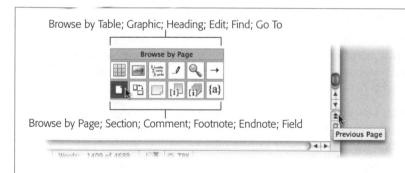

Figure 2-6:
The icons on the Select Browse Object palette (top) match the item types in the "Go to what" box. Once you've selected an item, you can click the Navigator buttons (lower right) to step directly to the next or previous one of the chosen item—Browse by Page in this example. This palette also has shortcuts to the Find and Go To dialog boxes.

As shown at the left in Figure 2-6, click the tiny round Select Browse Object button to choose *how* you want the Navigator buttons to take you through your document. Just click one of the icons (described below) in the pane that pops up.

Changing the browse object affects all open documents. If you've been browsing a big document by *sections,* and then switch back to a shorter one that you want to review by *page,* you need to change the browse object again.

Tip: You can check the current setting by positioning the cursor over one of the double-arrow buttons without clicking. A little pop-up label says "next page," "previous page," or whatever.

- **Browse by Page.** This setting is in force when you open a new document. With each click of a double arrow, you jump to the top of the next (or previous) page. (By contrast, the Page Up/Down keys scroll one *screen* at a time, even if that means you're jumping only half a page.)

- **Browse by Section.** When this setting is selected, the Navigator buttons take you from the top of one *section* to the next. Needless to say, it's most helpful if you've actually used section breaks in a document (see page 122).

- **Browse by Comment.** Word's Reviewing features (see Chapter 5) let you attach comments to a document, so that you can provide typed feedback to the author. Either way, this setting lets you skip from one such comment to the next, bypassing the remainder of the text. (It's a very good idea to use Browse by Comment before you send a document out into the world.)

- **Browse by Footnote, Browse by Endnote.** Similar to Browse by Comment, these settings take you directly from one note to the next. See page 220 for more on footnotes and endnotes.

- **Browse by Field.** When you've used the Mail Merge feature (page 262) or otherwise placed *fields* in your document (page 235), you can use the Navigator buttons to skip from one field to the next. This browse feature is really quite useful, since fields can look exactly like ordinary text and be easily missed. When browsing with this feature, Word helpfully highlights fields as it finds them.

- **Browse by Table.** This feature makes the Navigator buttons jump directly from one Word *table* (page 150) to the next.

- **Browse by Graphic.** Choosing this browse object does nothing unless your document has pictures, drawings, paintings, or scanned photographs. If it does, then the Navigator buttons move you from one graphic to another, skipping everything in between.

- **Browse by Heading.** This command is actually a two-in-one browse object. If you're working in Outline view, the Navigator buttons move the insertion point item by item, hitting each entry in your outline.

  This browsing method also works if your document's *styles* (see page 127) include any Heading styles. Use these preformatted font styles to set off chapter titles, captions, or subtopics. When you browse by heading, your insertion point skips from one heading to the next, bypassing all the mere mortal body text in between.

- **Browse by Edits.** Unlike the other browse objects, this one possesses a limited short-term memory. Word only remembers the last three places you clicked in your document. Check out the sidebar on the previous page for details.

Tip: Even though you've selected a browse object, you're not stuck with using the mouse to click the Navigator buttons. The keyboard shortcut ⌘-Page Up or Page Down takes you from one item to the next.

Finding and Replacing

When editing a document, sometimes you know exactly what you want to revise, but just don't know where it is. For instance, you want to go back and reread the paragraph you wrote about *mansions,* but you don't remember what page it's on. Or suppose you've found out that you misspelled Sarah's name all the way through an article. Now you have to replace *every* occurrence of Sara with Sarah—but how do you make sure that you've got them all?

That's where "Find and Replace" comes in.

GEM IN THE ROUGH

Back to Where You Once Belonged

The Go Back command is unique to Microsoft Word, and it's fantastically useful. No matter where you are in a document, this command scrolls directly back to the last place you clicked (usually the last place you edited text)—even if it was in another open document.

You'll find this command useful in a number of circumstances: after splitting and unsplitting the window, and then finding yourself deposited in the wrong part of a document; when you've just opened up a document that you were editing yesterday and want to return to the spot where you stopped; when reconsidering an edit after scrolling to a new location; and so on.

Better yet, Word doesn't just remember the last place you clicked; it remembers the last *three* places. Each time you use the Go Back command, your insertion point jumps among these four places—the last three edits and your current position—even if that means bringing different document windows forward.

You can trigger the Go Back command by pressing Option-⌘-Z, or Shift-F5, or using the Navigator buttons described above. If you fall in love with this feature, as you might, consider changing the keystroke to something easier to remember. (See Chapter 20 for instructions on changing a keystroke.)

Find

If you just want to find a certain word (or even part of a word), choose Edit → Find (or press ⌘-F). The "Find and Replace" dialog box opens, as shown in Figure 2-7. Type the word you're looking for, and then click Find Next (or press Return or ⌘-F).

Tip: If you turn on "Highlight all items found in Main Document," the Find Next button changes to say Find All. Now Word will select all occurrences of the search term simultaneously. At that point, you can bold them all, italicize them all, cut them all, or perform other kinds of neat global maneuvers.

Now Word searches for your search term, starting from the position of the insertion point. If it finds what you're seeking, it scrolls to and highlights each occurrence of that word or phrase in your document. (If it doesn't find any occurrences, an error message tells you so.)

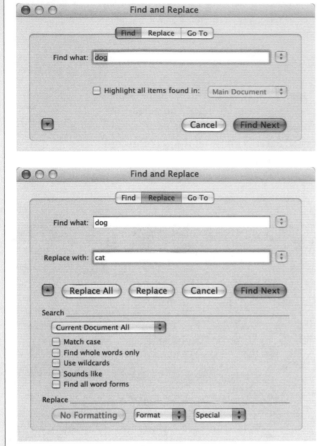

Figure 2-7:
Top: The Find dialog box.

Bottom: The expanded Replace box. The Format and Special menus at the bottom of this dialog box let you search for a font, typestyle, paragraph break, and so on. If you'd like to find all your italics and change them to boldface, or find all the dashes and delete them, these menus let you do it.

If Word finds an occurrence, but it's not the one you had in mind, you can keep clicking Find or hitting Return to find successive occurrences. When Word reaches the end of your document, it starts searching again from the beginning. When it finally wraps around so far that it finishes searching the whole file, another dialog box lets you know.

The Find box remains onscreen throughout the process, but don't let that stop you; you can pause and edit your document at any time. Just click in your document window, sending the Find box to the background. To resume your search, click the Find dialog box to bring it forward, then click Find Next.

Tip: The keystroke Shift-F4 (or Shift-⌘-Y) means "find the next occurrence of whatever I just searched for." The advantage is that it works even after you've closed the Find box altogether—and even if you performed your search hours ago (provided you haven't closed the document).

Replace

Although you can do edits and replacements in conjunction with the Find command as explained above, Word has a more streamlined process for making the same replacement over and over. Choosing Edit → Replace (Shift-⌘-H) opens the Replace tab of the "Find and Replace" dialog box.

Note: Before the dawn of Mac OS X, Word's Replace keystroke was just ⌘-H. Of course, Apple has now claimed ⌘-H as its universal Hide command, so Microsoft was forced to change the Replace keystroke to Shift-⌘-H.

It takes the Word veteran some time to unlearn ⌘-H for Replace. However, a few dozen shocks of seeing all your open Word windows disappear (and having to bring them back by clicking the W icon in the Dock) should train you to use the new protocol.

Once again, start by typing the word or phrase you want to replace in the "Find what" box. This time, however, you press Tab to jump into the "Replace with" box; now type the new, improved replacement text. When you click Find Next or press Return, Word searches the document and stops at the first match. Now there's a decision to make. After examining the highlighted phrase in context, click one of these buttons:

- **Replace.** This button means, "Replace this search term with my replacement text, then find the next occurrence of the search term."

Warning: If you simply click Find Next or press Return, Word doesn't make the replacement. You have to click the Replace button (or press ⌘-R) each time.

- **Replace All.** If you don't need this occurrence-by-occurrence interview, and you're sure you want to replace every occurrence of the search term in the entire document, click Replace All (or press ⌘-A).

  Be very careful, however: In most cases, it's safer to check each case to make sure the replacement is appropriate. For instance, if you're replacing "rite" with "right," Word will change even "criteria" to "crightria," giving quite an unexpected surprise to your editor, professor, or boss. Use Replace All only when there's little chance for that kind of confusion. Even so, you should proofread carefully afterward.

- **Find Next.** Suppose that, as you're searching for every occurrence of "Sara" to replace it with "Sarah," Word finds and highlights the first four letters of the word Saratoga. Clearly, you don't want Word to change this occurrence. In that case, just click Find Next (or press Return) to leave this occurrence alone and jump to the next one.

Advanced Find

Clicking the Expand button (the blue button with the down arrow on it) at the bottom of the Find or Replace tab makes the dialog box sprout an additional panel. (Pressing ⌘-M does the same thing.) It gives you the following precision controls for narrowing your search even further:

- The **Search** pop-up menu tells Word where to search. **Current Document All** starts the Find function from the very beginning of the document. **Current Document Down** and **Document Up** search forward and backward from the insertion point, and **All Open Documents** searches from the beginning of each document in the order that you opened them, moving automatically from one to the next.

- Turn on **Match case** when you want to find or change words only when they're capitalized a certain way; for instance, when you want to find the name Mike but skip over words like "mike."

- **Find whole words only** (⌘-Y) is a very powerful safety option. It tells Word to only look for the search term if it's separated from surrounding text by a space or punctuation mark—if it's a whole word unto itself, in other words. If you're searching for the word "men," for instance, turning on this box prevents Find from stopping on (or, worse, replacing) "menu" and "document."

- Checking **Use wildcards** (⌘-U) lets you use special characters to *stand in* for actual letters, in cases where you're unsure of the right letter or want to look for more than one spelling at a time. For example, ? stands in for any one letter or character. Entering *f?r* in the "Find what "box finds occurrences of "far," "for," "ferry," and so on. You can use * to represent any string of one or more letters (or other characters). Thus, entering *c*r* would find words like "car," "clear," and "quick brown."

When you'd settle for finding any one of several *specified* characters, put them in brackets. For instance, use *c[au]nning* to find all occurrences of both "canning" and "cunning" in your document.

Finally, an exclamation point indicates that you want to find any character *except* the one in the brackets. For example, *[!f]unk* finds "hunk," and "spunk," but not "funk."

Tip: There are several more wildcard characters in Word, which you can use—independently or in combination—to send Word on incredibly complex, convoluted searches. For a list of all wildcards, enter *wildcards* in the Word Help window's Search box.

- **Sounds like** (⌘-S). Turn on this box and enter a phonetic spelling for the word or words you're hunting for. Entering "thare" finds every occurrence of "there," and "their," but not "they're." Go figure. This option really comes in handy when you can't remember the spelling of a name; enter "lee" to find Ms. Li, for example.

- **Find all word forms.** This rather intelligent option finds all those irregularly spelled English nouns and verbs. For instance, if you're trying to find all the places where your article mentions running, type *run* and turn on this box. Word finds "ran," "runs," and "running"—but not "runner."

FREQUENTLY ASKED QUESTION

Converting Quotes from Curly to Straight, or Vice Versa

I need to convert all of Word's automatic, typographically correct "curly quotes" into Internet-friendly "straight quotes" before posting my work on a Web page or sending it by email. How do I do that?

As you've noted, Word converts your quotes automatically as you type, curling open and close quotes (and single quotes) as appropriate. To turn this feature off, choose Tools → AutoCorrect, click the AutoFormat As You Type tab, and turn off "Straight quotation marks with curly quotation marks."

You can also leave this feature turned on, while making the occasional curly quote straight—such as when you want a " mark to designate inches. The solution is simple: Just after typing the quote mark, press ⌘-Z or F1. Word straightens it instantly.

But to perform global surgery on an entire document, turning all curly quotes into straight ones, for example, choose Tools → AutoCorrect, click the AutoFormat As You Type tab, and turn off "Straight quotation marks with curly quotation marks." Click OK.

Now choose Edit → Replace. In both the "Find what" and "Replace with" boxes, type ' or ", and then click Find Next or Replace All. Word straightens all single or double quotes, as appropriate. (To curlify all straight quotes, repeat the procedure with the "Straight quotation marks with curly quotation marks" checkbox turned on.)

Finding by Format

Word is sometimes described as the Feature List That Ate Cleveland. Dozens or hundreds of features lie untapped by the vast majority of its owners.

But here's a buried feature that's well worth noticing: It's the Format pop-up button at the bottom of the Find dialog box, which lets you search for text according to its *formatting* (alone, or in combination with words typed in the "Find what" box). By opening this Format menu (or pressing ⌘-O), you'll see that Word lets you search for:

- **Font.** Finds occurrences of, say, Times or Palatino, as well as font *characteristics* like bold, italic, blue, 12-point, double-underline, shadow, and so on—in any combination.

- **Paragraph.** Locates paragraphs according to their indentation, line spacing, leading, outline level, page breaks, and so on.

- **Tabs.** Searches for tab stops by position and type.

- **Language.** Searches for text you've designated as being in a certain language (by highlighting the text and then choosing Tools → Language).

- **Frame.** Locates any *frame,* according to any of its attributes. (These days, most people use Word's text boxes instead of frames; see page 142.)

- **Style.** Lets you search for, or replace, any of your document's styles (see page 127).

- **Highlight.** Finds text you or a colleague has highlighted using the Highlighter tool on the Reviewing toolbar (page 168).

Tip: Once you've popped open the menu with ⌘-O, you can "walk" down its commands with the arrow keys. Press Enter when you've snagged the one you want.

This powerful feature is instrumental in dozens of situations. Sometimes it's useful when you just want to *find* something, like this:

- Type, for example, *the* in the "Find what" box. Choose Format → Style and choose one of the heading styles you've used in your document. (See page 127 for more on styles.) Word finds the word "the" only when it appears in a heading.

- Click inside the empty "Find what" box; choose Format → Font. In the resulting dialog box, click Italic, and then click OK. Word will now find every italicized word or group of words in the document, one by one.

The uses of this feature become even more amazing when you use the Replace function at the same time:

- Suppose that, in keeping with your newspaper's style guide, you decide to put Microsoft's company name in bold type, everywhere it occurs. Type *Microsoft Corporation* in the "Find what" box. Click in the "Replace with" box, choose Format → Font, choose Bold in the Font Style box, and click OK. Now, when you click Replace All, Word changes all occurrences of the phrase "Microsoft Corporation" to boldface.

Tip: You don't have to type *Microsoft Corporation* again into the "Replace with" box; if this box is empty, since you specified a format, Word assumes that you don't intend to change the text itself.

- You want to create a quick table of contents document. You decide that the easiest way is to remove all the words in your document that *aren't bold,* leaving behind only what appears in bold type (your headings, that is).

  Leave both the "Find and Replace" boxes empty. Click in the "Find what" box, choose Format → Font, click Not Bold, and click OK. By leaving the "Replace with" box empty, you're telling Word to *delete* every occurrence of the specified "Find what" item (in this case, text that's not bold). When you click Replace All, Word vaporizes all the body text of your document, leaving behind only the boldface type.

- Click in the "Find what" box and choose Format → Tabs. Word displays a dialog box similar to the one where you set tabs (see page 111). Type *.5* in the "Tab stop position" box and click OK. Use the radio buttons in the "Find Tabs" dialog box to tell Word what kind of tab you're searching for. Word won't find tabs if the alignment doesn't match. Click in the "Replace with" box, choose Format → Tabs, and type *1* in the "Tab stop position box."

Finally, click OK. Word finds all the paragraphs with half-inch tabs and changes them to one-inch tabs.

• Someone has given you an article that contains headings. But rather than using the Heading 1 *style* (see page 127), the author used simple boldface formatting for the headings. As a result, you can't use Word's Outline view to see just the headings.

The solution is simple: Click in the empty "Find what" box. Choose Format → Font, choose Bold in the "Font style" box, and click OK. Now click in the empty "Replace with" box; choose Format → Style, select the Heading 1 style, and click OK. Now, when you click Replace All, Word changes all bolded paragraphs to the Heading 1 style.

Your formatting selections are displayed just below the "Find what" box. Click No Formatting to erase them (in readiness for a different search, for example).

Note: If you've set up an elaborate string of formatting characteristics (Palatino, Heading 1 style, 12 point), there's no way to delete only one of them; you must click No Formatting to delete all of them and build the list again.

Finding Invisible Characters

The Special menu at the bottom of the "Find and Replace" dialog box lets you incorporate non-alphanumeric characters into your search. It also lets you search for document features that have nothing to do with words, such as column breaks, paragraph breaks, and hyphens.

When you choose one of these items from the Special menu, Word places its character code in the "Find what" box. You can use more than one of these choices and use them with wildcards, as described on page 58.

Tip: Once again, you can manipulate this list with the keyboard. Press ⌘-E to open the Special pop-up menu, and then use the arrow keys to highlight the commands on it.

The Special menu really demonstrates its power in "Find and Replace" operations. Some examples:

• Suppose your document is filled with typographically correct dashes, which may turn into gibberish if posted on a Web page or emailed. To convert them into double hyphens, click in the "Find what" box and choose Special → Em Dash (for a long dash, like this—) or En Dash (for a shorter dash, like this –). Click in the "Replace with" box and type two hyphens (--). When you click Replace All, Word replaces dashes with hyphens.

Tip: To replace both kinds of dashes in one pass, choose one after the other in the Special menu. Now place brackets around them in the "Find what" box.

- To take out column breaks and let the text reflow, click in the "Find what" box and choose Special → Column Break. Click in the "Replace with" box and choose Special → Paragraph Mark to ensure that the paragraphs in the newly joined columns don't run into each other.

- A Word document may look fine if there's just one press of the Return key after each paragraph, as the style in question may have built-in "blank lines" between paragraphs. But if you try to paste the document's text into an email message, you'll lose the blank lines between paragraphs.

  The solution is to replace every paragraph mark with *two* paragraph marks before copying the document into your email program. Click in the "Find what" box and choose Special → Paragraph Mark; then click in the "Replace with" box and choose Special → Paragraph Mark *twice*. Word replaces every paragraph mark (which Word represents with the code ^*p*) with two consecutive paragraph breaks (^*p*^*p*).

- To reduce typing, insert abbreviation codes into a Word document, then replace them with much longer passages of boilerplate text. Before searching, copy the replacement text to the Scrapbook, type the abbreviation code into the "Find what" box, click in the "Replace with" box, and choose Special → Clipboard Contents. Finally, click Replace All.

Tip: You'll see the Special → Clipboard Contents command only when you've clicked in the "Replace with" box. In other words, you can't search for something you've copied to the clipboard. That's unfortunate, since almost everyone, sooner or later, comes across a Word document filled with some strange symbol—little white squares, Symbol-font squiggles, or some other mysterious character. It would be nice if you could copy one instance to the Scrapbook, so that you could replace all instances with, say, nothing.

In such situations, you can usually get away with *pasting* the copied mystery symbol directly into the "Find what" box.

To undo selections you've made from the Special menu in the "Find and Replace" dialog box, select and delete the characters that Word placed in the "Find what" or "Replace with" boxes.

Spelling and Grammar

Whatever your document—term paper, resumé, or letter to the milkman—typos can hinder its effectiveness and sully your credibility. When you let mistakes remain in your document, your reader may doubt that you put any time or care into it at all. Word helps you achieve the perfect result by pointing out possible errors, leaving the final call up to you.

Tip: A spelling-related feature may have been benefiting you without you even noticing. When you incur a typo that even a Sominex-drugged reader would notice, such as *wodnerful* or *thier,* Word makes the correction automatically, instantly, and quietly. (Press ⌘-Z or F1 immediately afterward if you actually intended the misspelled version.) Technically, Word is using its spelling dictionaries as fodder for its Auto-Correct feature, as described on page 75.

As a bonus, the spell checker is smart enough to recognize run-together words (such as *intothe* and *giveme*) and propose the split-apart versions as corrected spellings.

There are two basic modes to Word's spelling and grammar features:

Check Spelling as You Type

Word's factory setting is to check spelling and grammar continuously, immediately flagging any error it detects as soon as you finish typing it. Each spelling error gets a red, squiggly underline; each grammatical error gets a green one. These squiggly underlines (which also appear in the other Office programs) are among the most noticeable hallmarks of Office documents, as shown in Figure 2-8.

If you can spot the problem right away—an obvious spelling error, for example—simply edit it. The squiggly underline disappears as soon as your insertion point leaves the vicinity. It's often more fun, however, to Control-click (or right-click) each error (see Figure 2-8), which opens a shortcut menu to help you handle the correction process. Here are the commands you'll find in this shortcut menu:

- **Help** opens the Word Help system, as described in Appendix B.

- The next segment of the shortcut menu lists spelling suggestions from Word's dictionary. It says "(no spelling suggestions)" if Word has none.

  If one of these suggestions is the word you were trying to spell, click it. Word instantly replaces the error in your document, thus evaporating the squiggly line.

- Choosing **Ignore All** from the shortcut menu tells Word to butt out—that this word is spelled exactly the way you want it. Once you've chosen this command, the underlines disappear from *all* occurrences of that term in *this* document. (If you use the same spelling in a new document, however, Word will flag it as an error again. To teach Word the word forever, add it to the custom dictionary, as described next.)

- As you've probably figured out by now, Word underlines a word not necessarily because it's spelled incorrectly, but because it's not on Word's list of correctly spelled words. Occasionally, you have to "teach" Word a new word. The **Add** command does exactly that.

  Word maintains word lists called custom dictionaries. When Word checks a word's spelling as you type it, the Add command on the shortcut menu

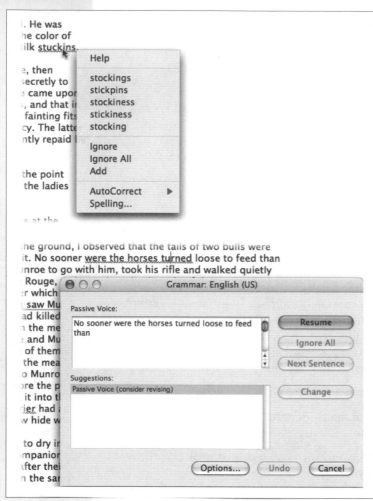

Figure 2-8:
Top: When Word is set to check spelling and grammar as you type, errors are underlined as you go. Control-clicking each error opens a shortcut menu that lists suggested spellings and commonly used "Spelling and Grammar" commands.

Bottom: Control-click a green underline and choose Grammar from the pop-up menu to display the Grammar window, where Word explains what it thinks is the matter with your prose. Press Return if you don't agree and want to move on to the next grammar error.

instantly adds that word to the current custom dictionary. (If the Add command is gray, you haven't yet created a custom dictionary. See page 71 to create a dictionary, and bring the Add button to life.) You can also edit a custom dictionary directly, as described on page 70.

- The **AutoCorrect** pop-up menu provides access to matching choices from Word's AutoCorrect list (see page 75). Often, but not always, these choices are the same as the alternate spellings from the custom dictionary.

- **Spelling** opens the Spelling dialog box and performs a spelling and grammar check on whatever you selected and clicked.

Checking Spelling and Grammar All at Once

If it annoys you when Word flags incorrect or unusual spellings as you type, there's something you can do about it. Turn that feature off, as described in Figure 2-10, and check spelling on demand—once at the very end, for instance. If that's the way you like it, choose Tools → "Spelling and Grammar" (or press F7, or Option-⌘-L) to open the "Spelling and Grammar" dialog box (Figure 2-9).

Word scans your document, starting at the insertion point, and displays errors one by one in the "Not in dictionary" box, as shown in Figure 2-9. As a courtesy, Word shows you the "error" in context, placing the whole sentence in the text box with the specific spelling error shown in red. Your options are as follows:

- Click **Ignore** (⌘-I) to skip over the error without doing anything. If you don't want Word to flag this particular error again (in this document), click **Ignore All** (⌘-G).

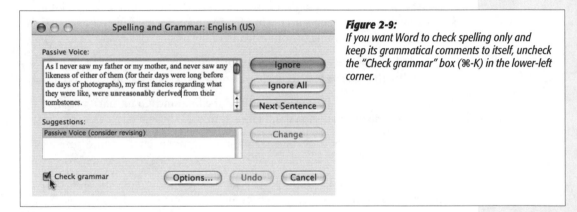

Figure 2-9:
If you want Word to check spelling only and keep its grammatical comments to itself, uncheck the "Check grammar" box (⌘-K) in the lower-left corner.

- As described under "Check spelling as you type," clicking **Add** (⌘-A) adds the highlighted word to the custom dictionary. From here on out, in every document, Word will understand this spelling to be a correct one.

- In the lower Suggestions list box, Word shows you some similarly spelled words from your main and custom dictionaries. Using the mouse or the up/down arrow keys, highlight one of them and click **Change** to accept that spelling just this once, or **Change All** (⌘-L) to swap all occurrences of the highlighted word—in this document only—with the selected suggestion.

- If you agree that something is misspelled, but you don't see the correct spelling in the Suggestions list, you can make the correction directly in the top text area, using any of Word's editing tools. (This is a handy trick when Word discovers a typo like ";lkjijjjjjj"—a sure sign that you'd fallen asleep on the keys. Just drag across the mess—right there in the dialog box—and press the Delete key to fix the error.)

  Then click Change or Change All, as described above, to apply your change to the document itself. You can also click **Undo Edit** (⌘-U) if you change your mind. (The Ignore button changes into Undo Edit as soon as you start typing in the window.)

- Whether you make a choice from the Suggestions window or make a change in the editing window, clicking the **AutoCorrect** (⌘-R) button tells Word to make the change from now on, using the AutoCorrect feature (see page 75). When you do so, Word enters your typo/correction pair to its AutoCorrect list, which you can view by choosing Tools → AutoCorrect and scrolling through the list. (See page 76 for more information on working with the AutoCorrect dialog box.)

- The **Undo** (⌘-U) button is a lifesaver for the indecisive. Once you've made a correction, after you've clicked Change, and even if you've created a new Auto-Correct pair, you can click Undo and take back your last change. Better still, the Undo command works even after you click Change, and Word has moved on to the next error. In that case, Word backtracks to the previous change and undoes it. In fact, you can keep on clicking Undo and reverse all the changes you've made since the beginning of your document.

  The Undo button is particularly valuable when you're spell checking rapidly and realize that you've just accepted one of Word's suggestions a bit too hastily.

- The **Options** (⌘-O) button opens the "Spelling and Grammar" panel of the Preferences dialog box, shown in Figure 2-10.

- **Close** (Esc) calls a halt to the spelling and grammar check and dismisses the dialog box.

  Over the years, Word's grammar checker has grown smarter and less likely to underline perfectly correct sentences or make incorrect suggestions. Some-times, however, you still need to rely on your own knowledge of grammar (and a healthy dose of common sense) in order to decide when to accept Word's suggested grammar changes—and when to click Ignore.

Spelling and Grammar Options

To tell Word how much (or little) help you need with your spelling and grammar, choose Word → Preferences; in the Preferences dialog box, click the "Spelling and Grammar" button. You'll find these options:

- **Check spelling as you type** turns on and off the red, wavy underlines that mark spelling errors in all Word documents.

- **Hide spelling errors in this document** turns off "Check spelling as you type" in the current document only.

- **Always suggest corrections** prompts Word to show you alternative spellings during spelling checks using the Spelling dialog box. Without this option, Word will flag errors without proposing suggestions.

Note: Control-clicking a squiggly-underlined word produces spelling suggestions regardless of the "Always suggest corrections" setting.

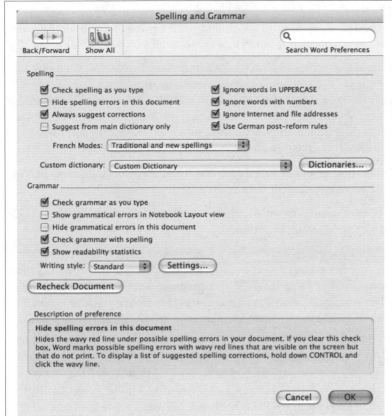

Figure 2-10:
*The Word → Preferences →
"Spelling and Grammar" panel is
command central for making
Word's spelling and grammar
features work for you. When you
click "Check spelling as you type"
or "Check grammar as you type,"
Word automatically unchecks the
"hide" choices. You can still turn
on "Hide spelling errors" or "Hide
grammatical errors" to
temporarily remove Word's
squiggly underlines on a
document-by-document basis.*

- **Suggest from main dictionary only** instructs Word to use only the list of words that came installed with it, ignoring your custom dictionaries. (See page 70 for more detail on custom dictionaries.)

- Turn on **Ignore words in UPPERCASE** if you frequently use acronyms or stock symbols (such as WFMI or ADM). Otherwise, Word interprets them as misspelled words.

- Turn on **Ignore words with numbers** if you'd like Word to leave words like 3Com and R2D2 alone.

- **Ignore Internet and file addresses** governs whether or not Word interprets URLs (*www.missingmanuals.com*) and file paths (Macintosh HD:Users:[user name]:Documents:Tests) as spelling errors. Because it's unlikely that most Web addresses are in Word's dictionaries, you'll usually want this option turned on.

- **Use German post-reform rules.** Turning on this box tells Word to use the new German spelling rules that were instituted in the 1990s—in Germany. (So if it works only on German-language Macs, why turn it on with English-language Macs? It actually helps with the spell-checking if some or all of the text is German.)

- **Custom dictionary.** See page 70 for a full explanation of this feature.

- **Check grammar as you type** turns on and off the green, wavy underlines that mark what Word considers grammatical errors in all Word documents.

- **Show grammatical errors in Notebook Layout view.** In Word's Notebook Layout view (page 181), many of your notebook ramblings are incomplete thoughts, little more than notes to yourself, stuff that you either don't need (or don't want) Word to check for grammatical correctness. If you don't want Word to check grammar in Notebook Layout view leave this box turned off. (Word still checks grammar in all the *other* views, just like normal.)

- **Hide grammatical errors in this document** turns off "Check grammar as you type" in the current document only.

- Turn off **Check grammar with spelling** to proceed through spelling checks without stopping for grammar issues.

- **Show readability statistics** may please educators and testers, but is probably of little value to anyone else. If you turn on this checkbox, Word applies a readability formula to the document. ("Check grammar with spelling" has to be on as well.) The readability formula calculates an approximate grade level based on the number of syllables, words, and sentences in the document. These statistics are displayed in a box at the end of the spelling and grammar check.

  Word uses one of two formulas to interpret the results. The *Flesch Reading Ease* score uses a scale of 0 to 100, with 100 being the easiest. A score of 60 or 70 indicates text that most adults could comfortably read and understand. The Flesch-Kincaid Grade Level Score, on the other hand, calculates grade level according to U.S. averages. A score of 8, for example, means that the document is on the eighth-grade reading level. For a general audience, that's a good level to shoot for.

  Either way, remember that this is a software program analyzing words written by a human being for specific audiences. By no means, for example, should you base somebody's entrance to a school on these scores—they're only crude approximations of approximations.

Writing Styles

Grammar can be very subjective. Contractions, for example, aren't incorrect; they're just appropriate in some situations and not in others. In an academic or medical paper, long sentences and the passive voice are the norm; in a glossy magazine article, they're taboo. On the other hand, other kinds of errors, such as writing the contraction "it's" when you mean the possessive "its," are things you *always* want to avoid. And when writing poetry or a play in dialect, the usual rules of grammar simply don't apply.

In other words, there are different writing styles for different kinds of documents. Word not only recognizes that fact, it lets *you* choose which one you want to use in a given situation. Better still, it lets you decide which specific grammatical issues you want flagged.

GEM IN THE ROUGH

Checking Foreign Language Text

The spell checkers in ordinary word processors choke on foreign terms. But not Word—it actually comes with different spelling dictionaries for dozens of languages. The program can actually check the English parts of your document against the English dictionary, the French portions against the French dictionary, and so on—all in a single pass.

This amazing intelligence works only if you've taken two preliminary steps. First, you must install the foreign-language dictionaries you intend to use (they're not part of the standard installation), using the technique described in Appendix A.

Second, you must tell Word which language each passage is in. To flag a certain word, passage, or document as Danish, for example, first highlight it. Then choose Tools → Language; in the resulting dialog box, select the language and click OK.

You've just applied what Microsoft calls language formatting—that is, you've flagged the highlighted text just as though you'd made it blue or bold. From now on, your spell checks will switch, on the fly, to the corresponding spelling dictionary for each patch of foreign language text in your document.

To select a writing style from Word's preconfigured list, choose Word → Preferences → "Spelling and Grammar". In the resulting dialog box, choose a writing style from the pop-up menu near the bottom of the box under Grammar.

To customize writing styles to your own needs, thus becoming your own grammar czar or czarina, click Settings. The Grammar Settings dialog box opens, as shown in Figure 2-11. (If the Grammar settings are dimmed in the dialog box, it's because the Grammar module isn't installed. See Appendix A for installation instructions.)

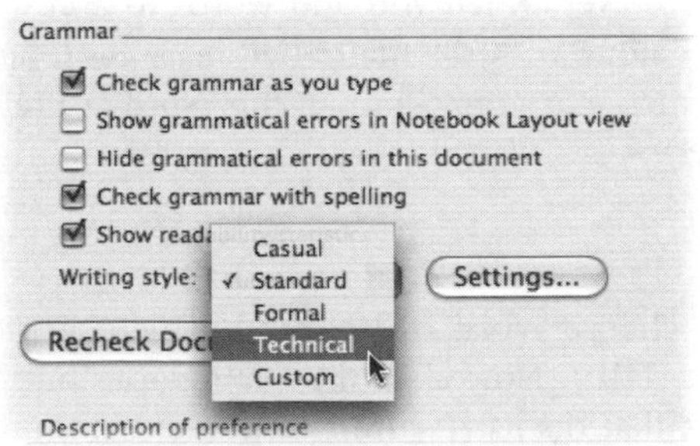

Figure 2-11:
You can modify existing writing styles (Standard, Casual, Formal, or Technical), or create your own combination of grammar standards (Custom), by turning options in the list on or off. Clicking Reset All returns the currently selected style to its original condition. (To restore all writing styles to their original settings, you have to reset them one by one.)

The choices you make from the pop-up menus under Require apply to all writing styles. Each menu gives you a chance to customize points of style that are more a matter of individual choice than grammar. Word doesn't automatically check for any of the three Require items listed here: whether you put a comma after the second-to-last item in a list (as in: *planes, trains, and automobiles*), whether punctuation goes inside or outside of quotation marks, or the number of spaces between sentences.

If you learned how to write in England, you probably put periods and commas *after* the quotation marks at the end of a quote. In the United States, punctuation is expected to go *before* the quotes. Choose "inside" or "outside" from the second pop-up menu to have Word check if you're doing it consistently, one way or the other.

If you're sending your text to an editor or layout person for desktop publishing, you'll probably be asked to put just one space between sentences; you probably learned how to type with *two* spaces after every period. You can choose 1 or 2 from the bottom menu to instruct Word to check the spacing for you.

You can create your own unique style by choosing Custom from the pop-up menu at the top of the box and turning on any combination of options. When you click OK, the custom style applies to your document; you can't name the style or create more than one custom style at a time.

Custom Dictionaries and Preferred Spellings

As noted earlier, Word maintains a list of thousands of words that it "knows" how to spell. When it checks your spelling, Word simply compares the words in your document to the words in the list.

To teach Word the words that you use frequently, you have two options: You can add them to a *custom dictionary,* or, if you have large batches of words that you only use for specific situations, you can create multiple custom dictionaries. Then choose which dictionary you wish to apply to the document you're currently working on.

You can't add words directly to Word's *main* (built-in) dictionary, which is permanently "hard-wired"—specially encoded for speed. In fact, you aren't even allowed to see the main dictionary. However, when you add words to a custom dictionary, Word uses them seamlessly along with the main dictionary (as long as you haven't turned on the "Use main dictionary only" box in the Word → Preferences → "Spelling and Grammar" panel).

Editing the custom dictionary

To add words to a custom dictionary, choose Word → Preferences, then click the "Spelling and Grammar" panel (Figure 2-10). Now click the Dictionaries button. In the Custom Dictionaries dialog box that opens (Figure 2-12), one custom dictionary is listed and checkmarked, meaning that it's currently in use. Any words that you've ever added to Word's dictionary during a spell check appear in this custom dictionary.

To review the list of words, click Edit. (If a message appears to warn you that Word will now stop checking your spelling, click Continue.) Suddenly, all your added words appear listed in a new Word document, which you're now free to edit. You can add, delete, and edit words using any of Word's editing tools; just remember to use the Return key to ensure each word is on a separate line.

Creating a new custom dictionary

In some cases, you may want to create a new custom dictionary for specific projects. For instance, suppose that you're writing something in a foreign language or a paper filled with technical terms. If you add these foreign or technical terms to the same custom dictionary that you use for everyday correspondence, they'll show up in spell checks and sometimes even create false errors.

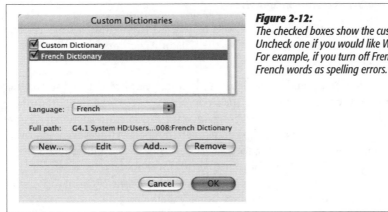

Figure 2-12:
The checked boxes show the custom dictionaries currently in effect. Uncheck one if you would like Word to stop using it in spell checks. For example, if you turn off French Dictionary, Word will interpret French words as spelling errors.

To create a new custom dictionary, click New in the Custom Dictionaries dialog box (Figure 2-12). Type a name for the new dictionary, and then click Save. Word saves the new custom dictionary in your Home folder's Library → Preferences → Microsoft folder.

Now you can add words to the custom dictionary in one of two ways:

- To add new words occasionally, in the course of your everyday writing career, click the name of the desired dictionary in the Custom Dictionaries dialog box. (Turn off any other dictionaries that may be listed in the box. Otherwise, Word will add newly learned terms to the default custom dictionary, for example, instead of your own foreign/technical one.) Then just go to work in your document. Whenever you check spelling, choose Add to place the unfamiliar term in your new custom dictionary.

- You can also add words all at once, by selecting the custom dictionary in the Custom Dictionaries dialog box and clicking Edit as described above. If there's a list of vocabulary words or technical terms in front of you, simply type or paste them into the text document that is the custom dictionary. Just make sure that each word is on a separate line before you click Save.

You can also copy and paste words from one custom dictionary into another. Thus, you can always copy the contents of the original custom dictionary into your specialized dictionary, so that you'll have constant access to all your preferred spellings.

Tip: When editing custom dictionaries, you can access them easily by going directly to the Library → Preferences → Microsoft → Office 2008 folder in your Home folder (although you could create and store a custom dictionary *anywhere*). You can open them easily in a program like TextEdit and edit away.

You can also rename these files. For example, if you've created new custom dictionaries, you may want to rename the default custom dictionary "original," "default," or "old."

Adding and removing custom dictionaries

After creating a new custom dictionary, you may decide to exclude it from certain documents. To do so, turn off its box in the Custom Dictionaries dialog box as described in Figure 2-12.

If you select a dictionary and click Remove, it disappears from this list and no longer appears in the pop-up menu in the Preferences → "Spelling and Grammar" panel. This is the way to go if you never again want this custom dictionary as an option and don't want anyone else to see it in Preferences. However, a removed custom dictionary doesn't go away forever. It remains in the Library → Preferences → Microsoft → Office 2008 folder (in your Home folder), or wherever you stored it on your Mac's hard drive. To return it to the Custom Dictionaries dialog box, click Add and choose it in the Add Dictionary dialog box.

Foreign language dictionaries

If your new dictionary is in a foreign language, there's an extra step. After creating the new custom dictionary, as described above, select the new foreign dictionary in the Custom Dictionaries dialog box. Then choose the appropriate language from the Language pop-up menu. Now Word will know to apply the correct spelling rules for that language.

Choosing custom dictionaries before spell checking

From now on, before you check spelling, you can specify which custom dictionaries you want Word to consider as it pores over your document. To do so, choose Word → Preferences → "Spelling and Grammar" panel, and then choose a custom dictionary from the pop-up menu.

Exclude dictionaries

As noted earlier, you can't edit the built-in Word dictionary. The previous discussions guide you through *adding* words to Word's spelling knowledge—but how do you *delete* a word from the built-in dictionary? After all, as noted above, the main dictionary is a hermetically sealed, specially encoded, untouchable entity that you can't edit using any tool known to man.

The answer: by creating an *exclude dictionary,* which is a special kind of dictionary document format that stores the words that you want Word to flag as spelling

---

errors. Whereas a custom dictionary "teaches" Word which words are spelled correctly, the exclude dictionary teaches Word what spellings are *wrong*, even though Word's main dictionary lists the spelling as correct.

For instance, say you prefer "focussed" to "focused." The second spelling, "focused," is the one that comes installed in Word. You should put the word "focused" into the exclude dictionary, so that Word will question that spelling during spell checks, giving you a chance to change it to "focussed."

To create an exclude dictionary, open a blank document. Type or paste in any standard spellings that you want Word to treat as errors. For instance, if you work for the Trefoil Theatre, you'll want to put "Theater" in the exclude dictionary. (The exclude dictionary is case sensitive; if you want Word to flag both "focused" and "Focused," for instance, you need to type both versions into the dictionary.)

When your list of excluded spellings is complete, choose File → Save As. In the Save box, navigate to the Home Folder → Library → Preferences → Microsoft → Office 2008 folder. Before saving, also do the following:

- Type a name for the exclude dictionary. "Exclude dictionary" is fine.

- Most importantly, you must choose a special format for this dictionary. In the Format pop-up menu, choose Speller Exclude Dictionary.

Click Save. You have to quit and relaunch Word for the exclude dictionary to take effect.

Five Ways to Type Less

At first glance, the Word window looks much like any computer screen. You type, and letters appear, just as in that classic Mac word processor, TextEdit. But there's actually much more to it than that. While you're typing, Word is constantly thinking, reacting, doing things to save you precious keystrokes.

As noted earlier, for example, Word corrects obvious spelling errors as you go along. But it also lets you create your own typing shortcuts, and even tries to anticipate your next formatting move, sometimes to the frustration of people who don't understand what the program's doing. The more you know what Word is thinking (it means well, it really does), the more you can let Word do the work, saving those precious brain cells for more important stuff—like writing or remembering to get the kids to soccer practice.

Click and Type

In olden days, our screens gave us a continually blinking insertion point, located in the upper-left corner of the screen. That's where you typed, no questions asked or answers given. If you wanted to type in the middle of the page—for example, to create a title page of a report—you couldn't just click there and start typing.

Instead, you had to take the ludicrously counterintuitive step of moving the insertion point over and down by tapping the Space bar, Tab key, or Return key until it was where you wanted it.

But in Word 2008, "Click and Type" assists location-challenged typists the world over by letting them reach their desired insertion point just by double-clicking. Here's how it works:

1. **Switch to Web Layout view or Print Layout view.**

   These are the only views where "Click and Type" is available; choose from the View menu to change views.

2. **Move the cursor around on the blank page, letting it hover for a second at the point where you'd like to place some text.**

   In some cases, you'll see the cursor change to indicate that Word is about to provide some free formatting help. If your cursor is near the left or right margin, Word assumes that you want your text to be left- or right-aligned; you'll see tiny left- or right-justified lines appear next to the hovering insertion point (see Figure 2-13). When you hover in the middle of the page, the insertion-point icon changes to centered text. If your cursor is near the top or bottom of the page, the cursor changes shape again to show that you're about to edit the document's *header* or *footer* (see page 209).

   If Word guesses wrong about the alignment, you can always adjust the text alignment later using the "Alignment and Spacing" tools in the Formatting Palette (page 106).

3. **Double-click.**

   The insertion point turns into a standard blinking bar, and you're ready to begin typing. (If the insertion point doesn't end up quite where you wanted it, just double-click again.)

Note: Behind the scenes, Word actually fills the page with Tabs and Returns, exactly as you did manually in the old days; that's how it gets your insertion point to the spot where you double-clicked. Knowing that (or *seeing* that, by clicking the ¶ button on the Standard toolbar) makes troubleshooting or adjusting Click-and-Typed text much easier.

To turn "Click and Type" on and off, choose Word → Preferences → Edit panel. Turn the "Enable click and type" box on or off.

AutoCorrect

Word seems psychic at times. You type *teh*, and Word changes it to "the" before you even have a chance to hit Delete. You start to type the name of the month, and all of a sudden today's date pops up on the screen—and you didn't even know what day it was.

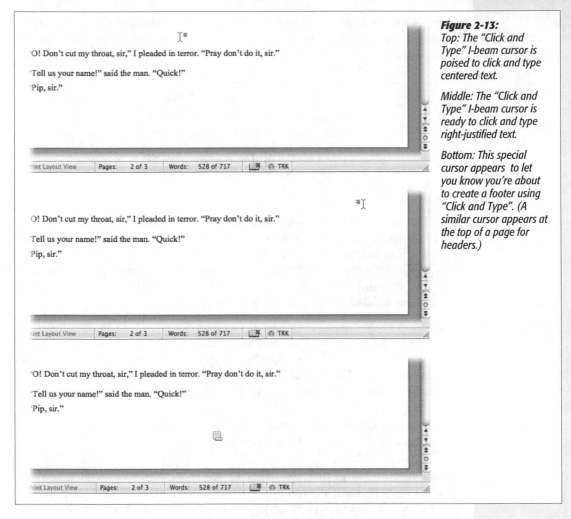

Figure 2-13:
Top: The "Click and Type" I-beam cursor is poised to click and type centered text.

Middle: The "Click and Type" I-beam cursor is ready to click and type right-justified text.

Bottom: This special cursor appears to let you know you're about to create a footer using "Click and Type". (A similar cursor appears at the top of a page for headers.)

You're witnessing Word's AutoCorrect and AutoType features at work—two of the least understood and most useful tools in Word's arsenal. They can be frustrating if you don't understand them, and a writer's best friend if you do.

Think of AutoCorrect as Word's *substitution* feature. All it does is replace something you're typing (the typo) with a replacement that Word has memorized and stored (the correct spelling). The correction takes place as soon as you type a space or punctuation mark after the incorrect word; no further action is required from you. And it happens so fast that you may not notice you've just been autocorrected unless you're watching for the blue bolt that slides under the word as Word analyzes it. If the correction isn't what you were expecting, hover your cursor under the word to reveal the AutoCorrect smart button, as shown in Figure 2-14.

Note: Crucial tip: If you retain one tip from this book's advice about Microsoft Word, remember this: *You can undo any automatic change Word makes,* under any circumstance, by pressing ⌘-Z or F1 just after Word makes it. That goes for automatic capitalization help, spelling help, formatting help, curly quote help, and so on. (It's also even faster than using the smart button shown below.)

Figure 2-14:
Hover your mouse over text Word autocorrects to display the AutoCorrect smart button. The provided options are contextual, but include undoing the action that Word has done, a heartfelt offer to stop doing it in the future, and a link to the AutoCorrect dialog box.

Word maintains a file of common misspellings and their corrections. That's why Word makes certain corrections and not others: Not all possible error/correction combinations that you need come installed on the list. To see this list, choose Tools → AutoCorrect and click the AutoCorrect tab (Figure 2-15). (Here you'll also find the most important checkbox in the world of AutoCorrect: the master on/off switch, called "Replace text as you type.")

The first three checkboxes cover capitalization errors; they save you from the errant ways of your pinky fingers on the Shift keys. When the first two boxes are turned on (see Figure 2-15), Word makes sure that you get a capital letter at the beginning of every sentence, whether you hold the Shift key down too long ("Correct TWo INitial CApitals") or not long enough ("Capitalize first letter of sentences").

Tip: Efficiency-addicted Word fans eventually stop capitalizing the first letters of sentences altogether. Word does it automatically, so why twist your pinkies unnecessarily?

If you turn on "Capitalize first letter of sentences," bear in mind that Word assumes every period is the end of a sentence. So why doesn't it auto-cap the first word after you type *U.N.* or *Jan.?* Because it's smart enough not to auto-cap after all-cap abbreviations (U.N.), and because it maintains a list of lowercase abbreviations that *shouldn't* be followed by capitals. (To see the list, choose Tools → Auto-Correct, click Exceptions, then click the First Letter tab; you can add your own abbreviations to this list, too.)

If you turn on "Automatically use suggestions from the spelling checker," Auto-Correct will go above and beyond the list of substitution pairs in this dialog box. It will use Word's main dictionary as a guide to proper spelling and automatically change words that almost, but not quite, match ones in the dictionary. (When Word can't decide on a match, it simply squiggly-underlines the misspelled word in the document.)

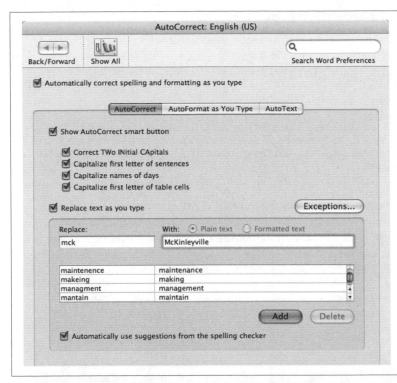

Figure 2-15:
You can open this dialog box by choosing Tools → AutoCorrect or clicking Control AutoCorrect Options whenever the smart button (see previous page) pops up. Feel free to add your own word combinations here, too. Put the typo in the Replace box, and the replacement version in the With box, then click Add. Think beyond typos, too—remember, you can make Word expand anything into anything. Make it replace "int" with "Internet," your initials with your full name, and so on.

WORKAROUND WORKSHOP

Telling AutoCorrect to Shut Up

Sometimes Word is more diligent in correcting errors than you'd like. What if you're trying to type a letter to a Mr. Porvide, and Word changes it to Provide? Or maybe you work for a company called Intelligence, and you're tired of changing the "e" to an "a" every time Word helpfully "corrects" it.

You don't want to turn AutoCorrect off, because you want Word to catch all your other typos. You could press ⌘-Z after Word makes each change, but that gets wearisome about the 35th time. Fortunately, there's a solution.

Click the Exceptions button on the AutoCorrect tab (see Figure 2-15). Then click the Other Corrections tab. Type your preferred spelling into the "Don't correct" text box and click Add. If you have many preferred spellings that you'll need to reeducate Word about, turn on the "Automatically add words to list" checkbox. Now, each time Word makes

an incorrect correction, click the Undo button on the Standard toolbar, choose Edit → Undo, or press ⌘-Z. Intelligence turns back into Intelligence, for example, and Word automatically adds your exceptional spelling to its AutoCorrect Exceptions list.

But you're not done yet, since the substitution pairs in the AutoCorrect dialog box (Figure 2-15) override the list in the Exceptions box. In other words, even though you've listed a preferred spelling as an exception, Word may still make the correction, and change Porvide to Provide, for example. The final step, then, is to delete the original AutoCorrect substitution pair. Choose Tools → AutoCorrect → AutoCorrect tab, scroll down until you find the offending correction pair, click to select it, and then click Delete. You may now Porvide to your heart's content.

AutoText: Abbreviation Expanders

AutoText is another Word feature that automatically changes what you've typed, once again delighting the expert and driving novices batty. In short, it's an abbreviation expander. Figure 2-16 shows AutoText in action.

Figure 2-16:
You're typing along. Suddenly you see a floating yellow screen tip just above the insertion point. That's Word's AutoText feature in action. It's proposing a replacement for what you just typed—a month, in this case. If you want to accept the suggestion, press Return or Enter; if not, just keep typing and pretend the screen tip never happened.

AutoText works by maintaining a preinstalled list of commonly typed terms and their replacements. You can also add your favorite terms to the list—the name of your company, your phone number, email address, and so on (see Figure 2-17). You can also add longer items—entire paragraphs, full addresses, lists, and even graphics, as described on page 80.

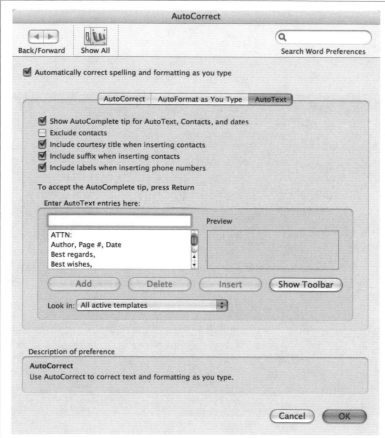

Figure 2-17:
This tab (Insert → AutoText → AutoText tab, or Tools → AutoCorrect → AutoText tab) is where you choose words, phrases, and fields to insert into your document without typing. You can also add your own items to the list by typing them into the "Enter AutoText entries here" box and clicking Insert. Select and click Delete to banish from your list any items you never use. You can also insert AutoText items into your document from this tab. Press the down arrow or Page Down key to scroll down until your desired entry appears in the Preview box (you can also use the scroll bar). Hit Return to drop the entry into your document; it lands wherever your insertion point has been blinking.

Setting up an AutoText entry

Word comes set up with dozens of ready-to-use AutoText entries. It completes not only the names of days of the week and months of the year, but also today's date and names from your Entourage address book (see Chapter 10).

But the real joy of becoming an AutoText addict is creating your own abbreviations. You can use AutoText to save form letters or contracts that go on for pages and pages, and then dump them into documents just by typing a few keys. If you're a lawyer, realtor, or medical professional who's not using AutoText to save time on boilerplate copy, you're missing out on a great timesaver.

To create a new entry, select a block of text (from a word or two to many paragraphs) and choose Insert → AutoText → New. (If the AutoText toolbar is visible—to make it so, choose View → Toolbars → AutoText—you can just click its New button.) Name your selection carefully, since the name you choose is the abbreviation that will trigger the expansion. Choose something easy to remember, but not something that you might type unintentionally. And, it has to be at least four characters long. Click OK.

Tip: If you've carefully formatted the paragraph you want to use as AutoText—with alignment, indentation, and line spacing, for example—you can preserve that formatting no matter what the style of the document you eventually use it in. Click the Show/Hide button (a ¶ symbol) on the Standard toolbar. Now when you select the text, select the ¶ symbol at the very end along with it; the selection's formatting will come along into AutoText.

Triggering AutoText entries

You can drop any item in the list into your document in one of two ways.

- **AutoComplete.** It doesn't get any less labor-intensive than this. When you type the first four letters of any word on the AutoText menu, AutoComplete, if turned on, shows you the full, expanded version in a pop-up screen tip (see Figure 2-16), hovering above the area where you're typing.

  To accept it, just hit Return; Word finishes the typing for you. If you don't want the choice that AutoComplete is giving you, just keep typing (or hit Esc). If you inadvertently accept a completion that you didn't want, just press ⌘-Z to undo it. You can also choose Edit → Undo AutoComplete.

  There's little downside to leaving AutoComplete turned on. After all, you can ignore all of its screen tip suggestions, if you dislike the feature. But to turn off even these suggestions, you'll find the on/off switch by choosing Tools → Auto-Correct → AutoText tab. It's the "Show AutoComplete tip for AutoText, Contacts and dates" box (see Figure 2-17).

- **Choosing from AutoText menu.** Choose Insert → AutoText. The current Auto-Text items are listed in the submenus that have arrows. Drag through the submenus until you find the entry you want to avoid typing, and click it to drop it

AutoText Toolbar

If you use AutoText frequently, or when you're first using Word 2008 and adding lots of new entries, consider keeping the AutoText toolbar visible at all times. Choose View → Toolbars → AutoText, or click Show Toolbar on the AutoText tab of the AutoCorrect dialog box (see Figure 2-17).

The first button on the toolbar, which looks like an A (representing text) and a mechanical cog-wheel (representing automation), calls up the AutoText tab, saving you several clicks.

All your AutoText entries are found under the All Entries menu, making them more easily accessible than the Insert → AutoText submenu.

The New button is usually grayed out. It's active only when you select a word, phrase, paragraph, or graphic. Clicking New brings up a dialog box where you can confirm, and name, your selection as a brand-new AutoText entry, never to be typed in full again. (The first four letters of the name entered here will trigger AutoComplete, so make sure to use the first four letters of what you want to type, or something equally easy to remember.)

into your document. Your choice appears whcrever you left your insertion point, and it inherits whatever text style and formatting is in place at that point (unless the AutoText includes paragraph formatting as described in the Tip on page 79).

AutoText graphics

Despite its name, AutoText can automate more than just text. It can easily store frequently used graphics, as well. Create a drawing in Word (see Chapter 18), or paste a graphic from another program into a Word document—a logo that you've created in a drawing or painting program, your scanned signature, or a favorite photograph, perhaps. Click the graphic to select it, then choose Insert → AutoText → New (or click the New button on the AutoText tab or toolbar).

You can't insert an AutoComplete graphic by typing. So, to drop it into a document, you have to choose its name from the Insert → AutoText submenu (or the AutoText toolbar).

AutoText fields

Some of the preinstalled AutoText entries are *fields*: placeholders that, when you print, Word fills in with the date, type, page number, and so on. Word lists them in the Header/Footer section of the AutoText submenu, because that's where you're most likely to use them.

For example, you can place a page number at the top of each page by putting a— *PAGE*—AutoText field in the header. To remind yourself (and everyone else) who wrote a particular document and when, place the "Author, Page #, Date" AutoText in the footer. (Word uses the name you entered when first setting up Office. To override that name, enter a different name in the Word → Preferences → User Information panel.)

AutoText for Polyglots

If you have the English version of Office 2008, and you never type in any language other than English, this sidebar is *not* for you.

But suppose you're typing a letter to your lover in Paris, only to realize—*sacre bleu!*—that the entries listed in the AutoText tab of the AutoCorrect dialog box are in English, and will do you no good at all.

Not to worry. Instead of using the AutoText tab, use the submenus on the Insert → AutoText menu, or the All Entries menu on the AutoText toolbar. Those menus reflect the language currently in effect at the insertion point, while the list in the AutoCorrect box always reflects the language of the version of Word that you've purchased.

How does Word know which language you're typing in? You told it so by highlighting the foreign language text, choosing Tools → Language, and then selecting a language in the dialog box that appears next. So, before typing your letter to Jean-Marie, choose Tools → Language, select French in the list that appears and click OK. *Et voilà!*—your choices on the AutoText submenus and AutoText tab are in French. (If you've already begun typing in French, be sure to select that text first. Otherwise, Word will think it's very poorly spelled English.)

Project Gallery Templates

When you launch Word, or when you choose File → Project Gallery, the Project Gallery appears, one of the two places in Office 2008 giving you access to a library of document templates and document-creation wizards (see Figure 2-18). (See Chapter 8 to learn about the other place: Office 2008's new Elements Gallery, which features Publication Templates when you're working in Word's Publishing Layout view.)

A *template* is like Word stationery: It's a special kind of document with formatting and preference options set the way you like them. A *wizard,* on the other hand, is Microsoft's term for a series of interview-style dialog boxes that request information from you, process your responses, and produce a document based on your answers.

The Project Gallery templates create not only Word documents, but documents for Excel, PowerPoint, and Entourage as well. Use the Show pop-up menu to narrow the field to only Word documents—and then use the Category list to display the type of the document you're after. With the advent of Word 2008's Publishing Layout view, several wizards have been put out of work. Only three remain: the Mailing Label Wizard, the Envelope Wizard, and the Letter Wizard.

Note: Many of these Word templates use the new Word Publishing Layout View—though you can't tell which by looking at their thumbnails in the Project Gallery. Choose one of these Publication Templates, and Word opens in Publishing Layout View, ready for you to begin replacing the template's placeholder text and pictures with your own. See Chapter 8 for the full story on Word's new page layout abilities.

The offerings in Office 2008's Project Gallery combine wizards and templates, with the ultimate aim of, once again, saving you much of the grunt work of typing and formatting. Here's how you might use one of these wizards to create a business letter:

1. **Choose File → Project Gallery.**

   The Project Gallery opens, as described on page 719. Except for Blank Documents and My Templates, all the Groups in the list box at the left have lists of built-in templates (Figure 2-18).

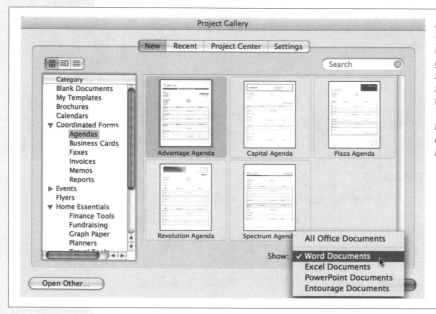

Figure 2-18:
Click the "flippy triangles" next to the groups to see a larger selection of templates. To see only the ones that work in Word, select "Word documents" from the Show pop-up menu at the bottom of the Project Gallery.

2. **Click Stationery.**

   Word displays a list of prefab stationery designs. (If you're not seeing the thumbnail images, click the icon-view button at the upper-left corner of the Project Gallery window and click the New tab.)

3. **Scroll down and double-click the Letter Wizard.**

   The Letter Wizard window appears (Figure 2-19). Here you choose a page design, a letter style, and whether or not to include a date or leave space for a preprinted letterhead. When you've made your selections, click Next.

4. **Fill in the blanks with the recipient's name and address—or click the address book icon to choose a name and address from your Entourage address book.**

   Continue by choosing the salutation style using the pop-up menu or the radio buttons marked Informal, Formal, Business, or Other. Click Next to move to the Other Elements tab.

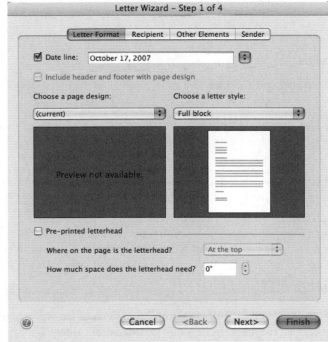

Figure 2-19:
Top: A template is a canned Office document filled with "dummy" text. You could, if you wish, simply drag through it and replace it with new text of your own.

Bottom: The Letter wizard, on the other hand, presents a series of dialog box tabs to fill in, partially automating the process of creating a letter.

5. **Use the checkboxes to include any of the optional elements such as Reference line or Attention, and then use the associated pop-up menu to choose the style for those elements.**

   Finish this section by choosing an address to include in the cc field, if desired, either by typing at in directly, or choosing an address by clicking the Address book icon. Then click Next again to move to the final Sender page of the wizard.

6. **Use the address book icon or the pop-up menu to add your (or the sender's) name and address.**

   Or turn on the Omit checkbox if you don't want to include the return address—for example, if you're sending the letter on preprinted letterhead.

7. **In the final section use the pop-up menus to add to your closing, a job title, company, or typist initials. Finally, turn on the checkbox for enclosures and enter a number in that field if you'll be enclosing other sheets with your letter.**

   At this point you've completed all the steps of the wizard—but you can still use the tabs at the top of the window to go back and make any changes to your setup.

8. **When the document looks the way you want it, click Finish.**

   Word transfers your setup to a new document in Print Layout view with the words *Type your text here* highlighted so you can immediately begin typing the body of your letter.

AutoFormat

Has this happened to you?

- You type a numbered list, and suddenly the next number in sequence appears on its own.

- You type a Web address, and suddenly Word turns it into a blue, underlined, working hyperlink (that you can't edit, since clicking inside it opens your Web browser).

- You type an email smiley—which looks like :)—and Word, on its own, decides to replace your punctuation symbol with an actual graphic smiley face, like ☺.

Tip: Remember: Just because Word steps in and formats something for you doesn't mean you're stuck with it. You don't even have to backspace over it; just press ⌘-Z or F1 (or choose the "change back" from the smart button menu). Whatever it is that Word just did—making a smiley face, turning a URL into blue underlined text, numbering a list—is restored to the way you originally typed it.

All of these behaviors—considered helpful by Microsoft and unspeakably rude by many Word fans—are triggered by a technology called AutoFormat. This tool doesn't have to be annoying. In fact, once you learn the workings behind AutoFormat, you can control and use it to your own advantage.

There are two ways to use AutoFormat: You can have Word autoformat words and paragraphs as you type them, or you can autoformat manually, in one pass, after the typing is complete.

Autoformatting as you type

To turn AutoFormat on and off, choose the Tools → AutoCorrect → AutoFormat As You Type tab. There they are: the master on/off switches for all of Word's meddlesome behavior (see Figure 2-20).

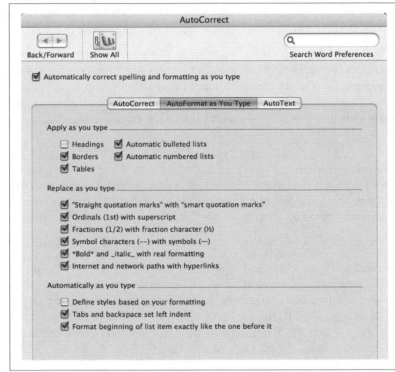

Figure 2-20:
The center tab of the AutoCorrect dialog box is called "AutoFormat as you Type". Here you can turn on and off the formatting-on-the-fly changes that Word offers to make. (As with the AutoCorrect feature described on page 75, this box may open when you click "Control Auto-Correct Options" on the smart button menu.)

To turn AutoFormat off completely, uncheck *all* the boxes and click OK.

You should also turn AutoFormat off if your document is destined for plain text, or if you're going to paste and format it in a different program anyway. Also, be aware that curly quotes and bullets can turn into funny characters when pasted into an email. (They look fine in Entourage email, but your recipient's email program may not translate them properly. And borders don't work at all.) Later, you can turn the same plain text into a nicely formatted Word document by conducting a single Auto Format pass, as described below.

There's a checkbox for each feature that Word can autoformat. Here's what each AutoFormat option does:

- **Headings.** If you type a short phrase with no ending punctuation and press Return twice, Word interprets it as a heading and applies a big, bold style (Heading 1) to it.

- **Borders.** Word draws a bold horizontal line across the page when you type three hyphens in a row (or three underlines) and press Return—a handy way to break up sections in a document, if that's indeed what you want.

  AutoFormat also creates a double line if you type three equal signs (===); a dotted line for asterisks (***); a wavy line for tildes (~~~); and a triple, picture frame-like line for number signs (###). (Press Return after the symbols.) Later, you can reformat the line or turn it into a frame by clicking in the paragraph and using the "Borders and Shading" tools on the Formatting Palette (page 114).

- **Tables.** This feature lets you create Word tables (see page 150) by using typed characters instead of the Draw Table tool. Type a plus sign (+) to start the table, a row of hyphens (---) to set the width for the first cell, another + sign to end the cell, more hyphens, and so on. The line has to begin and end with + signs. You can also switch to using Word's table tools to reformat or expand the table at any time.

Note: Because Word's table feature is so easy to use, it's hard to imagine why anyone would create a table using + signs and hyphens. The answer is that tables sent by email, as well as those posted on Web pages and newsgroups, *already* use this format. By pasting them into Word and performing an AutoFormat pass, you turn existing Internet tables into proper Word tables. Few people build a *fresh* table using this method.

- **Automatic bulleted lists.** When you type a common "bullet" character, such as *, -, >, or =>, and follow it with a space or a tab, then some text, and then press Return, Word changes the character to its proper bullet symbol (• or ❒, for example). It also switches to the ListParagraph style in your document's template (page 127). When you type a return at the end of a line, Word continues with the next bullet. Press Return twice to end the list.

  You can even use pictures as bullets; just choose Format → "Bullets and Numbering" → Bulleted, click one of the bullet thumbnails to modify, and click Customize. In the "Customize bulleted list" dialog box click Picture, choose a picture from your hard drive, and click Insert. The picture bullet appears on your page, scaled to match your font size, and ready to begin your list.

- **Automatic numbered lists.** When you type a number followed by a period (or a hyphen, close parenthesis, or close angle bracket [>]) and a space or tab, Word understands that you're starting a numbered list. After you press Return, Word automatically types the next number in the series and applies a ListParagraph style (page 127) from your document's template. Pressing the Return key twice in a row instructs Word to end the list.

- **"Straight quotes" with "smart quotes."** When you type a quotation mark (Shift-apostrophe), Word replaces the double-apostrophe straight quotes with more attractive, typographically correct curly quotes.

  Most of the time, this is a useful option. If you're going to email the document, however, turn this feature off. (See page 59 for details.)

- **Ordinals (1st) with superscript.** If you type "1st," Word instantly changes it to 1st.

- **Symbol characters (--) with symbols (—).** When you turn on this box, Word changes two hyphens to an em dash, like this—. It's a handy feature, especially because the keystroke for dashes is so hard to remember (Shift-Option-hyphen).

Tip: Typographically speaking, an en dash is used to indicate a range or gap in a sequence ("The poetry reading went from 6:30 p.m.–11:00 p.m., and featured a reading from pages 23–142 of *Letters My Father Never Wrote Me*"). The em dash is the real dash, which indicates a pause for impact ("I can't stand readings—especially poetry").

- ***Bold* and _italic_ with real formatting.** When Word encounters words bounded by asterisks and underscores, it changes them to boldface and italics, respectively.

  You may already be familiar with the use of asterisks and underscores for emphasis on the Internet. For the same reason, you can use this feature during a final AutoFormat pass (see below) to reformat text you've copied from an email or chat room. (Few people use this feature while typing, since it's easier to press ⌘-B for bold or ⌘-I for italics. Most people use it only when massaging text from the Internet.)

- **Internet paths with hyperlinks.** When this box is checked, Word changes URLs that you type (for instance) into working hyperlinks. Hyperlinks are usually formatted in blue and underscored, unless you change these settings in the Format → Style dialog box (see page 340).

- **Format the beginning of list item exactly like the one before it.** This option combines automation with the freedom of doing your own formatting.

  For example, suppose you want to start each item in your list with a Roman numeral, followed by a period and a space, followed by the first word in bold, followed by a period and the rest of the sentence in plain text. To begin, type the first item that way and press Return. Word starts a new list item every time you hit Return. Press Return twice to end the list.

  The key is to start the first item with a number or bullet to let Word know that you're starting a list. If you want the first word or words to appear in, for example, bold (like the first sentences in this bulleted list), you have to follow it with a period, colon, hyphen, dash, or other punctuation mark.

- **Define styles based on your formatting.** Here's the most powerful option on the AutoFormat tab. It tells Word to update the document's styles (see page 127), based on the formatting done directly in the document. For example, if you change your first heading to 14-point Helvetica Bold, Word applies that font to *all* occurrences of that style; you've just redefined the style, in fact. This option *overrides* any formatting you've done in the Styles dialog box, so use it with caution.

Tip: Consider memorizing AutoFormat "cues" for other AutoFormat options, too (in addition to using asterisks for bold and underlines for italic). For instance, if you frequently make bulleted lists, try to get in the habit of typing an asterisk for a bullet, knowing that Word will automatically change it to • (Or use a ListBullet *style*—see page 127).

Autoformatting in one pass

Even if you don't like Word making changes as you type, you can still benefit from AutoFormat—by running your finished document through what you might call its AutoFormat-O-Matic. For instance, you can take text that uses the Internet style for *bold* and _italic_ and have Word change them into proper **boldface** and *italics*. AutoFormat can also clean up a document by changing URLs into live hyperlinks or adding attractive bullets to lists, all at once.

First, choose Tools → AutoCorrect → AutoFormat As You Type and turn off all the boxes; now Word won't make any of these corrections *during* your typing.

When you're ready to autoformat, choose Format → AutoFormat → Options; the checkboxes here correspond, for the most part, to those described above. You're given only a couple of new ones here. They are as follows:

- **Other Paragraphs.** Ordinarily, Word's AutoFormat feature applies a Heading style to whatever it recognizes as a heading, and a List style to anything it recognizes as a list. But if you turn on this option, Word also applies other styles when autoformatting. For example, Word can format plain text to your default Body Text font and paragraph style.

  Word does this by comparing the text in the document to the styles in your Normal template (see page 230) and automatically applying the closest matching style. If this box is turned on and the document appears to be a letter, Word also applies letter features such as Inside Address.

- **Preserve Styles.** Turn on this box if you've already done some formatting of your own in the document *before* starting the AutoFormat pass. Word won't change the style of any text you've manually formatted.

When you click OK, you return to the AutoFormat dialog box. So far, you've just specified what happens when Word conducts its editorial pass through your document. To trigger that event later, choose Format → AutoFormat—which opens this dialog box. Choose a document type from the pop-up menu—General document, Letter, or Email—which tells Word what kind of document it's going to be auto-formatting. For instance, if the document is a letter, Word knows to apply letter styles such as Inside Address and Closing. If you choose Email, Word eliminates formatting options that usually don't work in email, such as first-line indents. (Clicking Options returns you to the AutoFormat tab described above.)

If you choose "AutoFormat and review each change," Word opens a dialog box showing each change Word is about to make; you can choose to accept or reject it. You can also click Style Gallery to apply one of Word's document templates (see page 227), with all its colors and fonts, to the finished document. If you choose "AutoFormat now," Word goes through the document and prepares all auto-formatting changes without pausing.

Formatting in Word

Formatting is a way to inject your style into the documents you create. Whether it's a newsletter for your college football fan club, or a white paper for your Fortune 500 business, formatting lets you transform that boring 12-point Times into something bold (pun intended) and exciting.

Word has independent formatting controls for each of four entities: *characters* (individual letters and words), *paragraphs* (anything you've typed that's followed by a press of the Return key), *sections* (similar to chapters, as described on "Inserting and Removing Section Breaks), and the entire *document*. Attributes like bold and italic are *character* formatting; line spacing and centering are *paragraph* attributes; page numbering is done on a *section-by-section* basis; and margin settings are considered *document* settings. Understanding these distinctions will help you know where to look to achieve a certain desired effect.

The Formatting Palette

The Toolbox, which is the envy of Windows fan the world over, puts Word's most commonly used tools and essential formatting commands within easy reach, including the popular Formatting Palette (Figure 3-1). If it's been hidden, reveal it by choosing View → Formatting Palette or click the Toolbox button on the Standard toolbar and click its Formatting Palette button. Both methods alternately hide and show the Toolbox.

The options on the Formatting Palette change depending on what you're doing. When you click a photo or drawing, for example, the palette changes to show the tools you need to work with graphics. Most of the time, however, the Formatting Palette displays the commands you most frequently need to work with fonts, paragraph formatting, and other elements of text.

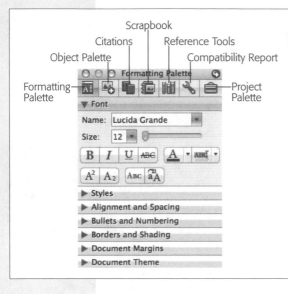

Figure 3-1:
In Word 2008, almost every conceivable formatting control resides in a single convenient window, a jam-packed command center called the Toolbox. Its row of navigation buttons open the Formatting palette, the Object Palette, Citations, Scrapbook, Reference Tools, Compatibility Report, and the Project Palette. The essential Formatting Palette is further subdivided into panes, including the Font panel, which lists the quickest ways to restyle your text. Clicking the close button sends the Toolbox genie back into its toolbar button.

Character Formatting

The Font panel of the Formatting Palette—the uppermost pane of the palette—deals mostly with the appearance of your letters, numbers, and other characters. You can also access most of these functions via the Formatting toolbar (choose View → Toolbars → Formatting if you don't see it).

Choosing Fonts

Installing Office 2008 adds 126 fonts to your Library → Fonts folder—an unannounced gift from Microsoft.

To change the font of the text you've already typed, select the text first, using any of the methods described on page 39. If, instead, you choose a new font in the middle of a sentence or even the middle of a word, the new font will take effect with the next letter you type.

Now, open the Font menu or click the Name pop-up menu in the Formatting Palette's Font pane to reveal your Mac's typeface names in their own typefaces (Figure 3-2). This what-you-see-is-what-you-get (WYSIWYG) font menu feature has a few interesting features, such as:

• If you have a very long list of fonts, you don't have to scroll all the way down to, say, Zapf Chancery. Once the menu (or Formatting Palette pop-up list) is open, you can *type* the first letter or two of the target font. The menu shifts instantly to that alphabetical position in the font list.

You can open the font list marginally faster if you *don't* use the WYSIWYG fonts feature. Pressing Shift when opening the Font menu or Fonts list in the Formatting Palette lets you see all the fonts listed in plain type. Honestly, though, unless you've got a really slow computer, the difference is negligible. But this Shift-key trick is a helpful solution when you're trying to figure out the name of a font that's showing up as symbols. (You can turn off the WYSIWYG feature for good by choosing Word → Preferences → General panel and turning off "WYSIWYG font and style menus," then clicking OK.)

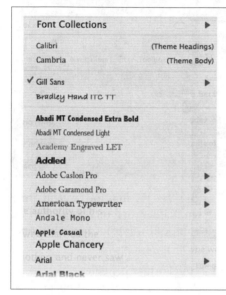

Figure 3-2:
Whether you pick from the Font menu or the Formatting Palette, you get to see what each font looks like. Fonts you've used most recently are conveniently grouped together at the top.

- Once you've turned off WYSIWYG font menus, you can still summon the WYSIWYG font when you *do* want it by pressing Shift when opening one of the Font menus.

Even the Formatting Palette doesn't have every possible font manipulation tool; for that, you'll need the Font dialog box, as shown in Figure 3-3. To open it, choose Format → Font or press ⌘-D. In the following pages, you'll read about both the Formatting Palette and the more complete controls available in the Font dialog box.

Font Sizes

Font sizes are measured in points. A point is 1/72 of an inch in letter height, but you don't need to know that; what you *should* know is that most text is printed at 10- or 12-point sizes.

Some fonts look too large at 12 point. Other fonts are almost uncomfortably small at 10 point. Print a test page to be sure, since the font size may look different on paper than on the screen, depending on your monitor's resolution. (If you have a

The First Rule of Fonts

Serifs are the little points or lines at the ends of the strokes that form certain kinds of typefaces. They're a remnant of the time before printing presses, when all type was inscribed by hand with a broad-tipped pen and ink. Over the past 500 years, type designers have retained serifs in these font designs—not out of a reverence for tradition, but because serifs make type more readable. Tests for readability have shown that serif-style typefaces—especially the *old-style* ones like Garamond, Palatino, and Times—are much easier to read in blocks of text than *sans-serif* typefaces. Most books, including this one, use a serif font as the primary typeface, and a sans-serif font for headlines, titles, and little informative boxes like this one.

Grab almost any book, newspaper, or magazine and you'll see the serif-for-body-copy rule in effect. Do your readers a favor by following this rule, whether you're writing a letter, a newsletter, or a doctoral dissertation.

For years Word used Times New Roman for its standard serif font, and Arial for its standard sans-serif font. But times change, and in order to improve the appearance of on-screen text—especially on LCD monitors—Microsoft demoted those two text troopers and replaced them with a pair of brand-new ClearType fonts, designed with the computer screen in mind, and bearing bizarre, made-up names. *Cambria* is the new standard serif font, and *Calibri* the new standard sans-serif font. Microsoft unveiled these new fonts in Office 2007 for Windows, and Office 2008 brings them to the Mac, along with their ClearType siblings: *Constantia, Corbel, Candara,* and *Consolas.*

high-resolution monitor, your tendency will be to make the font too large in order to achieve a comfortable size to read on the screen. Rather than increasing the font size, use the Zoom box [page 17] to verify that your font will print out in a proper size.)

To select a font size, choose one from the list in the Formatting Palette, type a size into the Size box in the Formatting Palette, or choose a point size in the Font dialog box (Format → Font or ⌘-D).

Tip: You can always bump selected text to a slightly higher or lower point size by pressing Shift-⌘-> (that is, period) or Shift-⌘-< (comma) for larger and smaller type, respectively. Each time you press the combination, the text grows or shrinks by the intervals listed in the Formatting Palette's Size box (from 12 to 14 to 16, for example).

Styles of Type

You can apply different type styles to your regular, unembellished font for emphasis or effect. Most font styles are available in the Formatting Palette with a single click; a few extra ones reside in the "Font style" box in the Font dialog box (see Figure 3-3, top). Those type styles, as they appear in the Font dialog box, are as follows:

- **Regular** denotes plain, unadulterated text. Not bolded, not underlined.

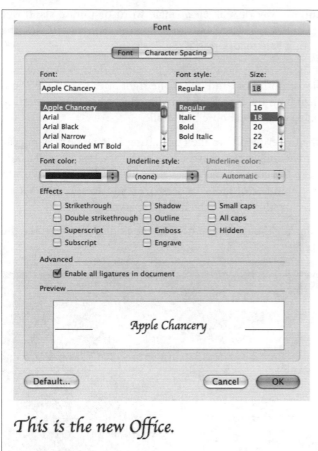

Figure 3-3:
Top: The Font dialog box (Format → Font or ⌘-D). It not only has more font style options than the Formatting Palette, it also gives you a preview at the bottom of the box. If you like what you see, click OK.

Bottom: The Advanced section of the Font dialog box has the checkbox to activate ligatures–those conjoined characters (shown in lower example) that improve the appearance of your text, as described on page 97.

Tip: You can return to plain text at any time without even opening the Font dialog box. Just highlight the text you've been playing with in your document and choose Edit → Clear → Formats or Clear Formatting from the Style menu in the Formatting Palette (*Keyboard shortcut:* Shift-⌘-N).

However, with an entire paragraph selected, the Clear Formatting command takes you all the way back to the Normal *style* (see page 127), which generally means your 12-point body type. (If you select less than a paragraph, it returns your text to the underlying *paragraph* style.) To strip font effects from a selected paragraph without changing its underlying style definition (such as 24-point Futura for a headline), press Control-Space bar instead.

- **Italic** is commonly used for foreign words and phrases, as well as the titles of books, movies, and magazines. *Shortcuts*: Click the capital I in the Formatting Palette, or press ⌘-I.

- **Bold** is the most common way of making a single word or phrase stand out from the surrounding landscape. Use bold for emphasis. *Shortcuts:* Click the capital B in the Formatting Palette, or press ⌘-B.

- **Bold Italic** is a beautiful effect for headings and headlines. Use either method described above to choose both bold and italic, one right after the other. You'll know you've got it when both the B and the I are highlighted in the Formatting Palette. In the Font dialog box, just choose Bold Italic.

- **Underline**. Clicking the underlined U in the Formatting Palette, or pressing ⌘-U (Shift-⌘-D for a double underline), draws a line under the text, as well as the spaces between words. In the Font dialog box, use the "Underline style" pop-up menu to choose from a number of fancy underscores, and to specify whether you want Word to underline the words only, not the spaces.

You can also choose a color for the underline itself in the Font dialog box; see the next section for more detail.

UP TO SPEED

What's Normal?

When opening a new blank document, notice the name in the Name box located in the Formatting Palette: Normal. Word's idea of normal, circa 2008, is black, 12-point Cambria.

But who's to say what's normal? You may prefer a soothing blue color. Or you may want to use boldface all the time, since you find it easier to read. You may want to make Sand your signature font—forget that stodgy Cambria! Fortunately, it's easy enough to specify your preferred typeface whenever you start a new document.

Choose Format → Font to open the Font dialog box. Now you can choose a font, color, size, or any of the other effects described in this section. When you've selected the font you want, click Default at lower left (shown at top in Figure 3-3). Word asks if you're sure that you want all new documents to use this font, as shown here. Click Yes. (Technically, you've just redefined the Normal style; see page 127 for more on the canned sets of formatting characteristics known as styles.)

Typing in Color

Color is a great way to liven up your documents—an increasingly valuable option in a world where many documents are read onscreen and nearly everyone has a color printer. Click the tiny "Font color" color swatch or pop-up menu in the Formatting Palette or the Format → Font dialog box to survey your selection of 70 colors, as shown in Figure 3-4. To choose a color, just click it.

Tip: When using Word to prepare a document for the Web, remember that colors look different on different computers. For example, someone viewing your page on a Windows machine or an older monitor may see your true colors very differently.

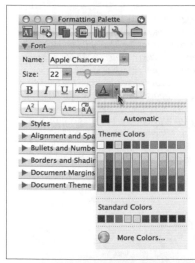

Figure 3-4:
From the Formatting Palette's font color button, Word gives quick access to 70 commonplace colors. To choose from a broader rainbow, click the More Colors button. Doing so opens the Apple Color Picker dialog box, which has several different ways to specify any color under the sun, as described on page 747.

POWER USERS' CLINIC

Ligatures: The Art of Linked Letters

Ligatures are pairs of letters that share common components when printed next to each other. Scribes writing with pen and ink in the Middle Ages originally created ligatures to save space on the parchment and increase writing speed—just like when you cross two "t's" in a word at once when you write, for example, "flutter." Typographers now create these special combination characters to improve the appearance of the printed text. The most common ligatures are ff, fi, fl, ffi, and ffl. (Believe it or not, the ampersand [&] is actually a stylized ligature for the letters *et*—Latin for *and*.)

Character Spacing

Occasionally, you may need to adjust the amount of space between letters, known to typographers as *tracking*. You use this control, for example, to expand or contract a headline to perfectly fit above a column. Used judiciously the effect is nearly invisible, yet it can make a big improvement to the appearance of your layout. Adjusting tracking by more than a few percent creates an odd appearance.

Office doesn't include this control in the Formatting palette—only in the Font dialog box. Select the text you want to adjust, choose Format → Font and click the Character Spacing tab (see Figure 3-5). Set the Spacing pop-up menu to Expanded—to increase character spacing—or Condensed—to decrease character spacing. Then use the up- and down-arrow button next to the By box to determine the percentage of expansion or contraction. Keep an eye on the Preview box to see the effect your changes will have.

If you turn on the "Kerning for fonts" checkbox and set the "Points and above" box for the size of text you want to affect, Office subtly adjusts the character spacing between each pair of letters for an even appearance. For example, applying kerning to the word TAP reduces the space between the T and the A, making the letter spacing appear more consistent.

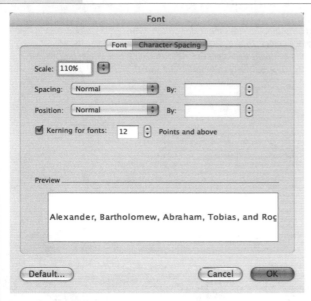

Figure 3-5:
The Character Spacing portion of the Font dialog box shows controls for the horizontal and vertical positioning of selected characters. Additionally the Scale control lets you stretch or shrink text horizontally—not the spaces between the letters, but the letters themselves—by selecting a percentage from the pop-up menu, or typing a percentage directly into the box. This control can create a bizarre appearance, but if you limit your adjustments to just a few percent, you can fine-tune the length of your lines of text invisibly.

While the Spacing control sets the horizontal position of the character, the Position control—otherwise known as *baseline shift*—sets the vertical character position. This adjustment comes in handy when writing chemical formulae or using the trademark (™) symbol. Use the up- and down-arrow button on the Position line to adjust the amount of shift while you watch the Preview panel.

Special Text Effects

Bold and italic give enough variety for most documents, but many more buttons await in the Formatting Palette, and still more choices in the Font dialog box. Some of them, such as Outline and Shadow, are clearly just for show (they usually look amateurish in printed documents); others, such as Subscript and All Caps, are invaluable tools.

Here are the options, in order, as they appear in the Font dialog box:

- **Strikethrough** and **Double strikethrough** indicate that something's crossed out, but you don't want to delete it outright. (Word's change-tracking feature adds strikethrough style to deleted text automatically; see page 171.) *Shortcuts:* Click the *ABC* button on the Formatting Palette (you can only apply the double strikethrough via the Font dialog box).

- **Superscript** and **Subscript** shift characters slightly higher or lower (respectively) than the other text on its line and slightly decreases their size—perfect for chemical formulas and exponents. (You don't need these effects for footnotes, as Word handles footnote formatting automatically, as described on page 220.)

You can make letters or symbols super- or subscripted, too, not just numbers—very handy if you like taking things to the Nth degree. *Shortcuts:* Click the A2 or A^2 in the Formatting Palette, or press ⌘-= for Subscript or Shift-⌘-= for Superscript.

- **Shadow** creates a heavier outline that makes the words appear slightly raised, and **Outline** reverses the color of the type, making the letter white and the outline black (or whatever text color you're using). Shadow Both was popular when the Mac first appeared, but seems dated now.

- **Emboss** and **Engrave** make letters appear slightly raised or carved out, as if with a chisel. They work best on a colored background, such as on a Web page. On a white background, the words gain a subtle drop shadow. (These infrequently used effects are available only in the Font dialog box, not on the Formatting Palette.)

Small Caps, All Caps

Word has several variations on the when-to-capitalize scheme you probably learned in English class. For example, you can apply either of these formats to text you've highlighted (or are about to type):

- **Small Caps** creates a formal look for headings and letterheads; all the letters are capped, but "lowercase" letters are shown in smaller capitals, SOMETHING LIKE THIS. *Shortcut:* Click the *ABC* button on the Formatting Palette.

- **All Caps** simply converts highlighted text to all capital letters. You can choose "All caps" in the Font dialog box, or click the "a → A" button in the Formatting Palette.

Even though the visual result is the same, there's a big difference between using the All Caps style and simply typing some words with the Caps Lock key down. Text you've formatted as All Caps is still, in Word's brain, actually mixed upper- and lowercase letters. It thinks you've applied the all-cap format just as a visual, the way you'd apply bold or blue or underlining. That is, by turning off the All Caps style, the text reverts to the capitalization you originally used when typing it—something you can't say about text you typed with the Caps Lock key.

You can therefore search for text in the All Caps style using the "Find and Replace" command, or define it as part of a *style* (see page 127).

Tip: To change the capitalization of words you've already typed—or to fix an email message that arrived IN ALL CAPITAL LETTERS—highlight the text and then choose Format → Change Case. By choosing from the list in the Change Case dialog box, you can make Word instantly "retype" the text as all lowercase (all small letters), all uppercase (all caps), Sentence case (where the first letter of every sentence is capitalized as usual), or Title Case (where the first letter of every word is capped).

(Unfortunately, these options aren't terrifically smart; Sentence case still leaves names and the word I lowercase, and Title Case doesn't leave small words like *of* and *the* lowercase.)

The most interesting (but least useful) choice here is tOGGLE cASE, which reverses the existing capitalization, whatever it may be.

Un-Typewriter Class

Even though most computer owners haven't touched a typewriter for years–if ever–many bad habits from that earlier technology persist. Here are a few of the more egregious examples of typewriter style that are obsolete in the computer age.

- **Underlining.** Although Word makes it simple to format text with underlining, don't use this style for emphasis. Use **bold** or *italics*, which are much more professional looking (and equally easy to apply). (When's the last time you saw something underlined in a magazine article?)

- **Spacing with the space bar.** Use the space bar only for spacing between words. Never use the space bar for aligning successive lines of text; when printed, those spaces will cause your text to tumble out of alignment. Instead, use Word's tab feature, as described on page 111.

- **Special characters and accents** are easy to produce correctly on a computer. Don't write resume if you mean résumé. Are you making copies or using the Xerox™? Don't put it off until mañana–take that vacation to Curaçao today!

To find out how to produce these special markings, use the Keyboard Viewer–but first you have to bring it out of hiding. Choose Apple Menu → System Preferences → International and click the Input Menu tab. Turn on the checkboxes for Character Palette, Keyboard Viewer, and "Show input menu in menu bar." From now on, you can open the Keyboard Viewer by clicking the International menulet–the little flag–at the right end of your Mac's menu bar and choosing Show Keyboard Viewer.

Use its pop-up menu to select the font you're using and watch the Keyboard Viewer as you press Option–with and without the shift key–to display these hidden characters. When you spot the character you're looking for, press that key on the keyboard or click it in the Keyboard Viewer to add it to your document at the insertion point.

When you press Option, the Keyboard Viewer highlights five keys–tilde, E, U, I, N–that you can use to add accents to letters using a two-step process. For example, to type the ü in über, type Option-u, followed by u. The same technique works to apply accents to ñ, é, and so on. After you learn a key combination, you won't need to open the Keyboard Viewer–until you need to type € or π.

You can only access the *complete* collection of special characters via the Mac OS X Character Palette; choose → Show Character Palette from the International menulet in the menu bar, or use Word's Insert → Symbol command. (See page 223 for more on symbols and special characters.)

Using two hyphens (--) to represent a **dash** is passé. What you want is an *em dash*–so called because it's the width of an upper-case M. Create it with the Shift-Option-hyphen key combination, or make sure you've configured Word's "Auto Format as You Type" feature to do it for you (see page 84).

Hidden Text

Word's Hidden Text feature can remove your personal notes and reminders from plain sight in a document. You can make the hidden text reappear only when you want to; you can also choose whether or not you want it to show up when printed.

To turn certain text invisible, first select it. Choose Format → Font → Font tab. (There's no button for hidden text on the Formatting Palette.) Turn on the Hidden box and click OK; the text disappears until you choose to show it. (To turn hidden text back into normal text, show the hidden text as described next, select it, choose Format → Font → Fonts tab, and turn off the Hidden box.)

Drop Caps

Have you ever wished you could duplicate those extra-large capitals that start the chapters of so many books? Unfortunately, just enlarging the point size of the first letter doesn't work. True drop caps, as they're called, are not only large, but they drop below the other letters on the line; hence the name.

But Word 2008 can do it. After typing the first paragraph of your chapter, choose Format → Drop Cap. Choose one of the drop-cap styles, then adjust the Options settings (font,

number of lines to drop down, and distance from text) until you've got the look you like. When you click OK, Word sends you into Page Layout view—if you weren't there already—where the drop cap appears as an independent graphic box that you can enlarge or drag as you would any graphic (see Chapter 19).

If you return to Normal view, you won't see the drop cap in its correct position; that's perfectly normal, so to speak.

When you want Word to display the text you've designated as hidden, use either of these techniques:

- Choose Word → Preferences → View tab. Turn on "Hidden text" and click OK.

- Click the Show/Hide button (¶) on the Standard toolbar (or the Document section of the Formatting Palette).

Either way, hidden text appears with a dotted underline to distinguish it from the rest of the text.

Tip: Whether or not hidden text prints is up to you. To print hidden text along with the rest of the document, choose Word → Preferences, click the Print button, turn on the Include with Document → Hidden Text box, and click OK.

Formatting

If you're in the business world, or even the business of organizing your thoughts, you can't go far without using numbered or bulleted lists.

Bulleted lists are an attractive way of presenting nuggets of information. Here's a great example:

- Each paragraph is indented from the left margin (like this one) and is preceded by a *bullet* (the round dot shown at left).

- Word comes with two automatic list-formatting features turned on to help create this kind of list: "Automatic bulleted lists" and "Automatic numbered lists." However, since many people can't figure out how to control this automatic behavior, it's one of the first things they turn off—once they figure out where the preferences are. They're at Word → Preferences → Auto Correct → AutoFormat as You Type, as discussed on page 84.

- You can always create a numbered list by typing a number at the beginning of each line, but it won't be nicely indented.

- You may know how to create a bullet (•) at the beginning of every line by using the keyboard shortcut Option-8. But again, that won't produce the clean left margin on your bulleted paragraphs.

- Furthermore, creating lists manually can get messy. For example, inserting an item between two existing ones in a numbered list requires some serious renumbering. And if you want your list indented, you'll have to fiddle with the indent controls quite a bit.

Word has partially automated the process. A quick way to start a numbered or bulleted list is from the Formatting Palette. Open the "Bullets and Numbering" panel by clicking anywhere on the "Bullets and Numbering" title bar, and then click one of the list icons (next to where it says Type, as shown in Figure 3-6). Word changes the paragraph *style* to ListParagraph (see page 127), promptly indents the paragraph containing the insertion point, and adds a bullet (or the number 1). Even the indenting is perfect: The second and following lines of a list item start under the first letter, not all the way back to the left margin. To start a new list item, just hit Return. When you're finished building the list, press Return *twice*.

Figure 3-6:
Click the "Bullets and Numbering" title bar to expand the panel. The panel provides a bucketful of listing options. For example, you may choose a type of list (numbered or not), its indent, and even the number to begin your numbered lists with. Or if you aren't in a bulleted state of mind, choose "none" to remove a bullet.

If you create a *numbered* list this way, Word does the numbering automatically as you go. Better yet, if you insert a new list item between two others, Word knows enough to renumber the entire list.

The pop-up menus and icons in the "Bullets and Numbering" panel control different aspects of how your list will look (the *entire* list, no matter which individual list line contains your insertion point).

- **Style** specifies the kind of numbering (Arabic numerals, roman numerals, and so on), or the size and shape of the bullet.

- **Start** tells Word what number to start the list with.

- The **Indent** icons increase or decrease your bullet's indent.

- The **Type** icons tell Word whether you want to start an unnumbered bulleted list (the Bullets icon) or a numbered list (Numbering icon). For more detail on bullets see below.

Extra Features in the Bullets and Numbering Dialog Box

The Formatting Palette is ideal for quickly designing a list, but the "Bullets and Numbering" dialog box has even more options. Open it by double-clicking a bullet or list number, or by choosing Format → "Bullets and Numbering" (see Figure 3-7).

Customizing a bulleted list

Bulleted lists as delivered by the Formatting Palette are fine, but there may come a day when simple black, round bullets just don't cut it for your radical new-age business plan. In such cases, click the Bulleted tab in the "Bullets and Numbering" dialog box. If one of the styles appeals to you, choose it by clicking; then click Customize to open the dialog box shown at the bottom of Figure 3-7. Watch what happens in the Preview box as you make the following changes:

- **Bullet character.** Choose an alternate bullet symbol, click the Bullet button to open the Symbol dialog box (see page 223), where you can choose any character in any font to become your new bullet, or click the Picture button to create your own bullet graphic (see the box on page 105).

- **Bullet position.** The indentation point of the bullet is measured from the left margin.

- **Text position.** The text indentation is also measured from the left margin. It's usually indented farther than the bullet; note how, in Figure 3-7, the text position indent is a larger number than the bullet position one.

Click OK to return to the "Bullets and Numbering" dialog box. The bulleted list style now appears as one of the eight list icons (see Figure 3-7), easily accessible if you want to use the same style of bulleting later in the document. Click OK again to apply the new bulleted style to the current paragraph.

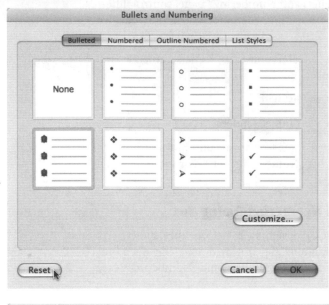

Figure 3-7:
Top: After you've customized a bulleted or numbered list (see below), clicking Reset returns a list icon to its original configuration.

Bottom: Clicking the Font button opens the Font dialog box (see page 95). You can then choose bold, italics, or even a different font altogether for your new bulleted list style. The Preview window shows you a representation of how your numbered list will look relative to the surrounding text.

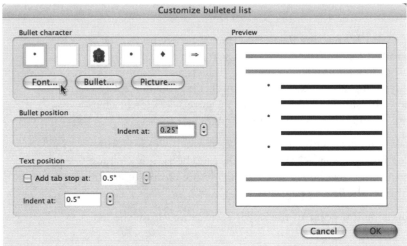

Customizing a numbered list

Like the Bulleted tab, the Numbered tab in the "Bullets and Numbering" dialog box presents a selection of eight preconfigured list styles (one of which is None). Click the one that suits your purposes, or at least comes the closest. Click Customize to open a dialog box much like the one at the bottom of Figure 3-7—but this one, of course, applies to numbers.

- **Number format.** You can't edit the number or numeral shown here, as it's determined by your choices in the "Number style" and "Start at" tools. You

GEM IN THE ROUGH

Picture Bullets

There is a host of bullets preinstalled in Word, both in the "Bullets and Numbering" dialog box and in the Symbol dialog box, as described on page 223. For added creativity, insert a picture bullet.

To do so, choose Format → "Bullets and Numbering" → Bulleted tab. Click one of the seven bullet-style thumbnails and then click Customize. The Customize bulleted list window appears. Click Picture. Now you can choose any graphics file on your Mac; Word starts you off with a folder full of its own preinstalled picture bullets. Choose one of those to

add the selected picture as a bullet to the current paragraph. Otherwise, navigate to your own picture file (something you've scanned, drawn, or downloaded from a Web site, perhaps), select the file in the list box, and click Insert.

It may sound like a lot of work, but you only have to do it once. When you press Return to make another list item, Word automatically continues using the edited picture bullet—and keeps it in the "Bullets and Numbering" line-up for later use.

can, however, type additional text into this window, such as the words *Figure*, *Item*, or *Commandment*—whichever word you want to appear before the number in each list item.

- **Number style.** This pop-up menu lets you choose Arabic or roman numerals, letters (*A*, *B*, *C*, and so on), or even words (*First*, *Second*, and so on).

- **Start at.** Usually, you'll start at 1, but you can also start at 0 or any other number by entering it in the box or choosing it with the arrows.

- **Number position.** Choosing Left, Right, or Centered from the pop-up menu aligns the number relative to the space between "Aligned at" and "Indent at."

- **Aligned at.** This is the distance from the left margin to the numbered item. For instance, if you choose Left from the number position menu and .5" for "Aligned at," the number itself will be placed half an inch from the left margin.

- **Text position.** This is the distance from the left margin to the text part of the numbered item. The larger you make this measurement, the farther from the number the text begins.

Click OK to return to the "Bullets and Numbering" dialog box; the custom numbered list style now appears as one of the eight list icons (see Figure 3-7). Click OK again to apply the new numbered style to the current paragraph.

Tip: If there's more than one numbered list in your document—if you're writing, say, a book about Office 2008 containing many numbered tutorials—you'll need a way to make the numbering start over at 1 for the second list. (Otherwise, Word will cheerfully keep your number sequence going all the way through a document.)

To tell Word to start over, click the first item in the *second* list and choose Format → "Bullets and Numbering". Click the radio button for "Restart numbering," or press ⌘-R. ("Continue previous list" gives the list item the next number in the series, no matter how many pages have elapsed since the first part of the list.) Click OK.

Paragraph Formatting

Beneath the Font and Styles panes of the Formatting Palette, you'll find "Alignment and Spacing", "Bullets and Numbering", and "Borders and Shading"—settings that affect entire *paragraphs*. Just as the Formatting Palette's top section provides the most useful controls of the Format → Font dialog box, its third section gives a subset of the Format → Paragraph dialog box (Figure 3-8, left).

And just as character formatting applies *either* to highlighted text *or* to text you're about to type, paragraph formatting applies to only a selected paragraph, several selected paragraphs, or the paragraph you're typing in (the one containing the blinking insertion point).

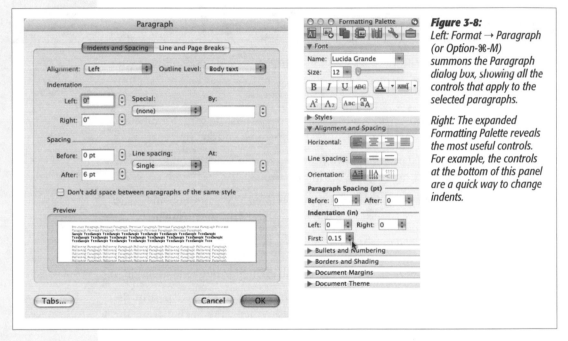

Figure 3-8:
Left: Format → Paragraph (or Option-⌘-M) summons the Paragraph dialog box, showing all the controls that apply to the selected paragraphs.

Right: The expanded Formatting Palette reveals the most useful controls. For example, the controls at the bottom of this panel are a quick way to change indents.

Alignment and Spacing

When you click the "Alignment and Spacing" title bar, the Formatting Palette expands to reveal all the commands that control how your text lies on the page (Figure 3-8, right).

Horizontal

These icons illustrate how your paragraph will be aligned with the left and right page or column margins: left aligned, centered, right aligned, or fully justified. (Justified refers to straight margins on both sides. Word automatically adjusts the spacing between letters and words to make the right margin come out even, exactly like a newspaper. Justification works best if you turn on hyphenation, too, as described on page 139.)

You may find yourself changing alignment frequently when writing something like a newsletter, where it's common to go from a centered headline to a left-aligned article to a justified column of classified ads. Fortunately, alignment is fully equipped with keyboard shortcuts: ⌘-R right-aligns the current paragraph, ⌘-L is for left alignment, ⌘-E centers the current line or paragraph, and ⌘-J justifies the current paragraph.

Line spacing

The amount of space between lines of text is called *line spacing,* or, in homage to the typewriter, single-, double-, or triple spacing. Since Word isn't constrained by the clicks of a typewriter's *platen* (the roller in a typewriter that guides the paper), you have much more line spacing flexibility.

Word's factory setting is for single-spaced lines, like the ones in this book. If you like more space between lines, or if you're required to use double-spacing for schoolwork or legal work, use these icons to change the spacing. The three line-spacing controls on the Formatting Palette correspond to single-spaced, one-and-a-half-spaced, and double-spaced text.

Note: In the olden days when printing presses used metal type, typesetters controlled line spacing by inserting thin strips of lead between the lines of metal type to give wider spacing. In the jargon of typesetters—and that of many desktop publishers—line spacing is still called *leading* (rhymes with "bedding").

Choosing Format → Paragraph → "Indents and Spacing" tab generates even more spacing options. As shown in Figure 3-8, you can choose a setting from the pop-up menu under "Line spacing" and, to get even more specific, type an exact number in the At box.

- **At least.** Choose this setting to add graphics or vary font sizes within a paragraph. In the box, type a minimum number of points (12 is a good size for single spacing). Word now will automatically adjust the spacing to accommodate any larger items in a line.

Tip: Here's a trick you can use in this or any Office 2008 measurement text box: You don't have to be content with *points* as the units. After typing the number you want, type *cm, mm, in,* or *pi* for centimeters, millimeters, inches, or picas, respectively. The software makes the conversion automatically.

- **Exactly.** Choose this setting for projects where you've been asked to use a specific line spacing in points. Enter the number of points in the box. (If any letters or pictures are too high for the spacing you've specified, they'll simply be decapitated.)

- **Multiple.** Use this setting to refine the double-single-triple spacing system. For instance, choosing Multiple and entering *1* in the At box denotes single spacing. Typing *1.3* in the At box tells Word to increase single-spacing by 30 percent. Specifying *3* in the At box creates triple spacing.

Finally, you can change line spacing using the keyboard: ⌘-1 tells Word to single-space the current paragraph, ⌘-5 is for one-and-a-half space (1.5, that is), and ⌘-2 results in double-spacing.

Widows, Orphans, and Paragraph Relationships

Ordinarily, when your text reaches the bottom of the page, Word chops a paragraph in half, if necessary, so that it continues on the top of the next page. The result isn't always especially good-looking, however; it may leave what publishers call a *widow* (the last line of a paragraph at the top of a new page) or an *orphan* (the first line of a paragraph all by itself at the bottom of a page). You can avoid these problems by highlighting a paragraph (or paragraphs), choosing Format → Paragraph → "Line and Page Breaks" tab, and turning on "Widow/Orphan control." This control instructs Word to allow no less than two lines at the top of any page before a paragraph break.

Similarly, to keep any paragraph or group of lines unbroken, just select any number of paragraphs or lines, choose Format → Paragraph → "Line and Page Breaks" tab, and turn on the "Keep lines together" box.

Another easily avoided typographical problem: a heading at the bottom of a page whose body text is split onto the next page. The solution: Select the heading, choose Format → Paragraph → "Line and Page Breaks" tab, and turn on "Keep with next." (It means, "Keep with next paragraph.")

Sure, these tools are useful when applied to individual paragraphs, but they're especially ideal for defining styles (see page 127). For example, you may as well turn on "Keep with next" for all of your heading styles, since it's never pretty when a heading appears on one page and its body text appears on the next.

Orientation

The Orientation icons on the Formatting Palette aren't actually paragraph-specific, like the other controls in their section. In fact, they work very differently depending on what you're editing:

- In a Text box, they rotate text inside the box (see page 143).

- In a table cell, they rotate the text in the selected cell (see page 159).

- If you've divided your document into sections (page 122), you can use one of these icons to rotate *entire pages* within a document—to get a couple of horizontally oriented (landscape) pages in a document whose pages are otherwise oriented vertically (portrait). Here's the trick: Before using the Orientation controls, insert a "Section Break (Next Page)" break before and after the pages you want rotated (page 134).

- If your document has neither tables nor section breaks, these icons rotate your *entire window* by 90 or 180 degrees. They don't affect how the document is *printed;* for that purpose, use the Orientation icons in the File → Page Setup dialog box. Instead, this feature rotates the image of your document onscreen to make it easier for you to edit the *text* that you've rotated 90 degrees, such as the vertical label of a table cell.

Paragraph Spacing

If you're in the habit of pressing Return twice to create space between paragraphs, it's time to consider the automatic alternative. The Paragraph Spacing tools on the Formatting Palette let you change the amount of space that appears, automatically, before and after the current or selected paragraph. (The same controls show up in the Format → Paragraph → "Indents and Spacing" tab, as shown in Figure 3-8.) When you click the arrows beside the Before and After boxes, the spacing increases and decreases in 6-point increments. For finer control, you can enter any numbers you wish into the boxes. (4 to 8 points is a good place to start.)

Change the spacing in the Formatting Palette or Paragraph dialog box at the outset of your document, or press ⌘-A to select all existing paragraphs first. The advantage of doing it this way is that the extra space is added automatically, with no danger of accidentally deleting any of the extra line breaks. Furthermore, if you change your mind about the extra space, you can press ⌘-A and readjust the paragraph spacing, without having to delete any extra line breaks.

POWER USERS' CLINIC

Formatting Revealed

In looking at a Word document, there are very few outward cues to tell you what's going on in terms of formatting— since you can't see the behind-the-scenes formatting parameters. However, when troubleshooting a formatting snafu, you might want to see exactly what Word is thinking.

You can. Choose View → Reveal Formatting. The cursor turns into a small word-balloon. If you click the balloon on any character, it opens into a larger balloon listing all of its font and paragraph formatting specifics: font, type style, indents, spacing before and after, and so on. You can click as many places as you like. As soon as you start to type again, or press the Escape key, Reveal Formatting turns off and the balloon goes away.

Indentation

To the horror of designers and typesetters everywhere, most people indent the first line of each paragraph by hitting the Tab key. Trouble is, Word's tab stops are automatically set at half-inch intervals—much too wide for professional use.

It's a far better idea (from the purist's standpoint, anyway) to use Word's dedicated indenting feature, which lets you specify individual *paragraph* margins (and first-line indents) that are independent of the document margins (see page 110).

Tip: If you do indeed press Tab to begin a paragraph, Word tries to guide you toward the proper way. It automatically moves the first-line indent marker (see Figure 3-15) to the first tab stop on your ruler. Now you've got a quick way to correctly indent your paragraphs. Adjust the marker (making the indent *smaller*, for best results) and then type away. All subsequent paragraphs will have the same first-line indent.

If you'd prefer that Word abandon this behavior, choose Word → Preferences → Edit panel and turn off "Tabs and backspace set left indent." Now the Tab key and indents are totally disconnected.

There are two ways to adjust indents for highlighted paragraphs: by dragging the indent markers on the ruler (Figure 3-9), or by setting numerical values (in the Formatting Palette or Format → Paragraph → "Indents and Spacing" tab). When you want to give a paragraph its own distinctive style, use one of these indents:

- **First line indent.** Drag the top-left marker (the first-line indent handle) to where you'd like the first line of each paragraph to begin. One-quarter inch is a typical amount. To set an exact measurement, adjust the First indent setting in the Formatting Palette (or choose "First line" from the Special pop-up menu in the Paragraph dialog box).

Figure 3-9:
Top: A paragraph with a hanging indent of a quarter-inch, and a right indent of a half-inch, as shown on the ruler.

Bottom: The Indentation settings on the Formatting Palette for the paragraph shown. To create a hanging indent, you have to type a negative number in the First box.

- **Hanging indent.** As shown in Figure 3-9, you create a *hanging indent* by dragging the lower, house-shaped marker. (The square left-indent marker moves along with it.) To set an exact measurement, type a negative number into the First box on the Formatting Palette (such as -.25"); or, in the Paragraph dialog box, click the "Indents and Spacing" tab and select Hanging from the Special pop-up menu.

- **Left and right indents.** Left and right indents are the internal left and right margins for a paragraph. Most people aren't aware of them, because they usually match the right and left margins of the *document*. But there are times when you want a paragraph to be narrower—either indented from the left margin or on both sides—such as when creating a *block quote*, for example (a longish quotation that you want separated from the rest of the text).

To adjust the paragraph margins for highlighted text, drag the left and right indent markers (identified in Figure 3-9) on the ruler, or change the Left and Right settings on the Formatting Palette. (The "Indents and Spacing" tab of the Paragraph dialog box have the same options.) The distances you specify here are measurements from the document's right and left margins, not from the edges of the paper.

Tip: You can also drag the first-line indent or left-indent marker *left*, into the margin, to make a line or paragraph extend into the margin. This is called a *negative indent*, which gives the effect of a hanging indent without changing the left margin. However, if you have a narrow left margin and use negative indents, you may get an error message when you print the document. That's because the negative indent is too close to the left edge of the page.

GEM IN THE ROUGH

Format Painter

It could happen to anyone. You finally have a paragraph exactly the way you want it. In fact, you want to use these settings for all the paragraphs you've previously typed.

Instead of going back to change them one by one, now is the time to use the Format Painter. Select the text you worked so hard to perfect. (If paragraph formatting is involved, just click somewhere in the paragraph; if it's just the font characteristics you want to copy, then select a few letters or a word.)

Once you've selected the text, click the Format Painter—the paintbrush icon in the Standard toolbar. Now you can perform the following:

Drag across the text that you want the new formatting applied to. As you let go of the mouse button, Word applies the formatting.

To copy the new formatting to a large amount of text or to nonadjacent paragraphs, double-click the Format Painter; it's now locked on. (A tiny + symbol on the toolbar icon alerts you that it's locked.) From now on, every paragraph you click or blurb you select will get the new formatting—that is, until you click the paintbrush again or press ⌘-period.

Press Esc or ⌘-period to cancel the Format Painter; press ⌘-Z or F1 (repeatedly, if necessary) to back out of what you've just done.

Tabs

To tell the truth, the era of the Tab key is fading. In the typewriter days, it was useful in two situations: when indenting a paragraph and when setting up a table. But in the Computer Age, newer, far more flexible tools have replaced the Tab function in both of those circumstances. The indentation controls described above are much better for paragraph indents, and the Table tool (page 150) is a far superior method of setting up tabular data.

Still, millions of people are more comfortable with the tab-stop concept than Word's newfangled tools. This section shows how those tools work (and assumes that you remember how tab stops work on typewriters).

Default tabs

Every Word document has a ruler (choose View → Ruler if you don't see it), which starts out with an *invisible* tab stop every half inch across the page. These are the *default* tab stops. You can prove that they exist by pressing Tab over and over again, watching as the insertion point moves from one to the next, exactly as on a typewriter.

But the default tab stops aren't permanent; they start to disappear when you do the following:

- Choose Format → Tabs to open the Tabs dialog box (Figure 3-10) and change their placement (in the "Default tab stops" box). You can do this by clicking the arrow buttons beside the box or by entering a new setting.

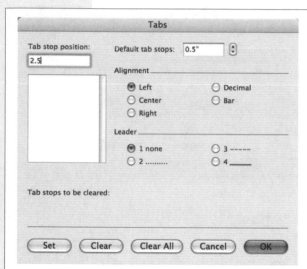

Figure 3-10:
You can change the spacing of the automatic tabs in the "Default tab stops" box (or by clicking the arrows next to it). You can also add a tab leader—that is, a dashed line, dotted line, or underline that automatically fills in the gap between the end of your previous typing and the tab stop.

- Set new tab stops, as described next. When doing so, all of Word's default tab stops to the *left* of your hand-placed tabs disappear. For instance, when you set a new tab at .75" from the margin, the default tab stop at .5" goes away; when you press Tab, the insertion point goes straight to .75". (All remaining default tab stops to the *right* of the new tab remain in place until you add more new tab stops.)

Setting tabs

The quickest way to set new tab stops is by using the ruler; just click anywhere in its tick marks to place a new tab stop. After tabs are set, you can reposition them by simply dragging them along the ruler. To delete one, drag it directly down *off* the ruler until it disappears into thin air.

To place tabs more precisely, choose Format → Tabs (or double-click any tab stop on your ruler) to open the dialog box shown in Figure 3-10. Any hand-placed tab stops are found in the list at the left, according to their distances from the left margin.

To create a new tab, type its location in the "Tab stop position" box, choose an alignment (described next), and click Set (or press ⌘-S). To delete a tab, click it in the list and then click Clear (or press ⌘-E). To change a tab's position, clear the existing tab and type the new position in the "Tab stop position" box. To delete all tabs in the list, click Clear All (⌘-A). Press Return or click OK when you're ready to close the Tabs box.

Tab types

When clicking a tab stop in the dialog box list, you'll be shown its *alignment*. As shown in Figure 3-11, pressing the Tab key doesn't necessarily align your insertion point with the *left* side of your tab stop. The following types of tab alignments help you arrange text on the page:

- **Left (⌘-L)**. This is the kind of tab stop you're probably used to. When you press Tab and then start typing, your text flows rightward from its origin beneath your tab stop.

- **Centered (⌘-N)**. The text is aligned with the tab stop at its centerline, creating a balanced effect that's ideal for things like invitations and brochures.

- **Right (⌘-R)**. When you press Tab and then start typing, your text flows *leftward* from its origin beneath your tab stop. Several of these rows together create a neat right margin.

- **Bar (⌘-B)**. This kind of tab stop isn't a tab stop at all. Instead, it's a method of producing a *vertical line* down your page, directly beneath the tab stop. You don't even have to press Tab to get this vertical line; any paragraph that includes this type of tab on the ruler continues the line down through the page. (Insert your own joke here about picking up the bar tab.)

- **Decimal (⌘-D)**. This behaves exactly like a right tab stop—until you type a period (a decimal point, in other words), at which point your text flows to the right. In other words, this very useful tab type lets you neatly align a series of numbers (such as prices), so that the decimal points are aligned from row to row.

You don't have to use the Tabs dialog box to change tab-stop alignment, by the way. If you click the *tab well* at the upper-left corner of the ruler (see Figure 3-11), you can choose a tab alignment from the pop-up menu. If you then click the spot on the ruler where you want the tab, you'll plant that tab type. For example, to set a left tab at 1/4", choose Left from the tab well's pop-up menu, then click at 1/4" on the ruler.

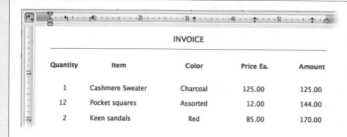

Figure 3-11:
Using different tab types, you can make your text align neatly from one line to the next. The columns in this example use a right tab, a left tab, a centered tab, and two decimal tabs.

Applying tabs to paragraphs and styles

When you set, clear, and move tabs, the changes apply to the paragraph containing your insertion point. Often, however, you'll want to use the tab settings for many paragraphs—or an entire document. Here are the ways you can do that:

- **Set the tabs before you start typing**. This is a common trick if, for example, you need to insert a little columnar table in the middle of a report. Every time you press Return to begin a new line, the same tab stops will be available.

- **Select all paragraphs**. If you've already done some (or a lot of) typing, select the paragraphs by dragging over them, or press ⌘-A to select the entire document. Set tabs as described above.

- **Make tab stops part of a style**. If you make your preferred tab stops part of a *style* (see page 127), you can apply them to any paragraph just by clicking that paragraph and choosing from the Style menu on the Formatting Palette. If you're *really* attached to certain tab stops, you can even make them part of your Normal style.

Borders and Shading

Black text on a white page is clear and easy to read, but it can get monotonous. When a little zest is required, try using borders, background shading, and fill patterns to emphasize various parts of your document. For instance, light gray background shading can highlight a useful list in the middle of your article. A plain border can set off a sidebar from the body of your text. And a fancy border can be part of an invitation.

Text and paragraph borders

To put a border around some text, first select the text in question; to put a border around an entire paragraph, just click anywhere in the paragraph. Click anywhere in the "Borders and Shading" title bar on the Formatting Palette to expand its panel, as shown in Figure 3-12. The controls are:

- **Type.** Clicking the square icon next to Type opens a palette of placement choices for your border: a square, a line above or below, and so on. Click the one you want. The light dotted line, No Border, automatically turns off the remaining controls described here.

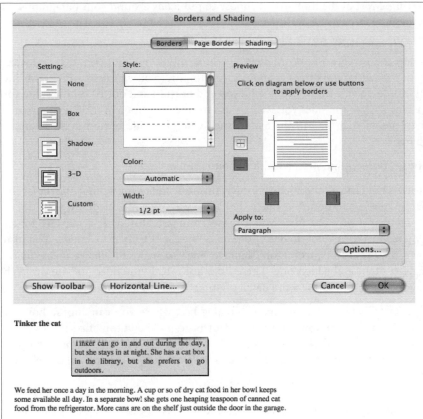

Figure 3-12:
Top: As you work, watch what happens in the Preview box at the right of the dialog box. The only way to see how the final result really looks, however, is to return to your document.

Bottom: Although Word gives you plenty of options for line styles and fill patterns, simpler is usually more effective. Here 10% gray shading and a one-half point drop-shadow border highlight a bit of vital information.

- **Style.** This pop-up menu shows a selection of solid, dashed, and multiple-line styles to apply to the border you've just specified.

- **Color.** Clicking the color square displays Word's standard palette of 70 colors. You can choose one, or click More Colors to use Office's color-picking tools, as described on page 747.

- **Weight.** This control denotes the thickness of the line in points (1/72 of an inch). The pop-up menu shows a variety of thicknesses ranging from 1/4 point to 6 points.

Extra features in the Borders and Shading dialog box

For more customization options than those available on the Formatting Palette, highlight the paragraphs you want to change and choose Format → "Borders and Shading". The dialog box shown in Figure 3-12 opens. When you click the Borders tab, you see these options:

- **Setting.** Most of the time, you'll choose to put a *box* around your paragraphs, as represented by one of the lower icons on the left (Figure 3-12). The shadow and 3-D options create a very professional, modern look.

  If you choose Custom, Word doesn't assume anything—not even that you want a four-sided box. As the Custom button implies, you can usse a different line style on each side of the box—solid top and bottom and dotted on the sides, for instance. Click the sides you wish to use from the buttons in the Preview panel, then design each one in the Style panel. Click the side button again to make changes.

- **Style.** Choose a line style, a width in points, and a color.

- **Horizontal Line.** Rather than a border, this tool adds a horizontal line *under* the paragraph in question. The line is actually a picture embedded into your document; that's why the lines you choose from are stored in a clip art folder (Microsoft Office 2008 folder → Office → Media → Clipart → Lines). You also have the option of turning on "Link to File" to make the line a *linked object* instead of an embedded one. These lines are mostly intended for use on Web pages. (See page 753 for more detail on linked and embedded objects.)

- **Options.** Clicking Options opens a dialog box where you can choose how far away from the text you want to set your border. The automatic settings are 4 points on each side, 1 point top and bottom. If you have room, consider increasing the amount of space between the text and border for a clean, elegant look.

Note: If your text is in a *text box* (see page 141), don't add a border around it—you'll just end up with two borders. Text boxes come with *built-in* borders, which you can format using the line tools on the Drawing toolbar and the Colors and Lines tab of the Format → Text Box tab.

That said, you *can* put borders on parts of the text *inside* text boxes. (If you also want to hide the border surrounding the text box, click the border, then choose No Line from the Line Color palette on the Drawing toolbar.)

Once your border is complete, click OK. You can now use the tools in the "Borders and Shading" section of the Formatting Palette (or the "Tables and Borders" toolbar) to make further refinements.

Page borders

When it's time to create a title page, certificate, or phony diploma, nothing says "professionally published" more than a handsome border around the edges of your page. To add one, choose Format → "Borders and Shading" → Page Border tab. (The Formatting Palette has no controls for adding a page border, but if you decide to add one at the last minute, you can add a quick and dirty border from the Print dialog box, as described on page 25.)

Most of the tools for designing a page border are the same as those for a paragraph border (described previously). But there are subtle differences: Page borders trace the page margins, regardless of the size or amount of text on the page, and the page border changes size automatically as you change the margins (page 120).

The Page Border tab lists a few extra features specific to page borders:

- **Art.** The Art pop-up menu has dozens upon dozens of small clip-art border motifs in repeating patterns (little marquees, banners, and—for those Halloween party invitations—black cats).

- **Apply to.** This menu on the Page Border tab lets you put a border on the first page of your document or section only. (Can you say "title page"?)

- **Options.** The Options button opens a dialog box with settings that control how the border frames the page, including the Margin settings described in Figure 3-13.

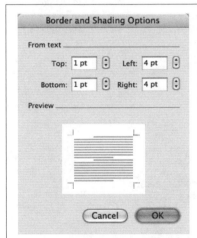

Figure 3-13:
The Margin settings control the distance of the text from the margin (or the paper edge, depending on what you choose from the "Measure from" menu). The border, however, still hugs the margins. In other words, when you increase the Margin settings in this dialog box, the text area will decrease as it moves farther in from the page margins. (Yes, some of the text may flow onto the next page as a result.)

"Align paragraph borders and table edges with page border" does more than align them; it actually *connects* them if they're adjacent. Thus, the side borders of a paragraph will extend out to and meld with the side borders of the page.

Turn on "Always display in front" unless you plan to place text boxes or images *over* the page border. (If you do so, you may want to give the border a lighter shading or lighter color.) The "Surround header" and "Surround footer" options determine whether the page border encompasses the header and footer (see page 209) along with the rest of the page.

Shading

When you decide to fill in a gray or colored background behind a paragraph or text box, the key words to remember are *light* and *subtle*. Patterns and shading can make text difficult to read, and the interference is often worse on the printed page than on the screen.

To put a fill or pattern behind text, you have to first select the text (or click anywhere in a paragraph). Click anywhere in the "Borders and Shading" title bar on the Formatting Palette to expand the panel, as shown in Figure 3-14, top.

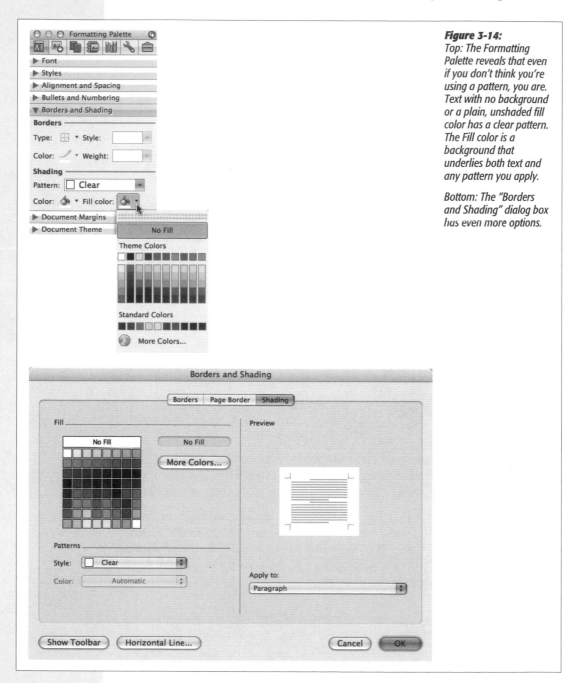

Figure 3-14:
Top: The Formatting Palette reveals that even if you don't think you're using a pattern, you are. Text with no background or a plain, unshaded fill color has a clear pattern. The Fill color is a background that underlies both text and any pattern you apply.

Bottom: The "Borders and Shading" dialog box has even more options.

- **Pattern**. The Pattern pop-up menu gives you a long list of choices, from Clear (no pattern), to a series of percentages of *halftone* shading (like newspaper photographs), to line patterns such as diagonal stripes. Most of the time, you're probably best off leaving this pop-up menu alone; use the "Fill color" control instead for a professional, even tint.

Tip: Choosing "Solid (100%)" from the Pattern pop-up menu results in solid black behind your text. Ordinarily, your black text disappears completely, but if you select some of the text, Word thoughtfully makes it white, producing an effect called *reversed type* like this.

- **Pattern color**. If you decide to choose a pattern, use the "Pattern color" pop-up menu to select its color. The color you choose here becomes the "black" color of the pattern you chose from the Pattern pop-up menu.

- **Fill**. This is the color that appears behind text or under any pattern you've chosen. You can choose from 40 colors and 24 grayscale shades.

Note: There's a difference between choosing No Fill and White fill color. No Fill is transparent, meaning when you layer a picture beneath text with no fill, you can see the picture. On the other hand, when you layer something beneath text with White fill, the fill blocks out whatever's below.

You can combine these options in fascinating and grisly ways. For example, any pattern you choose overlies the fill color of your paragraph, even if that's No Fill, in which case all you see beneath the pattern is the color of the paper. When you choose one of the percentage shadings from the Pattern pop-up menu, you're choosing a percentage of black or color to overlie the fill color.

Extra features in the Borders and Shading dialog box

A few extra features are available only in the Format → "Borders and Shading" dialog box. For example:

- You can control how far the fill extends beyond the text. For example, after choosing a fill color, choose Format → "Borders and Shading" → Borders tab. You'll notice that the None border setting is chosen. However, you can now click the Options button and adjust the "From text" settings, as described on page 117. The settings will apply to the boundary of the fill, as if it were an invisible border.

- Also in the "Borders and Shading" dialog box, the Horizontal Line button opens a "Choose a Picture" dialog box showing the decorative horizontal lines in Word's clip art gallery. Select one and click Insert to place the line across the text at the insertion point. (You can't make borders with these lines, just horizontals.)

Document Formatting

When you start with a blank document, Word provides a one-inch margin at the top and bottom of the page, and a stately one-and-a-quarter inch margin at each side.

Most people never change these settings. In fact, in its own, almost accidental way, Microsoft has dictated the standard margin formatting for the world's business correspondence. But if you learn how to work with margins—as well as paragraphs and indentation—you can give your document a distinctive look, not to mention fit much more text on a page.

Margins

You can adjust the margins of a Word document in either of two ways: by entering exact measurements (in the Formatting Palette or the Document dialog box), or by dragging the margins directly on the ruler.

To use the numeric option, choose Format → Document → Margins tab, or click the Document Margins title bar on the Formatting Palette. There you'll find individual boxes that let you specify, in inches, the size of the left, right, top, and bottom margins.

To set your margins by dragging, which produces immediate visible feedback, you need to be in Print Layout view (View → Print Layout) or Publishing Layout view (View → Publishing Layout).

- **Left, Right, Top, Bottom.** To set margins by dragging, point to the line where the ruler changes from white to blue, without clicking. (The blue area is *outside* the limits of the margin.) When the cursor changes to a box with double arrows, drag the margin line to any point on the ruler you wish (see Figure 3-15). Now you can change the margins on both the horizontal and vertical rulers.

Tip: You may find it extremely hard to adjust the left margin, since the trio of *indent* markers (Figure 3-15) lies directly on top of the blue/white boundary. Move the cursor slowly from one indent marker to the other until the Left Margin screen tip appears and the cursor shape changes as shown in Figure 3-13. However, you may find it much easier to just move the first-line indent handle out of the way while you adjust the margin.

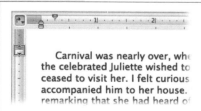

Figure 3-15:
The house-shaped controls in the top ruler set indents (page 109). This example shows a first-line indent. Drag the blue/white boundaries in either ruler to adjust the margins.

- **Header and Footer.** Headers and footers (see page 209) appear *within* the normal margins. For instance, if you've set the bottom margin for 1", you can have the page number (footer) appear a half-inch from the edge of the paper—half an inch below the bottom of the text. To do so, set the Footer margin for 0.5", as shown in Figure 3-15.

Tip: When you've got your margins just the way you want them, you can make that the setting for all new documents you open. Just choose Format → Document and click Default at the lower left of the Document dialog box.

Gutters and Mirrors

Word's *gutter* and *mirror* margin features make margins work when your document is destined to be bound like a book. In an open book, the *gutter* is the term for the inner margins where the pages attach to the spine. Usually, the gutters have to be wider than the outer margins to allow room for the binding and the spine. (You may want to talk to your publisher—the fine people at Kinko's, for example—to learn about margin requirements.) Word can add this extra space automatically. For instance, if you set a gutter space of 0.25", Word will *add* a quarter-inch to the gutter margin on each page.

Another useful tool for book margins is the *mirror margin* feature, which is designed to let you set up margins that are uneven on each *page*, but reflected on each two-page *spread* (see Figure 3-16).

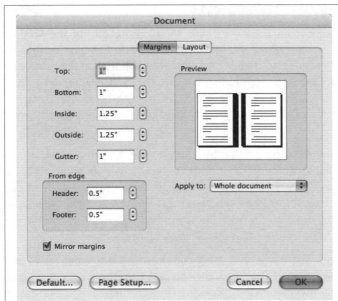

Figure 3-16:
A quick way to open this dialog box is to double-click the ruler located along the top-left side of the page. The gutter is an extra area for binding; the mirror margins feature is handy when you want the outer and inner margins to match on left and right pages.

Section Formatting

The Formatting Palette doesn't say anything about *section* formatting. In fact, most people have never even heard of it.

Still, section formatting is important in a few special circumstances, such as these:

- Sections allow you to divide a document into chapters, each with its own headers or footers.

- Sections let you change from, say, a one-column format for your opening paragraph to a three-column format for the body of the article. They also let you insert a landscape-orientation page or two into a paper that's primarily in portrait orientation.

- Sections give you flexibility in printing. You can print your title page on colored paper from a different paper tray on your printer, for example.

- You can set different margins for each section of your document. This might come in handy if your training manual includes multiple choice quizzes for which you could really use narrower page margins.

The bottom line: A section is a set of pages in your document that can have its own independent settings for page numbering, lines, footnotes, and endnotes. It can also have its own layout features, such as page borders, margins, columns, alignment, text orientation, and even page size. Finally, it can have its own printer settings, such as orientation and paper source.

Inserting and Removing Section Breaks

To start a new section, choose Insert → Break, then choose one of the Section Break *types*—depending upon where you want the new section to begin (relative to the current page). For instance, to change the number of columns in the middle of a page, choose Section Break (Continuous); to start the next chapter on a new page, choose Section Break (Next Page). If you're self-publishing a novel, remember that new chapters usually begin on a right-hand page; choose Section Break (Odd Page).

You'll see the change reflected right away. In Normal view, a section break shows up as two finely dotted lines labeled "Section Break (Next Page)" or whatever kind you inserted (see Figure 3-17). In Page Layout view, you see only the *effect* of the page break; if you chose the "Next Page" type, your text abruptly stops in the middle of one page and picks up again on the next. But if you click the Show (¶) button on the Standard toolbar, the breaks appear as double lines, just as in Draft view.

Choosing a section type may sound like a big commitment, but don't fret—you can always go back and change it. To do so, click anywhere in the section you want to *change*—that is, just after the section break itself—and then choose Format → Document → Layout tab. Choose a new section type from the "Section start" menu. (This menu has an additional section-break option: New column, which is useful solely if you're designing your document with multiple columns, as described on page 136. To make an existing column start at the top of the page, click it and choose "New column.")

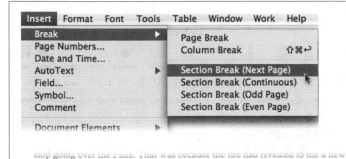

Figure 3-17:
Top: Create a section break by choosing from the Insert menu (there's no dialog box for it).

Bottom: An example of a "Next page" section break, shown here separating one chapter from another. You see the handy guides automatically in Draft view; in Print Layout view, turn on the Show/Hide ¶ button in the Standard toolbar to make them appear.

stop going over the Falls. That was because the fire had revealed to me a new passion—quite new, and distinctly different from love, grief, and those others which I had already discovered—FEAR. And it is horrible!—I wish I had never discovered it; it gives me dark moments, it spoils my happiness, it makes me shiver and tremble and shudder. But I could not persuade him, for he has not discovered fear yet, and so he could not understand me.————————Section Break (Next Page)————————

Extract from Adam's Diary ¶

¶

Perhaps I ought to remember that she is very young, a mere girl and make allowances. She is all interest, eagerness, vivacity, the world is to her a charm, a wonder, a mystery, a joy; she can't speak for delight when she finds a new flower, she must pet it and caress it and smell it and talk to it, and pour out endearing names upon it. And she is color-mad: brown rocks, yellow sand, gray moss, green foliage,

To remove a section break (in either Normal or Page Layout view) click the double dotted line and press Del (forward delete) on extended keyboards, or fn-Delete for PowerBooks. Or you can select the section break by clicking before it and dragging through it, and then pressing Delete.

Warning: Deleting a section break, or the last paragraph marker in a section (click ¶ to see it), also deletes its formatting. The section before the break will take on the formatting of the section *after* it. The sudden appearance of 24 pages of a two-column layout, for example, can be disconcerting if you're not prepared for it.

Formatting Within Sections

To change formatting or other settings within a section, such as page numbering or headers and footers, just click in the section and use the commands in Word's dialog boxes and toolbars. Settings like margins, alignment, columns, and page orientation, plus any feature involving numbering, such as page and line numbering, headers and footers, and so on, operate independently of the other sections in the document.

Page numbering across sections

When you use a header or footer and page numbers in your document, you can either number each section independently or number the document continuously from beginning to end. For example, suppose you've written a term paper with an introduction in its own section, which you want to number with Roman numerals. (You want regular Arabic numerals for the body of the paper.) Here's how you'd set things up:

1. **Click at the end of the introduction and choose Insert → Break → Section Break (Next Page).**

   The double lines appear, assuming you're in Draft view (click the Show button if you don't see them).

2. **Click anywhere in the introduction (*above* the section break) and choose View → "Header and Footer".**

   The header and footer areas of your page appear, as described on page 209. The "Header and Footer" pane appears in the Formatting Palette, too.

3. **Scroll down to the footer on one of the pages in the introduction and click in it, or click the Switch Between Header and Footer "Go To" button in the "Header and Footer" pane of the Formatting Palette.**

   The footer is labeled "Footer–Section 1."

4. **In the "Header and Footer" pane of the Formatting Palette, click Insert Page Number (the # icon), then click the Format Page Number icon (shown in Figure 3-18).**

   The Page Number Format dialog box opens, also shown in Figure 3-18.

5. **From the "Number format" pop-up menu, choose "i, ii, iii…"; click the "Start at" radio button. Click OK.**

   The number i appears in the box, which is right where the numbering for most introductions begin. (Type a different number if you want to use a different numbering system.)

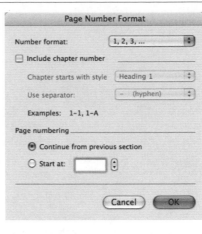

Figure 3-18:
Left: The "Header and Footer" pane of the Formatting Palette. Clicking the Format Page Number button opens a dialog box where you can tell Word exactly how you want the numbering to work. You can't do these kinds of edits directly in the document.

Right: Turning on the "Continue from previous section" radio button carries over the page numbering from the section before. You can start a section at any page number you choose by clicking "Start at" and entering a number in the box.

6. **In the Headers and Footers pane of the Formatting Palette, click the Show Next button (you've just done the same thing as clicking in one of the footers in the second section), then turn off the "Link to Previous" checkbox.**

   With Link to Previous turned off, you can format headers and footers—and therefore a page numbers—separately for each section.

7. **Back in the Headers and Footers pane of the Formatting Palette, click Format Page Number.**

   The Page Number Format dialog box appears once more.

8. **This time, choose the Arabic numerals (1, 2, 3, …) from the "Number format" pop-up menu. Click the "Start at" radio button; make sure *1* appears in the box. Click OK.**

Now, no matter how you add material to, or remove material from, the introduction and the body of your paper, the introduction will be numbered starting on page i. The numbering of the main body, meanwhile, will start over with 1. Should you change your mind and decide to number your paper consecutively from the intro to the end, you won't have to remove the section break. Just click one of the footers *after* the section break, click Format Page Number, and select the "Continue from previous section" radio button.

Styles, Page Layout, and Tables

After you've polished the *content* of your document, it's time to work on the packaging, and Word 2008 includes the wrapping paper, ribbon, and bows that can take you beyond simple word processing deep into the realm of page design and layout.

For example, an endless block of text running across the page is fine, but columns of text are more professional looking, easier to read—and much less boring. Or perhaps you'd like to add some well-placed borders, but you've never been sure how to work with them.

Note: This chapter builds on Chapter 3's formatting lessons and teaches finishing touches that give your document polish and flair. Yet to come, however, is Word 2008's new Publishing Layout view which takes Word's page-layout abilities to a whole other level. Its features make it more like a separate page-layout program than another document view, and you'll find it discussed in depth in Chapter 8.

Styles

Creating Word documents usually requires a small assortment of formatting styles, which you'll use repeatedly. In a short piece, reformatting your chapter titles (for example) is no big deal; just highlight each and then use the Formatting Palette to make it look the way you like.

But what about long documents? What if your document has 49 chapter headings, plus 294 (or even 394?) sidebar boxes, captions, long quotations, and other heavily formatted elements? In such documents—this book, for example—manually reformatting each heading, subhead, sidebar, and caption would drive you crazy. Word's *styles* feature can alleviate the pain.

A style is a prepackaged collection of formatting attributes that you can apply and reapply with a click of the mouse. You can create as many styles as you need: chapter headings, sidebar styles, whatever. The result is a collection of custom-tailored styles for each of the repeating elements of your document. Figure 4-1 makes all of this clear.

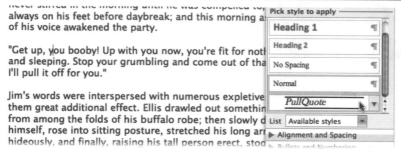

never stirred in the morning until he was compelled to, always on his feet before daybreak; and this morning a: of his voice awakened the party.

"Get up, you booby! Up with you now, you're fit for noth and sleeping. Stop your grumbling and come out of tha I'll pull it off for you."

Jim's words were interspersed with numerous expletive them great additional effect. Ellis drawled out somethin from among the folds of his buffalo robe; then slowly d himself, rose into sitting posture, stretched his long ar hideously, and finally, raising his tall person erect, stoo

Pick style to apply

Heading 1 ¶
Heading 2 ¶
No Spacing ¶
Normal ¶
PullQuote
List | Available styles
▶ Alignment and Spacing
▶ Bullets and Numbering

CHAPTER XXV

THE BUFFALO CAMP

No one in the camp was more active than Jim Gurney, and no one half so lazy as Ellis. Between these two there was a great antipathy. Ellis never stirred in the morning until he was compelled to, but Jim was always on his feet before daybreak; and this morning as usual the sound of his voice awakened the party.

"Get up, you booby! Up with you now, you're fit for nothing but eating and sleeping. Stop your grumbling and come out of that buffalo robe or I'll pull it off for you."

Jim's words were interspersed with numerous expletives, which gave them great additional effect. Ellis drawled out something in a nasal tone from among the folds of his buffalo robe; then slowly disengaged himself, rose into sitting posture, stretched his long arms, yawned

Figure 4-1:
Suppose you want to call special attention to a paragraph. This before-and-after shot shows the beauty of a style: With a single click in the Style pop-up menu on the Formatting Palette (top), you can apply a special font, style, and paragraph border all at once (bottom). Better yet, you don't have to remember how you formatted a similar paragraph earlier.

After creating your styles, just apply them as needed; they stay consistent throughout the document. During the editing process, if you notice an accidentally styled, say, headline using the *Subhead* style, you can fix the problem by simply applying the correct style.

You'll appreciate styles even more when it comes time to change the formatting of a particular style. If you change a style's description, Word changes *every occurrence* of that style in your document.

Styles aren't one of Microsoft's ease-of-understanding masterpieces, but they're getting better. Grasping how they work, where they're stored, and when they change explains many of Word's idiosyncrasies, and pays off handsomely in the long run.

Where Styles Are Stored

Every document has a collection of ready-to-use, built-in styles, whether you're aware of it or not. (To be more precise, every document is based on a *template* that stores a canned set of styles, as described on page 127.) Word opens each new blank document with the *Normal* paragraph style selected (unless you've made changes to your Normal template, as detailed on page 230).

The controls available to change the styles in your document reside in several places: in the Style panel of the Formatting Palette, the Formatting toolbar, and the Format → Style dialog box (see Figure 4-2).

Tip: There are many more styles in the Style dialog box than in the Formatting Palette or the toolbar menus, which have only a selection of the most useful styles. To see a more comprehensive list of styles without opening the Style dialog box, just Shift-click the Formatting toolbar's Style menu arrow, or choose All Styles from the Formatting Palette's Styles pane's List pop-up menu.

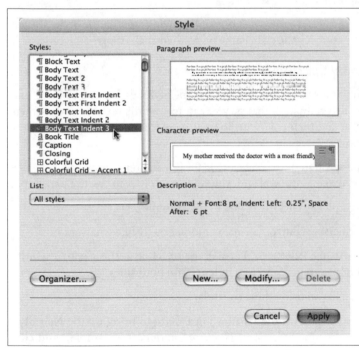

Figure 4-2:
Choose Format → Style to see the styles available in your document. Each document comes with a few styles, such as the Normal style and Heading 1, because every template has these starter styles built right in. (See page 224 for more on templates.) Starting from a different template might produce a different set of starter styles.

Applying Styles

To apply a pre-existing style to text you've already typed, highlight the text. For example, drag through some text, or click once inside a paragraph to select it. (You can also choose a style for a new paragraph *before* you begin typing it.)

Note: If you click twice to select a word, the style will only apply to that word. Clicking once within a paragraph, however, will apply the subsequently chosen style to the entire paragraph. No fuss, little muss.

Now choose a style from one of Word's style boxes, using one of the following methods (listed in descending efficiency order):

- Press Shift-⌘-S to highlight the Style menu in the Formatting toolbar (if it's showing—if it's not showing, this command displays the Formatting Toolbar) and then use the up and down arrow keys to step through the styles in the list until the one you're seeking is highlighted. Press Return to apply the style. You can also use the mouse to scroll through this list.

Tip: You can save time by typing the name of the style and then pressing Return. For this very reason, some people use very short style names when they format a style. For instance, if you name a style GX, you only have to press Shift-⌘-S, type *gx*, and Return to apply the style—never having touched the mouse. Better yet, give the style *two* names, separated by a comma—one in English for your own reference in using the Style menus, the other its "keystroke name." For example, your Sidebar style might be called *Sidebar, sb*.

- Use the scroll bar next to the Style list in the Formatting Palette, then click the style name to apply it.

- Choose Format → Style; double-click one of the style names in the Styles list box (see Figure 4-2)—or click the style name once, then click Apply.

Creating Styles by Example

There are two ways to create styles: You can use the Styles dialog box to build one, or you can "create by example"—that is, you can format the text in the document the way you want it, and then tell Word to memorize that formatting. The second method is usually easier.

For example, suppose you want to create a style for illustration captions. Start by typing out the caption, making sure you end with Return in order to create a paragraph.

1. **Select the paragraph (by clicking inside it, for example).**

   Now use the formatting controls to make it look exactly like you want it.

2. **Using the Formatting Palette or Format menu, choose the Century Gothic font, at 10-point size, italic, centered, indented on both sides.**

   Chapter 3 has details on using these controls.

3. **Click the New Style icon on the Formatting Palette to bring up the New Style dialog box, type the new style name (*Picture Caption*, for example), and click OK. (If the Formatting toolbar is open, you can simply type the new name in the Style box and then press Return.)**

   To apply this style more quickly in the future, consider assigning it two names separated by a comma—the second one can be an abbreviation (see the Tip above).

That's it…your style is now ready for use in your document.

Creating Styles in the Dialog Box

For more style control, use the Style dialog box. To use it, choose Format → Style and then click New (or press ⌘-N) or click the New Style icon in the Style pane of the Formatting Palette. The New Style dialog box opens, as shown in Figure 4-3.

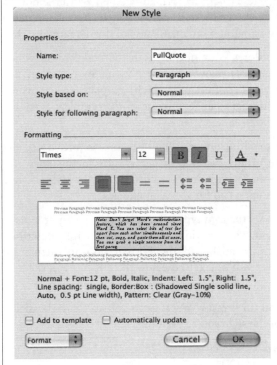

Figure 4-3:
As you develop your new style, the preview window in the middle of the New Style dialog gives you live feedback, so you can see exactly what you're creating. Below, the written definition of the style changes to indicate, in somewhat technical terms, the specifics of your formatting choices.

Use the various controls here to define this new style:

- **Name.** Give your style a name that reflects its usage: Headline, Sidebar, and so on.

- Style **based on**. Choose Normal or whatever existing style is closest to what you envision for the new style. Basing your new style on an existing one has two payoffs. First, it saves you time, since some of the formatting is already in place; second, when you modify the underlying style (such as Normal), all styles *based* upon it change as well, keeping your document design coordinated. For example, if you base Heading 1 on *(no style)*, and base other headings on Heading 1, then you can change the body text style without changing the headings. Or you could change the font of Heading 1, which automatically changes all the other heading styles—since they're based on Heading 1.

- **Style for following paragraph** is a big timesaver. Let's say the new style you're creating is a heading, and after each heading, you always return to typing in

Normal style. Instead of manually changing the font back to Normal after each use of the Heading style, just choose Normal here. Now, whenever you press Return after using the heading style, the font automatically returns to Normal.

- If you chose *Paragraph* in the **Style type** menu, the style will include the current settings for indents, tabs, and other aspects of paragraph formatting (as described in Chapter 3). If you chose *Character* formatting, then Word memorizes only the font and other type characteristics of your new style. You can apply a character-formatting style in a paragraph independently of the paragraph style.

- Turning on **Add to template** stores your new style in the *template* on which your document is based (page 224). Now, all new documents based on this template will include this style. (To find out which template you're using, choose File → Properties → Summary tab. The name of the template is shown near the bottom of the dialog box.)

- Turn on **Automatically update** with caution. When this box is turned on, any formatting change you make to any *one* occurrence of text in this style will change the style's definition—and with it, *every* occurrence of the style in your document. Great for global changes; bad for singular changes.

- The **Formatting** panel lets you set the font type, size, and color; paragraph justification; line spacing; and indent. These options, all of which are fully described in Chapter 3, have always been available in the Format pop-up menu (see below), but this new panel gives you quicker access to the settings you're likely to use most often.

Clicking the **Format** pop-up menu (or pressing ⌘-O) gains you access to the dialog boxes, where you actually format the style you're building:

- **Font** opens the Font dialog box, described on page 95.

- **Paragraph** opens the Paragraph dialog box, described on page 106.

- **Tabs** opens the Tabs dialog box, described on page 112.

- **Border** opens the Borders tab of the "Borders and Shading" dialog box (page 114).

- **Language** provides foreign language choices for your style, for the benefit of the spell checker and other proofing tools.

- Placing a **Frame** around a paragraph gives it some of the qualities of text boxes. (Frames are an early Word feature that most people have abandoned in favor of text boxes; see page 141.)

- **Numbering** opens the "Bullets and Numbering" dialog box described on page 103. The menu option's name, "Numbering," is only half accurate, since it's used for bulleted lists as well as numbered ones.

- **Shortcut Key** opens the Customize Keyboard dialog box (see page 768), where you can assign a keyboard shortcut to this style. For example, you can assign

Control-⌘-Z to your favorite heading style and apply it with a quick tap of the left hand. This feature is a godsend if you frequently change styles as you type along or have trouble using a mouse.

When you click OK after making changes in any of these formatting dialog boxes, you return to the New Style dialog box, where the description information tells you which characteristics you've assigned to this style.

When you click OK again to return to your document, the newly created style's name appears along with all the others in the Formatting Palette—ready to apply.

Changing, Deleting, or Copying Styles

There are several ways to change an existing style, but here are two of the quickest:

- Select text in your document and then, in the Formatting Palette, click the little triangle next to the style's name; choose Modify Style in the pop-up menu that appears. When the Modify Style dialog box opens (Figure 4-4), make your changes, and then click OK to update the style.

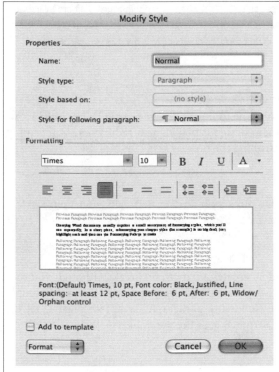

Figure 4-4:
To modify selected text, click the triangle to the right of the style's name in the Formatting Palette and select Modify Style from the subsequent pop-up menu. You get this nifty dialog box where you can do almost everything you can in the Format → Style dialog box, only more quickly. If you're already in the Style dialog box, click the Modify button to summon this window.

- Choose Format → Style; click the style's name in the Styles box; click Modify (or press ⌘-M); and use the Format menu to make changes to the font, paragraph, and so on, just as if creating a new style (as described above).

Deleting styles

To delete unwanted styles, choose Format → Style, then click the style in the Styles list box and click Delete.

Note: Word won't let you delete certain built-in styles (such as Normal, Heading 1, 2, and 3, and so on). If you click one of these styles, the Delete button is grayed out.

Transferring styles

Once you've cultivated a crop of magnificent styles, you may want to spread their sunshine to other documents. You can do so in the Organizer dialog box, described in the previous paragraph and on page 228, but that's a lot of trouble.

The sneaky, much faster way is to *copy* paragraphs formatted in the styles you want to transfer and then paste them into another document. Word automatically adds the pasted styles to the second document's list of styles. (If the document already has a style with the same name, it ignores the newly pasted one.)

Tip: If you're confused about which styles you've applied where, try this: in either Draft or Outline view, Choose Word → Preferences → View button. Set the "Style area width" to about one inch, then click OK. Now Word opens a new strip at the left side of your document window identifying the style of every paragraph!

Print Layout

Word automatically flows text from line to line and page to page. Nice, huh? However, an important part of document design is placing text right where you want it, breaking it up, and generally controlling the flow.

Inserting Breaks

A *break* is an invisible barrier that stops your text in its tracks, and then starts it again on a new line, column, or page.

Paragraph break

In Word, pressing Return (or Enter) creates a paragraph break. Although you may not have been aware of the term, they're created every time you end a paragraph. Unless you've chosen a different "following paragraph" style (see page 131), the new paragraph assumes the same formatting as the previous.

Line break

Pressing Shift-Return inserts a *line break*. It's similar to a paragraph break except that the text on the new line remains part of the original paragraph, and retains its style and paragraph formatting. No matter how you edit the surrounding text, the line break remains where you inserted it—until you remove it, of course.

Page break

Choose Insert → Break → Page Break (or press Shift-*Enter*) to force a *hard* page break. No matter how much text you add above the break, the text *after* the break will always appear at the top of a new page.

Use a page break when your want to start a new topic at the top of the next page. If you're writing a manual for your babysitters, for example, inserting a hard page break at the end of the *How to operate the home theater system* section that causes *The care and feeding of Tinker the cat* to begin at the top of the following page.

Tip: In Print Layout view, page breaks are generally invisible. The text just ends in the middle of a page and won't go any further, which can be disconcerting if you've forgotten about the page break you added.

To view the dotted lines that represent a page break, choose View → Draft, or click the Show ¶ button on the Standard toolbar.

Column break

To jump text to the top of a new *column* (in multicolumn layouts like those described in the next section), choose Insert → Break → Column Break. Word ends the current column and, when you start typing again, hops you over to the top of the next column at the top of the page.

If you choose this option when you're not using multiple columns (see page 136), it behaves like a hard page break. (On the other hand, if you later switch to a two- or three-column format, the column break behaves like a normal column break. If you plan to make two different versions of your document—one with columns and one without—you may therefore want to use column breaks instead of page breaks.) *Keyboard shortcut:* Shift-⌘-Return.

Section break

A *section* is like a chapter—a part of a document that can have formatting independent of the other parts. For example, each section can possess unique margins, page numbering, pagination, headers and footers, even printing paper size. See "Inserting and Removing Section Breaks" for more detail on sections.

To begin a new section, insert a section break by choosing Insert → Break and choosing the specific type of section break that you want (see page 122).

Warning: When deleting a break as shown in Figure 4-5, bear in mind that the usually invisible ¶ marker at the end of a paragraph "contains" the formatting for the paragraph that comes before it. If you join two paragraphs or sections together by backspacing until there's no break between them, they blend into one and take on the formatting of the *second* section or paragraph.

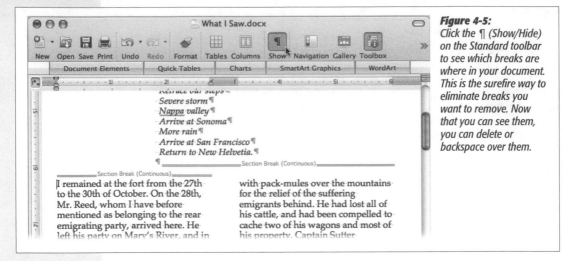

Figure 4-5:
Click the ¶ (Show/Hide) on the Standard toolbar to see which breaks are where in your document. This is the surefire way to eliminate breaks you want to remove. Now that you can see them, you can delete or backspace over them.

Working with Columns

If you're putting together, say, a newsletter, some classified ads, or the rule book for the computer game you've just designed, you can give your publication a professional look by pouring it into multiple parallel *columns* (see Figure 4-6). Newspapers and magazines, for example, use columns in their layouts because shorter lines are easier to read, and…well, they've always done it that way.

Tip: You can see multiple columns only in Print Layout view (View → Print Layout). Only one column per page appears in Draft view, much to the confusion of anyone creating columns for the first time.

Adding columns using the Standard toolbar

The quickest way to create columns is via the Columns button on the Standard toolbar, as shown in Figure 4-6 (top). If you want your entire document in columns, make sure nothing is selected; if you want columns for only part of the document, select that text.

Then click the Columns pop-up button on the Standard toolbar. Now drag downward and across to highlight the number of columns you'd like to use, as shown in Figure 4-6. If you need more than four columns, drag beyond their borders to expand the choices to five or six.

When you release the mouse, Word divides your text into columns of equal width. (If you highlighted only part of the document, Word automatically creates invisible *section breaks* above and below the selected portion; see page 122.)

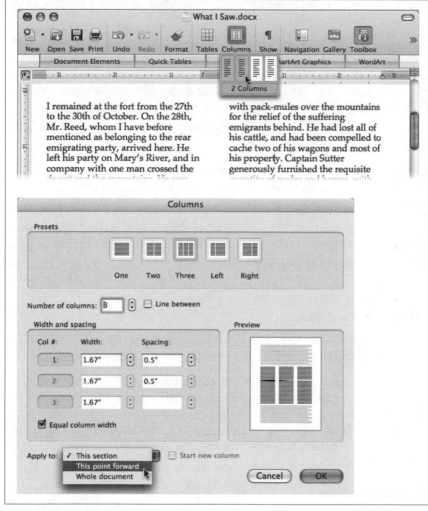

Figure 4-6:
Top: Use the Standard toolbar's Columns pop-up button to convert a document into multiple-column format immediately.

Bottom: For more control, choose Format → Columns. Here, you see the dialog box settings that will produce a two column format, with a narrower left column and a line between them. The menu at the bottom of the box lets you choose to apply the columns beginning at the insertion point, from the beginning of the document, or just to the current section.

Adding columns using the Columns dialog box

Although the Columns pop-up button on the toolbar is quick and easy, Word, as usual, gives you far more control if you're willing to visit a dialog box. To use this option, select text or click in your document and proceed as follows:

1. **Choose Format → Columns.**

   When the Columns dialog box opens (see Figure 4-6; bottom), the number of columns is preset to One, meaning that your text takes up the entire width of the page.

2. **Choose one of the icons at the top of the dialog box, or enter a number in the "Number of columns" box.**

The buttons labeled Two and Three create two or three columns of equal width. Left and Right mean, "Give me two columns (or the number of columns I'm about to specify in the 'Number of columns' box), but for some visual spice, make the first column half as wide, or twice as wide, respectively, as the other columns." Then change the "Number of columns" box if you want more than two.

3. **Click the arrow buttons next to the Width box for each column or the spacing boxes.**

Width boxes are available for the number of columns you've requested. The Preview box displays the results. To create columns of equal width at any point, check the "Equal column width" box.

4. **If you so desire, turn on "Line between" to draw a thin vertical line between columns (it only appears after you have written enough text to spill into your second column). Click OK.**

You return to the document, where the fancy columns are now in place.

How columns look and flow

After you finish a column, the text flows to the top of the next column. To end one column and move on to the next, choose Insert → Break → Column Break.

Columns start out left-aligned, with an uneven right margin. The general consensus, though, is that fully justified columns give the tidiest, most professional look. To justify columns, select all the text in your columns (⌘-A if that's your entire document), and then click "Alignment and Spacing" → Justification on the Formatting Palette. (Turn on automatic hyphenation, too, for better word spacing, as described in the following section.)

Adjusting column widths

You can resize columns by dragging the column margin markers on the ruler, as shown in Figure 4-7.

Using the Format → Columns dialog box to resize columns gives you better control over the measurements, and provides access to the "Equal column width" feature. If you turn on this box, the columns remain the same width no matter what; if you resize one of them using the arrow buttons, the others automatically grow or shrink to match.

If you don't turn on "Equal column width," you can resize each column individually; the other columns grow or shrink to fill the page width. You can also adjust the spacing with the arrow buttons (or by entering numbers in the boxes), and glance at the Preview pane to see the effects of your changes. The total width of the columns and spacing always equals the full text width on the page: the width between the left and right indents.

Figure 4-7:
The quickest way to adjust column widths is by eye. First choose View → Print Layout. Then place the cursor over the ruler near the column boundary you'd like to adjust (at the top of the page). When the cursor turns into a double-arrow box, drag to move the column margin.

Tip: If you're having trouble getting your column lengths to come out even at the bottom of the page, check the Paragraph Spacing (under "Alignment and Spacing" in the Formatting Palette). Leaving just a small amount of space before and after each paragraph makes it easier for Word to balance the columns.

Automatic Hyphenation

When you're using columns, the hyphenation feature (which automatically breaks longer words at the right margin) creates a straighter, almost even right margin. It also provides more regular spacing within each line in *justified* text (text that's stretched to be flush with both margins).

Word normally doesn't insert hyphens until you type them—or until you turn on the automatic hyphenation feature. To do so, choose Tools → Hyphenation, then turn on "Automatically hyphenate document" (see Figure 4-8). When you click OK, Word scrutinizes the document and hyphenates words where necessary, using its built-in dictionary as a guide to "legal" syllable breaks. Word will continue hyphenating automatically as you edit and add on to your document.

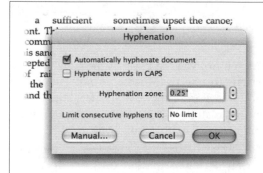

Figure 4-8:
By default, hyphenation is turned off; if a word is too long, Word moves it down to a new line. The result can be ugly gaps between words. Turning on "Automatically hyphenate document" can produce much better-looking spacing.

Hyphenation Settings

Before clicking OK, be sure to review the following hyphenation settings:

- Turning *off* "Hyphenate words in CAPS," leaves your acronyms whole; that's probably what you want it to do.

- The "Hyphenation zone" is the amount of space allowed at the end of a line before Word inserts a hyphen. The larger you set this number, the fewer hyphens you'll end up with in your document. The smaller the number, the more even the right margin will be—and the more hyphens you'll have.

- Set "Limit consecutive hyphens" to 2 or 3. If you set it to more than that, all the hyphens at the end of consecutive lines will look like a little ladder climbing up the page (a big no-no in professional publishing).

Undoing hyphenation is easy: Just choose Tools → Hyphenation and turn off the "Automatically hyphenate document" box. Word returns your document to its pristine, pre-hyphenated condition.

Manual Hyphenation

The automatic hyphenation feature is an all-or-nothing deal, in that it applies to the entire document, or not at all. If you'd like more say in Word's hyphenation propagation (say that three times fast with a mouthful of pickled peppers), use manual hyphenation. Doing so lets you say Yea or Nay to each word that Word wants to break up.

Here's how: Choose Tools → Hyphenation and click Manual. Word goes through your document, stopping at each word it wants to hyphenate, just as in a spell check. In the Manual Hyphenation dialog box that appears, you can click No (don't hyphenate), Yes (hyphenate at the blinking hyphen), or use the arrow keys to move to the point where you want Word to put the hyphen; *now* click Yes. Clicking Cancel dismisses the dialog box and ends manual hyphenation.

If you expect to be doing more editing to your document, then don't hyphenate manually. Unlike automatic hyphenation, manual hyphenation doesn't add or remove hyphens automatically as your text reflows during editing. (You can also rehyphenate only *parts* of the document by selecting the text before performing a manual hyphenation.)

Hard Hyphens

For the true control freak, Word gives you two ways to place hyphens right where you want them. These keyboard shortcuts are effective whether or not you use the manual or automatic hyphenation features. For example, if you feel your document has too many hyphens in a row, even after your manual hyphenation pass, you can still change a hyphenated word to have a nonbreaking hyphen.

- **Optional hyphen.** By clicking inside a word and then pressing ⌘-hyphen, you tell Word where to place a hyphen *if* the word needs to be hyphenated. As you edit the document, if the word moves away from the end of a line, the optional hyphen disappears, returning only if the word needs to be divided again.

- **Nonbreaking hyphen.** Click inside a word and then press Shift-⌘-hyphen. You've just told Word that you *do not* want to break this word up—ever.

To delete optional hyphens and the oxymoronic nonbreaking hyphens, click the Show/Hide (¶) button on the Standard toolbar. The invisible hyphens become visible (they look like an L-shaped bar and an approximately-equal sign, respectively) and are ready for you to delete.

Note: If Hyphenation is grayed out on the Tools menu, you may be in Outline view, where hyphenation is unavailable.

Text Boxes

Putting text in a box of its own, sitting there independently on the page, represents a quantum leap in text-flow management (see Figure 4-9). You can now format and color a text box independently from everything else on the page, as well as use drawing tools on it. In other words, text boxes let you think outside the box.

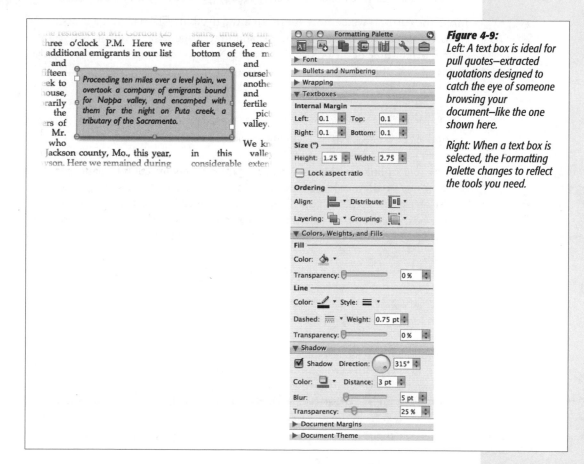

Figure 4-9:
Left: A text box is ideal for pull quotes—extracted quotations designed to catch the eye of someone browsing your document—like the one shown here.

Right: When a text box is selected, the Formatting Palette changes to reflect the tools you need.

Note: A text box is fundamentally different from a paragraph with a *border* around it, although text boxes can (and often do) have borders. For one thing, you can't drag to resize a bordered paragraph, or flow text around it, as you can with a text box. On the other hand, if all you want is a border and none of the other fancy features, then creating a border around a plain old paragraph is the easiest way to do it.

Text boxes also emulate the way desktop publishing programs such as Quark XPress and InDesign handle text. If you've never used professional desktop publishing software, consider this your initial training.

Note: Text boxes completely disappear in Draft view. To work with text boxes, make sure you're using Print Layout view (View → Print Layout) or Publishing Layout view (View → Publishing Layout)—or be prepared for some surprises when you first see the printout.

Creating Text Boxes

To create an empty text box in your document, choose Insert → Text Box. (Another avenue: If the Drawing toolbar is open [page 737], click the Text Box button.)

Move the cursor—which now sports an attractive blue "T" ball and a crosshair—to where you'd like the box to appear, and drag diagonally; Word shows you the rectangular outline of the box you're creating. The box is complete when you let go of the mouse, though you can always resize or move it later. To place text inside your new text box, begin typing or paste text you copied beforehand.

Tip: To enclose existing text in a text box, first select the text, then choose Insert → Text Box or click the Text Box button. Your text appears in a small text box, which you can then resize.

- **Link and unlink text boxes.** *Linking* text boxes sets up an automatic text flow from one to another, exactly as does InDesign, Quark XPress, or any newspaper on earth that makes you "Continue on page 12." As you add text to the first text box, overflow text falls into the second one, even if it's many pages away. Most people never suspect that Word is even capable of this page-layout feature.

Note: Word 2004's version of the Print Layout view (called Page Layout view) included a Text Box toolbar and more obvious text-box linking commands. With Word 2008's advent of the Publishing Layout view, Microsoft has shifted such page-layout features to the new view, and euthanized the Text Box toolbar in the process. Turn to page 295 for full coverage of text boxes in Publishing Layout view.

To link two text boxes, click the first box, type or paste text into it, and then click the box's forward link tab near its lower right corner. Your cursor again assumes the text box-drawing shape of the crosshair in the blue "T" ball. Use it to draw your next text box—which Word immediately fills with any of the overflow text from the first one. Repeat the process if you need more linked text boxes. Chapter 8 covers the process in depth, beginning on page 298.

Tip: There's nothing preventing you from repeating this process, linking three, four, or many more text boxes together into a continuously linked chain. You may drive your readers crazy, but you can do it.

- **Change text direction.** Choose Format → Text Direction, or open the Formatting Palette's "Alignment and Spacing" pane, click one of the text orientation buttons, and click OK. Word rotates the text within the box (and all others linked to it) to run vertically up or down the page—or back to horizontal again, as shown in Figure 4-10. (If you use this command when your insertion point is outside of a text box, Word rotates the text of your entire document.)

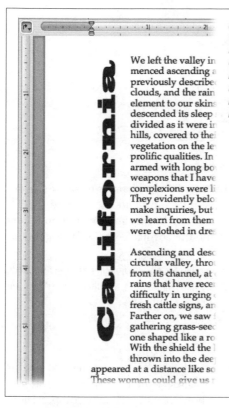

Figure 4-10:
Choosing Format → Text Direction or using the Orientation buttons in the Formatting Palette's "Alignment and Spacing" pane, lets you create eye-catching mastheads like this one. You can make text read top to bottom, bottom to top, or back to normal. (You can't turn text upside down.) Use this trick for creative layout effects for newsletter mastheads or letterheads, or for creating those tear-off tabs on the bottom of your lost-kitty poster.

Formatting Within Text Boxes

To format text within text boxes, just select the text first. The tools on the Standard toolbar and the Formatting Palette pertain to the text within a box, so long as the insertion point is in that box.

Tip: Choosing Edit → Select All or pressing ⌘-A, while the insertion point is in a text box, effectively selects all the text in that box *and* any boxes that are linked to it.

To adjust the margins within a text box (Figure 4-11), open the Formatting Palette's Text Box pane, or choose Format → Text Box. (This choice only appears when you've selected a text box.) Now click the Text Box tab, as shown in Figure 4-12. Alternatively, double-click the boundary of the text box. The settings you establish in these boxes control the distance between the borders of the text box and the text itself.

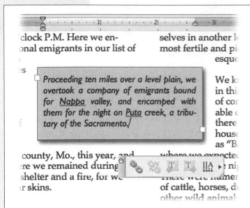

Figure 4-11:
Even if text boxes are linked, the internal margin settings (shown here in the ruler at the top of the page) apply only to the text box containing the insertion point.

Changing the background color or border style

When you've selected a text box, the Formatting Palette changes to show specialized controls for formatting its line thickness, line color, and background ("Fill") color or pattern. If you prefer, double-click the text box boundary or choose Format → Text box to access similar settings within the Format Text Box dialog box.

Tip: To use the drawing tools on a text box, make sure to select the box itself, not the text inside it. To do so, position the cursor on the box's outline until the cursor turns into a hand, and then click. (When you click *inside* the box, the tools on the Formatting Palette turn back to text tools.)

Sizing text boxes

If you can't see all the text in a box, you can either link it to another text box or just make the original box bigger. Here's how: Select the box by clicking it, and then drag any of the blue resize handles at its borders. Or, for numerical precision, use the boxes on the Formatting Palette's Size section; the relevant portions of the Formatting Palette are shown in Figure 4-9, right.

Working with Linked Text Boxes

Microsoft calls a group of linked text boxes a *story*. There's no limit to the number of text boxes you can link together—just keep creating new ones and linking them (page 298) until there's room for all your text.

Copying linked text boxes

You can copy or cut an entire story (or part of one) to paste into another document. To do so, select the text *box* (not the text) of the first box in the story and Shift-click any additional text boxes you want to copy. Once they're selected, you can copy or cut and paste the chain of boxes using any of the copy/paste methods described in Chapter 2. Use this method if, for example, you want to copy a series of text boxes and then change the text inside them. This saves you the work of creating and sizing new text boxes.

Note: Word can't link text boxes across documents in order to keep the text flowing "live" from one to the next.

To cut or copy the *text only* from a story, click in any box in the chain and choose Edit → Select All (or press ⌘-A). Now when you use the cut or copy and paste commands, you'll be pasting just the text, not the boxes.

Deleting one text box in a chain

If you delete one box in a story, the text remains intact, flowing from beginning to end through the remaining text boxes in the chain. Select the box that you want to delete by holding the cursor over the box's boundary until it changes into a four-arrow icon; click the box edge. Then choose Edit → Cut (or press Delete). If necessary, enlarge the remaining linked text boxes to show all of the story.

Grouping text boxes

You can *group* text boxes and then operate on them as a unit—the only problem is selecting them. As noted above, the trick is to click their *borders*; Shift-click to select the additional boxes that you want to group. Once they're selected, choose Group from the Grouping pop-up in the Ordering section of the Formatting Palette's Size, Rotation, and Ordering pane, or right-click and choose Grouping → Group from the shortcut menu. (If you change your mind, the Ungroup and Regroup commands are also on this menu.)

When you drag a grouped text box, they all move together. When you drag the sizing handles, they all grow or shrink by the same amount. Likewise, when you use the color and fill commands, they act upon all boxes in the group.

Text Wrapping and Layering

Whether you're creating a Web site or printed document, one of the most enjoyable parts is putting in a few images—photos, clip art, or drawings. But too often, the text and graphics don't harmoniously share the space. Many people find topics like *text wrapping* too intimidating to bother learning.

Don't be one of them. Word 2008's layout features are more intuitive than ever, especially for you, the wise and discriminating Mac fan.

Wrapping text around things

The "things" around which you can wrap text include pictures from your iPhoto library, clip art from Word's own collection (see page 734); charts from Excel, drawings you've made in Word or any drawing program, AutoShapes from the Drawing toolbar, WordArt, table, or text boxes. (See Chapter 19 for a review of the various graphic objects you can place into a Word document.)

The best way to configure the text around your text box or picture is with the Format dialog box. To get started, select the graphic or text box you want to wrap your text around. Ignore the text for now—just worry about getting the picture where you want it on the page. Then proceed as follows:

1. **Click to select the graphic or text box, then choose Format → whatever, or just double-click the graphic.**

   In other words, choose Format → Picture, Format → Object, Format → AutoShape, or Format → Text Box. The wording of the bottommost choice on the Format menu depends on the item you've selected. In any event, the appropriate Format dialog box now appears (Figure 4-12, top).

2. **Click the Layout tab. Choose one of the text-wrap styles by clicking its icon.**

   These wrapping controls correspond to those on the Formatting Palette, also shown in Figure 4-12. For example, choose Tight if you'd like the text to follow the outlines of an irregularly shaped object. Choose Behind Text to create a watermark, or choose Square for a neat, businesslike look.

3. **To keep the object right where you placed it on the page, click Other under "Horizontal Alignment."**

   The other buttons move the object to align with the left margin, center line, and right margin, respectively.

4. **Click Advanced.**

   The Advanced Layout dialog box appears (see Figure 4-13).

5. **Make the changes you want, as shown in Figure 4-13; click OK twice.**

Layering text with graphics

Most of the time, you'll want to wrap text *around* objects. But sometimes, for effect, you'll put text right *over* an object, or vice versa. To pull this off, use the "Behind text" or "In front of text" options shown in Figure 4-12.

If superimposing a graphic has made the text difficult to read, there are a couple of fixes. Either lighten the object beneath the text, or, if the text has a fill, change it to a clear or semitransparent fill.

- To lighten an object, select it. If it's a picture, open the Formatting Palette's Picture pane and adjust the Transparency slider.

Figure 4-12:
The wrapping controls in the Format dialog box (top) and the Wrapping pane of the Formatting Palette (bottom) lets you bend text to your will. Your text can leave a hole for the graphic (Square), hug its irregular sides (Tight), sit superimposed (Behind Text), hide beneath the graphic (In Front of Text), or treat it as just another typed character (In Line With Text).

- If the object is a drawing or AutoShape, you can use the Transparency sliders for Fill and Line on the Formatting Palette's Colors, Weights, and Fills pane to make it easier to see through.

Tip: You can even layer text with text—a great trick when using your company's name as a watermark on your letterhead, for example. To do so, make a text box containing the logo, apply a light color or light shade of gray to it in the Formatting Palette, and choose "Behind text" from the Style pop-up button in Formatting Palette's Wrapping section. Drag the logo into place.

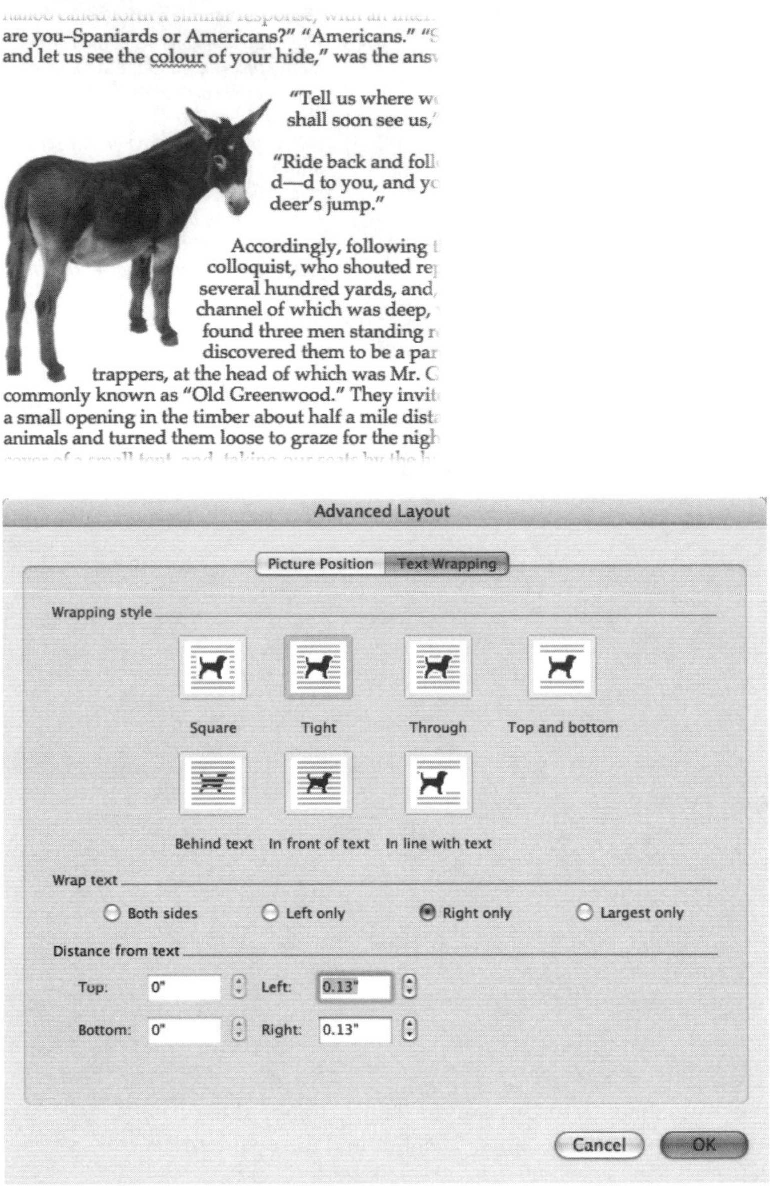

Figure 4-13:

Top: A Word clip art inserted into a document; left alignment, tight wrapping, one side only, 0.25" from text.

Bottom: The Advanced Layout tab has additional options. For example, you can wrap text on one side only, instead of both sides (if the text wrapping is down one side of a column, perhaps). "Largest only" wraps text only on one side—the side that has the most room, even if that changes in the middle of the object. This is a good choice for irregularly shaped objects. Distance from text lets you choose how close you want the text against the object it wraps—in hundredths of an inch.

Pictures and Drawings

Word comes with so many graphics features, "Microsoft Word and Picture 2008" might have been a better name for the program. More and more often, your skill using pictures, drawings, tables, and charts make your document the one that is read and understood.

The Insert menu has a long list of graphic objects you can pop onto a Word page: clip art, scans from a digital camera or scanner, drawing objects called AutoShapes, and so on. Because this Insert menu is available in most of the Office programs, its graphic commands are described in Chapter 20.

Inline vs. Page Graphics

Using graphics in Word entails only a few special pieces of knowledge. First, you can specify how the existing word processor text interacts with each graphic—whether it wraps around or passes over or under the image. (That's the purpose of the Text Wrap commands described earlier in this chapter.)

Second, it's important to understand that you can paste a graphic in either of two ways:

- As an **inline** graphic, one that sits right in the text. If you delete or insert text in preceding sentences, the graphic moves backward or forward as though it's just another typed character.

- As a **page** graphic, one that's married to a particular spot on the *page*. If you add or delete text, nothing happens to the graphic; it remains where you inserted or pasted it.

Note: Page graphics don't appear in Draft view or Outline view. To see them, you have to switch into Print Layout view, Web Layout view, Publishing Layout view, or the print preview.

The distinction between inline and page graphics has been a source of confusion since Word 1. And Microsoft continues to fiddle with the design of the controls that let you specify which is which.

In Word 2008, the scheme is simple, as long as you understand the technical difference between the two kinds of graphics that Word handles.

- **Drawing objects** always begin life as *page graphics*, floating on the page with no relationship to your text. (Drawing objects are graphics that *you make yourself*, right in Word, using the tools on the Drawing toolbar. They include AutoShapes, text boxes, arrows, rectangles, freehand lines, and so on.)

- **Pictures** begin life as *inline graphics*, embedded right in a line of text (unless you've changed your preference for inserting pictures in Preferences → Edit). (Pictures are images you import from other sources; they include Word's own Clip Art gallery, pictures from your iPhoto library, Photoshop files, and the like.)

Tip: See Chapter 19 for more detail on the distinction Word makes between drawing objects and pictures.

Converting Inline Graphics into Page Graphics

Just because drawings start out floating on the page and pictures start out hooked into your text doesn't mean they have to stay that way. It's easy enough to convert an inline graphic into a page graphic or vice versa. Select the graphic and open the Formatting Palette's Wrapping pane. Click the Style pop-up menu and choose In Line with Text to make it an in-line graphic. To turn it into a page graphic, choose any of the other wrapping styles in the menu.

If you prefer the dialog-box route, double-click the graphic, click the Layout tab in the Format dialog box, and click Advanced to access the same wrapping options (see Figure 4-13).

Word displays the graphic in its new environment: your former inline graphic is now floating on the page, or your former page graphic is now just another typed character.

Charts and Spreadsheets

Word's Insert → Object command lets you embed a variety of data—charts, equations, graphics, and other Office documents—from other Office programs right into a Word document.

You'll find a complete description of this feature, which technically is called Object Linking and Embedding technology (abbreviated OLE and pronounced "oh-LAY"—pass the tacos, please), in Chapter 18.

Tables

How do you use Word to create a résumé, agenda, program booklet, list, multiple choice test, Web page, or other document where numbers, words, and phrases need to be aligned across the page? In the bad old days, people did it by pressing the Tab key to line up columns. As Figure 4-14 illustrates, this method is a recipe for disaster. (Unfortunately, thousands of people *still* use this method—or, worse, they still try to line up columns by continuously pressing the Space bar.)

Using Word's *table* feature is light-years easier and more flexible. As shown in Figure 4-14, each row of a table expands infinitely to hold whatever you put into it, while everything else on its row remains aligned. Tables also have a few simple spreadsheet features.

Creating Tables

There are two ways to insert a table: You can let Word build the table to your specifications, or you can draw it more or less freehand.

Inserting a table

Office 2008's Elements Gallery introduces a new way to add tables, complete with background shading and borders. Click the Elements Gallery's Quick Tables Tab to display the Quick Tables gallery. Click the buttons at the left end of the gallery to view a selection of Basic tables with a variety of cell-shading styles, or Complex

Song	Album	Artist
Down to the River to Pray	A Wish	Wonderland Jazz Ensamble
Nuclear War	A Fireside Chat	Sun Ra Arkestra
Romance	The Myth of Red	Sasha Lazard
Super Life	Funk This	Chaka Kahn

Song	Album	Artist	
Down to the River to Pray/Lullaby of Forrealville Jazz Ensamble		A Wish	Wonderland
Nuclear War Arkestra	A Fireside Chat With Lucifer		Sun Ra
Romance	The Myth of Red	Sasha Lazard	
Super Life	Funk This	Chaka Kahn	

Song	Album	Artist
Down to the River to Pray/ Lullaby of Forrealville	A Wish	Wonderland Jazz Ensamble
Nuclear War	A Fireside Chat With Lucifer	Sun Ra Arkestra
Romance	The Myth of Red	Sasha Lazard
Super Life	Funk This	Chaka Kahn

Figure 4-14:
Top: If you use tabs to set up a table, things may look good at first—as long as every line fits within its space and you never plan to insert any additional text. Middle: Here's what's wrong with the tab approach: When you insert words into the columns, they push the text too far to the right, causing an ugly ripple effect.

Bottom: If you use a table, you never have this kind of problem. Just type as much text as you like into a "cell," and that row of the table simply expands to fit it.

tables laid out as calendars, an invoice, a quarterly report, and so on. Click one of the gallery's table thumbnails to insert the pre-designed table in your document (see Figure 4-15). Tables always enter your document as page graphics. The variations of Basic Quick Tables appear with three columns and eight rows. The size of the Complex tables varies depending on which design you choose. You can add, delete, or resize rows as described on page 157.

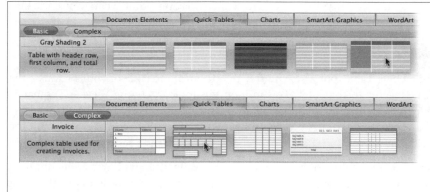

Figure 4-15:
Click the Quick Tables tab to display the Elements Gallery's collection of prefab table designs. The buttons at the left end display an assortment of basic (top) and complex (bottom) designs. As you move your cursor over the thumbnails, a brief description of the table appears at the left end of the gallery. Click one of the thumbnails to add it to your document.

To quickly add a plain table to your document use the Tables pop-up button on the Standard toolbar (see Figure 4-16).

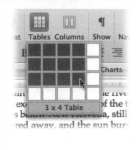

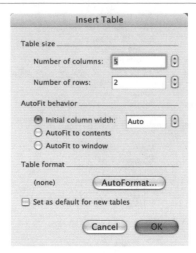

If the toolbar isn't visible, choose Table → Insert → Table. The Insert Table dialog box opens, also shown in Figure 4-16. After choosing the number of rows and columns you want (you can always add more later), click an AutoFit radio button to instruct Word how to size the columns across your table. If you know how wide in inches you'd like each column to be, click "Initial column width" and set a measurement in the size box. "AutoFit to contents" creates skinny columns that expand as you type into them, and "AutoFit to window" (the easiest way to go if you're not sure) spaces the selected number of columns evenly across the page. The table appears in your document at the insertion point when you click OK. Figure 4-17, top, depicts a small 5 × 3 table.

Drawing a table

Word's Draw Table tool gives you free rein to form the table of your dreams—the trick is learning to control it. To summon this toolbar, choose View → Toolbar → "Tables and Borders", or choose Table → Draw Table. The "Tables and Borders" toolbar opens and the cursor turns into a pencil. (Press Esc whenever you want the normal cursor back.)

When you drag the pencil horizontally or vertically, it draws lines; when you drag diagonally, it draws boxes. Using these techniques, you can design even the most eccentric, asymmetrical table on earth.

The tidiest way to begin drawing a table is to drag diagonally to create the outer boundary (Figure 4-18, top), then drag horizontal and vertical lines to create the rows and columns. Drawing your own table is a good option when you want a variety of widths in your rows and columns, as shown in Figure 4-18, rather than evenly spaced ones.

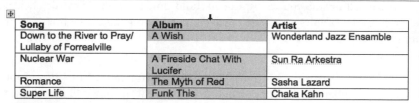

Song	Album	Artist
Down to the River to Pray/ Lullaby of Forrealville	A Wish	Wonderland Jazz Ensamble
Nuclear War	A Fireside Chat With Lucifer	Sun Ra Arkestra
Romance	The Myth of Red	Sasha Lazard
Super Life	Funk This	Chaka Kahn

Figure 4-17:
Top: Position your cursor at the very top of the column until the downward-pointing arrow appears—then click to select the whole column. Similarly, click just outside the table on the left to select an entire row. Now you can make a formatting change that applies to all the selected cells.

Bottom: The various panes of the Formatting palette can handle most of your table creation and formatting needs. For 2008, the buttons from the "Tables and Borders" toolbar are cloned in the Formatting palette's Table, and "Borders and Shading" panes. Use whichever you find more convenient.

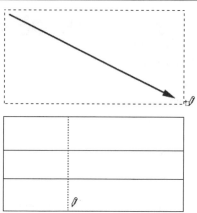

Figure 4-18:
Top: Drag diagonally to create the outer border of your table.

Bottom: The Draw Table tool lets you create rows and columns of any size and shape just by drawing them, but to be honest you can get similar effects, with much less drama, by using the Insert → Table command, as described on page 150.

To remove a cell or line you've just drawn, hold down the Shift key (or click the eraser tool on the "Tables and Borders" toolbar) and drag it across a line. The line promptly disappears. Be aware, however, if you erase the line between two cells, they merge.

When you're finished with your table's framework, you can dismiss the "Tables and Borders" toolbar. On the other hand, if you leave it open, you'll have buttons for sorting and formatting your table, or drawing more tables, ready at hand. Of course, you could also make use of the Formatting Palette's Table; "Borders and Shading"; and "Alignment and Spacing" panes, which have all the same buttons you'll find in the "Tables and Borders" toolbar. The insertion point is now blinking in your new table, all set to begin typing.

If you really make a mess of things, press ⌘-Z to undo what you've done, one step at a time. Alternatively, vaporize the entire table by clicking inside it and choosing Table → Delete → Table.

Typing into tables

To type into a table cell, click in that cell. You can use the up or down arrow keys to change rows; press Tab and Shift-Tab to jump forward or backward through the cells. (There's not much call for tabs within cells—after all, you've *already* aligned the text the way you like it. But if you need a tab character, press Option-Tab.)

Note: Pressing Return or Enter *doesn't* take you to the next cell; it puts a line break in the current cell instead. Get in the habit of pressing Tab to move on to the next cell.

You can also navigate like this:

Table 4-1. Keystrokes for Navigating Tables

To move to:	Press these keys:
First cell in the row	Control-Home
Last cell in the row	Control-End
Top cell in the column	Control-Page Up
Bottom cell in the column	Control-Page Down
Highlight whole table	Option-Clear
Next cell	Tab
Previous cell	Shift-Tab

As you type, text wraps within the cell, forcing the row to grow-taller as necessary. To widen the cell as you type, choose Table → AutoFit → "AutoFit to Contents". (Even then, the cell will widen only until the table reaches the edge of the page—then the text will start to wrap down.)

Of course, this automatic wrapping is the principal charm of tables. But if you find yourself wishing Word would *not* wrap text in this way, select the cells where you want wrapping turned off, and then choose Table → Table Properties → Cell tab. Click Options and uncheck the Wrap Text box. Click OK and then choose the Row tab and change the "Row height is" pop-up menu to Exactly. You can still enter as much text in a cell as you like, but the cell won't expand downward to show it— it'll just disappear beyond the cell boundary.

Selecting cells

To cut, copy, or drag material from cells in a table, you have to first select it, as with any other Word text. Because it's a table, however, you have the following options:

- To select multiple cells, drag the mouse—down, across, or diagonally over the cells.

- To select an entire column, click at the top of a column—the cursor changes into a downward-pointing arrow. Or, Option-click anywhere in a column. Likewise, to select an entire row, click at the left of a row—the cursor changes into a right-slanting arrow.

- To highlight a cell, click the thin, invisible *selection bar* at the left edge of a cell. (Double-click the selection bar to highlight a whole row.)

- To extend the selection by additional cells, rows, or columns, click one cell, row, or column, and then Shift-click another.

- To select the entire table, triple-click the cursor at the beginning of any row. In Print Layout, Publishing Layout, or Web Layout view, you can also click the table move handle (at the upper left) to select the entire table.

Sizing rows and columns

You can make a row taller or shorter, or a column wider or narrower, much the way you adjust Word's text boxes or margins. Click to place your insertion point inside the table, then point to any line or boundary of a table without clicking, and drag when the cursor turns into a double-sided arrow.

You can also rely on Word's own automatic table features to help you design the table. They include:

- **Balanced columns.** If a symmetrical, balanced look is what you crave, Word can automatically arrange the rows or columns across your table so that there's equal space between them. First select the rows and columns that you want to balance, then choose Table → AutoFit → Distribute Rows Evenly or Distribute Columns Evenly. (Corresponding buttons on the "Tables and Borders" toolbar and Formatting Palette can do all this with a single click; you can even Control-click [or right-click] and choose this option from the shortcut menu.)

- **Automatic sizing.** Often, you want the columns to stretch and shrink depending on what you type into them. Or, you just don't know in advance what size you want or need the columns to be. In such cases, choose Table → AutoFit → "AutoFit to Contents". As you work, the columns will stretch to just the width necessary to accommodate the contents. For maximum room, Table → AutoFit → "AutoFit to Window" stretches your columns—no matter how many of them there are—to fill the page from margin to margin.

  You can resize the table using the mouse at any time; doing so overrides and cancels the previous AutoFit setting. When you have the column widths right where you want them, choose AutoFit → Fixed Column Width. The same menu choices are available on the "Tables and Borders" toolbar (click the little arrow next to the Insert Table button) as well as the bottom of the Formatting Palette. Or simply Control-click (or right-click) and choose this option from the shortcut menu.

- **Numeric precision.** To set row and column sizes using exact measurements, select the rows or columns in question and then choose Table → Table Properties. The resulting dialog box (see Figure 4-19) has size boxes where you can enter exact measurements.

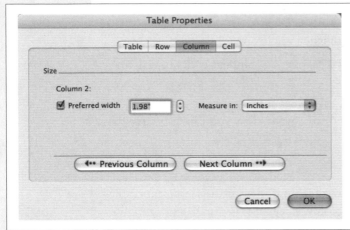

Figure 4-19:
When using the Table Properties dialog box, you can select a group of rows and columns and size them all at once, or you can use the Previous and Next buttons to work on each row or column one at a time.

For columns, you can also specify a percentage of the table width instead of a measurement in inches. For rows, you have the option of setting an exact measurement, or an "At least" measurement. When "At least" is chosen, the cells in that row will stretch downward to wrap text as you type—even if you've turned off "Wrap Text" on the Cell tab.

- **The whole table.** To resize the table as a whole, drag the lower-right corner. The rows and columns remain evenly spaced, or in whatever proportions you have chosen.

Adding rows and columns

If you run out of room and need more rows at the *bottom* of your table, it's easy to add more: Click the lower-right cell and press Tab. A new row appears, identical to the one above, ready for your typing.

To add a new row or column *anywhere* in your table, click in the table and then use the Table → Insert submenu. Choose one of the options from the menu that appears: "Insert Columns to the Left," for example. (These commands are also available in the Insert Table pop-up button on the "Tables and Borders" toolbar and the Formatting Palette.)

Adding multiple rows or columns at either end of your table, or anywhere within it, is a two-step process. First, highlight the *same number* of rows or columns as the ones you want to insert; to add two rows, select two existing rows. Next, choose Table → Insert, and one of the submenu options (Insert → Rows Below, for example). Word instantly creates the requested number of new, empty rows or columns.

Inserting individual cells works much the same way. Insert one cell at a time by choosing Table → Insert → Cells, or by using the Insert Table menu on the "Tables and Borders" toolbar. To insert multiple cells, select the equivalent number of *existing* cells at the desired location in your table before choosing from the menu.

Of course, you may find it more fun simply to click the Draw Table tool on the "Tables and Borders" toolbar and *draw* the extra columns and rows onto your table.

Deleting table parts

It's easy to dismantle a table in various ways:

- **Deleting cells.** Select one or more cells and choose Table → Delete → Cells. Word asks if you want to move the remaining cells up or leftward to fill the void; choose one and click OK (or press Return).

- **Deleting rows and columns.** Select them and choose Table → Delete → Rows (or Columns). You may find it faster to click anywhere in the row or column and choose Table → Delete → Cells, then choose a radio button to delete the *entire* row or column. Click OK or hit Return to confirm the deletion. You can also right-click and choose this option from the shortcut menu.

- **Deleting the whole table.** Click anywhere in the table and choose Table → Delete → Table.

Formatting Tables

When you click inside a table, the ever-responsive Formatting Palette sprouts a new set of formatting tools—a section called Table. In conjunction with the existing "Borders and Shading" section, you now have all the formatting controls you need.

To use them, begin by highlighting the cells, rows, or columns that you want to work on. Now you're all set to format any of these table elements:

- **Table border or gridlines.** The Borders tool lets you choose a line style (solid, dashed, and so on), color, and weight (thickness in points). Click the Type button to trigger a menu where you can choose which sides of the table you want borders to appear on. For instance, you may want only vertical lines inside the table and no outside border. Or you may want a heavier top border on the top row of cells only. (The same border formatting tools appear in the "Tables and Borders" toolbar.)

FREQUENTLY ASKED QUESTION

The Thin Gray Lines

I like the concept of a table, but I don't want thick black lines in my résumé (or Web page). How do I get rid of them?

You're right: Unless you intervene, these lines will actually print out. One of the quickest ways to delete the borders and gridlines is to click inside the table and then choose Format → "Borders and Shading". In the resulting dialog box, click None, then click OK.

Even then, however, you may still see thin gray lines. These don't print; they're just on the screen to help you understand the "tableness" of your table. You can hide even these lines, if you like, by choosing Table → Gridlines so that the checkmark disappears. If you do hide the lines, consider clicking the Show/ Hide (¶) icon on the Standard toolbar. The end-of-row and end-of-cell marks become visible, defining the bounds of your table.

Tip: You can also eliminate certain table lines entirely. Just click the eraser tool on the top row of the "Tables and Borders" toolbar, and drag along each line you want to disappear from the table. Doing so *merges* the table cells (page 161).

- **Background shading in cells.** Shading in a table is similar to a *fill* (see page 746), except that you don't use the Fill palette; you use the "Borders and Shading" pane in the Formatting Palette (or "Tables and Borders" toolbar). You can choose from 70 colors and shades of gray, or choose More Colors to use Word's color pickers (see page 747).

Autoformatting tables

With creative combinations of borders, lines, and shading, you can make a table look right for anything from Citibank annual reports to *Sesame Street*. When you're in a hurry, though, choose a Table AutoFormat for instant good looks.

Click anywhere in your table and choose Table → Table AutoFormat. There's a long list of potential formats in the list box of the Table AutoFormat dialog box. Simply click each for a preview. If you want to use *some* of the features in the format but not others (font, color, and so on), then just turn on the boxes for the ones you wish to use.

Tip: Turning on AutoFit is a good idea, since it ensures that the new format will exactly fit the existing information in your table, instead of vice versa.

Many of the formats have a different typeface or shading applied to the top (heading) row, first column, last column, and so on. The checkboxes in the "Apply special formats to" section control whether you accept those features with the rest of the format. For example, if you're not using the last row of your table for totals, don't turn on the "Last row" box.

Repeat table headings

For the purposes of Autoformatting, Word considers the first row of a table to be a heading. But what if your table is longer than a page? Wouldn't it be nice if Word could *repeat* the column titles at the top of each page? Well, it can, thanks to the Heading Rows Repeat feature.

Select the top row of your table (and any additional rows you want to repeat). Then choose Table → Heading Rows Repeat; that's all there is to it. When your table flows onto a new page (page breaks you insert yourself don't count), the heading will appear at the top of each new page of your table.

Cell margins and spacing

To enhance the look of your text in a table, adjust the gap between the characters and the borderlines. You can also put a little space around the outside of each cell—an especially attractive effect on Web pages (see Chapter 9).

Just select one or more cells and choose Table → Table Properties → Cell tab. Click Options, and set measurements in the size boxes for the distance between the text and the top, bottom, left, and right edges of the cell. The "Same as the whole table" box changes the margins of the selected cell to match the default cell margins for the table. To set the default margins for all cells in the table at once, choose Table → Table Properties → Table tab; click Options and enter measurements in the "Default cell margins" boxes.

To add more spacing around the *outside* of cells, click anywhere in the table and choose Table → Table Properties → Table tab. Click the Options button and turn on "Allow spacing between cells"; enter a setting in the size box. When you click OK, that amount of white space will surround each cell, simulating the effect of thicker cell walls. Usually .1" or less looks good. More space than that creates a waffle-like effect, as shown in Figure 4-20, top.

Text formatting within cells

Like text anywhere else in Word, you can change the direction and alignment of selected text in a table using the Format → Text Direction command—a terrific effect for row or column labels (Figure 4-20, right). In the resulting dialog box, choose the text orientation—horizontal, vertical, or bottom-to-top—and click OK.

Song	Album	Artist
Down to the River to Pray/ Lullaby of Forrealville	A Wish	Wonderland Jazz Ensamble
Nuclear War	A Fireside Chat With Lucifer	Sun Ra Arkestra
Romance	The Myth of Red	Sasha Lazard
Super Life	Funk This	Chaka Kahn

Figure 4-20:
Top: You can create some unusual table looks using, for example, .15" spacing between cells.

Bottom: Rotated text.

Sunny	Nuclear War	A Fireside Chat With Lucifer
Tommy	Down to the River to Pray/ Lullaby of Forrealville	A Wish
Chaka	Super Life	Funk This

You can also make the text in selected cells hug the left or right side of its cell, center it in the middle, or make it stick to the "floor" or "ceiling" of a cell. After selecting the cells, click the arrow button next to the alignment button on the "Tables and Borders" toolbar and choose the alignment pattern you seek. Align Top Left, for example, aligns text to the top and left margins of the cell, so that the text starts in the upper-left corner.

Table layout on the page

When you created your table, you probably dragged it where you wanted it, or built it starting from the insertion point. To position it exactly where it looks best on the page and apply advanced features like text wrapping, use the tools in the Table → Table Properties → Table tab, shown in Figure 4-21.

- **Size.** Use this box to set a width for the entire table. (It says "Preferred width" because it may change if you use the AutoFit feature, as described on page 156.)

- **Alignment.** Choose left, centered, or right alignment. "Indent from left" tells Word where to start aligning, measured from the edge of the page. (If your table already spans the page, margin to margin, you won't see any difference.)

- **Text Wrapping.** For large tables, you'll usually choose None. If you choose Around, the Positioning button becomes activated; clicking it opens a dialog box where you can use advanced layout features like those described on page 307.

Nested tables

A *nested table* is a table-within-a-table, or, more specifically, a table within a *cell* of another table. This feature is especially valuable when you're using Word as a

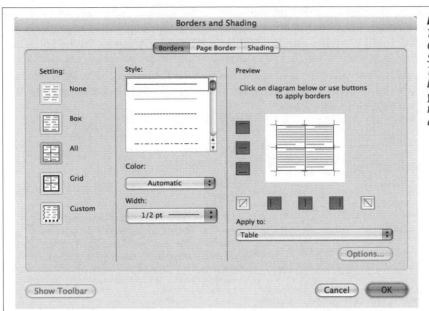

Figure 4-21:
The Table Properties: Clicking the "Borders and Shading" button in the Table Properties dialog box opens a box where you can choose lines and fills for the table, as well as page borders.

Web-design tool. For example, you can create a table with four large cells to divide your Web page into quarters, and put a smaller table in each one.

To create a nested table, click in the cell where you want the table to start, then click the Insert Table button on the "Tables and Borders" toolbar. Choose the number of rows and columns for your nested table. Now you can click in one of the nested cells and start typing. (Because the nested table has to remain within one cell, either resize the cell to hold the nested table, or choose Table → AutoFit and Distribute → "AutoFit to Contents" to allow the holding cell to expand.)

Merging and splitting cells

Merging and splitting are nothing more than ways of subtracting or adding columns en masse. Merging cells (or rows or columns) turns two into one, and joins their contents together as separate paragraphs in the merged cell. Splitting cells (or rows or columns) divides them, forcing their contents into the cell above or to the left of the split.

Start by highlighting the cells, rows, or columns you want to merge. Then choose Table → Merge Cells, or click the Merge Cells button on the "Tables and Borders" toolbar; the selected cells instantly merge. Another way to proceed: Use the eraser tool to remove the line dividing two cells, columns, or rows. This lets you see directly how merging cells works.

The quickest and most satisfying way to split cells is to draw new lines right smack across existing cells, using the Draw Table tool on the "Tables and Borders" toolbar.

If you need computer-aided precision, however, you can split cells, rows, or columns perfectly evenly by selecting them and then choosing Table → Split Cells (or click the Split Cells button on the "Tables and Borders" toolbar). In the Split Cells dialog box, choose the number of rows and columns you want your selection to be divided into. For example, the cells at the right in Figure 4-22 were split into two columns and one row; the one row that was selected stayed one row, and the two columns became a total of four.

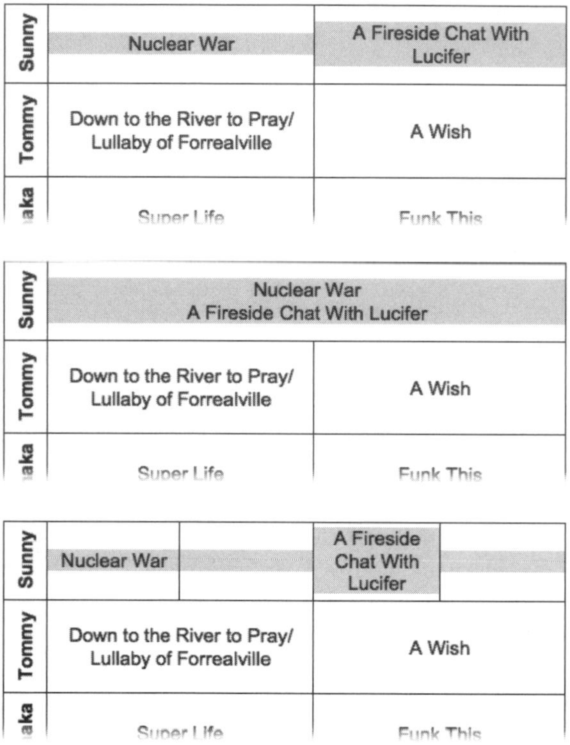

Figure 4-22:
Top: A simple table.

Middle: The same table after merging the two of the top cells.

Bottom: The table after splitting the same two cells in two. If the "Merge cells before split" box had been turned on in the Split Cells dialog box, A Fireside Chat with Lucifer would immediately follow Nuclear War in the top row.

Tip: You can also split a table, creating a blank line between its top and bottom portions—a great trick when you need to insert some regular text into the middle of it. Just click where you want the split and then choose Table → Split Table.

Converting text to a table

Sometimes you want to create a table from information that's already in Word, such as a table that a novice Word person (perhaps even a younger you) created by trying to line up text with the Tab key. Word is happy to be your obedient servant.

First, of course, select the desired text. Presumably, the text is a list, a number of words separated by tabs, or some other vaguely table-like blob of text. The key to turning highlighted text into a table is the Table → Convert → "Convert Text to Table" command. In the "Convert Text to Table" dialog box, start with the "Separate text at" settings. Choose the most logical place to divide your selected text into cells. If that's not a paragraph, comma, or tab, then click Other and press the key that represents your choice—Space bar, Return, period, and so on.

Word automatically suggests the number of columns you'll need to hold all the text, though you can also specify the number of rows and columns you want, too. You also have the chance to use the AutoFit and AutoFormat features now—or you can always save them for later. Click OK to begin the conversion process.

If the table doesn't look quite as you had hoped, examine it and learn how Word interpreted your choices in the "Convert Text to Table" dialog box. Then press ⌘-Z to undo the conversion and try again with different selections. Or just reformat your table using the tools described in this section.

Converting a table into text

You can also extract information from a table *without* maintaining its tableness. For example, suppose you want to import it into a page-layout program that doesn't understand Word tables. This kind of conversion is easy—simply click the table and then choose Table → Convert → "Convert Table to Text".

Your only decision is how to divide the contents of one cell from the next—you don't want them all to run together, of course. You have a choice of paragraph marks (each cell's contents will become a new Word paragraph), tabs, commas, or any other character you enter in the Other box by pressing its key. If you choose tabs, the result is what you've heard described as *tab delimited text*—that is, one tab separating each word or phrase that formerly occupied a cell on a single row, with a Return character at the end of each line.

Formulas in tables

Word isn't Excel, but Microsoft is at least aware that you may want to perform simple math from time to time. Fortunately, a table can carry out many of the most common spreadsheet tasks with the help of functions and operators. You can add up a column of numbers, for example, or have Word average them and display the results.

To add a column of figures, click in the bottom cell of the column (making sure that it's blank, of course) and click the AutoSum (Σ) button in the "Tables and Borders" toolbar or Formatting Palette (see Figure 4-23, top). Your answer appears immediately against a gray background (which doesn't print). This gray box indicates that you're dealing with a *field* (which you can only edit if you right-click and choose Toggle Field Codes, as explained on page 239).

Note: This kind of field doesn't update automatically. If your table numbers change, you have to select the total field and click the AutoSum button (or click the field and then press F9).

Quarter	Orders	Shipments	Total
Q1	654	546	$464,100.00
Q2	758	502	$426,700.00
Q3	891	856	$727,600.00
Total	2303	1904	$1,618,400.00

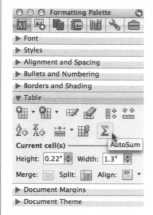

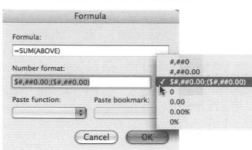

Figure 4-23:
Top: Clicking in the bottom cell and then clicking AutoSum adds up the numbers in each column.

Lower left: The Table pane of the Formatting palette shows the AutoSum button responsible for this magic.

Lower right: The Table → Formula command reveals that the AutoSum function does nothing more than insert the invisible formula =SUM(ABOVE) into the selected cell. You could have typed it in this dialog box yourself, if you had very little else to do.

For more complex formulas, click the cell where you want to place the results of your calculations and choose Table → Formula. Word's guess at what formula you're looking for already appears in the Formula window (see Figure 4-23). If that's not right, press Delete, type an equal sign to begin your formula, and build it with the following:

- **Cell references**. Cells in Word tables are named the same way as in Excel spreadsheets, except that you can't see the row letters and column numbers. The columns are named A, B, C, and so on, from left to right; the rows are numbered 1, 2, 3, and so on, from top to bottom. The upper-leftmost cell is A1.

  To refer to the entire column above the formula cell, use the expression (*ABOVE*); to refer to the entire row, use (*LEFT*). For a *range* of cells (a block of them), use a colon to separate the top-left and lower-right cells of the range, such as A1:B2 to name a four-cell range.

- **Operators**. *Operators* are symbols like + for addition, – for subtraction, * for multiplication, / for division, and > for greater than. Using operators in combination, you can set up a table cell to add sales tax (* 1.05) to a subtotal column, for example.

- **Functions**. Choose formulas from the "Paste function" list in the Table → Formula dialog box. These are the same as the Excel formulas described in Chapter 13.

• Click the arrow next to the **Number format** box to tell Word what you want the results to look like—AutoFormatted with a dollar sign, with commas, and so on.

Click OK to place the formula in the current cell. See Chapter 13 for much more on using formulas in Office 2008.

Sorting tables

If your table includes names, dates, or other listed items, you may want to arrange them in numerical or alphabetical order. Click one of the cells in the column containing the data you want to sort by, and choose either the Sort Ascending or Sort Descending button in the Table Toolbar or the Formatting Palette's Table pane.

To perform a more complex sort using up to three columns, click the table and choose Table → Sort. In the "Sort by" box, Word helpfully suggests that you start with "Column 1," the first column on the left. All the columns in the current table are listed in a menu; click the arrows to choose one. For instance, to sort chronologically, choose the column containing your dates. You can sort by Text (alphabetically), Number, or Date; just choose the one that matches your data.

You can choose second and third sort columns as well. For example, after the first column sorts by date, you may want to sort names alphabetically *within* each date. Use the "Then by" boxes to set up these second and third internal sorts.

Finally, choose one of the buttons at the bottom to designate whether your table has a header row or not—choosing "Header row" excludes that row from the sort.

Click OK to begin the sort. (Note that you can't sort columns—only rows.)

Working Collaboratively

Most of the time, you create documents in Word 2008 to send or show to other people. (The exception: Keeping your dream journal in Word. You know who you are.)

In the real world of business, publishing, and entertainment, more and more people find it valuable to be able to mark up and revise each other's documents. Thanks to the features described in this chapter, you, the original author, can peruse others' edits, and incorporate or delete them. Whether you're working with one partner or an entire team, Word's collaboration features make it easy to track the revisions and versions of the electronically transmitted documents that you or your teammates create.

Comments

Often when reviewing someone else's document, you'll want to add comments without making them a part of the text itself. You'll have a query for the author, an idea, a suggestion, or a joke—the kind of thing that you'd write in the margin or on a sticky note if you were working on paper. Fortunately, the days of typing boldfaced or bracketed comments directly into the text are long over.

Adding Comments

To add a single comment in Word, select the applicable text and then choose Insert → Comment (or press Option-⌘-A). Doing so triggers one of two things, depending on your selection in Word → Preferences → Track Changes. If you're in

Print Layout view or Web Layout view and you've turned on "Use balloons to display changes," your comment appears in a balloon at the side of the page. Otherwise, the Reviewing pane opens at the bottom of the document window, as shown in Figure 5-1, with an insertion point at the beginning of a new comment line marked with your name and the current date. Colored brackets (you can set the color at Word → Preferences → Track Changes) bookend the originally selected text. Type your comment, then press F6 to return to the main (upper) pane of the document window (or just click there).

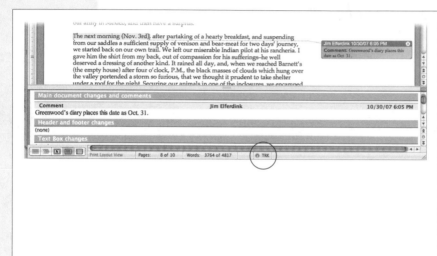

Figure 5-1:
A document showing the brackets that designate comments, the comment balloon, and the split-window Reviewing pane. If you prefer, you can turn off the balloon display in the Track Changes Preferences (see Figure 5-3). Then, when you point to a highlighted phrase, the comment appears at your cursor in a screen tip. Clicking the TRK indicator on the window's status bar (circled) represents a quick way to turn change tracking on and off. Clear means off; it turns blue when you click to turn it on.

If you plan to make more than a few comments, however, you may find it more convenient to open the *Reviewing toolbar,* which lets you add a comment with a single click. After selecting the text you'd like to praise, critique, or question, proceed as follows:

1. **Choose View → Toolbars → Reviewing.**

   The Reviewing toolbar opens.

2. **Click the New Comment button on the Reviewing toolbar (see Figure 5-2).**

   Word splits your window, showing the Reviewing pane at the bottom (unless you turned on comment balloons as described on the previous page).

3. **Type your comment; click back in the upper pane of the document window to return to it.**

   You can also press F6 to toggle between the two panes.

4. **When you're finished adding comments, close the Reviewing pane by double-clicking the separator above the Reviewing pane or by clicking its icon on the Reviewing toolbar.**

   If you're typing your comments into a balloon, just click outside the balloon or press Esc to return to the document's main body.

Word's reviewing toolbar (Figure 5-2), features several ways to access the reviewing features, which include both Comments and Change Tracking, described later in this chapter. The pop-up menu on the left of the toolbar provides the following viewing options:

- **Final Showing Markup.** If you've chosen to use balloons (as shown in Figure 5-2), and you're in Print Layout view, the text deleted by your reviewer/editor appears in balloons, and inserted text and formatting changes show up in the text itself. If not, the text and changes appear as indicated in Word → Preferences → Track Changes. Use this to quickly analyze what the editor has done to your precious prose.

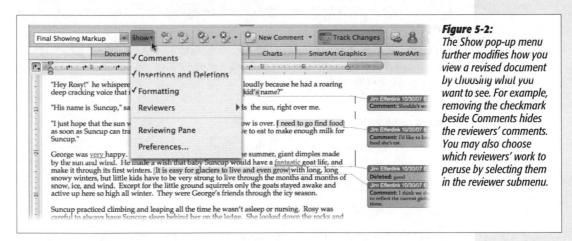

Figure 5-2:
The Show pop-up menu further modifies how you view a revised document by choosing what you want to see. For example, removing the checkmark beside Comments hides the reviewers' comments. You may also choose which reviewers' work to peruse by selecting them in the reviewer submenu.

- **Final.** This reveals how your document would look if you accepted all of your editor's changes and comments. Use this when it's just too darn painful to review them.

- **Original Showing Markup.** This is like Final Showing Markup turned inside out and viewed with a mirror. If you've chosen to use balloons, and you're in Print Layout view or Web Layout view, *deleted* text is shown in the document, and inserted text and formatting changes are pumped into the balloons. If not, the text and changes appear as indicated in Word → Preferences → Track Changes. This option is best for reviewing both the new and original text at the same time.

- **Original.** This displays your virginal document, before your editor or reviewer improved or destroyed it (depending on your point of view). Use this to see how the document would look if you rejected all changes.

Reviewing Comments

When you open a document with comments, the Reviewing pane doesn't automatically open. Instead, what you see depends on your document view. In the Draft, Outline, Publishing Layout, and Notebook views, you'll see brackets surrounding sections of text that have comments. Hovering your cursor over the brackets reveals the comment (except in Publishing Layout view). If you've turned on balloons in Print Layout view, you'll see the brackets connected to comment balloons in the document's margin, indicating the comments.

If you like, you can open (or close) the Reviewing pane, where all the document's comments are listed sequentially. To do that, choose Show → Reviewing Pane on the Reviewing toolbar, shown in Figure 5-2, or, if time isn't at a premium, click the Show pop-up menu on the Reviewing toolbar and choose Reviewing pane.

Note: Some folks don't like the Reviewing pane eating half their viewing space. If you're one of them, you may prefer to add comments in attractive text bubbles, instead of the Reviewing pane. To make it so, select Word → Preferences and click Track Changes at the left. At the bottom of the Track Changes panel, turn on "Use balloons to display changes." You can then see the balloons, but only in Print Layout view and Web Layout view.

If you've used Word for Windows, you may find these balloons look familiar. If you're a confirmed Machead, you may prefer the pop-up comment boxes from previous Word versions—in which case confine your reviewing to the Draft view.

Deleting comments

To delete a comment, do any one of the following:

- Control-click (or right-click) within the comment's bracketing and choose Delete Comment from the shortcut menu.

- Click the Reviewing toolbar's Reject Change/Delete Comment button.

- Select the comment or the comment's title bar in the Reviewing Pane, and then Control-click and select Delete from the shortcut menu.

- Click the "X" button in the comment's balloon.

Navigating Comments

The main document pane and the Reviewing pane have independent vertical scroll bars. You can move around in each one using any of Word's usual navigation tools (see page 50). You can also use the Previous Comment and Next Comment buttons on the Reviewing toolbar (Figure 5-2), or the Navigator Buttons described on page 53, to hop from one comment in the document to the next. (The main document window scrolls automatically to keep up.)

If the Reviewing pane isn't visible, choose View → Toolbars → Reviewing, or Control-click (or right-click) the group divider (the vertical dotted lines) on any toolbar and choose Toolbars → Reviewing. Now you can edit comments—yours or anyone else's—or click Delete Comment (on the Reviewing toolbar) to do away with a comment completely.

Change Tracking

When it's time to mark up a document for revision, many people who otherwise use their Mac for everything still turn to paper, red pen, and highlighter. After all, marking up a printout lets you see both the original and your handwritten edits at a glance. And when you collaborate with others on a paper or project, you can use different colored ink to differentiate the various editors.

The problem with the paper method is that you eventually have to retype the document, incorporating all the handwritten comments, into Word.

To avoid all that hassle, you can simply edit onscreen in Word. Word has tools that highlight text in a multitude of colors and see at a glance who made what changes. Even better than paper, Word can automate the process of comparing and merging edited documents. On the downside, it's tough to make origami from your monitor—unless it's one of the new *really* flat screens...

Getting Ready for Change Tracking

In order for Word's change-tracking tools to work properly, you need to tell Word how you want your name to appear (when it's used to "sign" comments and changes) and how to display the changes.

Identify yourself

Especially if you're working with others, Word needs to know who you are so that your name can be attached to your version and your changes. To ensure that Word knows your inner scribe, choose Word → Preferences → User Information panel. If your name isn't already there, fill in the panel. Word will use the name in the author box to identify and label any changes and comments you add to the document. Click OK when you're finished.

Note: The User Information tab and your own address book "card" in Entourage are linked; that is, when you change User Information, you also change your Entourage "this is me" card, and vice versa. (You tell Entourage which set of contact information is yours by opening the card with your info and choosing Contact → This Is Me.)

Turning on change tracking

Suppose you receive a document from a colleague who's asked you to help clean up the prose. If you just dive right in, editing away, she'll have no way of spotting the changes you made. When you intend to review a document, whether it's your own draft or a Word document given to you by someone else, you have to ask Word to track your changes *before* making them. Here are three ways, presented in order of speed:

- By far the easiest way to activate change tracking is to click the Track Change button on the Reviewing toolbar. If the Reviewing toolbar isn't visible you need either (a) another cup of coffee or (b) to turn it on by selecting View → Toolbars → Reviewing.

- Turn on the tiny TRK button on the status bar at the bottom edge of your document window (Figure 5-1). (The button turns blue when you click it.)

If you prefer the third and longer way, you can go the dialog box route and gain some additional options, as described next.

1. **Choose Tools → Track Changes → Highlight Changes.**

   The Highlight Changes dialog box opens, as shown in Figure 5-3, bottom.

2. **Turn on "Track changes while editing".**

   You also have the option to turn "Highlight changes on screen" on or off. If it's *off,* you won't see any of the distracting special markings as you edit the document; the usual coloring and other annotation formatting won't appear. You'll feel as though you're editing a Word file *without* change tracking turned on. (The only difference: Every now and then, Word will abruptly refuse to let you backspace any farther than you have. That's because your insertion point has collided with a deleted word—which you can't see because it's currently invisible.)

   Behind the scenes, though, Word will indeed record every change you make. At any time, you or a collaborator can choose Tools → Track Changes → Highlight Changes and turn "Highlight changes on screen" *on* again to make them show up.

   Now proceed as described in "Making Changes," below.

Making Changes

After turning on change tracking, edit the Word document as usual. Use any of the tools described in Chapter 2, including inserting text, formatting it, and deleting large blocks of text or even entire pages. Word keeps track of it all, as shown in Figure 5-4.

Changing tracking options

The Track Changes dialog box in Figure 5-3 (top) and the sample document in Figure 5-4 shows Word's factory settings for onscreen changes, which are as follows:

- Word places a thin vertical line in the margin where *any* kind of change has been made.

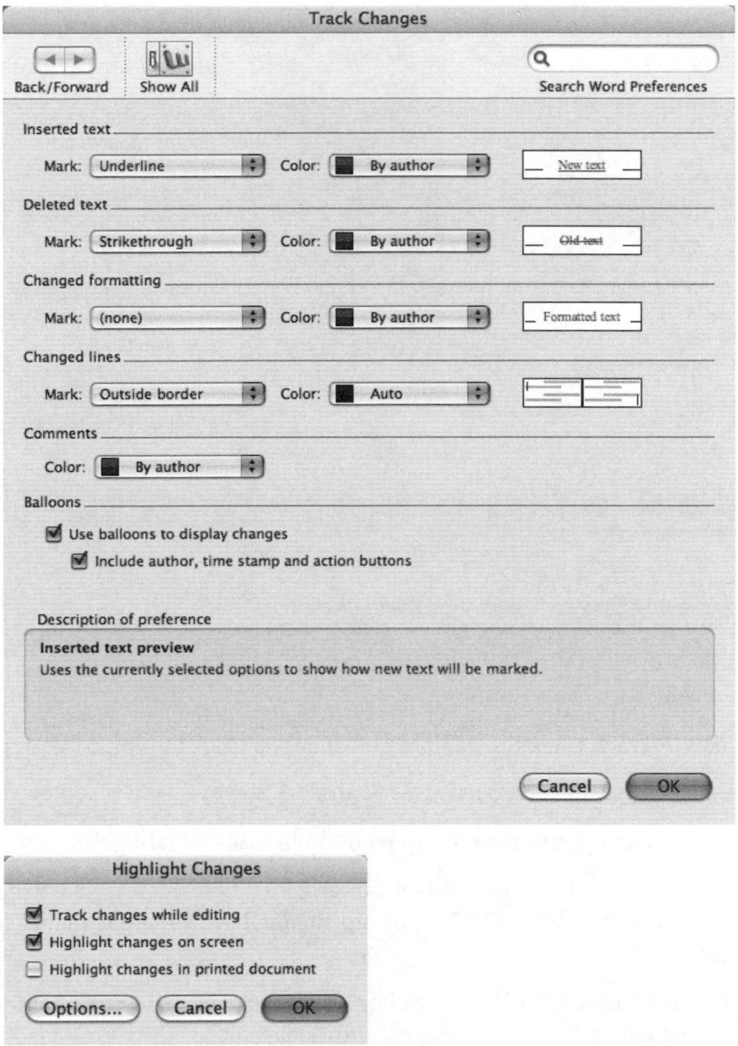

Figure 5-3:
Top: Use this box, which you see after clicking Options in the Tools → Track Changes dialog box, to specify what colors or other formatting Word should use to indicate text that's been added, deleted, or changed.

Bottom: Turn off the "Highlight changes in printed document" checkbox to hide all your changes during printing. This way, you can have a hard copy of the document with the edited text, but no deletions or highlighted insertions. Of course, if you do want to see all that in the printout, leave the checkbox turned on.

- Text you've inserted is underlined and color-coded by author. Text typed by the first person to review the document appears in red, the second author in blue, the third in pink, and so on, for up to eight authors. Then Word starts over again with red.

- Deleted text is changed to strikethrough and color-coded by author.

- Formatting changes (to boldface or italic, for instance) don't leave any visual trace (bolding and italicizing aside) except for the thin margin line (unless you're using Print Layout view or Web Layout view, where text balloons also describe the change). You can change this setting, however, as described next.

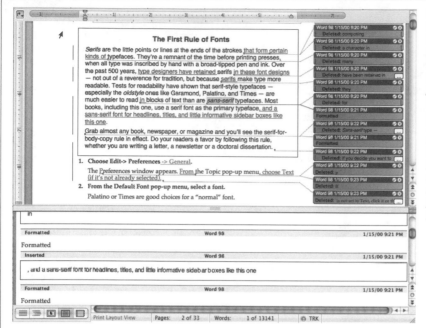

Figure 5-4:
If your work comes back heavily marked up by your editors, feel lucky. Keep in mind two things: (a) The changes are probably for the better, and (b) your editors are actually doing their job. You can see the annotations both in the text itself and in the Reviewing Pane. (You can open this pane by clicking the pane-like button at the far right of the Reviewing toolbar.)

Here is how to work with these options:

1. **Choose Tools → Track Changes → Highlight Changes. Click Options.**

   The Track Changes dialog box opens (see Figure 5-3, top).

2. **For each kind of change, use the pop-up menu to indicate a highlighting style.**

   For instance, you could choose "strikethrough" for "Deleted text" so that it looks like it's been crossed out. The pop-up menus have different marks for each context.

3. **If you don't want to use Word's "By author" color system, as described above, choose different colors for "Inserted text" and "Deleted text."**

   Unless everyone in your work group can agree on a different color scheme, it's probably best to stick with Word's color choices. Having different editors in the same document can get confusing, and Word does an efficient job of keeping track of the colors.

4. **Choose different colors for reformatted text ("Changed formatting") and the changed lines ("Outside border") only if you want to make these items more obvious.**

5. **Click OK.**

Reviewing Changes One by One

When reviewing a Word document edited using the tracking feature, it's easy to examine the changes one by one, accepting or rejecting each proposed revision, until you finish with a normal, clean-looking document. (For documents with multiple authors or editors, see "Merging Tracked Changes" below before proceeding.)

To get started, open the document.

Reviewing changes: light edits

If there's only light editing, the easiest way to approve or reject each change is simply to Control-click the changed text; from the contextual menu, choose Accept Change or Reject Change. When you accept a change, Word removes the color and marking and turns the change into normal text. When you *reject* a change, Word removes the marked or colored text and restores the original.

Reviewing changes: heavier edits

If there are many changes, you may as well pull out the heavy artillery—the Reviewing toolbar. Choose View → Toolbars → Reviewing to display the Reviewing toolbar which has everything you need. From here you may choose how to view your reviewer's edits, page through the edits and comments, and attach the document to an instant message or email.

1. **Click at the beginning of the document; click the Next icon on the Reviewing toolbar.**

   Word scrolls to the first change and highlights it.

2. **Click the Accept Change icon (with the checkmark) or the Reject Change icon (with the x) on the Reviewing toolbar.**

   Again, when you accept a change, Word turns the change into normal text. When you reject one, Word restores the original.

   If you change your mind after accepting or rejecting a change, press ⌘-Z to undo it.

3. **Click the Next Change icon and continue the process.**

   If change tracking is turned on, any new editing you do—when you make a change to your editor's changes, for example—will be highlighted on the screen with your author color. If you're doing the final pass on the editing—and have the final say—there's no need to track these last-minute changes. Click the Track Changes button on the Reviewing toolbar to turn it off, or turn off the TRK indicator in the Status bar at the bottom of the document. If the Status bar isn't visible, click Word → Preferences → View, and turn on Status Bar (under Window).

   When you reach the end of the document, but have missed reviewing some changes along the way, Word asks if you want to return to the beginning.

4. **Click OK.**

Word scrolls back up to any changes you missed along the way.

Accepting or Rejecting All Changes

If you trust your editors completely, you can accept or reject *all* changes in a document, all at once. You don't even have to look at them first (although you should, unless you're sure your editors are *much* better at writing in your unique voice than you are). Word also makes it possible to view the document as a whole, with or without all changes. Select what you want to see from the Display for Review pop-up menu at the left end of the Reviewing toolbar or choose Tools → Track Changes → Accept or Reject Changes to open the dialog box. You can also accept or reject all changes from the Reviewing toolbar. Just click the arrow next to the Accept Change icon, and choose "Accept All Changes in Document" from the pop-up menu.

1. **Choose a way to view the document.**

    If you choose Tools → Track Changes → Accept or Reject Changes, the dialog box that appears is small for a reason: It's designed to be moved aside, so that you can survey the document before making the radical move of accepting or rejecting all of the edits that have been made to it.

    To help you with this pursuit, you're given three radio buttons. They let you see the document with all changes highlighted (as shown in Figure 5-5), as if all changes were accepted ("Changes without highlighting"), or in its original state before any changes were made. These humble-looking radio buttons are one of the most powerful aspects of the change-tracking feature.

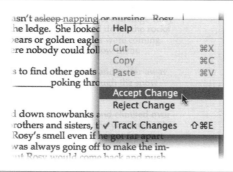

Figure 5-5:
You can accept or reject a proposed edit (such as here, where asleep has been changed to napping) by Control-clicking it.

2. **To go ahead and make all proposed changes, click Accept All. To return the document to its original condition, click Reject All.**

    Word asks if you're sure before proceeding. Remember, even after accepting all or rejecting all, you can change your mind by clicking Undo.

3. **Click Close.**

Merging Tracked Changes

One of the most common scenarios for using change tracking is to email or otherwise transfer the same original document out to several reviewers, each of whom peppers it with edits and comments. If they all came back on paper, it would be quite a challenge to sort through and incorporate all the good ideas.

In Word, it's easy to merge the edited documents together, one by one. To do so, open the original file—or any one of the edited documents—and proceed as follows. Choose Tools → Merge Documents.

1. **Word opens the "Choose a File" dialog box, where you'll choose the first file into which to merge the currently open document.**

   When you find the file, double-click it.

2. **Word begins the merging process.**

   When it's over, the file you chose contains both its own tracked changes *and* those merged in from the original, but will only display one set of formatting changes on the same text (although both are listed in change balloons in the Print Layout view). Word will, however, ask you which to display. The changes from different authors appear in different colors.

3. **If you have more files to incorporate, repeat steps 1 and 2.**

   When all the documents are merged, place your insertion point at the beginning of the document and review the changes as described on the preceding pages.

UP TO SPEED

Quicker Document Dispatch

Word 2008 lets—nay, encourages—you to email or Instant Message (IM) your documents right from the Reviewing toolbar. Granted, you could always attach a document to an email in Entourage or send a file via your MSM chat window—but the Reviewing toolbar makes these moves much easier. To email a document, click the paper-with-envelope-with-arrow icon in the Reviewing toolbar. Doing so pops open an email message in your default email program with the document already attached (that's *so* cool). Type your message, select a recipient, and then click Send.

To send the document via IM, you (and your recipient) need a Windows Live Messenger account (available at *www.microsoft.com/mac*). Click the IM icon (a blue Weeble-like person), select the file recipient, and your document is now prepped for sending. Once your intended target accepts the file, it zips across the Internet. It's all part of the evil empire's desire to keep you in the Office/MSM loop for all your work and play. (Well, maybe not *all* your play.)

Of course, if you prefer insatnt messaging with iChat, you can use it to transfer files, too. Just drag the icon of the file you wish to transfer from the Finder right into the iChat text-entry box where you usually type your message.

Comparing Documents

The merging process described earlier in this chapter works well if *all* documents have been edited using Word's change-tracking feature. But often enough, you wind up with two drafts of a document, one of which has been edited (by you or somebody else). Word's Compare Documents feature can help you see where edits have been made—a feature that has saved the bacon of more than one lawyer in back-and-forth contract negotiations.

To use it, round up both the edited version and your original or master copy and proceed as follows:

1. **Open the changed copy of the document. Choose Tools → Track Changes → Compare Documents.**

   Word opens the "Choose a File" dialog box. Here's where you select the *original* document—the one you want to compare the edited version to. The original could be the one that's never been edited, or one that's been edited with change tracking, or even one that's been merged. Just make sure that you've reviewed it and accepted or rejected all tracked changes before you begin the comparing process.

2. **When you locate the original version of the document, double-click it.**

   Word compares the two documents and creates a *new* document based on the *second*—a.k.a. original—document, with tracked changed inserted as if the *first* document were created by editing the second (original).

If there were already tracked changes in either of the documents, Word ignores them and gives priority to the actual, unmarked text. If either of the documents has untracked changes, Word asks before proceeding with the comparing process. Usually, you'll want to click OK and go ahead. The unmarked changes may be edits you made to the document while you were writing it, before you started the reviewing process.

UP TO SPEED

Preparing to Send a Reviewed Document

If someone else will be merging the reviewed documents, there are a few things you can do when you send your edited copy to make her job easier:

- **Make changes visible.** Choose Tools → Track Changes → Highlight Changes before you send your

document off. That way, the recipient can see immediately that it's been edited.

- **Change the document's name.** Add your initials to the file's name in the Finder, for example, so that it won't be confused with the original during the merging process.

Working with Notebooks, Outlining, and Master Documents

Have you ever sat down at your Mac and pounded out a polished white paper, 25-page essay, or complete novel in one smooth pass, your words flowing logically from start to finish? Probably not. Thoughts often come in fragments, and these shards of logic form the foundation for annual reports, term papers, and books. Microsoft understands, and provides tools for better capturing and organizing those thoughts. Enter Word's Outliner and its spin-offs the Document Map, Master Documents, and the Notebook Layout view.

Outlining is simply a way of organizing your ideas, and Notebook view is a great tool for capturing those ideas, rearranging them, and even voice-recording your thoughts. As your document grows and reaches completion, the Document Map— which resides in Word's Navigation Pane—lets you fly through it, easily locating the page you're looking for from among the other 147, and Master Document lets you and your co-workers create the mother of all documents.

Note: Notebook layout is a curious hybrid to be sure. On one hand, it appears that Microsoft wanted to make a utility that works as the human brain does—a way to capture your stray thoughts on "paper." Unfortunately, it lacks the ease of use and advanced features of a full-fledged note-taking and organizational tool, like Circus Ponies' NoteBook, or the depth of word processing ease available in other Word views. But hey, it's a step in the right direction.

Notebook Layout View

From its binder-like appearance to its ability to take "dictation," Notebook Layout view is Microsoft's attempt to let your computer work as you do. To that end, they designed something where you can take notes quickly and rearrange them as you wish.

Opening Your Notebook

Choose File → Project Gallery, click the Word Notebook icon, and begin typing. Each new block of text starts out as Note Level 1, as you can see by a quick glance at the Formatting Palette. By hitting Tab, you can indent text under a heading to indicate that it applies to, and should be grouped with, that header, as shown in Figure 6-1. This is great stuff when taking notes in class, at a meeting, or just capturing concepts from your head. Additionally, you can click the little button to the left of each block of text and move it wherever you want on the page.

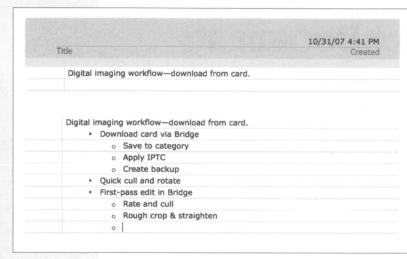

Figure 6-1:
Top: As you type into a freshly created Notebook document, text flows onto the page automatically set to Note Level 1.

Bottom: After you finish the sentence or thought, press Return, and then Tab, to indent the next section of text, shown at center. Pressing Shift-Tab moves the indent back toward the left–promoting the line to a higher level of importance.

If you already have a non-Notebook Word document in front of you, select View → Notebook Layout to open Notebook Layout view. Alternately, you can click the Notebook Layout view Icon (it's the right-most of the view icons) at the bottom left of your page. Or, for the keyboard- and shortcut-crazed among you, Option-⌘-B also takes you to the Notebook Layout view. However you invoke the view, the first thing you see on your Notebook Layout view journey is the pop-up message shown in Figure 6-2.

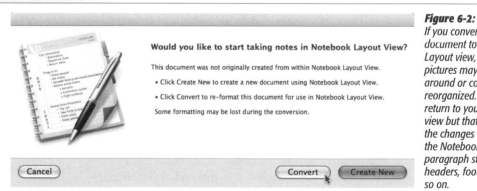

Figure 6-2:
If you convert a regular document to Notebook Layout view, inserted pictures may get sloshed around or columns reorganized. You can return to your previous view but that won't undo the changes wrought by the Notebook view to paragraph styles, headers, footers, and so on.

Where Did My Formatting Go?

Notebook Layout is a possessive view, and doesn't take kindly to other intruding views. It likes it best when you begin in Notebook Layout and stay there. When you change from other views to Notebook Layout, several things happen. Right off the bat Word asks if, in essence, you're really sure you want to do this. It opens a box asking if you wish to start a new, Notebook Layout view document, or convert the existing one (Figure 6-2). It then adds, almost in a whisper, "Some formatting may be lost in the conversion."

You don't say.

Pictures and text boxes will frequently get shoved about by the conversion. Even more important, much, if not all, of the template formatting and paragraph styles in your non-Notebook Layout view document will be lost. In other words, all those carefully crafted headers, bullet lists, and captions will morph into plain, everyday text. So, before you convert, make sure it's something you really want to do. Otherwise, it's best just to start from scratch in Notebook Layout view. That way you know what you're getting.

However you get there, once you arrive in Notebook Layout view, you see a clean new sheet (assuming you're starting with a new document) of lined notebook paper. Kinda makes you want to take a pen to your computer screen, doesn't it? But please, despite the temptation, don't scrawl "Timmy likes Sally" or "Mr. Quackenbush is a nerd," on your computer screen. Replacing computer screens gets real expensive, real quick.

Like much of Word 2008, the Notebook Layout view is intuitive. As you type, words dance (or spew—mood depending) onto the page. You'll notice, however, that each paragraph, block of text, or picture is marked with a clear/gray bubble to its left. The bubble is similar to the little rectangle you see in Word's Outline view (page 191), but much easier to use. Furthermore, you can take that bubble and drag (it turns blue) your text wherever you like on the page. In fact, there's much more you can do with your text than reposition it, and most of those capabilities reside on the aptly named Notebook Layout view Standard toolbar, as shown in Figure 6-3.

The Notebook Layout Toolbar

The Notebook Layout view significantly changes the Standard toolbar into something that's tailored to the view at hand. Everything you need waits for your click on the toolbar or folds neatly into the ever-useful Formatting Palette.

Note: In addition to the transformation of the Standard toolbar, you'll notice that most of Word's other toolbars become completely unavailable when you're in Notebook Layout view. Check the View → Toolbars menu—they're just not there. Apparently, Microsoft wants to get all possible distractions out of your way when you're taking notes. On the other hand, if you're used to using Word's more advanced features like Change Tracking or even Style formatting, you may find Notebook Layout view more of a hindrance than a help.

Figure 6-3:
When you enter the world of Notebook Layout view, the Formatting Palette morphs to provide the appropriate commands. Here you can adjust the indent level, the font, bullets and numbering, and "paper" style; sort your notes or add a footer; and add checkboxes to your notebook items or even turn them into Entourage tasks.

- **Appearance.** Click here to choose the "paper" style for your notebook. If you find those binder rings get in your way while you're writing (left-handed, perhaps?), select one of the Without Notebook Rings styles.

- **Scribble.** A pen icon represents the Scribble tool. Click here to turn your mouse into a pen with which you can draw on your document. The cursor changes to look like a pen. Press and hold the mouse button to draw.

  Scribble's convenient for drawing quick graphical marks, such as arrows, or circling important sections of your document, but it's a tad too cumbersome to write more than a word or two. The pop-up menu beside the Scribble icon presents thickness options for your pen's point, and you can also choose an ink color on the palette that pops beside each pen thickness. The Scribble pop-up menu has the following options:

— **Fine Point**. Draws a thin line. You can also click the arrow to the right and choose a color.

— **Very Fine Point**. You guessed it—draws an even thinner line. Again, click the arrow to the right for your color perusing enjoyment.

— **Medium Point**. The point of choice for those who like fat pens.

• **Eraser**. The Eraser removes AutoShapes drawn with the Scribble tool. It's very simple. Click the Eraser, and then click the object to remove it. Faster than a Red Sox World Series sweep, and way easier.

• **Select Objects**. Click the Select Objects icon, and drag over an area to select any objects within it. You'll find this especially useful when you need to select a group of objects or when you've sent an object behind the text, making it difficult to select.

• **Audio**. Clicking the microphone displays the Audio Notes toolbar. Using this toolbar, you can make your computer take dictation. For more details, see page 187.

• **Quick Search**. As described in Figure 6-4, the Quick Search is a very useful tool that cuts the clicks from thought to located word.

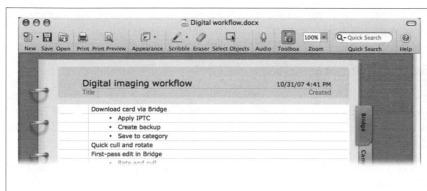

Figure 6-4:
When you're notebooking it, the Notebook Layout view's Standard toolbar replaces Word's Standard toolbar. One of its most convenient tools is the Quick Search window. Click in the window, type in your search terms, press Return, and Word buzzes through the document, rooting out every occurrence in this section.

Organizing Your Notes

Notebook Layout view comes into its own when you're either taking notes on your laptop during a meeting or trying to get your arms around that huge project that you and your fellow visionaries brainstormed. It's not a view you'll often use when

What's That Pen Doing?

The pen actually draws a shape that you can subsequently select and drag to new locations or even resize. On the one hand that's great, giving you gobs of flexibility. On the other hand, it's not so great. Since the shape is, in essence, a hand-drawn picture, Word treats it as one. For example, if you circle a word, you'll find that the word disappears because the shape is now in front of it. To place it behind, Control-click (or right-click) the shape and choose Arrange → Behind Text from the shortcut menu; or choose Format → AutoShape, click the Layout tab, and then move the shape "Behind Text." A bit counter-intuitive, no? Of course,

if you have the AutoShape's Fill properties set to "no fill," you won't have these problems. You'll be able to spot the word through your circle.

The shape you've drawn is like any Word AutoShape—it's a drawing object, and you can format it like one. To format the shape, choose Format → AutoShape. The Format dialog box (see page 307) opens, where you can choose how text will flow around the shape, whether it will reside in front of or behind the text, and all the other familiar formatting features.

composing your romance novel. But that's okay; Notebook does what it does pretty darn well, by automatically and clearly applying outline levels to every thought you type.

The cool thing about all this leveling business is the flexibility it provides when you're viewing and organizing your Notebook document. If a heading, any heading, in the document has *subheadings* beneath it, Word tags the heading with a big blue flippy triangle, as shown in Figure 6-5. You can click this triangle to expose or hide the subheadings.

Note: Levels are kind of like golf. The lower the number, the better (more important) the level. Level 1 is the highest level, level 2 is next, and so on.

Setting Text Levels with the Keyboard and Mouse

You can set text levels with various combinations of the Tab key, as described below. You can, of course, highlight text and drag it with the mouse, just like any other text, but you may find it quicker to learn a few shortcuts and never take your hands off the keys as the ideas come gushing out.

- **Tab** or **Control-Shift-Right arrow.** These commands *demote* the text one level of importance and tuck it neatly beneath the text above it. You can also use your mouse to drag the note bubble to the right.

- **Shift-Tab** or **Control-Shift-Left arrow.** These commands *promote* the text one level, moving it back out toward the margin, where items of greater importance reside. You can also use your mouse to drag the note bubble to the left.

- **Control-Tab.** Indents the first line of text one tab without changing the level.

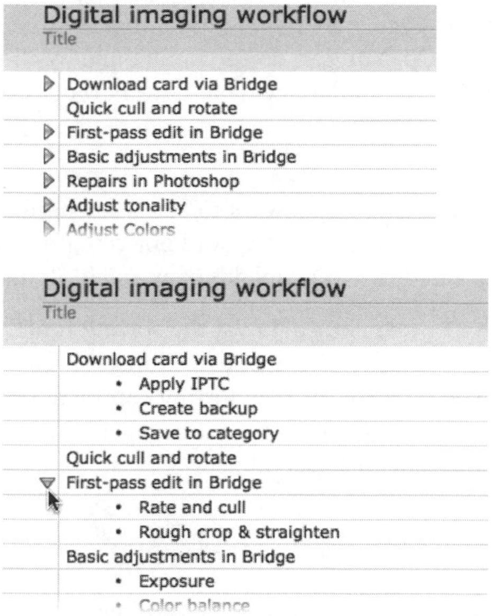

Figure 6-5:
You can expand or collapse the subheadings in your Notebook. At top, headings are collapsed, displaying only the top-level text. After clicking the flippy triangle, the subheadings pop out, as shown at bottom. As you can see here, it's possible to have several levels of embedded headings. Wherever there are subheadings, you'll see the renowned flippy triangle—though it disappears once you click it to expand the topic. Mouse over that topic again, and the triangle reappears.

- **Control-Shift-Up arrow.** Moves the selected paragraph up. Note that this keystroke physically moves the paragraph; it may change its note level as well, depending on the paragraph above it.

- **Control-Shift-Down arrow.** Moves the selected paragraph down, again without changing its note level.

- **Control-Shift-A.** Expands *all* text under *all* headings. Great if you want to see *everything* you've written.

- **Control-Shift-<number>.** Displays the selected note level. For example, Control-Shift-1 displays all the Level 1 notes.

Setting Text Levels with the Formatting Palette

If you prefer clicking buttons to elevate or reduce the importance of text the Note Levels section of the Formatting Palette is at your disposal. To open Note Levels, click the Note Levels title bar.

To promote text (raise it's level), click anywhere in the text line, and then click the Promote icon. To demote the text, click in the text line and click the Demote icon. If you need to demote or promote text several levels, it's easier to use the level pop-up menu on the Note Level section. Just click the arrow to the right of the level window and then click the level you desire. You can also press Tab (to demote) or Shift-Tab (to promote), as described earlier. Keep pressing until you reach the desired level. (Additionally, you can press Tab or Shift-Tab *before* typing a heading.)

The Move Up and Move Down icons don't change a level's level, so to speak, but rather alter the position of the text on the page, one line at a time. If you want to move the text up, select it and click Move Up. You can do the same thing by clicking on the clear/gray bubble to the left of the text and dragging it to the new position.

Sorting Headings

As you've probably gathered by now, there are myriad ways to sort your headings and organize and reorganize your notes. You can drag notes (and objects), promote and demote headers, and move them up and down. It's cool, it's easy, and it's fast.

What's even faster is Notebook's ability to sort your data via the sorting function that's added to the Formatting palette whenever you work in Notebook Layout view. Select the section (see page 122) you wish to sort (the sorting commands sort a section or a selection, not the entire document), open the Sorting pane by clicking Sorting title bar, and click either Ascending or Descending.

Note: Unless you collapse a header before sorting, Word moves the header without its subheadings.

- Ascending sorts from the top of the page to the bottom, 1 through 9, then A through Z. For example, it would place a heading beginning with "Aplomb," before a heading beginning with "Zealot."

- Descending sorts from the top of the page to the bottom, Z through A, then 9 through 1.

Placing Notes Beside Your Notes

Okay, you've organized your notes into some form of logic. Everything to do with the company party is listed under the Level 1 heading of Company Party, and all things pertaining to the boss's favorite client is tucked under the client's name. But what if you have some questions about items in both categories, need to remind yourself to order the party food, and prepare a report for that number one client, and just keep in mind what is what, and set priorities for both? There are two ways of quickly transforming your notes into a to-do list: the Note Flags feature in Notebook Layout view, or by marshalling the forces of Entourage.

Flagging Action Items

The Note Flags panel of the Formatting Palette has a pop-up menu that lists checkboxes and other items for just about every flagging purpose. Place a flag in the margin next to anything in your notebook by first clicking the text (anywhere in the text line), and then selecting the flag from the list. To remove the flag, select it again in the Formatting Palette.

Note: You can't apply a flag to a graphic. If you select a graphic, the Formatting Palette no longer includes the Note Flags section. You may, however, click a line near the graphic and place your flag there.

The obvious checkboxes are great for placing beside items on your Notebook list. Once placed, you can click the box to place a check in it. So, after you've finished that step in the project, you can check it off. Instant gratification!

Important Enough to Track in Entourage?

Pretty icons beside your notes are all well and good, but what if you want to take your reminder out of Word and into the real world? If you use Entourage to organize your life, you could launch that program and start a new task. Fortunately, there's no need to subject yourself to that kind of strain. Just click Create Entourage Task in the Note Flags section of the Formatting Palette. Doing so opens a dialogue box where you can set the date and time when you wish to be reminded of the selected task.

This cross-program feature is a great timesaver and an ideal way to follow up on the notes that you took at yesterday's meeting. Simply click in the line of text you wish to remember, let's say "Prep sales report for Olsen by Tuesday noon," click Create Entourage Task, and set an appropriate reminder, for, say Tuesday morning.

Typing Less with Audio Notes

Hey, that's what everyone wants to do. Spend a little less time clacking on the keyboard and a little more time living a private version of the Corona commercials. Well, Notebook Layout view can't deliver a cold one to your hammock, but it can get your hands off the keyboard with the Audio Notes toolbar and its capabilities. For example, you're sitting in that three-hour, Monday night sociology class. Just call up Word, open a new document in Notebook Layout view, turn on Audio Notes, and let it run. Then, as you type notes, Word automatically inserts icons that link to an audio snippet of whatever it was recording when you were typing.

The beauty of this arrangement is that you don't have to worry about typing every word the professor drones. Just type main points; you can click and listen to the recording to refresh your memory later. You can also link audio notes to previously written text—something that's convenient if you wanted to connect a complex description to a point that you briefly touched on in your written notes. This feature is really designed for laptop Notebook note-takers, but works on any Mac with a built-in mic (like iMacs) or with an attached external mic (like a Mac Pro). Just be sure to grab a chair near a power outlet when you cart your Mac Pro into class. Here's how to enter your audio notes and listen to them later.

Entering an Audio Note

To enter an audio note, click in the text where you wish to insert the audio note, click the microphone to display the Audio Notes toolbar, click the Record button, and start speaking (or you may need to *stop* talking so that your microphone can hear the important stuff). Or, just click the microphone and type away. Word automatically creates new audio notes every few lines. Click Stop (the blue square on the Audio Notes toolbar) when you wish to stop recording. When you pass the cursor over the text, the blue speaker pops into the left margin.

Note: Choose Word → Preferences → Audio Notes to adjust the recording quality for your notes. Word's standard setting of Medium quality produces monaural MP4 files at a relatively low sample rate—perfect for voice recording or lecture notes. If you require higher quality, or have attached a stereo microphone (the built-in mic in your laptop is mono), you may want to increase the quality settings. However, higher-quality means your notes take up more—perhaps much more—space on your hard drive.

Listening to an Audio Note

To listen to a note, click the blue speaker icon, which pops up in the left margin of the page as you mouse over notated text. Your recording fills the air, and if you wish it to fill a little more or less, you can adjust your Mac's output volume using the volume control near the right end of your menu bar or by choosing System Preferences → Sound → Output. You'll find more playback controls in the Audio Notes toolbar, conveniently described below. To display the toolbar, click the Audio toolbar icon. The toolbar, as shown in Figure 6-6, inserts itself beneath the standard toolbar.

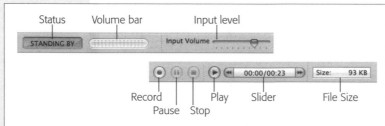

Figure 6-6:
The Audio Notes toolbar (shown here divided in half to fit on the page) provides the controls needed to insert sound into your document. Keep an eye on the Size measure as you record: larger files take longer to save and email.

Tip: Perhaps you'd like to share your captured verbal brilliance with someone who doesn't have access to your computer. Don't worry, Word 2008 has you covered. You can export your audio notes to another medium. Choose Tools → Audio Notes → Export Audio. Word exports *all* the audio in the notebook document as an MP4, AIFF, or WAV file (depending on your Audio Notes Preferences settings) to a location of your choosing. After you've done that, you can burn the file to a CD or transfer it to your iPod and take it wherever you like. It's a dream come true for those folks who truly like to hear themselves talk.

The Audio Notes Toolbar includes several functions:

- **Recording Status**. Located on the far left of the toolbar, the status bar shows whether you're in Standing By (or playing) or Recording mode.

- **Volume**. The Volume bar measures how loudly the computer hears you (or whatever it's hearing). For example, if you clap, the bar spikes (swings to the right). If you get really quiet, centering yourself in that peaceful place that only you know, the bar settles to the left…at least until your kids storm exuberantly into the room.

- **Input Volume.** The input volume slider sets the input volume. Move it to the left if you're loud (or a close talker), move it to the right if you have a soft voice or are recording your professor in a classroom.

- **Recording Button.** As you might expect, the recording button starts the recording process. Click it to start recording the lecture, or talk normally (unless your "normally" means whispering or mumbling). Watch the size display on the right of the toolbar as you talk to see how much hard-drive space you're eating up.

- **Pause Button.** Pauses the recording. Use it if you either wish to return later to add to your audio note, if the cat has your tongue, or if your professor launches into one of his interminable digressions about how things were when he was in college. Pausing the recording lets you add more material to the same recording when you resume. If you click the Stop button, you'll need to start a new recording.

- **Stop.** Stops the current recording.

- **Play.** The Play button plays the selected recording. A small speaker that appears as you pass your mouse over it designates an audio note. Select an audio note and click Play to hear it. Double-clicking the speaker also starts playback.

- **Slider.** This small bar tracks the progress of the currently playing audio note. You can also slide the slider anywhere in the window to begin the audio note at that point. That trick can be quite useful if you left a contact phone number at the very end of a 30-second message. Skip to it straight away—just place the slider near the end and click Play.

Tip: Although the blue speaker pops up whenever you pass your mouse over an audio note, it's much easier to draw attention to the note with a line of text such as, "Monday meeting," or whatever. Click Show All Audio Markers in the status bar at the bottom of the window to display all the speaker icons. Now you can spot them without mousing around.

Manipulating Notebook Sections

By now you're a pro at putting words onto notebook pages. It's also important to understand how to manipulate the pages themselves, specifically how to make changes to entire sections by adding improvements such as headers, footers, or removing the characteristic lined paper look. Notebook Layout view pages, referred to as sections, are an important organizational tool.

Note: Notebook pages really aren't—pages, that is. The Notebook Layout's sections are continuous sheets of paper, kind of like a Web page. In fact, you can't insert a page break into a notebook. If you convert the notebook to a different Word view, such as Draft or Print Layout, you'll see that, behind the scenes, Word delineates each tabbed section with a section break (page 135).

Labeling Sections

A title resides at the top of each section. Initially—because Word 2008 can't read your mind—it's blank (the title, not your mind), but you can fill it in by clicking in the title block (as shown in Figure 6-7), and typing whatever you wish. This label doesn't, however, change the title on the tab located on the right of the notebook page. To change these tab titles, double-click the tab, type your new tab title, and press Return.

Reordering the sections of your notebook is simple. Click on a section tab and drag it to its new location.

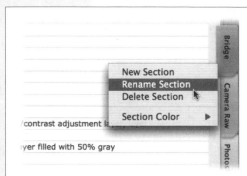

Figure 6-7:
It's a good idea to rename your sections to something useful. Dates are a good idea, as are categories. Control-click a tab to bring up this menu for adding, deleting, renaming, or color coding your section tab—or just double-click a tab and start typing to rename it.

To Line or Not to Line

Notebook Layout view's factory settings include lined paper. It's a curious, if understandable, decision by Microsoft. Curious, because on a computer, you don't need lines to keep your writing even; understandable, because it's a notebook view, and the lines make your computer screen look like a notebook.

Text is positioned exactly between the lines, so if you increase the space between the lines (using the Rule Lines pane of the Formatting Palette), you'll increase the space between each line of text.

You can choose whether the lines appear on the page or not in the Rule Lines section of the Formatting Palette. You can choose Standard or None from the Style menu.

- **Standard.** This factory setting gives each page lines that look like notebook paper, with text spaced between the lines. It's great most of the time you're in Notebook view, because it reminds you you're supposed to be, well, taking notes.

- **None.** Removes all the lines. If the lines bug you, choose this setting and get a clean sheet of paper on which to type.

A separate menu, **Distance,** sets the spacing between the lines, in points (page 93). Obviously, the larger the number, the greater the spacing.

Numbering Pages

Oddly enough, you can choose to number your notebook pages in a footer, even though you'll only see this page number when you print your notebook, click Print Preview, or switch to another view, such as Print Layout view. Numbering is a good idea if you intend to print your document, so you'll know you've got all the pages in the correct order.

To include page numbers, click the flippy triangle next to Footer in the Formatting Palette. The footer options are either None (no footer), or Page Numbers. Choosing Page Numbers plops them at the bottom of your pages. You can also choose to have Word begin renumbering the pages with each new tabbed section.

Outline View

Your teachers were right: The more time you spend on the outline, the less work you'll have to do when it comes time to write your actual paper, article, or book. Word's automated Outline view frees you from the drudgery of keeping track of all the letters and numbers in an outline, while encouraging you to categorize and prioritize your ideas.

Note: Before Notebook Layout view, Outline view used to be the only way to organize your thoughts with levels. And it's still a darn good way to do so. Although you can't use audio notes in Outline view, it does give you access to more of Word's other features. For example, you can't insert hyperlinks in Notebook Layout view, but you can in the Outline. Neither can you apply Styles to the Notebook (that's one of the reasons it sloshes around your intricately formatted documents), but you can in Outline view.

Building an Outline

To outline your document from the beginning, open a blank document and choose View → Outline, or click the second tiny icon at the lower-left corner of your document window. (You can also apply Outline view to an existing document, which is described later in this section.)

Whenever you switch to Outline view, the Outline toolbar appears (see Figure 6-8). When you first start typing, your words are formatted as Heading 1— the highest level in the outline hierarchy. (Outline headings correspond to Word's built-in heading styles.)

Now you're ready to build your outline. Press Return after each heading. Along the way, you can create the subheadings using either the mouse or the keyboard, as described next.

- **Promoting and demoting**. Moving topics out toward the margin (toward Heading 1, making them more important) or inward (less important) promotes or demotes them, identical to the same functions in the Notebook Layout view (page 184).

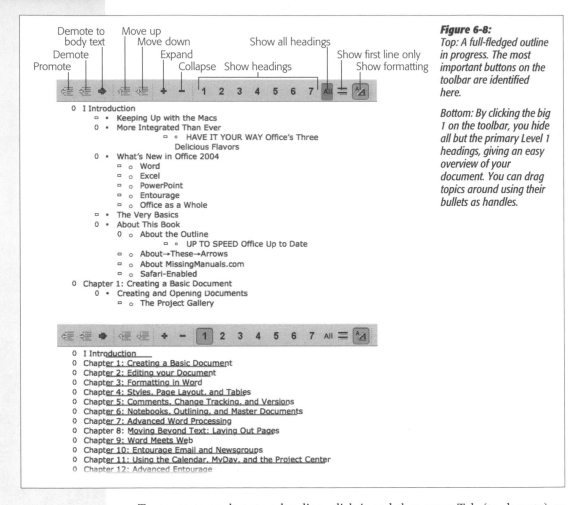

Figure 6-8:
Top: A full-fledged outline in progress. The most important buttons on the toolbar are identified here.

Bottom: By clicking the big 1 on the toolbar, you hide all but the primary Level 1 headings, giving an easy overview of your document. You can drag topics around using their bullets as handles.

To promote or demote a heading, click it and then press Tab (to demote) or Shift-Tab (to promote). Keep pressing until you reach the desired level. (You can also press Tab or Shift-Tab before typing a heading.)

Or, if you're a mouse-driven kind of person, click the Promote and Demote buttons at the left of the Outline toolbar (see Figure 6-8). Keyboard Shortcuts: Shift-Control-left arrow to promote; Shift-Control-right arrow to demote. You can also drag with the mouse, as shown in Figure 6-9.

Tip: You can promote or demote an entire batch of headings at once. Drag through an outline to select certain headings, or neatly select a heading and all of its subheadings by clicking the + symbol. (To eliminate subtopics from the selection, first click the + sign, then Shift-click where you want the selection to *end*.)

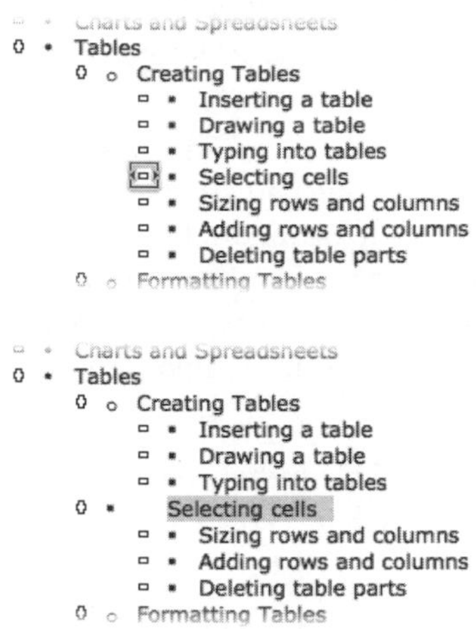

Figure 6-9:
Top: You can promote a heading just by dragging it. As you drag the icon next to a paragraph, the cursor turns into a box with arrows. Now drag the margin line out to the desired level.

Bottom: When you release the mouse, you've just promoted the heading. A paragraph of body text turns into a heading using the same technique.

- **Inserting body text.** You wouldn't impress many people if you wrote nothing but headlines. Fortunately, you can flesh out your headings with regular body text by clicking the double-arrow icon on the Outline toolbar. (It stands for Demote to Body Text, which actually demotes the text to the Normal style.) Use this style, denoted by a tiny white square in Figure 6-9, for the actual, longer-than-one-line paragraphs and thoughts that constitute the main body of your writing. *Keyboard shortcut*: Shift-⌘-N.

- **Rearranging headings.** To move topics up and down on the page without promoting or demoting them, just drag them by the + and – handles (see Figure 6-9). Alternatively, you can select the topic or topics and click the Move Up and Move Down arrows on the Outline toolbar. *Keyboard shortcuts*: Control-Shift-up or -down arrow.

- **Breaking up headings.** You'll probably come across instances, especially when outlining an existing piece of writing (see below), where you need to separate one sentence from the previous one in order to make it a new topic. Just click before the first letter of the sentence and then press Return to put it on a new line.

Collapsing and expanding an outline

The whole point of creating an outline is to organize the topics you're presenting, to ensure that all the major points are there, and to arrange them in a logical order. Therefore, it's helpful to see just your main points at a glance, unencumbered by the minor details. Here are ways you can control how much you see:

- **To show only Level 1 headings:** To get a quick "big picture" view of your outline, click the large numeral 1 on the Outline toolbar, or press Shift-Control-1; now Word shows *only* your Level 1 headings, the real main points of your document. Everything else is temporarily hidden.

Similarly, clicking 2 (or pressing Shift-Control-2) shows heading Levels 1 *and* 2, so you can check how your subtopics are looking, and so on. (Figure 6-8 shows this trick in action.)

- **To collapse only one section of an outline:** Double-click the puffy + sign next to it. All subtopics of that heading disappear, leaving just a gray bar behind as evidence that something's been hidden. To expand it again, double-click the + again. (Double-clicking a minus sign doesn't do anything, since there's nothing to collapse.) This trick is helpful when you're closely examining a small portion of a long outline and just want to move some minor details temporarily out of your way.

- **To view first lines only:** Click the Show First Line Only button on the Outline toolbar, or press Shift-Control-L, to make Word hide everything but the first line of every paragraph—whether it's a heading or body text.

- **To hide all body text:** You can collapse all the material that you've relegated to body text so that only headings are visible by clicking the All button on the Outline toolbar (or pressing Shift-Control-A).

- **To expand everything:** In an outline where you've collapsed at least one heading somewhere, the All button takes on a different role. Clicking it now expands any headings or body text that have been collapsed. Click All or press Shift-Control-A to get everything out in the open and return to work. (If you click All again at this point, it hides all body text and returns to its role as body-text toggle.)

Tip: If the heavy boldface type and dark fonts make your outline hard to read, click the Show Formatting button on the toolbar. It displays all headings in plain, unformatted type.

Outlining an Existing Document

Say you've been typing away on your latest essay or annual report, and you're stuck. You've run out of ideas, and the ones you did have no longer look so clear now that you see them onscreen. It's still not too late to apply the organizational power of an outline. Just choose View → Outline; Voilà! Word displays your document in outline format, using your own line breaks, indents, and headings as a guide. Now you can use the navigational tools described to reprioritize and clarify your thoughts.

Numbering an Outline

If what you remember about outlining came from high school English class, you may be wondering about the I's and a's and funny little iii's that you were taught to use as outline numbers. Not only can Word number your headings and subheadings automatically, but it can also automatically renumber the outline as you move topics around.

To add numbering to an outline, select the whole outline (Edit → Select All or ⌘-A) and choose Format → "Bullets and Numbering" → Outline Numbered tab. Then choose an outline style as shown in Figure 6-10. Now continue working as usual with your outline. Even if you drag topics around or insert new ones, Word automatically updates the numbering.

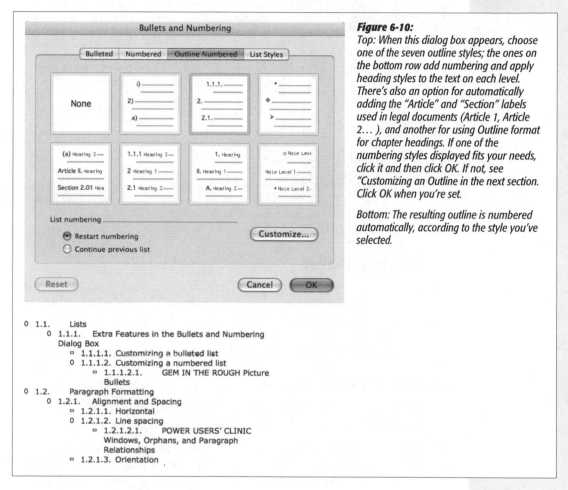

Figure 6-10:

Top: When this dialog box appears, choose one of the seven outline styles; the ones on the bottom row add numbering and apply heading styles to the text on each level. There's also an option for automatically adding the "Article" and "Section" labels used in legal documents (Article 1, Article 2…), and another for using Outline format for chapter headings. If one of the numbering styles displayed fits your needs, click it and then click OK. If not, see "Customizing an Outline in the next section. Click OK when you're set.

Bottom: The resulting outline is numbered automatically, according to the style you've selected.

Renumbering a numbered outline

You can't edit a numbered outline in your document; when you click the numbers or letters, nothing happens. But what if you're starting a new section with a completely different outline in it, and want the numbers to start all over again? Double-click the number or letter, or click the heading whose number you wish to change and choose Format → "Bullets and Numbering" → Outline Numbering tab, and click Customize. To change the number of the current heading, you have to first change the number in the "Start at" box, as shown in Figure 6-11. Any numbered headings following this one will be numbered in a continuing order.

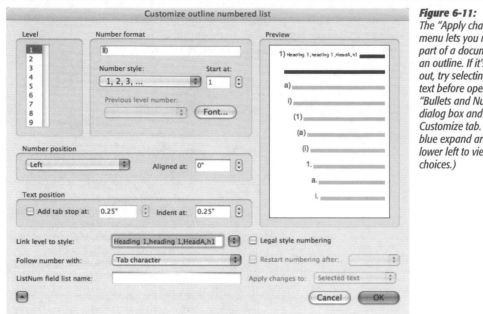

Figure 6-11:
The "Apply changes to" menu lets you make only part of a document into an outline. If it's grayed out, try selecting some text before opening the "Bullets and Numbering" dialog box and the Customize tab. (Click the blue expand arrow at lower left to view these choices.)

Customizing an Outline

The seven built-in numbering formats cover most purposes, especially if you're creating the outline for your own benefit. But if you've been asked to turn in a document in outline format, if you're using Word to create a legal document, or if you're one of those people who can always see improvements through tinkering, you may need to tinker with the outline's formatting to get just the right result.

Using the Custom Outline dialog box

To set up an unusual numbering style for your outline, choose Format → "Bullets and Numbering" → Outline Numbered tab, and click Customize.

When the Custom Outline dialog box first opens, as shown in Figure 6-11, the settings you see pertain to the numbering style you've chosen in the "Bullets and Numbering" dialog box, and to the current heading level at the insertion point.

In the Level box at the left, choose the outline level you want to tailor. For instance, you can live with Word's built-in typeface for chapter titles, but want your secondary headings to look different. In that case, leave Level 1 alone and click the 2 in the Level box. The Preview box presents an example of the current numbering; it changes as you make changes in the Custom Outline dialog box.

- The **Number Format** panel shows the numbering style—letter, Roman numeral, and so on—for the current level.

- Word generally begins counting headings with the number 1. But if you want to print out an outline that's supposed to be a continuation of another document, you may want its numbering to start with, say, 17. That's the number you type into the **Start at** box.

- Choose from the **Previous level number** menu when you want to display level numbers together. Ordinarily, the title might be numbered 1, and the three sub-headings a, b, and c. But if you want the subheads numbered 1a, 1b, and 1c instead, choose Level 1 from this menu. This numbering tactic is useful when your outline has long paragraphs, since it'll keep you from getting lost in the levels.

- The **Font** button lets you choose a font and typeface for the outline *number* only. (To change the font for the heading *text*, use "Link level to style" as described below.)

- The **Number position** panel is where you can choose left, centered, or right alignment, relative to the distance between the text (see below) and the left margin. The **Aligned at** box is where you set the left indent. Watch what happens in the Preview box as you click the arrows.

- The **Text position** box sets the distance of the text from the left margin. It operates independently of the number position.

Advanced outline customization

If you click the blue arrow button, the dialog box expands, sprouting a handy fold-out panel showing even more intimidating-looking options.

- In the **Link level to style** menu, you can choose to apply any of the styles in the current document template (see page 127) to the level that you're formatting.

- The **Follow number with** menu lets you insert a tab, a space, or nothing at all between the number and the text. (You do it here because you can't directly format outline numbers in your document, not even in Outline view.)

- The **ListNum field list name** box lets you lets you name the outline list template. Then you can insert a ListNum field that references that outline number list by name.

- Check the **Legal style numbering** box to apply legal style (no letters, no capital Roman numerals) to any numbering style. This box grays out the "Number style" menu and gives Legal style numbering complete control.

- When you choose a new level in the Level box, the **Restart numbering after** box is turned on automatically. That's because each subtopic is numbered from the beginning, under the main topic that contains it (1a, 1b; 2a, 2b)—unless you take a unique approach to counting, you wouldn't want your headings to go 1a, 1b, 2c, 2d, for example. Thus, under subheading (a), sub-subhead numbers start again with i, ii, iii, and so on, as shown in Figure 6-11.

Click OK to close the Customize box and apply your selections from the "Bullets and Numbering" dialog box. If you plan to always use the outline in Outline view, you're done; otherwise, consider switching into Draft or Print Layout view for further refinement. You'll discover that the nice, even indenting of your various headings in Outline view may not exist in Draft or Print Layout view. As a result, you may have to adjust the indentation of your various heading styles to make the indenting levels correspond in the other views.

The Document Map

The Document Map doesn't actually look like a map. It looks like a portable table of contents that's open as you read. This unusual view can save you hours of tiresome scrolling (see Figure 6-12).

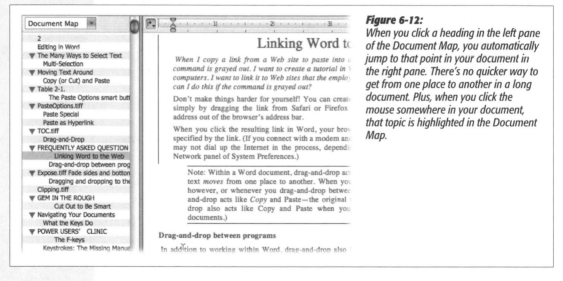

Figure 6-12:
When you click a heading in the left pane of the Document Map, you automatically jump to that point in your document in the right pane. There's no quicker way to get from one place to another in a long document. Plus, when you click the mouse somewhere in your document, that topic is highlighted in the Document Map.

What's in the Document Map

In essence, the Document Map is a navigating pane revealing just the headings in a document. A heading, in this case, can be any text in one of Word's built-in heading styles, a style you've *based on* one of the built-in heading styles, or text to which you've applied an *outline level*.

Viewing and Navigating the Document Map

To see the Document Map, you need to open the Navigation Pane. You can do that by either choosing View → Navigation Pane or clicking the Navigation Pane icon on the Standard toolbar. A narrow panel with its own vertical scroll bar opens on the left side of your document window. From the little menu at the top of the pane, choose Document Map. (Your other choice—Thumbnails—is described on page 286 and in Figure 6-13.)

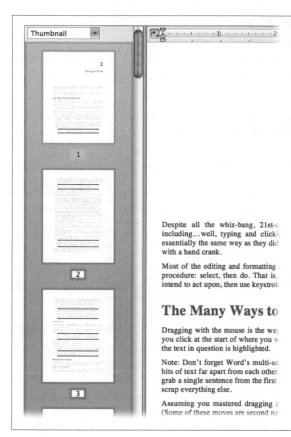

Figure 6-13:
For truly visual creatures, Word has a great way to hunt for pages in a long document—the Navigation Pane's Thumbnail view. To use it, click the pop-up menu at the top of the Navigation Pane and choose Thumbnail view. The Thumbnail view displays a miniature picture of every page in your document. To go to the page, just click its thumbnail. If a page isn't visible, use the scroll bar to move to it.

The Document Map doesn't have a horizontal scroll bar at the bottom; if you can't read the full text across the Document Map pane, drag the narrow bar—the resize bar—to widen its pane. However, you can read the full text of any topic without resizing: point the cursor at any line of text, and a screen tip appears, revealing the full text.

The flippy triangles in the Document Map work just like those in any Finder window: Click one to reveal or conceal all its subtopics. If you're a fan of contextual menus, you can also Control-click (or right click) a heading in the Document Map, and choose Expand, Collapse, or any of the level headers that you'd like to see.

Because the items shown in the Document Map have levels, like headings and outline topics, you can collapse or expand the entire "outline" so that, for example, only the Level 1 and Level 2 headings show up, exactly as you can in Outline view. To do so, Control-click in the Document Map pane and choose a heading level from the contextual menu (as mentioned above). If you choose Show Heading 4, for instance, the Document Map displays only Levels 1 through 4, hiding everything else.

To dismiss the Document Map, choose View → Navigation Pane again, double-click the resize bar, or click the Navigation Pane icon in the Standard toolbar.

Customizing the Document Map

The Document Map automatically shows up as black Lucida Grande text with blue highlights. To jazz up the Document Map font (or just make it less ugly), choose Format → Style and choose Document Map in the Styles list box. Click Modify to bring up the Modify Style box.

Now choose Font from the Format menu. Whatever font, color, size, case, or text effect you specify now will apply to all text in the Document Map.

Tip: At this point, you can even change the highlight color, which appears when you click a heading in the Map. Click OK; then, from the Format pop-up menu, choose Borders. Click the Shading tab in the resulting dialog box. Choose a new fill color as described on page 746.

Click OK, OK, and Close when you're satisfied. (Clicking Apply changes the current paragraph in your main document to the Document Map style; that's probably not what you want to do.) If you have a change of heart at this point, press ⌘-Z to restore the Document Map to its original, bland condition.

Master Documents

In the beginning, there was Word 5.1. It had fonts, sizes, styles, tables, and graphics. But the people weren't satisfied. They wanted to bind together many different chapter documents into a single, unified book. They wanted to knit together files written by multiple authors who had edited their respective sections simultaneously on the network. They wanted to print, spell check, or find-and-replace across dozens of different Word files at once, or generate tables of contents, indexes, and cross-references for all component Word files at once.

On the sixth day, Microsoft created the Master Document. (Really, it looks like they created it on the fifth day. They saved the sixth for Notebook Layout view and Zune.) Notebook is perhaps the simplest form of outlining, while Outline view is more capable, more complex. Finally, Master documents are the Mother Lode of document organization.

But on the 2008th day—or version—Microsoft decided that this might be just too much for the average Word fan to comprehend and hid access to this feature behind an innocuous button in the Outlining toolbar. No longer would the multitudes be mystified by Master Document in the View menu.

Without a doubt, a Master Document looks much like an outline. However, each heading in the Master Document can refer to a section or an entirely different *Word file*. As in the Document Map, you click these headings in Master Document view to travel directly from one part of the overall document to another.

In essence, a Master Document is a binder containing the individual Word files that comprise it (which Microsoft calls *subdocuments*). Each subdocument can be formatted independently, moved or removed, split up, or combined with another

---

subdocument—all while remaining safely under the umbrella of the Master Document. The Master Document concept is slightly alien, difficult to understand, and sometimes a bit flaky; but if you're putting a book together, Master documents may be the only way to go.

Warning: Master documents are sometimes a cause of document corruption. When you're using this feature, back up your work even more frequently than usual.

Creating a New Master Document

To start building a Master Document, open a new document, choose View → Outline, and click the button at the right end of the Outlining toolbar. The Master Document toolbar appears, and your document is set up for outlining (see Figure 6-14).

Setting up your über-document is exactly like creating an outline (see page 191), in that you use all the same techniques. Each heading, however, will eventually become the name of a separate file on your hard drive. Because a Master Document will wind up as a herd of individual files, you'd be wise to save it on your hard drive in a folder of its own; the subdocuments will wind up there, too.

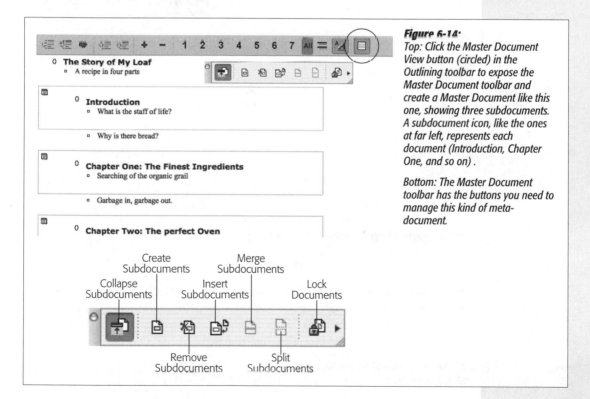

Figure 6-14:
Top: Click the Master Document View button (circled) in the Outlining toolbar to expose the Master Document toolbar and create a Master Document like this one, showing three subdocuments. A subdocument icon, like the ones at far left, represents each document (Introduction, Chapter One, and so on).

Bottom: The Master Document toolbar has the buttons you need to manage this kind of meta-document.

Spinning off a document

To spin off a particular heading as a subdocument, click it and then click the Create Subdocument button on the Master Document toolbar (see Figure 6-14). (You can also highlight several headings [and text, if desired] at once before clicking the Create Subdocument button. Just make sure the first heading is at the level you'll want represented as subdocuments.)

A light gray box that defines the boundaries of the document appears onscreen; you can type or paste into it. Behind the scenes, you've just created a new, linked file in your Master Document's folder (Figure 6-15). You or your network comrades can edit these individual files independently; whenever you open up the Master Document, you'll see the changes reflected.

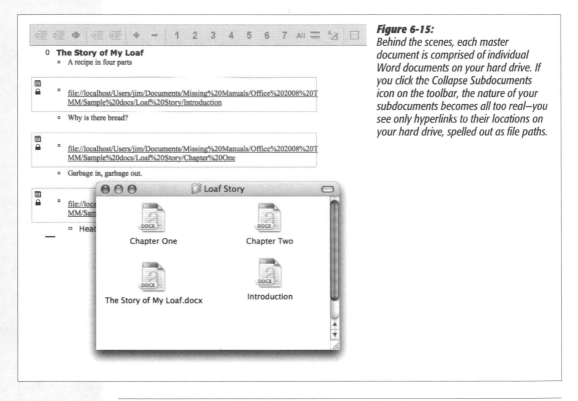

Figure 6-15:
Behind the scenes, each master document is comprised of individual Word documents on your hard drive. If you click the Collapse Subdocuments icon on the toolbar, the nature of your subdocuments becomes all too real—you see only hyperlinks to their locations on your hard drive, spelled out as file paths.

Note: Subdocument files are stored in the same folder as the Master Document and behave like perfectly normal Word files. But don't drag their icons to another folder; rename them by clicking the icon's name, and so on. If you do, the Master Document won't be able to find them. Instead, move and rename subdocuments using the techniques described later in this section.

The safest way to copy a Master Document and all its subdocuments to another location is to select them all and move them all at once. Better still, just move the folder containing them.

Incorporating a document

You can turn an existing Word document on your hard drive into a new subdocument, too. Just click the Insert Subdocument icon on the Master Document toolbar to open its dialog box. When you navigate to and select a file and click Open, the contents of the document appear in your Master Document as a subdocument, just like all the others.

Viewing Master Documents

Master Documents look and act vastly different in each of Word's views. If you can remember to switch into the correct view, you've won more than half of the Master Document game. Here's what each view does to a Master Document:

- **In Draft view**, subdocuments become *sections* (see page 122), with a section break separating each. Use Draft view to type and edit your document. Be careful not to remove the section breaks. Removing them will inadvertently combine the Word documents that make up your Master.

  If, in Draft view, your document looks like a series of hyperlinks, with no other text, you have two choices: Click on a hyperlink to open that subdocument in a new window, or choose View → Outline, click the Master Document View button, then click the Expand Subdocuments button on the Master Documents toolbar. Now when you return to Draft view, the text in your Master Document will flow continuously, with a section break between subdocuments.

- **Web Layout, Print Layout, and Publishing Layout views** function just as they normally do. Your document appears to be a seamless whole, with no visible breaks between subdocuments.

- **Outline view** turns the Master Document into one big outline; here too, if you see hyperlinks instead of text, expand the subdocuments as described above. This view is useful for organizing your document at any stage of the process because it's so easy to drag-and-drop. In Outline view, subdocuments are represented by continuous section breaks.

- If you convert your Master Document to **Notebook Layout** view (page 181), you get a beautiful notebook with each subdocument in a tabbed section of its own.

Note: If you sense a pattern here, you're right. A subdocument in Master Document view and a tab in Notebook Layout view are both represented, in Draft view, by continuous section breaks (page 122).

Working with Master Documents

In Master Document view, not only can you see all your subdocuments, you can also open them, arrange and organize them, and control access to them.

Opening and expanding subdocuments

When you click the Collapse Subdocuments button (first on the Master Document toolbar), something odd happens: Each subdocument is listed as a blue, underlined hyperlink, with only its heading visible (Figure 6-15). The rest is collapsed, exactly as in an outline. The text of the hyperlinks can look unfamiliar to you, since they're the *folder path* and *file name* of the subdocument. Clicking a link opens the subdocument in its own window.

You also see a padlock icon next to each collapsed heading. It's a persistent bug; that document isn't, in fact, locked in any way. If you double-click the heading (to open the file into its own window) or expand it, you'll find that it's easily editable.

Tip: You *can* lock a subdocument so that it's protected from errant mouse clicks in Master Document view; just click in the expanded subdocument and click the padlock icon on the toolbar. Even so, double-clicking its small subdocument icon or its collapsed heading opens it into its own window, which is easily editable. In other words, the Lock function doesn't give what you'd call government-level security.

But when you open a subdocument into its own window, the padlock in the Master Document indicates that you (or anyone else) can't edit the same document in Master Document view. The lock feature is really effective only when sharing a Master Document over a network, where it prevents two people from editing the same document at the same time.

Once you've collapsed your subdocuments, you can drag their little document icons up or down to rearrange them (or press Delete to remove them).

When you then click the Expand Subdocuments button on the Master Document toolbar (the very first icon again), the subdocuments open within the Master Document window. A light gray box outlines the contents of the subdocument in outline form.

Moving and renaming subdocuments

Don't rename or move a subdocument in the Finder; if you do, the Master Document will no longer be able to find it. If you really want to rename or move one of these documents, do so from within the Master Document, like this:

1. **Open the subdocument using any of the methods described above, and choose File → Save As.**

2. **Type a new name for the subdocument and, if desired, choose a new location for it. Click Save or press Return.**

With these two steps, you've updated the Master Document's *link* to the subdocument. The next time you open the subdocument from within the Master Document, the one with the new name and location will open. (The subdocument with the old name and location is still there, sitting on your hard drive as an independent Word document. You can delete it, unless you have some further use for it.)

Splitting and combining subdocuments

Suppose you want to chop a long chapter into two shorter ones. Or perhaps two people who were collaborating on a report have had a big fight, requiring you to solve the problem by giving them individual assignments. Fortunately, the process of dividing a subdocument in two, which Word calls *splitting*, is comparatively painless.

To do so, expand the subdocuments in Master Document view. Click where you want your split-off document to begin, and then click the Split Subdocument button on the Master Document toolbar.

At other times, you may want your subdocuments to meld together. For instance, you may want to combine two short chapters into one longer one, without restarting the pagination. You could cut and paste text from one subdocument into another, but there's a more elegant way, which Word calls *merging*.

To perform this task, move the subdocuments that you intend to merge so that they're next to each other in your outline. Highlight them, and then click the Merge Subdocument button on the Master Document toolbar.

The new, merged subdocument carries the name of the *first* subdocument that you combined. The original, unmerged versions of the second (and other) subdocument files remain in their original folder locations on your hard drive, but they're no longer connected to the Master Document.

"Removing" a subdocument

The Remove Subdocument button on the Master Document toolbar doesn't actually delete it (for that, see below). Instead, this function brings the document's contents into the Master Document itself, so that it's no longer linked to an external file on your hard drive. For example, you might use it when, for formatting reasons, you want your introduction to be part of the Master Document, instead of giving it a subdocument of its own.

To do so, expand the subdocuments. Click the subdocument icon, and then click Remove Subdocument on the Master Document toolbar. The contents of that subdocument now appear in the body of the Master Document. (You can delete the old subdocument file, which is now orphaned on your hard drive—unless you want to keep it as a backup.)

Deleting subdocuments

Deleting a subdocument from a Master Document is easy: With the subdocument expanded and unlocked (see page 206), click the subdocument icon to select it and then press Delete. (When you delete a subdocument, you only remove it from the Master Document; you don't actually delete its file. The original subdocument file is still in the same folder where you left it, and where it will stay until you Trash it.)

Master Documents and Formatting

Like all Word documents, every Master Document is based on a template (see page 224). Not surprisingly, all subdocuments have the same template as the Master Document. What is surprising, and potentially confusing, is the fact that a subdocument can have its *own* template, independent of the Master Document—and yet it can still take on the Master Document template when you want it to.

In Master Document view, all subdocuments share the same Master Document template—its styles, headers, footers, and so on. When you print *from this view*, all subdocuments print in the styles of the master template, resulting in a very consistent look. But when you open a subdocument *in its own window*, the subdocument's own independent template applies—with its own type styles, headers, footers, and so on. All the template parts listed on page 228 can operate independently in the Master Document and its subdocuments.

Master Document Security

Master documents were designed for sharing. The fact that two different people can simultaneously work on subdocuments of the same Master Document makes collaboration easy. When the individual subdocuments are done, you can review and print the finished product in Master Document view, ensuring that the formatting is consistent throughout. An added challenge, however, is keeping people from messing with subdocuments that they shouldn't, whether or not they're doing it maliciously.

Locking and unlocking subdocuments

The simplest (and most easily foiled) way of keeping someone from tampering with a subdocument is to lock it, as described on page 204. When a subdocument is locked, you can open and read it, but you can't edit or change it.

Fortunately, anytime someone is working on a subdocument, it gets locked automatically when viewed by anyone else on the network. It remains locked until its editor finishes and closes it.

Assigning passwords

Unfortunately, locking a subdocument by using the Lock Subdocuments button is a good way to prevent others from making accidental changes to it, but it doesn't actually lock out those who know about the Lock Document button. For true security, Master Documents and subdocuments need to be password-protected just like any other document. As always, you can password-protect either the Master Document or (if you've opened one into its own window) a subdocument; either way, the instructions on page 10 apply.

Sharing a Master Document on a network

One of the most popular uses for Master Documents is file sharing. For instance, members of a public relations department can each work on a separate section of their company's annual report. The report is a Master Document, and each section is a subdocument.

Here are a couple tips for successful Master Document file sharing:

- Choose one person to be team leader. That person will format the Master Document, assign and keep a safe record of the passwords, and oversee the final proofreading and distribution of the completed document.

- Make sure all Macs involved are networked and set up for file sharing. If any team members aren't familiar with file sharing, arrange consultations with the network administrator. To learn more about setting up file sharing, choose Help → Mac Help in the Finder and search for *file sharing*, or consult *Mac OS X: The Missing Manual*.

Editing Long Documents

Word is an almost unfathomably deep program. Most people use it to type reports, write letters, take notes during class, and little else. That's fine—Microsoft intended the program to be easy for even novices to use. But take a plunge beneath its placid surface and Word rewards you with footnotes and endnotes for the research-minded; autosummaries and data merges for the time-challenged; and captions, tables of contents, and indexes for those creating something meatier than a letter to the editor.

This chapter takes you deep into the dimly lit realm of Word's power-user features, well beneath the easy-to-use surface used by millions of everyday, casual word-smiths. The material you'll find here is at your disposal when you need to write a dissertation, craft an annual report, draft a full-length book, or create any other complex, structured document.

Headers and Footers

A header or footer is a special strip showing the page number—as well as your book title, chapter title, name, date, and other information—at the top or bottom of every printed page in your document (or a section of it).

Creating Headers and Footers

Adding headers and footers to your document is now easier than ever thanks to Word 2008's assortment of preconfigured Document Elements. Click Document Elements in the toolbar to reveal the Elements Gallery (if it's not already showing),

Page Numbers: The Simple Method

Page numbers are the most popular use of headers and footers. That's why Word provides buttons for adding and formatting them right on the "Header and Footer" pane of the Formatting Palette (see Figure 7-1, top).

But there's an even easier way to number your pages in Word: Just choose Insert → Page Numbers. The Page Numbers dialog box opens, as shown in Figure 7-2, bottom. Watch the Preview window change as you adjust the controls found here, such as Alignment (which includes Inside or Outside, for use when you're setting up bound-book pages); "Show number on first page" (turn it off if your document has a title page); and the Format button, which opens a dialog box where you can specify what kind of numbering you want (1, 2, 3; i, ii, iii; a, b, c; and so on).

When you turn on "Include chapter number," Word includes the chapter number along with the page number—in a "Chapter 1, Page 1" scheme. In the "Chapter starts with style" menu, choose the heading style that you used for the chapter number (you have to use one of Word's built-in headings—or a style based upon one of them—to make this numbering feature work). Then, choose a separator (a hyphen, dash, or whatever).

Figure 7-1:
Word 2008's new Elements Gallery lets you insert a header or footer by choosing one of the preformatted styles. Set the pop-up menu at the left to determine which pages receive your header or footer, then simply click your style choice to make it so.

and then click the Header or Footer button. As shown in Figure 7-2, Word displays its gallery of preformatted header or footer styles. Use the pop-up menu to determine whether this header or footer will appear on odd pages, even pages, or all pages. Then click one of the thumbnails in the gallery and watch as Word inserts it in your document and switches to "Header and Footer" view.

Word treats the header and footer as a special box at the top or bottom of the page. To view these special text areas, choose View → "Header and Footer". Word switches to Print Layout view (if you weren't there already) and a blue line appears separating the header and footer areas from the rest of your document. Meanwhile, back in the document body, the rest of your text fades to gray. (If you find that faded representation of your body text distracting, hide it by clicking the Show/Hide Document Text icon on the "Header and Footer" pane of the Formatting Palette.)

Tip: If you're already working in Print Layout view, you don't have to bother with the View → "Header and Footer" command. Just move the cursor to the top or bottom of the page; when the cursor turns into this shape 📄 double-click. The header and footer outlines appear.

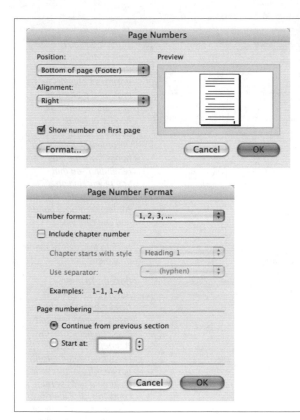

Figure 7-2:
Choose Insert → Page Numbers for the shortcut method using this dialog box (top). Click the Format button to summon the Page Number Format dialog box (bottom) to fine-tune your numbering style or to choose a starting number other than 1.

If you haven't used the Elements Gallery to start with, fill your header or footer by typing inside it and clicking icons in the "Header and Footer" pane of the Formatting Palette. If you have begun with one of Words preformatted styles, now's your chance to modify that formatting to your taste. For your convenience, Word places a centered tab stop in the middle of the typing area, and a right-aligned tab stop at the right. You can choose View → Ruler and adjust these tab stops, of course (see page 111), but they're especially handy when you want to produce a header like the one shown in Figure 7-3.

1. **Make sure the cursor is at the left margin. Type the chapter title.**

   After typing Chapter 1: The Beginning, you can highlight and format it; for example, italicize it by pressing ⌘-I.

2. **Press Tab.**

   The cursor jumps to the center-aligned tab in the middle of the header or footer.

3. **Insert the date.**

   Click the Insert Date icon on the Formatting Palette, as shown in Figure 7-4. (Word inserts the date as a *field,* which is continuously updated; whenever you open this document, the date will be current.)

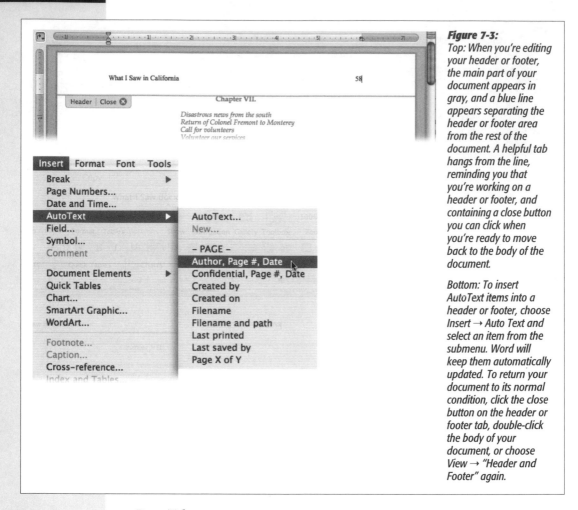

Figure 7-3:
Top: When you're editing your header or footer, the main part of your document appears in gray, and a blue line appears separating the header or footer area from the rest of the document. A helpful tab hangs from the line, reminding you that you're working on a header or footer, and containing a close button you can click when you're ready to move back to the body of the document.

Bottom: To insert AutoText items into a header or footer, choose Insert → Auto Text and select an item from the submenu. Word will keep them automatically updated. To return your document to its normal condition, click the close button on the header or footer tab, double-click the body of your document, or choose View → "Header and Footer" again.

4. **Press Tab.**

   Now your cursor is aligned at the right margin.

5. **Type *Page,* and a space; insert the page number by clicking the Insert Page Number icon on Formatting Palette (Figure 7-4); type *of;* insert the total number of pages by clicking the Insert Number of Pages icon.**

   (Of course, most people don't use the "Page X of Y" notation; if you want just the page number to appear, simply click the Insert Page Number icon and be done with it.)

   Word inserts placeholder fields (indicated by a nonprinting, gray background) into your header or footer, so that it says *Page 3 of 15,* for example. When you print or scroll through your document, you'll see that each page is correctly labeled in this way.

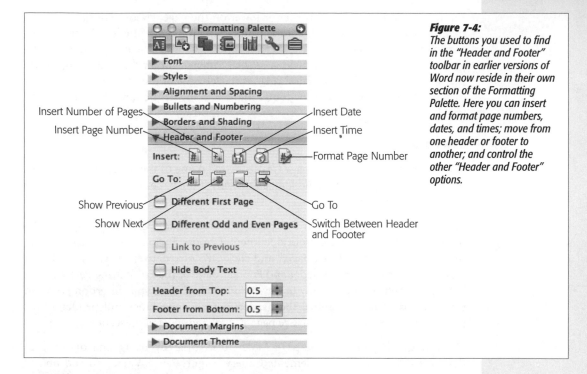

Figure 7-4:
The buttons you used to find in the "Header and Footer" toolbar in earlier versions of Word now reside in their own section of the Formatting Palette. Here you can insert and format page numbers, dates, and times; move from one header or footer to another; and control the other "Header and Footer" options.

Tip: If you need help identifying an icon on this palette, point to it without clicking. As usual in Office 2008, a screen tip appears to identify it.

---

6. **Double-click the dimmed body portion of your document (or click the Close button on the toolbar) to exit the header/footer editing area.**

   If, at this point, you want more control over page numbering, click the Format Page Number button on the "Header and Footer" pane of the Formatting Palette In the dialog box that appears, you can specify how you'd like the page numbers to appear (*a, b, c,* or in Roman numerals, or with chapter numbers included). You can also indicate that you'd like them to begin with some number other than 1, which is ideal when your document is the *continuation* of a document you've already printed.

Tip: Headers and footers don't appear or print when you save your Word files as Web pages. But leave them in–they'll appear and print (if you chose the "Save entire file into HTML" option) if you return to using the same file as a Word document.

Positioning headers and footers

Headers and footers automatically extend from the left margin to the right margin. To make them wider than the text and extend them into the margins, give the header or footer a *hanging* or *negative indent* (see page 110).

To move a header or footer higher or lower on the page, choose Format → Document → Margins tab; adjust the numbers in the "From edge" boxes. (Higher numbers move the header or footer text closer to the middle of the page.) Alternatively, you can adjust it visually by clicking in the header or footer and then dragging its margin up or down in the vertical ruler at the left side of the page. This adjusts the distance between the header or footer and the body of the text. If the ruler isn't visible, click Word → Preferences → View → Window → Vertical Ruler.

Cover pages

If your term paper has a title page (featuring the name of the paper centered on an otherwise blank page), it would look a little silly if the paper's title also appeared in a footer at the bottom.

Fortunately, you can give your first page a different header or footer—or none. To do so, go to the first page of your document. Choose Format → Document → Layout tab, click "Different first page," and click OK. Alternatively, click the Different First Page button on the "Header and Footer" pane of the Formatting Palette. (The "first page" setting applies only to the *section* that contains your insertion point. In other words, you can control the header/footer's appearance independently for each section in your document. See page 122 for more detail on sections.)

Or, you can bypass the title-page footer-formatting by using one of the pre-designed title pages in the Elements Gallery (Figure 7-5). When you add one of these pages to your document, Word knows you don't want headers and footers on that page and makes the change to the Document Layout dialog box for you.

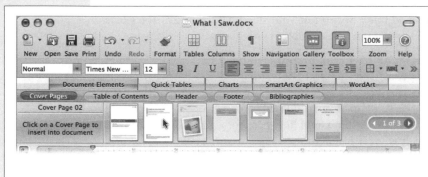

Figure 7-5:
Click Document Elements to reveal the Elements Gallery, then click Cover Pages to display the variety of title-page designs Word puts at your disposal. No matter what page you're on when you make this choice, Word always inserts the cover page at the beginning of the document.

Now you can edit and format the unique header and footer for your first page, or just leave them blank. (You can also apply this technique to the first page of each *section* of your document; see page 122.) If you haven't formatted the header and footer for the rest of the document, click the Show Next button on the "Header and Footer" toolbar; Word takes you to the second page, where you create the headers and footers for the rest of the pages.

Bound-book pages

If your document is going to be bound like a book, you'll probably want different headers and footers on odd and even pages, exactly like those on these book pages (book name on left-side pages, chapter name on right-side pages).

To create these mirror-image headers and footers, choose Format → Document → Layout tab, click "Different odd and even," and click OK. (Alternatively, click the Different Odd and Even Pages icon on the "Header and Footer" pane of the Formatting Palette.) Then edit the headers and footers for the odd and even pages in your document; when you edit *any single* odd or even page, Word applies the changes to *all* of them. If you began your header or footer foray in the Elements Gallery, then you made this pagination choice back then. If you have a change of heart, you can use this technique to change it.

Different headers (and footers) for different sections

If you've divided your document into *sections* (see page 122), you can type, for example, different chapter names or numbers in the headers and footers for each section—a very common technique when you want to break your document into chapters.

By default, all headers and footers in a document are the same, even when you insert section breaks, so the trick is to *sever* the connection between the headers and footers in consecutive sections. For instance, if you want a different header in each of your document's three sections, go to a page in the *second* section and choose View → "Header and Footer". Click in the header and click the Same as Previous button in the Formatting Palette's "Header and Footer" pane. (This button breaks or rejoins the header/footer connection between each section and the one before it. You can use it to restore the header and footer connections if you change your mind, and once again make them uniform throughout the document.)

Repeat the process for the third section, and so on.

Citations

When you need to refer to another work—a book, journal article, Web page, or interview—you have to cite the source accurately and succinctly. Loved and loathed by scholars the world over, the citation, that indispensable and unavoidable footnote to any kind of serious research, provides a standardized style for these vital scraps of information. However, getting all those commas, colons, quote marks, italics, and underlines in just the right places has driven many great minds to near distraction—and created employment for many grad students as publication deadlines loom.

One standard format for citations is called MLA (Modern Language Association) style, and it looks like this:

> Smith, Charles D. "The 'Crisis of Orientation': The Shift of Egyptian Intellectuals to Islamic Subjects in the 1930s." International Journal of Middle East Studies 4 (1973): 382–410.

Note: The three biggies in the style world are MLA, favored by humanities scholars; APA (American Psychological Association), favored by psychologists and sociologists; and CMS or Chicago (Chicago Manual of Style), favored by historians. For more information visit any of their Web sites: *www.mla.org,* *www.apastyle.org,* and *www.chicagomanualofstyle.org*.

Word 2008's Citations feature can make even the most staid academics utter a subdued "Ye haw!" The Citations Palette occupies prime real estate in the Toolbox, two tabs to the right of the Formatting Palette. It's essentially a mini database dedicated to tracking every possible form of reference citation (Figure 7-6).

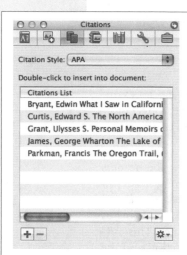

Figure 7-6:
Word 2008's new Citations palette lets you build a database of all your reference citations, and then insert them into footnotes, bibliographies, or the body of the text by double-clicking an item in this list. Use the plus-sign button to add a new item. You can select an item and use the minus-sign button to remove it from your collection unless you've inserted it within your document's body text.

The Citations palette lets you assemble a list of references and then select and insert them—in perfectly formatted style—into a footnote, endnote, bibliography, or anywhere else. Here are the steps:

1. **Open the Citations palette, choose your favored style from the Citation Style pop-up menu: APA, Chicago, MLA, or Turabian, and then click the plus sign button at the bottom.**

   The Create New Source window appears, ready for you to begin filling in the salient bits of data for this particular source (Figure 7-7).

2. **Use the Type of Source pop-up menu to narrow the data fields to what's needed, for example, for a book, article, or interview.**

   Depending on your choice of citation style, the most vital fields display asterisks next to their names. Use the tab key to move through the fields, noting the Example pane at the bottom of the window showing the correct format for each entry.

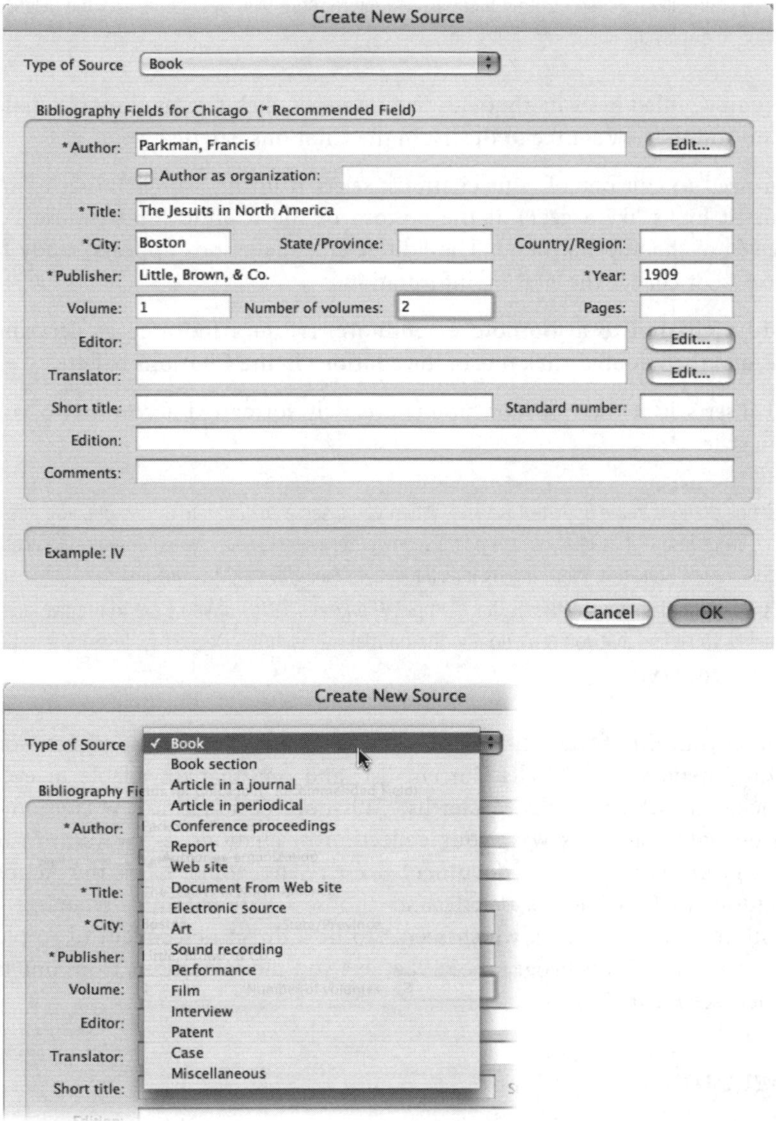

Figure 7-7:
Top: The Create New Source dialog box lets you track a huge number of data fields for each citation, but only those marked with an asterisk are required for your chosen citation style.

Bottom: Use the "Type of Source" pop-up menu to choose just what type of document, artwork, or interview you're dealing with.

3. **Enter each name in the Last, First and Middle fields, and then click the Add button.**

Word adds the name to the box at the bottom of the window. Repeat the process to add more names and if necessary use the Up, Down, or Delete buttons to get your list in the proper order. Click OK, and Word adds the multiple-name listing to the Create New Source window—punctuated just so, according to your selected style.

Tip: If any of your author, editor, or other name fields require more than one name, click the neighboring Edit button to display the Edit Name dialog box.

4. **Once you've filled in as many fields as you need, click OK to close the dialog box and add the new source to the list in the Citations palette.**

    If you need to edit one of your citations, select it in the list, click the Actions button (it looks like a gear) at the bottom of the window, and choose Edit Source from the pop-up menu. The Edit Source dialog box appears, ready for you to add or change the citation information.

5. **To add a citation to a footnote or endnote, create a footnote as described above, and then double-click one of the citations in the Citations palette.**

    Word inserts it at the insertion point, precisely formatted according to your chosen style.

Note: Deleting citations in the body text is tricky. When you insert a citation into a footnote, endnote, or bibliography, Word inserts it as text you can edit like any other text. However, when you insert a citation into your document's body text, Word inserts it as a text field (see page 235) containing the author's last name and publication date in parentheses, for example, *(Parkman, 1910)*. If you want to remove one of these text fields, you'll find that you can't do it in the normal way with the Delete key. Instead, select the field and choose Edit → Cut.

As you build your list of citations, Word actually saves this list in two places—one for the document, which it calls Current list; and one that's available in every Word document, which it calls Master list. Whenever you add a new citation, it ends up on both lists. This way, your collection of citations is always available when you begin writing a new document on a related topic. Click the Actions (gear) button in the Citations palette and choose Citation Source Manager to access both lists. This window, which seems to be a direct descendent of Apple's venerable Font/DA Mover program of 1984, lets you move citations from one list to the other (see Figure 7-8).

Bibliographies

Word also makes use of the Citations database to help you create a one-click bibliography. If you want your bibliography to appear on separate page, position your insertion point at the end of your document and choose Insert → Break → Page Break. Make sure you're looking at your document in Print Layout view, click Document Elements in the Elements Gallery, and then click Bibliographies. Click the Bibliography or Works Cited thumbnails to instantly create your bibliography at the insertion point (Figure 7-9).

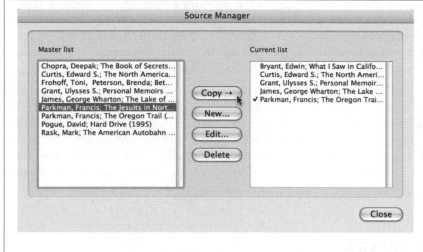

Figure 7-8:
If you're creating a new document and need to use citations you've created before, choose Citation Source Manager from the Citations palette's Actions (gear) button to open Word's citations clearinghouse. Select previously created citations in the Master list (⌘-click to select more than one) and click the Copy button to move them to the Current list, making them available in the Citations palette. Conversely, if you're opening a document containing citations created on a different computer, select them in the Current list and click Copy to move them into your Master citations collection. A checkmark indicates a citation you've used in the document's body text (see the Note on page 218).

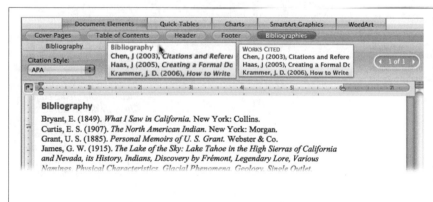

Figure 7-9:
Create an instant bibliography (assuming you've entered your reference data in the Citations list) by clicking the bibliography thumbnail in the Elements Gallery. Word creates a bibliography using the Citation Style shown in the pop-up menu—which matches the style you've used elsewhere in your document. If you try to change the style here, Word warns you that doing so will change the citations style for the entire document.

Whichever you pick, Word creates the list—using your selected Citation Style—from the entire contents of your Citations List as it appears in the Citations palette, inserting it as a field in your document. In other words, if you have a reference listed in your citations list but you never actually referred to it in your document, it still appears in the Bibliography or Works Cited list when it appears in your document.

If you click the bibliography field once it appears in your document, Word displays a Smart button with which you can choose to Update Citations and Bibliography (to reflect recent additions to your Citations list), or Convert Bibliography to Static Text (so you can edit, format, add or delete text from the bibliography). For example, if you Convert Bibliography to Static Text, you may be able to improve readability by selecting the entire bibliography and adding some space between paragraphs using the "Alignment and Spacing" pane of the Formatting Palette (see page 106).

Footnotes and Endnotes

Footnotes, as any research scholar can tell you, are explanations or citations located at the bottom of each page, referred to by a small superscript number or symbol in the main text. (See Figure 7-10 for an example.) *Endnotes* are similar, except that they're listed together in a clump at the end of the document, instead of on each page. Word can handle each kind of annotation gracefully. Here's how to insert a footnote or endnote into your document:

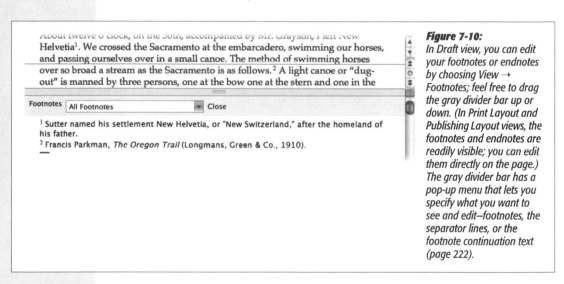

Figure 7-10:
In Draft view, you can edit your footnotes or endnotes by choosing View → Footnotes; feel free to drag the gray divider bar up or down. (In Print Layout and Publishing Layout views, the footnotes and endnotes are readily visible; you can edit them directly on the page.) The gray divider bar has a pop-up menu that lets you specify what you want to see and edit—footnotes, the separator lines, or the footnote continuation text (page 222).

1. **Click at the exact point in your document where you want the superscript note number to appear; choose Insert → Footnote or press Option-⌘-F.**

   The Footnote pane appears, proposing a footnote. (Press the keystroke ⌘-E, or click Endnote, for an endnote instead.)

If left to its own devices, Word will number your footnotes sequentially (1, 2, 3…). If you'd rather use a symbol (such as an asterisk), click "Custom mark" and type the desired symbol, or click the Symbol button and choose one from the various palettes.

2. **If you want nonstandard numbering, click Options.**

If you're some kind of radical, you may prefer Roman numerals, letters, symbols, or something else. In the resulting dialog box (see Figure 7-11), you can also choose where to place footnotes and endnotes: at the bottom of the page or immediately after the text, for instance. Click OK to close the box.

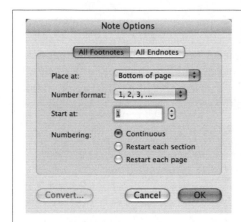

Figure 7-11:
The radio buttons on the All Footnotes and All Endnotes tabs let you choose where to start and restart the numbering. For instance, if you choose "Restart each page," the first footnote on each page will be marked "1."

3. **Click OK to close the Footnote and Endnote dialog box.**

In Draft view, Word opens up a pane at the bottom of the document window, where you can type the actual text of the note. To toggle between displaying and hiding the note pane in Draft view, choose View → Footnotes; in Print Layout view, no such shenanigans are necessary—the notes simply appear at the bottom of the page, separated by the main text by a line. You can edit them directly.

Word usually draws a horizontal line, a third of the way across the page, above your footnotes, as you can see in Print Layout view. If you'd like to edit this line, however, you have to switch to Draft view, and then choose Footnote Separator or Endnote Separator from the Footnotes pop-up menu (in the bar at the top of the note pane). Now edit the text (or line) that you find there. You could even make the line a different color, for example, or delete it entirely by clicking it and pressing Delete.

4. **Type your footnote.**

You can type any kind of clarifying prose in a footnote, but what you'll often want to include is a *citation*—a reference to a specific book or article that provided your information. See page 215 to learn about Word's new Citation tool.

5. **Repeat from step 1 to add more footnotes, or click Close to move the Footnotes pane out of your way.**

   Each footnote is marked in your text by a small number or symbol, as specified by you. At any time, you can jump back and forth between the footnote symbol (in the main window) and the Footnotes pane by pressing F6.

Tip: You can combine footnotes and endnotes in a single document. For example, footnotes might contain explanations and elaborations of text, while endnotes might contain citations.

Deleting Footnotes and Endnotes

To remove a footnote or endnote, select the superscript number or symbol in your text (not in the Footnote pane) and press the Delete key. The number and the entire note disappear, and Word renumbers the remaining notes as necessary. (Deleting the note number in the footnote or endnote itself, or in the Footnote pane, works no such magic. All you do is delete the little superscript number before the note. The rest of the note, and the number in your text, stay right where they are.)

Tip: You can convert footnotes to endnotes, or vice versa—a blessing for the indecisive. In Print Layout view, select the note, Control-click (or right-click) it and select "Convert to End Note" or "Convert to Footnote" from the pop-up menu. In Draft view, choose View → Footnotes, choose All Footnotes or All Endnotes from the pop-up menu in the gray divider bar, select the notes you want to convert, and Control-click the selection. Choose "Convert to Endnotes" or "Convert to Footnotes" from the shortcut menu.

Controlling Footnote Flow

If your footnotes are too long to fit on their "home" page, they flow into the footnote section of the next page. (Endnotes flow to the *top* of the following page.) As a courtesy to your reader, you may want to add something to the separator line— "Continued on next page," for example. Word, being equally thoughtful, lets you do exactly that.

Open the note pane as shown in Figure 7-6 and choose Footnote (or Endnote) Continuation Notice from the Footnotes pop-up menu. Type your thoughtful text, ("See next page," or what have you), and click Close.

Tip: Word positions endnotes immediately after the document or section's text, according to your specification. To put them on a separate page for printing, click in front of the first endnote and choose Insert → Break → Page Break. If you have numerous endnotes, you may want them to start on a new page so they're easier to check against your paper.

Inserting Symbols

You can use hundreds of different symbols in Word 2008—both Unicode symbols like those you can get from Mac OS X's Character Palette and those in Word's own Symbol dialog box. The following terms, for example, all depend upon symbols for correctness and clarity: 98.6°, Oscar®, ¿Que pasa?, and so on. Larger symbols called dingbats let you do cool things like put a ☎ next to your phone number. High-tech dingbats, like those in Microsoft's Webdings font, come in handy on Web pages, like ✉ to indicate an email link.

To enter the wonderful world of symbols, choose Insert → Symbol. The Symbol dialog box appears, giving you a palette of symbols in the Symbol font. Drag your cursor across them for a closer look.

If you don't see the symbol you're looking for, choose another symbol font from the Font menu. If you want a standard typographical symbol, such as © or ®, choose "Normal font" from this pop-up menu (or just click the Characters tab, where you'll find a cheat sheet of such common symbols and the keystrokes that produce them).

When you've finally highlighted the doohickey you want, click Insert (or press Return) to place it into your document at the insertion point.

If there's a symbol you wind up using frequently—you're a Valentine's Day consultant, for example, and you use the ❤ symbol about 20 times a day—you can set it up for easier access in either of two ways.

First, you can assign a keyboard shortcut to it. To do so, click the ❤ in the Symbol dialog box (in the Zapf Dingbats font, for example), and then click Keyboard Shortcut. In the resulting dialog box, press the keys you want to trigger this symbol (Control-H, for example). If you choose a key combination that's already assigned to another Word function—which is fairly likely—you'll just get an alert sound. Keep trying until you stumble onto an unassigned combination. Use the pop-up menu at the bottom of the window to choose whether to save this keystroke just in the current document, or as part of the Normal template (see page 230), so it'll work in all documents based upon it.

But you may find it easier to use a word or letter combination to insert a symbol. For instance, if you want an to appear every time you type Apple, or your favorite dingbat (say ✿) to appear when you type a code like *xq*, click the symbol and then click AutoCorrect. The AutoCorrect dialog box opens, showing your chosen symbol in the Replace With box. Type the word or code you want to trigger the appearance of the symbol and then press Return twice.

Line Numbers

If you're a lawyer, Bible scholar, or aspiring Hollywood scriptwriter, you're already familiar with *line numbering:* tiny numbers in the left margin every 5 or 10 lines (see Figure 7-12). But even in everyday business, they're occasionally useful; you could email a press release to your boss and ask, "Let me know if I come on too strong in lines 5–8," for instance.

Line numbers show up only in Print Layout and Publishing Layout views (choose View → Print Layout or Publishing Layout, or click the Print Layout or Publishing Layout button on the bottom left of the page). To add them to your document, select the text whose lines you want numbered. If it's a single section, for example, click anywhere in that section; if it's the whole document, choose Edit → Select All or press ⌘-A. If you're at the start of a new document and want to start numbering immediately, read on.

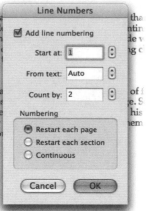

George was worried. He was getting sm[...] tha[...]
now, but he used to fill up the whole vall[...] ntin[...]
year, century after century he crept down [...] de [...]
out its floor. He even ripped pieces right [...] g c[...]
himself and taking them with him down [...]

George lives under tall headwall cliffs tha[...] of [...]
him from the cliffs all day long. Then tho[...] e. S[...]
the huge crack called a *bergschrund* where[...] his [...]
down to become part of the bottom layer [...] em[...]
derneath and spits them out as finely gro[...]

"Melt and freeze, melt and freeze,

Melt and freeze and crack and cleave.

Rocks on my bottom, rocks on my top,

I slip along and grind the crop.

Winter snow's my weight and power,

Line Numbers

☑ Add line numbering

Start at: 1

From text: Auto

Count by: 2

Numbering

⦿ Restart each page
◯ Restart each section
◯ Continuous

Cancel | OK

Figure 7-12:
When you're comparing documents with others or reading through a script, line numbers are indispensable. Add them by choosing Format → Document → Layout tab and clicking Line Numbers to summon this dialog box. If you'd like Word to not number specific paragraphs, highlight them and choose Format → Paragraph → "Line and Page Breaks" tab and turn on "Suppress line numbers." Here, for example, that option was used for the quotation, so the numbering skips over that part.

Tip: By choosing Format → Paragraph → "Line and Page Breaks" tab and turning on "Suppress line numbers," you make Word skip over the selected paragraphs in its numbering. Keep this checkbox in mind when defining a style, too, since you can use it to ensure that your captions are *never* numbered, for example.

Choose Format → Document → Layout tab. If you've selected text as described above, choose "Selected text" from the "Apply to" menu at the right; click Line Numbers. Turn on "Add line numbering" and set the following (see Figure 7-12):

- **Start at** tells Word what line to start counting with. Select 2, for instance, if you want Word *not* to include the heading at the top of the page.

- **From text** is the distance from the left margin of the text. Auto is a good start unless a certain distance has been specified.

- **Count by** tells Word: "Show numbers only on every _th line." The most common settings are 5, 10, and 20.

- Numbering, when it's **continuous,** begins at the first line and goes all the way to the end of the document. You can also tell Word to start over on each page, or after each section break.

To delete line numbers, just select the text again, choose Format → Document → Layout tab, and turn off "Add line numbering".

Templates

This chapter may cover the most advanced features of Microsoft Word, but nothing you've read so far can touch the exasperating—yet exhilarating—complexity of *templates,* the system of special files that Word uses to store your keystrokes, Auto-Text entries, styles, and dozens of other preference settings. There are two kinds of templates—global and document. Because you can simultaneously load more than one template, sometimes they interact in complex ways, including switching your text to radically different formatting.

When using Word as a basic word processor, you can safely ignore templates. Millions of people use Word every day, in fact, unaware that lurking behind the scenes of every single document is one critical global template called Normal. Every setting they change, every keystroke they redefine, every style they apply—everything gets stored in this template file. Most people, in other words, never need step behind the curtain to view the knobs and levers controlling the template.

Learning about templates, however, can pay off in spades in certain situations. For example:

- If you collaborate with other people, you can send them a template you've created containing an officially sanctioned set of styles, so that all your documents will have a consistent look.

- Similarly, your boss or network administrator may give *you* a template file, filled with styles, so that your corporate correspondence will resemble everyone else's.

- Or maybe you plan to use your laptop, and want to ensure that all of the custom keystrokes, AutoText entries, and styles that you've carefully worked up on your desktop Mac are in place on the laptop.

The following pages take you through this insanely challenging topic with as few migraines as possible.

Document Templates

In any normal program, a template is simply a stationery pad, a locked icon in the Finder that, when opened, automatically generates a blank, untitled copy of the original. If you frequently (or even occasionally) need to create documents that incorporate certain standard elements, such as the top of your letterhead or boiler-plate text on a contract, document templates can save you a lot of time.

Word has something like this kind of template, too. You see dozens of these templates, called document templates, whenever you choose File → Project Gallery. These are regular Word documents—brochures, labels, newsletters, and so on—that have been saved in a special, self-duplicating format. You can read more about the Project Gallery in Chapter 18.

Creating a document template

It's very easy to create your own document template: Just prepare a Word document. Then dress it up with graphics, font selections, dummy text, tables, forms, whatever you like. It's very important to understand that you can also customize this document with Word's more advanced features, such as:

- Styles

- AutoText entries

- Margins and tab settings

- Customized menus and toolbars

- Page layout (columns, for example)

- Headers and footers

Then choose File → Save As, choose Document Template from the Format pop-up menu, and Word jumps to the special My Templates folder automatically. Office 2008 moves that folder into a special user folder found at User → Library → Application support → Microsoft → Office → User Templates.

Name the file and then click Save.

Using a document template

From now on, whenever you'd like to peel off a copy of that template, choose File → Project Gallery, click My Templates (or whatever folder you selected inside the Templates folder), and double-click the name of the corresponding template. It's just like opening a regular Word document, except that instead of appearing as a blank, stripped-down document, it comes complete with a number of predefined elements. The keystrokes you defined in the template, the styles you set up, the AutoText entries, dummy text, and so on will all be ready to use. All you need to do is save the new, untitled document and name it.

If you send a copy of this document template to another person or another machine, all of these preference settings will similarly be ready to use any time they open it. (If a Windows person might be the recipient, remember to add *.dotx*— or *.dot* if you're saving it as a Word 97-2004 Template—to the end of the file's name; otherwise, Windows won't recognize what kind of file it is.)

However, the settings, keystrokes, macros, toolbars, and so on, won't be available in any other Word document—only new ones "peeled off" from the document template will be available. You or your colleague may wind up longing for a method of making these customizations available universally, to any Word document, including existing ones. That's perfectly possible—and it's the purpose of *global* templates.

Global Templates

Every Word document, even a new blank one that you've just opened, is based on a template; that's why you see a list of styles available in the Formatting Palette of even a brand new file. Behind the scenes, every Word document is based, at the minimum, upon a template called Normal.

Normal is what Word calls a *global* template, meaning that it's available to all documents all the time. Exactly as with document templates, a global template determines which styles, toolbars, page layout elements, AutoText entries, and other features are available when you use the document—but you don't have to go through the Project Gallery to open one, as you would with a document template.

Note: There's no technical difference between a document template and a global template—the same template file can serve as either one. The only difference is how you *load* it. If you use the Project Gallery, the template affects only a single document; if you use the Templates and Add-Ins command, as described on page 232, the template affects all documents.

Modifying a Template

No matter how hard you try to create a template the way you want it, the time comes when you have to go back and change it. You want to make your heading sizes smaller, or you have a new logo, and so on.

In a nutshell, you make such changes by opening the template file (choose File → Open, navigate to the Applications → Microsoft Office 2008 → Office → Media → Templates folder for built-in templates; or to Home → Library → Application support → Microsoft → Office → User Templates for templates you've created, and open the template you want to modify). Make whatever changes you want to the document—adjust the styles, margins, zoom level, default font, whatever—and then choose File → Save. From now on, all new documents you spin off from that template will reflect your changes.

Note: When you modify a template, the changes don't automatically ripple through all *existing* documents you peeled off of it before the change. You can open each of those older files, however, and force them to update their styles, macros, keystrokes, and so on, to reflect the changed template. To do so, choose Tools → "Templates and Add-ins". Turn on "Automatically update document styles." Click OK.

Attaching a Document Template

It happens sometimes that 20 minutes into working on a new document, you realize that there's a template that would be just perfect for it. Fortunately, Word lets you *attach* a new template to a document, even if it began life as the offspring of a different document template. For instance, you begin a letter and decide that the Normal template looks a little too plain. You can look through the Project Gallery, find a letter template whose styles appeal to you, and attach it.

Here's how to attach a new document template:

1. **Choose Tools → "Templates and Add-ins".**

   The "Templates and Add-ins" dialog box appears.

2. **Click Attach. In the "Choose a File" box, navigate to, and open, the template you'd like to attach, as shown in Figure 7-13.**

   The file name of the newly attached template appears in the "Document template" box of the "Templates and Add-ins" dialog box.

3. **Click "Automatically update document styles"; click OK.**

The Normal *style* in your document (which, confusingly, is unrelated to the Normal *template*), along with other built-in styles (Heading 1, Heading 2, and so on),

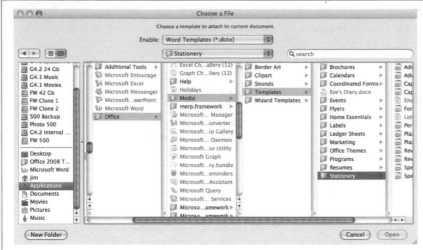

Figure 7-13:
The templates that come with Office 2008 are stored in the Applications → Microsoft Office 2008 → Office → Media → Templates folder, but you can use this dialog box to navigate to a template anywhere on your Mac. Remember that any document, template or not, in a folder in your Templates folder is automatically treated as a template, and shows up in your Project Gallery.

changes to match those in the template you just attached. Moreover, your document now uses any AutoText entries, custom toolbars, shortcut keys, and custom menus that were stored in the attached template. (If you want to use the customizations without changing styles, do *not* click "Automatically update document styles" in step 3.)

Note: Boilerplate text and graphics from the newly attached template don't suddenly appear in your document. Styles from the template don't appear either, unless the current document has styles whose names match. If you still want the new template's styles imported into your document, you have to copy them into your document using the Organizer (see below) or the Format → Style dialog box.

Word only allows one document template to be attached at a time. This is one of the ways that document templates are different from global templates, which you can gang up simultaneously.

The Organizer

Any style, AutoText entry, or custom toolbar that you create and save to a document becomes part of a template (either the Normal template or a document template). Because of a little-known but very timesaving Word feature called the Organizer, you never have to create one of those custom items more than once. The Organizer, which works just like the Citation Source Manager described above, lets you transfer these items from file to file (see Figure 7-14).

To use the Organizer, proceed like this:

1. **Choose Tools → "Templates and Add-ins"; click Organizer.**

   You can also get to the Organizer by choosing Format → Style and clicking Organizer. The Organizer dialog box opens, as shown in Figure 7-14.

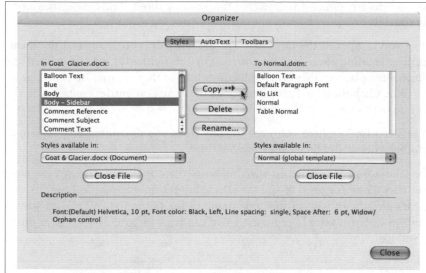

Figure 7-14:
*When you click an item
in either list box, the
direction of the arrow on
the Copy button changes
accordingly. As always
when offered lists on
your Mac, you can Shift-
click to select a number
of consecutive list items,
or ⌘-click to select (or
deselect) nonconsecutive
items in the list.*

2. **Inspect the file names above the two list boxes.**

   The left box represents the currently open document or document template if there is one; the right box represents the current global template. However, it doesn't matter which is which. You can move a style, AutoText entry, or toolbar from any document or template to any other, in either direction.

3. **Set up the two lists so that the files you want to copy to and from are visible.**

   If you don't see the document or template that has what you want, click Close File below one of the boxes. When the button changes to Open File, click it again. The "Choose a File" dialog box opens; use it to navigate to, and open, the template or document that has the features you want.

Tip: To save frustration, note that the Enable pop-up menu at the bottom of the "Choose a File" dialog box is automatically set to *Word Templates.* In other words, if you're looking for a standard Word file that has styles you like, it won't be activated in the "Choose a File" dialog box until you choose Enable → All Word Documents.

   If you began this exercise with the destination document (target document) open on the screen, it should already be listed on the left side of the Organizer. If not, however, it's easy enough to click its Close File/Open File button so that the correct destination file is also listed.

4. **Click the appropriate tab at the top of the Organizer dialog box, depending on the kinds of items you want to copy.**

   For example, suppose you created some terrific AutoText entries while working on a different Mac, and now you want to use them on your home-based Mac.

So, you cleverly emailed yourself the file, sending those AutoText entries along for the ride.

Now you've opened the Organizer; on the left side, you've opened the document containing the AutoText entries. On the right side, you've opened the Normal template, so that Word will autocomplete those entries on *your* Mac all the time. Click the AutoText tab to see all the AutoText entries contained in the files on both sides.

5. **When you find an item you want to copy from one document or template to another, click it and then click Copy.**

   See Figure 7-14 for advice on selecting more than one entry. In any case, after you click Copy (or press ⌘-C), the selected items now appear in both lists. (If there's already an item of the same name in the target file, Word asks you to confirm that you want to replace it.) You can copy in both directions, as much as you like.

Tip: You can also use the Organizer to *rename* template items, such as styles and macros. Just click one and then click Rename. Enter the new name in the adorable little dialog box that appears and click OK.

If you ever want to *delete* items—AutoText entries that pop up too often, for example—the Organizer is a good place to do that, too (although you may also go to Tools → AutoCorrect → AutoText and delete them there too). Select the item in one of the list boxes and click Delete.

---

6. **Click Close.**

   Word asks if you want to save the changes you made to your documents; click OK. You return to your document, where the changes you made in the Organizer are now in effect.

Normal and Global Templates

Every Word document is based on a document template. As noted earlier, 99 percent of all Word documents are based on the Normal global template, usually unbeknownst to their authors. In fact, the very first time you launch Word and click the icon for a blank document, you're using the Normal template.

The Normal template

Because Word documents are based on the Normal global template, the very first document you ever created (and probably most of them since that time) came set up to use certain default settings—the automatic font style (Cambria, 12 point), nine heading styles, standard margins, and so on. Whenever you create new styles (as described on page 127), they wind up being saved as part of the document template, so that they'll appear in the Formatting Palette Style list of any other Word document based on the Normal template.

But what if you want to change the default page margins, or change the Normal font to something a little less, well, normal?

The easiest way is simply to choose File → Open, navigate to the Home → Library → Application Support → Microsoft → Office → User Templates folder, and double-click the Normal template. Make whatever changes you want—to the Normal font style (choose Format → Style); to the paragraph containing the blinking insertion point, which all subsequent paragraphs will inherit (Format → Paragraph); to the document margins (Format → Document); and so on. Save and close the document. Your modified Normal template will now determine the specs of any subsequent documents you create.

Tip: The default setting that most of the world's Word fans want to change is the *font.* Experienced Word veterans—and most readers, for that matter—wouldn't mind if they never saw Cambria 12 again. For this reason, Microsoft provides a shortcut to modifying the default font in the Normal template—a method that protects the novice from even having to know about templates.

It's the Default button. Choose Format → Font, choose a typeface, and then click Default; click Yes to confirm. Any new documents you create using the File → New command automatically reflect your changes.

This useful Default command also appears when you're modifying your margins (Format → Document), proofing language (Tools → Language), page setup (File → Page Setup—choose Save As Default from the Settings pop-up menu)—all of which represent the most popular default formatting changes. In this way, you can change the Normal template on the fly, without opening it.

Loading a template as global

Suppose someone has sent you a Word template containing AutoText entries, custom toolbars, shortcut keys, and custom menus you'd like to use frequently. Instead of re-creating them, you can turn that person's document into a *global* template, and use those settings at will. To do so, open the document and proceed as follows:

1. **Choose File → Save As. Navigate to the Home → Library → Application Support → Microsoft → Office → My Templates folder. Click Save.**

   Word saves the document as a template.

2. **Open a new blank document. Choose Tools → "Templates and Add-ins".**

   The "Templates and Add-ins" dialog box opens, as shown in Figure 7-15.

3. **Click Add. Navigate to the My Templates folder; open the template you just saved.**

   The template now appears in the list box as checked, (see Figure 7-15).

4. **Click OK.**

Loading a new global template has a similar effect to attaching a new document template (macros, AutoText, custom menus, and shortcut keys are transferred to your document), but because it's a *global* template, these items are available in all documents—until you either unload the template or quit Word, that is.

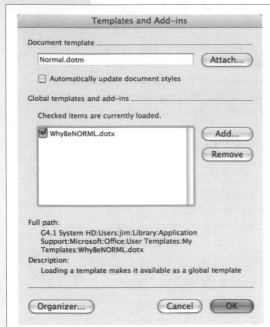

Figure 7-15:
You can make the custom items in any Word template available in every Word document by loading the template as a global template.

Note: You don't get a global template's *styles* when you attach it in this way. You can transfer them into your document using the Organizer, as described on page 228, or attach the same template as a document template.

Unloading a global template

To unload a global template you no longer need, choose Tools → "Templates and Add-ins" and uncheck it in the list, or click Remove.

AutoSummarize

Imagine this scenario: Five minutes to get to the professor's office, and you suddenly remember that she wanted you to include an abstract (a summary) at the beginning of your thesis. Or this one: You proudly plunk your report on your boss's desk and he says, "I'm not reading all this. Give me the 15-minute version." Word's AutoSummarize feature just may come to the rescue.

Unfortunately, Word doesn't actually read your document and then write a well-crafted summary. (Maybe in Word 2028.) What Word does is scan the document for frequently used words, then string what it believes to be the key sentences together into a summary. ("Key sentences" are those that include those most common words.) In other words, you're best off setting fairly low expectations for this feature. Think of AutoSummarize as something that helps you come up with a *rough* summary; you can (and should) edit the summary later.

Using a Template as a Startup Item

Word automatically unloads any global templates you load (other than the Normal template) when you quit Word. When you open Word again, the Normal template is the only global template automatically loaded.

If you want to make the AutoText entries and other attributes of another global template available all the time, you can pursue one of these two avenues:

- Copy them into the Normal template using the Organizer, as described on page 228.

- Turn the additional global template into a startup item.

To do the latter, navigate to the template on your Mac's hard drive; it's probably in the Home → Library → Application Support → Microsoft → Office → User Templates folder → My Templates. Click the template's document icon to select it and choose File → Duplicate. Drag the copied file to the Microsoft Office 2008 → Office → Startup → Word folder (to make it available to everyone who uses your Mac), or to your Home → Documents → Microsoft User Data folder if you want this template to pertain only to your account.

From now on, this startup template is automatically loaded to every Word document you open. In other words, this global template isn't automatically unloaded when you quit Word.

Creating an AutoSummary

Open the document you wish to summarize; choose Tools → AutoSummarize. Word immediately gets to work, compiling a list of key words in your document and flagging the sentences that contain them. Since it may take some time, especially in a long document, kick back and watch some TV. If nothing's on, you can press ⌘-period to cancel the process.

When Word's behind-the-scenes work is done, it presents you with a dialog box like the one in Figure 7-16.

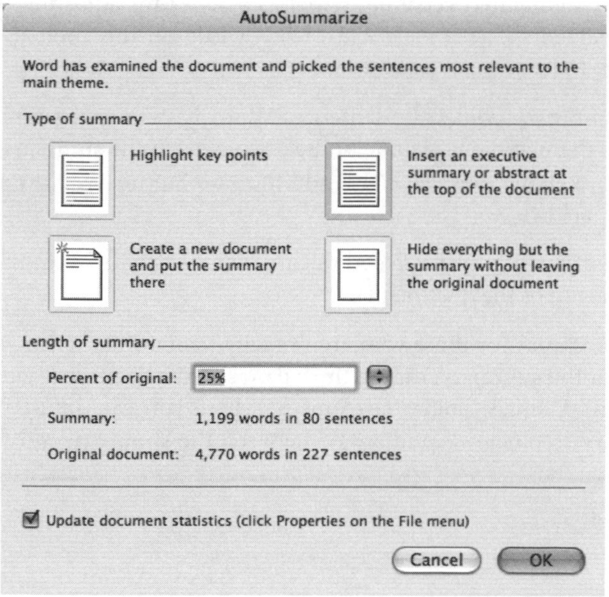

Figure 7-16:
If you've filled in the Keywords and Comments boxes on the File → Properties → Summary tab, uncheck the "Update document statistics" box here. Otherwise, Word will replace your keywords and comments with its own keywords and summary.

Type of summary

The icons under the "Type of summary" heading let you choose how you want Word to display the summary it has generated:

- Click **Highlight key points** if you'd like to scroll through your document and see which sentences Word flagged as being key points for inclusion in the summary as in Figure 7-17. This option is an effective way to see how Word has interpreted your document.

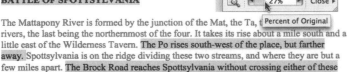

BATTLE OF SPOTTSYLVANIA

🔍 ◀ 27% ▶ Close ▶

Percent of Original

The Mattapony River is formed by the junction of the Mat, the Ta, rivers, the last being the northernmost of the four. It takes its rise about a mile south and a little east of the Wilderness Tavern. The Po rises south-west of the place, but farther away. Spottsylvania is on the ridge dividing these two streams, and where they are but a few miles apart. The Brock Road reaches Spottsylvania without crossing either of these streams. Lee's army coming up by the Catharpin Road, had to cross the Po at Wooden Bridge. Warren and Hancock came by the Brock Road. Sedgwick crossed the Ny at Catharpin Furnace. Burnside coming by Aldrich's to Gates's house, had to cross the Ny near the enemy. He found pickets at the bridge, but they were soon driven off by a brigade of Willcox's division, and the stream was crossed. This brigade was furiously attacked; but the remainder of the division coming up, they were enabled to hold their position, and soon fortified it.

About the time I received the news of this attack, word came from Hancock that Early had left his front. He had been forced over to the Catharpin Road, crossing the Po at Corbin's and again at Wooden Bridge. These are the bridges Sheridan had given orders to his cavalry to occupy on the 8th, while one division should occupy Spottsylvania. These movements of the enemy gave me the idea that Lee was about to make the attempt to get

Figure 7-17:
The only way to really interpret Auto Summarize's results is by using the "Highlight key points" summary. This way, you can see Word's summary in context as you flip through the document. This view displays a tiny toolbar (upper-right) that lets you switch between the highlighted view and the Hide everything view, and adjust the percentage of the original included in the summary.

When you click OK, your document appears with yellow highlighting on certain sentences. You also get a tiny toolbar containing a button for toggling between the summary and the highlighted version, as well as a slider for adjusting the length of summary percentage (see page 235). Click Close on this toolbar to return your document to its original condition.

- **Insert an executive summary** copies the sentences Word has chosen as representative and displays them at the *beginning* of the document. If the summary is either too long or too sketchy, press ⌘-Z to undo the AutoSummary. Now see "Length of summary" below.

- **Create a new document** opens a blank Word document and puts the summary there (instead of at the top of the document).

- **Hide everything** is the choice for those who aren't ready to commit. When you click OK, it shows you the summary, hiding the balance of the document without actually closing it. A small toolbar also opens, where you can adjust the length of the summary (see below), and toggle between the summary and the full document.

- Under **Length of summary** at the bottom of the dialog box, Word shows you the length of the summary relative to the full document. The default setting is 25 percent, which means that the summary is exactly one-quarter the length of the document as a whole. When you change the percentage and then click OK, the AutoSummarize dialog box goes away, and Word re-creates the summary according to your whims.

Fields

The concept of *temporary placeholders* is one of humankind's greatest inventions. When your car has a flat, the spare acts as a somewhat undersized stand-in for the tire, supporting the car until the new tire is in place. When technicians set up the lighting for a particular Hollywood movie scene, a low-paid extra models patiently, so the highly paid star doesn't have to while the technicians fiddle with shadows. When a magazine designer doesn't yet have the photo that will go on page 25, he'll simply place a box there in the correct size and label it FPO (for position only), with the intention of replacing it with the finished photograph when it's ready.

In Word, *fields* are temporary placeholders that stand in for information that may change or may come from another location on your hard drive—the current date, a page number, a place you've bookmarked, the name of a Word file, and so on. Fields, in fact, are the basis of some of Word's most powerful features. They let you:

- Create form letters and address labels, and merge them with your contact information (see page 262).
- Create indexes (page 255) and tables of contents (page 249).
- Create invoices that calculate their own totals (page 238).
- Create cross-references (page 246) and captions (page 242).

Inserting Fields

You can't *type* a field into a document. You have to ask Word to create it in one of the following ways:

- Choose a command that creates a field. These are usually found on the Insert menu, such as Insert → "Date and Time".
- Choose Insert → Field and choose one of the available field types from the Field dialog box (see Figure 7-18).
- Press ⌘-F9 and type the field *code,* if you know it. (The field code is a short piece of code that tells Word what kind of information will go there.)

You may never have to create a field manually. Most of the time, fields are built right into a Word feature or another command. For instance, when you choose Insert → "Date and Time", Cross-reference, Bookmark, Footnote, or Caption, Word uses a field to define the location and content of these features.

However, there are hundreds more fields at your disposal in Word, and inserting them is as easy as choosing them from a list in the Field dialog box.

Building fields in the Field dialog box

To place a field where the insertion point is located, choose Insert → Field to open the Field dialog box as shown in Figure 7-18. Because there are so many fields in Word, the program displays them in category groups. When you click a category in the left box, the list of fields in that category appears in the right box.

When you click a field name on the right side, the field code appears in the "Field code" box below (DATE in Figure 7-18 example). A more complete description appears in the Description panel near the bottom of the dialog box. You can learn a lot about fields just by clicking and reading the descriptions.

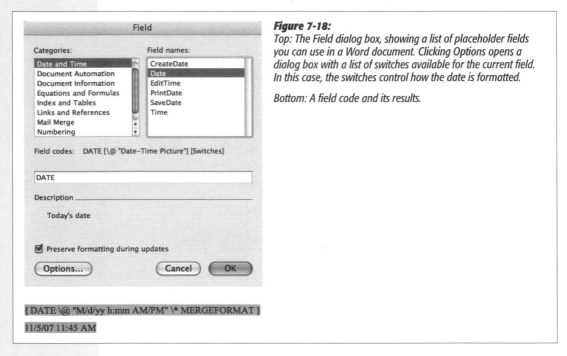

Figure 7-18:
Top: The Field dialog box, showing a list of placeholder fields you can use in a Word document. Clicking Options opens a dialog box with a list of switches available for the current field. In this case, the switches control how the date is formatted.

Bottom: A field code and its results.

Modifying Fields with Switches

The Field dialog box has an Options button that lets you specify in more detail how you want a field to look and act. When you click it, the Field Options dialog box displays any applicable *switches* (software options), as shown in Figure 7-19. Like the Field dialog box, the Field Options dialog box has a Description panel below the "Field code" box; as you click each option, its description appears. You can read more about switches in the following tutorial.

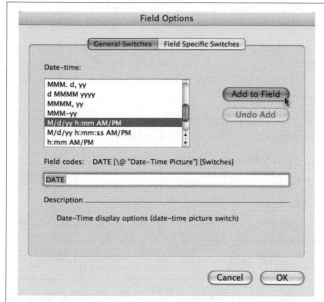

Figure 7-19:
Depending on the field you're modifying, the Field Options dialog box may show one Options tab or, as shown here, or two Switches tabs. A switch is an instruction that modifies the field results. In this case, Date-Time switches tell Word how to display the current date and time. Click "Add to Field" to add the selected item to the Field code.

As you build a field by adding switches or other options, you see the field code grow in the "Field code" box at the bottom of the Field dialog box. (Field veterans can type directly into this box, using the syntax shown above the box as a guide.)

Tip: If you know a thing or two about field codes, you can also edit them directly in the document. Just Control-click in the field code, choose Toggle Field Code, and edit away.

When you've selected any options or switches, click OK (or press Return) to dismiss the Field and Field Options dialog boxes. Word returns you to your document, now containing the newly minted field. If you click it, Word highlights the field in dusky gray. The highlighting alerts you to the fact that you're looking at a field rather than normal Word text, and disappears when you click somewhere else.

Tip: If you'd rather see fields highlighted at all times, you can make them permanently gray. (The high-lighting doesn't show up when you print.) Choose Word → Preferences → View button. Choose Always from the "Field shading" menu. Caution: If you choose Never, it will be much harder to tell where fields are. And since you can't edit field text as ordinary Word text, confusion may ensue.

What a Field Does

A field is a bit of computer code that, in one way or another, processes information. For instance, a Caption field remembers what number a caption is supposed to be, and displays that information (see page 242). The field code has all the computerish instructions that tell Word how to figure out the Caption number and then format it. In another example, a Merge Field code (see page 235) tells Word what piece of information to grab from a database. Finally, a Date field retrieves the date from your Mac's System Preferences and places it in your document.

For example, suppose you're creating a fax cover sheet you plan on using every day. Since you keep forgetting to date your faxes, you want to create a document with a Date field in it. That way, when you fax your daily dispatch, it's automatically dated. Here's the process:

1. **Open a blank Word document and begin typing your fax cover sheet. Click wherever you want to place the date. Choose Insert → Field.**

   The Field dialog box opens, as shown in Figure 7-18.

2. **Click "Date and Time" in the Categories box (left) and "Date" in the Field Names box.**

   You actually have two options here. *CreateDate* inserts today's date, which is what you'll always see. *Date* updates automatically; it inserts the current date each time the document is printed. In this case, you obviously want the current date each time.

3. **Click Options. Choose your favorite Month/Day/Year combination from the list box, as shown in Figure 7-19.**

   The date codes aren't exactly in common English, but there is a logic to them. In general, a single letter in one of these codes (M) stands for a number (1 for January, and so on), and a repeated letter (MMMM) stands for a full version (*January* spelled out).

4. **Click "Add to Field", and then click OK twice.**

   The date appears in your document. When you click it, it appears highlighted in gray to indicate that it's a field, not a typed-in date.

5. **Save your document.**

   You could also save this document as a template. The Date field works either way.

Working with Fields in a Document

Once again, Word 2008 lets you have it your way about how field text looks, updates, locks down, and prints out. To change the text formatting for a field, select the entire field by dragging across it (either the field results or the field code, whichever is showing at the moment), and then use any of Word's formatting commands: press ⌘-I for italics, choose a font or font color from the Formatting Palette, and so on.

Tip: If you format fields this way, make sure that the "Preserve formatting during updates" box is turned on in the Field dialog box (see Figure 7-18, top). Otherwise, the field will revert to its original formatting whenever you *update* it (see below).

Displaying fields

When you look at a field in your document, you may see one of two things: the field code (which looks like intimidating gobbledygook) or the result of the field code (see Figure 7-18, bottom). For example, when you insert the DATE field into a document, it might show up either as {DATE\@"m/D/YY"*MERGEFORMAT} (the field code) or simply *5/25/09* (the result).

If you're seeing one of these but you'd rather see the other, Control-click the field and choose Toggle Field Codes from the shortcut menu.

Or, to switch *all* fields in your document from field codes to their results, press Option-F9.

Updating fields

Because fields are just placeholders, the information that eventually fills them will change from time to time. The date changes, for example, or you may change your user information (which affects AUTHOR fields).

Word doesn't automatically update fields *while a document is open.* In other words, if you leave a document open for two days, the date fields in the documents won't reflect the actual date. However, if you close that document, Word updates the date fields upon opening. To update fields in open documents, press ⌘-A (selecting an entire document automatically selects all the fields in it) and press Shift-Option-⌘-U. A quick way to update a single field is to Control-click it and choose Update Field from the shortcut menu.

Tip: If you like, Word can update your fields automatically each time you print. The secret is to choose Word → Preferences ▸ Print tab and turn on the "Update fields" box.

Locking, unlocking, and unlinking fields

There will be times, especially when you send someone else a copy of your document, when you really don't want anyone to change your carefully planned field codes. To protect a field from changes, click in it and press ⌘-F11. This keystroke *locks* the field, meaning that you can't update the field or edit its code. You can still format the field results, however. (To lock all fields in the document at once, press ⌘-A, then ⌘-F11.) To unlock a field, thus enabling updating and editing again, select it and press Shift-⌘-F11.

If you *really* want closure on a field, you can end its life as a field—freeze it in time forever with its current results. To do so, click in the field and press Shift-⌘-F9. Unlinked from its code, the field is now ordinary Word text; it's no longer a field, and will never be automatically updated.

Field printing options

Normally, you'll want to print your document with the field results; you want people to see a date, not { DATE MMMMd, yyyy *\ MERGEFORMAT }. However, it is possible to print out a copy that shows the field codes, so that a technical-type person can look them over, for instance. To do so, choose Word → Preferences → Print panel and turn on the "Field codes" checkbox (under "Include with document").

Bookmarks

Bookmarks in Word are the digital equivalent of folding down the page's corner or underlining a paragraph that you want to refer to later. You can use bookmarks in long documents as you write them, perhaps to mark places that need more work later. They're also useful in Word documents you get from others, to mark places that you have questions about, or pages that you're going to use most often. And because you give each digital bookmark a *name,* it's easy to jump to specific spots in a long (or even short) document.

Adding Bookmarks

Select the word, phrase, or paragraph you want to bookmark, or just click in the text at the appropriate spot. Choose Insert → Bookmark (or press Shift-⌘-F5), and assign your bookmark a name in the "Bookmark name" box (see Figure 7-20). When creating a name, adhere to these parameters: Be descriptive and specific; use underlines instead of spaces (Word, in its ornery way, doesn't permit spaces in bookmark names); use numbers, if you like, but not as the first character; and don't exceed 40 characters.

Click Add or press Return when you're done.

Deleting Bookmarks

To delete one or more bookmarks, press Shift-⌘-F5 or choose Insert → Bookmark, click the name of the bookmark you want to discard, and click Delete. Of course, your other option is to delete the text or graphic object (if any) that the bookmark is attached to. When the text or image goes away, the bookmark goes with it.

Navigating by Bookmark

After you've scattered bookmarks throughout your document, you're ready for the fun part: leapfrogging from one bookmark to another, skipping all the extraneous stuff in between. Your choices are to take Word's word for it that you're at a bookmark, or make all bookmarks visible on the Preferences → View panel, as described above.

Note: What you see when you leap to a bookmark depends on what you did when you created it. If you had highlighted text or graphics before choosing Insert → Bookmark, that text or object is selected when you jump to it. If you had only clicked in some text *without* highlighting anything, you get a blinking insertion point at the bookmark when you jump to it—that's all.

- **Use the Bookmarks dialog box.** To go directly to a bookmarked location, press Shift-⌘-F5 or choose Insert → Bookmark; the Bookmark dialog box lists all the bookmarks you've created. Double-click the name of a bookmark. The insertion point moves to the selected bookmark; the Bookmark dialog box remains open so that you can repeat the process. Press Return (or click Close) to dismiss it.

- **Use the Go To command.** Another way to travel to a particular bookmark is to press F5, ⌘-G, or choose Edit → Go To. Each of these actions opens the Go To tab of the "Find and Replace" dialog box (see page 53). In the "Go to what" list box at left, click Bookmark and choose a bookmark name from the menu at right. Click Previous and Next to jump around by bookmark.

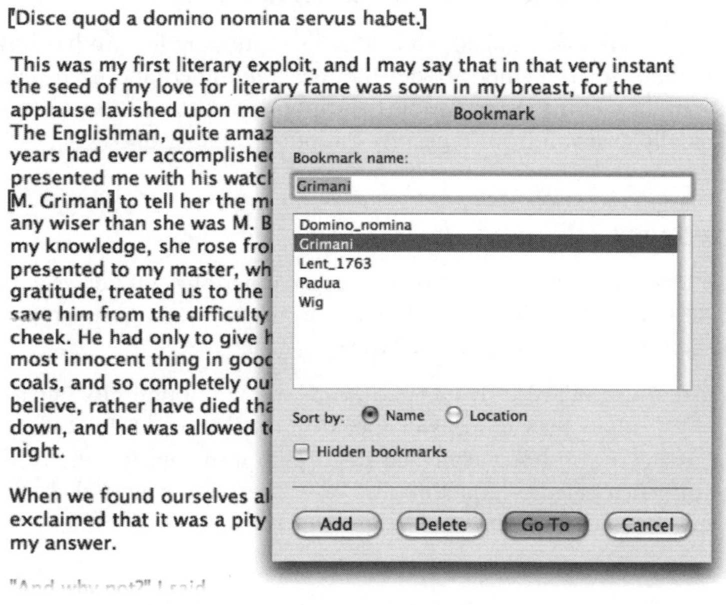

[Disce quod a domino nomina servus habet.]

This was my first literary exploit, and I may say that in that very instant the seed of my love for literary fame was sown in my breast, for the applause lavished upon me

Bookmark

Bookmark name:

Grimani

Domino_nomina
Grimani
Lent_1763
Padua
Wig

Sort by: ● Name ○ Location

☐ Hidden bookmarks

Add   Delete   Go To   Cancel

Figure 7-20:
Back: Bookmarks in a document are represented by heavy brackets if you've turned on that option in the Word → Preferences → View panel.

Front: All bookmarks you've inserted appear in the Insert → Bookmark dialog box, which is also where you name new bookmarks. (If the Add button is grayed out, you've typed an invalid name; backspace and try again.)

- **Use the Navigator buttons.** Start by using the Go To procedure described above to jump to the first bookmark. Now you can close the Find box and use the Navigator Buttons (page 53) to move forward and backward through your bookmarks, or press the keyboard shortcuts, Shift-page down and Shift-page up, instead.

Tip: When using the Bookmark dialog box, checking the Hidden Bookmarks box adds cross-references (see page 246) to the bookmark list. Now you can use the Bookmark dialog box and the Go To feature to browse your cross-references.

Viewing Bookmarks

Bookmarks are invisible; even the Show/Hide (¶) button on the Standard toolbar or Formatting Palette doesn't uncover them. If you really want to see where they lie on your document, choose Word → Preferences → View tab; turn on the Bookmarks checkbox. (To hide them again, just turn off the box.)

When visible, text bookmarks are surrounded by thick brackets; location bookmarks appear as big, fat I-bars.

Captions

Captions are labels that identify illustrations, tables, equations created by Microsoft Equation Editor, and other objects by number (see Figure 7-21).

Most people type in captions manually, but Word's captioning feature has huge advantages over the manual method: It can number, renumber, and even insert captions automatically. Letting Word handle the captions not only saves you time, but could potentially save you from repeating a caption number or leaving out a caption entirely.

Inserting Captions

To caption an item—table, picture, text box, or some other object—first select it, then choose Insert → Caption. Instead of typing a caption, you *build* it using the Caption dialog box, as shown in Figure 7-21, top.

- **Caption, Label.** You can't directly edit the words in the Caption box (such as "Figure"), which is how the caption will appear in the document. Instead, this box reflects whatever you select from the Label pop-up menu. If none of the three labels provided (Figure, Equation, Table) strikes your fancy, click New Label and type your own—*Illustration* or *Chart,* for instance—and hit Return.

- **Position.** This pop-up menu lets you choose one of the two most popular places for the location of your caption: above or below the captioned item.

- **Numbering.** Word numbers your captions automatically; this feature, after all, is the whole point of the exercise. Use the Numbering dialog box, as shown in Figure 7-21, middle, to choose a number format (Roman numerals or whatever).

  If you choose to include the chapter number in the captions (perhaps before the hyphen—"Figure 7-20," as in this book, for example), you need to tell Word how to *find* the chapter numbers. A couple of conditions apply: All the chapters need to be within the same document, and you have to use one of Word's built-in chapter-heading styles (see page 127) for the chapter headings.

Caption

Caption: Figure 1-1 Giacomo Casanova 1725 – 1798

Options

Label: Figure ⬍   New Label...

Position: Below selected item ⬍   Delete Label

Numbering...

AutoCaption...   Cancel   OK

Caption Numbering

Format: 1, 2, 3, ... ⬍

☑ Include chapter number

Chapter starts with style: Heading 1 ⬍

Use separator: – (hyphen) ⬍

Examples: Figure II–1, Table 1–A

Cancel   OK

Figure 7-21:

Top: Select a graphic and then choose Insert → Caption to call up the Caption dialog box. Word inserts the label and number; you type the rest of your caption text.

Middle: If the chapter headings in your document use one of Word's built-in heading styles, you can make Word automatically number your figures 1-1, 1-2, 1-3, and so on by turning on the "Include chapter number" checkbox. The Examples line shows what the caption will look like on the page.

Bottom: A caption in place. Note that if you're planning to import your Word document into a desktop publishing program, you'll probably lose your captions. The text of the captions may appear, but the numbering will likely be lost.

nazed at my answer, said that no boy of eleven
hed such a feat,
, and presented
other, inquisitive
Griman] to tell her
but as the abbe
he was M. Baffo
. Surprised at my
n her chair to get
d presented to my
g how to express
ed us to the most
in order to save
f paying her a
her cheek. He had
of kisses, the
ocent thing in
oor man was on
mpletely out of countenance that he would, I

Figure 1-2 Giacomo Casanova
1725 – 1798

For instance, suppose you've formatted all your chapter headings using the Heading 1 style. Furthermore, suppose you've autonumbered them as described on page 103: you chose Format → "Bullets and Numbering" → Outline Numbered tab and selected one of the numbering styles with Heading 1, Heading 2, and so on. Now, when you turn on the "Include chapter number" box and choose Heading 1 from the pop-up menu, your captions include the correct chapter number. (And your chapter headings are automatically numbered, to boot.)

When you finish creating the caption, click OK. The caption (numbered 1) appears in a separate paragraph above or below the selected object. As you insert more captions, Word will number them in order. (*Deleting* or rearranging captions is another matter, however, as described below.)

Adding Text to Captions

If the caption for your bird picture reads "Figure 1," you can simply click after the 1 and type a description, such as *Blue-footed Booby.*

If you accidentally type over or delete the label or caption number, hit ⌘-Z (or choose Edit → Undo Typing) to restore order. If it's too late to Undo, then your only alternative is to delete and reinsert the caption. The document's captions may then need to be updated (see below).

Tip: A neat way to add supplementary text to captions is to click the caption and choose Insert → Caption; you can then type the extra text in the Caption window itself. This technique produces a caption that you can't edit in the document itself.

Deleting and Editing Captions

To delete a caption, select it and press Delete. To change a single caption—for example, to change "Figure 1," to Table 1 and leave all the other Figure captions untouched—you have to delete the caption and insert a new one as described above.

Word's captioning feature makes it exceptionally easy to change *all* captions of the same label at once. For example, if your document has a series of captions labeled "Figure 1," "Figure 2," and so on, you can easily change them to the more descriptive Photo 1.1, Photo 1.2, and so on. Just select any of the captions (be sure to select the *entire* caption) and choose Insert → Caption to open the Caption dialog box. Now you can choose a different label, create a new label, pick a different numbering system, and so on. Any changes you make will apply to *all* captions under the original Figure label.

Note: Technically, captions are *fields,* which are described in full on page 235. So if you've used captions in your document, you may start to see strange-looking codes like { SEQ FIGURE *ROMAN } instead of the caption. Don't be alarmed—and don't delete them! What you're seeing is Word's *field code*—its own, internal geek instructions for creating the caption. You need to tell Word to display the field *results*—the caption itself—instead. To do that, Control-click the field code and choose Toggle Field Codes from the shortcut menu. Or, to return *all* caption field codes to normal, press ⌘-A (or choose Edit → Select All), Control-click any single field code, and *then* choose Toggle Field Codes. (Be sure to press Control *before* clicking, otherwise you'll undo the Select All.)

Updating Captions

When it comes to automatic caption numbering, Word's fairly good at counting—but not infallible. When you delete a caption or drag one out of sequence, the others don't get renumbered automatically. If you want your figures numbered sequentially, you have to *update* the captions after making such a change.

To update a single caption, select it by selecting all of its text; then press Shift-Option-⌘-U. (Alternatively, Control-click the caption and choose Update Field from the shortcut menu.) Updating all captions in a document at once couldn't be easier: Just press ⌘-A (Select All), then Shift-Option-⌘-U.

AutoCaptioning

Inserting captions is easy enough, but you can make it downright effortless. Word's AutoCaptioning feature can automatically add a caption to any chart, equation, or table whenever you add one to your document. Here's how it's done:

1. **Choose Insert → Caption; in the dialog box, click AutoCaption.**

   In the AutoCaption dialog box, you're presented with a list of checkboxes for the kinds of objects Word can automatically create captions for—an equation, a table, a Microsoft Organization Chart, and so on.

   Note· AutoShapes are *not* on the list. Captions for AutoShapes and other drawing objects have to be inserted manually; fortunately, Word still numbers them correctly along with all those created automatically.

   ---

2. **Turn on the boxes—as many as you wish—for the kinds of graphics you want captioned.**

   You can have more than one kind of label in your document, and you can choose different object types for each one. For example, use "Table A" for tables and "Figure 1," for pictures and charts. To do so, turn on the "Microsoft Word Table" box and go onto step 3; choose "Table" for the labels. Then repeat the procedure, turning on the boxes for the items you want the "Figure" label applied to. You can have as many kinds of labels AutoCaptioned at once as you like, provided you can keep them all straight in your head!

3. **Using the pop-up menus, choose a label and a position for the captions.**

   When you check a box as described in step 2, you may notice that the Label menu changes. Word is suggesting a label for that type of object. You can override it by making a different choice from the Label menu.

   The label and position choices here work as described on page 275; as always, you can create new labels by clicking the New Label button.

4. **Choose a numbering style for the AutoCaptions.**

   If you're using more than one type of caption label, each can have a different numbering style.

5. **Click OK.**

Now insert the pictures or tables in your document. The captions will appear automatically.

Turning AutoCaptions Off

To turn AutoCaptioning off, choose Insert → Caption, click AutoCaption, and uncheck the boxes for the captioned objects. Existing captions stay put, but no new ones will be added automatically.

Cross-References

Long, technical, or scholarly documents—or computer manuals—frequently contain phrases like "see Chapter 12" or "see Figure 8, on page 112." These are *cross-references*—words that refer the reader to another place in the document. Of course, you can always type your own cross-references—but what a mess you'll have when you decide to cut a few pages from the first chapter, and all 1,424 of your cross-refs now point to the wrong page numbers!

Word stands ready to create smarter cross-references that update themselves no matter how you edit your document. What starts out saying "See page 24" will change automatically to say "See page 34" after you insert a 10-page introduction.

Remember these two principles as you start on the road to cross-reference nirvana:

1. **Word thinks of cross-references as pointing to *objects* in your document, not places.**

   In other words, a cross-reference has to be connected to a figure, a bookmark, or a heading.

2. **Cross-references can only refer to something within the same document.**

   If you're creating a document with multiple chapters, you have to combine them into one Master Document (see page 200) before working with cross-references.

Inserting Cross-References

When creating a cross-reference, start by typing appropriate lead-in text into your document: *See, Turn to, As shown in,* or whatever you like. Then it's time to get Word involved.

Here, for example, is how you might build a cross-reference that reads, "See Figure 1, below" (see Figure 7-22).

1. Type *See Figure;* then choose Insert → **Cross-reference.**

   The Cross-reference dialog box appears.

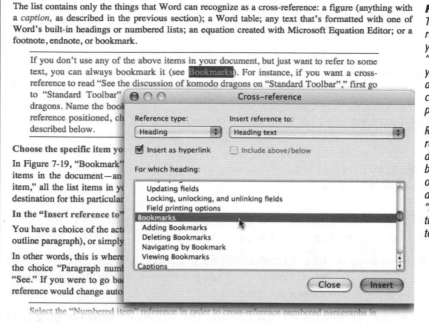

The list contains only the things that Word can recognize as a cross-reference: a figure (anything with a *caption*, as described in the previous section); a Word table; any text that's formatted with one of Word's built-in headings or numbered lists; an equation created with Microsoft Equation Editor; or a footnote, endnote, or bookmark.

If you don't use any of the above items in your document, but just want to refer to some text, you can always bookmark it (see Bookmarks). For instance, if you want a cross-reference to read "See the discussion of komodo dragons on "Standard Toolbar"," first go to "Standard Toolbar" [...] dragons. Name the book[...] reference positioned, ch[...] described below.

Choose the specific item yo[...]

In Figure 7-19, "Bookmark"[...] items in the document—an[...] item," all the list items in y[...] destination for this particular[...]

In the "Insert reference to"[...]

You have a choice of the act[...] outline paragraph), or simply[...]

In other words, this is where[...] the choice "Paragraph num[...] "See." If you were to go ba[...] reference would change auto[...]

Select the "Numbered item" reference in order to cross-reference numbered paragraphs in

Figure 7-22:
Top: A clickable cross-reference in place. When you click the phrase "Field Printing Options," your document scrolls automatically to the corresponding paragraph.

Right: The Cross-reference dialog box displays all the headings, bookmarks, figures, or other landmarks in your document. Clicking the "Insert as hyperlink" box turns the cross-reference text into a clickable link.

2. **Make a selection from the "Reference type" pop-up menu.**

   The list contains only the things that Word can recognize as a cross-reference: a figure (anything with a *caption,* as described in the previous section); a Word table; any text that's formatted with one of Word's built-in headings or numbered lists; an equation created with Microsoft Equation Editor; or a footnote, endnote, or bookmark.

Tip: If you don't use any of the above items in your document, but just want to refer to some text, you can always bookmark it (see page 240). For instance, if you want a cross-reference to read "See the discussion of komodo dragons on page 30," first go to page 30 and bookmark the paragraph where you talk about komodo dragons. Name the bookmark "komodo dragons." Now go to where you want the cross-reference positioned, choose Bookmark in the "Reference type" menu, and continue as described below.

---

3. **Choose the specific item you're cross-referencing in the "For which" list box.**

   In Figure 7-22, "Heading" is the chosen reference type; the "For which" box lists all the heading items in the document—a computer software manual in this case. If you had chosen "Numbered item," all the list items in your document would appear, and so on. From this list, choose the correct destination for this particular cross-reference.

4. **In the "Insert reference to" menu, specify what type of item you want the reference to point to.**

   This is where you tell Word what you want the cross-reference to *say*. In Figure 7-22, the choice "Heading" places the selected heading text in the cross-reference after the typed word "See." If you were to go back and rewrite that heading in the manual, the text in the cross-reference would change automatically.

Note to attorneys: Select the "Numbered item" reference in order to cross-reference numbered paragraphs in legal documents. The "Paragraph number (no context)" and "Paragraph number (full context)" options in the "Insert reference to" menu were created just for you. "Full context" names a cross-referenced paragraph by the entire string of outline numbers: 1. (a) (i), and so on. Use "no context" to refer to the same paragraph simply as (i).

   You have a choice of the actual text (of the caption or paragraph), the number (of the page, list item, or outline paragraph), or simply "above" or "below."

   If *above/below* isn't one of the choices on the "Insert reference to" menu, turn on the "Include above/below box" to add "above" or "below" to the end of the cross-reference, as shown in Figure 7-22.

   Thereafter, no matter where you move the referenced item—as long as it's within the same document—Word will change "above" to "below," or vice versa, as necessary.

5. **Click Insert or press Return when you're done creating the cross-reference.**

   Word inserts the cross-reference field in your document; it appears as *See Figure 1, below* in a gray box, an indication of its field status.

Modifying and Deleting Cross-References

To change a cross-reference (perhaps you've changed a figure or divided your document into two shorter ones), just select it, choose Insert → Cross-reference, and modify the settings. You can, for example, change a cross-reference to "Figure 2" instead of "Figure 1".

To delete a cross-reference, select it and press Delete. (When selecting a cross-reference, drag over only the shaded part, as shown in Figure 7-22; don't include any additional text you've typed.)

Note: You can't create a cross-reference to anything inside a text box (see page 141).

Like captions, cross-references are a type of *field* (see page 235), and also like captions, cross-references can sometimes spontaneously combust. Similarly, you fix them as you would broken captions. For example, if you see some cryptic characters like { REF_Ref372221765\r\p } instead of the cross-reference you were expecting, Control-click the shaded part of the cross-reference and select Toggle Field Codes from the shortcut menu.

Again like captions, Word sometimes misses a few—despite the fact that the program updates cross-references automatically when you move text in your document. Therefore, as part of the finishing touches on any document where you've used cross-references, press ⌘-A and then press Shift-Option-⌘-U. You've just signaled Word to update all cross-references (and captions, for that matter).

Creating a Table of Contents

Word's Table of Contents (TOC) feature saves you time and helps organize your document. Once you've built a table of contents in Word, you can use it to navigate your document (just as you might with the Navigation Pane); you can custom format it to get just the look you want; you can save yourself the task of updating page numbers if you add or delete text from your document (which can be a major pain); and you can use it as a Web site map, because in Online and Print Layout views, a Word Table of Contents is automatically hyperlinked.

TOC the Easiest Way: Using Built-in Headings

If you have a well-organized document, and you've used Word's outliner or one of its built-in heading styles (Heading 1, Heading 2, and so on) to introduce each new topic, Word's TOC feature was made for you. Go directly to step 1 below.

If you wrote your document without headings, on the other hand, insert them before creating the table. (Use Word's built-in heading *styles,* as shown on page 129.) Be descriptive when you design the headings; instead of just "Chapter 10" or "Advanced Techniques," use "Chapter 10: Underwater Architecture" or "Advanced Card-Counting."

When you're ready to deliver a TOC to the first page of your masterwork, proceed as follows:

1. **Click where you want the TOC to begin.**

   To put the TOC on the first page, click at the very beginning of the document. (You can also insert it after a title page or introduction.)

2. **Switch to Print Layout view and click Document Elements in the Elements Gallery to access Word's preformatted text elements, and then click the Table of Contents button.**

   The Elements Gallery displays the thumbnails for pre-designed tables of contents (see Figure 7-23).

3. **Make sure the "Create with" button is set to Heading Styles, and then click one of the thumbnails.**

   Word generates the table of contents and drops it into your document at the insertion point—complete with page numbers (see Figure 7-24).

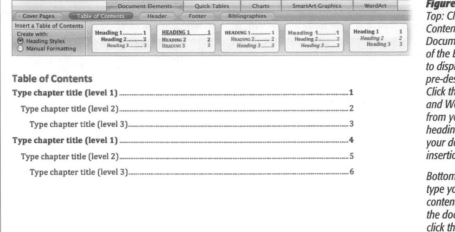

Figure 7-23:
Top: Click the Table of Contents button in the Document Elements tab of the Elements Gallery to display a variety of pre-designed TOC styles. Click the one you like, and Word generates it from your document's headings and places it in your document at the insertion point.

Bottom: If you'd rather type your own table of contents instead of using the document headings, click the Manual Formatting button at the left end of the Gallery, click one of the thumbnails, and replace the dummy text that Word puts in your document with your own.

If you desire more control over the display of your table of contents then the automated Document Elements provide, Word is more than happy to put you in the driver's seat. As before, the first step is to place the insertion point where you want the table of contents to begin and then continue as follows:

1. **Choose Insert → "Index and Tables" → Table of Contents tab.**

   You should now be staring at the "Index and Tables" dialog box shown in Figure 7-24.

2. **Choose a style in the Formats box, as described in Figure 7-24, top.**

   If none of the format styles thrills you, choose "From template" and see "TOC the Harder Way: Using Other Styles" on page 252.

3. **Decide how many levels you want to show, using the "Show levels" control.**

   For example, you may want your table of contents to show only chapter titles; in that case, choose 1 in the "Show levels" box. If you've divided your document into many levels of detail, each with its own heading level, you may want to show only the first two or three levels to keep the table from getting too long. (The table of contents in this book, for example, shows chapter titles and the first- and second-level subject headings.)

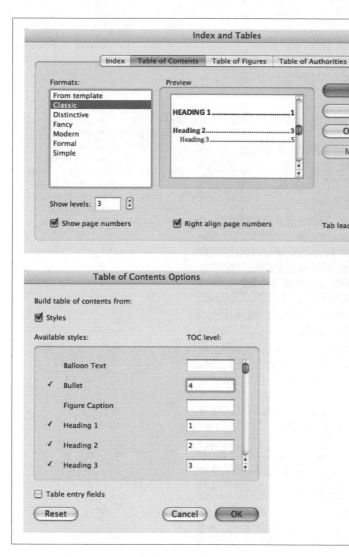

Figure 7-24:
Top: The "From template" format uses the styles in the current document template and results in a consistent appearance with the rest of your document. (See page 127 for more on styles.) Click each one and look in the Preview window; choose the one that makes the best impression.

Bottom: The Options dialog box lets you build your table of contents from styles you've used in your document other than Heading 1, Heading 2, and so on. For instance, you can add the Bullet style to the list and assign it a level so that important list items will appear in the table of contents.

4. **Format the page numbers.**

   Most printed tables of contents include page numbers, of course, but if you're preparing a document for the Web where page numbering is irrelevant, then turn off "Show page numbers."

   If you elect to use page numbering, you can also indicate whether you want them to be right-aligned (as in the Preview window in Figure 7-24, top) and what style of Tab leader you want (the dots, dashes, or lines that connect each title with its page number). The Preview window in Figure 7-24 shows a dotted line, but the "Tab leader" menu offers several other choices.

5. Click OK.

You now return to your document. If you switch into Draft, Print Layout, or Publishing Layout view, you'll see the table of contents, complete with page numbers (see Figure 7-25).

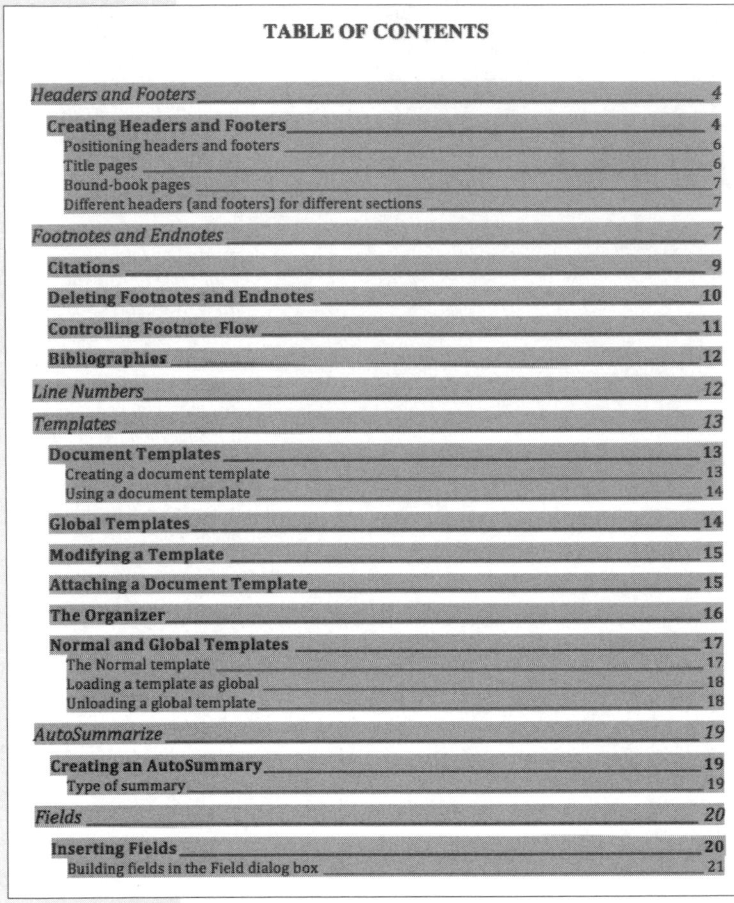

TABLE OF CONTENTS

Headers and Footers 4
Creating Headers and Footers 4
Positioning headers and footers 6
Title pages 6
Bound-book pages 7
Different headers (and footers) for different sections 7
Footnotes and Endnotes 7
Citations 9
Deleting Footnotes and Endnotes 10
Controlling Footnote Flow 11
Bibliographies 12
Line Numbers 12
Templates 13
Document Templates 13
Creating a document template 13
Using a document template 14
Global Templates 14
Modifying a Template 15
Attaching a Document Template 15
The Organizer 16
Normal and Global Templates 17
The Normal template 17
Loading a template as global 18
Unloading a global template 18
AutoSummarize 19
Creating an AutoSummary 19
Type of summary 19
Fields 20
Inserting Fields 20
Building fields in the Field dialog box 21

Figure 7-25:
A table of contents created from the headings in an actual Word document. The gray doesn't print; it simply informs you, the editor: "These are fields, and I, Microsoft Word, will be responsible for maintaining and updating them. Don't try editing anything here yourself."

TOC the Harder Way: Using Other Styles

Life is easiest if you use Word's built-in heading styles (Heading 1, Heading 2…) when preparing your manuscript—but that's not your only option. If you've arranged your document using other styles, whether built-in or ones you've created, you can use those as the basis for your table of contents headings instead. For example, suppose every major section of your document begins with a style you've called FancyHeadline, you can create a table of contents that lists just those headlines. To do so, choose Insert → "Index and Tables" → Table of Contents tab. Follow steps 1 through 5 on page 250, and then click Options.

In the Table of Contents Options dialog box, you see a scrolling list of all styles in your document (see Figure 7-24, bottom). If you scroll down, you'll see that Heading 1, 2, and 3 have been assigned to corresponding TOC levels. Delete the numbers from these heading styles and type new TOC level numbers (1, 2, and so on) into the boxes next to your own styles.

Click OK and return to the Preview box to check your work.

Tip: You can even type each level number next to more than one style. For instance, if you want your captions to be listed in the table of contents under each main topic, like your Level 3 headings, just type *3* in the box next to Caption (as shown in Figure 7-24).

In fact, you don't even have to use different levels. If you make *every* heading style Level 1, every item in your Table of Contents will have equal weight—no indents or typeface changes.

Updating or Deleting a Table of Contents

Like many Word features, TOCs rely on self-updating, noneditable blocks of gray-background text called *fields,* as described earlier in this chapter. If, during an evening of sleepless creativity, you decide to rewrite the names of the different sections in your thesis, it may come as something of a shock to discover that your table of contents still shows the original section names. And if you cut out that 31-page digression into the mating habits of the Venezuelan beaver, you may be surprised to discover that the table of contents page numbers haven't been updated to reflect the new, shorter status of your paper.

The solution is simple: After editing your document and before printing or sending it, update the Table of Contents by *updating* its fields. To do so, click at the left side of the first line of the TOC, and then press Shift-Option-⌘-U.

Tip: The field-editing process *wipes out* any formatting or editing you've done to the text in your table of contents—which is an excellent argument for formatting your TOC using the dialog boxes as described on page 251 instead of formatting them by hand.

To dispense with a TOC, click at the very beginning of the first line of the Table of Contents. Press Option-F9 to display the TOC field code against its gray background ({ TOC\o"1-3" }, for example). Select the entire field code, brackets and all, and press Delete. You've just vaporized all remnants of the Table of Contents.

Tip: You can change the typographical look of your TOC headings just as you would any style (see page 127 for more on styles). Just choose Format → Styles, click the TOC1 style name, click Modify, and proceed as described on page 133. Click OK to return to the Style dialog box. Click the next TOC heading level, click Modify again, and repeat until you've designed a table of contents to call your very own.

Table of Figures and Table of Authorities

Creating a table of figures or table of authorities is very much like creating a table of contents. Word takes captions (for the Table of Figures) or citations (for the Table of Authorities) and compiles them into a table. You can custom design type styles just as in a TOC, and you can update and delete these tables exactly as described above. There are only a few differences.

Table of figures

A table of figures is a list of captions, as opposed to headings. If you've inserted captions for pictures, tables, graphs, or equations in your document, Word can list them, along with their page numbers and tab leaders, just as in a table of contents. The steps for creating one are precisely the same as for creating a table of contents (page 249), except that you click the Table of Figures tab in step 2 instead of Table of Contents.

Table of authorities

Lawyers, legal secretaries, and paralegals: This section is for you. In fact, nobody else is likely to know what a table of authorities *is*. A table of authorities (TOA) doesn't automatically use existing document styles like headings or captions. You have to mark each citation (case, statute, or document) that you want the TOA to use. To create a table of authorities in Word, follow these steps:

1. **In your document, select a citation.**

   For example, you might highlight "Title 37, Code of Federal Regulations, Section 1.56(a)."

2. **Choose Insert → "Index and Tables" → Table of Authorities tab; click Mark Citation.**

   The keyboard shortcut, for the nimble-fingered, is Shift-Option-⌘-I.

3. **Select the current citation type in the Category menu.**

   If you want to use a category that's not shown, click one of the numbers (8 through 16) in the menu. Click Category; then type the new category name in the "Replace with" box. Click Replace, and then click OK.

4. **Edit the text of the citation in the "Selected text" box.**

   Do so only if you want the citation to appear differently in the Table of Authorities. For example, add boldface or underscores.

5. **Type an abbreviated version of the citation in the "Short citation" box.**

   In the next step, Word is going to search for the next occurrence or occurrences of this citation. If you used a specific abbreviation in your document, use that here as well—"Title 37," for instance.

6. **Click Mark or Mark All.**

If you want to go through your document and find citations individually, click Mark and then click Next Citation. To let Word find, and automatically mark, all long and short versions of the current citation, click Mark All. Word marks citations with TA *field codes* (see page 235).

7. **After marking all your citations, click Close.**

The Mark citation box goes away.

When you're done marking the citations, it's time to create the Table of Authorities itself.

8. **Click where you want the Table of Authorities to begin. Choose Insert → "Index and Tables" → Table of Authorities tab. Choose from the category menu.**

You can make a table of authorities for all citations, or create a separate one for each category. If you formatted citations in the "Selected text" box (step 3 above), be sure to turn on the "Keep original formatting" box.

9. **Choose a design in the Formats box and continue formatting your Table of Authorities.**

See the box on page 261 for more detail on formatting.

10. **Click OK.**

If you add a new citation after completing the Table of Authorities, it's easy. Just select the new citation, press Shift-Option-⌘-I and follow steps 3 through 7 in the first set of instructions above.

To update a Table of Authorities, click at the very beginning of the table and press F9. The same rules apply as described in "Updating or Deleting a Table of Contents," on page 253.

Indexing

Although Microsoft may hate to admit it, even with its new Publishing Layout view, few people actually use Word to publish books. Most "real" books may be *written* in Word, but they're usually then poured into a page-layout program like Quark XPress or InDesign for the rest of the process.

That doesn't stop Microsoft from wishing its word processor were up to the challenge, though. As evidence, here's Microsoft's indexing feature, which can spew forth a professional-looking index for a document, complete with page numbers, subentries, and the works. (The operative word, however, is *can;* indexing involves considerable patience and tolerance on your part. As you'll soon find out, indexing often involves a descent into Word's sub-basement of field codes—a pseudo-programming language that's not intended for casual experimentation.)

Phase 1: Create Index Entries

As smart as Word 2008 is, it can't read your document and ascertain what the important topics are; you have to tell it which concepts you want indexed.

You do so by reading over each page of your document. Each time you come to an important point that you want included in the index, perform the following steps:

1. **Select the word or phrase that you want to index.**

   For instance, in a book about birds, you might want to create an index entry for *eggs*. So you'd highlight the word *eggs* in the manuscript.

2. **Press Shift-Option-⌘-X.**

   You could also choose Insert → "Index and Tables" → Index tab and then click Mark Entry in the dialog box—but life's too short.

   Shift-Option-⌘-X is a keystroke well worth learning (or redefining to something easier—see page 768), since you'll be using it often. It opens the Mark Index Entry dialog box with your selected word in the Main entry field, as shown in Figure 7-26. This field represents exactly how it will appear in the index, so, for example if you want your entry capitalized, or not, make it so here.

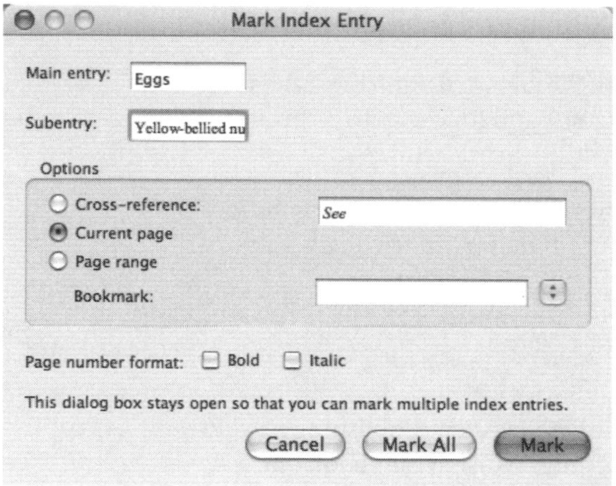

Figure 7-26:
The index entry for the term you highlighted doesn't have to match the text you highlighted. If you'd rather have this index entry say Omelettes instead of Eggs, for example, feel free to type right over the proposed "Main entry" text here.

3. **Choose Bold or Italic for the page number, if you like.**

   Use this feature to make the principal mention of the indexed term boldface or italic. This will make it stand out from the rest of the page numbers for the same term—to indicate a page where an illustration appears, for example (Eggs, 9, 11–13, *34*, 51–52).

4. **Specify a subentry, if applicable.**

   For instance, if the material on the current page is mainly about yellow-bellied nut hatch eggs, you may want the index to show "yellow-bellied nuthatch" as a subentry under "eggs" (see Figure 7-26). Type *Yellow-bellied nuthatch* in the Subentry box. Word assumes that you want this particular phrase indexed as a subentry under "eggs" (or whatever your main entry was in step 1).

5. **Click Mark to create an index entry for your selected word or phrase.**

   If you click Mark All instead, Word creates an index entry for *every* occurrence in the document of the word or phrase you selected in step 1. (The fact that it flags only the *first* occurrence in each paragraph is actually beneficial, since the entry maybe repeated frequently in a paragraph. The purpose of the index is to direct the reader to the correct paragraph or page; to index each occurrence would create an overly long, cumbersome index.)

Note: Mark All is case-sensitive. In other words, Mark All will create entries for each occurrence of *eggs,* but not *Eggs.*

---

6. **Highlight the next entry in your document.**

   Unlike just about any other dialog box you've ever run across, this one remains open even after you click Mark or Mark All. However, to move on to the next entry, you have to select another word or phrase and then press Shift-Option-⌘-X again.

7. **Proceed through your entire document, marking each entry you want in the index by highlighting it and then pressing Shift-Option-⌘-X.**

   A *field code* (see page 235) appears in your document after each term you've indexed. Because these fields are formatted as *hidden text* (see page 100), Word automatically turns *on* the Show/Hide button on the Standard toolbar. That's why you see line breaks, paragraph breaks, and any other hidden text in addition to the index field codes.

8. **Click Close.**

   Now you're ready to build the index as described on page 259.

Cross-references

A cross-reference in an index looks like this: "Eggs, *See reproduction.*" It tells your reader: "*You* may be looking under Eggs, but actually I've listed all of these entries under Reproduction." (Of course, if you create a cross-reference for "reproduction," you have to actually create index entries for that topic!)

To create a cross-reference, follow the steps above, but before clicking Mark Entry in step 3, type the cross-referenced term into the "Cross-reference" box. The word "See" already appears in the "Cross-reference" box; you can type text after it (or over it). For instance, you can change it to "See also" or just "also."

Page range entries

Occasionally, the information related to your index entry spans several pages, like this: "Eggs, 9–19." Unfortunately, Word requires that you *bookmark* the range of pages before creating the index entry. To do so:

1. **Select the entire block of text that you want indexed, even if it's many pages long. Choose Insert → Bookmark; name the bookmark in the "Bookmark name" box, then click Add.**

   You can name the bookmark anything, because this name doesn't affect the index entry name. If this is the first mention of eggs in the document, for example, you could call it *Eggs1*. After you click Add, the Bookmark dialog box closes. (See page 240 for more on bookmarking.)

2. **Back in your document, click at the end of the selected bookmark text.**

   This tells Word where to mark the index entry field. (If you don't see the bookmark brackets around the text, turn on Bookmarks on the Word → Preferences → View panel.)

3. **Press Shift-Option-⌘-X.**

   The Mark Index Entry dialog box appears.

4. **Type the index entry, but then click "Page range." From the pop-up menu, choose the name of the bookmark you just created.**

   This menu lists all the bookmarks you've created so far in the document you're indexing.

5. **Click Mark and continue creating index entries, if you wish.**

When you later create the index, the range of pages you bookmarked will appear next to the index entry.

Phase 2: Editing Index Field Codes (Optional)

Like many Word features, Word's indexing feature relies on *fields* (invisible placeholders, as described on page 235). Because index entry fields are marked as hidden text (page 100), you can only see them when the Show/Hide (¶) button located on the Standard toolbar (or Formatting Palette) is on. At that point, the indexing codes show up, looking something like this: { XE "eggs-FIXME(WDEND)eggs1" }. In other words, if you'd like to see the field codes—so that you can delete them, edit them, or just see where they are—click ¶ on the Standard toolbar or the Document section of the Formatting Palette.

Once you've made your field codes visible, you can edit or delete them. To delete an index entry, select it by dragging over its field code (including the brackets), and then press Delete. Unless you want to fool around with editing field codes, deleting an entry is also the easiest way to *edit* an entry; after deleting the faulty field codes, simply create a new replacement entry, as described on page 256.

If you're unafraid to edit field codes directly, however, here's how to edit the four kinds of index field codes:

- **Single page entry (eggs, 234)**. The field code looks like { XE "eggs"\b }. If you mis-spelled the main entry, made an error in capitalization, or whatever, you can edit the word between the quotation marks. But be careful not to disturb any other part of the code, including the spaces. Also, in this example, the *b* after the back-slash indicates boldface; an *i* here stands for italic. To change a boldface page number to plain text, for example, delete both the letter *b* and the backslash.

- **Cross-reference entry (eggs, *See* reproduction)**. The field code looks like { XE "eggs"\t "*See* reproduction" }. In addition to editing the main entry, you can also change the cross-reference (reproduction) or the additional text (*See*). Again, be careful not to disturb any other part of the code.

- **Page range entry (eggs, 234-236)**. The field code looks like { XE "eggs-FIXME(WDEND)Eggs1" }. This one's tricky to edit, because in order to change the range bookmark name (see "Page range entries" on page 258), you have to type in the *exact* name of the bookmark. However, you can change this into a single-page entry by deleting the bookmark name with its quotes, the back-slash, and the *r*. And, of course, you can edit the main entry name.

- **Subentries (eggs, robin's, 21)**. The field code looks like { XE "eggs:robin's" }. The main entry is before the colon, the subentry is after. You can edit either one, and also create additional layers of subentries just by adding another colon followed by another subentry, and so on.

Phase 3: Building the Index

Once you've marked index entries in the document you're indexing, you can generate the index itself, as follows:

1. **If the field codes in your document are showing, turn off Show/Hide by clicking ¶ on the Standard toolbar to hide them.**

   This step ensures that your document is paginated correctly. When field codes are showing, they take up room just like extra words and throw off the page numbers.

   Most of the time, you'll want to insert a page break or section break just before the index, so that the index will begin at the top of a new page. Then:

2. **Click in your document where you want the index to begin. Choose Insert → "Index and Tables" → Index tab.**

   The "Index and Tables" dialog box opens, as shown in Figure 7-27.

   Choose a Type radio button to specify the layout of your subentries.

   If you click Indented, each subentry appears indented under the main entry. If you click Run-in, all entries in the index are flush left. (Watch the Preview window for an example of each.)

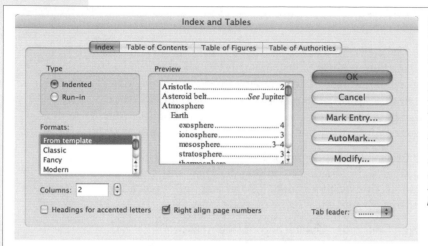

Figure 7-27:
The "Index and Tables" dialog box previews the index you're about to create. If the Preview in your copy of Word–or, indeed, the final index itself–shows text that's cramped and hard to read, you need to click the Modify button and adjust the Index1, Index2, and Index3 predefined styles to clearer fonts and paragraph spacing.

3. **Choose a Format from the Formats list.**

   If you choose "From template," Word uses your current template's *styles* (page 127). To see what the other canned index designs look like (Classic, Modern, and so on), click each and view the results in the Preview window.

4. **Choose a number of columns in the Columns box by clicking the arrows or entering a number.**

   You can choose one, two, three, or four columns per page. To save space, most indexes use a multiple-column format. If your document already *has* columns, choose Auto to make your index match the same number of columns.

5. **Turn on "Right align page numbers" to move the page number out to the right margin of the page or column.**

   Turning this on affords you the option of using a *tab leader* (dots or dashes between the entry and its page number), as shown in Figure 7-27. Choose it from the small pop-up menu at the lower right.

6. **Click OK.**

   Word creates an index. This will take a few minutes, especially if your document is long. You can stare at the watch icon or go get a snack.

Phase 4: Cleaning Up the Index

Once Word has finished building the index, you can edit it as you would any text. You can also revisit it in any of these ways:

- **Reformat the index.** Click the index and choose Insert → "Index and Tables"; in the resulting dialog box, you can change any of the options on the Index tab, as described above. (Because you clicked the index first, any changes you make will apply to it, even though this dialog box normally creates a *new* index.)

AutoMarking Long Documents

If your document is very long, reviewing it can be an exercise in tedium. Although the Mark All button helps, Word's AutoMark feature can accelerate the process even further. However, this feature is only worth using on very long documents—maybe 100 pages or more—because it entails an extra step that has its own brand of tedium: creating a concordance file.

A concordance file is a Word document with a two-column table that you create yourself from a blank document. In the first (left) column, you type the text you want Word to look for and mark in your document. In the right column, you type the index entry itself, which may not necessarily be the same term. (Using this technique, you can index, under printing, five pages of discussion about dot-matrix printers, laser printers, fonts, and ink cartridges; the actual word printing may never appear in the text.)

Another example: You could type egg, eggs, Egg, laying, reproduction in the left column (each in its own cell), and

eggs directly across from each in the right cell (as shown here). (To create a subentry, use a colon, also depicted in the illustration.) At the end of this exercise, Word will find each word in the left column and index it under the term you've specified in the right column—all of the sample terms shown here, for example, will be indexed under "eggs."

After logging each important term in your document this way, save and close the concordance file. Then open the manuscript document. Click at the end of the document, and then choose Insert → "Index and Tables" → Index tab.

In the resulting dialog box, click AutoMark. Navigate to your concordance file and open it. Word automatically places index entry fields in the document; you can see them highlighted as you scroll through it. If you missed any major topics, just create another concordance file and repeat the process. Now build your index as described on page 259.

- **Update the index (Shift-Option-⌘-U).** If, after sleepless nights of soul-searching, you decide to edit your document by inserting or deleting text, Word doesn't automatically update your index; all of its page numbering is now off. Similarly, if you decide to add, delete, or edit some index entries themselves, they won't be reflected in the index you've already generated.

  The solution, either way, is to click in your index and press Shift-Option-⌘-U. Word updates the index; as when you created the index, this will take some time.

- **Deleting an index.** To remove an index from your document, click it and press Option-F9 (it will be represented as a field code). Select and delete the entire field code to delete the index.

Tip: Deleting the index doesn't delete the index *entries* you've marked in your document. Usually, leaving them in place does no harm, since they're marked as hidden text and generally don't print or show up onscreen. But if you need a genuinely clean document, use the Replace command described on page 57. Using the Special pop-up menu, choose Field and replace it with nothing. Word will neatly extract them from your file.

Mail Merges

If the term *mail merge* is new to you, it may be because "mail merge" is a kinder, gentler euphemism for its result: *form letters.* Or maybe it's because you're familiar with Microsoft's previous name for this function: data merge. In any case, a mail merge grabs information from a database and uses that information to automatically fill in the blanks of a Word file, as in, "Dear <<name>>, As a fellow <<city>> resident, I thought you might be interested in contributing <<income>> to our fundraiser." In this example, a mail merge can effectively churn out what seem to be personal, individually written letters. Merging data can also create labels, envelopes, or a catalog.

Having Office 2008 on your Mac puts you at a definite advantage: You get to use all of Word's document-beautifying features (see Chapter 3) to write the placeholder letter, and you have your choice of programs to organize the data. You can use an existing Excel file, your Entourage Address Book, a FileMaker Pro database, or a Word table to supply the data you want plugged into the generic letter.

The placeholders Word uses when you write the letter are *fields* (see page 235). And because fields can process information like computer code, Word mail merge documents are very powerful. For example, you can set them up to prompt you for information before proceeding with the merge ("What dollar amount to ask for?").

To make these interactive functions easier to use, Office 2008 offers the Mail Merge Manager. Just as the Formatting Palette consolidates dozens of different formatting features, so the Mail Merge Manager also collects and automates the features you need for four of the most popular merges: form letters, labels, envelopes, and catalogs.

Preparing Data Sources

Before you begin your mail-merge experience, decide what computer document will contain the *source data*—the names and addresses for your form letters and envelopes, for example, or the items and prices in your inventory database that you'd like to merge into an attractive catalog.

The most common data source is a database of names, addresses, and other personal information. Office 2008 can grab data from Word tables, tab-delimited text files (such as ASCII), Excel files, the Entourage address book, or FileMaker Pro databases.

As you delve into merges, you'll need familiarity with two important pieces of database terminology: *records* and *fields.* A *field* is a single scrap of information: a phone number or a shoe size. (This *database* field isn't quite the same thing as the gray-text placeholder *Word* fields described earlier in this chapter—although the database kind of field will indeed be represented by a Word field in your form letter.) A *record* is the complete set of fields for one form letter, mailing label, or envelope—the name, address, phone number, and so on.

Tip: Whether you create a new database for your merge or use an existing one, make sure that each record is set up the same way. If you're using a database where the first and last names are in separate fields in some cases and together in others, you're going to have trouble getting the merge to work properly.

Creating a New Data Source

Let's say you have a bunch of application slips filled out by kids signing up for your hockey lessons, and you want to write each student a welcome letter. However, you don't have the database in electronic format yet. The easiest way to start a data source file is to launch Word and choose Tools → Mail Merge Manager. What you'll see is something like Figure 7-28.

The list of database fields you'll need depends on what you plan to say in the form letter. In the example in Figure 7-28, the coach realized that she'd need the date, first and last name, address, shoe size, school grade, the instructor name, and the entrance where the student's hockey class would gather for its first meeting. A few fields already in the database for other purposes—phone number, for example—won't be used in this letter; that's OK.

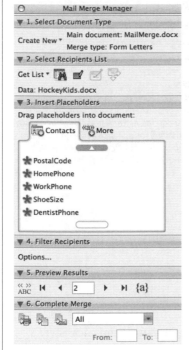

Figure 7-28:
The mail-merge feature of Word isn't a shining example of simplicity. But the section structure of the Mail Merge Manager palette, which looks a lot like the Formatting Palette, at least makes the steps sequential. The file name and main document type appear here—in this example, it's called MailMerge.docx (see it near the top?). So does the database you've selected (see it in the Select Recipients List?). At the very bottom are the controls you use to actually perform the merge. If you want to abandon the main document and start again, choose Create New → "Restore to Normal Word Document" on the Mail Merge Manager.

To create a data source for your project, proceed as follows:

1. **Open the main document.**

    "Main document" means the file that will contain the letter itself—the text that won't change from one printout to the next. Choose Tools → Mail Merge Manager, if the palette shown in Figure 7-28 isn't already open.

2. **On the Mail Merge Manager's top pane, marked "1. Select Document Type," choose Create New → Form Letters.**

    Along with form letters, Word also lets you create labels, envelopes, or a catalog. Continue working your way down the numbered panes of the Mail Merge Manager.

3. **On the Mail Merge Manager's Select Recipients List section, choose Get Data → New Data Source.**

    As you can see from the pop-up button, Word comes ready to access information from your Office (Entourage) Address Book, a FileMaker database, or other data file—or to create a new list of data from scratch. That's what you'll be doing in this example.

    The Create Data Source dialog box appears, as shown in Figure 7-29. It has a list of suggested fields for form letters. Edit the list of fields by adding and changing fields you need, or removing fields you don't, also as shown in Figure 7-29.

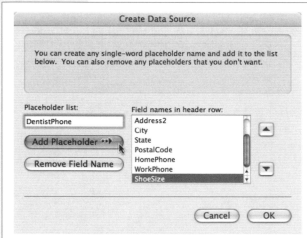

Figure 7-29:
Scroll through the "Field names in header row" box and click "Remove Field Name" for any you don't plan to use. To add fields you'll need for your hockey letter (DentistPhone, for instance), type them in the "Field name" box and click Add Field Name. Note that Word doesn't permit spaces in field names.

4. **Click OK. Name the database (*Hockey Kids*, for instance) and click Save.**

    You've just created a Word document with a table containing the fields you created in step 3 above, that will hold all your data.

Now you're confronted with a Data Form window like the one shown in Figure 7-30. It's time to play fill-in-the-blanks; use this dialog box to type in the information for each kid in your class. (Alternatively, you can choose File → Open, open your Hockey Kids document, and add rows to the Word table you'll find there. See page 150 for full details on working with tables).

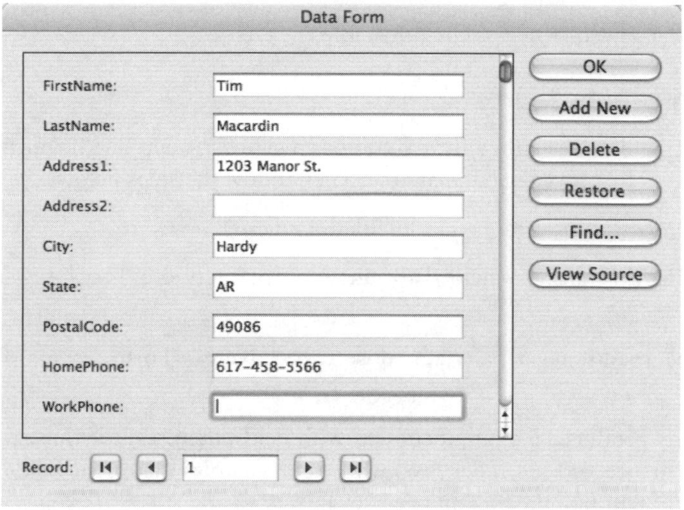

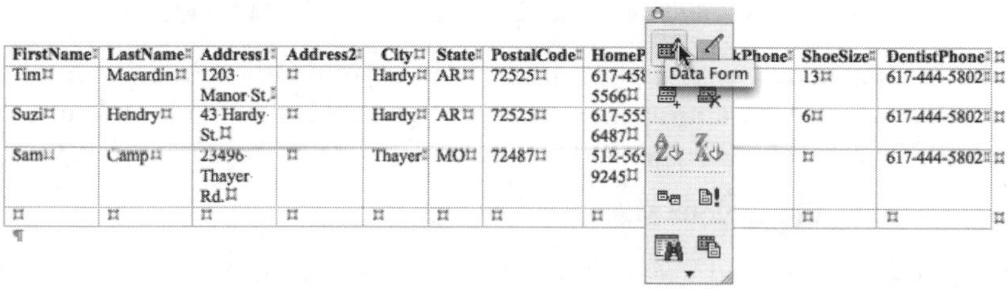

Figure 7-30:
Top: When entering data in a Data Form you can click View Source at any time and see all your data in table form. This data source is a regular Word document you can see any time by choosing File → Open.

Bottom: When working on the data source document you can return to the Data Form dialog box at any time by clicking the Data Form button on the Database toolbar.

5. **Enter the first kid's name, address, and other bits of information, pressing Tab to jump from blank to blank. Click Add New to save the first record and clear the form for the next set of data.**

   Click Delete to "backspace" over the record you just entered; click Restore to bring it back. The counter at the bottom reminds you where you are; use the navigation buttons to move backward and forward through the records.

6. **When you're finished typing in the data, click OK.**

   A list of the fields you've created appears on the Mail Merge Manager (see Figure 7-28).

To add more records to your data source at a later time, you have two alternatives. As mentioned above, you can open your Hockey Kids document, and add rows to the Word table you'll find there. You can also click the Edit Data Source button in the Select Recipients List section of the Mail Merge Manager palette, to pull up the Data Form shown in Figure 7-30, top. Once the data source is open, you can use the Database toolbar to sort and edit it. (If you don't see this toolbar, choose View → Toolbars → Database.)

You're ready to perform the merge; skip ahead to page 270.

Using an Existing Data Source

To merge an existing database into a form letter or envelopes, say in FileMaker Pro or Excel, you have to first save the database file. Then follow the steps below:

1. **Open your form letter (or create a new blank document).**

   If the Mail Merge Manager palette isn't already open, choose Tools → Mail Merge Manager.

2. **On the Mail Merge Manager palette, choose Create New → Form Letters (for this example).**

   If you've already produced a main document with fields, then add to your existing database a first record (a header row) whose entry names match the fields in your main document (see the box on page 267).

3. **On the Mail Merge Manager, choose Get List → Open Data Source.**

   If the existing database is in FileMaker Pro or your Office Address Book in Entourage, choose the appropriate command from this pop-up button instead. (You need a copy of FileMaker Pro on your Mac for that option to work.)

4. **Navigate to the file on your Mac and click Open.**

   You're ready to proceed. If you haven't written your form letter yet, go to the next section. When both your form letter and data source are ready, go to page 269.

Creating the Main Document

When you're ready to write the actual form letter, you have a choice—like thousands of Publishers' Clearinghouse Sweepstakes form letter writers before you. You can either use an existing Word file as the body of the Mail letter, or start from scratch.

To showcase the power of fields in a mail merge document, here are the steps used to create the letter shown in Figure 7-31, bottom. In the Mail Merge Manager, make sure the flippy triangle next to Insert Placeholders is pointing downward and click the Contacts tab, so that you can see the fields available in your data source. (If you haven't selected or created a data source, see "Creating a new data source" on page 263 or "Using an existing data source" above.)

Header Rows and Header Sources

To set up a mail merge, you have to insert fields from a database called the *data source* into the form letter or document. The data source usually takes the form of a table where each column's name appears at the top (Name, Address, Phone, and so on). In fact, that's exactly what the steps described on page 263 do—they lead you through the construction of a correctly formatted Word table. (You could just as easily make your own Word table by hand, as long as the first row contains the field names and subsequent rows contain the records you want to merge.)

To know where to place what data, Word relies on the table's column names (like First, Last, and Phone), located in the header row. In other words, when Word comes to the FirstName field in the main document, it plugs in the next name from the FirstName column of the data source.

When creating a data source and main document from scratch, as described on page 266, your header row automatically matches the fields in your main document. If you're using an existing data source with a main document that already has fields, you can change the top row or first record of the data source to match—usually. But if you can't edit—or don't want to edit—the existing database, you can still make it match the fields in your main document by creating a separate header source.

To do so, choose Get Data → Header Source → New Header Source. Word opens a dialog box just like the Create Data Source box. The difference is, Word uses the field names you enter here as a substitute top row for your existing database. For example, if the first names are stored in the second field of your database, make FirstName the second field in the separate header source, even if the field is called something else in the database. The header source has to have the same number of fields as the database, even if you don't plan to use them all in your merge.

FirstName	LastName	Address1	HomePhone	ShoeSize	DentistPhone
Tim	Macardin	1203 Manor St.	617-458-5566	13	617-444-5802
Suzi	Hendry	43 Hardy St.	617-555-6487	6	617-444-5802
Sam	Camp	23496 Thayer Rd.	512-565-9245	11	617-444-5802

Figure 7-31:
This data source (top) was created in Excel, and the form letter, ready for merging (bottom), was created in Word. The first row of the spreadsheet is the header row, displaying the field names.

«FirstName» «LastName» ¶
«Address1» ¶
¶
Dear «FirstName», ¶
¶
It's hockey time again. I know that, despite the problem with the parents fighting on the ice, you all are looking forward to the coming season. ¶
¶
We will be practicing at the National Guard Armory (they have agreed to provide security) on Tuesdays and Thursdays at 6:00 p.m. Please come equipped with your gear, your proof of dental insurance, and make sure that your parents have lots of money to pay for all the fundraisers. ¶

1. **Open a new Word document. Type the date, if you like, and then press Return two or three times.**

   You're about to insert the first addressee's mailing address, as is customary in a standard business letter. But you don't want to have to *type* that information— that's *so* 1985. You want Word to fill it in for you, not just on this letter, but on every one of the 44 letters you're about to write and print.

2. **Drag-and-drop merge fields from the Mail Merge Manager palette to place the mailing address into the letter, as shown in Figure 7-32.**

3. **Type** *Dear* **and a space, and then drag-and-drop the FirstName field.**

   Word represents the field (which, when you print, will be replaced by somebody's *actual* first name) using brackets. You should now see, in other words, *Dear <<FirstName>>*.

   If your data source has a field for titles (such as Mr., Ms., or Dr.), you can insert it instead, add another space, and then drag the LastName field: *Dear <<Title>> <<LastName>>*.

4. **Continue writing the letter, drag-and-dropping merge fields as appropriate.**

   See Figure 7-32 for an example.

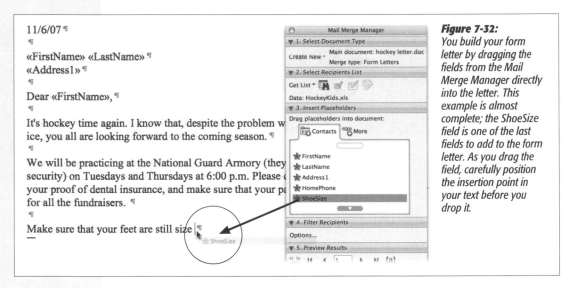

Figure 7-32:
You build your form letter by dragging the fields from the Mail Merge Manager directly into the letter. This example is almost complete; the ShoeSize field is one of the last fields to add to the form letter. As you drag the field, carefully position the insertion point in your text before you drop it.

5. **Insert an Ask field to collect the instructor's name for the letter.**

   Our hapless hockey coach *still* doesn't know who the instructor will be. In fact, she won't know until it's almost time for the letters to go out. Therefore, she'll fill in the instructor's name during the merge itself.

   Here's where the *Fill-in field* comes in. On the Insert Placeholders section of the Mail Merge Manager palette, click the More tab, drag "Fill-in" to the point in the letter where the instructor's name should go. A dialog box appears; in the Prompt box type *What's the instructor name?*, or something else that will help you (or whoever's filling in the forms) remember what was supposed to go there.

   This dialog box also gives you a chance to specify a fallback entry—default text that will appear in the letter in case you don't get the instructor list on time ("name to be determined," for example). If you turn on the "Ask once" box, Word will ask you once for the missing information, then merge it into *all* the letters.

Tip: You may be tempted to use the Fill-in field with abandon, so that Word will ask you, in the process of printing out the form letters, to fill in personalized information for each record. But you can't *see* the records *during* the merge, so you won't have any way of knowing which information should be filled in for each person's letter.

The way to customize the Fill-in field is with a *query* (page 270). For instance, filter the student database by grade and then conduct a separate pass for each, so that you can type a different instructor name for each batch of letters.

---

6. **Finish typing the letter and save the document as usual.**

   Word has inserted field codes for all the merge fields you've just drag-and-dropped. If you'd like to see them, choose Preview Results and click the View all placeholders button ({a}) on the Mail Merge Manager.

Previewing, Formatting, Preparing to Merge

After you've prepared a main document and inserted merge fields, you can see how the document will look with the actual data.

On the Preview Results section of the Mail Merge Manager palette, click the View Merged Data button (ABC). Word shows you the first finished form letter, complete with *Dear Garfinkle* (or whatever the FirstName is in the first record from your data source). Click the arrows in the box on the Preview Results pane of the Mail Merge Manager to browse the other merged records.

In Preview mode, you can make formatting changes to the main document as well as to the merge fields. Just select text or fields in the usual way and use the Formatting Palette to add bold, italic, or other formatting. (When you reformat a field, the change applies to that *entire* field—for *all* documents in the merge.)

Once you've filled and prepared a data source, designed a main document, and outfitted it with merge fields, you're ready to merge. Check the top two panels of the Mail Merge Manager to ensure that the file names of your main and database documents appear correctly. Use the Preview Results feature as described above. Proofread your main document carefully, especially if you have numerous records in your database—you don't want a tiny mistake copied many times over! Finally, do a final save on your main document and your data document.

When everything looks good, Word stands ready to merge your data and your form letter in any of three ways: sending it directly to the printer, merging into a new Word document, or merging into outgoing email messages.

Merging Straight to the Printer

If you've already previewed your merge, simply click the Print button (on the Standard toolbar) or the Merge to Printer button in the Complete Merge pane of the Mail Merge Manager (Figure 7-28). Specify the number of copies you need in the print dialog box and hit Return. Word prints the merged documents on your labels or paper.

Customizing merge printing

The pop-up menu in the Complete Merge pane of the Mail Merge Manager is automatically set to All, meaning that Word will print a merged document for *all* records in your chosen data source. The other choices are Current Record (to print just the record you're currently previewing in the document window) and Custom.

When you click Custom, you can use the From and To boxes below it to specify a range of records to merge. For example, if you have sticky laser labels that come 30 on a sheet, and you just want to print the first page of labels, enter *1* and *30;* Word will print only the first 30 records (that is, one page of labels). For the second page, enter *31* and *60,* and so on.

Query Options

If you want to print nonconsecutive records, use the Mail Merge Manager's Query Options. This feature lets you *filter* your records before merging (choose only the records that meet certain criteria) or sort them into a certain order.

With your main and data source documents chosen in the Mail Merge Manager, turn your attention to the fourth pane labeled Filter Recipients and click Options. The dialog box shown in Figure 7-33 appears. Let's say you want to send a special letter to clients in Baltimore, letting them know that you're going to be visiting their city next month. Your data source contains *all* your clients, even those in San Francisco, whom you obviously don't want to receive the same letter.

Since you're filtering by city, choose the City field on the Query Options → Filter tab and type in *Baltimore* in the "Compare to" box. Set the Comparison pop-up menu to "Equal to". As you can see in Figure 7-33, there are lots of filtering options. You've just completed a query that states, "If the City field is equal to Baltimore, then include this record."

You can even apply more than one query. For example, you could set the second line to read "Or, City, Equal to, Washington." By choosing Or from the first pop-up menu, you also added your clients from Washington to the list—since they're near enough to visit you in Baltimore. When you use the Or pop-up, you're adding more records to your first batch—when you use And, you're further filtering the results of your earlier query. For example, you can filter out the people who have a work phone number *and* who live in your state. You can filter out people who live in Baltimore *or* Washington *and* have a shoe size greater than nine (perhaps you're a traveling hockey skate salesman). Filtering specificity is limited only by your imagination and the data fields you have to choose from.

You may want to use a second Query Option—Sort Records—before printing your merge documents so that the pages that emerge from your printer in some sort of order. For example, you might want them sorted by state for bulk mailing purposes, or sorted by city if you're a traveling salesman.

Click the Sort Records tab in the dialog box Query Options and select up to three sorting criteria by choosing data fields from the Sort by pop-up menus and clicking Ascending or Descending to determine the sorting order (see Figure 7-33).

Click OK when you're done; now you can print the merged documents as described earlier.

Merging to a New Document

Instead of sending your form letters (or mailing labels) to a printer, it's often more useful to have Word generate a brand-new Word document, looking exactly as though a tireless secretary had painstakingly typed up a copy of each form letter with the correct addresses inserted. This is the only way to go if, for example, you want to tweak the wording, adding a personal touch to each outgoing letter independently. You can always print the thing *after* looking it over and editing it.

Creating a new mass form-letter document is easy: After setting up your main document and data source, click the Merge to New Document icon in the Complete Merge pane of the Mail Merge Manager palette. Word churns for a moment and

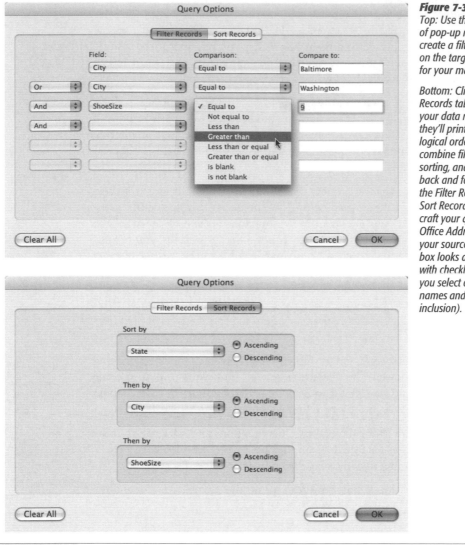

Figure 7-33:
Top: Use this collection of pop-up menus to create a filter to home in on the target audience for your mail merge.

Bottom: Clicking the Sort Records tab lets you sort your data records so they'll print out in a logical order. You can combine filtering and sorting, and you can click back and forth between the Filter Records and Sort Records tabs as you craft your query. (If the Office Address Book is your source, this dialog box looks a bit simpler, with checkboxes that let you select only certain names and addresses for inclusion).

then produces the document (with a page break automatically inserted after each copy of the letter). Save the merge document to your hard drive. Edit, add your personal flourishes, print, or duplicate it just as you would any Word document.

Merging to Email

All this talk about mail merging to a printer using actual paper is so old school—nowadays form letters just as often end up as email messages. And of course Office 2008 comes with a feature that lets you send out form letters by email. Here's how this feature works:

1. **Create a form letter main document and a source document as described on the previous pages.**

   For best results, don't use complex formatting, since some people can only view email as plain text (see Chapter 9).

2. **Click the "Generate e-mail messages" icon on the Mail Merge Manager's Complete Merge.**

   If the button is dimmed, it could be that Entourage isn't selected as your default email program. Open Apple's Mail program, choose Mail → Preferences → General and choose Microsoft Entourage from the Default email reader pop-up menu. Quit Mail and start again from step 1.

   If all is well, the Mail Recipient dialog box opens—as shown in Figure 7-34.

Figure 7-34:
You can choose to send mail-merged email as plain text, formatted text, or as an attachment to a blank message. If you send the letter as a file attachment, the name of your attachment will be the same as the file name of your main document. You may want to rename it for the benefit of your recipients, especially if you have a tendency to give documents unflattering names, like Damn Hockey Season Again.

3. **Using the To pop-up menu, choose the field containing the email addresses. Type a subject for your email message.**

   For example, *Hockey time!*

4. **Using the bottom pop-up menu, specify how you want to send the letter. As text (that is, plain text in the body of the email), as an attachment (which creates a Word attachment on a blank email message), or as an HTML Message (formatted text in the body of the email). Click Mail Merge to Outbox.**

   The Mail merge proceeds as usual: Word asks you to type Fill-in fields, and so on. Entourage opens automatically, and you can watch the boldface digits next to its Outbox skyrocket as Word crams newly generated messages into it. There they wait until you click Send (or until a scheduled Send runs). There's no preview, but you can open any of the merged emails in the Outbox and look at or edit them.

Labels and Envelopes

Two of the most common Word mail merges are automated for you: address labels and envelopes. Either way, this is an extremely powerful feature that lets you combine the database flexibility of your Entourage Address Book with the formatting smarts of Word. Whether you're the local Scoutmaster or an avid Christmas card sender, letting Word prepare your mass mailings beats addressing envelopes by hand any day.

Prepare for one of these data merges as follows:

- Prepare a data source, as described on page 262.

- Know the size of the labels or envelopes you're going to use. Have some on hand as you begin the process. (You can buy sheets of self-adhesive labels at Staples or any other office supply store; Avery is one of the best-known names and the Avery label style numbers are the gold standard of mail merging mavens everywhere. These labels come in every conceivable size and shape; the 30-per-page version—Avery 5160—is the most popular.)

- Set aside some time for trial and error.

Merging onto labels

Make sure that the labels you buy will fit into your printer and feed smoothly— buy inkjet or laser labels, for example, to match your printer.

To create labels, open a new blank Word document and proceed as follows:

1. **Choose Tools → Mail Merge Manager.**

   The Mail Merge Manager palette appears.

2. **On the Mail Merge Manager, choose Create → Labels.**

   The Label Options dialog box appears (see Figure 7-35, top). Unless you're that rare eccentric who uses a dot matrix (impact) printer, leave "laser and inkjet" selected.

3. **From the "Label products" pop-up menu, select the brand of labels you have.**

   Word lists every kind of label you've ever heard of, and many that you haven't.

Tip: If you've bought some oddball, no-name label brand not listed in Word's list, click New Label. Word gives you a dialog box, complete with a preview window, for specifying your own label dimensions. (But before you go to that trouble, look carefully at the fine print on the package, where it probably says something like "Equivalent to Avery 5164.")

---

4. **Inspect your label package to find out what label model number you have; select the matching product in the "Product number" list box. Click OK.**

   The main document becomes an empty sheet of labels. It's time to start dragging field names from your source document.

5. **On the Mail Merge Manager, use the Get List pop-up button to select the database or file containing your addresses.**

   For example, to use your Entourage Address Book, choose Office Address Book from this menu. If your addresses are stored in an Excel spreadsheet or a tab-delimited text file, choose Open Data Source instead (then navigate to your database or data source file and open it).

   If you haven't set up your database yet, choose New Data Source and follow the steps on page 263.

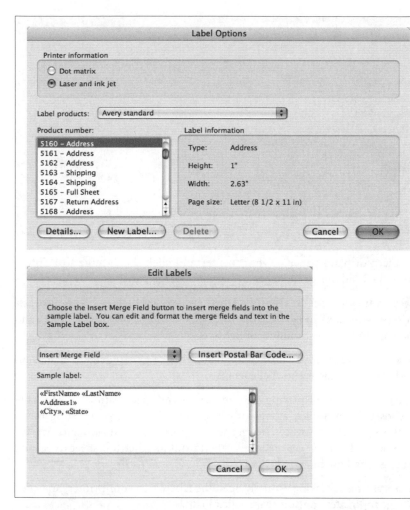

Figure 7-35:
Top: Avery 5160 is one of the most popular label products; it comes with 10 rows of three labels each.

Bottom: If you're assembling a bulk mailing and therefore need to bar code your own envelopes, click "Insert Postal Bar Code." Word asks you to select the name of the merge field where your Zip codes are, then prints the corresponding bar code on each envelope or label. Your mail is likely to reach its recipient faster if you use these bar codes.

6. **In the Edit Labels dialog box that appears, choose field names from the "Insert Merge Field" pop-up menu to build your address.**

    As shown at the bottom of Figure 7-35, use the Space bar and Return key as you go. For example, choose FirstName, insert a space, choose LastName, then press Return to start a new line. Choose City, type a comma if you like, and then choose State; add two spaces before choosing Zip code. (If you want to change the font and other formatting at this point, see the box on page 276.)

7. **Click OK.**

    You return to your main document window, where placeholders for your labels now appear. (Click the <<abc>> icon on the Mail Merge Manager's Preview Results pane to preview the actual names and addresses as they'll be printed.)

    If you want to further format individual labels, you can do so now using the Formatting Palette. Just select the text or the field placeholders to format them.

WORKAROUND WORKSHOP

Formatting Label Text

You can format your labels' text when you're in the Edit Labels dialog box—although it's not immediately apparent how because the formatting palette and menu items are grayed out while this dialog box is opened. But since you committed some of the basic keyboard commands to memory as suggested on page 51, Word stands ready to assist you. Select any or all of the fields—be sure to include the quote marks enclosing each field—and press ⌘-B for bold or ⌘-I for italic.

If your formatting desires extend beyond the basic bold and italics, take heart. Again, select the field or fields you wish to format and then press ⌘-D to summon the Font formatting window. Now you can go to town using all of Word's character-formatting options: font, font style, size, color, character spacing, and so on. Click OK to dismiss the Font formatting dialog box and see your changes displayed in the Edit Labels window. Use the same technique with ⌘-option-M to invoke Word's Paragraph formatting dialog box if, for example, you have a hankering for right-aligned labels.

8. **Load a piece of plain paper in your printer and click the "Merge to Printer" button in the Mail Merge Manager's Complete Merge pane.**

    This way, you can check to see if the labels are properly aligned without wasting an expensive sheet of labels. Hold the paper printout over a label sheet and line them up in front of a window or light.

9. **If you need to tweak your labels' alignment, choose Create New → Labels on the Mail Merge Manager and click Details.**

    A dialog box pops up, displaying the dimensions and specifications of your currently chosen label model, along with boxes and arrows for adjusting them. Adjust the Top margin or Side margin to shift the text up, down, and side-to-side in order to better fit on the labels. Then print another test sheet to be sure your changes had the intended effect.

    When everything's working properly, load the labels into your printer, and click the "Merge to Printer" button again. Click Print.

Tip: Take advantage of the Merge → Custom pop-up menu (see page 270) if you have a long mailing list. Some printers tend to jam if you try to print too many pages of labels at once.

Editing labels

You can edit a label document by opening it, just like any main document. But because of the unique problems involved in changing a sheet of labels, Word provides a couple of special tools. To make changes to an existing label document, proceed as follows:

1. **Open the label document.**

    Word opens the document and the Mail Merge Manager. (If not, choose Tools → Mail Merge Manager.)

---

2. **Click the "Add or remove placeholders on labels" button.**

   It's the third icon in the Select Recipients List section of the Mail Merge Manager palette. The Edit Labels dialog box opens, as shown in Figure 7-35.

3. **Make changes to the label format.**

4. **Add or remove merge fields or change text formatting, for example, by selecting the merge fields and using the Formatting Palette. Click OK and proceed with the merge.**

Yet another way to format labels

You can also edit labels right in the main document, which you may find easier than using the Edit Labels dialog box. The secret is in the "Fill in the items to complete your document" button on the Mail Merge Manager (the fourth icon in the Select Recipients List section of the Mail Merge Manager palette). Here's how to use this method of label editing:

1. **Open the label document; click the *first* label on the page.**

   Word opens the document and the Mail Merge Manager. (If the Mail Merge Manager isn't open, choose Tools → Mail Merge Manager.)

2. **Edit the label document.**

   For instance, you can drag merge fields from the Mail Merge Manager, type additional text, and format the text or field placeholders (font, color, and so on). Remember, you're doing this only in the first label.

3. **Click the "Fill in the items to complete your document" button on the Mail Merge Manager.**

   Word changes all labels on the sheet so that they match the changes you just made in the first label.

   When you're satisfied with the way things look, merge and print the labels as described on the previous pages.

Merging onto envelopes

Printing envelopes on computer printers has always been an iffy proposition; in essence, you're trying to cram two or three layers of paper through a machine designed to print on sheets only one layer thick.

If your printer has guides for feeding envelopes and is envelope-friendly, so much the better. Additionally, you may find that some brands of envelope fit your printer better than others.

When you're ready to begin, open a new blank document and follow these steps:

1. **Choose Tools → Mail Merge Manager, and then choose Create New → Envelopes.**

   The Envelope dialog box opens, as shown in Figure 7-36. If you don't care for Helvetica, Arial, or whatever, click Font to call up a Font dialog box. You can use any of Word's fonts and effects.

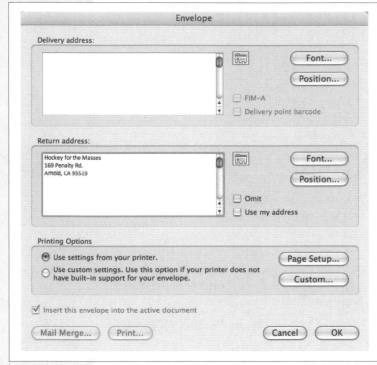

Figure 7-36:
If your return address doesn't automatically appear in the Return Address window, type in the address you want to use in the "Return address" box. Or, you can check the "Use my address" box to pull up the name and address you entered when you set up Office 2008. Turning on Omit will print the envelopes with no return address at all—so you can use preprinted envelopes or use up your supply of stick-on labels from Amnesty International.

2. **Leave the Delivery address box empty, but include a return address if you want one.**

   Type your return address, or turn on "Use my address" to import your address from Entourage, or turn on Omit to leave the return address blank.

3. **Click Position. In the Address Position window, click the arrows to move the return and delivery addresses around on the envelope, if necessary.**

   If the return address is too close to the envelope edges, for example, or the delivery address is too low, now's your chance to fix it.

4. **Click Page Setup.**

   Word opens your printer's usual Page Setup dialog box. Choose the envelope size from the pop-up menu and click OK. (If you don't see the correct size, click Cancel; under Printing Options, click the "Use custom settings" button, then click Custom. In the Custom Page Options dialog box, choose an envelope size and tell Word how you plan to feed it into the printer.)

5. **Click OK, and then OK again to dismiss the Envelope dialog box.**

   Your chosen envelope format appears in the main document; it's time to "type in" the addresses you want to print.

6. **If you want to print just one address from your Entourage Address Book, click the Address Book icon at the upper right of the Delivery Address window, and proceed as shown in Figure 7-37.**

   If you want to run an actual mass printing of envelopes, however, do this:

7. **On the Mail Merge Manager, choose Data Source → Get Data → Open Data Source; select and open your database.**

   Again, Excel spreadsheets, FileMaker databases, and tab-delimited text files are fair game. If you haven't set up your database yet, choose New Data Source and follow the steps on page 263.

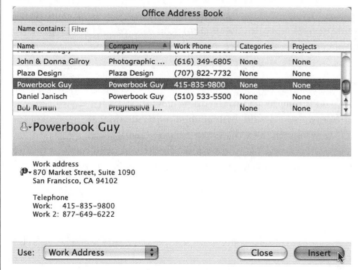

Figure 7-37:
Choose the desired name and address from your Entourage address book, and then click Insert as shown. Close the Address Book to return to the Envelope dialog box, where you can format the envelope.

8. **Drag field names from the Merge Field panel of the Mail Merge Manager into the address box of the envelope in the main document.**

   Add spaces and line breaks in the usual way, as shown in Figure 7-36.

9. **Prepare your printer's feed for envelopes; click Merge → "Merge to Printer". Click Print.**

   If the envelope gods are smiling, your printer now begins to print the envelopes perfectly. (If they're not, then you may discover that you'll have to rotate the envelopes in the paper slot, or worst case, remove the envelope with a pneumatic tool borrowed from your local garage). Depending on your printer model, you may have to print one envelope at a time—if so, choose Current Record from the drop-down menu at the bottom of the Mail Merge Manager.

Macros

A *macro* is like a script: a step-by-step series of commands that Word performs, rapid-fire, each time the macro is run. Although the vast majority of Office fans live quite happily without ever invoking a macro, many power users revel in the efficiency a well-designed macro brings to their computer life, automating a variety of repetitive, tedious tasks. If that describes you, sit down and take a deep breath because Office 2008 brings you some bad news—and some good news.

When Microsoft rewrote Office 2008 as a Universal Binary program—one that will run efficiently on the new Intel Macs as well as the older PowerPC Macs—they had to make some very basic changes to the way the program operates. Most obvious is the new XML file format introduced by Office 2007 for Windows. Less obvious, but much more shocking to some, is the fact that Office no longer uses Visual Basic for Applications, or VBA—the programming language that controlled the wizardry of Word macros. In its place is AppleScript—Mac OS X's system-wide scripting language—support for which is better than ever in Office 2008. With AppleScript, you can do nearly everything you could do with VBA. Additionally, AppleScript extends scriptability to the system and the rest of your programs, allowing multi-application macros. (See page 769 for much more about Apple-Script, VBA, macros, and Office automation.)

You'll still find Tools → Macros in Word 2008. Choose it to open the Macros dialog box. But instead of the macro recorder you may be looking for if you're used to earlier versions of Word, you'll find instead just a list of dozens of Word commands. Here you'll find commands to, for example, change text alignment, add borders, draw shapes, check spelling, and so on. Select the macro name, read what it's supposed to do in the Description box, and then click Run to perform it.

Moving Beyond Text: Publishing Layout View

From the beginning, Word's mission as word-processor extraordinaire has been to put text elegantly on the page—with a modicum of page-layout ability. Word 2008 inaugurates a new era. Apparently having mastered text, Word is moving on to master the page.

Word's new persona debuts as the Publishing Layout view—a way of approaching pages as an assembly of objects instead of a flow of text. Word isn't trying to take over the job of professional page-design software like Quark XPress or Adobe InDesign. Instead, it aims to fill the gap between those programs and Word's regular word processing abilities. Reach for Publishing Layout view anytime you need to put together a stylish newsletter, classy brochure, or quick poster.

By starting with one of dozens of professionally designed templates, you can plug in your own text and pictures and have a polished document in a short time. You can change as much or as little about the templates as you choose to—or start with a completely blank page. You can also incorporate sounds and videos if your document is destined to be viewed on a computer instead of the printed page.

Note: Pushing pages full of pixels around in Publishing Layout view can tax the processing power of any Mac—notably G4 systems. You'll notice this especially when resizing or repositioning text boxes or pictures: the response on screen can lag behind your cursor inputs by several seconds. Make the best of your old G4 by quitting unnecessary programs, and installing as much RAM as you can afford. On the other hand, if you're looking for a reason to upgrade to one of the new Intel Macs, Word 2008 gives you a good one.

Templates: Ready-to-Use Page Designs

For artists, writers, and page designers, nothing is as frightening as a blank page. Thanks to Word's Publishing Layout View templates, fear of the blank page is a thing of the past. (Good riddance vacansopapurosophobia!) Although you *can* start with a blank canvas when the creative juices are raging, don't be shy about reaching for one of Word's templates to give you a jump-start (see Figure 8-1).

JULY 2008

CSU
Summer Arts

Fresno State University, July 7 – 25, 2008

Hot? Not!

Yes, it's true—Fresno State is now air conditioned! Gone are the fans and swamp coolers and in their place state-of-the-art air-conditioning systems that keep every indoor space at a comfy 59 degrees.

Summer + Fresno + Photoshop = A Lot of Hot Shots

Yes, it does get warm in Fresno in the summer, but the heat has never wilted the spirits of the students attending one of Mark Larson's whirlwind photography workshops!

This year magazine photographer Alfred Eisenstaedt shares his tips for getting the best candids—and his conversion to digital.

The second week features lab work with Photoshop guru Edward Weston, who will reveal his 15 favorite plug-ins!

Of course the air conditioners actually make the air outside much hotter and create a Fresno-sized hole in the ozone layer, but you'll forget all about that once you're inside swaddled in sweaters and long underwear.

Hot Fun in the Summertime!

Candids	Photoshop	Printing
Week One	**Week Two**	**Week Three**
Shooting great candids with available light isn't easy. Alfred Eisenstaedt opens up a stop.	Unravel the mysteries of filters, blend modes, and layer masks with Edward Weston.	The cry of *"Laissez le bon temps rouler"* means printmaster Dominic Effers is in da house!

Figure 8-1:
With Word's Spring Newsletter as the starting point, this kind of page is easy to put together. All you have to do is replace the placeholder text and pictures, making some font changes, and changing the picture size.

Tour of a Template

The next few pages present an overview of choosing and using Word's Publishing Layout view templates—and the Publishing Layout view itself. The rest of the chapter fleshes out the topic in depth, including starting a document from scratch and saving and sharing your own templates.

Choosing a Template

You can open a new Publishing Layout view document template from the Project Gallery or—if you're already working in Publishing Layout view—from the Elements Gallery (see Figure 8-2).

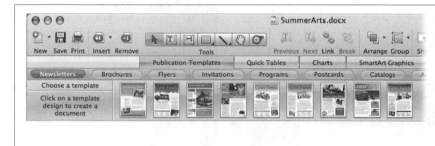

Figure 8-2:
The Publication Templates section of the Elements Gallery displays thumbnail views of all available templates. Choose the type of document you want to create by clicking the buttons for newsletters, brochures, flyers, invitations, and so on; then click one of the thumbnail images to open a new document based on the template.

1. **To open the template from the Project Gallery, choose File → Project Gallery.**

   The Project Gallery appears. Click the New tab, and then click the various categories in the list to display their document thumbnails. Click the flippy triangles that appear next to some of the categories to reveal their subcategories. The categories leading to Publishing Layout view are Events, Flyers, Marketing, Newsletters, Calendars, CD Labels, and Programs.

Tip: If you're already in Publishing Layout view, click the Elements Gallery's Publication Templates tab just below the toolbar to reveal the publication templates thumbnails—arrayed in the Elements Gallery (Figure 8-2). Or, to start from scratch with a blank document, choose the Blank Documents category and click the Word Publishing Layout thumbnail.

---

2. **Double-click one of the Template thumbnails to open it. (To follow along with the example on these pages, choose the Spring Newsletter.)**

   A new document based on the template opens in Publishing Layout View, displaying the workspace, content tabs, and toolbar that are unique to this view (see Figure 8-3).

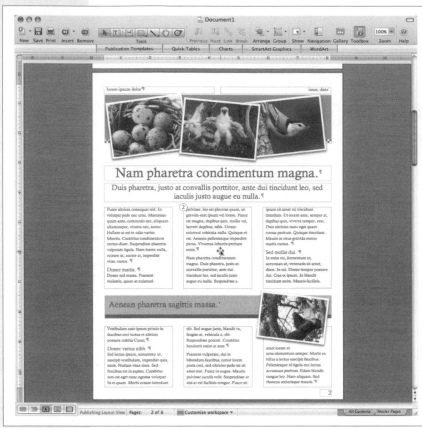

Figure 8-3:
By choosing View → Show → Outlines, you can keep better track of your text-box layout. This page uses a set of six linked text boxes; the cursor is over the second box in the series, which temporarily displays a number indicating its position in the lineup. The Status bar at the bottom of the window shows what page you're on and has the pop-up menu for customizing the workspace—the "worktable" on which the pages lie—as well as the tabs to shift from the normal All Contents view to the Master Pages view (page 312).

If you're used to word processing with plain text, your first glimpse of one of Word's carefully designed page layout templates can be a shocker. Although the eye-catching layout looks like the product of a skilled designer using a professional page-layout program like InDesign or Quark, it's actually created entirely in Word by harnessing the power of the new Publishing Layout View.

Similar to its Notebook Layout cousin, Word's Publishing Layout view displays its pages the way they might look in real life—on an attractive tabletop background with the look of real wood. If you don't like designing your pages while they're laid out on oak, click the Customize Workspace pop-up menu at the bottom of the window and choose a different background. If you want the least conspicuous background, choose Industrial, Aluminum, or Titanium.

Word's designers created the first page of the Spring Newsletter by using background images, text boxes, photographs, and a photo with a transparent background. You can get a better idea of how they constructed the page by choosing View → Show → Outlines (see Figure 8-3).

The layout outlines reveal that this page is composed of a collection of text boxes arranged on top of a couple of background graphics (which are actually on the Master Page, described on page 312). All three of the photos are JPEG graphics, rakishly rotated to give the newsletter an informal look. Two of the pictures display a white border or stroke (page 749), the flower has a transparent background (page 311) and overlaps one of the other photos (page 308), and they all sport drop shadows (page 751) to help give the two-dimensional newsletter a three-dimensional feel. Finally, the "Save the Date!" text box uses a color fill.

Lorem Ipsum Dolor?

Besides the design, the first thing you'll notice about this template is that this newsletter seems to be about spring-time in ancient Rome. Actually, the text used in this template–and in all Publishing Layout view templates–is *placeholder text,* intended to be replaced by whatever text you wish to place there. Typesetters call this kind of place-holder "Greek text"–even though the standard filler is derived not from a Greek text but from a 2000-year-old *Latin* treatise on ethics by Cicero, *De Finibus Bonorum et Malorum (The Extremes of Good and Evil).*

Designers use this dummy text when creating layouts so that (non-Latin) readers aren't distracted by the content of the text–but instead pay attention to the design of the page. This practice goes back to the 1500s when lorem ipsum first appeared in a type specimen book–and it continues to this day, using that same chunk of text.

Adding template pages

All of the newsletter templates (and many other templates) are multi-page, designed to match and work together in the particular document you're creating. If you're designing a newsletter, for example, you probably want a front page that shows the headlines and masthead, a variety of inner pages designed differently, and perhaps a back page that lets you fold and mail the newsletter without an envelope. In fact, that's the exact arrangement of the Spring Newsletter template's six pages. Click the Navigation button in the toolbar (or choose View → Navigation Pane) to reveal the Navigation Pane (Figure 8-4) and use its scroll bar to view all the template pages.

Although Microsoft's designers have provided a complete newsletter package of six pages, your newsletter can be any length at all—and you're free to reorder or remove pages. To remove a page, highlight it in the Navigation Pane and then click the Remove button in the toolbar, or choose Insert → Remove Page. Word dutifully withdraws the page from your document. If the Navigation Pane isn't showing (Figure 8-4), clicking the Remove button removes whichever page contains the insertion point.

Note: You don't *have to* have the Navigation Pane visible while you're adding or removing pages–but it certainly helps keep you "on the same page" with Word while you do so.

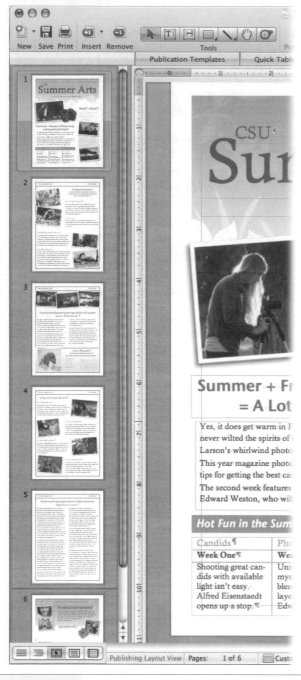

Figure 8-4:
Click the Navigation button to reveal the navigation pane, a strip of thumbnails showing your page order. In this document, a double line between pages 5 and 6 indicates a section break where the Master Page design changes (page 312). You can reorder pages by dragging them into a new position and remove a page by selecting it and pressing Delete or clicking the Remove button in the toolbar.

Adding a page is just as easy. Click the Insert button in the toolbar (or choose Insert → New Page) and Word creates a new blank page following the selected page in the Navigation Pane (or following the current page if the Navigation Pane is hidden). To add another template page—instead of a blank page—choose the page style you want in the Navigation Pane and use the Insert button's pop-up menu to choose Duplicate Page (or choose Insert → Duplicate Page). Word creates an exact duplicate of the page—layout, text, pictures, the works.

Adding your own words

With a few exceptions, the "Greek" text in the template is placeholder text, intended to show you the document's design, as described in the box on page 285. You can't edit this placeholder text—in fact, it disappears when you click it. When it vanishes, start typing and your words begin to fill up the space. With the placeholder text out of the way, you're back in the world of normal word processing.

To get started, for example, scroll back to the first page, click "Lorem Ipsums," and then type your own name. (If your name is much longer than Lorem Ipsums, it forces the headline onto two lines. Select your name, open the Formatting Palette, and use the Size slider in the Font pane to decrease the size and keep the headline on one line.)

Next, click one of the text boxes and start typing—or paste in text from another document. The placeholder text disappears, replaced by your words. Whenever you click a text box, your first click selects the whole *box*, displaying its eight light blue handles. Your second click (or simply starting to type) takes you inside the box—into text-editing mode—where you can add or edit text using all of Word's usual word processing features.

Double-click the orange "Save the Date!" Headline text box and type your own headline. When you're done adding text, leave the editing mode and select the text box by clicking one of its corners or clicking outside and then back on the text box—making its corner handles reappear. If it's not already open, click the Toolbox button in the toolbar and open the Formatting Palette's Colors, Weights, and Fills pane. Then click the Color pop-up menu and choose a different color for the text box fill. (Since the text is white, or reversed, stick with the darker colors.)

If you decide this document's a keeper, choose File → Save, give it a name, choose a destination, and then click Save. When you're working with templates, the document you work on is always a clone of the template. You can modify the document and save it, and still go back to the Elements Gallery and find the template there, unchanged, and ready for another use.

Adding pictures

Similar to the dummy text in the text boxes, two of the pictures on this page are placeholders—the flower is a regular picture, not a placeholder (the difference will soon become obvious). If you find the "template people" irresistible, you can keep their pictures. Otherwise, drag some of your own photos onto the placeholder to replace the template family with your own—the size, border, rotation, and other attributes of the placeholder picture remain the same. Just click the Object Palette button in the Toolbox and then click the Photos tab to display a folder of your own pictures or your iPhoto library (see page 291). This shortcut gives you access to any picture folders on your computer—all from within Word. Scroll through your images and drag any one of them onto one of the template's picture place-holders. Word replaces the template's version of a perfect family with your own.

You don't *have* to use the Object Palette's view of your photos. You can drag a pic-ture file directly from a folder, or a thumbnail directly from iPhoto, Adobe Bridge, Microsoft Expression Media, or from most any other photo organizing software. You can also add pictures to your document without using picture placeholders: Just drop the picture into your document at the approximate place you want it to appear. Word inserts small pictures at full size and scales down large pictures so they don't take over the whole page. Then you can click the picture and drag one of its resizing handles to adjust the picture size (see Figure 8-5).

To remove a photo, click once to select it, then press delete.

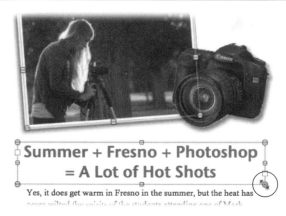

Figure 8-5:
Click any picture or text box once to select it, and then use the corner or side handles to adjust its size. When you move your cursor over one of the handles, it assumes a double-headed arrow shape (circled). Pictures feature an additional handle sprouting from the top edge. Drag this handle to rotate the picture. Text boxes display two additional squares you can click to link one text box to another (see page 298).

Building Pages with Objects

To perform its page-layout wizardry, Word views the various elements you can incorporate on your page—pictures, movies, text boxes, shapes, tables, and so on—as *objects*. Word approaches objects in two ways:

- **In-line objects** behave like a text character in a line of text. If you add more text to your document in front of this kind of object, it gets pushed along with the text, always remaining tied to the words next to it. You'll find in-line objects a good choice for text boxes containing a small image that needs to stay con-nected to the surrounding text. See Figure 8-6 for an example.

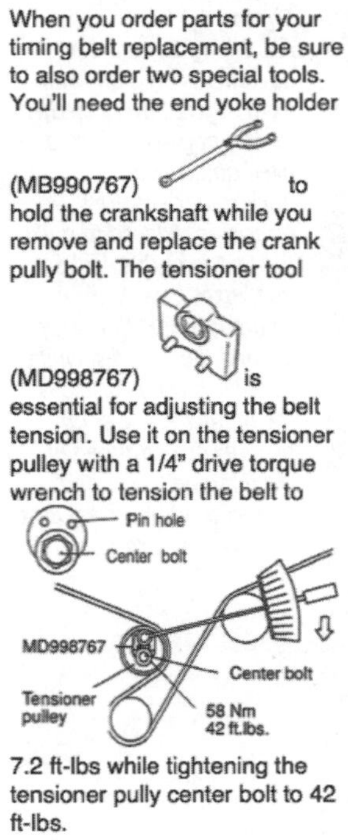
When you order parts for your timing belt replacement, be sure to also order two special tools. You'll need the end yoke holder
(MB990767) to hold the crankshaft while you remove and replace the crank pully bolt. The tensioner tool
(MD998767) is essential for adjusting the belt tension. Use it on the tensioner pulley with a 1/4" drive torque wrench to tension the belt to
Pin hole
Center bolt
MD998767
Center bolt
Tensioner pulley
58 Nm
42 ft.lbs.
7.2 ft-lbs while tightening the tensioner pully center bolt to 42 ft-lbs.

Figure 8-6:
These three in-line objects stay connected to the surrounding text, even if you remove or add text earlier in the document.

- **Fixed objects** are standalone entities. Instead of being tied to the document's text, they're bolted into the page at a specific spot. Most people prefer fixed objects when they're adding pictures or charts to the page layout. Adding text to the page doesn't affect the objects' placement, and you can drag and resize these kinds of objects to precisely position them on the page (Figure 8-7).

When you insert a fixed object on a text-filled page, you can determine whether the text flows under the object, over the object, or *wraps* around it—flowing around the object so the text neither overlaps the picture nor is hidden by it (see page 306).

Since fixed objects are separate items, you can stack them in *layers*—just like you can arrange paper snapshots on a scrapbook page. One picture is on top, overlapping portions of other pictures underneath. Besides shifting the position of each object, you can also shift its layer—moving it in front of or behind other objects it overlaps.

Tip: You choose an object's fixed or in-line status when you add it to the page, but you can convert it from fixed to in-line or vice versa at any time (see page 294).

In-line objects always remain on the same layer as the text in which they're embedded. When you adjust the arrangement of layers in your document, you can only move *fixed* objects in front of or behind the text layer. Unlike scrap-booking with paper snapshots, Word also lets you adjust the opacity of each object, so you can see through to the objects in the layers below (see page 749).

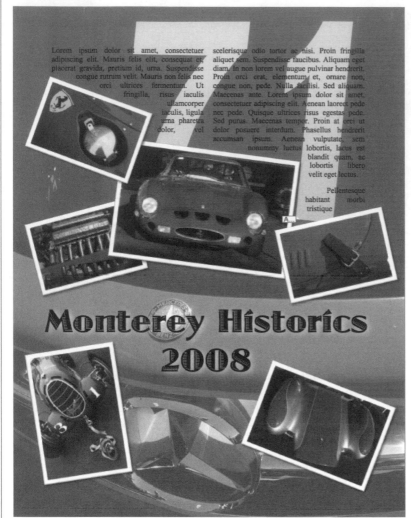

Figure 8-7:
Publishing Layout view documents are built with fixed objects. Every element on this page is, in fact, a fixed object. The background picture's opacity is reduced to make the text readable. Linked text boxes have two columns of text that wrap around the pictures, while another text box displays the headline. The small pictures are arranged in overlapping layers and feature white borders, drop shadows, and rotation.

After you place objects on the page, you can crop, resize, rotate, and layer them on top of one another. You can add shadows, adjust their opacity, or group several objects together in order to reposition them simultaneously. For the full story on object manipulation, see "Moving Objects Around" on page 300.

The Toolbox Redux

The Publishing Layout View is no different from other Word views when you adjust various parts of your document—just use the Toolbox. Along with the Formatting Palette's familiar text controls, Publishing Layout view makes use of the Wrapping, Text Box, Colors, Weights, and Fills, and Shadow panes. (These controls are covered in depth starting on page 306.)

The Object Palette

The four tabs of the Object Palette let you drag to place shapes, clipart, symbols, and photos onto your page (see Figure 8-8).

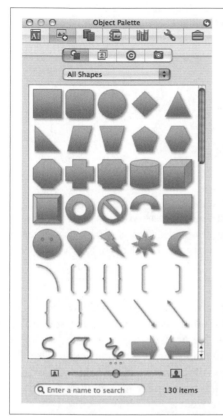 

Figure 8-8:
The Object Palette's four tabs provide a quick way to insert shapes (left), clip art, symbols, and photos (right) by simply dragging a thumbnail into your document. Use the slider at the bottom to control the thumbnail size; narrow down your choices by using the pop-up menu at the top or by typing into the search box.

Shapes. The Object Palette's first tab provides easy access to AutoShapes (which you can also access from the Drawing toolbar or from the Insert → Picture → AutoShapes command). Use the palette's pop-up menu to view all the shapes or to narrow your view down to a certain type, like Lines, Stars and Banners, Arrows, and so on. Place one of these shapes on your page by dragging it in. Word inserts the shape at a standard size, which you can then resize to your liking. Alternatively, click your desired shape in the Object Palette and move your cursor back to your document—where it now appears as a crosshair. Start dragging, and the shape appears—stop dragging when it's about the right size. You can constrain the proportions of a shape—to draw a perfect square or a perfect circle, for example—by pressing Shift while you drag a shape's corner handle.

Many of the shapes have one or more yellow, diamond-shaped adjustment handles that control one of the shape's attributes—like the sharpness of a star's points, the shape of a bracket, the angle of a triangle, or the smile or frown of a smiley face. Figure 8-9 shows a couple of examples.

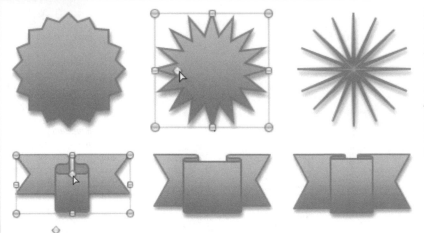

Figure 8-9:
If a shape features a yellow, diamond-shaped handle, you can drag it to adjust the appearance of the shape, dulling or sharpening a star's points, or reshaping a ribbon, for example. By experimenting, you can achieve radically different looks.

Tip: When you choose Callouts from the Object Palette's pop-up menu, you access a special variety of shape that acts like a mini text box. You can type inside these shapes, using all of Word's font-formatting controls, in order to add explanatory notes to pictures or diagrams, or cartoon-like thought and speech bubbles to your photographs.

Clip Art. Click the Object Palette's second tab for access to Word's collection of clip art and stock photos. You can access the much more complete and searchable Clip Gallery by choosing Insert → Picture → Clip Art (see page 734), but the Object Palette gives you a quick and easy way to access your clip art collection. Use the pop-up menu to view the entire collection of all images, or choose one of the categories like Business or People. Drag one of the thumbnails into your document to place it, and then use the corner handles to resize it.

Symbols. The Object Palette's Symbols tab lets you insert special characters right into your text—musical notes, Greek letters, fractions, and Currency symbols, among others. As with all of the Object Palette tabs, you can use the pop-up menu to view all of the symbols, or only certain categories, such as Math, Shapes, Checkmarks, and so on. Just click one of the symbols to place it in your document at the insertion point. (Unlike shapes, clip art, and photos, Word inserts symbols as text characters—not objects.)

Photos. The final tab in the Object Palette gives you a peek into your photo collection, be it in iPhoto or some other folder (see page 291). The pop-up menu lets you choose from recently used folders or select any other iPhoto library or folder on your computer or network. Drag a thumbnail into your document and then use the corner handles to resize it. If you drop a photo into a picture placeholder, it assumes the placeholder's attributes—size, border, shadow, rotation, and so on.

Note: When you add clip art or photos to your Word document, Word makes a copy of the picture and makes it part of that document's file. Thus, if you move that document to another computer, Word displays all the pictures you've added.

Plan Ahead

Having Word's assortment of document templates at your fingertips is a boon for the hurried or harried. But even before you choose a template, run through some of the basics of document set-up to ensure that your end product comes out the way you want it to. What paper size will you print on? Will it be a vertical (portrait) or horizontal (land-scape) layout? Will the document be folded, printed on both sides of the sheet, or bound? Is it going to require page numbers, sections, or a table of contents?

Keep these requirements in mind as you choose your template and make adjustments using Page Setup and Format → Document before you begin entering text and inserting pictures.

Inserting Fixed and In-line Objects

After you decide *what* to insert in your document, the next question is *how*: as a fixed or an in-line object. Fixed objects are glued to a spot on the page (although you can always move them later) while the text flows around or over them, whereas in-line objects are attached to the text and move along with it.

In-line objects

Think of in-line objects like another character or word in a sentence. In-line objects enter the page at the insertion point—just like a typed character. Although you can use in-line objects in Publishing Layout view, they're usually more useful in longer text documents, where you want a picture to remain close to a certain paragraph no matter how much editing you do to the document before that paragraph.

To create an in-line object, double-click the text box containing text where you want to insert it, so you see its blinking insertion point. Then drag a photo or clip art thumbnail from the Object Palette (or drag an image file from a folder) into the text box. As you move your cursor over the text box, the insertion point follows along at the tip of the arrow. Guide the insertion point to the spot in the text where you'd like the in-line object to appear, and release the mouse button.

Word then copies the image to your chosen point in the text box. Click the image to display its selection handles, and drag any of them to resize the image.

You can also add an in-line object by first placing your insertion point at the spot you want it to appear, and then choosing Insert → Picture → and choosing Clip Art, or From File, from the submenu. (AutoShapes is another choice, but they always appear in your document as fixed objects.) Choosing Clip Art opens the Clip Gallery, from which you can choose a picture (page 734), while choosing From File summons the Open dialog box, allowing you to navigate to any picture file on your computer.

Fixed objects

Fixed objects are married to a spot on the page rather than within a line of text. To add a fixed object, first make sure you're not inside a text box. Clicking the margin of the document or the "virtual tabletop" around the document is a reassuring move that closes any text boxes and deselects any objects. Then drag the image or file into your document. Click the image to call up its selection handles and drag any of them to resize it. Click inside the picture to drag it into position.

You can also add fixed pictures via the Insert → Picture menu: clip art from the Clip Gallery, pictures from any file, or AutoShapes from their tiny toolbar.

Converting object style

After you insert an object in your document you can change it from an in-line to fixed object or vice versa. Double-click the object to open the Format dialog box, click the Layout tab, and choose "In line with text" or one of the other fixed object wrapping styles.

Note: Tiger fans beware: The wrapping controls in the Format dialog box won't let you convert the object style. Instead, select the picture and choose Edit → Cut (or press ⌘-X). Then, to convert it to an in-line object, place your insertion point within a line of text and choose Edit → Paste (or press ⌘-V). To convert it to a fixed object, make sure the text-editing insertion point is *not* present inside a text box, and choose Edit → Paste.

Inserting Movies and Sounds

The Object Palette provides a quick way to insert shapes, clip art, and photos—the type of objects you'll often want in a printed document. However, Word's mixed-media abilities also let you include sounds and movies in your page layout if your oeuvre is destined to be viewed on a computer.

Insert a movie or sound in your document by dragging the video or sound file from a folder onto the page. Movies appear on the page displaying their first frame—and the usual object selection handles which you can use to change the size. Sounds appear on the page as a loudspeaker icon (see Figure 8-10). Both movies and sounds display a small filmstrip icon in the lower-left corner. Clicking it brings up the movie controller for starting and stopping the movie or sound, and adjusting the volume.

Word uses QuickTime to display movies and sounds, so any format that QuickTime can handle is fair game: MOV, Flash, MP3, MPEG-4, AAC, AIFF, and lots more. If you open a movie in iMovie, you can also drag individual clips from iMovie into your Word document.

Figure 8-10:

Top: Movies appear like a picture in your document, except they bear a filmstrip icon in the lower-left corner. Double-click this icon to bring up the playback controls. If your movie starts with a black frame—as many do—you can use QuickTime Pro to set a different frame as the poster frame, the frame that displays before the movie plays.

Bottom: Sound files display a loudspeaker icon and the same QuickTime filmstrip. They also respond to a double-click by displaying the playback controls.

Tip: Word doesn't let you drag a song or sound file into your document directly from iTunes. You can avoid the tedium of navigating deep into iTunes' folder structure to insert a sound by dragging it from iTunes to the desktop (which copies it to the desktop) and then dragging it into your Word document. Tidy up when you're done by trashing the redundant sound file on the desktop.

If you prefer, you can use the menus instead of drag-and-drop to insert audio and video files. Choose Insert → Movie, navigate to the movie or sound file you want to insert, and double-click it (or click once to select it and then click Choose) to bring it into your document.

Making Text Boxes or Sidebars

Text boxes, callouts, pull quotes, and sidebars are common elements of page-layout design. These kinds of text boxes are useful for highlighting or isolating some text from the rest of your document. In Word's Publishing Layout view, all text resides in text boxes—even if it's a full page of text.

Editing in iTunes

You can use iTunes to select just a part of a song or sound file to use in Word. You may find this technique handy when you're discussing sections of songs in your essay on the birth of bebop, for example.

1. Select a song in your iTunes library and determine the starting and ending time of the segment you want. To do so, play the song and watch the elapsed time display above the progress bar at the top of the iTunes window. (You can switch between total, elapsed, and remaining time by clicking the time display.)

2. With the song selected, choose File → Get Info, and click the Options tab. Type the Start Time and Stop Time in the appropriate boxes. Doing so also turns on the checkbox for the start and stop time. The iTunes elapsed-time display only shows minutes and seconds, but you can add a decimal in these boxes to set the start and stop times with thousandth-of-a-second precision.

3. Click OK. iTunes now *plays* only the portion of the song you've selected—but if you export the song or drag it into Word, you'll still get the full-length version.

4. Choose Advanced → "Convert Selection to AAC". (This menu command changes depending on how you've set iTunes' importing preferences. It may say "Convert Selection to MP3" or to Apple Lossless, for example.)

iTunes creates a new song in the library, and displays its shortened length in the Time column. Rename the song with a distinctive title so you know this is the edited version, say, *A Night in Tunisia-intro*.

Now you can insert the newly edited song into your bebop document, *Deconstructing Diz*.

Sidebars usually hold a paragraph or several paragraphs that are related to, but not really part of, the flow of your main text. Sidebars can stand alone as a little chapter or chunk of information. (This book, for example, uses gray sidebars to hold these kinds of digressions.)

Callouts or *pull quotes* highlight an important point in the main text. Since they relate directly to part of the text, they need to be placed near the relevant text. Magazine articles often have pull quotes to add visual interest to the page and break up columns of plain text.

You can insert a new text box in a document by choosing Insert → Text Box, or by clicking the Text Box icon in the toolbar, or by pressing ⌘-2. Voilà—your arrow cursor sprouts a crosshair and a blue ball labeled T—for text. Start dragging, and a text box outline appears. When it fills as much space as you need, release the mouse button; the insertion point begins blinking within your new text container. That's your signal to begin typing or to paste in the text box's contents. If you type more than the box can hold, a clipping indicator appears at the bottom of the box to show you that some of your text is clipped off or hidden (see Figure 8-11). Resize the box to reveal the hidden text or link it to another text box (see page 298).

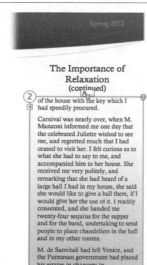

The Importance of Relaxation

M. de Malipiero passed a remark upon my cheerful looks and the dark circles around my eyes, but I kept my own counsel, and I allowed him to think whatever he pleased. On the following day I paid a visit to Madame Orio, and Angela not being of the party, I remained to supper and retired with M. Rosa. During the evening Nanette contrived to give me a letter and a small parcel. The parcel contained a small lump of wax with the stamp of a key, and the letter told me to have a key made, and to use it to enter the house whenever I wished to spend the night with them. She informed me at the same time that Angela had slept with them the night following our adventures, and that, thanks to their mutual and usual practices, she had guessed the real state of things, that they had not denied it, adding that it was all her fault, and that Angela, after abusing them most vehemently, had sworn never again to darken their doors; but they did not care a jot.

A few days afterwards our good fortune delivered us from Angela; she was taken to Vicenza by her father, who had removed there for a couple of years, having been engaged to paint frescoes in some houses in that city. Thanks to her absence, I found myself undisturbed possessor

Continued on page 6

The Importance of Relaxation
(continued)

of the house with the key which I had speedily procured.

Carnival was nearly over, when M. Manzoni informed me one day that the celebrated Juliette wished to see me, and regretted much that I had ceased to visit her. I felt curious as to what she had to say to me, and accompanied him to her house. She received me very politely, and remarking that she had heard of a large ball I had in my house, she said she would like to give a ball there, if I would give her the use of it. I readily consented, and she handed me twenty-four sequins for the supper and for the band, undertaking to send people to place chandeliers in the hall and in my other rooms.

M. de Sanvitali had left Venice, and the Parmesan government had placed his estates in chancery in consequence of his extravagant expenditure. I met him at Versailles ten years afterwards. He wore the insignia of the king's order of knighthood, and was grand equerry to the eldest daughter of Louis XV., Duchess of Parma, who, like all the French princesses, could not be reconciled to the climate of Italy.

The ball took place, and went off splendidly. All the guests belonged to Juliette's set, with the exception of Madame Orio, her nieces, and the procurator Rosa, who sat together in the room adjoining the hall, and whom I had been permitted to introduce as persons of no consequence whatever.

On the following day I paid a visit to Madame Orio, and Angela not being of the party, I remained to supper and retired with M. Rosa. During the evening Nanette contrived to give me a letter and a small parcel. The parcel

Continued on page 8

Figure 8-11:
Linked text boxes display a number in their upper-left corner indicating their position in the chain of linked boxes. Additionally, the link tabs near the upper-left and lower-right corners display an arrow if the text box is linked from one to another. Clicking one of those arrows takes you directly to the previous or next text box in the series. To help you track multiple sets of linked text boxes, Word paints the selection rectangles of linked text boxes with matching colors.

Tip: Word can automatically create a text box from copied text. Copy some text from another document or from another place in the current document. Click the margin of the document to be sure nothing is selected, then choose Edit → Paste Special, and choose Unformatted Text. A new text box appears in the upper-left corner of the current page, filled with the contents of your clipboard in your document's default body text style—just waiting for you to drag it into position.

When you're typing in a text box, click the border of the text box to switch from text-entry mode back to object mode, and then drag the box to reposition it or drag one of its handles to resize it. If you're not typing in a text box, a single click selects the box so you can resize or reposition it, while a double-click takes you into its text-entry mode.

Tip: If you like to use shapes to contain text for callouts or captions—a favored method—you'll find that only some of the shapes allow you to fill them with text. Only shapes in the Callout category are ready and willing to act as specialized text boxes. But actually, creativity rules: you can use any of the other shapes as text boxes by Control-clicking (or right-clicking) the shape and choosing Add Text. From now on that shape behaves just like one of the official Callout shapes.

Linking text boxes

If you have more text than will fit in one text box, want your text to flow from one column to another, or want to break up a sidebar into two or more portions, Word can *link* the text boxes to the text flows from one to another. Linked text boxes can be on the same page or on several different pages. Magazines often use this technique for a running sidebar that occupies, for example, the right column on the right page for several pages running. Linked text boxes behave as one virtual text box—if you add extra text to the first box any displaced text flows into the next linked text box. Or, if you use Select All, Word selects the text in all the linked text boxes.

To make a linked text box, create the first text box and type or paste text into it; then click the box's forward link tab (see Figure 8-11). Your cursor again assumes the text box–drawing shape with a crosshair and the blue "T" ball. Use it to draw your next text box—which Word immediately fills with any of the overflow text from your first box. Repeat the process if you need more linked text boxes. Once you've created a link, Word changes the color of the linked box's outlines, using different colors for each set of linked boxes. Additionally, the text box's two linking tabs reveal if the box is linked *to* another text box (an arrow in the right-side link tab), or linked *from* another text box (an arrow in the left-side link tab). When you hover your mouse over a linked text box, Word briefly displays a number in the upper left corner of the box indicating its position in the linking line-up.

You can create a chain of as many linked text boxes as you require. When Word creates a linked text box, it establishes that box's order in the chain for the flow of text. But Word doesn't prevent you from dragging linked text boxes into any order you want within your document—though your readers may wish it had.

You can select all the text in a series of linked text boxes to change font formatting or to copy the text to another document, for example, by placing the insertion point in any of the text boxes and pressing ⌘-8 (or choosing Edit → Select All).

If you need to move a set of linked text boxes at once, press Shift as you click the other boxes in order to select the whole set. Then you can drag them to a new location in your document. Have patience, however, when dragging text boxes. Even on a fast computer, it can take several seconds for the boxes to catch up with your cursor, especially when dragging from one page to another. Eventually they'll arrive at their new destination, links intact.

Tip: If you need to drag linked text boxes to a spot in your document several pages away, use the Zoom control in the toolbar to reduce your view to 25 or even 10 percent. Then you can carefully drag your text boxes to a distant page, return your zoom control to its normal setting, and get back to work.

If you're relocating an individual text box or any other kind of object, you'll find it more convenient to use cut and paste. Select the text box or other object, and then choose Edit → Cut. Scroll to the page in your document where you'd like to relocate the object, click that page's margin to be sure nothing is selected, and then choose Edit → Paste. The text box or object reappears. This method works with multiple objects as well, but not with linked text boxes.

You can also create a link to a text box that already exists. Select the first text box and then click the Link button in the toolbar. Your cursor sprouts a blue ball emblazoned with a chain link icon. Click an empty text box to create a link to it. (In an effort to help you keep your prose under control, Word only lets you link to empty text boxes.)

If you've created a link and wish you hadn't, you can unlink the text box, removing all the text from any boxes farther down the chain. To do so, select a text box which links forward to another, and click the Break icon in the toolbar. Doing so breaks the chain and removes any text from the boxes you've linked to. That text reverts to being overflow text for the first text box—which you can expand or link to another text box to contain it.

Tip: If you're a mathematician, you'll notice that the Insert → Object → Microsoft Equation command is missing in Publishing Layout view. Don't let that stop you. Open the Equation Editor directly by choosing Applications → Microsoft Office 2008 → Office → Equation Editor. (If you use equations regularly, save your sanity by adding the Equation Editor to your Dock.) Create your equation, then copy it from the Equation Editor and paste it into your page layout. Once you've added an equation in Publishing Layout View, you can double-click it to bring the Equation Editor back in case you need to modify your math. (See page 754 for more on the Equation Editor.)

Formatting text boxes

Think of text boxes as little documents within your document. And just like a word processing document, you can fill a text box with plain text, or you can dress it up at will with a background color or image, borders, shadows, tables, charts, pictures, and so on (Figure 8-11).

You can add a solid color, a gradient (a fill color that gradually blends one color into another), or an image to the background of the text box; you can also choose to have border, a drop shadow, or adjust its opacity. The Formatting Palette's Colors, Weights, and Fills, and Shadow sections provide controls for most of these options. Or choose in Format → Text Box to someone the Format Text Box dialog box, the headquarters for all text-box formatting options.

You can add other objects—images, shapes, or tables—within a text box as in-line objects. To do so, place the insertion point in the text at the spot you want to insert the object, and choose a type of object from the Insert menu or from the Object Palette.

You can use fixed objects within a text box as well, but when you do, you're actually creating two or more layered objects on the page. To add a fixed object, click the margin of the document so the insertion point disappears, and then choose the type of object from the Insert menu or from the Object Palette. Resize the object and drag it into the text box. If necessary, open the Formatting Palette's Wrapping pane to adjust the type of wrapping and the wrapping margin (see page 306). You can attach the object to the text box—so it moves along with it if you reposition the text box—by grouping the two objects. Select the object, hold down the Shift key, and then select the text box. With both items selected, choose Group from the Group button in the toolbar. Now if you move the text box the object comes along for the ride.

Note: When you group a text box with another object, you can't resize the box without also resizing the object it contains. In order to independently resize either the text box or the object inside it, select the group object, choose Ungroup from the Group button in the toolbar, and then make your changes. To tie them together again, select both items and choose Group from the toolbar Group button.

Word controls the way text in the neighboring text boxes wraps around a text box just as it does with other objects. You can adjust those settings in the Formatting Palette's Wrapping section.

The way Word displays the text inside a text box depends on the normal font and paragraph formatting controls. However, you need to visit the Formatting Palette's Text Box pane to adjust the box's *Internal Margin*—the space between the text box's text and the border of the box. Word lets you set the four side margins independently.

Moving Objects Around

When you're working in Publishing Layout view with pictures, text boxes, shapes, tables, and so on, Word sees them all as *objects* and handles them in similar ways. Once you master resizing, rotating, and text wrapping around, say, a picture, you're ready to do the same operations on shapes, tables, text boxes, and other objects.

Selecting objects

Select an object by clicking it. Its selection handles appear, in effect saying, "I'm ready and waiting—mold me to your whim!" The most basic object maneuvers are *moving* and *resizing*.

Moving objects

You can drag fixed objects anywhere on the page or to another page on your document. In-line objects, however, refuse to be dragged anywhere. Instead, select the in-line object and choose Edit → Cut (or Control-click the object and choose Cut from the pop-up menu), reposition your insertion point within the text where you'd like the picture to appear, and choose Edit → Paste (or Control-click and choose Paste from the shortcut menu).

If you have to move an object very far—to another page or to the other end of your document—use this same cut-and-paste method. You can shift-click to select more than one object to move at the time.

Note: This cut and paste method won't work with multiple linked text boxes (see page 298).

Resizing objects

When you place your arrow pointer over one of an object's six selection handles (tables only have two), the cursor changes into a double-headed arrow, which means you can resize the object by dragging that handle. When you drag one of the square handles in the center of each side, you can stretch or squish the object—even if it's a photograph. However, if you use the round corner handles, Word preserves the picture or movie's aspect ratio as you drag, preventing you from accidentally stretching or widening your subject's natural proportions. You're free to alter the proportions of other objects—like shapes and tables—while you drag their corner selection handles. Or, to force Word to preserve their proportions, hold down the Shift key while you resize.

If for some reason you want to change this behavior, making a picture stretchable with its corner handles or preventing a carefully designed AutoShape from being stretched, open the Formatting Palette's Size, Rotation, and Ordering pane and turn off or on the "Lock aspect ratio" checkbox.

While you're in that part of the Formatting Palette, you'll notice the other method of changing an object's size: numerically, by entering numbers in the height and width boxes or by using the up- and down-arrow button to gradually change those numbers. This ability is especially useful when you need to match the dimensions of two or more pictures. Select two or more objects and enter the width and/or height measurements. Presto: All your selected objects are now the same size. (If "Lock aspect ratio" is turned on you can enter only one of the dimensions; turn off that checkbox in order to enter both.)

Aligning objects

The static alignment guides—Word's virtual T-square—help you to precisely align objects with text and with each other. You can create as many non-printing vertical or horizontal alignment guides as you need. To do so, click and drag from either ruler onto the page. Word changes your cursor to a double-bar between

---

double arrows, displays the blue alignment guides, and a box showing the distance from the edge of the page to the guide. Drop the guide when you get it into the correct position.

Page alignment guides show only on one page. You can reposition them by dragging—your arrow cursor again takes on the shape of the double bar with arrows, indicating it's ready to reposition the guideline. When you're done lining things up, remove a guide by dragging it back to the ruler or off of the page. Or remove all guides from the page by choosing View → Show → Clear Static Guides.

Objects also have *built-in* alignment guides. Alignment guides appear when you drag an object so that its center crosses the horizontal or vertical center of the page. Alignment guides also show up *between objects* as you drag one object, causing its center to align vertically or horizontally with the center of another object on the same page. In addition, guides appear when you drag an object so that one of its *edges* crosses the horizontal or vertical center of the page, or aligns vertically or horizontally with the edge of another object on the same page. All this alignment guide stuff is a little difficult to conceptualize if you've never seen these kinds of guidelines in action. But guidelines are worth learning because they can be enormously helpful if you're trying to place an object just so; Figure 8-12 shows how these lines work and what they look like.

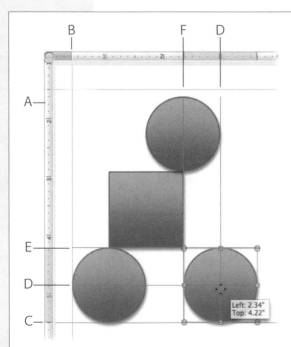

Figure 8-12:
Drag from any spot on the ruler into the document to add alignment guides wherever you need them (A). Choose View → Show and turn on Static guides, Dynamic guides, and Margin Guides to create the most alignment options. When you drag an object, its alignment guides appear whenever it aligns with another object. The left circle's left edge is aligned with an alignment guide (B). The selected circle's bottom edge is aligned with the automatic half-page guide (C); its center is aligned with this the center of the circle to its left, and with the edge of the circle above (D); its top edge is aligned with the bottom of the square and the top of the neighboring circle (F); and its left edge is aligned with the edge of the square and the center of the upper circle (F).

Finally, you can turn on a rectangular alignment guide to display your document's margins. Choose View → Show → Margin Guides to turn this feature on or off.

All of these various guidelines exhibit a magnetic attraction that makes them snap to one another. As you drag an object, and its invisible center or edge guidelines approach another guideline—the page center guidelines, another object's edge or center guidelines, or alignment guides you you've added to the page—the object's alignment guides appear and the object snaps into position, perfectly aligned with the guideline.

Sometimes however you may need to position an object very close to, but not exactly on, a guideline. In this case, Word's guideline magnetism thwarts your positioning efforts. Temporarily turn off this feature by pressing ⌘ while you drag, and you can position the object as you wish, without fear of it snapping to a nearby guideline.

Tip: The best way to carefully position fixed objects doesn't involve the mouse at all. Instead, select the object, and then use the four arrow keys to jog it one pixel at a time in any direction.

Automatic alignment

Word can automatically align two or more objects either by their edges or their center lines. To align several objects, select them, open the Formatting Palette's Size, Rotation, and Ordering pane, and choose one of the options in the Align button's pop-up menu. The Left, Center, and Right commands align the objects vertically along their left side, vertical center lines, or right sides. The Top, Middle, and Bottom commands align objects horizontally along their tops, horizontal centerlines, and bottom sides. Figure 8-13 shows the effect. If you turn on the Align to Page option at the bottom of the menu and then choose one of the other menu commands, the selected objects align to the centerline or edges of the page.

Distributing objects

Sometimes being spaced out is a *good* thing. Perhaps you have four objects and you want them evenly spaced across the page. Drag the objects into the approximate arrangement you want, placing the first and last objects in the series precisely. Click one object and then press Shift as you click to select each of the others. When you've selected all of them, open the Formatting Palette's Size, Rotation, and Ordering pane, and choose Distribute Horizontally or Distribute Vertically from the Distribute pop-up menu. Word adjusts the objects, equalizing the space between them. Finish up by using the Align command described earlier to straighten out the line. If you turn on the Aligned to Page option at the bottom of the menu and then choose one of the Distribute commands, Word distributes the selected objects evenly, centered on the page.

If you're distributing objects horizontally (or left to right), they don't have to be aligned vertically (or up-and-down), and vice versa. Figure 8-13 shows the situation.

Figure 8-13:
You can perfectly align and space a group of objects horizontally or vertically. Insert them into the document in their approximate positions. Place the two end objects where you want the row to begin and end—in this case the left side and the right side. Select all the objects and choose Align Middle from the Align button's pop-up menu to first get them all in a straight line. Next choose Distribute Horizontally from the Distribute button's pop-up menu to space them equally between the two end objects.

Rotating objects

Word always adds new objects (except lines) to the page so that they're perfectly aligned with the rectangular margins of your document. If you've ever had to lay out a document the old-fashioned way—using paste or wax to hold pictures and columns of text in place—this feature alone is cause for a few hosannas. Yet there are times you prefer a picture, table, or shape to appear on your document at a jaunty angle—instantly imparting an air of excitement, action, or even intentional sloppiness. Or perhaps you'd like to run your newsletter's headline vertically along the side or put an answer to this week's anagram upside down at the bottom of the page. All this is possible, but the method you use to accomplish the task differs depending on the type of object involved.

Pictures and clip art arrive on your page ready to rotate—simply drag the green handle that extends from the top of their selection box. Alternatively, double-click the picture or clip art to open the Format Picture window. Click Size in the list and use the Rotation knob, or its up- and down-arrow button, or enter an angle measurement in the box directly. Instead of spinning the Rotate knob with your mouse, you can also just click the knob to move its angle indicator to that position. Unlike a compass where zero degrees occupies the top (North) position, Word puts the zero degrees indicator at the right (East) position to indicate horizontality.

Tip: You'll find it very difficult to use the Rotation knob precisely with your cursor right on the knob. However, you can twist the knob with one-degree precision if you start rotating with your cursor on the knob, and then move the cursor several inches away from the knob—in effect creating a much larger knob that you can adjust more precisely.

To rotate a shape, select it and then open the Size, Rotation, and Ordering pane of the Formatting Palette. Choose Free Rotate from the Rotate pop-up menu. Word replaces the standard selection handles with four green ones, and changes your arrow cursor into a rotate icon. Use it to grab one of the green handles and drag to rotate the shape. You can also use the Rotate Left or Rotate Right commands in this menu to rotate in 90° increments. The Rotate menu also houses commands to flip the object vertically or horizontally, so you get a mirror image of the original.

Note: Once you add text to a shape, Word sees it as a text box and refuses to rotate it. See page 306 for the workaround.

When you rotate a shape using the Rotate menu, or a photo or clip art using the rotate handle, you can hold the Shift key to rotate in 15 degree increments.

Rotating text

Word lives up to Microsoft's reputation of being a rather straight-laced, button down, all-business software company when it comes to rotating text—you can't. You can run text horizontally or vertically—but that's it. At least, those are the only clear options Word provides. However, by utilizing a sneaky workaround, you can rotate and even flip text to your heart's content.

Using the Microsoft method, select a text box and then use the Orientation buttons in the Formatting Palette's "Alignment and Spacing" pane to twist the text 90° to the left or right, running it vertically up the page or down the page. When you choose one of the vertical text directions, the horizontal text alignment buttons also swivel—becoming, in effect, vertical text alignment buttons—allowing you to align to the top of the text box, the bottom, the center, or to justify. When a text box is vertically oriented, all the rest of the paragraph formatting controls—line spacing, paragraph spacing, indentation, and so on—continue to work in this vertical world.

In order to rotate text other than just 90° to the left or right, you have to think outside the box—the text box, that is. Since Word refuses to rotate text boxes, you have to transform the text box into a picture—which is exactly what happens when you paste a text box *inside* another text box.

1. **Start by creating your text box exactly as you want it to appear when it's rotated.**

   Do all your font formatting, line spacing, borders, fills, shadows, and so on. However, don't include any Returns—they don't make the transition.

2. **When you're satisfied with the look of your text box, select the box (not just the text, the whole box) and choose Edit → Copy or press ⌘-C.**

   When you copy a text box, Word actually copies an image of the box.

3. **Click the Text Box tool in the toolbar or choose Insert → Text Box and draw a new text box considerably larger than the one you just copied.**

   You need to make this text box—which will become the container for your rotated text box—large enough to hold the other text box after you've finished rotating it.

4. **With the insertion point blinking in your new text box, press ⌘-V or choose Edit → Paste.**

   Word pastes your first text box inside the empty container text box.

5. **Click once on the text to select the inner text box, which is now a picture, and therefore sports the green rotating handle at the top. Drag that handle to rotate the text.**

Note: Word has one other type of rotatable text container: *WordArt*. Creating a bit of WordArt text results in a drawing object that you can flip or rotate like any other drawing object. However, all the WordArt text styles are designed for eye-catching display purposes, not for body text. If you can find a style that's not too garish, WordArt can work well for headlines, labels, or short captions. See page 741 for the full WordArt story.

Wrapping

When you use objects—whether in-line or fixed—on a page containing text, you have to determine if and how that text is going to flow or wrap around the object. You can choose to have the text run directly over the object—not wrapping at all—or wrap tightly, loosely, just on the top and bottom, or just on one side of the object. The Formatting Palette's Wrapping pane and the Format → Picture or Object dialog box provide a veritable "wrappers delight" of options for controlling this effect (Figure 8-14).

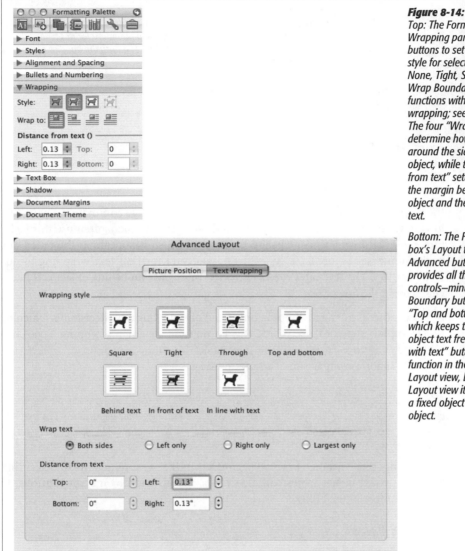

Figure 8-14:

Top: The Formatting Palette's Wrapping pane features buttons to set the wrapping style for selected objects: None, Tight, Square, and Edit Wrap Boundary (which only functions with Tight wrapping; see Figure 8-15). The four "Wrap to" buttons determine how the text flows around the sides of the object, while the "Distance from text" settings let you set the margin between the object and the surrounding text.

Bottom: The Format dialog box's Layout tab has an Advanced button which provides all the same controls—minus the Edit Wrap Boundary button and plus a "Top and bottom" button which keeps the sides of your object text free. The "In line with text" button doesn't function in the Publishing Layout view, but in the Print Layout view it lets you change a fixed object into an in-line object.

To wrap or not to wrap: that is the question Word asks of every object in your document. Answer it by selecting an object, opening the Formatting Palette's Wrapping pane, and choosing from among the Style and "Wrap to" buttons. Word handles text wrapping differently on in-line and fixed objects. All the wrapping adjustments in the Formatting Palette apply only to fixed objects. If you click the first of the wrapping style buttons, you turn wrapping off—the picture floats on top of the text, obscuring whatever's underneath. You might choose to not wrap text around a fixed object when you're using an image as a background on

Figure 8-15:
Use the Tight wrapping style for irregularly shaped objects with transparent backgrounds. You can further adjust the wrapping boundary for this type of object if you click the Edit Wrap Boundary button and drag the handles of the invisible wrapping boundary.

the page, for example—in which case you'd use the Arrange command (see the following section) to move the picture behind the text. Designers often use this technique with an image whose opacity is set very low, so it appears as the faded out background (see Figure 8-7). By contrast, you can't turn off text wrapping for an in-line object. The text can't run over the top of it, since an in-line object acts like a character in the line of text.

If you choose to use text wrapping on a fixed object, your next decision is which of the wrapping styles to use. Click the Formatting Palette's wrapping Style and "Wrap to" buttons in turn to see their effect on the text around or object (see Figure 8-16 for a comparison of wrapping styles).

Note: Word gives you just one wrapping style for in-line objects. The object always sits on the baseline in the line of text, just like any other text character—and stays tied to its neighboring text, as would a text character. If you want to move the object up out of its line of text, just add returns before or after the object.

You can use the "Distance from text" controls in the Wrapping pane to determine how tightly text wraps around an object. Use the up and down arrow buttons or enter a number in the boxes.

Arranging objects

After you've garnished your document with objects—modified, resized, positioned, and wrapped them—you may still not be finished with object manipulations. Word offers a few more options to control how an object relates to the page and to other objects around it.

Layering objects. Anytime objects overlap one another, or whenever a fixed object appears within a block of text, one object has to be in front of the other. Word manages multiple objects by placing each object, and each text box, on its own invisible layer. In this way, objects are free to overlap one another—even obscure underlying objects completely—without harming the individual objects.

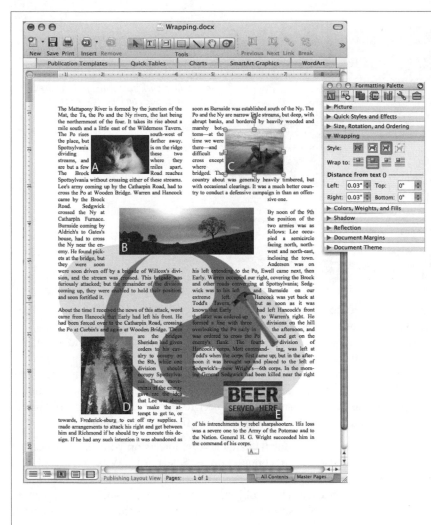

Figure 8-16:
You can determine exactly how text wraps around objects—or have your text ignore objects completely and plow right over them—using controls in the Formatting Palette's Wrapping pane. The low-opacity background image (yin-yang) lies behind the text with wrapping turned off. Two pictures (A, B) use the standard wrapping style, where the text flows around all sides of the object. Use the "Distance from text" settings to wrap the text tightly or loosely. The next two of the "Wrap to" buttons allow you to wrap text around only the left or right side of an object (C). The fourth of those buttons wraps the text to whichever side of the object has more space (D). To keep the column free of text on both sides of the object (E) set the left and right measurements of the "Distance from text" as high as you need to—or use the Advanced Layout tab of the Format Picture dialog box to choose "Top and bottom."

As you add objects to your document, Word places them on the top layer; the new object covers up any portion of another object it overlaps. Text boxes (which also contain any in-line objects) occupy a layer just like any other object. You can move objects forward or backward through the layers by visiting the toolbar and using the Arrange button's pop-up menu to choose Bring Forward or Send Backward (see Figure 8-17). Move a selected object all the way to the front or back of the pile by choosing Bring to front or Send to back from the Arrange button's menu. Better yet, Control-click a selected object (or right-click) and from the pop-up menu choose your preferred layering style. Or, if you're Formatting Palette–inclined, open the Size, Rotation, and Ordering pane and use the Arrange pop-up menu.

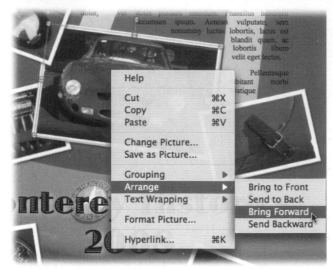

Figure 8-17:
Control-click (or right-click) and choose one of the four commands in the Arrange submenu to move an object in front of or behind other objects. Parts of eight layers are visible in this document: a background image, text boxes, and pictures, each on their own layer.

If you add an object to a text box and turn off wrapping (page 306), Word places the object on top of the text. However, you can move objects behind the text—to run text over a background image, for example—by selecting it and using the arrange commands. But once you place an object behind the text, it's difficult to select the object in order to resize or reposition it, since clicking it only selects the text in the layer above it. You can circumvent this problem by temporarily sending the text box to the back, returning your object to the land of the clickable where you can modify it as you wish and then send it to the back once more.

Should you decide to make a global change to the objects on your page, select one object and then press ⌘-A (or choose Edit → Select All). With all the objects selected you can, for example, delete them all, or shift their position using the arrow keys. If you Shift-click several objects of the same type—pictures, or shapes, for example—you can make simultaneous adjustments of their object properties such as transparency, shadows, or reflections.

Grouping objects. After going to the trouble of precisely positioning fixed objects relative to one another, you may find it useful to move, rotate, or copy them as if they were a single object. Word gives you the power to *group* objects in this way—and later, if you need to adjust them individually, *ungroup* them.

Hold down the Shift key as you click the objects you want to group, selecting them all (all objects have to be on the same page). Control-click (or right-click) and choose Grouping → Group from the pop-up menu (or use the toolbar's Group menu). Word replaces the individual selection handles with just one set enclosing the whole group (Figure 8-18).

Alpha Channels

Some image files have an invisible stencil called an *alpha channel* that designates certain parts of the image as transparent. Only certain graphic file formats—such as Photoshop, TIFF, or PDF—recognize this kind of transparency. Many clip art graphics use alpha channels so that irregularly shaped objects aren't always surrounded by a rectangular area of white space.

You can add alpha channels to graphics by using pricey image-editing software like Adobe's Photoshop or Illustrator. But you can also create alpha channels—and save yourself several hundred dollars—by using that essential $35 shareware program GraphicConverter, from Lemke Software (*www.lemkesoft.com*).

The exact procedures used in the various programs differ, but essentially you create a transparent background region—instead of a white one—and designate it as an alpha channel. Word provides a rudimentary tool to create an alpha channel in the Formatting Palette's Picture pane. Click

the Transparent Color button and then click the color in your picture you wish to make transparent. Because there's no way to adjust the threshold on this tool, it really only works for solid colors—and even then it doesn't do a very good job with edges. However, it may be all you need to quickly turn a plain background transparent.

Once you've found or created an alpha-channel graphic, insert it in Word like any other graphic and use the Formatting Palette's Wrapping pane to adjust its wrapping options. Use the Square button to ignore the alpha layer, instead wrapping to a rectangular border around the object. The right Tight button activates the alpha layer, wrapping text into the transparent regions of the object. One more option exists in the format Object or Format Picture dialog box. Choose the Layout tab and click the Advanced button to access the Through wrapping style, which allows the text to show through any transparent region, even through a hole in a donut, for example.

Figure 8-18:
When you Control-click (or right-click) two or more selected objects and then choose Grouping → Group from the pop-up menu, Word staples the two together and they become a single object you can manipulate as one. Grouped objects lose their rotation selection handle, but you can still rotate them using the Formatting Palette's Rotate menu—or ungroup them and manipulate them individually.

Tip: If you group pictures, you'll notice the green rotate handle disappears. Fear not—you can still rotate by using the Formatting Palette's Size, Rotation, and Ordering pane's Rotate menu. However, if you group a text box with a picture you'll lose that ability since text boxes are fundamentally non-rotatable.

When you group items, even if they're all pictures, Word turns off the "Lock aspect ratio" option in the Formatting Palette's Size, Rotation, and Ordering pane. So when resizing, keep grouped pictures in proportion by either turning on that checkbox in the Formatting Palette or just press Shift key while you drag one of the corner handles.

Select an object group and Control-click (or right-click) and choose Grouping → Ungroup to restore the objects' individuality so you can, for example, resize or delete one of the group members. When you're ready to tie the group together again, select any one of the group members and use the Regroup command. Word remembers which objects were in that group and binds them together for you. You'll also find the grouping commands in the Formatting Palette's Size, Rotation, and Ordering pane's Grouping menu.

Once you create a group, Word sees it as a single object—meaning that you can add it to another group, and on and on—wheels within wheels.

Master Pages

Word reserves a special foundation layer for Publishing Layout view documents. The *Master Page* contains objects that appear on every page of your document, or on every page of a section if you've broken your document into sections (page 122). You'll find master pages very useful in order to do things like place a watermark, logo, or background image—usually at a very reduced opacity—on every page. Master pages are also the place to insert headers and footers in your Publishing Layout view document.

Click the Master Pages tab in the lower-right corner of the document window. Word hides all the page content that's not part of the master page and displays a tag in the upper left corner of each page to remind you that you're working on the master page and show what type of master page you're looking at.

A Master Pages pane appears in the Formatting Palette with the three checkboxes you can use to determine master page attributes:

- **Different First Page.** Choose this option if your document or section's first page is a title page or cover page and you'd like it to display different master objects than the rest of your document or section. For example, title pages usually don't have headers and footers.

- **Different Odd and Even Pages.** Turn on this checkbox if your document will be printed and bound and you want different master objects on the left and right pages.

- **Same As Previous.** If you've broken your document up into more than one section, Word makes this option available. Turn it on if you want the master objects from the previous section to continue through the current one. If you also turn on Different First Page, then the first page of the current section matches the first page of the preceding one.

You can add objects and text boxes to master pages just as you would normally. The only difference is that they'll show up on the first page, or *every* page, of that section.

To add headers or footers to a Master page, turn on the margin guides (View → Show → Margin Guides) and add text boxes outside of the margins. Choose Format → Document → Margins if you need to adjust the margins to accommodate a taller header or footer.

After making changes to your master pages, click the All Contents tab in the lower-right corner of the document window to return to the normal document view, showing the regular page elements plus the master page elements. When you're in All Contents view, you can't select any of the Master page objects. To do so, just click the Master Pages tab again.

Tip: You can easily transfer an object from the normal page to the master page by selecting it and choosing Edit → Copy. Then switch to the Master Pages tab and choose Edit → Paste. Word places the object in the same position on the Master page. The same technique works in reverse to move an object from the master page to a normal page.

Creating Templates

By now, you've undoubtedly used—and come to appreciate—Word's time-saving templates. They range from the very simple, like the Personal Letter, to the complex, multipage Publishing Layout view templates. But whether plain or intricate, they all share a common purpose: to get you started on the document quickly, with a large part of the formatting already in place—so you can concentrate on the content instead of the layout. This section shows you how to make your own templates so you can add them to Word's Project Gallery, where they'll appear alongside Microsoft's templates, ready and eager.

You can create your own templates either by starting from scratch with a blank page, or by modifying one of Word's templates. After you make all your changes to the document, choose File → Save As and choose Word Template (.dotx) from the Format pop-up menu, give the template a name, and click Save. From now on when you open the Project Gallery you'll find the new template listed in the My Templates section.

Modifying an Existing Template

Open a template as a starting point for your own template-modification endeavors. For example, you might decide to use the Event Poster as a basis for a standard poster design for your band—one you could easily modify with the date and venue for each new performance.

1. **Open a template.**

   Use the Project Gallery or the Elements Gallery to choose the Event Poster.

---

2. **Click the Master Pages tab at the bottom of the window and make any changes you want to appear on every page of the document (see Figure 8-3).**

   In this case, the document is only one page, but perhaps you'd like to lighten up the background image a bit to make the poster less dark and formal-looking. Select a background image and use the Transparency slider in the Colors, Weights, and Fills section of the Formatting Palette to lighten the image (Figure 8-19).

Figure 8-19:
You can modify one of Word's templates to make it your own—adding, removing, or modifying any of its elements before saving it as a template. Starting with the Event Poster (left), you can add your own picture, name, and text—including text-box reminders were you'll fill in the appropriate event information for each concert (right).

3. **Click the All Contents tab at the bottom of the window and change the text boxes to reflect your band's boilerplate text: your name, description, and a blurb, for example.**

   Insert any text that you'd like to appear on every version of this document, and enter reminders in those text boxes that need to be filled with specific information. Change the position, font, color, shadow, anything at all. And of course, add your own picture or artwork.

4. **Add or delete any other elements to transform the Microsoft template into your own.**

   Add other images, delete or resize text boxes. Use any of the object modification techniques described in the preceding pages until you're delighted with your design.

5. **Choose File → Save and choose Word Template (.dotx) from the Format pop-up menu, give your new template a descriptive name, and click Save.**

   Unless you choose a different destination, Word saves the template in your My Templates folder (Home → Library → Application Support → Microsoft → Office → User Templates → My Templates), making it available to the Project Gallery—also in the My Templates section. You can save the template in any folder and it functions just fine—it just won't appear in the Project Gallery.

Creating Templates from Scratch

If you're a real do-it-yourselfer, you can create templates from scratch, by starting with a blank sheet and building up a sample document exactly the way you want it. Start by opening a new blank Word Publishing Layout document from the Project Gallery or by choosing File → New Blank Publishing Layout Document if you're already working in the Publishing Layout view. This document becomes the model document you'll build up to create a template. Choose File → Save right off the bat and give it a title—something like *Company Newsletter Model*. Then as you work on it, periodically press ⌘-S to save your work. After you're all done creating the model document, you save it as a template.

Begin by choosing File → Page Setup and selecting the paper size and orientation, choose Format → Document → Margins to adjust your document margins (.5 inch in this example), and then begin the actual document design.

1. **Click the Master Pages tab in the lower-right corner of the document window.**

   The Master tag in the upper-left corner of the window reminds you you're now looking at the Master page—the place for any standard elements you want to appear on every page of your document (see page 312). Master pages are also great place for alignment guides (page 301) so they'll display on every page of the document, to help you maintain a consistent layout from page to page.

2. **Drag the vertical alignment guides from a Left ruler onto the page to provide column guides.**

   Divide the page into as many columns as you like—or three columns if you're following along with this tutorial. Use the ruler to help you create equal-width columns, placing alignment guides at 3 inches and 5.5 inches—representing the center of each column margin (Figure 8-20).

3. **Add any background images or text you want to appear on every page, such as a company logo—in this case, a large screw—and a company motto.**

   You want this logo as a background image which text can flow over and still be readable, therefore set its transparency to a relatively high 75% and set the wrapping style to none (page 306). Follow up by adding a text box containing the company motto at the bottom of the page.

4. **Click the All Contents tab in the lower-right corner of the document window to close the Master page view and return to the normal page view.**

   Now you can add picture drop zones and text placeholders to the document so that pictures and text you add each month will maintain a consistent appearance.

5. **Insert a picture by dragging it from the Object Palette, for example (page 291).**

   Use any of the picture formatting techniques to reposition, resize, rotate, add shadows or borders, and so on (page 744).

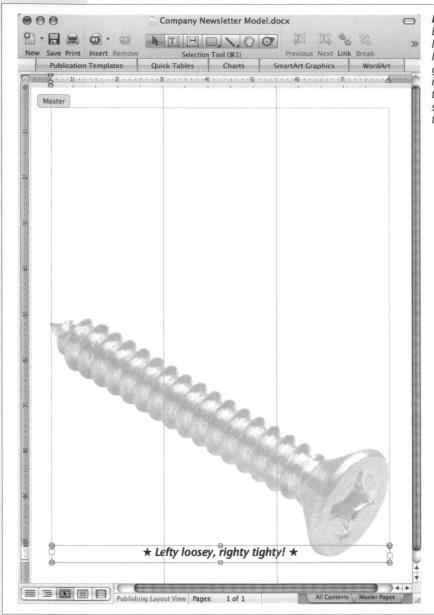

6. Convert the picture into a drop zone by double-clicking the picture to open the Format Picture dialog box. Click the Layout tab and then click the Advanced button. Click the Picture Position tab and at the bottom of the window turn on the checkbox marked Picture Placeholder. Click OK twice to close both parts of the Format Picture dialog box.

By transforming the picture into a drop zone, any picture you drop onto it assumes all of its formatting attributes: the size, rotation, Borders, shadows, and so on will match from one issue of your newsletter to the next (see Figure 8-21).

7. **Add a sample headline to the top of your document and format it with your headline style. Then transform it into a text placeholder by choosing Format → Text Box → Layout, clicking the Advanced button, clicking the Picture Position tab, and turning on the Text Placeholder checkbox near the bottom of the window. Click OK twice to close both parts of the Format Text box dialog box.**

Add more text boxes, if you like, for the columns of text for your articles. Add some sample text to each of them, or create linked text boxes filled with sample text, and transform them into text placeholders as well. Now when you use the template, anytime you click in a text box containing placeholder text, the placeholder disappears and whatever you type takes its place, assuming the formatting of the placeholder text—just like the Microsoft templates.

Tip: If you want to add your own Greek placeholder text, grab some from one of the Lorem Ipsum generators on the Web, like *www.lipsum.com*.

8. **Create additional pages for your newsletter if you desire (page 285).**

   Consider breaking your document into sections in order to have more than one master page (page 312) for different sections of your document.

9. **Save your document as a template by choosing File → Save As and choosing Word Template (.dotx) from the Format pop-up menu. Give your newsletter template a unique name, and click Save.**

   Word offers to save the template in your My Templates folder (Home → Library → Application Support → Microsoft → Office → User Templates → My Templates), making it available to the Project Gallery—also in the My Templates section. A better choice, however, is to save it in the My Publication Templates folder (which you'll find right next to the My Templates folder in the User Templates folder). This way your template shows up not only in the Project Gallery, but also in the Elements Gallery. (You can save the template into any folder and it functions just fine—it just won't appear in the galleries.)

Organizing Templates

Once you start creating your own templates, sooner or later you'll need to create new categories in the Project Gallery or delete templates you no longer need. Word doesn't show "New Folder" or "Delete Template" commands in the Project Gallery; you have to manually make new folders and trash templates.

Word keeps all the templates you've created separate from its assortment of stock templates. If you save your templates in the standard location, you'll find them in the My Templates folder by following the path Home → Library → Application Support → Microsoft → Office → User Templates → My Templates. Drag any templates you no longer need from the My Templates folder to the trash.

To add a new category to the Project Gallery, create a new folder next to My Templates in the User Templates folder. Name it for your new category, drag templates from the My Templates folder into it, or choose it when saving new templates.

Sharing Templates

You can share templates with other Word fans and let them take advantage of your hard work—and your creative brilliance—by sending a template as an email attachment, burning it on a CD-ROM, copying it to a USB flash drive, and so on.

But first you have to *find* the template file you want to share. One way is to dig deep into your hard drive to find Word's template storage vault and make a copy of one of your templates. As noted previously, they're in Home → Library → Application Support → Microsoft → Office → User Templates → My Templates.

A much easier way, however, doesn't involve any hard drive excavation at all. Open the Project Gallery and create a new document from the template you want to share. As soon as it opens, choose File → Save As and choose Word Template (.dotx) from the Format pop-up menu. You have to rename the template, and then choose an easy-to-find destination—say your desktop—and click Save. You've just created an exact clone of the template which you can now easily share with others.

Tip: Templates can be a bit hefty in the file-size department. If you want to email a template, compress it first. Control-click (or right-click) the template icon and, from the pop-up menu, choose "Create Archive of [file name]". Your Mac creates a compressed .zip archive of the file.

Word Meets Web

Nowhere is computerdom's speed-crazed evolution more obvious than on the Web. New ways of harnessing the Web's power and presenting information seem to appear daily. For developers of Web-page design software, the "you snooze, you lose" rule is especially apropos. Unfortunately for those who wish to live their entire life within the confines of Microsoft Office, the programmers responsible for Word's Web capabilities have been napping for years.

Office 2008's Web-page creation abilities are essentially unchanged since Office 98. You can still convert your PowerPoint slideshows, Excel spreadsheets, Entourage calendars, and Word documents into Web pages. And if you start with a simple Office document, there's a good chance it will translate into a decent Web page. Just don't try anything fancy. If you're serious about creating Web pages, then by all means get yourself a dedicated Web-design program like Dreamweaver, Go-Live, RapidWeaver, or iWeb.

Word as HTML Reader

According to legend, once upon a time a few people actually used Word as a Web browser. Earlier versions of Word had the ability to open Web pages; there was even a Web Toolbar with forward and back buttons and a Favorites menu. But there haven't been any confirmed sightings of these individuals for years, and in Word 2008, Microsoft quietly deleted its Web-browsing abilities. Word's ability to read documents written using the HTML Web-design language, however, is unaffected.

Opening Web Pages from Your Hard Drive

Documents written using the HTML Web-design language aren't confined to the Internet anymore. Because they're relatively small, include formatting, and open with equal ease on Macs, Windows PCs, and every other kind of computer; HTML documents are now a common exchange format for Read Me files, software user manuals, and the like. (You know when you have one because its file name ends with *.htm* or *.html.*)

Tip: When you open any kind of HTML document—like a Web page you've saved to your hard drive or a Word document you've saved as a Web page—in Word, it automatically opens in *Web Layout* view. If you can't see images, background colors, or other Web features in your document, you've probably somehow gotten into the wrong view. Choose View → Web Layout.

Word can open such documents directly: Just launch Word and choose File → Open, make sure that you have All Documents selected in the Enable pop-up menu (if you don't, Word won't let you select and open HTML files), then navigate to the file on your Mac and click Open. The file opens into Word's Web Layout view. Hyperlinks work, but otherwise the file acts more like a Word document than a Web page. For example:

- Scrolling text (see page 327) doesn't scroll.

- Animated GIFs don't work.

- Movies designed to play automatically (and anything else requiring a Web-browser plug-in) don't work.

- Text flow and the positioning of images on your page will probably be different in Word than in a browser. Using a table for layout alignment (see page 328) results in more consistency between Word and browser views.

Viewing HTML Code for a Web Page

When you open an HTML document, Word does its best to show you the images and text of that document just as though you're viewing it in a Web browser. In other words, you see the *results* of the HTML programming, not the HTML code itself.

If you're comfortable working in the HTML language, however, Word is only too happy to show you the underlying code:

1. **Open the Web page in Word. Choose View → HTML Source.**

   If that menu choice is grayed out, save the Web page document first. The Web page opens as a document full of HTML code. A tiny, one-button toolbar (Exit HTML Source) also opens.

2. **Edit the HTML in Word. Click Exit HTML Source when you're finished.**

   Word returns you to Web Layout view, which reflects the changes you just made.

Creating a Web Page in Word

As mentioned before, most people who are serious about creating Web pages use programs like Dreamweaver or GoLive. But Word can convert any of its own documents into a Web page, ready to "hang" on the Internet. Make no mistake: Professional Web designers will sneer at your efforts, since Word fills the resulting behind-the-scenes HTML code with acres of unnecessary computer instructions that can make a Web page take longer to load into visitors' browsers. Furthermore, they can also render your design layout imprecisely. But when you need to create only the occasional simple Web page, or when saving money and a short learning curve are more important to you than impressing professional Web designers, Word can suffice.

Designing a Site Map

Before you start working on your Web page in Word, it's a good idea to have a plan of action. Take a blank piece of paper (really—paper and pencil work *great* for this!) or Word document, draw a box for each page of your Web site, and label them to figure out how many Web pages your site will have, and how they'll be connected by navigational links. For instance, you might have a home page, an FAQ (frequently asked questions) page, a page of scanned photos, a long article on a page of its own, and a page with your contact information. Figure 9-1 shows an example sketch.

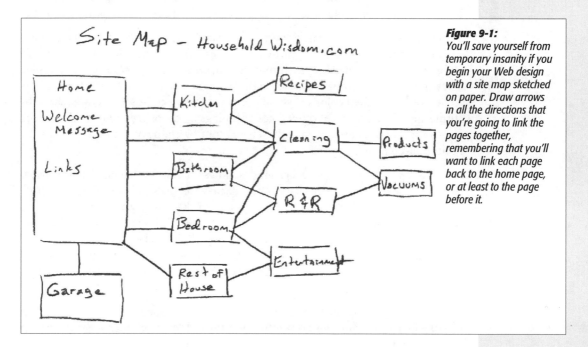

Figure 9-1:
You'll save yourself from temporary insanity if you begin your Web design with a site map sketched on paper. Draw arrows in all the directions that you're going to link the pages together, remembering that you'll want to link each page back to the home page, or at least to the page before it.

Basic Web-Page Layout

Once you've figured out which Web pages you'll need, create individual Word documents to represent those pages. You may need to use Word's advanced graphics and design tools—especially tables and hyperlinks—much more in a document that will ultimately become a Web page than, say, a run-of-the-mill memo. But otherwise, editing and designing a Web-bound Word document is similar to editing and designing any other Word file.

Tip: The following pages assume that you're interested in designing your Web pages essentially from scratch. If you have Web page templates from an earlier version of Word, feel free to add them to your Home → Library → Application Support → Microsoft → Office → User Templates → My Templates folder, making them available via the File → Project Gallery command. If the Web page you have in mind fits one of those basic styles, by all means use the template to save time. See page 721 for more on the templates.

Themes

Keep your site's graphic design simple. Although Word's Web tools let you use a riot of background and font colors, nothing looks cleaner and more readable on the Web than black type on a plain, light background. Still, Word 2008 comes with a laundry list of canned presets for Web pages (and other documents), called Themes. Each theme incorporates professionally coordinated choices for font, bullet graphics, horizontal lines, headings, background colors, and other elements.

To review your options, click the flippy triangle next to the name Document Theme in the Formatting Palette (see Figure 9-2). Use the buttons above and below the six thumbnails representing the Theme's font and color combinations. Click one of the thumbnails to select a theme. Each theme has a *color scheme*, a collection of coordinated colors. If you'd prefer a different color scheme, you can substitute any of the dozens of other color groupings by choosing one from the Colors pop-up menu. Similarly, change the Theme font by choosing a new one from the Fonts pop-up menu.

Word doesn't display the background settings in the Document Theme pane. Instead, choose Format → Background to display the Background palette (see page 325). As you make these changes, Word applies them to your Word document, where you'll notice major differences only if you used Word's built-in heading styles, picture bullets, horizontal lines, and hyperlinks. (These are the elements a theme can affect.) If you've already saved the document as a Web page, or if you're in Web Layout View, you'll also get the full effect of the background pattern, picture, or color.

Finally, after applying the theme and returning to your document, you can tailor it to your liking. Just use the Formatting Palette and Word's other tools to change the font color, border style, and so on.

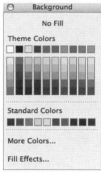

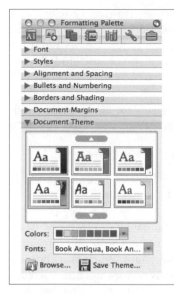

Figure 9-2:
Left: The Document Theme pane of the Formatting Palette lets you choose from the dozens of pre-designed themes displayed here as thumbnails.

Right: Choose Format → Background to open the Background palette in order to adjust background color or fill. If you use the Colors or Fonts pop-up menus or the Background palette to make changes to one of the existing themes, click Save Theme to preserve this combination in your My Themes folder. From now on it will be available at the top of the scrolling theme thumbnails, separated from the stock themes by a gray line.

Backgrounds

Although a white or very light background is your best bet for Web page legibility, Word lets you choose anything, from graceful to hideous, as the backdrop for your page. It can be a solid color background, a pattern or gradient, or a picture (see Figure 9-3). If you don't specify a background color, your visitors' Web browsers will use a default color, which is usually white or light gray.

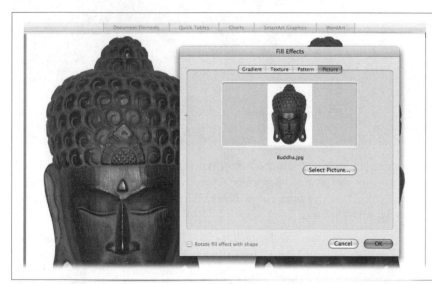

Figure 9-3:
Click Fill Effects on the Background palette, click the Picture tab, and then click Select Picture to choose a picture file from your hard drive. If you choose a large picture it fills your Web page; if you choose a small picture, Word tiles the image across the page.

To choose a background color for your Web page, choose Format → Background; in the Background color palette, click one of the color blocks to make it the background color. You can choose a different color by clicking More Colors and using one of Word's color pickers as described on page 747. If you choose No Fill, your background will be the default color of your reader's Web browser.

Note: When you're adding a background color to a Web page template that already contains a background *pattern*, the color overrides the pattern. To remove the color and restore the pattern, click No Fill on the Background color palette.

You can also click Fill Effects on the Background palette; you'll be shown a wide range of fancy backdrops, from burlap to shimmering gradients. (See Chapter 19 for more on these options.) Most of them are much too busy for a Web page that you actually expect people to read. For the sake of humankind, please use background textures, patterns, pictures, and gradients sparingly—with only very light colors—or not at all. In Web page design, less is truly more. When you choose a color, it appears instantly as the background of your Web page document. Word automatically switches into Online Layout view, if you weren't there already.

Font colors

You specify the color for the text of your Web page just as you would in any Word document—for example, using the Font Color button on the Formatting Palette.

POWER USERS' CLINIC

Automatic Color

When you open the Font Color section of the Formatting Palette, you'll notice that your first choice is Automatic Color. If you choose Automatic Color for text in a Web page, your reader will see it in whichever color she's chosen for her Web browser. (In Safari, for example, you can specify your default text color by choosing Safari → Preferences →

Appearance and then click either of the Select buttons for standard or fixed-width fonts. The Mac OS X Font window appears where you can change the font style, size, and color.)

Choosing No Fill for your background color and Automatic Color for your font is the ultimate in consideration for your reader. It does, however, limit your creativity.

When choosing a font color, the most important thing to remember is how it will show against your background. Remember, you want a lot of contrast between the background color and the font color. Black, blue, and red are good font color choices for light backgrounds.

White text on a black background sounds elegant, but it's not a good choice when working on a Web page in Word, since the black background shows up only in Web Layout view. When you switch to Normal view, you'll get white text on a white background—the 21st century version of invisible ink without the whole lemon-on-paper-held-up-to-a-light thing. You lose the ability to print your page from Draft view for the same reason.

Also, be aware that some people, in a vain attempt to load Web pages faster, turn off graphics in their Web browser. (In Safari, for instance, you do this by choosing Safari → Preferences → Appearance and turning off the checkbox for "Display images when the page opens.") Because background pictures and patterns are, in fact, graphics, readers who've turned graphics off won't see them. Instead, they'll simply see your text against their browser's automatic background color, which is usually white or light gray—yet another reason why black, red, and dark blue are safe font colors for Web pages.

Other text effects

You can use any of Word's text formatting—such as different fonts, typefaces, and paragraph formatting—in documents you'll be saving as Web pages, but bear in mind that they may look different, or be lost completely, depending on your reader's browser. (See Chapter 3 for more detail on text formatting.)

Word also has another special effect for use on Web pages: scrolling text. Use it with caution—since animated text, as noted earlier, strikes many Web denizens as extremely annoying. Scrolling or marqueeing text is, unfortunately, a very popular text effect on Web pages. As shown in Figure 9-4, a single dialog box lets you determine all aspects of how the text looks and scrolls.

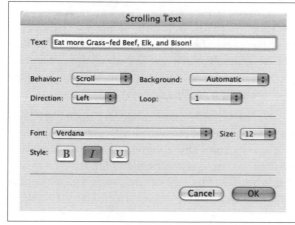

Figure 9-4:
The Font pop-up menu in the Insert → HTML Object → Scrolling Text dialog box lets you apply scrolling to text in any Word font. Scrolling or "marqueeing" text rolls across the width of your Web page from one side to the other like your very own CNN news crawl.

To open this box, highlight the text you want to scroll and then choose Insert → HTML Object → Scrolling Text. Choose a font, size, and typestyle in the lower panel of the dialog box, a different background color from the Background pop-up menu, and an animation style from the Behavior, Direction, and Loop pop-up menus.

For example, *Scroll* makes the text roll across the screen just like the letters on the marquee of a Broadway theater. (Use the Direction pop-up menu to specify whether it starts from the left or the right.) It goes all the way across until it disappears, then reemerges at the opposite edge and starts over again. From the Loop menu, choose the number of times you want the scrolling action to take place: one through five times, or Infinite.

Slide scrolls the text to the opposite edge of the page, and then stops. *Alternate* means that the text bounces back and forth across the screen as though in a slow-motion game of Pong. See how easy it is to be annoying?

Note: Please use the scrolling text feature with caution. It's difficult to read, and often adds little to your page. People browse the Internet for information, not to exercise their eyes as they attempt to track scrolling text.

To edit your scrolling text, select the text and choose Insert → HTML Object → Scrolling Text. Make any changes in the Scrolling Text dialog box. You won't see any text animation in Word; you have to save the result as a Web page and then open it in a Web browser.

Tip: A quick way to look at your Web page in a browser as you work on it is to save the Word document, then drag the proxy icon—the little icon in front of the document name in the document window's title bar—to your open browser window or the browser's icon in the Dock. Using this method, you can view the page in browsers that aren't set as your default browser. It's always a good idea to view your page in various browsers to be sure the page appears properly no matter which browser your viewer is using. To open your page in your default browser, choose File → Web Page Preview, as described on page 336.

Tables in Web page layout

These days, it's a very rare Web page whose design is nothing but a single river of text running down the middle of the page. Most professional Web pages, including those at *www.macworld.com*, *www.nytimes.com*, and *www.missingmanuals.com* are composed of several parallel columns. Each can contain an independent flow of text, as well as such standard elements as a graphic or navigation bar.

To create this effect in Word, use a Word *table*, as described in Chapter 4. Aligning objects using HTML alone is notoriously difficult. But if you compose your Web page with a table, you can use its rows and columns to align the text and graphics on your page. If you hide the borders, as described in Figure 9-5, your visitors won't even be aware that they're viewing a table. (You can still view the gray gridline indications in Word, but they won't show when the finished Web page is viewed in a browser.)

A single cell of your table can be extremely tall, if necessary. If yours is like a typical Web page, in fact, the entire page may be composed of a single row of the table, whose cells stretch the full height of the page. That's perfectly OK, and it's a clever way to get two or three parallel columns with independent text flows. (See page 150 for information on creating Word tables.)

Tip: Consider using *nested* tables for the smaller objects in your Web page. For example, create a table eight cells long by two cells wide to hold a list of links. Fill the table, then drag it into a large cell in your main table. The main table will help align the list relative to the rest of the page. (See the list of links in Figure 9-5, for example.)

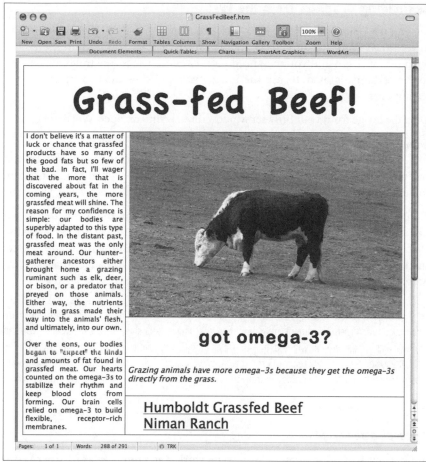

⊖ ⊖ ⊖   🗎 GrassFedBeef.htm

Figure 9-5:
A simple Web page laid out in a Word table. The table gridlines properly line up the text blocks, bullets, and links with each other. To make the black lines disappear, choose Table → Table Properties; click the "Borders and Shading" button; click None, OK, and OK. You can also select the entire table and choose No Border on the "Borders and Shading" panel of the Formatting Palette.

Graphics, Sounds, and Movies

Both Word's Clip Art Gallery and the Web itself are brimming with images that you can use to adorn your Web pages. You can also use any of Word's drawing tools, such as AutoShapes, SmartArt Graphics, and WordArt (see page 737), in the Web pages you create. When you save the Web page, Word saves the graphic in the Web page's folder as a GIF file (see the sidebar box on page 331).

Graphics do enhance your Web page's appearance. Keep in mind, however, that pictures take much longer to download than the text surrounding them. Try to strike a balance, only using a couple pictures per page for the typical information-focused Web site. Remember, about 20 percent of Web denizens are still using dial-up, narrow-band (56 kpbs) connections.

Downloading Graphics from the Web

When you see a picture you love on a Web site, you *can* easily download it and use it on your own Web site—but be aware that much of what you find on the Web is covered by copyright and you may need permission to use it (see the Note below). If you're certain it's okay to use the image, you can download it in one of the following ways:

- Drag the image from your browser window directly into an open Word document.

- Drag the image out of the browser window and onto your desktop or into the folder where you're keeping downloaded images. Let go of the mouse button when the outline of the image appears on the desktop or when the destination folder appears highlighted.

- Control-click (or right-click) and *hold* the hand cursor on the image that you'd like to copy. From the shortcut menu, choose Save Image to the Desktop (Safari). In Firefox, choose Save Image As and in the resulting dialog box, select the folder on your hard drive where you like to keep downloaded images. Click Save.

Note: You may be able to legally use certain copyrighted materials under the *fair-use* doctrine; for example when used for criticism, comment, news reporting, teaching, scholarship, or research. Often, you can find out whether images are copyrighted, free to use as long as you give credit, or whatever, right on the Web site. If you see the words "Creative Commons," then you can usually use the image for any purpose, with credit. When in doubt, ask permission from the copyright owner before using a photograph or other artwork.

Text wrapping and graphics

Wrapping text around images on Web pages works the same way as in other Word documents, as described on page 306. If you're using a table to lay out your Web page, you can even use text wrapping within a table cell.

The instructions for wrapping text around a graphic image are exactly as described on page 306—with one difference. In HTML, you can place graphics over text, behind text, with text above and below it, or wrapped around either side of it. What you can't do, however, is wrap text around *both* sides of a centered graphic. Thus, in Web Layout view, that option is grayed out on the Wrapping section of the Formatting Palette. To activate the choices on the "Wrap to" menu, drag the graphic to either side of the table, cell, or page.

Inserting Clip Art

Clip art gives you an effective way of "punctuating" your Web page and keeping its layout organized. Large, uninterrupted blocks of text make for difficult reading on the Web, so you can prevent eyestrain by using small graphic elements to break up your text—a benefit for both you and your readers.

Graphics Formats on the Web

Like Safari, Firefox, and other modern Web browsers, Word lets you use images for Web pages in any of three formats: GIF, JPEG, and PNG. If you place any other kinds of images in your Web page, such as PICT or bitmap, Word converts and saves them in one of the three compatible formats listed above, based on the following criteria:

- Photographs are saved in JPEG format. (JPEG graphics use a compression system that's especially effective with photographs.)

- Clip art, drawing objects, and PICT files are saved as GIF files. (GIF images are limited to 256 colors, but download very quickly. In other words, they lend themselves to drawings and other simple images.)

- If you've chosen "Enable PNG as an output format" in Preferences (see below), Word saves all images in PNG—Portable Network Graphics format. PNG is an improvement over both JPEG and GIF. PNG works equally well for both simple images and photographs. If you save all your Web page images as PNG, your Web page will load faster, take less storage space on your Mac, and work on most Web browsers.

To do so, choose Word → Preferences → General panel and click Web Options. Click the Picture tab and turn on "Enable PNG as an output format." Because PNG is gradually replacing GIF as the most popular Web graphics format, the only reason not to use it is that certain older browsers won't recognize such images.

Word now features two methods for finding and inserting clip art: the traditional Clip gallery, and Word 2008's new—and easier—Object Palette. Click the Toolbox button (if the Toolbox window's not showing) and then click the second button from the left at the top of the Toolbox window to reveal the Object Palette (see Figure 9-6). Click the ClipArt tab and use the scroll bar to see all the available clip art. Narrow your choices by using the category pop-up menu to select, for example, people, or animals. When you find the one that strikes your fancy, drag it into your document window.

Or you can use Word's traditional Clip Gallery. Either way you're accessing the same collection of clip art.

1. **Choose Insert → Picture → ClipArt.**

   The Clip Gallery appears. (See page 734 for more on this feature.)

2. **In the Category list in the Clip Gallery, scroll down to find the category you desire.**

   Use the scroll bar in the thumbnail pane to see all images in the category.

3. **Click the image you want, and then click Insert.**

   You return to your document, where the newly placed graphic appears.

Whichever method you use to insert clip art, once it appears in your document, you can resize it by clicking once to select it, and then dragging one of the corner handles. Use the corner handles to maintain the image's proportions—use the side handles if you want to stretch or squish the image.

Photos

Web pages can be a dreary place without photos. Most people would rather see a picture than read a thousand words. As your potential readers click their way through cyberspace, it's often the pictures that catch their eye and make them want to hang around your site a bit longer.

Indeed, many of the images in the Clip Gallery are photos. But Word 2008 now gives you access to your entire iPhoto library—and any other folder full of pictures on your computer—via the Object Palette. Open the Toolbox and click the Object Palette button—the second from the left. Then click the Photo tab, the rightmost of the four tabs. Word immediately starts filling in the palette with your images. The first time you use it, it displays the contents of your iPhoto library. (Subsequently, it shows you the picture folder you used the last time you opened the Photo tab.) Use the pop-up menu to choose which photos it displays (see Figure 9-6).

- **Photos** displays your entire iPhoto library.

- **Albums** displays photos from one of your iPhoto albums when you choose its name from the submenu.

- **Rolls** displays photos from one of your iPhoto rolls—or photo-importing sessions—when you choose its name or date from the submenu.

Figure 9-6:
When you click the Object Palette's Photos tab, Word opens a wormhole directly into your iPhoto library—or any other folder containing images. You can use the zoom slider at the bottom of the window to control the size of the thumbnails—helpful when you need to zoom in for a quick preview before selecting an image. When you find the perfect picture, drag it directly into your document.

- **Other Library or Folder** displays an "Open Library or Folder" dialog box, so you can choose any other folder of pictures on your computer or network. If you have more than one iPhoto library, click the "Show iPhoto libraries" button at the bottom of the dialog box, navigate to that folder, and then click Choose. For any other folder, click the "Show image folders" button, navigate to the folder, and then click Choose.

Note: The Object Palette can display photos in jpeg, .tiff, and .png formats, but not those in Photoshop (.psd), pdf, or RAW format.

The Object Palette's Photos pop-up menu remembers the last five folders you visited, making it easy to return to one of them by choosing its name from the menu. If you know the file name—or even just part of it—type it in the search box, and Word narrows down your selection of images as you type. Once you locate the image you want to use, just drag it into your document. (See page 291 for more on using photos in Word documents.)

Inserting Horizontal Lines

Inserting a horizontal line between sections is another great way to break up text on a Web page. If you started your Web page by choosing a theme, then Word has a line in a coordinating color and pattern already picked out for you. To insert one, proceed as follows:

1. **Choose View → Toolbars → "Tables and Borders".**

   The "Tables and Borders" toolbar opens.

2. **Click the arrow button next to the Borders button on the "Tables and Borders" toolbar. Choose Horizontal Line from the pop-up menu (see Figure 9-7).**

   Word inserts the line for your theme at the document's insertion point.

Figure 9-7:
Click the tiny arrow button next to the Borders button on the "Tables and Borders" toolbar to access the horizontal line command. When the line appears in your document, you can use its corner handles to resize it or even make it thinner or thicker.

You can also insert a horizontal line in any Web page by choosing Insert → Picture → Horizontal Line. The "Choose a Picture" dialog box opens, showing you the contents of your Mac's Applications → Microsoft Office 2008 → Office → Media → Clipart → Lines folder. Select a line (based on what you see in the preview window) and click Insert. Word places the line across your Web page document at the insertion point. When you choose a line in this fashion, it overrides your Theme line style, so the next time you insert a line using the "Tables and Borders" toolbar as described above, Word uses this new line style.

Movies

Web pages created in Word can store and play digital movies in any of several formats: QuickTime, QuickTime VR, MPEG, and some AVI files. (Word converts AVI to QuickTime when you save the Web page.) You can use any such movie that you have on your Mac—whether you downloaded it or made it yourself—in a Web page you create in Word.

To use a movie from the Web in your Web page, you need to download it onto your Mac. If you just click a link to watch a movie, that doesn't necessarily download a copy for you. You have to Control-click (or right-click) the link and then, from the shortcut menu, choose either Download Linked File (Safari), or Save Link As (Firefox). Either way, you'll get a chance to name the file and choose a folder location for it on your Mac, such as the desktop or your Documents folder.

Then:

1. **Choose Insert → Movie.**

   You have to be in a Word document, not an .htm document, and you should be in Print Layout or Web Layout view. The Open File dialog box appears. (If you use the Insert → Movie command in Draft view, Word automatically switches to Print Layout view.)

Note: If you can't find the Movie command on your Insert menu, see the sidebar on page 335 for a workaround.

---

2. **In the Insert Movie dialog box, navigate to the movie file on your hard drive and double-click it.**

   The movie appears on your page, where you can drag it anywhere on your Web page, wrap text around it, and resize it just like any Word picture—all using the Formatting Palette.

Note: Word 2004 gave you the ability to set a poster frame—a still picture shown when the movie's not playing. Unfortunately, during the transition to the new XML file format, Office 2008 has lost this ability. When they're not playing, movies display their first frame—which is often black. Until Microsoft patches things up, the workaround is to purchase QuickTime Pro for $30 (*www.quicktime.com*) and use it to set a poster frame before bringing the movie into Word.

Removing a movie

Deleting a movie is easy: Click the icon or poster frame to select it and press the Delete key.

Tip: Your movie won't play on the Web unless each visitor to your page has installed the QuickTime plug-in. Not all Mac people have the most recent version, and Windows types may not have it at all. You can help them by giving them a link to the Web site where Apple gives downloads of a free version for both Windows and Mac. For example, you might add this text somewhere on your Web page: "You need the free QuickTime plug-in for Mac or Windows to view the movies on this Web page. Download it at *www.apple.com/quicktime/download/.*" (See page 336 for more on inserting hyperlinks.)

WORKAROUND WORKSHOP

The Crazy Movie Workaround

Bizarrely enough, you can't put a movie on a Web page in Word when you're in a Web page. If you're working in a document that you've saved as a Web page—that is, a .htm document—you can look at the Insert menu all you want; the command is just not there. Only in a standard Word document does the Insert → Movie command appear.

You'll have to design most of your Web page in a standard Word document, taking care to insert all your movies before saving the document as a Web page. You can play, reposition, format, and set a poster frame for movies after you've saved the document as a Web page, but you can no longer add new movies. To add movies again, choose File → Save As and save your document back into Word Document format. Then save it as a Web page when you're done. (Your other alternative, of course, is to buy a copy of Dreamweaver or GoLive.)

Inserting Sounds

If your movies, background pictures, and animated text aren't enough multimedia to satisfy your need to annoy your visitors' and stall out their modems, don't give up—Word also comes with a library of sounds that play as your reader views your Web page. You can use one of them, or any sound you've downloaded in the WAV, AIFF, or MIDI format.

Note: Word's Web pages viewed in Safari or Firefox don't play their sounds. It's apparently another victim of the XML file format transition—and perhaps a blessing in disguise. Good ol' Internet Explorer, however, has taken no such vow of silence.

---

1. **Choose Insert → HTML Object → Background Sound.**

   The Background Sound dialog box appears.

2. **Click Select; navigate to the sound file and double-click it.**

   The standard installation of Office has a starter set of sound effects in the Microsoft Office 2008 → Office → Media → Sounds folder.

3. **Choose the number of times you'd like the sound to play from the Loop menu, and then click OK.**

   When your viewer opens the Web page, the background sound plays the number of times you chose to loop it.

To remove a sound, choose Insert → HTML Object → Background Sound. The name of the current background sound file is shown at the top of the dialog box. Click Clear to remove it from your Web page.

Web Page Preview

As you build your Web page, you'll need to preview your work-in-progress from time to time. Yes, choosing View → Web Layout shows what your document will look like in a Web page; but you won't be able to see your animated text and certain other browser-only features. Fortunately, the File → Web Page Preview command actually shows it in your Web browser, which provides a much more accurate preview.

The document name in the title bar may not match the file name that you gave the document when you saved it. That's because Word takes the Web-page name from the title box on the File → Properties → Summary tab. In other words, if you'd like to change the name that appears in the Web browser's title bar when opening your Word document as a Web page, simply choose File → Properties → Summary tab and change the title.

Hyperlinks

Hyperlinks—buttons, graphics, or text phrases that, when clicked, take you to a different document—are what Web sites are all about. In Word, you can make just about any kind of link you've ever dreamed of—links to Web pages, to other documents or pages you've created, to movies or sound files, or to a point in the same document or another document.

Note: The Edit Hyperlink dialog box, which you'll use in this section, has a Document tab that's supposed to let you create a hyperlink to a document anywhere on your computer. But, as of this writing, it's exceptionally flaky and doesn't function at all using Tiger (10.4). In Leopard (10.5) it works, but opens a linked Word document in Draft view–which can be disconcerting since the page appears completely blank if it's actually a Publishing Layout view document.

Linking to Another Place

If your document is long, you may want links to help your reader navigate it. For instance, on a Web page (or even a senior thesis), you can place a link called "Back to top" at the bottom of your page, or a list of links at the top of the page that link to paragraphs farther down. Either way, this can save your reader lots of scrolling.

If you've used Word bookmarks (see page 240) or its built-in heading styles in the target document, you can use them as anchors—the targets—for your links, like this:

1. **Select the text ("Back to top," for example) or graphic that will be the hyperlink; choose Insert → Hyperlink.**

   The Insert Hyperlink dialog box opens, as shown in Figure 9-8. The text you selected in your Web page document appears in the Display box. If a graphic will serve as the link, then <<Selection in Document>> appears in the box.

Tip: Microsoft doesn't kid around about the Insert → Hyperlink command; it has about 731 alternate methods of triggering it. For example, you can also Control-click the selected text or object and choose Hyperlink from the shortcut menu, or click the Insert Hyperlink button on the Standard toolbar, or press ⌘-K.

2. **Click the Document tab, then click Locate.**

   The "Select Place in Document" dialog box appears.

3. **Choose the bookmark or heading, click OK, and then click OK.**

   If you haven't successfully created any bookmarks or used one of Word's built-in heading styles, Top of the Document is the only available choice. If you do have headings and bookmarks in the document, click the flippy triangles to view the entire list.

After you click OK to close the Insert Hyperlink dialog box, the text you selected in step 2 turns into a blue, underlined hyperlink. To test it, just click the link; the document scrolls so that the heading or bookmark anchor jumps to the top of the screen.

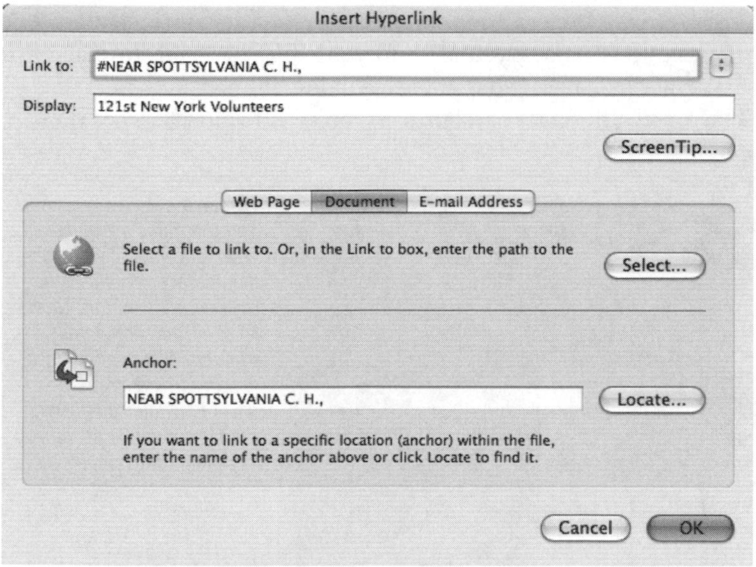

Figure 9-8:
The Insert Hyperlink dialog box has a tab for each of the three types of Word hyperlinks. Click ScreenTip to edit the pop-up screen tip that appears when somebody points to your link without clicking.

Linking to Another Web Site

If you're designing a Web site, of course, the link you're probably most interested in creating jumps to *another* Web page. That's why Word provides so many different ways of creating a hyperlink to another page on the Web.

By typing a URL

As many an annoyed Mac fan can tell you, Word comes factory set to turn *any* Web address you type into a living hyperlink. Creating Web pages with Word is the one time you'll actually be grateful for this behavior. Just type the Web address into your Web page document, beginning with *www* and ending with *.com, .org*, or dot-whatever. Word automatically creates the hyperlink (unless you've turned off this feature in Word's Preferences, as described on page 87).

By dragging a URL

You don't have to memorize and type a URL in order to place a hyperlink in your document. All you have to do is find it on the Web; then you can drag and drop the Web address into your Web page (although what appears on the page depends on the browser you're using).

Open your Web browser and visit the Web page that you'd like to link to. Switch back to Word, and then drag the icon next to the Address window from the browser into your document, as shown in Figure 9-9. If you're using Firefox, Word adds the Web address as plain text—*not* a hyperlink. Also, due to Word's penchant for pasting formatted text, use the Paste Options button that appears next to your pasted address and choose Match Destination Formatting from the shortcut menu—or just copy the Web address and paste it into your document by choosing Edit → Paste Special and selecting Unformatted Text. Then, to make Word turn it into a hyperlink, place your insertion point immediately after the Web address and then press the Space bar. Finally—you've got yourself a hyperlink.

Figure 9-9:
You can make a Web link in a Word document by dragging the address icon out of the address bar in Safari. These kinds of links aren't only useful in Web pages, they'll function in any Word document, launching your Web browser and taking you straight to that page.

If you're using Safari or (for old times' sake) Internet Explorer, Word creates a hyperlink *field* without any of the previous rigmarole. If you see the field code (see page 235) instead of the title of the Web page, select the entire field code and press Option-F9. In Safari, the field displays the actual Web address; in Internet

Explorer, the hyperlink in your document will be the Web page's title (as seen in the title bar of your browser window), not the URL itself. If you want to see the underlying URL, point to the Web-page name without clicking to make the identifying yellow screen tip appear.

If you'd like to use different text than the Web page's real title or address for the hyperlink, edit the hyperlink as described on page 340. For example, if the Web page you're linking to is titled "Actor Bio 2," you might want to change it to the more descriptive "Brando: The Early Years."

Note: Although there is an Anchor box on the Web Page tab in the Insert Hyperlink dialog box, the page has to have HTML anchor tags or Word bookmarks, as described on page 240 in order for this feature to work.

Email Hyperlinks

An *email* hyperlink, also known as a *mailto* link, opens a new, preaddressed message in your default email program (or the program of whoever clicks the link). When you create a Web page, it's common practice to include an email hyperlink to yourself, so that your readers can contact you with questions, comments, or orders. To do so, just follow these steps:

1. Type and select the text ("Contact me") that will become the email hyperlink.

   As with any other hyperlink, you can use a graphic, but you should also include some text to make it clear what the link does.

2. **Choose Insert → Hyperlink. In the Hyperlink dialog box, click the Email Address tab. In the To box, type the email address you want the link to mail to.**

   The Recent Addresses list contains a list of email addresses for which you've recently created hyperlinks (not necessarily ones you've actually used). To look up an address in your Entourage Address Book instead, click Launch Email Application. No matter what your default email program, Entourage launches. There's no further integration with Entourage, however, so you'll have to manually copy and paste the address you want out of its Address Book.

3. **Press Tab; type a subject line, if you wish.**

   In other words, when your visitor clicks the "Contact me" link, his email program will automatically open. When it does, an outgoing blank email message will appear, preaddressed to you *and* with the Subject line already filled in. Including a subject line can help you keep track of emails that come from this particular Web page. However, not all Web browsers, or all email programs, work with the subject-line-in-an-email-hyperlink feature.

4. **Click OK.**

   The email link is ready to click.

Note: If all you need is a simple Web or email hyperlink, just type it into Word. Word creates the hyperlink instantly (if, that is, you haven't turned off this feature in the Tools → AutoCorrect → AutoFormat As You Type dialog box). Later, should you want to change the link to read "Contact Me" or something more elegant-looking than your plain old email address, edit the link as described next.

Likewise, for simple addresses like *www.apple.com*, just type the URL into your document. You can always go back and change the text later, as described next.

Selecting and Editing Hyperlinks

When you click a hyperlink in Word, Word follows the link, even if that means launching your Web browser. But if clicking triggers the link, how are you supposed to *edit* the hyperlink text?

The easiest way is to Control-click (or right-click) the link and choose Hyperlink → Edit Hyperlink from the shortcut menu. The Edit Hyperlink dialog box opens; here you can change the URL, email address, display text, screen tip (see the box below), anchor, and so on.

If the dog ate your Control key, you can also highlight the link by carefully dragging across it or moving the insertion point into it with the arrow keys, then pressing ⌘-K (or choosing Insert → Hyperlink) to open the Insert Hyperlink dialog box. In fact, if all you want to edit is the display text for a hyperlink, just drag carefully across it (or Control-click it and choose Hyperlink → Select Hyperlink) and then retype.

Similarly, you can edit graphic links without triggering them; once again, the trick is to select the link without activating it—by Control-clicking it. After editing the image using the Formatting Palette or the Drawing or Picture toolbars, press Esc or click elsewhere to deselect the object and avoid inadvertently making further changes.

Hyperlink colors

In Word, text hyperlinks appear in blue type until they're clicked, whereupon they change to purple. You can change these colors, if you like; the trick is to change the Hyperlink *style*, just as you'd change any Word style (see page 133 for instructions).

If you can't stand to work with colors that aren't your own, you can even change the color that clicked hyperlinks change *into* after being clicked. Just modify Word's built-in Followed Hyperlink style.

These new hyperlink colors override default hyperlink colors when the page is opened in your Web browser. If your colors don't work, it's because your visitor has changed his browser preferences to override the color choices that have been programmed into Web pages.

Removing Hyperlinks

To remove a hyperlink you no longer want, you have two options:

- Drag over the hyperlink text and press Delete or position your insertion point after the link and press the delete key until you've expunged it. Both the hyperlink and the display text or object are deleted.

- To cancel out the link while leaving the display text or object in place, Control-click the link and choose Hyperlink → Edit Hyperlink on the shortcut menu. Click Remove Link.

Web Forms

If you've ever searched a Web site, taken a poll, or made a purchase online, you've used a Web *form*. Web forms comprise pop-up menus, checkboxes, and little text boxes. They're designed to collect information from the Web site visitor and save it on a server for processing.

You can build a Web form in Word, but you'll need the help of a Web programmer to write the necessary CGI scripts to make the form work. (CGI stands for *common gateway interface*, a software convention for transferring and processing data between Web pages and servers.)

To build a Web form, you have to insert various *form controls* in your page—checkboxes, radio buttons, pop-up menus, buttons, and so on—that your visitors will use for submitting the information and resetting the form. You'll find them in the Insert → HTML Object submenu. With a programmer at your side, select settings and values from the resulting dialog box.

Saving Web Pages

If you started your Web page from a blank Web page, as described at the beginning of this section, all you have to do to save it is press ⌘-S or choose File → Save or Save As. However, you can also save a standard Word document or template as a Web page, like so:

1. **Choose File → "Save as Web Page".**

   The Save dialog box opens, as shown in Figure 9-10

2. **Click one of the radio buttons depending on how you'd like to save the file.**

   The **Save entire file into HTML** option creates a dual-purpose document. It stores the information *both* for display on the Web *and* for returning to it as a Word document. Such word processor–only elements as headers and footers, comments, page numbers, and page breaks will reappear when you open it again in Word.

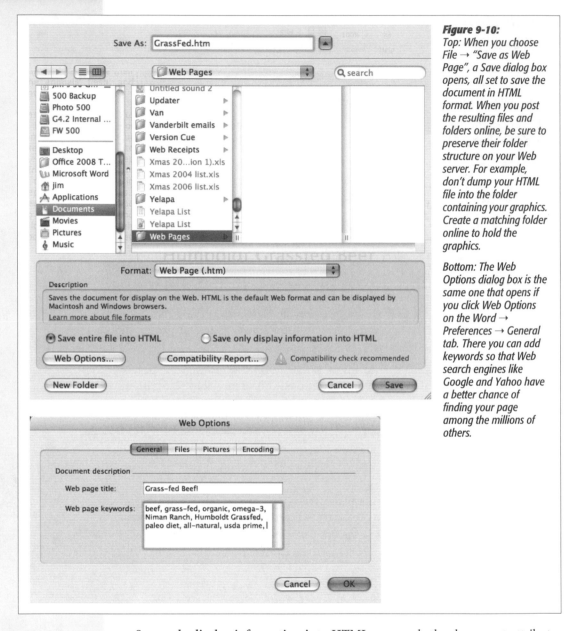

Figure 9-10:
Top: When you choose File → "Save as Web Page", a Save dialog box opens, all set to save the document in HTML format. When you post the resulting files and folders online, be sure to preserve their folder structure on your Web server. For example, don't dump your HTML file into the folder containing your graphics. Create a matching folder online to hold the graphics.

Bottom: The Web Options dialog box is the same one that opens if you click Web Options on the Word → Preferences → General tab. There you can add keywords so that Web search engines like Google and Yahoo have a better chance of finding your page among the millions of others.

Save only display information into HTML saves *only* the document attributes that work in a Web browser. Other information, such as page and section breaks, columns, and headers and footers will be lost. This option makes a smaller, more compact HTML file, which is a good thing if your Web service provider charges based upon how much server space you use.

Tip: If you choose this option, use Save As first to save a copy with all the normal Word elements intact; you may decide to use the document in Word again.

3. **Click Save.**

   Word takes longer than usual to save the document. When it's finished, you can switch to Web Layout view (if you weren't already there) to see the Web page as it will appear online.

Web Options

When you click Web Options in the Save dialog box (see Figure 9-10), you can specify special Web features that would normally require mucking around in HTML code.

- The Web page *title* you enter on the **General Tab** appears in the title bar in a Web browser. The Web page *keywords* are the terms that search engines like Google and Yahoo spot when searching. (In HTML, these words are known as *meta tags*.)

- "Update links on Save" in the **Files** tab comes already turned on. If you've changed or moved any of your Web page's supporting files, such as bullets, graphics, or background patterns, Word updates the links so the page will work when you reopen it. The "Save only display information into HTML" checkbox turns on the corresponding radio button in the Save dialog box (see above).

- Checking "Enable PNG as an output format" on the **Pictures** tab saves all the images in your Web page in Portable Network Graphics format, as described on page 331. The "Screen size" pop-up menu shows just about every screen size and resolution combination your Web page visitors are likely to have. 1,024× 768 is the smallest screen most people use today, and therefore a pretty safe bet.

   The "Pixels per inch" box, is another vestige of the olden days of Web browsers. Leave it set at 72 and forget about it.

- The menu on the **Encoding** tab displays all the foreign languages and browser formats Word can use for saving your Web page. If your page contains text in a different alphabet system (such as Cyrillic or Japanese), choose it from this menu.

Tip: As you complete your Web page, consider testing it in different Web browsers. Text may wrap differently, colors and graphics may look different, and movies and marquees may not operate the same way, if at all, in different browsers.

If you have a copy of the America Online program, for example, open your page using its File → Open command. Try the same experiment in Firefox. You'd do well to also check your Web page on a Windows PC running Internet Explorer.

Lost in the Translation

Despite all its Web-savvy trappings, Word, when you get right down to it, isn't actually an HTML editor. The Web pages it creates capture the spirit of the original Word document you prepared, but not the letter, since you lose quite a bit of its look in the conversion to a Web page. Among the casualties: text boxes; fancy text effects like embossed type, shadow, and strikethrough; drop caps; page numbering; margin settings and page borders; headers and footers; multiple columns; and styles. All of these Word features drop out when the document is converted to HTML. Fields (see page 235) *sort of* carry through; the resulting Web page shows the field information (such as the date), but it's no longer self-updating. Tabs aren't reliable, either, since Word converts them into HTML tabs, which, in some Web browsers, turn into spaces. (Use tables wherever you're inclined to use tabs.) Footnotes, on the other hand, perform beautifully. The superscript numbers turn into hyperlinks that scroll to the notes at the bottom of the page.

POWER USERS' CLINIC

HTML Text Styles

The HTML styles in the Format → Style dialog box let you transform a saved Web page into an attractive Word document. For example, suppose that someone at your company created an online training manual, but no one made a paper version. Or maybe you want to download an article from the Web and create a printed version (with permission, of course).

These Web pages are HTML documents, and the text in them is formatted using HTML codes. For instance, one HTML code creates a first-level heading, another denotes an address or citation, and another creates hyperlinks. These labels are listed in the Styles list box in the Format → Style dialog box; except for Hyperlink and Followed-Hyperlink, their style names all begin with the letters HTML.

You can format and redefine these styles as you would any Word styles; when you do, Word will use them for HTML-formatted text whenever you open a Web page in Word. You may want to make all hyperlinks match your Normal style, for example. (Headings in HTML are automatically changed into your Word heading styles.)

To convert a Web page into a Word document, open the Web page in your browser. Choose File → Save or Save As; save the page onto your Mac in HTML format. Open the page in Word by choosing File → Open and navigating to the Web-page file. You will see the text in the document, but not the images (they don't get saved along with the rest of the page).

Posting Your Web Site Online

Creating HTML documents is only the first step in establishing a Web presence. The final step is uploading them to a *Web file server*—a computer that's always on and connected to the Internet. You have several options:

- **Use your own Mac.** If you have a full-time connection (cable modem or DSL) and a *static* IP address (which you usually have to pay extra for), you can use the built-in Web Sharing feature of Mac OS 9 or Mac OS X to make your Web site available to the Internet at large. Your Web address won't be very memorable (along the lines of *http://192.168.34.2*), the speed won't be great, and not very many people can visit your site at once, but the price ($0) is right. The Mac's online help and *Mac OS X: The Missing Manual* have instructions.

- **Use your ISP.** Most Internet service providers (ISPs) give you somewhere between 10 megs and 1 gig of free space to hold your Web pages as part of your monthly fee. Into that space, you can upload your Web pages directly, making them available for public browsing. Your ISP takes care of keeping its computer up, running, and connected to the Internet.

- **Use the Apple HomePage feature.** Apple gives every Mac fan 10 GB of Web space, for a $100 yearly fee, in the form of the Sites folder on your iDisk—a virtual hard drive. (Visit *www.mac.com* for details.) Just put the HTML documents you've created—name your home page *index.html* for best results—and graphics into the Sites folder of your iDisk. (Don't bother using the Mac Home-Page-building tools; Web pages you've designed using Word don't show up. But if you just drag them into your iDisk's Sites folder, they're instantly available on the Internet.)

UP TO SPEED

Naming and Nesting Folders

If you've had experience creating Web pages using a real HTML editing program, you know about the headache of creating sets of folders to organize all the pages and picture files that compose your Web site. If the various HTML documents (the individual Web pages) and their graphics (your picture bullets, background patterns, and so on) aren't on your hard drive and on the Internet in precisely matching folder hierarchies, you'll get dead links, missing graphics, and worse. You also need to save the graphics files (for picture bullets, background patterns, and so on) in folders.

When you save a Word document as a Web page, you create one document (whose name ends in .htm) containing the text, and an accompanying folder containing all of the graphics, sounds, and movies. All you have to do is post them online in the same relative folders.

If you're making a large Web site with many pages, you may want to nest folders within one larger folder to help keep things organized.

Part Two: Entourage

2

Email, Address Book, and Newsgroups

Life is complex. Just keeping up with the daily flow of information can be a full-time job. There are schedules to keep, phone numbers and addresses to file, tasks to track, long range plans to make—and an unending avalanche of email to sort, file, and reply to. Who wouldn't long for a personal assistant to help keep life and business on track? Make that a couple of assistants—or perhaps...an entourage? Takin' care of business with an entourage like Elvis's can get expensive—even if you don't reward them with jewelry and Cadillacs. But when it comes to managing your computer life, Office 2008's Entourage can TCB with the best of them. (And that can make you feel like the King.)

Much more than an email program, Entourage can help you schedule meetings, track your to-dos, and scope out your calendars. Since Office 2001, Entourage has sought to be a Mac fan's personal information manager (PIM) and email program all in one, as well as being a vehicle to tie together all the individual programs. The Project Center, described in Chapter 11, is the nexus for this informational synergy.

Note: If Entourage is your personal assistant, Office 2008 introduces an under-assistant in the form of My Day. This diminutive, standalone program lets you keep tabs on the vital tasks and events of the day, and helps save you from falling into the black hole of your email when all you really need to know is the time of your haircut appointment. You'll find My Day described in Chapter 11 also.

In addition to its organizational capabilities, Entourage is at heart a first-rate email program. Entourage handles email and newsgroups with ease, as you'll see in this chapter. For the first time, Entourage 2008 cooperates with Mac OS X's Spotlight search to help you find any information you have in Entourage—even in message attachments. And since junk email won't go away by itself, improved junk mail filters help shield you from the bad, while letting through the good.

The Big Picture

The Entourage main window is divided into three main areas: buttons for Entourage's main functions at top left, a list of folders for your email on the left, and a big viewing area for your messages, calendars, tasks, and so on, on the right (Figure 10-1) What you see in the main viewing area depends on which Entourage function you're using; see the box on page 351. Like changing stations on a car radio, you can switch among Entourage functions by clicking the six buttons at the upper-left.

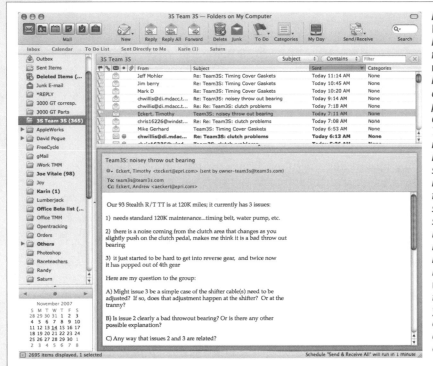

Figure 10-1:
When you're using Entourage's email function, the standard window displays a folder list, a list pane showing all of the messages in a particular folder, and an email-specific toolbar. There's also an information bar at the bottom of the screen that shows how many messages are in a chosen folder, how many are selected, and what schedules (if any) Entourage has on deck. Don't miss the Fonts tab in Entourage → Preferences → General, where you can specify the type size and style you prefer for reading and printing your email and other Entourage components.

Entourage Functions

When you first launch Entourage and complete the Setup wizard (described in a moment), the Mail button at the upper left is already selected. But mail is only one of Entourage's functions. The six big icons at the upper-left corner of the Entourage screen correspond to the following features:

- **Mail.** This, of course, is the big workhorse feature: email. This chapter covers the Mail feature in detail.

- **Address Book.** Your electronic "little black book"—home to not just the email addresses in your social entourage, but also phone numbers, home addresses, and so on. The Address Book also features predefined Address Book *views* that let you find subsets of your data—every member of your family, for example. You'll find the complete details starting on page 412.

- **Calendar.** Plan your day, your week, your month…if you dare, plan your year! You can manage your schedule and track important events using the Entourage Calendar. Once again, a set of views can quickly show you only work- or family-related events, recurring appointments, or whatever. See page 444 for details.

- **Notes.** Memo-pad-like musings that you can attach to names in your address book, tasks in your to-do list, and so on. See page 489 for details.

- **Tasks.** Your to-do list. When you click this button, the right side of the screen shows the list of tasks you've set up for yourself. See page 462 to read everything about Tasks.

- **Project Center.** The master control center from which you can track the email messages, documents, notes, pictures, tasks, and calendars associated with your current projects, and begin new ones. It's your one-stop project clearing house (see page 475 for details).

POWER USERS' CLINIC

The Mighty Morphing Interface

You don't have to be content with the factory-installed design of the Entourage screen. You can control which Entourage panes are visible, how big they are, and which columns show up in list views.

Some people like to read email messages in separate windows, while others like to use the Preview pane at the right side of the window, which displays the current message right in the main Mail window. To turn on Entourage's Preview pane, choose View → Preview Pane and select On Right, Below List, or None.

Another way you can individualize your Entourage experience is by organizing your email and newsgroup message using *groups*. This feature lets you divide and conquer your messages in the list window according to project, subject, date sent, priority, and more. (See the box on page 375 for full detail.)

You can hide or show the toolbar or the folder list using the View menu. For example, to hide the toolbar, choose View → Hide Toolbar.

To change the size of a pane, drag its border, as shown in Figure 10-2. You can drag any border that has a tiny dot in its middle. (You don't have to drag right on those dots, though.)

Entourage also lets you decide what columns appear in Mail view's list pane. If you don't care about seeing the Categories column for your email, for example, you can hide it, leaving more space for name, Subject, and Date. To switch columns on or off, choose from the View → Columns submenu.

You can also rearrange the columns, which can be handy if you'd rather see the Subject column first instead of the Sender, for example. Just drag the column's header horizontally; release when the vertical dotted line is where you'll want the column to wind up. To make a column wider or narrower, drag the short black divider line between column names horizontally.

When you change Entourage views—from Mail, to Address Book, to Calendar, and so on—you'll see even more interface changes. Although the basic layout of the window remains constant—folders on the left, toolbar on top—the contents of the main window pane changes to display the current function's info; and the collection of toolbar icons also changes to match that function.

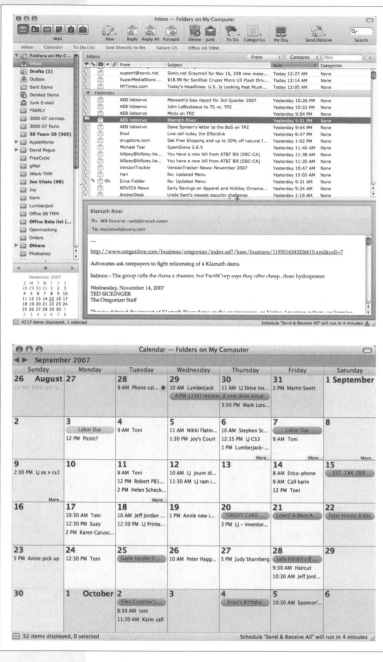

Figure 10-2:
Top: Drag any of the window dividers to resize the panes according to your needs.

Bottom: If you prefer to see the main information in the largest view, use the View (or Calendar) menu to hide everything that can possibly be hidden. This option is especially effective when you've opened multiple Entourage windows, as described in the box on page 353.

The Toolbar

Unlike Word, Entourage has only one toolbar (see Figure 10-3), which changes to reflect your current activity. For example, if you're working with email, the toolbar's buttons all pertain to email functions; if you click the Calendar button, the

Multiplying Windows

When you launch Entourage the first time, it's set to display each major function—Mail, Address Book, Calendar, and so on—in the main window when you click the appropriate icon in the top-left corner. Whichever feature you choose takes over the main Entourage window and hides the others. But what if you want to see your calendar and your email at the same time?

You can—by opening them in separate windows. To do so, choose File → New → Open New Main Window. Now you can see two views simultaneously, such as your Calendar and Notes, two Mail windows, your Address Book and Tasks, and so on. Just click the view buttons in the top left corner to choose what to display. If you are fortunate enough to be staring at a 30-inch display, don't stop at just two Entourage windows—make as many as you like!

toolbar gains calendar-appropriate commands. You'll encounter these commands in the context of the email, newsgroup, calendar, address book, notes, and task discussions in this and the following chapters. The six Entourage view buttons at the left end of the toolbar persist through every view.

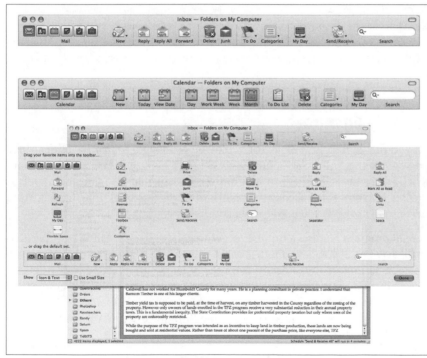

Figure 10-3:
Entourage's toolbar commands change to match the Entourage function you're using, for example, switching from email icons (top) to calendar icons (middle). Control-click the toolbar to choose the display options or open the Customize Toolbar palette (bottom), and its complete catalog of available toolbar buttons.

Entourage 2008, for the first time, lets you customize its toolbar. If you find that you never use the Categories button or frequently need to forward messages as attachments, for example, consider customizing the toolbar so you only see the buttons you really need. Control-click (or right-click) the toolbar and choose Customize Toolbar from the shortcut menu to display all the possible buttons for the current Entourage function. Drag new buttons onto the toolbar or drag unwanted buttons off it. Along with buttons, you'll find spaces and separators to help you perfect your toolbar.

If you find yourself getting carried away with adding buttons—or just need to maximize a small screen—choose Use Small Size from the toolbar's Control-click menu. This menu also gives you an option for displaying the buttons as Icon Only, Text Only, or Icon & Text—otherwise known as right brained, left brained, and information overload.

If you're a keyboard-command maven, you may prefer the ultimate toolbar customization—removing it entirely. That way, since there are keyboard commands for virtually every button in the toolbar, you can keep your hands on the keyboard, and minimize onscreen clutter. Choose View → Hide Toolbar to liquidate the button bar and give yourself another vertical half inch of screen real estate. Alternatively, click the little oblong button in the upper-right corner to hide or reveal the toolbar.

Note: The Toolbar control button, lodged in the upper-right corner of nearly every Mac OS X window, is a cause of great confusion for many otherwise-savvy Mac fans. Apple added this button when they moved the two buttons that had been in that corner to the left to join the Close button. You'll find this button in all Office document windows, where it toggles between showing and hiding the toolbar. In Finder windows it hides the toolbar *and* the Sidebar—and regularly instigates frantic tech-support phone calls after an inadvertent mouse click.

Setting Up Entourage

When you first launch Entourage (or when you create a new *identity*, as described on page 495), the Entourage Setup Assistant presents itself. The Setup Assistant presents a long series of question-and-answer screens that give you the opportunity to set up your email accounts, import your address book information from whatever mail program you used to use, and so on.

Any email program requires a number of technical details that define your particular email account. If you have another email program that's been working fine, you may be able to import all the details from the older program, along with your collection of saved mail and addresses. It's easier to import from some programs than others. If you're bringing in mail from Apple Mail or Eudora (version 5.0 or later) it's a cinch—just follow the instructions in the Entourage Setup Assistant. If you're importing from other email programs, see the box on page 355.

If you've never used your Mac for email before, however, or if you're using a Mac that doesn't have a functioning email program, you'll need to type these email settings into Entourage directly. Unless you're quite a technical person, your sole source of this information is your Internet Service Provider's help line (or instruction sheet). You need the account information your ISP gave you in order to receive or send email, so have this info on hand as you set about getting Entourage ready.

The Import Business

With the advent of Office 2008, Entourage's automated import capabilities are seriously diminished. The Entourage Setup Assistant offers only two choices beside earlier versions of Entourage: Apple Mail and Qualcomm Eudora version 5 or later. Entourage 2004 could import those two as well as Netscape Communicator, Outlook Express, and Claris Emailer. Much of that was possible because those older Mac OS 9 programs could run under Classic, thereby letting Entourage interact with them.

With Mac OS X 10.5 Leopard, Classic is no more, and Entourage's email import capabilities are limited to messages saved in the MBOX format. Luckily, most Mac OS X email programs—including Thunderbird, Eudora, and Mailsmith—make use of this format.

When you're ready to make the switch, export your mailboxes from your current program in the MBOX format. You'll end up with one or several files with the .mbox extension. Then turn to Entourage and choose File → Import to launch the Import assistant. Click "Contacts or messages from a text file" and then click the right arrow. Then click "Import messages from an MBOX-format text file" and again click the right arrow. Navigate to your exported .mbox file and click Import. Repeat this Import assistant procedure if you have more than one .mbox file to import.

Although this folder-by-folder method is a bit tedious, it ensures you'll also get the mail included in any *subfolders*. If the mailboxes you exported from your previous mail program had no subfolders, then you can import them the easy way: Create a new folder in Entourage (choose File → New → Folder) and drag the .mbox file into it.

Then let the Setup Assistant take you by the hand like this:

1. **Import your calendar, address book information, and email from your older programs, if you like.**

   As part of Entourage's campaign to serve as the only communication and organization program you'll ever need, the Setup Assistant now offers to import email and address book information from another email program, calendar program, or address book program that you *used* to use before the great day of Entourage's arrival.

   This feature saves you astronomical amounts of time. Since all of your familiar data is instantly available, you can get comfortable with Entourage—your new email/calendar/address book program—in record time.

   The assistant gives you three choices: to import nothing at all; to import information from an earlier version of Entourage; or to import from another program.

   If you choose to import from another program, the Setup Assistant presents you with a short list of email programs from which it can import information: Apple Mail or Qualcomm Eudora (5.0 or later). You can also tell Entourage that your email program isn't listed, at which point it explains that Entourage can import mail messages in the MBOX format; or contacts from a comma- or tab-delimited text file.

   Finally, you'll choose from a list of individual items to import: your mail messages, addresses, account information, filters, signatures, calendar items, tasks,

When it comes to email, there are three flavors of accounts: POP (also known as Post Office Protocol or POP3), IMAP (also known as IMAP4), and Web-based. Although the lines between them are often blurry, each has its own distinct nature, with different strengths and weaknesses.

POP accounts are the most common kind. This type of account usually transfers your incoming mail to your hard drive before you read it, which works fine as long as you're using only one computer to access your email.

If you want to take your Entourage email world along with you on the road, you have to copy the Documents → Microsoft User Data folder on your desktop Mac's hard drive—or, at the very least, the Documents → Microsoft User Data → Office 2008 Identities folder—into the corresponding location on your laptop's hard drive. Then, when you run Entourage on the laptop, you'll find your messages and attachments already in place.

(Another travelers' tip: Entourage can leave your POP mail on the server, so that you can read it while on the road, but still find it waiting on your home Mac when you return. See page 362.)

IMAP accounts are most often found among educational institutions and corporations, but are becoming more popular for personal use because of services like .Mac and Gmail. Unlike POP, where your mail is stored on your hard drive, IMAP keeps your mail on the remote server, downloading it only when you want to read or act on a message. Thus, you can access the same mail regardless of the computer you use. IMAP servers remember which messages you've read and sent, too.

The downside to this approach, of course, is that you can only work with your email when you're online, because all of your mail is on an Internet mail server, not on your hard drive.

Web-based servers are similar to IMAP servers, in that they store your mail on the Internet; you use a Web browser on any computer to read and send messages. Although Web-based accounts are convenient, most free Web-based accounts put ads in your email, and you may find it awkward to compose and manage messages using a Web browser. The notable exception is Google's Gmail service, which is ad free, works great on a Mac, and has a POP and IMAP settings so you can use it with Entourage.

The only downside to POP and IMAP accounts is that if you switch ISPs, you have to switch your email address as well. To prevent this problem, you can use Gmail or Apple's .Mac service, which give you a permanent email address. If your "real" email address changes, these services simply forward your mail to whatever new address you specify. That way, you'll never have to send out a change-of-email-address again.

notes, and so on. Your choices vary depending on the program you're importing from. Once you've selected the items to import, click the right arrow to start the process, which can take a long time depending on the volume of your saved messages. (Better grab a snack.)

When the importing is complete, click Finish. If you didn't previously indicate that you wanted Entourage to be your default email program, the Setup Assistant will ask you again. Tell this eager-beaver software Yes or No.

Once you've successfully imported your email account's settings, you're ready to start using Entourage. Skip to the next section.

If you didn't import settings from an existing email program, however, or if the importing didn't go smoothly, you may now have to type in the email settings for your account.

2. **Tell Entourage your email address.**

Type your email address in the box provided. Click the right arrow to continue.

Note: If you're part of a large organization, your email account may run on Exchange server, a centralized system that keeps track of email, calendars, and contact information on a centralized server. That way, you can access it from any computer and share calendars and other information with your coworkers. Turn on the checkbox for "My account is on an Exchange server" if this applies to you, and ask your network administrator for the Exchange server settings you'll need to complete the Setup Assistant.

If your email account is on a popular system that Entourage has in its memory banks—like EarthLink, Hotmail, or Gmail—it automatically fills in the mail server settings for you and displays a window saying "Automatic Configuration Succeeded." It also reports that you can verify these settings in the next window by clicking the right arrow.

If Entourage is *not* familiar with your email provider, the Assistant's window says "Automatic Configuration Failed" and alerts you that you'll have to manually fill in the rest of the account settings after you click the right arrow to continue.

The Set up Assistant displays its "Verify and Complete Settings" window (Figure 10-4). If Entourage recognized your email account in the last window, your job is just to check its work and type your password in the appropriate field. Otherwise, continue with the following steps to enter your account information.

Note: For years AOL existed in its own private universe, forcing you to use only AOL software to access its email. But in recent years AOL realized that if it was going to continue to compete in cyberspace, it would have to open its email portals. Now you can set up AOL for either POP or IMAP.

Figure 10-4:
If you don't import your settings from another email program or an earlier Entourage, the Entourage Setup Assistant walks you through the process of entering the pertinent information. If, for security reasons, you'd rather enter your password every time you check for email, then turn off the option to save your password in the Mac OS X Keychain.

3. **Type the name you want to use to sign your email and newsgroup messages.**

   The "Your name" text box probably already contains the name that you entered in Word as your user name, but you can put any name you like here—*Buddha Boy,* if you like. (Again, though, read up on etiquette on page 410.)

4. **Enter your email account ID and password.**

   In this step, you'll need to enter your *email account ID* and the password for your account. Your account ID is usually the portion of your email address that comes before the @ symbol, although some email systems require your complete email address in this box.

   Entourage is willing to store your password in the Mac OS X *Keychain* (a handy Mac OS X feature that memorizes all of your email and file-sharing passwords for you). Turn off the "Save password in my Mac OS X keychain" box only if you want to have to type your password every time Entourage checks your email—which gets old very quickly but may be comforting if shady characters have access to your computer.

5. **Tell Entourage what kind of incoming mail server you'll be using, and type in your incoming and outgoing mail server addresses.**

   As noted above, you need to consult the account information your ISP gave you when you signed up (or ask your network administrator, if you're on a corporate network) to figure out what settings to use. The choice here in the pop-up menu for the incoming mail server type is between POP and IMAP.

   Not shown in this Setup Assistant window are the advanced server options for alternative ports, security, and authentication. If your ISP requires them, you'll have to enter those manually after you complete the Setup Assistant (see page 360). Click the right arrow button to continue.

6. **Click Verify My Settings.**

7. **Assuming you're connected to the Internet, Entourage tests the server settings you've just entered and shows what it finds out in the Results box. Click the left arrow if you need to go back and change any of your settings. Otherwise, click the right arrow to continue.**

8. **Name your account.**

   Entourage needs a name for your brand-new account, such as *Earthlink Account* or *Comcast Account.* Turn on the top checkbox to enter this email address in your "Me" contact card in the Entourage Address Book.

   A word about the other checkbox here: The Entourage toolbar has a button called Send/Receive. If you have more than one email account, clicking this single button can check *all* your email accounts. Turn off the "Include this account in my Send & Receive All schedule" option on this screen if you *don't* want this account to be checked automatically. Additionally, you can configure Entourage to Send & Receive All on a schedule—every five minutes for example. This checkbox also determines whether the account is included in those scheduled connections.

Note: On the other hand, you may also select which account you wish to send and receive email from the pop-up menu beside the Send/Receive button.

9. **Click Finish to wrap things up.**

    Entourage now has all the basic information it needs to start work. Its final question is whether you'd like to make Entourage your default email program. If you click the Make Default button, Entourage opens whenever, for example, you click an email link on a Web page or in a program's online help.

Tip: If you decide later that you'd prefer to use a different email program, you have to open Apple's own Mail program, choose Mail → Preferences, and then select your default mail reader. Not surprisingly, Apple runs the show—so you have to use this procedure even if you don't want to use Mail.

GEM IN THE ROUGH

Using Your .Mac Address with Your ISP

If you're looking for an email address with a little Macintosh cachet, or if the address your ISP has given you is hopelessly hard to remember, check out Apple's mac.com email service.

.Mac can forward mail from your .Mac address to your ISP, but you can also send and receive mail directly via your .Mac address. This can avoid confusion: your correspondents simply use your .Mac address, and your messages appear to come from your .Mac address rather than a hard-to-remember ISP address. No one needs to know about your ISP. In fact, as noted earlier, you can change ISPs and continue using your .Mac mail without anyone having to update their address books.

All this .Mac fun isn't free, though. In order to get your nifty email address, you have to sign up for the whole .Mac package, which costs $100 a year—really not so bad considering you get a bunch of other features like 10 GB of server space for Web site hosting, backup, or file transfer purposes; and some free software to boot. (Check out Gmail.com for a free alternative—albeit without the .Mac address and other .Mac goodies.) Visit *www.mac.com* to learn all about it, to subscribe, or to sign up for a free 60-day trial. Then configure Entourage to use it as described in "Setting Up a Second Email Account" below.

Setting Up a Second Email Account

The Account Setup Assistant just described is a relatively painless procedure for setting up your main email account. But if you have additional accounts to set up, you can return to the Setup Assistant like this:

1. **With Entourage open, choose Tools → Accounts.**

    This brings up the Accounts window, the central point for dealing with email, newsgroups, and directory services accounts in Entourage.

2. **With the Mail tab selected, click the New button.**

    Entourage's Account Setup Assistant reappears. Continue with step 6 of the previous instructions.

Note: If you have more than one email account set up in Entourage, one of these accounts is the *default
account.* The default account is the one that's automatically used to send and receive mail, unless you
specify otherwise. To specify the default account, choose Tools → Accounts and click the Mail tab in the
resulting window. The current default account is shown in bold. Select the account that you want to make
the default, click Make Default, and close the window.

Configuring Your Account Manually

If you've got all the necessary settings for a new account on a slip of paper in front of
you, then the screen-by-screen assistant may seem unnecessarily slow; or you may need
to add some advanced mail-server options that the Account Setup Assistant didn't
offer. Here's how to create a new email account without any setup assistant help.

Choose Tools → Accounts to open the Accounts window. Then, with the Mail tab
selected, click New. When the Account Setup Assistant appears, click Configure
Account Manually. Entourage now asks what kind of account you want to set up:
POP, IMAP, Exchange, or Windows Live Hotmail. Choose the account flavor you
want from the pop-up menu, and click OK (or click Set up Assistant if you wish to
go back to Entourage's step-by-step hand-holding). The Edit Account dialog box
opens displaying three or more tabs (depending on the account type you've chosen)
where you can enter all of your relevant information (see Figure 10-5).

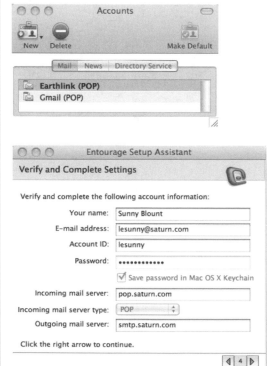

Figure 10-5:
*Top: Choose Tools → Accounts to summon the Accounts
dialog box. Use the toolbar buttons to create or delete an
account, or double-click an account to edit its settings.*

*Bottom: The Account Settings tab of the Edit Account window
has the same basic information as the Account Setup
Assistant, but in a much more compact form.*

Note: Setting up an account manually has another payoff: It gives you advanced control over how Entourage sends and receives mail. These are options most people can and should ignore (unless your ISP requires them).

Under the Account Settings tab (see Figure 10-5, bottom), click "Click here for advanced receiving options." You get a window where you can specify a secure connection, choose a different port for your POP or IMAP connections, or force Entourage to use a secure password.

If you click the Options tab (Figure 10-6, top), you can specify the default *signature* for this account (page 405), additional *headers* you want added (for geeks only), and whether you want to limit message sizes (page 371).

If you have an IMAP account, you're also given some additional options, which are described on page 363.

Warning: Other than the name you give your account, there's absolutely no room for creativity in any of the account settings. Misplaced punctuation, an erroneously capitalized password, or an invisible space at the beginning of your account ID or mail server address will put the kibosh on your email account. If you're troubleshooting email problems, it's often helpful to select the entire contents of the field and re-enter it—removing any invisible spaces in the process.

Sending and Receiving Mail

All of the careful setup you've done up till now leads up to your goal: telling Entourage to check for incoming mail and send any outgoing mail. The basic process is easy, but several subtleties can make your email experience more satisfying.

Tip: You can also set up Entourage to check your email accounts automatically according to a schedule, as described on page 365.

Send and Receive All

When Entourage opens for the first time, you've got mail; the Inbox contains a message for you from Microsoft. It wasn't actually transmitted over the Internet, though—it's a starter message built into Entourage just to tease you. Fortunately, all your future mail comes via the Internet.

You get new mail and send mail you've written using the Send & Receive command. You can trigger it in any of several ways:

- Click the Send/Receive button in the toolbar.
- Choose Tools → Send & Receive → Send & Receive All (or choose from the submenu *which* account you wish to send and receive email from).
- Press ⌘-K.

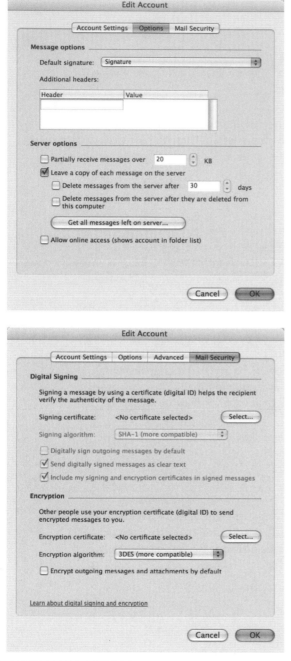

Figure 10-6:
Top: Clicking the Options tab reveals a slew of options that aren't available through the Account Setup Assistant. For example, if you have a slow connection, you can choose to just partially receive large messages, and if you'd like to access your mail from more than one computer, you can choose to leave a copy of the messages on the server.

Bottom: The Mail Security tab lets you choose email-specific security options.

Now Entourage contacts the mail servers listed in the account list, retrieving new messages and downloading any files attached to those messages. It also sends any outgoing messages and their attachments.

Configuring IMAP Options

IMAP accounts offer lots of flexibility—but as usual in the software world, that means that they also offer lots of complexity. To find Entourage's staggering array of IMAP options, choose Tools → Accounts; double-click the name of your IMAP account; and click the Options tab. Here you'll find special options, in addition to those described at the end of this chapter:

- **Always download complete message bodies.** Normally, when you connect to an IMAP account, Entourage grabs only the message's headers—its size, subject line, sender's name, and date. The body of the message stays on the server until you preview or open the message, at which time Entourage retrieves the whole thing. If you turn on this box, however, Entourage downloads both the headers and the message contents to your Inbox, making them instantly available. This option, in other words, makes your IMAP account behave a lot like a POP account.

- **Root folder.** If you haven't heard from your IMAP account administrator that this is something you need to fill in, ignore it.

- **Live Sync (stay connected with server).** These options let you choose how Entourage manages its connection to IMAP servers—for example, whether it tries for a connection as soon as Entourage is launched, how long it should stay connected, and whether it should connect to all of your mail folders or just the Inbox.

- **Check for unread messages in subscribed folders.** If you've subscribed to IMAP folders, turning on this option makes Entourage check them for new mail automatically. Turning it off means you'll have to look inside the folders yourself.

If you're an especially technical IMAP fan, you can also tweak the Advanced tab in the Edit Account window. There, you'll be able to fine-tune two sets of preferences:

- **Special folders.** Ordinarily, an IMAP account stores your incoming, deleted, and filed messages on an Internet server. Messages you've sent or haven't yet sent (because they're in your Drafts folder), however, remain on your hard drive. If you turn on "Store special folders on IMAP server" and then turn on the corresponding folder checkboxes, Entourage stores the contents of the Sent Items and Drafts folders on the server, too, so that you'll have access to them from anywhere. (You'll need to specify a server's folder path for these items, should they be named anything but "Sent Items" and "Drafts.") You can also choose a folder to collect the junk mail that hits your IMAP account, as determined by Entourage's junk mail filter. (If you disagree, click the "junked" message and click the Junk button in the Entourage toolbar—which now changes to Not Junk.)

- **Delete options.** This feature has nothing to do with wiping out stock holdings. Instead, it has to do with how your IMAP Internet server processes a message that you delete: It can either delete it outright or move it to its own Deleted Items folder. You can also indicate here when deleted messages are actually deleted—when you quit Entourage, after messages reach a certain age, or when you close an IMAP folder.

Tip: After it's done, Entourage tries to communicate its success or failure by playing a cheerful chime—one for "You've got mail," a different one for "You've got no mail," and so on. You can change these sounds, opt to have Entourage flash the menu bar instead, elect to have Entourage bring itself in front of your other open Mac programs when there's new mail, or even choose a completely different sound *set*. All of this fun awaits in the Entourage → Preferences → General Preferences → Notification tab. Oh yes, you can also turn off notifications altogether.

In the list on the right side of your screen, new messages appear in bold type. Folders *containing* new messages show up in bold type, too (in the Folder list at the left side of the screen). The boldface number in parentheses after the word "Inbox" lets you know how many of its messages you haven't yet read.

Finally, after downloading the messages, Entourage applies its filters—what it calls *Rules*—to all new messages, putting mail from mailing lists into specific folders, for example. You'll find more on rules on page 396.

The Progress window

While it's connecting to the Internet and transferring messages, Entourage reports briefly on its activity at the bottom of the main window. If you'd like more detail, open Entourage's Progress window, as shown in Figure 10-7, by choosing Window → Progress or pressing ⌘-7.

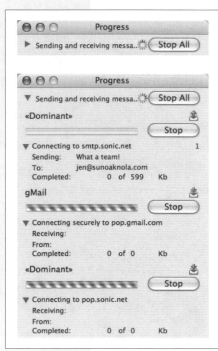

Figure 10-7:
Top: The progress window first appears as a small window with a flippy triangle on the left side.

Bottom: When you click it, the window shows you all of the details as it makes a network connection: what server has been checked, the number of messages left to be downloaded, where they're coming from and how much of each message is left to be downloaded.

Checking a specific email account

You don't have to check *all* of your email accounts whenever you want to get mail. Suppose, for example, you're having a holiday weekend at home and don't really care to see any email from your work account, but to want to see any messages that come to your personal account.

You can exclude an account (or several accounts) from the "Send & Receive All" routine easily enough. Open the Accounts window (Tools → Accounts), double-click the account's name, turn off "Include this account in my 'Send & Receive All' schedule," click OK, and close the Accounts window.

But suppose you *usually* want to check all accounts, but *occasionally* want to check only one of them. On such an occasion, choose that account's name from the Send/Receive menu button on the main Entourage window. (Alternatively, choose the account name from the Tools → Send & Receive submenu.)

Advanced Mail-Getting Features

Hundreds of thousands of people are perfectly content using Entourage for email just as it comes out of the box. But if you're willing to open the hood and modify a few technical options, you can unleash some awesome variations on the "Click a button to download mail" routine.

Automatic checking on a schedule

Stop pressing a button to check your email. You can set up Entourage to check your email according to a regular schedule. To be sure, this is an advanced feature, which may force you to think, just for a moment, like you're a computer. But there's no debating the convenience of receiving messages throughout the day, moments after your correspondents click their send buttons. (On the other hand, some folks enjoy the uninterrupted peace and quiet of their workday, and prefer to take a virtual walk to the post office once or twice a day.)

To create a schedule, choose Tools → Schedules to bring up the Schedules window (Figure 10-8, top). Click the New button in the window's toolbar, which brings up the Edit Schedule window with an untitled schedule (Figure 10-8, bottom). (If you want to edit an existing schedule—for example, Send & Receive All might be the only schedule you really need—double-click it in the Schedules window.)

In this window, you can set three options: the schedule's name, when it happens, and what happens. To give the schedule a name, just type it in the Name field at the top of the window.

The *When* portion of this window lets you determine when a schedule runs, using a pop-up menu:

- **Manually.** Nothing happens automatically. To run the schedule, you'll have to choose its name from the Tools → Run Schedule submenu. In other words, it's not a schedule.

- **At Startup.** Entourage runs the schedule whenever you launch the program.

- **On Quit.** Entourage runs the schedule when you *quit* the program.

- **Timed Schedule.** You can set specific times and days for schedules to run. That is, you can set a schedule to run every Thursday and Sunday at 12:20 p.m., if you like.

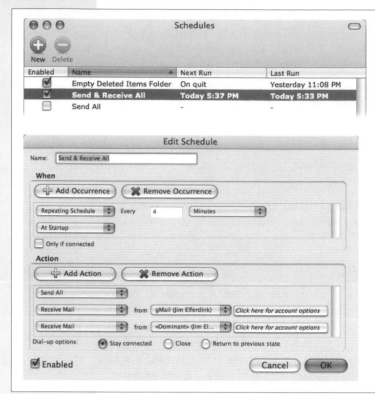

Figure 10-8:
The Entourage Schedules window (top) shows all of the schedules available in your copy of Entourage. When you click the New button to create a new schedule (or double-click an existing schedule to edit it), the Edit Schedule window appears (bottom). Here you direct Entourage what to do and when to do it.

- **Repeating Schedule.** Unlike with a timed schedule, you can set a schedule to run at regular intervals, such as every 5 minutes or every hour.

- **Recurring.** This option lets you use a schedule to run in a recurring pattern over a defined period of time—such as monthly on the 21st day of each month for a period of three months, starting two months from today. (Somewhere someone needs this option.)

For Timed schedules and Recurring schedules, you can set the particulars by clicking the button next to the pop-up menu, which opens a window where you can set exact days, hours, and minutes for schedules to run.

By clicking the Add Occurrence button, you can add up to three "triggers" for this automated action. For example, you might set up a Timed Schedule, an At Startup schedule, and an On Quit and schedule, so that, for example, your email gets checked once when Entourage is launched, then every 10 minutes, and once again when Entourage quits.

Tip: If you connect to the Internet with a modem, turn on "Only if connected," to prevent Entourage from trying to connect to the Internet to run the schedule (dialing furiously and seizing control of your phone line over and over again). Instead, Entourage will trot off to the Internet only if your Mac is already connected.

Now that you have specified *when* your schedules are to be run, you need to determine *what happens* when a schedule is run; Entourage can do much more on a timetable than check your mail. Control these options in the Action section of the Edit Schedule window. The pop-up menu has eight options:

- **Receive Mail.** Entourage connects to a mail server and downloads any waiting mail. This is an ideal action to schedule at startup.

- **Receive News.** If you want to download the latest newsgroup postings (see page 429), you can tell Entourage to download that information—another one that's useful in a startup schedule.

- **Send All.** This action sends all waiting mail—a useful one to schedule for when you quit Entourage. That way, you can make sure that all of your outgoing mail goes out before you walk away from your Mac.

- **Run AppleScript.** AppleScript scripts can be made to do just about anything— they're especially good for integrating functions of several programs, not just email (for additional details see page 769). For instance, you could tell Entourage to run a script that backs up your Documents folder onto a different hard drive when you quit Entourage. (AppleScript is a programming language—an easy one to master, but still a programming language. Information and links to online resources are also available at Apple's AppleScript Web site, *www.apple.com/ applescript*. You can also read all about it in *AppleScript: The Missing Manual*.)

- **Delete Mail.** Trashes Entourage mail from your Deleted Items folder, which might be something that you want to do whenever you quit the program.

- **Delete Junk Mail.** Empties your junk mail folder—this is another cleanup chore you might want Entourage to do when it quits. If you do, however, you're getting rid of a safety net for good mail sorted into the junk mail folder by mistake.

- **Launch Alias.** This schedule item opens an alias to any document or program on your hard drive—powerful stuff if you want to launch, say, your Web browser whenever you launch Entourage.

- **Excel Auto Web Publish.** This item has to do with Excel's Save As Web Page feature, which lets you publish an Excel workbook as a Web page automatically.

So why is an Excel option showing up in an Entourage dialog box? When you set a workbook to publish on the Web on a recurring basis, Excel hands the task off to Entourage's scheduling feature, where it appears as a schedule. Once it's in Entourage, you can further customize *when* the automatic publishing of that workbook takes place. When Entourage executes an Auto Web Publish schedule, it opens the workbook in Excel and saves it as a Web page. (This option isn't available unless you've already created an autopublishing workbook in Excel.)

Once you've selected one of these options, you can also select parameters for it. For example, if you choose Receive News, you can specify which subscribed newsgroups (see page 429) you want to read.

You can add dozens of actions to take place in a single schedule. To add an action, click the Add Action button. A new pop-up menu appears. (To delete one, too, click its line in the dialog box and then click the Remove Action button.) At the bottom of the dialog box, the Enabled checkbox lets you turn this schedule on or off—as does clicking the same-named checkbox in the Schedules window (Figure 10-8, top).

Entourage comes with three prefab schedules you can edit to meet your own ends: Empty Deleted Items Folder, which deletes all messages in the Deleted Items folder; Send & Receive All, which sends all outgoing mail and receives any waiting mail for all the accounts you've set up; and Send All, which sends all outgoing mail without checking for *incoming* mail. You can run these schedules, as well as any you've set up yourself, by choosing from the Tools → Run Schedule submenu.

The cabin-in-the-woods feature: online accounts

As noted earlier in this chapter, the world's most common email account types are POP (in which your messages are transferred from the Internet to your hard drive) and IMAP (in which your messages always remain on your mail server rather than your computer). The kind of account you have depends on your ISP.

But like other hip email programs, Entourage can let you use POP accounts almost as if they *were* IMAP accounts—that is, you can grab your messages without removing them from your Internet server. Better yet, the program can download only the *headers* of the messages, which takes but an instant, even over a slow (or expensive) connection. Once you have the headers, you can survey the subject lines or the names of the senders, and choose which messages you want to download in their entirety.

This feature is ideal for use when you're staying in a remote getaway cabin, dialing your Internet account over a slow modem connection, for two reasons. First, you're spared the tedium of downloading a bunch of messages and attachments you don't really need while on retreat. Second, the mail stays on the server until you delete it manually; it'll still be there when you return home, when you can again download the messages, this time onto your main Mac.

Note: Most Internet service providers allow you to accumulate only 5 or 10 megabytes' worth of mail. Beyond that limit, incoming messages get "bounced" back to their senders. In other words, you can't delay downloading your messages indefinitely, and attachments can easily consume a lot of your quota. Unfortunately, there's no way within Entourage to see how much space your mail is using on your ISP's server. Depending on your ISP, you may be able to see that information if you logon to your email account via Web-mail.

Microsoft calls this feature *online access,* by which it means that you'll access mail in this account only via the Internet, rather than downloading it to your hard drive. To set up your account this way, choose Tools → Accounts, which brings up the Accounts window. Double-click the account that you want to make available for online access.

In the resulting Edit Account window, click the Options tab and turn on "Allow online access," as shown in Figure 10-9. You wind up with a new icon in the Folder Items pane: the online representation of your account, bearing the same name.

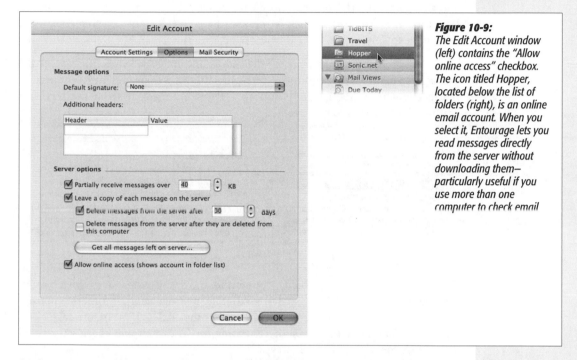

Figure 10-9:
The Edit Account window (left) contains the "Allow online access" checkbox. The icon titled Hopper, located below the list of folders (right), is an online email account. When you select it, Entourage lets you read messages directly from the server without downloading them— particularly useful if you use more than one computer to check email

Setting up an account for online access doesn't remove its mail or folders from your hard drive. It just sets up an additional, different way of accessing the account, as represented by a new icon in the Folder List for that account. (Yes, this is confusing.)

Tip: When you set up an account for online access, it's usually a good idea to turn off Entourage's Preview pane (View → Preview Pane). You'll see why in a moment.

To make Entourage check the mail server for new messages sent to this account, click this icon in the Folder Items list—just one click. Entourage starts by downloading only the *header information* of the waiting messages: subject lines, sender names, date and time the message was sent, and so on. It doesn't download the messages themselves.

If you see a message whose subject line or sender looks promising, click it. If Entourage's Preview pane is showing, Entourage downloads the message and shows it there. If not, double-click the message to make Entourage download it and display it in the message window.

Either way, the message also remains on the mail server—that's the big difference between using the online access feature and using the Send & Receive command for that account.

To delete mail from an online account, select the messages that you want to delete, and then press the Delete key. (Now you see why it's a good idea to turn off the Preview pane—when you click a message to delete it, you simultaneously tell Entourage to *download* it if the Preview pane is on the screen.)

The message doesn't move, but a "deleted online message" icon appears in the message's Online Status column (see Figure 10-10). When you next connect to that account in online mode, Entourage deletes the message from the server, if you're still connected to the Internet.

Figure 10-10:
Online messages that you've deleted still show up in the message list, bearing an icon that looks like a red X. The next time that you connect to an online account, any messages that are marked for deletion will be shown the door. If you change your mind, you can click the deleted online message icon and choose "Leave Message on Server".

On the other hand, if you change your mind and want to *keep* a message you've marked for deletion, click the deleted online message icon. From the pop-up menu, choose Leave Message on Server, so that the "deleted online message" icon disappears. The message will be there waiting for you when you check your email account in one of the "normal" ways.

WORKAROUND WORKSHOP

Don't Bug Me

Advertisers—and spammers—are increasingly using *Web bugs*, which are references to tiny, 1-by-1 pixel graphics that come embedded in HTML-formatted email messages. Web bugs exist purely for tracking purposes: If your email program downloads a Web bug, a corresponding entry appears in the advertisers (or spammer's) Web server log. Now they know where and when someone viewed the message.

There's no way to tell if an HTML-formatted message contains a Web bug (at least not without examining the HTML source). But if you tell Entourage not to "Display complex HTML in messages" (choose Entourage → Preferences → Security, and turn off the appropriate checkbox), you preserve a little more privacy. Even with this setting turned on, Entourage doesn't download pictures, which, after all, could be Web bugs, until you click the "Download Pictures" link at the top of the preview window. If you're the happy medium type, turn on the checkbox on the same panel that automatically downloads HTML images only from senders in your Address Book (whom, presumably, you trust).

Restricting download sizes

For road warriors stuck with slow modem connections, you can tell Entourage to grab only the first portion of a message, so that you don't have to sit through an hour-long modem connection to download that "You Want It When?" cartoon that your aunt thought was just *so* funny.

To do this, select Tools → Accounts and then open the account for which you want to limit the size of downloaded messages. Click the Options tab at the top of that window, and then turn on "Partially receive messages over _ _ _ KB." You can set how much of a message you want to grab (see Figure 10-9). If you decide that you want to download the entire message, click the broken-envelope icon; choose "Receive Entire Message at next Connect" from the menu that pops up (Figure 10-11).

Note: It's crucial to remember to turn this option *off* once you get home, or you'll be wondering why Entourage keeps chopping off your messages and giving you half-downloaded, inoperable attachments.

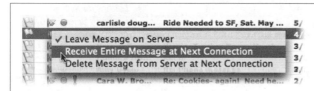

Figure 10-11:
Messages that Entourage has only partially retrieved show a half-completed picture of an envelope in the Online Status column.

Offline access

When you're in the plane or riding the Greyhound, you probably don't have an Internet connection. In such situations, you may want to read your email and write replies—but you'll undoubtedly be annoyed that, every 15 minutes or so, Entourage tries vainly to get online, triggering an avalanche of error messages.

To return serenity to Entourage world, choose Entourage → Work Offline. A checkmark appears next to the menu item and "You are working off-line" appears in the lower right corner of the main window. From now on, you can read and write replies to your email without interruption. In fact, if you click Send & Receive, Entourage asks if you're sure you want to go online before it attempts to make a connection. (Choose Entourage → Work Offline again to remove the checkmark from the menu item and return to the normal "connect when ready" mode.)

Reading a Message

Seeing a list of new messages in Entourage is like getting wrapped presents; the best part is yet to come. There are two ways to read a message: using the preview pane, and opening the message in its own window. Most email maestros prefer using the preview pane for most email reading. You can quickly scan through your messages using the up-and down-arrow keys, seeing entire short messages and the top part of longer messages in the preview pane. Then when you come across a message you really want to see—like one containing a large photo of your granddaughter—you can open the message in its own window (Figure 10-12).

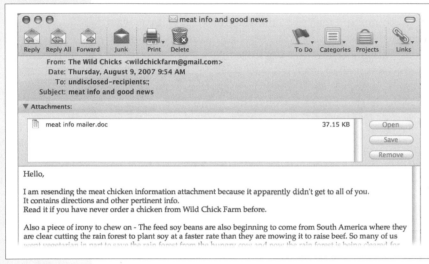

Figure 10-12:
When you open an email message by double-clicking it, you may see several things in addition to the text of the message: the attachments and the attachment control buttons, basic information (such as who sent the message, when it was sent, and its subject), and an email toolbar complete with buttons for Reply, Forward, Delete, and so on.

To preview a message, first make sure the preview pane is showing. Choose View → Preview Pane and choose whether you want the Preview Pane to the right of your message list (⌘-\) or below it (Shift-⌘-\). The Entourage main window splits in half and the preview pane opens either to the right of the message list or below it. When you click a message's name in the message list, the body of the message appears in the preview pane. Don't forget that you can adjust the relative sizes of the list and preview panes by dragging the gray border between them.

POWER USERS' CLINIC

Where Are the Headers?

As a favor to you, and to make Internet email look less intimidating, Entourage normally hides the blobs of technical-looking text known as Internet headers. This information shows all the email servers a message has visited on its way to your Inbox, along with dates, times, and other data.

Sometimes this information can be enlightening or helpful in troubleshooting or reporting a problem to an ISP. To view the header information choose Message → Internet Headers (Shift-⌘-H). Entourage displays the detailed routing information in a separate window.

To open a message into a window of its own, double-click it in the list pane, or press Return to open the selected message. An open message has its own toolbar, with essential buttons for replying, forwarding, deleting, and so on.

Tip: When a sender's name or the email subject is too long to display in the message list, Entourage trims it, and adds an ellipsis (…) to let you know there's more to this item. You can, if you like, resize Entourage's columns to make more room for this text: just drag the border between the columns. You can also point to a particular bit of abbreviated text without clicking. A small, yellow tooltip appears, revealing the entire, unabridged text.

Regardless of your viewing preference, any attached pictures, sounds, or movies *also* appear in the body of the message. You can even play those sounds and movies in the email message itself. (Entourage displays and plays any kind of file that QuickTime can understand—JPEG, GIF, PICT, Photoshop files, and so on—and can also call on Mac OS X's graphics smarts to preview Acrobat PDF documents.)

Tip: If the text of a message is too small to read, Control-click (or right-click) and choose Increase Font Size from the pop-up menu. If a message's text is too *big* (for a narrow window or a laptop screen, say), choose Decrease Font Size from the pop-up menu.

Once you've read a message, you can view the next one in the list either by pressing ⌘-] (press ⌘-[for the previous message) or by clicking it in the list pane. (If you're using the preview mode, and haven't opened a message into its own window, you can also press the up or down arrow keys to move from one message to the next.)

Tip: To mark a message that you've read as an *unread* message, so that its name remains bolded, choose Message → Mark as Unread (Shift-⌘-T), Control-click (Windows refugees can right-click) the message and choose Mark as Unread from the shortcut menu.

If you're a neatnik and prefer not to see the messages you've already read—but don't want to throw them away—you can *hide* them. Just choose View → Unread Only (Shift-⌘-O). To bring the hidden messages back, choose View → Unread Only again. This setting applies to the currently selected folder only. If, on the other hand, piles of paper and stacks of mail give you a sense of comfort, don't freak out if all your messages have disappeared. You've probably inadvertently applied this command; choose View → Unread Only to remove the checkmark from that menu item and restore your missing messages.

Icons in the message list

After you've received some messages in Entourage, you'll notice that some of those messages have icons at the left side of their list-view lines. These badges or flags give you useful information about the messages:

- **To Do Flag.** This leftmost column always shows a gray flag icon, but it turns red (🚩) if you click it (or click the To Do flag button in the toolbar) to designate this message as one requiring action—and to add it to your to do list. When you check it off your To Do List or click the flag icon a second time, Entourage replaces the red flag with a green check mark (✔). See page 386 for more details about flagging messages.

- **Links.** A chain-link icon here (⚭) indicates that a message has been *linked* to another message, calendar event, task, note, or the like. (See "Flagging messages" for more on linking.)

- **Online Status.** An icon that looks like an emaciated folder (▯) indicates that a message has only been partially retrieved—a dead giveaway that you've turned on the "Partially receive messages over" option described on page 371. A red X through it (✖) indicates that the message has been deleted from the server in an *online account* (page 368). Finally, an icon with a superimposed clock face indicates that the message will be fully downloaded the next time that you connect.

- **Status.** The status column shows the status of particular messages. A blue bullet next to a sealed envelope (✉ ●) means that the message has been received but not yet read. A curved blue arrow facing left (↰) denotes a message that you've answered. A purple, angled arrow facing right (↱), on the other hand, indicates that you've *redirected* the message (see page 383). An orange arrow facing right (➭) denotes mail that you've forwarded to someone else.

Note: Unfortunately, Entourage displays these last three icons only after your replies, forwards, and redirects have actually been sent, rather than when you write the reply, or choose to forward or redirect a message. As a result, it can be difficult to determine whether or not you've processed a message if you don't happen to be connected to the Internet.

If you modify the text of a message you've received (see page 380), the status column shows a pencil and notepad icon (🖉). If a message is associated with a calendar event (or invites you to an event—see page 454), the message status icon shows a small calendar (📅). (Caution: the calendar status overrides things like the symbols for forwards and replies.)

- **Priority.** This column's icons indicate a message's priority: a red exclamation point (❗) for Highest priority; an orange one for High priority; a dark blue downward arrow (⬇) for Low priority; and a pale blue downward arrow for Lowest priority. No icon means Normal priority.

Note: You see a priority icon only when your correspondents used their email program's priority-labeling feature, or if you change the priority of a message once you've received it. After all, what Bob at the office thinks is wildly important may not even be a blip on your radar.

- **Attachments.** If a message has one or more files attached (see page 389), a paper-clip icon (📎) appears in this column.

- **Digital signing.** If you see a padlock icon (🔒) in this column, it means the message has been *digitally signed*. That is, the sender added a certificate that helps verify that the sender is indeed who he says he is, and the message hasn't been tampered with in transit (see page 362).

- **Groups.** If you're using Entourage's groups view of email or newsgroup messages (see the box below), the group title bar displays a flippy triangle (▶) at the left: click the triangle to expand or collapse the list of messages in the group.

How to Process a Message

After you've set up your Entourage email account, and email starts arriving, the fun really begins. Assuming you want to do more than just watch your Inbox fill up, you'll have to do something with those messages in the following ways:

Deleting messages

Sometimes it's junk mail, sometimes you're just done with it. Either way, it's a snap to delete a message that's before you on the screen, whether it's in a preview pane, in its own message window, or just highlighted in the message list: simply press the Delete key. Alternatively, you can:

- Press the forward-delete key, if your keyboard has one.

- Press ⌘-Delete.

- Click the Delete (trash can) button on the toolbar.

- Choose Edit → Delete Message.

- Control-click (or right-click) the message in the list, and choose Delete Message.

GEM IN THE ROUGH

Where Are My Threads?

Entourage Email and Newsgroups used to be all about the threads. For the uninitiated, threads were strings of related emails, usually with the same subject. Utilizing threads made it very easy to track all the messages relating to, say "Wastegate control solenoid removal." Starting with Entourage 2004, Microsoft replaced threads with *groups*, which is a way of sorting messages by various criteria.

Entourage's standard view is actually a grouped view: messages are organized into groups by the date received (for example, Today, Yesterday, or Last Week). You can, however, change this to suit your needs. To do so, select View → Arrange By → Show in Groups and then choose your favorite. Instead of using this menu command, a quicker way is to just click the column heading: From, Subject, Sent, and so on.

For instance, if you click the Subject column heading, your messages group by subject—the next best thing to a thread. For example, all the Wastegate messages will cling together under the Wastegate title bar, and so on. You can scroll through the message list to find the subject you're looking for, and see all the messages and replies with that subject line.

Or perhaps you want to track who sent the message. This works great for folks who can remember who wrote something, but can't remember when they wrote it or what the subject of the message was. Just click the From column heading, and Entourage groups the messages in the active folder by the sender's name. Every person who has sent you email gets a header bar, with all her messages listed underneath it.

Click any of the column headings a second time to reverse the display order.

You can also delete a batch of messages at once by highlighting them or their group header and then using the delete button, menu command, or keystroke.

Tip: If you're viewing a message in a separate window, and you want to delete it and move to the next in one easy step, press Option-⌘-]: that's the same as the key command for moving to the next message (⌘-]) plus the Option key. If you want to delete the current message and move to the *previous* message, press Option-⌘- [instead.

Either way, the message or messages don't actually disappear, just as moving a file icon to the Mac's Trash doesn't actually delete it. Instead, these commands move the messages to Entourage's Deleted Items folder. If you like, you can click this icon to view a list of the messages you've deleted. If you spot something in there you'd like to preserve, you can rescue messages by dragging them into any other mail folder (such as right back into the Inbox, as shown in Figure 10-13).

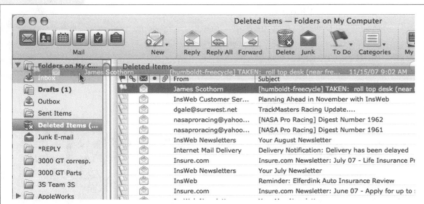

Figure 10-13:
By dragging an item out of the Deleted Items folder, you can save it from certain doom. On the other hand, you can delete messages by dragging them into the Deleted Items folder.

Selecting Messages

When you want to process a group of messages simultaneously—to delete, move, or forward them, for example—you need to master the art of multiple message selection. To select two or more messages that appear consecutively in your message list, click the first message, then Shift-click the last. This trick selects every message between the two that you clicked.

To select two or more messages that aren't adjacent in the list (that is, skipping a few messages between selected ones), ⌘-click the messages you want. Only the messages you click get selected—no filling in of messages in between.

After using either technique, you can also deselect messages you've managed to highlight—just ⌘-click them again.

Entourage doesn't truly vaporize messages in the Deleted Items folder until you "empty the trash." You can empty it in any of several ways:

- Control-click the Deleted Items folder. Choose "Empty Deleted Items" from the shortcut menu.

- Control-click (or right-click) the Deleted Items folder and choose Empty Deleted Items from the pop-up menu.

- Choose Tools → Run Schedule → Empty Deleted Items Folder.

- Click a message, or a folder, within the Deleted Items Folder list and then click the Delete icon on the toolbar (or press ⌘-Delete). You'll be asked to confirm its *permanent* deletion.

- Set up a schedule to empty the folder automatically when you quit Entourage, for example, or to delete only messages that are older than, say, 60 days. See page 365 for instructions.

Replying to messages

To reply to a message, click the Reply button in the toolbar, choose Message → Reply, or press ⌘-R. Entourage creates a new, outgoing email message, pre-addressed to the sender's return address.

To save you additional time, Entourage pastes the entire original message at the top of your reply, complete with the > brackets that serve as Internet quoting marks (Entourage indents quoted text in HTML messages). (It's also a feature you can turn off; choose Entourage → Mail & News Preferences, click the Reply & Forward tab, and turn off "Include entire message in reply.") Entourage also tacks *Re:* ("regarding") onto the front of the subject line, a long-standing convention of Internet email, and prefixes the quoted message with a one-line label indicating who originally wrote it, and when it was written.

Tip: If you need to quote only *part* of a message in your reply, select the text you want to quote before you choose Message → Reply (or simply press ⌘-R). Entourage creates a reply that includes only the text you selected as the "quotation." See page 381 to find out why keeping your quoted material brief is a thoughtful gesture for your correspondents. (This same technique lets you *print* only a portion of an email message as well.)

Meanwhile, if you want to include text you've copied from some other source—a Word file, for example—as a quotation, click in your message where you'd like the text to appear, and choose Edit → Paste Special → Paste As Quotation (or press Control-⌘-V). Entourage inserts the text in the clipboard as it would any other quoted material in your email message.

Your cursor appears at the bottom of the message area, below any quoted text; you can begin typing your reply. (If you'd rather see your insertion point above the quoted text, choose Entourage → Preferences → Reply & Forward and turn on the checkbox marked "Place insertion point before quoted text.") You can also do any of the following:

- Add recipients to the message by adding email addresses in any of the recipient fields (To, Cc, or Bcc).

- Remove one or more recipients (by clicking their names and then clicking the Remove button in the window that appears, or pressing the Delete key).

TROUBLESHOOTING MOMENT

Fixing the Entourage Database

Entourage keeps all of its messages in a single, gigantic database file on your hard drive. It's called Database, and it sits in the Documents → Microsoft User Data → Office 2008 Identities → Main Identity folder in your Home folder (in the Finder, choose Go → Home).

As you add and delete hundreds of messages from this database over time, some digital sawdust gets left behind, resulting in peculiarities when addressing messages, or general Entourage sluggishness. You also wind up with massive Entourage files, which can consume hundreds of megabytes of disk space. That's a particular bummer if you like to copy your message database to your laptop when you go on a trip, or if you back up your data every day. A more pressing need for database maintenance arises when you observe any of the following more serious problems:

- Entourage doesn't open, stops working, or quits unexpectedly.

- Entourage items don't open or the item that you click isn't the one that opens.

- Blank lines appear in the message list.

- Address Book entries don't display properly.

- Clippings disappear from the Scrapbook.

- Calendar events or contacts disappear.

- When you perform an Entourage search, the results don't match your search criteria.

- A blank Office Reminders window appears.

Fortunately, it's easy enough to rebuild the database, a procedure that cleanses, repairs, organizes, and purges your message files. You wind up with a much more compact and healthy database. To do so, quit Entourage and any other Office 2008 programs you're running. If you're using a laptop, plug in the power adapter. Then hold down the Option key while launching Entourage. The Database Utility window appears (see Figure 10-14) listing the Entourage databases on your computer (if you have more than one) and giving you four choices of possible actions to take:

- **Verify database integrity.** Choose this option first if you're having any kind of trouble with your Entourage database. The utility checks the database for corruption, and if it finds any gives you the option of rebuilding the database. If it the database is working properly, it makes no changes.

- **Compact database.** If you're not having any trouble with Entourage but just want to tidy up the database, making it as compact as possible, select this option.

- **Rebuild database.** If you suspect trouble with your database or if you ran the Verify database integrity check and it identified problems, then this command creates a backup copy of the database for safekeeping, then repairs and compacts it.

- **Set database preferences.** Choose this item to determine how the Database Utility goes about performing the Database integrity check (the first of the four options in this window). If you turn on the checkbox in the following window marked "Perform Database integrity check in the background" then the Database Utility continually monitors your database's health and reports any problems as soon as they appear. A note in this window also advises you that you can't perform a Database integrity check on a laptop running on battery power—because a corrupt database could result from a loss of power during the check. In other words, plug in your laptop before using the Database Utility.

You'll now find two Identity folders in your Microsoft User Data folder. The newly rebuilt one, bearing the same name as the Identity you started with; and the backup copy with the words "Backed up" and the date and time appended to the folder name. You can throw the "Backed up" older identity away after you've confirmed that the new database is working.

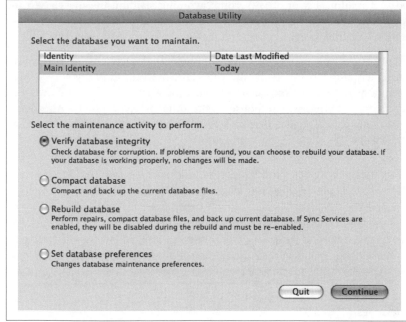

Figure 10-14:
If Entourage is acting strangely, or you'd just like to compact its database to make it a smaller, more efficient file, then hold down the Option key while you launch the program to summon the Database Utility.

- Edit the Subject line or the original message.

- Use the Return key to create blank lines within the bracketed original message in order to place your own text within it. Using this method, you can splice your own comments into the paragraphs of the original message, replying point by point. The quoting brackets preceding each line of the original message help your correspondent keep straight what's yours and what's not.

- Attach a file (see page 407).

Note: If the original message came with an attached file, Entourage doesn't fasten the attachment to the reply.

There are two basic kinds of replies. Create them by choosing commands from the Message menu, Control-clicking (or right-clicking) the message in the list and choosing from the shortcut menu, or by using the toolbar buttons.

- A **standard reply** (click the Reply button) goes only to the sender of the message. If that sender is a mailing list (see the box on the facing page), then the message may be sent to the *entire* mailing list—which may not be what you intend. Check the To address to make sure you're sending a message to the right place!

- **Reply To Sender** (available in the Message menu) creates a reply that goes to the person who wrote the original message (or posted the message to a newsgroup; see page 435). Use this option if you'd like to reply privately to a message posted to a mailing list or a newsgroup, avoiding sending the message to the entire mailing list or group. (If you use this command on a message that *didn't* come from a mailing list or a newsgroup, Entourage treats it as a standard reply.)

- The **Reply To All** command addresses a message to *all* recipients of the original message, including any Cc recipients. This is the button to use if you're participating in a group discussion; all six of you can carry on an email correspondence, always sending each response to the other five. (Reply To All doesn't send the reply to anyone who may have been in the secret Bcc field, as described on page 399.)

Tip: Entourage starts out placing the insertion point at the bottom of any quoted text in a reply. As mentioned above, you can put your response *above* the quotation, by choosing Entourage → Preferences → Reply & Forward and turning on the "Place insertion point before quoted text" checkbox. However, if you use a signature (page 405) Entourage still places your signature at the very bottom of the message—where it may never be seen beneath all the quoted material. Keep your reply *and* your signature above the quoted material by clicking the button in the same preferences window marked, "Place reply at top of message and include From, Date, To, and Subject lines from the original message."

Editing messages

Entourage lets you edit a message somebody *else* wrote. For once in your life, you can edit down some overly loquacious person without hurting his feelings.

Just double-click a message to open it into a window, and then choose Message → Edit Message. (If it's HTML formatted, it becomes a plain-text message.) Feel free to delete or rewrite the text. When you close the window, Entourage asks if you want your changes preserved. After you click Save, a pencil and notepad icon appears next to the message's name, a reminder of your meddling.

Reformatting messages

Some messages are forwarded and replied to about 900 times. With each round, more quoting brackets get added at the beginning of each line. Sooner or later, these messages become almost illegible (see Figure 10-15, top). Fortunately, Entourage can usually clean up a message's text. It can, for example, make a message's text all uppercase or all lowercase, increase or decrease its quoting levels (those multiple brackets >>>), or even straighten out curly quotes (which often arrive at the other end of Internet email as gobbledygook).

The most useful of these tools is Rewrap Paragraphs. When you have a badly wrapped message, the Edit → Auto Text Cleanup → Rewrap Paragraphs command (or click the Rewrap Text icon) does its best to remove all those funky line breaks so that the message is clean and legible once again.

> To: Jim Elferdink <<u>macintosh@sunra.com</u>>
> Subject: Re: THIS IS A VERY IMPORTANT MESSAGE-PLEASE READ
>
>>>>>>>>>>>>>>>>>>> Subject: Fwd: THIS IS A VERY IMPORTANT MESSAGE-PLEASE READ
>>>>>>>>>>>>>>>>>>>
>>>>>>>>>>>>>>>>>>> This e mail was sent to me from a good friend and rliable
source in
>>>>>>>>>>>>>>>>>>> Connecticut.
>>>>>>>>>>>>>>>>>>>
>>>>>>>>>>>>>>>>>>> Alert: I checked with Norton Anti-Virus, and they are
gearing up for
>>>>>>>>>>>>>>>>>>> this virus so I believe this is real. I checked snopes.com
and this is
>>>>>>>>>>>>>>>>>>> for real. Get this sent around to your contacts ASAP...we
don't need
>>>>>>>>>>>>>>>>>>> this spreading around.
>>>>>>>>>>>>>>>>>>>
>>>>>>>>>>>>>>>>>>> READ AS SOON AS POSSIBLE. PLEASE FORWARD THIS WARNING
AMONG
FRIENDS,
>>>>>>>>>>>>>>>>>>> FAMILY, AND CONTACTS:
>>>>>>>>>>>>>>>>>>>
>>>>>>>>>>>>>>>>>>> You should be alerted during the next days: Do not open any
message
>>>>>>>>>>>>>>>>>>> with an attached filed called "INVITATION", regardless of who
sent it.
>>>>>>>>>>>>>>>>>>> It is a virus that opens an Olympic Torch which "burns" the
whole hard
>>>>>>>>>>>>>>>>>>> disc C of your computer.. This virus will be received from
someone who
>>>>>>>>>>>>>>>>>>> has your e-mail address in his/her contact li st, that is wh

-0800 To: Jim Elferdink <macintosh@sunra.com> Subject: Re: THIS IS A VERY
IMPORTANT MESSAGE-PLEASE READ

Subject: Fwd: THIS IS A VERY IMPORTANT MESSAGE-PLEASE READ

This e mail was sent to me from a good friend and rliable
source in Connecticut. Alert: I checked with Norton
Anti-Virus, and they are gearing up for this virus so I
believe this is real. I checked snopes.com and this is for
real. Get this sent around to your contacts ASAP...we don't
need this spreading around. READ AS SOON AS POSSIBLE.
 PLEASE FORWARD THIS WARNING AMONG FRIENDS, FAMILY, AND
CONTACTS: You should be alerted during the next days: Do
not open any message with an attached filed called
"INVITATION", regardless of who sent it. It is a virus that
opens an Olympic Torch which "burns" the whole hard disc C of
your computer.. This virus will be received from someone who
has your e-mail address in his/her contact li st, that is wh
y you should send this e-mail to all your contacts. It is
better to receive this message 25 times than to receive the
virus and open it. If you receive a mail called
"invitation", though sent by a friend, do not open it, and
shut down your computer immediately. This is the worst Virus
announced by CNN. It has been classified by Microsoft as the
most destructive virus ever. This virus was discovered by
McAfee yesterday, and there is no repair yet for this kind of
virus. This virus simply destroys the Zero Sector of the Hard
Disc, where the vital information is kept. SEND THIS E-MAIL
TO EVERYONE YOU KNOW. COPY THIS E-MAIL AND SEND IT TO YOUR
FRIENDS AND REMEMBER: IF YOU SEND IT TO THEM, YOU WILL
BENEFIT ALL OF US.

Figure 10-15:
*Top: You can see how forwarding
email multiple times can badly
mangle the text.*

*Bottom: After choosing Edit → Auto
Text Cleanup → Remove Quoting,
and Rewrap Paragraph commands,
the message's lines are neat and
tidy—though the virus hoax message
may still not be worth reading.*

Tip: When you use the Rewrap Paragraphs command on a message you've received, Entourage asks if you want your changes to the original made permanent. Sometimes that's just fine, but other times you may want to keep the original (bad) formatting around, just in case Rewrap Paragraphs messed up a chart or specially formatted text like song lyrics.

No biggie: You can have *both* the original and the cleaned-up version. Just make a duplicate of the message (select the message, choose Edit → Duplicate Message), and then use Entourage's formatting tools on the copy.

About Mailing Lists

It doesn't take long after venturing into the world of email to come across something called a mailing list. Mailing lists come in two general forms: discussion lists where members of the mailing list contribute to a group discussion via email, and broadcast-only lists that transmit messages to subscribers. For example, a group of jazz music fans might have an email discussion list where members write about anything jazz-related they like, but a particular jazz artist might have a broadcast list to announce concerts and albums to fans who've signed up for updates. By searching Yahoo (*www.yahoo.com*) or Google, you can turn up mailing lists covering just about every conceivable topic.

Many Internet discussion lists are unmoderated, which means you can send a message to all members of the group instantly, without someone filtering the messages for content or relevance to the group. That's why you have to be careful when you just want to reply to one person in the discussion group; if you accidentally reply to the list address and not to a specific person, your message may be distributed to everyone on the mailing list—sometimes with embarrassing or disastrous consequences.

Forwarding messages

Instead of replying to the person who sent you a message, you may sometimes want to *forward* the message—pass it on—to a third person. You can do that in one of two ways: pass the message along as is, or package it up in an attachment to a new message.

To send a message off just as it came, click the Forward button in the toolbar, choose Message → Forward, or press ⌘-J. A new message opens, looking a lot like the one that appears when you reply. But first you have to address it just like you would any other outgoing message. Once again, before forwarding the message, you can edit the subject line or the message itself. (For example, you may wish to precede the original message with a comment of your own, along the lines of: "Kate: I thought you'd be interested in this joke about Mozart.") Entourage inserts one-line labels indicating what part of your message is the forwarded content, which helps eliminate confusion.

When you forward a message this way, Entourage puts the insertion point at the top of the message, and inserts labels—"Forwarded message" and "End of Forwarded Message"—to indicate where the forwarded message starts and stops. You can also tell Entourage to use Internet-style quote characters (">") before the forwarded text: choose Entourage → Mail & News Preferences, select the Reply & Forward pane, and check "Use quoting characters when forwarding." (You can also change the starting position of the insertion point from this panel—though be aware that these preferences control replying and forwarding.)

If you have a long message that's like a document in itself, you might want to keep it separate from the text you're adding, so you can have Entourage turn the mail into an attachment. This method also keeps the material safe from prying eyes until your recipient chooses to open the attachment. To do so, click Message → "Forward as Attachment", and take it from there.

Note: If the original message contained an attachment, this time, Entourage *does* retain the attachment (unless you delete it first).

Redirecting messages

A *redirected* message is similar to a forwarded message, with one extremely useful difference: when you forward a message, your recipient sees that it came from *you*—just as if you'd written the whole thing yourself. But when you *redirect* a message, your recipient sees the *original* sender's name as the sender; the message bears almost no trace of your involvement. In other words, a redirected message uses you as a low-profile relay station between two other people.

Treasure this Entourage feature; plenty of email programs, including Microsoft's own Outlook and Outlook Express for Windows, don't have a Redirect command at all. You can use it to transfer messages from one of your own accounts to another, or to pass along a message that came to you by mistake. You might use it when, for example, you, a graphic designer, receive a question from a customer about the sales tax on his bill. You could redirect it to someone in the accounting department, who could respond to it directly just by clicking Reply. You'd then be mercifully insulated from *any* ensuing discussion of sales tax.

To redirect a selected message, choose Message → Redirect, or press Option-⌘-J. Entourage presents an outgoing copy of the message for you to address. You'll notice that unlike a forwarded message, this one lacks quoting brackets. You can't edit a redirected message; the whole idea is that it ends up at its destination unaltered. If you need to make a comment to the new recipient, use Forward or Forward as Attachment instead.

Note: When you redirect a message, you do leave some electronic fingerprints on it. If the recipients look at the Internet *headers* of a message you've redirected, they'll see information Entourage inserted indicating who resent the message, and there may be other clues. Entourage inserts these details both to help avoid confusion and to prevent abuse.

Printing messages

To print a message choose File → Print or press ⌘-P; the Entourage Print dialog box pops up, so that you can specify how many copies you want, what range of pages, and so on. Finally, click Print.

Tip: If you know you just want one copy of a message using the default print settings, choose File → Print One Copy, or press Option-⌘-P. Entourage will zap a single copy of the current message to your printer, with no need for any additional dialog boxes.

Filing messages

Organizers take note—Entourage lets you create as many new folders in the Folder list as you need. Then, by dragging messages from your Inbox onto one of these folder icons, you can file away your messages into appropriate topics. You might create one folder for family messages, another for order confirmations when shopping on the Web, another for correspondence relating to an important project, and so on. In fact, you can even create folders *inside* these folders, a feature beloved by the hopelessly organized: your Family folder might have subfolders for each branch of the family tree.

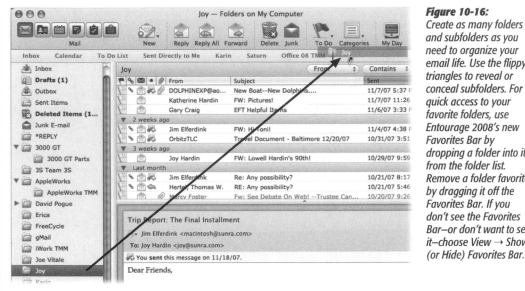

Figure 10-16:
Create as many folders and subfolders as you need to organize your email life. Use the flippy triangles to reveal or conceal subfolders. For quick access to your favorite folders, use Entourage 2008's new Favorites Bar by dropping a folder into it from the folder list. Remove a folder favorite by dragging it off the Favorites Bar. If you don't see the Favorites Bar—or don't want to see it—choose View → Show (or Hide) Favorites Bar.

To create a new folder, choose File → New → Folder, press Shift-⌘-N, or choose New Folder from the New menu button on the Entourage toolbar. A new folder appears in the Folder list, sporting the imaginative moniker "untitled folder." Just type a new name and then press Return.

Tip: To rename a folder you've created, click it once to select it, and then click its name. Now rename the folder as you would any Macintosh icon. You can't rename or delete Entourage's built-in folders (Inbox, Drafts, Sent Items, and so on), but your own folders are up for grabs.

You can move a message into a folder in any of three ways:

- Drag it out of the list pane onto the folder icon. You can grab any part of a message in the list as a handle. You can also select and drag a bunch at once.

Figure 10-17:
Whenever you reply, forward, flag, or do something else to a message, Entourage keeps a record of it and displays your most recent actions in the yellow box at the top of the message (top). If it has further information about this message's past life, it displays the History link at the right side of the yellow box. Click it to reveal the rest of the story of this message's existence (bottom).

GEM IN THE ROUGH

The Entourage Email "Paper Trail"

As a sensational convenience to you, Entourage keeps track of what you've done with a message—replied, forwarded, or redirected. It displays your message's history in a yellow banner at the top of the original message, as shown here at top, identifying what was done, and when.

You can also see the actual contents of the reply, forward, or redirect—that is, open a copy of the message in question—by clicking the Show link in that banner.

Only the most recent action you've taken on a message fits in the yellow banner, however. If you want to look at the entire history of actions performed on a message, click the History link at the right end of the banner to bring up a small pop-up window listing all the actions, including the date they were performed. Once again, you can click any of the links to open the corresponding messages for your reference. (Note: This paper trail is also accessible via a message's Links; see page 388.)

Tip: If you *Option*-drag a message into a folder, you make a copy of the message in that folder, leaving the original message where it was.

- Highlight a message in the list pane, or several, and then choose Message → Move To and select the folder from the submenu. Alternatively, press Shift-⌘-M to open a window listing all the folders in the Folder list. Highlight the folder you want (by clicking or typing the first couple letters of its name). Then press Enter or Return (or click Move).

- Control-click a message (or one of several that you've highlighted); from the resulting shortcut menu, choose Move To and select the folder from the submenu.

Note: At the bottom of the folder pane, below any folders you create, you'll find Mail Views. Although they appear in the folder pane, they're not folders. They're actually Saved Searches, formerly known as Custom Views—one-click message filters that help you zoom in on different aspects of your message collection. You can't drag messages into these pseudo-folders. See page 390 for more particulars on Mail Views.

Exporting and Archiving Email

Believe it or not, at some point you'll probably want to get some email out of Entourage. Perhaps you'd like to give a collection of messages to someone who uses a different email program (without forwarding them all), or perhaps you'd like to keep years-old correspondence around for posterity's sake, but would prefer not to keep it forever in Entourage's ever-growing, monolithic database. Or maybe you just want to back up some of your email separately from Entourage.

Fortunately, Entourage makes it easy to extract a bunch of messages for storage or transfer: just collect (or copy) the messages you wish to export into a single mail folder, and then drag that folder to the Mac OS X desktop. Entourage saves all the messages in a standard, text-only .mbox format. Virtually every email program (including Entourage)

for any Mac, Unix, or Windows machine, can open and import these files, making them ideal for transferring messages between programs. Note that Entourage doesn't include subfolders in these exports—if you want to export a group of folders, you have to do so one at a time and then reorganize them when you bring them back into Entourage or another email program.

If the messages you export have attachments, Entourage includes encoded versions of those attachments in the .mbox file. You may not want to include attachments in your exports, and other email programs or computers may not be able to understand some of the attachments. If you don't want to include attachments in your export, your only choice is to delete them from messages before you export them.

Tip: When you click a flippy triangle in the Folder list (or highlight a folder and press ⌘-right arrow), you get to see any folders within that folder, exactly as in the Finder's List view. You can drag folders inside other folders, nesting them to create a nice hierarchical folder structure. (You can drag a nested folder back into the list of "main" folders—just drag it to the "On My Computer" item at the top of the folder list.)

You can also drag messages between folders. Just drag a message from the message list onto the desired folder at the left side of the screen.

This can be a useful trick when applied to a message in your Outbox. If you decide to postpone sending it, drag it into any other folder (like Drafts). Entourage won't send it until you drag it *back* into the Outbox.

Flagging messages

Sometimes you'll receive an email message that prompts you to some sort of action, but you may not have the time (or the fortitude) to face the task at the moment. ("Hi there…it's me, your accountant. Would you mind rounding up your expenses for 1993 through 2006 and sending me a list by email?")

That's why Entourage lets you *flag* a message, summoning a little red flag in the Status column next to a message's name *and*—new in Entourage 2008—automatically adding that message to your To Do list. Since all flags are now To Do items, all flags also have due dates. The quickest way to add a To Do flag is to click the message's gray flag icon in the message list. When you do so, Entourage creates a To Do item with your standard due date. (You can set your standard To Do due date by choosing Entourage → Preferences → General Preferences → To Do List and selecting one of the intervals from the pop-up menu: Today, Tomorrow, This Week, Next Week, or No Date.)

To choose a different due date, select one or more messages, and then click the pop-up menu next to the flag button in the toolbar and choose from the pop-up menu (see Figure 10-18), or Control-click (or right-click) the message and choose from the To Do submenu. If you select Choose Date, the Dates and Reminder window appears. Here you can specify the Start date (when you want the item to appear in your To Do list), the Due date (when the item is actually due), and a reminder (an Office Reminder window that pops up on your screen to help jog your memory).

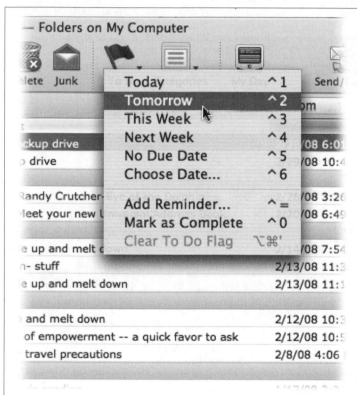

Figure 10-18:
Use the To Do Flag's pop-up menu to choose exactly when you need to respond to the selected message. If you do a lot of flagging, consider learning the keyboard equivalents listed in the menu (the chevron symbol stands for the Control key). Add a reminder to any flag, mark the item as completed, or clear the flag entirely using the final commands in this menu.

To view the messages you've flagged, you can do one of three things: Choose View → Flagged Only to display all the flagged messages in the current folder, click the Flagged search icon (page 350) in the Mail Views folder at the bottom of the folders pane, or switch to Entourage's Tasks function (page 462) and examine your To Do List.

Linking messages

Email messages can be much more valuable when they're linked to other bits of Entourage information, such as other messages, calendar events, notes, and so on—yet another payoff of having an email program with built-in calendar and address book info. For example, you can link a message to a calendar event; thereafter, you'll be able to click the link in the appropriate calendar day square to consult the original message (because it contained directions, for example).

Entourage creates some links for you automatically: for instance, when you reply to a message (or forward or redirect it), Entourage automatically creates a link between the original message and your response. That's how the message history feature works (see Figure 10-19). When flagging a message for follow-up (see page 386), you create a reminder that links to the original message.

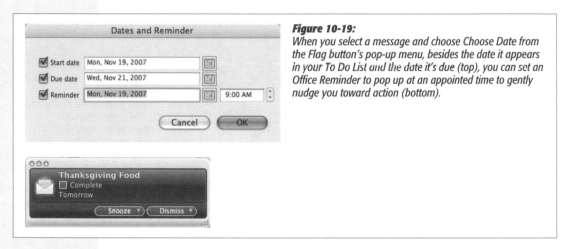

Figure 10-19:
When you select a message and choose Choose Date from the Flag button's pop-up menu, besides the date it appears in your To Do List and the date it's due (top), you can set an Office Reminder to pop up at an appointed time to gently nudge you toward action (bottom).

Chapter 13 has full details on links. In the meantime, here's a summary that's specific to email:

In addition to responding to messages, you can link messages in three other ways: by opening the links menu, creating a link to an existing item, and creating a link to a new item.

- **Open Links.** To open the Links window, choose Tools → Open Links or click the Link button in the toolbar (if you've added that button by customizing your toolbar—see page 353). In the Link To window for the selected message, you can create or remove links to existing or new items. You can also open the item on the other end of a link.

- **Link to Existing Item.** You can create a link to one of seven kinds of existing Entourage info-bits: another (email) Message, a Calendar Event, a Task, a Note, a Contact (address book entry), a Group, or even a File on your hard drive. (This last feature can be extremely handy. You might link a message about the date of your Macworld Expo talk to, for example, the Word document containing your outline.)

To link to an existing item, choose the kind of link you want to make from the Tools → Link to Existing submenu, and then select the item to which you want to link. You can also create such a link from the Link To window.

- **Link to New Item.** You can also link a message to a Message, Calendar Event, Task, Note, Contact, or Group that you're *about* to create—that is, you can simultaneously create a link *and* the item it's linked to. This is handy when you suddenly get the inspiration to create a link, but you haven't yet created the item on the other end of that link. Perhaps an email message from your epicurean friend contains a recipe for garbanzo bean stew and makes you think, "Ooh, I need to remember to bring a dish to Hari's potluck next week!" you can create a link from that message to a new calendar item, then create the event using Entourage's Calendar feature.

  To create a link to a new item, choose the kind of link (and new item) that you want to create from the Tools → Link to New submenu. Once you've created a link, a small chain-link icon appears in the Links column in the message list.

To remove a link, open the Link To window (choose Tools → Open Links, choose Open Links from the Link pop-up button in the toolbar, or click the link column next to the message in question). Once the Link To window is open, select the link, and then click the Remove button at the top of the window.

Prioritizing messages

You can set one of five priority levels for messages that you send or receive: Highest, High, Normal, Low, and Lowest. Once you've assigned priorities to your messages, Entourage can sort them so that the most important messages appear at the top.

To set a message's priority, highlight its name in the List pane and then choose from the Message → Priority menu. To sort messages by priority, click the Priority column header (the exclamation-point icon at the left side of the List pane). The first time you click, Entourage sorts your messages from highest priority to lowest; the second time, it lists them from lowest to highest importance.

Note: You're not the only one who can set a message's priority. Sometimes incoming messages have their priority already set–invariably to Highest (for those who think their messages are vital) or Lowest (for those considerate about sending out genuinely unimportant mail). You can change this setting for a received message according to your priorities by choosing from the Message → Priority submenu.

Opening Attachments

Sending little text messages is fine, but it's not much help when somebody wants to send you a photograph, a sound recording, a Word or Excel document, and so on. Fortunately, enclosing such items as *file attachments* is one of the world's most popular email features.

POWER USERS' CLINIC

Custom Arrangements

Custom arrangements let you design your own, carefully configured manner for displaying messages. Consider the following scenario: Every day you find yourself searching for various file attachments you've received. So you click the attachment column heading to group the attachments together then start scanning the From column as you try to remember exactly who sent it to you. Or do you find that you arrange your Mail window quite differently when you have 4,365 unread messages and need to ferret out the most important work-related ones than when you're keeping up with everyday correspondence? Either way, you have to spend time rearranging the Entourage window before you get to your actual work.

The Custom Arrangements feature was made for you. Once you set up one of these complex email-management schemes, which are based on the Groups feature (page 375), you can recreate it anytime just by choosing its name from the View → Arrange By submenu. Don't waste another minute.

Choose View → Arrange By → Edit Custom Arrangements and follow these steps:

1. Click New to display the Edit Custom Arrangements dialog box (see Figure 10-20).

2. In the Custom arrangement name box, type a name.

3. Choose the options you want from the pop-up menus. The various options let you decide exactly how you wish to display and order the messages. For example, if you group the items by Subject and then sort the groups by Sent, all the messages with the same subject will be sub-divided into groups based on who sent the message. You can also decide whether you wish to sort from A to Z or Z to A. By the same token, your chronological order can begin with the most recent or the oldest.

4. The bottom pop-up menu determines if you want Entourage to display your message groups collapsed (so you can easily see all the groups) or expanded (so you can see all the messages in each group without having to click its flippy triangle).

5. After you're finished, click OK.

Once you've created an arrangement, you can easily edit it by choosing View → Arrange By → Edit Custom Arrangements and double-clicking the arrangement in the list. Entourage whisks you back to the Edit Custom Arrangements dialog box, where you can rename or otherwise alter the custom arrangement. To clear away old, unused arrangements from the menu, choose View → Arrange By → Edit Custom Arrangements, select the arrangement and click Delete.

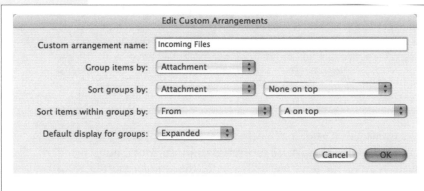

Figure 10-20:
In order to sort and display your mail differently depending on the task at hand, you can create several custom arrangements and quickly switch between them by choosing View → Arrange By. The oddly named secondary "Sort groups by" pop-up menu determines whether the chosen group ends up at the top of the list or not.

When you receive an email message with an attachment, you may notice that it often takes much longer than usual to download from the Internet. That's because attached files are typically much larger than email messages. (For more information on attaching files to send to others, see page 407.)

When you've received a message with an attachment, a small paper-clip icon appears in the attachments column at the far left of the List pane.

Unlike, say, America Online or Eudora, Entourage doesn't store downloaded files as normal file icons on your hard drive. Instead, they're stored in the Entourage database—a big, specially encoded file on your hard drive. To extract an attached file from this mass of data, you first have to open the message (either in the Preview pane or by opening the message into its own window). Now you'll see a new section in the window labeled Attachments, as shown in Figure 10-21, listing any files that came along with the message.

If you expand the flippy triangle to the left of the word Attachments, you see a list of the files, complete with their icons, plus three buttons: Open, Save, and Remove. At this point, you can proceed in any of several ways:

- Click one of the file icons (or Shift-click to select several, or click one and then press ⌘-A to highlight them all), and then click Save. The Save Attachment dialog box appears, so that you can specify the folder where you want to save the files on your hard drive.

- Drag a file icon (or several selected ones) clear out of the message window and into a folder or onto any visible portion of your desktop, as shown in Figure 10-21.

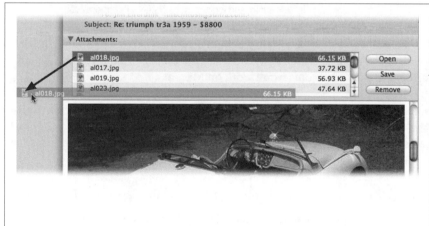

Figure 10-21:
When you receive an attachment via email, you see it represented just above the message text. Nearby buttons let you open, save, or remove the attachment. But when you drag an attachment's icon onto your desktop (or into a folder) you copy the file out of the Entourage world and into your Macintosh world, where you can file it, trash it, open it, or manipulate it as you would any file.

- Double-click the attachment's icon in the message (or highlight it and click Open). If you were sent a document—a photo, Word file, or Excel file, for example—it now opens in the corresponding program (Photoshop, Word, Excel, or whatever).

Warning: After the attachment is open, if you make any changes to it, use the *File → Save As command* to save the file into a folder of your choice. Otherwise, your changes evaporate immediately.

- Highlight an icon (or several) and click Remove. You've just detached and discarded the file.

Tip: It's easy to set up Entourage to save *all* incoming file attachments into a particular folder on your hard drive—or onto your desktop for easy retrieval—saving you the step of manually saving or dragging them. (This arrangement should sound familiar to America Online, Eudora, and Claris Emailer fans.)

The trick is to use the message rules described in the next section. One of them has an option to save all file attachments (or only those from certain senders) automatically into a folder you specify.

When attachments don't open

Several factors may be at work if you're unable to open a file attachment. For starters, your correspondent's email program may have *compressed* or *encoded* the file to make it take less time to send. If you're having trouble getting a file to open, therefore, your first step should be to drag the attachment's icon onto that of StuffIt Expander, a free program that you can download from *www.stuffit.com*.

StuffIt Expander can gracefully decode and decompress just about any compressed or stuffed file, including those with file name suffixes like .sit, .cpt, .hqx, .gz, .z, .arc, .uu, and .zip.

Tip: Of course, Mac OS X generally hides these extensions, but you can always see a file's hidden extension by highlighting it, choosing File → Get Info, and looking in the Name & Extension section.

If the file still won't open, even after being decompressed, then you may be dealing with a file from a Windows PC. Some you can open relatively easily; some require more work, and some won't work on Macs at all.

Warning: Although there are no Mac OS X viruses, Mac fans *can* fall victim malicious bits of code—*malware*—on the Internet in the form of *Trojan horses*. These aren't technically viruses, since you have to download and install them. But you're not installing what you think you are—hence the term "Trojan horse." But so far, none of these have caused trouble for more than a handful of people

The best clue is the three-letter *file name extension* on the file's name. For example:

- **.doc, .xls,** and **.ppt.** These extensions identify Microsoft Office documents created before the advent of Office 2007 for Windows and Office 2008 for Mac—Word, Excel, and PowerPoint, respectively. You can usually open these documents with Office 2008 by double-clicking them, but if that doesn't work, drag the document to the icon of the appropriate Office program.

Viruses by Email

I'm scared of attachments. Won't I get a virus?

The media periodically gets breathless and wide-eyed about new viruses and worms (programs that have been deliberately written to gum up a computer). These little programs often come attached to, or masquerade as, ordinary files or messages sent to you—sometimes inadvertently by people you know. When you try to open or save an attachment, Entourage sometimes warns you of the possibility of viruses and gives you an opportunity to chicken out. (Entourage doesn't warn you if you drag the attachment out of the message to your desktop.)

Fortunately, there are still no viruses that can affect Mac OS X, so infecting your computer via email is currently impossible. Furthermore, Office 2008 eliminates another source of viruses—macro viruses written with Office's former VBA programming language and embedded into Word and Excel documents. Since Office 2008 doesn't work with VBA, macro viruses can't affect Office 2008 programs.

Although Mac OS X isn't vulnerable to emailed viruses now, there's no reason to assume that will always be the case. It's always a good idea to delete attachments, without opening them, from people you don't know. If you receive unexpected attachments from people you do know, check with them before opening any files, particularly if the message is brief or out of character, or if that person uses Windows.

In fact, with more than 100,000 viruses for Windows floating around, Microsoft is belatedly attempting to improve the legendarily leaky security on the Windows platform by implementing all kinds of new protections. In a misguided effort to protect Mac fans from malicious attachments, Entourage 2008 completely blocks a host of file types including .exe, .mpkg, and .webloc. You can neither send nor receive files that are on this "blacklist" of potential threats. (For the complete list of file types that Microsoft's Department of Computerland Security has profiled as potential threats, search for "unsafe attachments" in Entourage Help.) Microsoft's inconvenient workaround asks you to compress or archive files (Control-click the file and choose Create Archive) before attaching them to a message—and request that people sending you such attachments do the same.

- **.docx, .xlsx,** and **.pptx.** These extensions identify the new style of Word, Excel, and PowerPoint documents created in the XML file format. They open with no ado in Office 2008.

- **.mpg.** You've been sent an MPEG movie, and you can usually play it using QuickTime Player.

- **.wmf, .wma, .wmv.** You've been sent a file encoded in Windows Media Format—a Microsoft media format similar to QuickTime. You can play these files in QuickTime player with the addition of a special component called Flip4Mac. Go to *www.flip4mac.com* and look for the Get WMV Player Free button.

- **.mp3, .wav,** and **.aif.** MP3 files are compact, great-sounding music files. They're what Apple's iTunes and iPod are all about. If an MP3 file doesn't play when you double-click it, drag it onto the iTunes icon.

- **.ra, .rm,** or **.ram.** This file is an audio, video, or streaming media item in Real-Player format. Neither QuickTime nor Windows Media Player can play these items. Get a copy of RealPlayer at *www.real.com*.

- **.bmp.** This is a Windows Bitmap file. You should be able to open this type of graphic using Mac OS X's Preview program, or Word 2008.

- **.tif** or **.tiff.** TIFF graphics files are common in desktop publishing. (The graphics in this book, for example, are TIFF files.) If you can't open it by double-clicking, the Mac OS X Preview program can show it to you. Word can also open TIFF images.

- **.psd.** A Photoshop document. You can view these in Preview if you don't have Photoshop.

- **.exe.** This extension denotes an *executable* file for Windows—like a Mac program is executable on a Mac. By itself, your Mac can't run Windows programs, just as Windows computers can't run Macintosh programs. But you can run .exe files and any other Windows programs on an Intel Mac running Windows with BootCamp or Parallels.

- **.bat, .pif, .scr,** or **.com.** These are other kinds of Windows programs, which you can't run on the Mac (unless it's an Intel Mac running Windows). They're also, unfortunately, often associated with email-based worms and viruses. They can't harm a Mac, but delete them anyway, so that you don't pass them along accidentally to a Windows-using friend.

- **.jpg** or **.gif.** You can open these graphics files in Word, PowerPoint, Preview, or Safari. In fact, you often see these images or photographs right in the body of the email messages that brought them to you.

- **.pdf.** This downloaded item is probably a manual or brochure. It came to you as a portable document format file, better known as an Adobe Acrobat file. Entourage generally shows you a preview of the PDF file right in the email message, but you can also open the document with either Preview or the free Adobe Reader (*www.adobe.com*).

- **.html** or **.htm.** A file whose name ends in .html or .htm is a Web page. In the beginning, Web pages hung out only on the Internet. These days, however, you're increasingly likely to find that you've downloaded one to your Mac's hard drive (it may be a software manual for some shareware, for example). To open the Web page, double-click in the attachment area of the message to open it in your Web browser, or drag the document to the visible area of a Web browser window, if you already have one running.

- **.vcf.** You've got yourself an electronic "business card," called a vCard, containing contact information that you can add to your Entourage Address Book. See page 421.

- **.rtf.** RTF stands for Rich Text Format, and indicates a formatted word processing document as described on page 45. Word 2008 opens this kind of file with ease.

- **.wps.** This file was created using Microsoft Works, an all-in-one software suite that's something like AppleWorks. Unfortunately, Office 2008 can't read these files; ask your correspondent to export the file as RTF, plain text, or another format if possible. For a greater feeling of self-reliance, buy a file-conversion program like MacLinkPlus (*www.dataviz.com*).

- **.wpd.** This suffix denotes a WordPerfect document. Several years ago, Word-Perfect was the dominant word processing program for PCs. (The file name extension *.doc* "belonged" to WordPerfect files, in fact, until Microsoft co-opted it for use with Microsoft Word—one of many actions that caught the Justice Department's attention over the years.) Office 2008 can't open WordPerfect files directly. Here again, reach for MacLinkPlus or ask your correspondent to export the document as RTF, HTML, or plain text.

- **.fp5** and **.fp7.** These are FileMaker Pro databases (*www.filemaker.com*).

If you were sent a file with a three-letter code not listed here, you may well have yourself a Windows file that can be opened only by a Windows program that you don't actually own. You might consider asking your correspondent to resend it in one of the more universal formats described above.

GEM IN THE ROUGH

Using the Junk Mail Filter

The Entourage Junk Mail Filter scans your incoming messages for some telltale signs of junk email (spam), and then moves suspect mail to a folder called Junk Email, thus keeping your Inbox relatively clean of worthless come-ons.

To use the Junk Mail Filter, choose Tools → Junk E-mail Protection, and then, in the dialog box that opens, choose the level of protection you desire.

By clicking the Safe Domains tab, and typing domain names in the space provided, you can specify certain domains (companies or entities, as indicated by everything after the @ sign in the email addresses) to exclude from the filter—such as stuff arriving from your work domain. Messages from addresses in your Address book are never identified as junk, and the Junk Mail Filter never targets mailing lists you're managing using the Mailing List Manager feature. Conversely, click the Blocked Senders tab and enter addresses or domains that you *always* want filtered out as junk mail.

Entourage's Junk Mail Filter is good, but it *does* make mistakes, letting junk mail slip through into your inbox, and occasionally routing good messages into the Junk Email folder. It's a good idea to occasionally scan through the Junk Email folder in order to check up on the filter and retrieve any good messages before finally deleting all the spam.

Entourage provides two toolbar buttons: Not Junk—to move a message from the Junk E-mail folder back to the Inbox—and Junk—to move messages into the Junk E-mail folder. However, unlike junk filters in some other email programs (Apple Mail, for example), Entourage's Junk Mail Filter doesn't actually learn from the mistakes you correct in this manner. When you use the Not Junk button it only offers to add the sender to the Entourage Address Book, or add the sender's domain to the Safe Domains list—or just move the message back to the Inbox.

Using Message Rules

Once you know how to create folders, the next step in managing your email is to set up a series of *message rules* (or *filters*) that file, answer, or delete incoming messages *automatically* based on their contents, such as subject, sender, or size. Message rules require you to think like the distant relative of a programmer, but the mental effort can reward you many times over; message rules turn Entourage into a surprisingly smart and efficient secretary.

Setting up message rules

Select an email message of the type you're creating a rule for *before* you start setting up the rule. That way, Entourage fills in the appropriate text (see step 4, below) as you choose the filtering criteria. Then follow these steps:

1. **Choose Tools → Rules.**

   The Rules dialog box appears, as shown in Figure 10-22, top. As you can see, the tabs here let you set up different rules for each kind of email account (POP, IMAP, Hotmail, Exchange), plus separate rules for newsgroups (page 429), and outgoing messages.

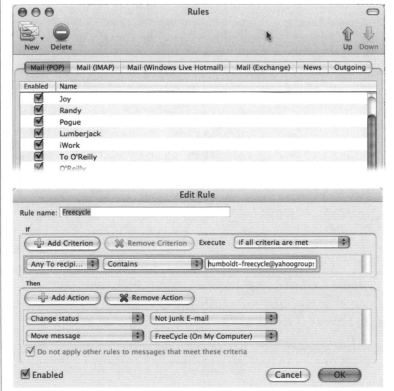

Figure 10-22:
Top: Mail rules can help file your messages, serve as an email autoresponder, or call important messages to your attention. Choose Tools → Rules and click the appropriate Mail tab to create or view your rules. Select a rule to see what it does, and use the Up and Down buttons (or just drag the rule) to specify the order in which Entourage runs the rules.

Bottom: Double-click a rule to open the Edit Rule dialog box, where you can specify or modify what the rule does.

2. **Click the tab you want to work with, and then click New.**

The Edit Rule dialog box appears (Figure 10-22, bottom).

3. **Use the top options to specify how Entourage should select messages to process.**

For example, if you'd like Entourage to watch out for messages from a particular person, you would set up the first two pop-up menus to say "From" and "Contains," respectively.

To catch messages pertaining to your eBay buying and selling hobby, set the pop-up menus to say "Subject" and "Contains."

If you click Add Criterion, you can set up another condition for this message rule. For example, you can set up the first criterion to find messages *from* your uncle, and a second that watches for messages from your cousin in order to sort them both into the Family folder.

If you've set up more than one criterion, use the "Execute" pop-up menu to indicate whether the message rule should apply if *all* the conditions are true, or if *any* one of them is true.

You can also set up catch-all rules that do their thing *unless* any or all criteria are met. For instance, if you're using an account purely for internal email at your company, you can set up a rule for that account that files away (or deletes) all mail *except* messages from an address containing your company's ".com" name.

4. **Specify *which* words or people you want the message rule to watch out for.**

After you've used the two criterion pop-up menus, a text box appears. Into this box, type the word, name, or phrase you want Entourage to watch out for—a person's name or email address, or *eBay,* in the previous examples.

5. **In the lower half of the box, specify what you want to happen to messages that match the criteria.**

If, in steps 1 and 2, you've told your rule to watch for mail containing eBay in the Subject line, here's where you can tell Entourage to move it into, say, an eBay folder.

With a little imagination, you'll see how the options in this pop-up menu can do absolutely amazing things with your incoming email. Entourage can delete, move, or print messages; reply, forward, or redirect them to somebody; automatically save attachments into a downloads folder you've set up; or when you receive messages from some important person, play a sound, animate the Entourage icon in the Dock, or display a dialog box.

6. **In the very top box, name your mail rule. Click OK.**

Now the Rules dialog box reappears (Figure 10-22, top). Here, you can manage the rules you've created, choose a sequence for them (those at the top get applied first), and apply them to existing messages.

Tip: Entourage applies rules in the order they appear, from top to bottom, in the Rules window. If a rule doesn't seem to be working properly, it may be that an earlier rule is intercepting and processing the message before the "broken" rule even sees it.

To fix this problem, try moving the rule up or down in the list by selecting it and then clicking the Up or Down buttons or by just dragging the rule up or down the list. When troubleshooting rules, it may help to selectively turn preceding rules on or off.

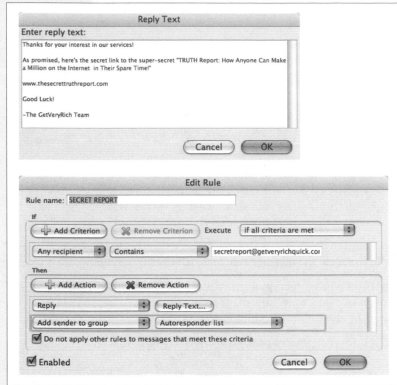

Figure 10-23:
In this example, if Entourage receives an email message to a specified address—one you set up specifically to collect sales leads, for example—it sends an email reply using the text you create after clicking the Reply Text button (top) and adds the sender's address to a special group (bottom) in your Entourage Address Book (see page 412).

Writing a Message

To create an email message in Entourage, use one of these tactics:

- Choose File → New → Mail Message.

- Press ⌘-N. (If you're using an Entourage function that has nothing to do with email—the Calendar or Tasks, for example—press Option-⌘-N instead.)

- Click the New button on the toolbar or choose Mail Message from its pop-up menu.

In each case, an empty email message window appears, filled with email composition tools.

Using Directory Services

You're all set to send someone an email message, when it hits you: You don't know her address. In the good old days, several Web services (such as Bigfoot and four11) served as free "email phone books," and Entourage's Directory Services could connect to them an attempt to find email addresses for you. But that lasted only as long as it took these companies to figure out this was a service people were willing to pay for. On the other hand, in these times of increasing privacy concerns, the lack of free email directories is probably a good thing.

Entourage's Directory Services still works great for companies that provide their own email directory (via an electronic phone book known as an LDAP server). In that event,

choose Tools → Accounts, click the Directory Service tab, and then click the New button in the window's toolbar. The Account Setup Assistant now walks you through a two-step process of entering your company's server information. (Get it from your network administrator.)

While you're in the Accounts window, you can choose which LDAP account you'd like as your main directory; select the account's name and then click the Make Default button in the toolbar. Entourage displays your default service in bold, and uses this service when you're addressing an email message and choose Directory from the pop-up menu in order to search for an address.

Step 1: Addressing the message

The first thing you'll see when you create a new email message is the address pane, a pop-up window with four buttons, three address fields, and a list of addresses from your Entourage Address Book (see Figure 10-24). The fields here are labeled To, Cc, and Bcc, each of which has its own purpose:

- **To.** Most of the time, you'll type your correspondent's email address here. If the recipient's email address resides in your address book, Entourage can autocomplete it for you after you start typing. Just keep typing until it narrows it down to the one address you want—or scroll through the suggestions until you find the correct address, and double-click it or press Enter.

- **Cc.** Cc stands for *carbon copy;* the name harks back to the days of typewriters, when creating a copy of a document required inserting carbon paper between two sheets of typing paper. In email terms, putting someone's email address in the Cc area means, "No reply required; just thought you'd want to see this." People listed in the Cc field receive a copy of the message, but aren't the primary recipients.

- **Bcc.** A *blind carbon copy* is a secret copy. This feature lets you send a copy of a message to somebody secretly, without any of the other recipients knowing that you did so. The names in the To and Cc fields appear at the top of the message for all recipients to see, but nobody can see the names you type into the Bcc box.

  You can use the Bcc field to quietly signal a third party that a message has been sent. For example, if you send your co-worker a message that says, "Chris, thanks for staying late last night and helping Mr. Harris—I wish everybody at this office showed the kind of dedication to the job that you do," you could Bcc your boss or supervisor to clue her in to this outstanding employee without embarrassing Chris.

The Bcc box is useful in other ways, too. Many people send email messages (containing jokes, or press releases, for example) to a long list of recipients. If the names are in the To or Cc fields, then everybody gets to see everybody else's address—a definite no-no among privacy advocates.

But if the sender used the Bcc field to hold all the recipients' email addresses, none of the recipients will see the addresses of any of the others.

Tip: After addressing a message, you can drag the addresses back and forth among these three blanks: from the To box into the Cc box, for example.

If you want to send a message to more than one person, click the Add button and type in a second (or third, or fourth) email address, or just press the Tab key or click in an empty area of an addressing box and start typing. As in most dialog boxes, press the tab key another time to jump to the next field (to proceed from the To field to the Cc field, for example).

You don't have to remember and carefully type out all those email addresses, either. As you type, Entourage compares what you're typing with the names in your Entourage Address Book. If it finds a match—that is, if you've typed *ton* and your Address Book contains the name *Toni Martin,* for example, Entourage sprouts a list of that and any other *ton* matches. The more letters you type, the closer Entourage zeroes in on your intended addressee. Entourage also remembers the last 200 addresses you've sent mail to and received mail from that *aren't* in your address book, which can be handy when you think of something you'd like to add to a recent exchange. (You can turn this feature off or simply clear out the list in Entourage → Preferences → Mail & News Preferences → Compose if it bothers you.)

You can choose from this list of proposed addressees either by pressing Return when Entourage highlights the correct name, by pressing the up- or down-arrow key to highlight a name, and then pressing Return, or by clicking a name. If none of Entourage's guesses are correct, just keep typing; Entourage quietly withdraws its suggestions.

Alternatively, you can access your address book by clicking the Address Book button just above the To field (see Figure 10-24).

Tip: The tiny icon that appears in front of each email address that you've entered indicates Entourage's understanding of the address. If you see a tiny humanoid figure, (similar to the MSN Messenger icon) you've input an address that's in the Entourage Address Book; if you see a blue circle/button symbol, you've typed an address that's not in your Entourage Address Book. (Of course, you can always add one of these addresses to your Entourage Address Book just by Control-clicking it and choosing "Add to Address Book" from the shortcut menu.)

A green question mark indicates Entourage doesn't understand the address, probably because it isn't a correctly formed email address—you may have included a space in the address by mistake, for example.

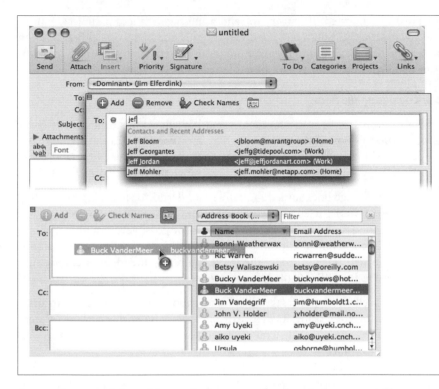

Figure 10-24:
*Top: As you type an
address, a pop-up menu
of matching names from
your address book
appears. Click the one
that you want, press Tab
to accept the highlighted
name and enter another
one. Or press Return to
use the highlighted
name, close the
addressing window, and
move to the Subject line.*

*Bottom: Click the
Address Book icon in the
Address pane's toolbar,
scroll up and down your
list of contacts, and drag
addresses into the To,
Cc, or Bcc panes. If you
just double-click a name
it goes directly into the
To pane. Repeat the
process to add more
names.*

Across the top of the address window are a few handy buttons. Add opens up a
new empty row in the current addressing field, where you can specify an additional address. The Remove button removes a selected recipient's row. Check
Names is handy if you don't know a coworkers email address and you're connected to your company's LDAP address directory (see page 399) in hopes of turning up the correct address.

Tip: You can use the Tab key to move between address fields, subject line, and the message's body text.

If you have more than one account set up in Entourage, a From pop-up menu
appears above the message's addressees. Choose from that pop-up menu to pick
the account you want to use to send the message.

Step 2: The Subject line

Some people, especially in the business world, get bombarded with email. That's
why it's courteous to put some thought into composing the Subject line (use
"Change in plans for next week" instead of "Hi," for example). Then press the Tab
key to make your cursor jump into the large message area. Don't make your subject too long: remember, most people will see it in a list with other information like
your name and the date and time you sent the message, and the subject may get

compressed or truncated. If you try to send a message without a subject, Entourage will warn you this isn't a very good idea, but it's not a fatal one either. You can go ahead and send it. Entourage will automatically insert "<no subject>" as a subject line. And your recipient's spam filter may possibly delete it.

Step 3: Composing the body

After you've addressed your message and given it a subject, it's time to write your message. To do this, just click (or Tab into) the message area and start typing. You can use all the standard editing techniques, including selection, drag-and-drop, and the Cut, Copy, and Paste commands, to rearrange the text as you write it.

As you type, Entourage does something rather wonderful (or alarming, depending on your point of view): it checks your spelling as you go, using a red squiggly underline to mark questionable spelling. To check for possible alternative spellings for a suspect word, Control-click the red-squiggled word; a list of suggestions appears in a shortcut menu. Choose the word you really intended, or choose Add to add the word to the Office 2008 dictionary.

If you want to spell-check a message all at once, choose Tools → Spelling (or press Option-⌘-L) after composing it. (To turn off automatic spell checking, choose Entourage → Preferences → General Preferences → Spelling tab, and turn off "Check spelling as you type.")

Tip: You can use the same keyboard shortcuts in Entourage that you use in Word (such as ⌘-right arrow to move the cursor one word to the right)—a great timesaver. Just choose Entourage → Preferences → General Preferences → General tab, and make sure that "Use Microsoft Office keyboard shortcuts for editing text" is turned on.

That same preference tab lets you make Entourage resemble Word in other ways, too. It lets you turn on automatic whole-word selection, "smart cut and paste" (spaces are automatically added or removed as necessary when you insert or delete text), and a Font menu that shows fonts in their own typefaces. Similarly, the Spelling tab in the General Preferences dialog box gives the same control over spell-checking options that Word does.

All of this should sound familiar; it's precisely the same basic mechanism that Word 2008 employs when it looks for spelling mistakes on the fly, as described on page 63.

Tip: If you're composing a long email message and need a break, or it's one you don't want to send until later, choose File → Save or press ⌘-S to save the message in your Drafts folder. To reopen a saved draft, click the Drafts folder in the Folder list, and then open the draft that you want to work on from the list on the right.

Step 4: Choosing a format (HTML or plain text)

When it comes to formatting a message's text, you have two choices: *plain text* or *HTML* (hypertext markup language). Plain text means that you can't format your text with bold type, color, specified font sizes, and so on. HTML, on the other hand, lets you use formatting commands such as font sizes and bold text.

But there's a catch: although nowadays nearly all email programs can read HTML-formatted email, they don't always handle it the same way. An HTML message that looks fine for you may be incomprehensible for someone using another email program. HTML messages can also be much larger (and therefore slower to download on slow Internet connections) than plain-text messages, especially if you include pictures, sounds, or other multimedia elements.

So which should you choose? Plain text lends a more professional, old-hand feeling to your messages—but, more important, it's the most compatible. Whether your recipient uses a high-end workstation, a Web browser, a cell phone, or a 20-year-old terminal in a dusty university basement, a plain-text message almost *always* gets through intact. (There are some exceptions: accented characters and language encodings may complicate the issue.)

HTML-formatted messages, on the other hand, may not arrive intact. Your recipient may see a plain-text version of the message, which Entourage includes as a courtesy, but some email programs can't even display *that* neatly.

In general, you're better off using plain text for most of your messages, and sending HTML only when you need it and you're sure your recipients can see it. To specify which format Entourage uses for all outgoing messages (plain text or HTML), choose Entourage → Preferences → Mail & News Preferences → Compose, and select a format from the "Mail format" pop-up menu.

You can also change formats on a message-by-message basis. For example, if you generally like to send plain-text messages, you can switch one particular message into HTML mode by clicking the Use HTML button to the left and just above the body text area (see Figure 10-25), or choose Format → HTML. Either action activates the HTML toolbar, which you can use to add pizzazz to your messages. This toolbar is broken up into six sections:

- **Fonts.** The two controls in this section let you choose a font and font size for your email.

Note: If your message's recipient doesn't have the font you specify in this toolbar section, her email program substitutes some other font. To avoid such problems, stick to common cross-platform fonts like Arial, Courier, Times New Roman, or Verdana.

- **Styles.** Just as you'd expect in a word processor, you can choose Bold, Italic, Underline, or Teletype (which puts the selected text into a fixed-width font) styles for your text.

Figure 10-25:
HTML-based email lets you exercise some control over the layout of your email messages, including font, color, and text alignment. The HTML toolbar, shown just above the message body, is similar to what exists in many word processing programs. With it, you can turn plain text into an HTML-formatted masterpiece. But please remember, formatting exists to clarify communication, not obfuscate it.

WORKAROUND WORKSHOP

The Lowdown on "Complex" Markup

If you've created Web pages using the HTML language, you're probably scratching your head as you read about Entourage HTML email features. Where are tables? Where are forms? Where is JavaScript? Heck, how do you even embed a link into text instead of spelling it out as an ugly URL?

The short answer is: You don't. Entourage's HTML features are meant to enhance typical email communication, not to produce sophisticated Web pages.

Fortunately, you can call on another Office 2008 program for assistance. Open Word, type the email of your dreams, including links, pictures, tables, or whatever. When you're

finished, choose File → Send To → Mail Recipient (as HTML). Doing so opens Entourage and imports the document into an email message. Just address the message, give it a subject, and set it free. Entourage doesn't interpret the HTML perfectly—sometimes your pictures and tables may be sloshed about a bit—but hey, it's quick and it's all there.

Since you're probably not going to all this trouble for a casual message, be sure to send it to yourself as a test (and maybe also to some friends who use a variety of email programs) before setting your message loose on the world. You'll find that creating HTML that works in email programs is a different art from creating HTML for a Web site.

- **Alignment.** Lets you choose left, center, or right paragraph alignment.

- **Numbering, Bullets and Indents.** Lets you put the selected text in a bulleted or numbered list. It also lets you set the indent level of the selected text for some good organizational formatting.

- **Color.** These two controls let you choose a text color and a background color for your email messages. You can choose from one of 16 prefab colors, or you can mix your own (see page 747).

- **Rules.** There's only one button here, the Horizontal Line button, which puts a horizontal rule (in other words, a line) at the insertion point.

Remember: when it comes to email formatting, less is more. If you go hog-wild formatting your email, you may make the message hard to read, especially for people using email programs that interpret the HTML codes differently than Entourage does.

Tip: All of the HTML toolbar's commands are also accessible in the Format menu.

You can also insert pictures, sounds, or movies into HTML email messages. Type your message, place the insertion point where you'd like the item to appear, and then choose the appropriate command from the Message → Insert menu. Entourage asks you to locate and double-click the file you want to insert.

Tip: You can also drag the icons of graphics and movies right into the window of an outgoing HTML email message, where they appear at the insertion point. For sounds and background graphics, on the other hand, you have to use the Message → Insert menu.

Note that Entourage automatically converts TIFF and PICT images into JPEG format when you add them to HTML messages. If you need your recipient to receive these files unaltered, send them as standard file attachments instead of inserting them or dragging them into the window.

Once you've inserted a media item into a message, you can only move it around by inserting Returns and spaces in front of it. To delete a picture, sound, or movie, backspace over it, or select it and then press the Delete key. To remove a background image, select Message → and Remove Background Picture.

Tip: Just as file attachments can make an email message enormous, images, sounds, and movies can mean that your message will be measured in megabytes. That's fine if all your recipients have fast connections like cable modems. But if one of them is trying to check email using a dial-up connection, your ultra-cool inline images, movies, and sounds will become a giant headache.

Step 5: Adding a signature

Signatures (or "sigs") are bits of text stamped at the bottom of your email or newsgroup messages. Signatures began as a way to provide contact information without having to type it out in every message. But as online culture evolved, signatures became personal statements. A signature may contain a name, a postal or email address, a memorable quote, or even art composed of typed characters.

To create a signature, choose Tools → Signatures, which brings up the Signatures window. In it, you'll see something called the Standard signature. You can edit this signature by double-clicking it, or you can create any number of new signatures by clicking the New button. Either way, you get an editing window where you can type your new signature. (Your signature can be either plain text or HTML-based, as described in the previous section.)

Sig and Ye Shall Find

As cool as signatures are, don't go overboard. Few things are more annoying than downloading a two-line message followed by a full-screen signature. On mailing lists and newsgroups, a big signature is likely to get you drummed out of town. When making signatures, follow these guidelines:

• Keep signatures to four lines of text or less, focusing on essential information.

• Consider including a hyperlink to a Web page where people can find out more about who you are and what you do.

• Avoid potentially offensive material or blatantly commercial come-ons (although a brief pointer is OK,

particularly if it's to something you're personally involved with).

• Protect your privacy: consider not including email addresses, phone numbers, postal addresses, and other personal data, especially when sending messages to public forums like mailing lists and newsgroups. There's no telling where that information may go or who may get their hands on it. (See the box on page 409.)

If you really like flamboyant signatures for your email to your regular correspondents, great! But please, also create a simple, bare-bones sig just for mailing lists, newsgroups, and people outside your circle of friends.

Note: If you format your signature with HTML, Entourage automatically converts it to plain text when you write a plain-text message. Be sure your signature looks good in either format!

Once you've created one or more signatures, you can tack them onto every outgoing message or on a message-by-message basis:

• **Always append a signature.** Choose Tools → Accounts. In the Accounts window, double-click the account in question. (You can have a different standard signature for each account.)

In the resulting window, click the Options tab to reveal a pop-up menu of signatures. Select the signature that you'd like to have at the bottom of every email message created using that account. (You can always override this choice on a message-by-message basis.)

Tip: If you turn on the Random checkbox, Entourage will randomly select one of these gems to grace the bottom of every email message that you send. This is the way to rotate your pithy quotes from, say, *The Secret* without seeming repetitive to your correspondents. (Select Tools → Signatures, and then click the Random checkbox to turn on this feature.)

• **Message by message.** After writing your message, choose the signature you want from the Signature pop-up button (the little pen) in your message's toolbar. Entourage pastes the signature at the location of your insertion point.

Step 6: Add any file attachments

You read about *receiving* attachments earlier in this chapter; *sending* them some-times involves a little extra brainwork.

To attach a file or files to an outgoing email message, Microsoft, in its usual fashion, gives you several different methods to choose from:

- **Drag-and-drop.** If you can see the appropriate Finder window or item on the desktop behind the Entourage window, you can drag file or folder icons directly off the desktop and anywhere into the outgoing email message window, or to Entourage's icon on the Dock.

Tip: If you drag the *alias* of a file or folder, Entourage is considerate enough to ask you whether you mean to send the alias file itself (which will probably be worthless to your correspondent) or the file that opens when you double-click the alias.

- **Add button.** Click the Attach button in the message's toolbar, or click the Add button in the Attachments section of the outgoing email window. Either way, the Choose Attachment dialog box appears. Navigate to, and highlight, the file or folder you want to send, and then click Open.

- **Use a menu.** Choose Message → Add Attachments (or press ⌘-E) to do the same thing.

Once you've attached files, their names appear in the message's Attachments section, seen in Figure 10-26.

Attaching files is the easy part; knowing how to *encode* those files can be tricky. Not all computers (including the mail servers that transmit messages) can understand Macintosh files. Furthermore, a few email servers still mangle anything that isn't a plain-text message. Encoding your attachments is the solution to both problems.

Unfortunately, different computers recognize different file-encoding schemes. Encoded improperly, the file turns into gibberish and can't be opened on the other end.

To make matters even more complicated, files can also be *compressed* (as StuffIt or ZIP archives, for example) to make them smaller and reduce the amount of time it takes to send and receive them.

Fortunately, Entourage uses an encoding scheme called *AppleDouble,* which both Macs and Windows PCs can reconstitute. And it compresses your files only if you attach an entire folder (not individual files). It uses ZIP compression in that case, which Macs and PCs can decompress with no trouble.

There may be times, however, when you want to change these options. For example, you may want to turn on the ZIP compression for a single large file. Or you may have trouble sending files to someone using the factory settings, so you want to try different settings.

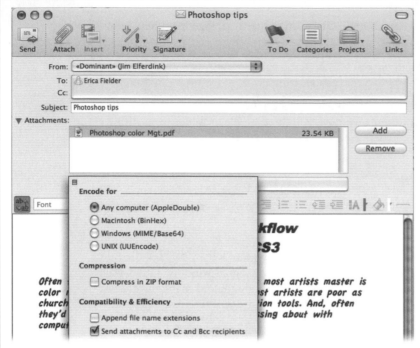

Figure 10-26:
A file's icon appears in the attachment section of the message window; click the "Encode for…" button below that panel to change the encoding, compression, and compatibility options. By clicking a couple of radio buttons and checkboxes, you can be sure that your recipients can open the attachment each and every time. The "Append file name extensions" is an incredibly valuable option, especially when sending files to Windows fans. If you failed to add the .doc, .xls, or .ppt to the end of their names, Entourage can do it for you at this stage.

Tip: However you choose to encode your file, be considerate of the recipient's time. About half of the email users in the United States still connect to their email servers with a dial-up connection. Sending attachments larger than a couple of megabytes can tie up their connection for a long time while it downloads. If you have a really large file to send, it's best to check with the recipient before sending. If it's just too big, you might have to put it on a CD-ROM and snail-mail it.

To change encoding and compression options, click the gray "Encode for" button just below the Attachments window (see Figure 10-26). A little pop-up window appears where you can change the encoding, compression, and compatibility options:

- **Any computer (AppleDouble).** This encoding scheme flattens a Mac file into something that other kinds of computers can read, including mail servers and Windows machines.

- **Macintosh (BinHex).** This encoding method is for Mac-to-Mac transfers only. Use it only when you've tried sending a file to another Mac fan using the AppleDouble setting and had no luck.

- **Windows (MIME/Base64).** This encoding method is for sending files to Windows and some Unix computers. Again, use it only when you've had no luck using AppleDouble.

FREQUENTLY ASKED QUESTION

Canning Spam

Help! I'm awash in junk email! How do I get out of this mess?

Spam is a much-hated form of advertising which, despite legislation and continual hand-wringing, isn't diminishing. While there's no instant cure for spam, you can take certain steps to shield yourself from it.

- Don't publicize your email address on the Internet—don't put it on your Web page or in your newsgroup signatures, and don't allow it to be listed in any public place—like a newsgroup. Spammers have automated software robots called trawlers that scour every public Internet message and Web page, automatically collecting email addresses they find, and then sending spam to those addresses or selling them to other spammers.

- Get a second email address you can use for Web sites, software registration, and mailing lists. At least if this address "leaks" to spammers, your primary address hasn't been compromised.

- When filling out forms or registering products online, always look for checkboxes requesting permission for the company to send you email or share your email address with its "partners." Just say no. If the company doesn't explicitly post its privacy policy on the Web site, assume no information you provide will be kept private.

- Use the Entourage Junk Mail Filter (page 395).

- Create message rules to filter out messages containing words and phrases most often found in spam such as "casino," "search engine placement," "herbal Viagra," and so forth. (You'll find instructions on page 396 in this chapter.)

- Consider paying $30 and installing SpamSieve, an exceptionally talented spam filtering software that takes the place of Entourage's Junk Mail Filter (*www.c-command.com*).

- Ask your ISP what kind of anti-spam services they offer. (It may be a free part of your service—and they may already be filtering spam from your mail.)

If you really have a spam problem, get a new email address. Give it to people you trust. Use the old address only for junk mail, and check it for messages only infrequently.

- **Unix (UUEncode).** UUEncode (which stands for Unix-to-Unix Encode) is the best thing for sending to a Unix or Linux fan. (It's also useful when you don't know *what* email program or operating system your recipient is using and AppleDouble doesn't work; UUEncode has been around so long that almost any email program can open UUEncoded messages.)

- **Compression (Compress in ZIP format).** As noted earlier, Entourage automatically compresses your attachments when they're included in a *folder*. Both Mac and Windows fans can easily unzip these archives.

Tip: When sending a file to a Windows PC, Entourage has the potential to end your "they can't open my files" headaches forever. Just remember to follow three steps in the Encoding window shown in Figure 10-26: Use no compression; use AppleDouble encoding; and turn on the "Append file name extensions" checkbox. Your Windows friends can open Office for Mac files easily, as long as they have Office on their computer. However, in order to open Office 2008's XML format files (the ones with .docx, .xmlx, and .pptx extensions) they need Office 2007 for Windows—which many Windows fans still don't have. Play it safe by sending your Office files in 97/2004 format (which bear the file extensions.doc, .xml, and .ppt), unless you're certain your recipients are completely up to date, Office-wise.

To remove an attachment, select its icon in the expanded Attachments window and press the Delete key (or click Remove). (*Dragging* an attachment out of the Attachments window doesn't remove it from the message. Instead, it makes a copy of the file where you drag it—unless you drag it to the Trash can in the Dock.) You can also remove all attachments in one fell swoop by choosing Message → Remove All Attachments.

Step 7: Send your email on its way

Once your message is put together properly, you can send it in any of several ways:

- Click the Send button in the message's toolbar.
- Press ⌘-Return (Send Message) or ⌘-K (Send & Receive All).
- Choose Message → Send Message Now.
- If you want to wait until the next time Entourage is connected before sending the message, choose Message → Send Message Later, press Shift-⌘-Return, or Shift-⌘-K.

When Entourage finishes sending the message, it disappears from your Outbox, and reappears in the Sent Items folder for your reference. (If you're a person of steely nerve and impeccable memory, you can turn off this feature; choose Entourage → Preferences → Mail & News Preferences → Compose, and turn off "Save copies of sent messages in the Sent Items folder.")

Email Netiquette

Different companies, organizations, and groups have different email cultures, so email norms might vary from place to place. But over the years, general rules of Internet etiquette—that is, netiquette—have evolved. Knowing a little netiquette not only saves you embarrassment in public forums like mailing lists, but also makes your messages more understandable.

Most of these items apply to newsgroup postings as well as ordinary email, but a few points of netiquette apply strictly to newsgroups:

- **Use your real name.** Entourage lets you enter anything you like for your name when you set up an account (see page 358). But using your real name gives you more credibility and lets your friends and correspondents more easily manage mail from you.

Note: An exception to this rule would be a newsgroup or mailing list where the privacy of participants is very important, such as online support groups. For these cases, consider using another email address managed via a separate Entourage account. The account can use whatever pseudonym (and signature) you like. (See page 359 for information on setting up multiple accounts.)

- **Write clearly.** Since email is a written medium, good writing can make you look *really* good. You don't have to be Shakespeare or even sound like a professional author. But make sure your message includes all the information your correspondent may need, check your grammar, and use Entourage's spell checker. Also, make allowances for people whose writing seems awkward or difficult to understand: English may be the most common language on the Internet, but it's not the primary language for millions of Internet users.

- **Be civil.** Some people write things in email that they would never dare say to your face. No matter how offended you might be, responding in kind just makes things worse. The best response to rude email is no response at all.

- **Quote sparingly.** When quoting another message, only quote enough material so your correspondent knows what you're talking about. Quoting the entire message makes it harder for your correspondent to understand what *you're* saying. You can also put your responses in between bits of quoted text, which makes it obvious what you're replying to.

- **Use blank lines.** Nothing is less inviting to readers than a solid page of text, devoid of paragraphs. Insert blank lines between paragraphs and quoted material in your message.

- **Put angle brackets around URLs.** If you put a Web address (URL) in a message, surrounding it with angle brackets <like this> turns it into a live, double-clickable link in a wide range of email programs.

- **Avoid all caps.** Capital letters are difficult to read on computer screens and MAKE YOU LOOK LIKE YOU'RE SHOUTING.

- **Write specific subjects.** Remember that the subject of a message is one of the few things (besides your name) that your correspondents see in a typical mailbox listing. Make your messages easy to find later by using specific subjects. "Lunch at Little John's Monday at 12:30?" is a better subject line than simply "Psst! You hungry?"

- **Don't forward chain letters.** It's okay, you're not going to have bad luck if you don't forward that message to 10 people. Virtually all chain letters—even those claiming to help a sick child, stop an Internet tax bill in Congress, report a dangerous new computer virus, or contain best wishes from the Dalai Lama—are hoaxes. They display your gullibility, waste time, and annoy a lot of people. If you hanker to send on one of these messages, check it out first at *www.snopes.com* or *www.hoaxbusters.org*.

Mailing list etiquette

The following points are particularly relevant to mailing lists:

- **Don't use HTML formatting.** There's bound to be someone—or a lot of someones—on a mailing list who can't handle, or can't abide, HTML-formatted messages. Furthermore, many mailing lists are available as *digests* where all the messages each day are sent as one large message late at night, rather than as individual messages throughout the day. HTML-formatted messages often don't come across in digests at all.

- **Don't send file attachments.** It's almost always wrong to send a file attachment to a mailing list, even if it's small. If you *must* make a file available to a mailing list, put it up on a Web or FTP site for interested members to download (Apple's .Mac service is perfect for this sort of thing). Then all you have to do is put a URL in your message.

- **Keep your sig short!** Your signature (page 405) should be four lines or less.

- **Stay on topic.** Most mailing lists are devoted to a particular subject, and your messages should be reasonably "on topic" for that list. It wouldn't be appropriate to discuss sports cars on a mailing list dedicated to acoustic guitars, or ask questions about Apple's latest Mac models on a mailing list devoted to 1970s television sitcoms. On the other hand, there's probably an appropriate mailing list for almost anything you want to discuss (and lots of things you wouldn't be caught dead discussing)!

- **Keep private conversations off lists.** Sometimes it's more appropriate to reply to a particular list member privately rather than the entire list. In those cases, just write a private email to the person.

- **Trim the quoting down to the essential.** When you send a reply to somebody's posting, trim out all of the >quoted >portion except the part in question. Nobody needs to read the entire treatise again.

Finally, as tempting as it may be to send out flurries of advertising about your products or business using the Internet, it's a bad idea. Spam isn't only illegal in many jurisdictions (meaning you can be sued), it's guaranteed to get your Internet account shut down without notice. It's fine to keep in contact with current customers via email if they've given you permission, but quite another to use the Internet as a means to harass others.

Address Book

Even if you're still living under the delusion that Entourage is only good for email, you can benefit from its built-in Rolodex function that saves all your email addresses and also full contact information, such as name, address, phone number, and photo.

But make no mistake: The names and accompanying information don't just stay locked away in storage. No, they're a hardworking lot that often offer their services as you work in Office's other programs. For example, once your Address Book contains a few names, Entourage offers to automatically complete addresses as you start typing in the To field of email messages. It can also fetch the phone numbers of people you're inviting to events that you schedule in Entourage's calendar. You can also easily include address book information in Word, Excel, or

PowerPoint. You can also assign your contacts to Entourage projects (see Chapter 11). From then on, when you open up the Project Palette anywhere in Office, you'll see all the contacts that have anything to do with the project listed there.

The Address Book isn't a separate program that you double-click when you want to look up something; it's just one module of Entourage. You view it by clicking the Address Book icon in the upper left of Entourage's main window, by choosing View → Go To → Address Book, by pressing ⌘-2 (and probably in dozens of other ways).

A Tour of Address Book World

The Address Book interface (Figure 10-27) parallels Entourage's Mail view, which shows a list of messages above, the body of the highlighted message below. In the Address Book, when you click someone's name in the list above, you get a detailed view below, of whatever information you've recorded about that person. Sometimes that's only a name and email address; sometimes it's the whole shebang—postal addresses, anniversary, astrological sign, shoe size, and so on.

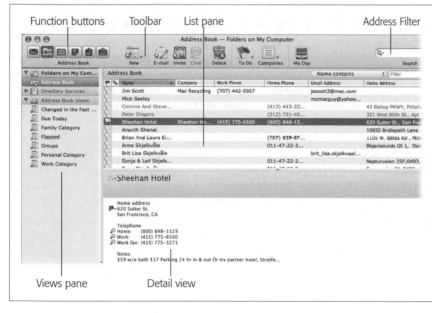

Figure 10-27:
Much like the Entourage Mail view, the Address Book window has a preview pane showing a list up top, detailed information down below. It reveals a plethora of other information about this person, depending on which columns you choose to display using the View › Columns menu. Like the Mail view, the Address Book view has a quick-find filter in the upper-right corner. To find a certain person's information quickly, type a few letters of his name into this box.

You also manipulate the Address Book list view much like email. For example, you navigate the list and highlight selected names exactly the same way (see page 371). And you manipulate the various columns of address information just as you would with email messages. The columns give you at-a-glance information about your acquaintances—name, company, phone numbers, email address, category, and whether there are any links or flags.

Tip: Entourage can show you more than 40 columns of information about each person in your address book. Unless you have either a 70-inch monitor, or an extreme obsession with detail, you can probably get by with fewer. To specify which columns show up in the list view, select them from the View → Columns submenu.

Creating Contacts

Suppose you're already looking at your Address Book list. To open a new "Rolo-dex card" for somebody you know—a new *contact,* in Address Book lingo—click the New button or press ⌘-N. (If you're not already in Address Book view, choose File → New → Contact, or choose Contact from the New pop-up menu.)

Entourage presents the Create Contact window (Figure 10-28, top). You can use this window to enter basic data about new contacts, such as names, addresses, email addresses, and phone numbers.

Tip: If someone has sent you contact information via email using a vCard (usually appearing as an email attachment with a ".vcf" extension), you can drag the vCard directly to Entourage's address list. Entourage creates a new contact record for you automatically. See page 421 for more details.

Three of the fields—email, the address field, and one of the phone fields—have pop-up menus next to them for labeling the information you've recorded. You can use these to specify whether the address or email address you've just typed in is home or work, or whether a phone number is mobile, fax, or whatever. It's not necessary to click inside each field before typing into it. As in any dialog box, you can press Tab to move the cursor to the next field (from the First [name] to Last [name] field, for example), or Shift-Tab to jump back to the *previous* field.

Tip: Don't bother with parentheses and hyphens in phone numbers—Entourage adds them for you. You'll find the controls for turning this feature on and off (and specifying the punctuation you prefer) by choosing Entourage → Preferences → General Preferences → Address Book → Format phone numbers.

In an unusual, uncharacteristic Microsoftian feature lapse, Entourage doesn't automatically capitalize names. Nor is there any way to use information in a previ-ously created contact as a starting point for a new contact. In other words, if you know 30 people who work for Microsoft and you want to enter their contact infor-mation in Entourage, you'll have to type (or paste) *Microsoft* 30 times.

Tip: Although Entourage lacks some built-in timesaving features, it is *scriptable.* If you're familiar with AppleScript, you can create a simple script that handles such repetitive tasks automatically. Easier yet: you can download some excellent, ready-to-run Entourage scripts from *www.scriptbuilders.net.*

Once you've filled out the information in this window, you can either close the win-dow, (saving your new contact information and returning to the master Address Book screen) or click More to expand the form into the long form (Figure 10-28, bottom), which has places for more exhaustive information on your contacts.

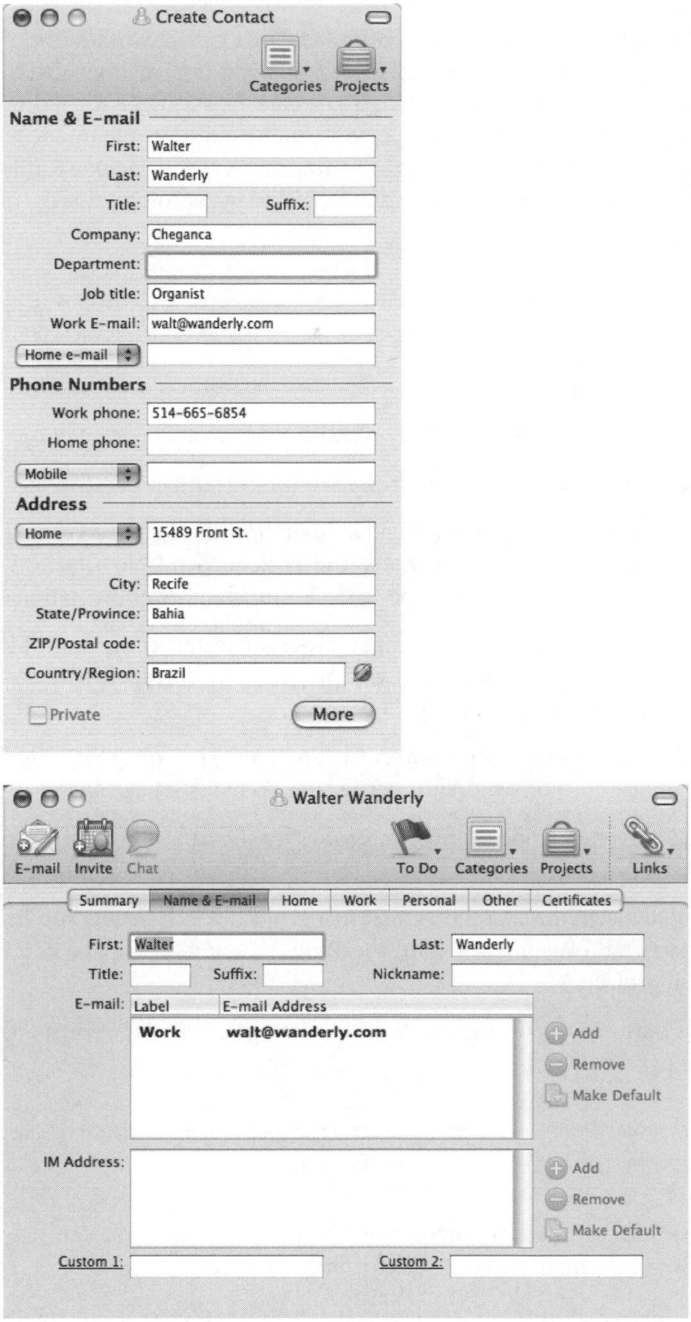

Figure 10-28:
The Create Contact window comes in two flavors—the short form (useful for casual contacts, shown at top), and the long form (useful for people you either know very well or need to keep a complete dossier on, shown below). Click the More button to expand the short form into the longer one (bottom). (Once you do, however, there's no returning to the simpler form. When you reopen a contact in the future, you can only access to the long form.)

The long form

If you click the More button at the bottom of the Create Contact window, you've moved into *long form* country, where the detail-oriented and information-obsessive roam (sung to the tune of "Home on the Range"). While the short-form window is great when all you need in a contact is a person's name, address, email address, and/or phone number, the long form turns Entourage into a giant personal information database, where you can enter a contact's birthday, astrological sign, and even a photo.

Tip: You open the expanded version of the Contact dialog box whenever you double-click an existing contact in your address book. You can also reach the expanded form by highlighting a name and pressing ⌘-O or choosing File → Open Contact.

The long form has its own toolbar featuring several contact-related commands:

- **E-mail.** Creates a new email message addressed to the currently open contact.

- **Invite.** Click this button to open a Calendar invitation dialog box. Fill in the subject, date and time, write a quick note, and click its Send Now button to email the invitation to this contact. (See page 454 for much more on invitations.)

- **Chat.** If you have the Microsoft Messenger program installed on your Mac, clicking here opens an instant message window with the current addressee—assuming they're also running Messenger.

- **To Do.** Click this button to add the contact to your To Do list, or use its pop-up menu to determine a time or set a reminder for the To Do (see page 462).

- **Categories.** Lets you choose one or more categories for the currently open contact (see page 474).

- **Projects.** Lets you assign the current contact to a project, which means you'll see it in the Contacts tab of your project in the Project Center. (See page 475 for more details on projects.)

- **Links.** Use this button to view or create links to messages, calendar events, tasks, and so on (see page 500).

Note: Control-click (or right-click) the toolbar and choose Customize Toolbar to access a few more buttons you'll find useful if you often print or delete contacts from this window.

This long form window also sports seven tabs along the top that you can use to enter and view more information about the currently open contact:

- **Summary tab.** Shows all of the information that you've entered about the person. If you haven't entered any contact information yet, this window is blank. The bottom of the Summary tab also displays when you last sent or received a message from the contact.

- **Name & E-mail tab.** Lets you enter complete naming information about your contact, including a title, nickname, and suffix, if any. It also lets you enter a slew of email and instant message addresses.

  This window also has *custom fields*—Custom 1 and Custom 2—where you can store other kinds of information about this contact's name and email addresses, such as what email address a person prefers to use while on vacation.

  If you use one of this person's email addresses most of the time, select it and click the Make Default button to the right of the Email field. From now on, when you type that person's email address in a new message, Entourage will suggest that address first as the primary address.

Note: Curiously, Entourage doesn't directly offer a place for middle names or initials. You'll just have to enter them as part of the First Name. (Just watch out if you use your Address Book to fuel a mail merge!)

- **Home tab.** Shows the person's home address, Web page, and telephone numbers, along with two more custom fields—Custom 3 and Custom 4—where you can enter your own kinds of data (perhaps the person's garage color or favorite lawn fertilizer).

  If you turn on the Default address checkbox in this window, this address becomes the *default* address for that contact, the one that Entourage goes to first when you don't have a choice of addresses—for example, when you choose Contact → Map Address.

- **Work tab.** Shows the contact's work address, employer's Web page, and work telephone numbers. It also includes the contact's company, job title, and department. Once again, you get a couple of custom fields—Custom 5 and Custom 6—to handle any extra information.

- **Personal tab.** Here, you can enter your contact's birthday. It's worth typing in a couple of friends' birthdays, if only to see the raw power of Microsoft software at work: Entourage automatically calculates the astrological sign and age for your pal, saving you the trouble.

  There's also room here for recording a spouse's name, the names of any children, your contact's anniversary, and any interests of note.

  You can probably guess the function of the "Drag and drop image here" box. Yes, it's a place to paste in, or drag in, a graphics file that depicts this person for handy visual reference. If you have a digital photo of one of your contacts, you can drag the graphics file right out of a Finder window or a Web browser and into the well in the Personal tab's right side. Entourage accepts most standard graphics formats—even Photoshop files. You can use any size picture, but keeping it small is wise from a disk-space and memory perspective. If you can't remember names but never forget a face, this feature's for you. From now on, this picture appears at the top of any message you receive from that person.

Tip: The tiny calendar icon to the right of the Birthday and Anniversary fields is a pop-up menu. It has commands to summon a pop-up calendar for easier date selection, inserting today's date, or adding a birthday or anniversary to your Entourage calendar so that you don't forget to buy a gift.

- **Other tab.** Lets you enter notes about your contact such as, "Hates email—prefers telephone," and provides still more custom fields—Custom 7 and Custom 8, plus Custom date 1 and Custom date 2—to provide places for any data that Microsoft may have missed.

- **Certificates.** Click here to choose the encryption certificate that you wish to use when sending an email to this contact. If you don't have one, you can get one from a digitally encrypted message sent by this contact, or by importing their encryption certificate. This security feature lets you send and receive emails that only you and the recipient can open and read. The certificate acts as the "key" to unlocking these digitally safety-sealed messages.

Tip: To change the name of a custom field, click its label and type in a new field name in the window that results. Click OK or press Enter—but note that you're changing this field's label for *all* "cards" in your Address Book.

When you finish entering all of this information about your contact, you'll have quite an impressive dossier. Click Save (or press ⌘-S) to commit it to your hard drive. When you first try to close without saving, Entourage asks you if you want to "Always save changes without asking." If you click No, you'll be seeing this message a lot in the future. If you click Yes, Entourage saves all contacts without bugging you first. (If you should ever want to get this and similar warning messages back again, click the "Reset Confirmation Dialogs" button in Entourage → Preferences → General Preferences → Notification panel.)

POWER USERS' CLINIC

Instant Contact

When you're processing email, you can add someone's email address to your Address Book without having to bother with all of the dialog-box shenanigans described in this section. Whenever you're looking at an open email message—or even a closed one in a list of messages—Control-click (or right-click) the sender's email address and choose Add Sender To Address Book from the shortcut menu. Entourage instantly creates a new Address Book entry

for that person, featuring the email address and the person's name (if they supplied it with the email message). Adding the other details is up to you.

To add information from a *directory service* search (see page 399), select the address in the search results window and click the Add to Address Book button.

Working with vCards

You've probably received plenty of email messages that come with strange little files attached whose names end in .vcf—but unless you pay very close attention to email conventions, you may not know what they are.

They're vCards, which were invented as a way of exchanging business-card information via email, sweeping away the drudgery of manual input forever. Although they sound like a good idea, vCards haven't really caught on; primarily because they're typically incomplete and poorly implemented (most people don't enter all of the pertinent information). Furthermore, they litter your hard drive with annoying attachments.

To pull the information out of a vCard and into the Entourage Address Book, drag the .vcf attachment onto your open Address Book. The contact information nestles itself nicely among your other contacts. If the .vcf file is on your hard drive (rather than attached to an email message), drag it into your Address Book window instead.

To send contact information as a vCard (which could be either your own electronic business card or any of your contacts'), drag a name from your open Address Book (or an entire row in a list view) anywhere onto a waiting email message. (Alternatively, highlight a name in your Address Book and then choose Contact → Forward as vCard.) Either way, your outgoing message now displays the .vcf file attached. If you want to create individual vCard files, just drag contacts from your Address Book to the Mac OS X desktop.

When using vCards, remember there's no way to choose what information Entourage includes in a vCard: nearly everything goes in, including birthdays, notes, complete home and work contact info, and even a photo if you've entered one. (A photo can make the vCard enormous, and in any case is only likely to get through to other Entourage fans.) So before you send a person's vCard to someone else, be certain it's appropriate to send along everything you've recorded about the contact.

Your correspondent will be able to incorporate that Address Book "card" into her own address book, and will appreciate your timesaving gesture—if she's even heard of vCards, that is.

Opening, editing, and deleting contacts

To edit a contact you've already entered into Entourage, double-click the appropriate row of the Address Book list, or click once and then choose File → Open Contact (⌘-O). Entourage presents the Summary window shown in Figure 10-29. Click the appropriate tab to edit the details on it, just as you did to begin with.

If someone is no longer part of your life—or you wish it were so—click the Delete button in the toolbar, choose File → Delete Contact (⌘-Delete), or just press the Delete key if the contact is selected in the list view. Entourage asks if you're sure you know what you're doing (there's no way to undo such a deletion).

Creating groups

As you might expect, collections of contacts fill *groups*. They make it easy to send an email message to everyone in a group in one fell swoop—just address it to the group instead of entering a bunch of single email addresses.

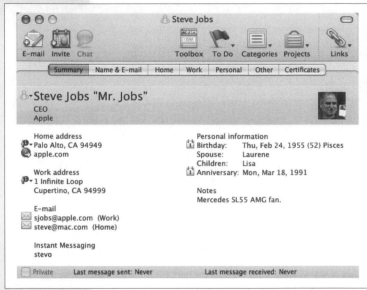

Figure 10-29:
Once you've gone through the trouble of entering complete information about your contact, you'll know more than you probably should. Click the Summary tab to gaze admiringly at the expansive data screen.

Here are three fascinating tidbits about groups:

- You can enter an email address into a group without having to enter it first as an independent Address Book card. This feature may come back to haunt you, however. You may one day start to address an email message by typing *McGi*, frustrated that Entourage refuses to complete *McGillicuddy*, even though you're certain you entered Bob McGillicuddy into the Address Book. What's probably happened is that you entered old Bob into a group without first creating an independent address book card for him. (People whose names exist only in a group aren't eligible for Entourage's AutoComplete feature.)

- Someone can be a member of more than one group.

- A group can nest in another group.

To create a new group when you're viewing the Address Book, choose Group from the New menu button—or choose File → New → Group.

Now the Group window appears. Once you've typed in a name (*MLM Team, Newsletter List,* or *Pass Jokes On,* for example), creating a group is easy. You can add people's names to the group by dragging them in from the Address Book window (Figure 10-30).

If you'd rather type than drag, you can type an email address from your Address Book (which Entourage automatically completes for you), or you can enter a completely new email address as part of the group. Simply click the Add button on the toolbar, which adds a blank space in the group, ready for you to type in an email address.

Tip: You can quickly create a group by ⌘-clicking or Shift-clicking any number of contacts in the Address Book, and then choosing File → New → Group to create a new group from those contacts.

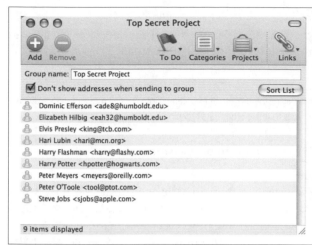

Figure 10-30:
By dragging addresses to a group window, you can quickly create a group. Turn on "Don't show addresses when sending to a group" to protect the privacy of members of that group. That way, the individual email addresses won't show on the message; however, your group's name and your own address will appear on both the From and To lines of the message. This configuration, unfortunately, makes the message vulnerable to certain spam filters, including, ironically, Entourage's own Junk Mail Filter.

Importing Contacts

If you haven't used Entourage before, there's a good chance that you keep your addresses on the Mac in another program, such as the Apple Address Book, Now Contact, Palm Desktop, or even Netscape Communicator. "No problem," says the ever-confident Microsoft. Entourage can import contact information from these programs and several more.

Furthermore, if your little black book resides in something like a FileMaker Pro database, an Excel spreadsheet, or some obscure off-brand address software, Entourage can grab contact information from a *tab-* or *comma-delimited text file.* Most databases, and many address book programs, can save their contents in these intermediary formats, precisely to make it easier for you to transfer your life from one such program to another. If you opened up one of these files in a word processor, you'd see that a press of the Tab key (Bob → Smith → 23 Main Street → Chicago, and so on) or a comma separates each piece of information, and that a press of the Return key separates each "card's" information.

The method you use to import your address book depends on what program you're importing it *from.*

Importing vCards

If your current contact program uses the vCard format, simply export your contacts as vCards and drag the vCard or cards into the open Entourage Address Book. If you're using the Apple Address Book, for example, you can drag a group of contacts to the desktop where they appear as a group vCard. Then drag that card into the Entourage Address Book to import the contacts. Or you can save time and a mouse click, while helping to keep your desktop tidy, by just dragging contacts directly from the Apple Address Book into the Entourage Address Book.

The Import Assistant

If you're importing contacts from an earlier version of Entourage or Qualcomm Eudora (5.0 or later), or from a text file, the Import Assistant helps automate the process.

Note: The File → Import command begins the process of importing contacts, mail messages, *and* calendar events, so you may see some references to those other data types on the Import Assistant's screens.

1. **Choose File → Import to summon the Import Assistant.**

   The Begin Import window gives you three choices for importing contacts. If you choose "Entourage information from an archive or earlier version," you'll then be asked which version—2001, X, 2004, or archive (.rge). Choose "Information from another application," and you can choose between Apple Mail (which doesn't have contacts) and Qualcomm Eudora (5.0 or later). If you choose "Contacts or messages from a text file," you'll be asked to locate a tab- or comma-delimited text file. This process may feel familiar; it's similar to the Entourage Setup Assistant you saw when setting up Entourage for the first time.

2. **Choose the program you'll be importing from by clicking one of the radio buttons and then clicking the right arrow to continue.**

   If you choose to import information from one of these programs, Entourage asks you what information you would like to grab—such as contacts or calendar events—and then proceeds to inhale that information.

   If, on the other hand, you choose to import contacts from a text file, Entourage asks you for the location of that text file. Then it opens the Import Contacts window (see Figure 10-31).

3. **Align the fields in the list so that they match up with the corresponding tidbits of address info by dragging them up or down, using the ribbed rectangular handle that appears on each line.**

   If there are *unmapped* fields—fields from your older address book software that Entourage isn't sure *what* to do with—you can drag them from the "Unmapped fields" section into the proper place on the left side of the window.

   Once you've lined up all the fields correctly, click Import (or press Enter) to bring your social circle into its new software home.

Exporting Contacts and Archives

Entourage lets you export contacts in either the time-honored tab-delimited text file or to an Entourage archive, which you can subsequently save, store, and import into another copy of Entourage (like the one on your PowerBook). What makes the Entourage archives so cool is that they can encompass so much more than tab files—not just contacts, but also emails, tasks, notes, and even calendar events.

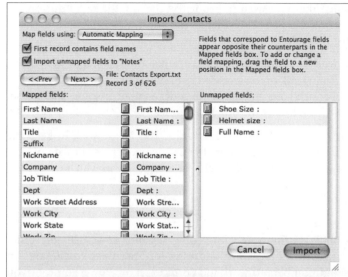

Figure 10-31:
In this window, Entourage asks you to match up the fields from the text file with the Entourage Address Book fields. Here's where you get the chance to match up first names in the file with the First Name field in Entourage, last names with the Last Name field in Entourage, and so on.

WORKAROUND WORKSHOP

Cross-platform Contact Imports

If you're moving an address book from a Windows-based program to Entourage, you won't encounter much trouble. Just export the contact list either as vCards or as a tab-delimited text file, which you can transfer to the Mac via network, email attachment, or disk. Then, in Entourage, choose File → Import and proceed exactly as described on these pages.

To move contacts in the opposite direction—from Entourage to a PC—export your contacts as a tab-delimited file, and then hand them off to your PC. Don't forget to append the required Windows suffix .txt to the end of your file's name. (When naming the file, use standard letters and numbers; Windows doesn't accept such wacky characters

as the vertical bar or the asterisk.) Or, if your Windows program handles vCards, drag contacts out of Entourage to the desktop where they'll become vCards—then transfer these to the PC.

Finally, note that the invisible character that ends each line in a text file is different in Mac OS X (and other Unix operating systems), and Windows. If a Windows program doesn't understand your text file, you may have better luck if you send it to the Windows machine via email (which should convert the line endings), or switch the file to Windows line endings using a program like the free Text-Wrangler (*www.barebones.com*) or the text-processing utilities you can find at *www.versiontracker.com*.

If you want to export your contacts to a tab-delimited file—for example, to use in Excel—choose File → Export Contacts and then turn on "Export contacts to a list (tab-delimited text)." As you proceed through the assistant, choose a folder location for the file, and then click Save.

If you wish to create an Entourage archive, choose File → Export Contacts and turn on "Export Items to an Entourage archive." Then, under the archive header, choose either contacts or any other Entourage items (those in a specific project, in a category, or all items) that you wish to export by clicking the radio buttons. If you want to choose items in a project or category, a pop-up menu lets you choose *which* project or category.

You can also choose what Entourage items (tasks, email messages, and so on) you wish to archive by turning off or on the checkboxes next to the item type. For example, you may only want your contact list in order to mail greeting cards. If so, remove the checkmark from beside the other categories.

After you make your archiving decisions, Entourage asks if you wish to keep the archived items in Entourage or delete them after archiving. Err on the side of caution and keep a backup in Entourage. Next, choose a directory in which to save the items, and click Save.

Using Contacts

Once your Address Book is brimming with people, it's time to actually *do* something with all that data. Besides providing addresses for Entourage email, you can put all those names and numbers to work in Word, Excel, or PowerPoint, or you may assign them to projects, where they will show up along with your project in the Project Center. Here are a few of the ways you can reap the benefits of your Address Book.

Sending email to someone

Chapter 11 covers the various ways you can address a piece of outgoing email from within the email portion of Entourage. But you can also summon a preaddressed piece of outgoing email from within the Address Book itself. For example:

- Click a name in the Address Book and choose Contact → New Message To.

- Control-click someone's name and then choose New Message To from the shortcut menu that pops up.

Either way, Entourage whips open a new email message addressed to that lucky individual.

Flagging a contact

It's useful to flag someone's name in a number of different situations. For example, flagged contacts bubble up to the top of a list when you sort it accordingly (by clicking the Flag column in the Address Book list), which makes flags an excellent way to denote important contacts. And when you print your contacts, you can print just the flagged ones.

In Entourage 2008, flagged contacts become To Do items, complete with due dates and reminders if you so desire. So you can just flag a contact, putting that name in your To Do list to remind you, for example, to prepare for your niece's visit. See page 462 for all the To Do details.

To turn that little gray flag to the left of a contact red, just click it. To flag multiple contacts, select them and click the To Do button. Click the red flag to turn it into a green check mark, checking it off of your To Do list. Choose Clear To Do Flag from the To Do button's pop-up menu to return the flag to its shadowy gray, un-tampered-with appearance.

Using contacts in Word

Suppose you're writing a letter to someone listed in your Address Book. As you start to type the person's name in Word, a floating yellow AutoComplete tip balloon appears, as shown in Figure 10-32, showing the contact's full name. If Word has correctly guessed what you're trying to do, press the Return key while the AutoComplete tip balloon is showing. Word obligingly completes the person's name for you.

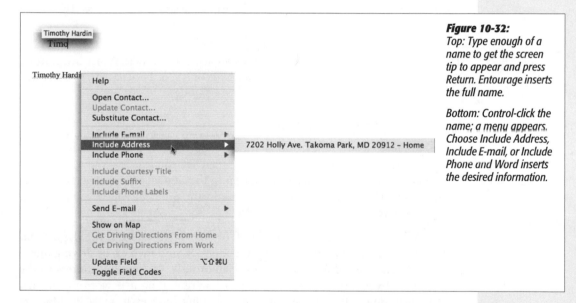

Figure 10-32:
Top: Type enough of a name to get the screen tip to appear and press Return. Entourage inserts the full name.

Bottom: Control-click the name; a menu appears. Choose Include Address, Include E-mail, or Include Phone and Word inserts the desired information.

If you *don't* intend to type a name—that is, if you've typed *will,* but Word's AutoComplete tip balloon proposes William Shakespeare (a name it found in your Address Book), just continue typing without pressing Return. The box goes away. (This behavior springs from Word's AutoText feature, described on page 78.)

As Figure 10-32 points out, you can Control-click an inserted person's name if you'd like to add her phone number, mailing address, and so on. The resulting shortcut menu gives you several choices:

- **Open Contact.** Opens the contact in its own window, where you can get more information or even edit the contact info, without having to launch Entourage.

- **Update Contact.** You'd use this command when editing a Word document you wrote some time ago. The command consults the Entourage Address Book and updates the name, number, or address (if it's been changed in Entourage since you first created the Word document).

- **Substitute Contact.** Brings up your contact list, so that you can substitute a different person's information. You might use this command when, for example, sending an existing letter out to a different person.

- **Include E-mail, Include Address, Include Phone.** Pastes the contact's email address, postal address, or phone number into the document. These commands are only available if, in fact, you've specified that information in Entourage. If the contact has several emails—perhaps one for work, one for home— you get to choose which to paste.

Note: Office programs only draw contact information from the currently active Entourage *identity* (more on identities in Chapter 11).

This auto-insert feature isn't the only example of Entourage/Word integration. You also encounter it when doing a Mail Merge in a Word document, as described on page 262.

Five Very Impressive Buttons

When you're viewing the expanded address book screen for somebody in your Address Book, Entourage has five buttons that let you harness the data you've input in clever ways. These five icons appear in the contact's Summary tab, among other places. Here's a look at what they do, in the order in which you see them shown in Figure 10-33:

- The **Address Actions** icon sits to the left of every street address. It hides a menu that, when clicked, offers to consult the Internet for a map of, or driving directions to, the selected address (or, less glamorously, to copy the address to the Clipboard, ready for pasting into a letter you're writing in a word processor). Not surprisingly, Entourage only uses mapping services from MSN Maps & Directions, a Microsoft Web site.

- The globe-like **Open Web Page** icon appears next to any URLs (Web addresses) you've entered onto somebody's card. When you click this button, your Web browser opens the associated Web page.

- When you want to dial a contact's telephone number, click the small **Magnify Phone Number** icon to the left of it. Doing so doesn't *dial* the phone for you. It does, however, magnify that telephone number so that it's big enough to see from several feet away (Figure 10-33, top).

- The **Send Mail** icon sits next to the contact's email address. When you click it, Entourage creates a new email message addressed to that contact.

- The **Add to Calendar** icon appears to the left of the Birthday and Anniversary fields. Clicking it adds a recurring event to your Entourage calendar—handy insurance against missing important birthdays or anniversaries.

Printing the Address Book

Thanks to some fine attention to detail by the Entourage programmers, you can print the Address Book in a variety of formats, specifying just the details you want to have on paper.

Start by clicking the Address Book icon at the upper left of the Entourage main window. Then choose File → Print to bring up the Print window (Figure 10-34). In addition to a print preview, it has four other small sections:

- **Print.** This pop-up menu lets you select what to print: All Contacts, Flagged Contacts, or Selected Contacts (that is, names you've highlighted by clicking, Shift-clicking, or ⌘-clicking, as described on page 39).

- **Style.** This pop-up menu lets you choose whether you want to print a full address book (with lots of contact information per page) or a simple phone number list.

- **Layout.** The Layout button opens the Print Layout window, where you can specify how contacts are sorted, whether first names or last names are printed first, whether cut lines and punch holes are printed, and what other bits of contact information are printed (such as company name and personal information).

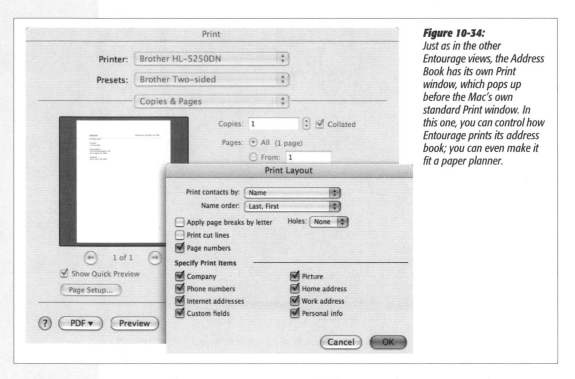

Figure 10-34:
Just as in the other Entourage views, the Address Book has its own Print window, which pops up before the Mac's own standard Print window. In this one, you can control how Entourage prints its address book; you can even make it fit a paper planner.

- **Form.** If you use a Day-Timer or similar paper planner, you can choose a template from this pop-up menu, corresponding to the most popular precut paper types available at office-supply stores. You can also use the Add, Edit, and Delete buttons to create and delete your own paper designs.

Newsgroups Explained

Newsgroups (also known as Usenet) began back in the Internet Dark Ages as a way for people to have discussions via a bulletin-board-like system, where a message gets posted for all to see, and anyone can reply to that posted message. These public discussions are divided into categories called newsgroups, which cover the gamut from naval aviation to navel contemplation.

These days, newsgroups have a certain reputation as a place to exchange photos of scantily clad pets, cartoon characters, and even humans, not to mention pirated software, music, and video files that carry doubtful copyright pedigrees or even viruses.

Even so, there are tens of thousands of interesting, informative discussions going on, and newsgroups are great places to get help with troubleshooting, exchange recipes, or just see what's on the minds of your fellow Internet jockeys.

Although using newsgroups is like using email in Entourage, it's important to remember that anything you see or post in a newsgroup is public, and will probably remain so for years to come. (Sites like Google maintain searchable newsgroup archives going back to the mid-1980s, complete with email addresses!) Think before you post, especially if you have aspirations to run for Congress someday.

Newsgroups

Newsgroups don't necessarily contain news; in fact, they're Internet bulletin boards collectively referred to as *Usenet* (which stands for *user network*). Usenet started way back in 1980—about 10 years before the World Wide Web appeared—and has been growing ever since. There are well over 100,000 newsgroups on every conceivable topic: pop culture, computers, politics, and every other special (and *very* special) interest. More than 100 of them are just about the Macintosh. Fortunately, in addition to being an email and calendar program, Entourage is also a *newsreader*. You can use Entourage to read and reply to newsgroup messages almost exactly as though they were email messages.

In fact, Entourage lets you use multiple *news servers* (bulletin-board distribution computers), subscribe to individual newsgroups, filter messages in your newsgroups using Rules, and post and read messages (complete with attachments, if needed). See Figure 10-35.

Tip: Be wary of arachnids when posting to newsgroups. Email retrieval robots called *spiders* comb the Usenet for email addresses and gather them up by the millions. The spider's owner then slaps the addresses on a CD and sells them to spammers. Does that mean you shouldn't use newsgroups? No, but it does mean you should exercise caution when posting. One method to avoid unwanted spam is to create a Web-based Hotmail or Yahoo email account and use it only for newsgroups. Spiders can still retrieve this address, but at least you aren't handing them your main email address. Additionally, both Hotmail and Yahoo have sophisticated spam filters, capable of filtering most of the junk the spammers send.

Figure 10-35:

If you've been using Entourage for email, the newsgroup portion should look familiar.

Top: Click the News server, which you'll find listed below all your mail folders. All of newsgroups on the server appear in a massive list to the right. Use the quick filter at the top of the pane to help locate your topic.

Bottom: Double-click the list name to open a new window listing the messages in the selected newsgroup, and a Preview pane showing the text of the highlighted message.

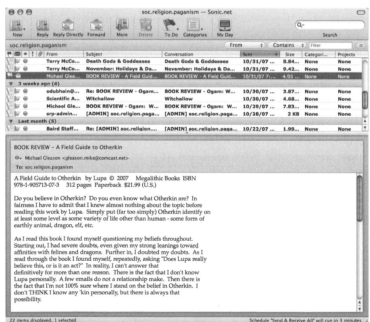

Setting Up an Account

Setting up a new news account is similar to setting up a new email account; the adventure begins by contacting your Internet service provider and finding out its *news server address.* Depending on how your ISP runs its news service, you may also need your user name and password.

Next, choose Tools → Accounts. Choose News from the New pop-up button in the resulting Accounts window. You can either enter news server information manually, or click the Setup Assistant button to have the Account Setup Assistant step you through the process of creating a news account like this:

1. **With the Account Setup Assistant open, select the email account you want to use and enter your organization.**

   Entourage needs an email address because every newsgroup posting has an email address associated with it.

2. **Click the right arrow. Enter your news server address, and indicate whether that server requires you to log on with name and password.**

   In this step, you'll need to enter the address of your news server. Sometimes you get newsgroup access (and the necessary settings) from your ISP. If your ISP doesn't provide newsgroup access, you'll have to subscribe to a news service. They run about $10 a month, and they're generally more reliable than news servers run by ISPs. Check out *www.easynews.com, www.supernews.com,* or *www.newsguy.com* for such services.

   If you're directed to do so by your ISP, turn on "My new server requires me to log on" and enter your user name and password.

3. **Click the right arrow. Enter your Account ID and password.**

   If you told Entourage that you needed to log into your news server, you'll have to provide the details in this step. The password is optional—if you want Entourage to save it, turn on "Save password in my Mac OS keychain." If you don't enter it here, you'll have to type it every time you connect to your news server.

4. **Click the right arrow. Give your account a name.**

   You can give it any name you want, such as *Earthlink Newsgroups.*

5. **Click Finish.**

   An icon for your new account shows up in the folder list.

Note: If you prefer to enter all of the news server particulars in one step, rather than using the Account Setup Assistant, you can skip the assistant entirely, or bail out of it at any time by clicking the "Configure Account Manually" button in the lower part of the assistant window.

Download the List of Newsgroups

When you first click a news server icon, Entourage asks you if you want to download a list of newsgroups. Click Receive (see Figure 10-36, top).

Entourage goes to work downloading the list, which can be quite long—tens of thousands of entries, in most cases—and takes several minutes if you connect to the Internet with a dial-up modem. Once that's done, though, you don't have to do it again. You should occasionally update the list, however, by selecting the server's icon in the folder list and clicking the Refresh button (or choosing View → Get New Newsgroups). New newsgroups appear on a more-or-less constant basis, and unused newsgroups sometimes even disappear.

The number (and nature) of newsgroups available on a particular server is up to its operators. For example, Entourage comes preconfigured to connect to the Microsoft News Server. Instead of carrying tens of thousands of newsgroups on every conceivable topic, the Microsoft News Server carries about 2,300 newsgroups, all related—surprise!—to Microsoft products. (Incidentally, these aren't bad places to learn about Office 2008 programs: check out the newsgroup called *microsoft.public.mac.office.entourage.*)

Even the big ISPs rarely carry *every* available Usenet group. Furthermore, they may not keep individual newsgroup postings around for very long, since the storage required to do so is enormous, and the number of people who actually want to read many of these newsgroups can be very small. (Honestly, do you think you'll be a regular contributor to *alt.alien.vampire.flonk.flonk.flonk?*)

Furthermore, many ISPs refuse to host newsgroups that carry stolen software, music, video, and other materials. In fact, your ISP may simply deny access to the *alt.* hierarchy, which is where the most free-wheeling (and most dubious) activities take place. That's not to say *alt.** newsgroups are fundamentally bad, but if there's one you want to read (*say, alt.guitar.beginner*), you might have to ask your ISP to specifically turn it on.

Figure 10-36:
Top: After you create a newsgroup account, Entourage offers to fetch the list of every newsgroup on the server.

Bottom: Enter the text that you want to look for in the newsgroup's Filter (such as mac). If you turn up an appealing topic in the gigantic list beneath, select the group and click the Subscribe button in the Entourage toolbar, to subscribe to it so that Entourage will download the latest messages on that topic every time you connect.

Warning: Like certain Web sites, plenty of newsgroups aren't suitable for children. Similarly, because newsgroups are public, spammers tend to litter newsgroups with their cheesy schemes and material many would find offensive. No one regulates newsgroups, and no one has complete control over what can and can't be posted there.

Finding Newsgroups and Messages

If you're looking for a particular topic—guitars, for example—you can view a list of those discussions by typing a phrase into the "Display newsgroups containing" field at the top of the window. Entourage hides any newsgroups that don't match that text (see Figure 10-36, bottom).

Try different criteria—typing in *mac* will show you many Macintosh-related newsgroups, but will also turn up newsgroups devoted to Fleetwood Mac, macho trucks, and GNU emacs. Typing *garden* shows a number of newsgroups related to gardening, but may also show newsgroups devoted to the band Soundgarden.

Reading Messages

Once Entourage has downloaded a list of available newsgroups, it's up to you to sift through them and select the discussions you want to keep up with.

Fortunately, Entourage makes it easy to follow the raging Internet discussions with a feature called *subscriptions*. To subscribe to a newsgroup, select its name in the list, and then click the Subscribe button in the toolbar. An icon for that newsgroup now appears under the server's name in the folder list, where it acts like a nested folder.

The next time you connect to the Internet, Entourage downloads all of the messages in the discussions to which you've subscribed. (There may be just a few messages, or several hundred. They may go back only a few days or a couple of weeks, depending on how much "traffic" there is in each discussion and how long your news server keeps messages available.)

Tip: Entourage keeps copies of newsgroup messages in a Newsgroup Cache file located in your Office 2008 Identities folder. Over time, you'll realize that most newsgroup messages are ephemeral things you don't necessarily want taking up space on your hard drive. To clean out Entourage's local cache of newsgroup messages, Control-click the name of your news server in your Folder list and choose "Clear Cache" from the shortcut menu. Entourage purges its local cache of newsgroup messages.

To read the actual messages in a newsgroup, double-click its name in the newsgroup list—which opens its list of messages in a new window. It takes just a few seconds as Entourage downloads a list of articles in that newsgroup.

You read messages in a newsgroup exactly as you read email messages. Since you're probably reading the newsgroup to expand your knowledge of a certain topic, you may want to choose View → Arrange By → Show in Groups and choose Subject from the same submenu to gather the messages into groups according to their subject lines. (As discussed in the box on page 375, Entourage 2008's groups provide a multitude of ways to organize your messages.)

As with normal email messages, newsgroup messages that come with file attachments appear in an Attachments section inside the message; you can save those attachments just as you would email attachments. (Exercise extreme caution with any attachment downloaded from a newsgroup.) Some particularly large attachments in newsgroups get automatically divided into multiple segments. If you're having trouble saving a multipart attachment to your hard drive, make sure that you've selected the message containing the *first* part. Even then, you may find that joining multipart newsgroup messages isn't one of Entourage's strongest features.

Tip: To help sift through the spam that clogs newsgroups, you can set up *news rules* by choosing Tools → Rules, clicking the News tab, and then clicking the New button. Exactly as with the message rules described on "Using Message Rules you can set up rules that screen out messages from certain people, messages with certain phrases in their subject line, and so on.

Composing, Forwarding, and Replying to Messages

Working with newsgroup messages is very similar to working with email messages. You reply to them, forward them, or compose them exactly as described earlier in this chapter (see Figure 10-37). As with email, you can use either plain text or HTML formatting, attach files, and clean up text that may have been wrapped badly somewhere along the way.

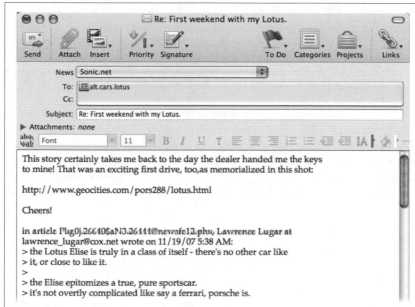

Figure 10-37:
A full-blown message ready for posting features a newsgroup address, a subject line, and a message text. This one also links to an image readers can view in a Web browser if they're interested. The message will be uploaded to the news server when you click the Send button.

Usenet Netiquette

Although newsgroups are anarchic places, they also have traditions and general norms. Many of the points in "Email Netiquette" (see page 410) apply to composing messages for Usenet, but newsgroups have a few considerations of their own:

- **Lurk before you post.** When you read a newsgroup but don't post messages to it, you're considered a "lurker." There's no shame in lurking. In fact, you *should* lurk in a newsgroup for at least a few days, to get a sense of what topics are commonly discussed and who the most active participants are. Many newsgroups have cultures of their own—newcomers are always welcome, but it's best to avoid stepping on anyone's toes, so learn the dance.

- **Read the FAQ and search the archive.** Many newsgroups have a FAQ ("frequently asked questions") document available on a Web site or posted periodically to the newsgroup. These documents contain the questions most often asked by newcomers to the group—and, even better, answers to those questions! Before posting a question you suspect may have come up before, check to see if the newsgroup has a FAQ, or search a Usenet news archive (like *http://groups.google.com*) to see if the topic's been covered recently.

• **Newsgroups are not billboards.** Don't post advertising to newsgroups. If you're an established member of a newsgroup, a brief announcement of something relevant to the group is fine—for instance, if you're a regular in a guitar-oriented newsgroup, you might mention that your little brother just released his first finger-style guitar CD. Similarly, a pointer in your signature to your company or your products is fine. But anything above that scale is likely to incite derisive comments or even result in abuse reports to your ISP.

• **Avoid extensive cross-posting.** Posting a message to more than one newsgroup is called *cross-posting*. It's OK to post to a handful of newsgroups if you genuinely aren't sure where your question or message is most appropriate. But widely cross-posting a message isn't much different than spamming, and so your message will be treated much like spam: derided, ignored, or even reported to your ISP.

• **Avoid HTML formatting.** Due to Usenet's text-based nature, millions of people access newsgroups using old computers, old software, and slow connections. HTML-formatted newsgroup messages are frowned upon because they take longer to download and don't look good in a wide variety of newsreaders. If the major participants in a particular group all use HTML and no one objects when they do it, then posting HTML-formatted messages is probably fine. Otherwise, always use plain text.

• **Avoid "me-too" messages.** As a general rule, don't respond to messages if you're only going to agree with or restate what has just been said. (If you absolutely *must* say "I second that!" at least refrain from quoting the entire previous message in your response.)

• **Neither a troll nor a flamer be.** Tossing out provocative or insulting statements just to stir up other newsgroup participants is called *trolling,* and it's frowned upon. On the other hand, don't respond to abusive or deliberately provocative messages. You may incite a *flame war,* in which a newsgroup degenerates into increasingly vitriolic exchanges and insults. When a flame war erupts, reasonable people tend to abandon the newsgroup, sometimes never to return. If a particular person in a newsgroup always pushes your buttons, create a rule (see page 396) so you never see newsgroup messages from that person.

Tip: Although Entourage is an OK newsreader, some of its newsgroup features are limited and awkward. If you find yourself participating in Usenet newsgroups regularly, consider a separate newsreader program that offers more comprehensive features—full threading, message scoring, FAQ retrieval, and more. A good newsreader can vastly improve your Usenet experience.

You can find good lists of Mac newsreaders at *www.newsgroups.com* and *www.macorchard.com/usenet/*. In particular, check out Thoth or one of the numerous descendents of NewsWatcher.

Mail and News Preferences

Entourage keeps track of two sets of preference settings: one covering how email and newsgroups are handled, and one handling Entourage's general behavior. The following section details the email and newsgroup options.

You can view the mail and news preferences by choosing Entourage → Preferences and looking under Mail & News Preferences in the lower part of the preferences list. The Mail & News Preferences section, shown in Figure 10-38, is divided into four panels: Read, Compose, Reply & Forward, and View.

Figure 10-38:
In the Compose section of Entourage's Mail & News Preferences you'll find the options for creating and sending messages. You might find it helpful to turn on "Append file name extensions" so that your attachments always bear their telltale file type for the aid of your PC-using correspondents.

Read panel

The controls under this section govern what happens when you read your email, and they're divided into three parts: Messages, Languages, and IMAP. As you'll soon discover, some of them are intended exclusively for the technically minded.

- **Messages** governs what happens to open messages that you delete or file (such as whether Entourage closes the message window or opens the next message in line). You can also specify how many seconds have to elapse, with a message open in front of you, before Entourage considers it as having been read, and therefore no longer displays its name in boldface type. For example, if you've set the "Mark message as read after displaying for _ seconds" option to 3, Entourage waits three seconds before considering an open message as having been read. This feature can be useful if you like to skim through your messages, glancing for just a few seconds at each, without changing their unread status.

- **Languages** lets you select a *character set* (including non-Roman alphabet sets like Cyrillic, Greek, or Korean) for messages that arrive without a specified character set. Set this option to the character set that you read most often—usually your primary language group.

- **IMAP.** If this box is checked, deleted IMAP messages don't show up in your message lists. If this box *isn't* checked, IMAP messages marked for deletion will still be visible in their respective folders, with a red X displayed next to the message and a red strike-through line through the message.

Compose panel

This set of preferences controls what happens when you're writing messages. It's divided into three parts: General, Attachments, and Recent Addresses.

- The **General** checkboxes govern whether Entourage checks the names of your addressees against your default directory service (which is generally only useful if your company organization runs its own; see page 399) and whether or not you like to keep copies of sent messages in the Sent Items folder.

  You can also govern whether the HTML Formatting toolbar is visible when you're composing mail, and you can specify your preferred format for mail and news messages—plain text or HTML.

- **Attachments** lets you set up how Entourage processes file attachments—how you want such files to be compressed and encoded, and whether or not you want Windows file name suffixes added automatically.

  This dialog box also controls whether or not Entourage sends file attachments to addressees in the Cc and Bcc fields, on the assumption that you may sometimes want to send the *file* only to the primary recipients, but send the *message* to a long list of other people (whose addresses are in the Cc or Bcc fields)—the most common way of doing business.

- **Recent Addresses** controls whether Entourage offers to autocomplete the last 200 email addresses you've sent or received (ones that *aren't* in your Address Book) when you're addressing messages. Some people find this feature annoying and turn it off, but others find it useful to be able to quickly re-enter email addresses without first having to create an address book entry for them.

Reply & Forward panel

These controls govern replies and forwarded messages:

- **Include entire message in reply.** When you reply, this option adds the text of the original message, for your recipient's reference. Unless the original message is short, you'll want to edit down the original as you compose your reply.

- **Use quoting characters when forwarding.** This option adds quoting characters to each forwarded message's text. The > symbols are an Internet convention used to make it clear that *you* didn't write the bracketed text. If you turn off this box, Entourage will instead insert tags above and below the message to indicate where quoted text starts and stops.

- **Reply to messages in the format in which they were sent.** If this box is turned on, Entourage chooses the message format (HTML or plain text) according to the formatting of the *original* message. Uncheck this box to use the format you've specified on the Compose tab of the Mail & News Preferences dialog box.

- **Reply using the default account.** If this box is turned on and you have more than one email account, Entourage always uses your *default* (primary) account to send replies—even if the original message was sent to a different account.

- **Mail Attribution.** If you like, Entourage can tack on some stock text that introduces a message you're answering. As you can see in the edit box, Entourage can even incorporate the sender's name and/or email address, or the date the original message was sent, into this boilerplate text. As with signatures, some people get clever with these lines, coming up with introductory lines like this: "On [DATE], [NAME] is thought to have uttered:"

- **Place insertion point before quoted text.** This little checkbox puts the cursor at the *top* of the email message when you create a reply or a forwarded message. Turn this option *on* if you like your reply to appear *above* the original message text, and *off* if you like to type your reply *below* the quoted text.

Tip: On the Internet, the most accepted practice is to put replies *below* any quoted material. In the business world, however, an email culture has arisen in which replies go *above* any quoted material—thanks to the predominance of Microsoft Outlook, which comes set to do it that way.

- **News Attribution.** Like the Mail Attribution option, the News Attribution option automatically fills in some basic information when you reply to a newsgroup message. This attribution can display the message's author, the date, the time, and the article ID of the message to which you're replying.

View panel

These controls manage how Entourage displays messages, subscriptions, and quotes:

- **Show unread messages as bold.** This checkbox is responsible for displaying the names of unread messages in bold type in the message list.

- **Show messages using these colors.** Lets you choose colors (instead of—or in addition to—bold text) to indicate which messages have been read. After turning on this box, click the color swatch next to the words *Unread* and *Read* to choose from a menu of 16 different colors. (Or choose the 17th option, Other, which opens the Mac OS X color picker for a seemingly infinite variety of color choices.)

- **Show attached pictures and movies in messages.** Entourage generally displays picture or movie attachments right in the message window, saving you the trouble of opening them. This option can, however, make such messages take longer to appear on the screen.

- **Show contact picture in message header.** If you've added a picture to a person's contact in your Address Book, choose this option to display their smiling face (or whatever picture you've chosen to represent them) at the top of each of their messages.

- **Show newsgroups and IMAP folders using these colors.** When turned on, this option lets you color-code the names of newsgroups and IMAP mail folders to which you've subscribed or haven't subscribed to.

- **Color Quoting.** In this multihued box, you can change the color given to various levels of text quoting—levels one through four, at least.

  For example, suppose you write to your boss: "How does it look?" She writes back to you, "How does WHAT look?"—and you see your own original query bracketed (>) and in blue type. When you reply to her, your original question now appears with *double* brackets (>>) and in the second-level color you choose here. This color-coding can make it simpler to follow a protracted discussion taking place via email or a newsgroup.

  Anything higher than level-four quoted text takes on the same color as level-four quoting. To change a color, click one of the text strings in the box and select a new color from the menu that pops up.

Exchange Server

Microsoft's Exchange Server is like a virtual file box that people on all the computers in a corporation can access. Among a vast number of other talents, it lets everyone store (and share) email messages, contacts, calendar items, tasks, and notes. People using Outlook in Windows world have been using Exchange Server for years (whether they know it or not), but Entourage mavens couldn't "talk" to their Windows brethren on a common Exchange Server as full Exchange Server clients until Entourage X 10.1.4 came along.

You use the Account Setup Assistant to hook up with your company's Exchange Server. If everything goes as smoothly as Microsoft envisioned, you need only type in your email address, and Entourage does the rest. (If not, it's time to call in the system administrator.) After setup, you'll be able to:

- Send and receive Exchange-based email messages.

- Address messages by using the Global Address List, a centralized address book housed on the common server.

- Share your Inbox, contacts and calendar information.

- See whether other folks using the server are on "free" or "busy" status.

- View and share information through public folders— a feature of Exchange Server that provides an effective way to collect, organize, and share information with others in an organization.

- Use the Out of Office Assistant to reply to messages automatically when you're away.

Unfortunately, it's not always so easy, and covering the Microsoft Exchange Server in detail is beyond the scope of this book. You can, however, find more details in the Microsoft Office 2008 for Mac Resource Kit at www. microsoft.com/mac/.

Calendar, Tasks, and the Project Center

Computers are supposed to be ultra-efficient timesaving devices—and perhaps they are—yet everyone's life is just as wonderfully full and busy as ever. There are reports to be written, projects to coordinate, shopping to be done, vacations to plan, and kids to take to soccer. Although Entourage can't drive your kids to practice, it can remind you when to take them, and it can help you take control of the rest of your day. Entourage is a willing and able partner in keeping track of the million things you need to do and the information you need to get them done.

Entourage means email, contacts, and calendar to most people. And the objective- and goal-oriented can't live without its Tasks feature. But many have yet to catch on to the Project Center, a virtual Entourage command center that first appeared in Office 2004. It gives you one-stop access to all the email messages, appointments, to-do items, Word documents, Excel spreadsheets, and other files connected to a certain project. A project can be a major work-related goal, but it can also represent your volunteer work, New Year's Eve party, kids' soccer camp, financial planning—actually any life pursuit. All you have to do is create a project and tell Entourage which items to "file" under it. From then on, everything relating to that project is at your mousetip.

This chapter shows you how to use all of Entourage's organizational goodies, starting with the Calendar and Tasks features, then pulling them all together under the umbrella of the Project Center, and finishing up with a few vital components addressing the entire ball of Entourage wax: synchronizing, searching, linking, and categorizing.

The Calendar

You can open the Entourage calendar either by clicking the Calendar view button in the upper left of the Entourage main window, choosing View → Go To → Calendar, or pressing ⌘-3. No matter how you open it, your calendar shows up with all scheduled events listed on the appropriate days at the appropriate times (see Figure 11-1). In fact, it can display anything from a single day to six weeks on a single screen.

If you have the folder list showing (Calendar → Show Folder List) you get a second miniature overview calendar in the lower-left corner. (Click the tiny arrow button in the lower-left corner if you don't see this mini-calendar. Drag the divider bar above the overview calendar to adjust the number of months it shows.)

Figure 11-1:
Entourage's Calendar view provides an overview of adjacent months and a big view of the current month. You can also choose to display the current week, work week, or day. Holidays and other special days (which you have to import from a separate file; see the box on page 459) appear in the large detail calendar. At the top of the window, Entourage has a calendar-specific toolbar for changing the view, opening your To Do list, categorizing appointments, and so on.

Working with Views

Entourage has three kinds of views: a *month view*, which looks like every wall calendar you've ever seen (see Figure 11-1), a *column view*, which displays up to seven days' worth of events as vertical time lines, and a *list view*, which displays only your scheduled events or appointments (see Figure 11-2).

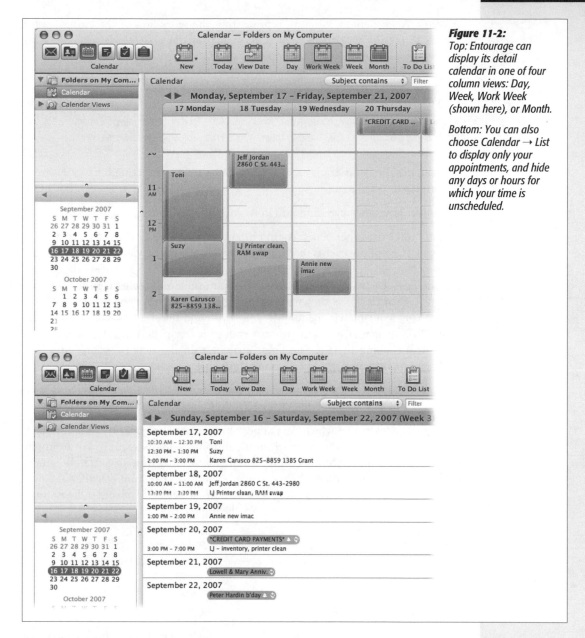

Figure 11-2:
Top: Entourage can display its detail calendar in one of four column views: Day, Week, Work Week (shown here), or Month.

Bottom: You can also choose Calendar → List to display only your appointments, and hide any days or hours for which your time is unscheduled.

Displaying days, weeks, and months

To control what the main calendar window shows, use the following buttons on the Entourage toolbar or commands on the Calendar menu:

- **Day** shows the appointments for a single day in the main calendar area, broken down by time slot.

- **Work Week** depicts columns, representing the workdays of the current week according to your settings in the Entourage preferences—five days per week for most people, two or seven for others.

Tip: If you enjoy an eccentric work schedule, you can redefine which days constitute your work "week" by choosing Entourage → Preferences → General Preferences → Calendar, and changing the days-of-the-week checkboxes. When you choose "Work Week" using the toolbar or the Calendar menu, Entourage happily displays columns for only Tuesday, Thursday, and Friday (or whichever days you work).

- **Week** fills the main display area with seven columns, reflecting the current week (Sunday through Saturday).

- **Month** shows the current month in its entirety.

- **List,** unlike the other views, doesn't offer a vertical grid of time slots. Instead, it creates a list of the events that you were looking at in the view you just switched from. For example, if you were perusing Day view, then List view shows that same day's events—in List format. These are the events scheduled for the current day (or days), as shown at top in Figure 11-2. Unlike the other views, List view isn't available via the toolbar unless you add that button yourself (see Figure 20-3 on page 764), but you can choose it from the Calendar menu or by Control-clicking (or right-clicking) anywhere in the detail calendar area and choosing List from the resulting shortcut menu.

- **View Date** lets you choose a specific date to examine. The chosen date is displayed onscreen in Day view, and highlighted in Work Week, Week, or Month view.

You can also determine which days appear in the detail calendar by selecting them in the mini calendar at the lower left of the Entourage main window. For example, to make the calendar show nothing but an important three-day stretch, simply drag the cursor across those three calendar squares in the mini calendar at lower left (Figure 11-3). You can even drag across up to six weeks to maximize the number of days you can see in month view and get the big picture.

Tip: Entourage provides a quick way to access the current day's date: Choose Calendar → "Go to Today", or press ⌘-T. If you're in Month, Week, or Work Week view, the command highlights today's date.

Recording Events

Most of Entourage's calendar is intuitive. After all we've been using calendars of one kind or another successfully for centuries.

In many ways, Entourage's calendar isn't very different from those analog versions we leave hanging on our walls for months past their natural life span. But Entourage has several advantages over paper calendars. For example:

- Entourage can automate the process of entering repeating events, such as weekly staff meetings, birthdays, anniversaries, or Pilates classes.

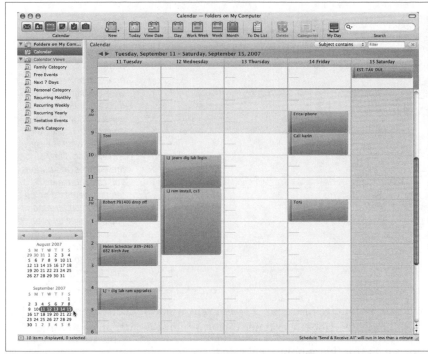

Figure 11-3:
When you drag the cursor across a set of dates in the mini calendar, the main calendar shows nothing but those days. You can select as many as six weeks worth using this method. Just drag from the first date to the last date you want to see— you can even drag across months. Entourage displays today's date in red and underlined on the mini calendar in an effort to keep you from coming unstuck in time.

- Entourage can give you a gentle nudge (with an Office Reminder in a pop-up dialog box) when an important date is approaching.

- Entourage can automatically send invitations to other people to let them know about important meetings. (Let's see one of those "Humboldt Honeys" calendars do *that!*)

- Entourage's calendar integrates with the Project Center by placing important project—or email follow-up, or task—dates on your calendar if you so desire.

You can record an appointment using any of several methods, listed here in order of decreasing efficiency:

- When viewing a column view, such as a day, week, or work week, drag vertically through the time slots that represent the appointment's duration, and then double-click within the highlighted area (see Figure 11-4).

- Double-click a date in any of the calendar views.

- Click the New toolbar button.

- Choose File → New → Calendar Event (or press ⌘-N).

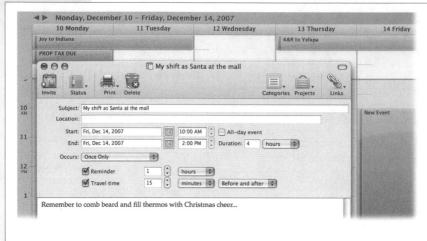

Figure 11-4:
You can open a window that creates a new event by double-clicking a highlighted swath of hours on any column view (background). With the help of the calendar event window, shaping an event to do exactly what you want is easy. By twiddling a few of these knobs and buttons, you can change a 10-minute event into an all-week extravaganza; and you can invite all your closest friends and co-workers, and set a reminder so it you don't miss it.

In each case, Entourage brings up a New Event window, depicted in Figure 11-4. Here's an unusually elaborate example of how you might enter an appointment:

1. **Type a name for this appointment into the Subject line.**

   For example, you might type *Pebble Beach Concourse.*

2. **Press Tab to jump to the Location field. Specify where this event is to take place. For example,** *Carmel.*

   This field makes a lot of sense; if you think about it, almost everyone needs to record where a meeting is to take place. You might type a reminder for yourself like *My place,* a specific address like *212 East 23,* or some other helpful information like a contact phone number or flight number.

   You can also leave this field empty if it's not important to you.

3. **Press Tab. Specify the starting date, if necessary.**

   If you began this entire exercise by double-clicking a date in Entourage's month view, or by dragging through time slots on one of the Entourage calendar displays, then skip this step, since Entourage has automatically filled in the date you indicated. Helpful, no?

   Otherwise, you can change the date here in two ways. First, you can edit the date displayed here, using this format—12/12/02—to specify the date. (If you omit the year, Entourage assumes you mean this year.)

   Or you can prefer to click the tiny calendar button next to the Starting Date field. A mini calendar window appears; move to the month you want by clicking the arrows at the top, and then click the date you want (or the Today button) to close the mini-calendar. You've successfully filled in the Start and End date fields.

Tip: When editing a date, pressing the + key moves the date one day forward, and pressing − moves the date one day backward. The + and − keys on the numeric keypad work great for this.

4. **Press Tab. Specify the ending date.**

Most events, thank goodness (unless it's a week of swimming with dolphins in Bimini), start and end on the same day. Entourage saves you time by making that assumption, and setting both Start and End dates to match. (The only time you have to type the ending date manually is if it's later than the starting date.) Entourage lets you type an ending date earlier than the starting date for an event, but complains only when you actually try to save the event.

5. **Turn off the "All-day event" checkbox, if necessary, and then specify the Start and End times.**

If you opened this dialog box by dragging through time slots on the Entourage calendar, then skip this step. Like the ideal administrative assistant that it is, Entourage has already filled in the Start and End times for you.

Otherwise, turn off "All-day event" (unless, of course, this event really *will* last all day; we've all had meetings like that). Doing so prompts the Start and End time boxes to appear. You can adjust the times shown here by typing, clicking buttons, or a combination of both. For example, start by clicking the hour, then increase or decrease this number by clicking either of the arrow buttons or by pressing your up and down arrow keys. (Of course, you can also type a number.) Press Tab to highlight the minutes, and repeat the arrow buttons-or-keys business. Finally, press Tab to highlight the AM/PM indicator, and type either *A* or *P* to change it, if necessary. (You can also press the up or down arrow keys to toggle between AM and PM.)

Tab once again to highlight the End time field.

By now, you're probably exhausted just reading the steps required to set up, say, a lunch meeting. That's why it's usually quicker to begin the appointment-entering process by dragging vertically through an Entourage calendar column display; it spares you from having to specify the date and time.

6. **Use the Occurs pop-up menu if an event will recur according to a predictable schedule.**

The Occurs pop-up menu contains common options for recurring events: once a week, on a particular day of every month, on a particular day each year, Every Day, or Every Weekday. You can select any of these items, or move immediately to the Custom option, which opens the Recurring Event window (Figure 11-5). Use the Recurring Event window to indicate how often the event recurs (Daily, Weekly, Monthly, or Yearly). Once you've clicked the appropriate button, an additional set of controls appears, offering such plain-English variations as "Every January 14," "The second Tuesday of January," "The third Tuesday of every _ months," and so on.

Figure 11-5:
If you've indicated a Weekly repeat, you can specify that this event takes place more than once a week by turning on the days-of-the- week checkboxes. This event—a running workout—takes place Sunday, Tuesday, and Thursday of each week, rain or shine.

The bottom part of the box lets you indicate how long this event will keep repeating. If you click "No end date," you'll be stuck with seeing this event repeating on your calendar until the end of time (a good choice for recording, say, your anniversary—especially if your spouse consults the same calendar). You can also turn on "End after _ occurrence(s)," a useful option for the kids' springtime soccer practice. You can also turn on "End by", and specify a date that will cut off the repetitions; use this option to indicate the last day of school, for example.

Click OK when you've finished setting up the repetition. To the right of the Occurs pop-up menu, there should be a plain-English summary of the options you set up.

7. **Set a reminder, if you like.**

   The Reminder section of the dialog box lets you set a reminder that pops up on your screen at a preset time. (Office Reminders have to be turned on for reminder windows to appear; for more about Office Reminders, see page 469.) You can specify how much advance notice you want for this particular appointment. For your favorite TV show, you might set up a reminder only five minutes before air time; for an important birthday, or anniversary you might set up a 10-day warning to allow yourself enough time to buy a present, mail a card, or book a flight to Puerto Vallarta. (Entourage starts out proposing 15 minutes in advance for every reminder. You can change this setting in Entourage → Preferences → General Preferences → Calendar.)

   If the event requires getting to the church on time, for example, turn on "Travel time" and then enter the amount of cushion you want to leave yourself for traffic and the like.

Tip: If a reminder pops up when you're concentrating on something else, click the Snooze button (Figure 11-6) to erase the reminder from your screen for the default snooze time (which you can change in Entourage → Preferences). Use the Snooze button's pop-up menu to eradicate this reminder for some other period of time. If you've already taken care of this event or just decided that you don't like your computer bossing you around, click the Dismiss button—or if you're being bugged by several reminders on your screen at once use the Dismiss button's pop-up menu and choose Dismiss All.

Figure 11-6:
The Office Reminders program, which comes with Office 2008, handles reminders for events and tasks. When a reminder comes due, Office Reminders pops a little window in front of whatever else is on your screen. You can then choose to deal with the matter immediately, and drop what you're doing to run out the door—or perhaps first click the calendar icon to open the event and check the details.

8. **Press Tab. In the white, empty notes area, type or paste any helpful text.**

   Here's your chance to customize your calendar event. You can add any text that you like in the notes area—driving directions, contact phone numbers, a call history, or whatever. Several pages' worth of information can fit here.

   If you choose to use the Invite feature described on page 454, Entourage includes the text you place here in the email invitations you send out.

9. **Specify a category or project for this appointment, using the pop-up menu at the right end of the toolbar.**

   See page 473 to read more about categories. For now, it's enough to note that Entourage's color-coded categories are helpful in distinguishing your calendar events at a glance. Family events might show up in blue, for example, and work events in red.

   For more information on the Project Center, see page 475. The short story: Assigning an event or appointment to a project displays the appointment with the project, and color-codes the appointment with a circle in the color you assigned to the project.

10. **Close the event window if you've previously instructed Entourage to always save your appointments. Otherwise, press ⌘-S, then close the event window (by pressing ⌘-W, for example).**

    Your newly scheduled event now shows up on the calendar, complete with the color coding that corresponds to the category you've assigned. (In month views, the text of the event itself reveals the color; in column views, the block of time occupied by the event reflects its category color.) Appointments that last longer than one day (such as vacations) appear as category-colored banners that stretch across squares on the month view; in column views, they appear just beneath the date at the top of the column (see Figure 11-7).

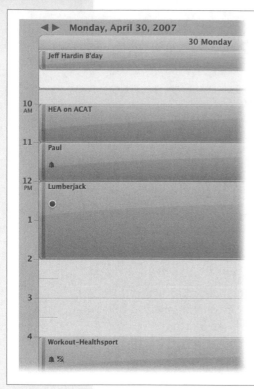

Figure 11-7:
After you've created your event, it dutifully appears in your daily calendar nestled among your other calendar events. This column view shows All-day events (or banner events) at the top of the calendar, above the start of your day. Then, each event shows up as a colored box in the column. If an event has a reminder, a small bell icon appears in the box; if the event contains a note, it shows a notepad icon; if the event is recurring, it shows two arrows in a yin-yang arrangement; and if you've assigned an event to a project, a colored bullet alerts you to its status. (Events that are 30 minutes or less don't have room to display these icons.)

What to Do with an Appointment

Once you've entrusted your agenda to Entourage, you can start putting it to work. Microsoft Entourage is only too pleased to remind you (via Office Reminders) of your events, to reschedule them, to print them out, and so on. Here are a few of the possibilities.

Editing Events

To edit a calendar event, open its event window either by double-clicking its name on the calendar or by highlighting it and choosing File → Open Event (⌘-O) or pressing Return. The calendar event pops up in its window, exactly as shown in Figure 11-4. Alter any of its settings as you see fit.

Tip: When changing only an appointment's category, bypass the event dialog box. Instead, just Control-click the appointment's block or its name, and choose Categories from the resulting shortcut menu. (Or select an event and use the Categories button's pop-up menu in the toolbar.) Click a category to assign the event to that category. Note that it's perfectly OK for an event to have more than one category. You can unassign an existing category by clicking it again.

You don't have to bother with this, however, if all you want to do is reschedule an event, as described next.

Rescheduling Events

If an event in your life gets rescheduled to a new date that's currently visible on the screen, then you can simply drag it to that new date to officially reschedule it (see Figure 11-8).

Tip: If you'd like to duplicate an event—if you had so much fun having lunch with that old flame that you'd like to do the same thing the day after tomorrow, for example—press Option while you drag the original appointment.

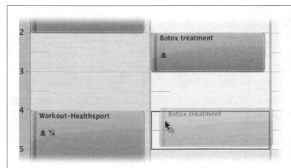

Figure 11-8:
You can drag an appointment vertically in its column to make it earlier or later in the same day, or horizontally to another date. If you invited people to an event that you're editing, Entourage asks if you want to send an update to your invites, so that they're always kept in the loop.

Alas, Entourage doesn't let you copy, cut, or paste calendar events. If something is postponed for, say, a month or two (that is, to a calendar "page" that would require scrolling), you have no choice but to double-click its name and then edit the Starting and Ending dates or times.

Note: When rescheduling a recurring event, Entourage applies the change *only* to the event you've moved, leaving the rest of the recurring events intact. If you want to change the time or date of the whole series, open the event for editing. Only then does Entourage ask whether you want changes applied to just the event you opened, or all the recurring events.

Lengthening or Shortening Events

If a scheduled meeting becomes shorter or your lunch hour becomes a lunch hour-and-a-half (proven to boost productivity!), changing the length of the representative calendar event is as easy as dragging the top or bottom border of its block in any column view (see Figure 11-9).

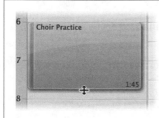

Figure 11-9:
You can resize any Entourage calendar event by dragging its border. As your cursor touches the top or bottom edge of a calendar event, it turns into a horizontal line with the arrows above and below. You can now drag the border to make it encompass more or less time on your calendar. As you drag, Entourage displays a helpful reminder of the event's total time.

Printing Events

Entourage has a user-friendly way of committing your calendars to paper. To get there, choose File → Print, or press ⌘-P.

In this window, you can exercise control over how Entourage prints your calendar by changing the control settings you'll find grouped near the middle of the window: Print, Start and End dates, Layout, and Form.

- The **Print** pop-up menu presents four options regarding what to print: a Daily Calendar, a Calendar List, a Weekly Calendar, and a Monthly Calendar (see Figure 11-10).

- **Start** and **End** let you specify start and end dates for the printout.

- **Layout** lets you choose which portions of the calendar to print. You can select Events or Tasks, or only certain kinds of tasks, or only items from a certain project or category. It also lets you specify whether *cut lines* or "punch holes here" indicators appear on each sheet, for trimming and punching your pages to fit a day planner (described next).

- **Form.** If you use a paper-based, binder-style day planner (such as a Franklin-Covey, Day-Timer, or Day Runner), you're in luck. Entourage lists canned layouts for the most popular formats in the Form pop-up menu.

- **Standard print options.** The other options are identical to those presented in Chapter 1. You may choose your printer, presets, number of copies, and the page setup. Then you can preview the print job, save it as a PDF, or fax it.

Deleting Events

To delete an appointment, first select it, then simply press the Delete key or Control-click (or right-click) the appointment and choose Delete Event from the pop-up menu. (There are other ways, if you're looking to waste time: select the event and click the Delete button in the toolbar, choose Edit → Delete Event, press ⌘-Delete). In the confirmation dialog box, click Delete (or press Return).

Note: If you delete a recurring event (like a weekly meeting), Entourage asks if you want to delete just that particular instance of the event or the whole series. Unlike Entourage 2004, Entourage 2008 deletes the *one* occurrence of the event rather than the series when you press Return, so if you're fast-fingered you won't lose the entire series. You're welcome.

Sending Invitations

At last it's time for you to harness Entourage's combined calendar/email/address-book power. Thanks to a cross-platform data-exchange standard called *iCalendar*, you can send invitations or meeting requests to others and, if they have an iCalendar-aware email/calendar program (such as Entourage, Outlook, iCal, Lightning, or Sunbird), they can easily reply to accept your invitation.

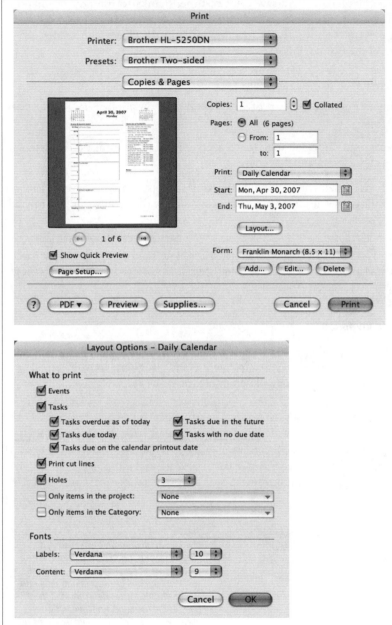

Figure 11-10:
Not surprisingly, you press ⌘-P to invoke the Print dialog box—though it now features the many printing options for Entourage calendars (top). As shown here, you can even shape them to fit paper planners. If your planner brand isn't listed in the form section, click Add Form to set the margins so that they fit your printer. Click the Layout button to open the Layout Options window (bottom) where you can control which calendar elements you wish to print.

If you click the Invite button in an event window's toolbar (see Figure 11-4), Entourage sprouts an Invite field. Use it just like the "To" field in an email message, as described in Chapter 10; that is, specify the email addresses of anyone that you'd like to invite to the event. If they're already in Entourage's address book (covered in Chapter 10), you save a lot of time, thanks to the pop-up menu of contacts and recent addresses that match the few letters you've typed. Type the invitation message you want your invitees to see in the blank white notes area at the bottom of the Event window.

Sending the invitation

Once an invitation becomes part of an appointment, the toolbar sports these new buttons:

- **Send Now** sends an email message to everyone on the guest list (complete with the subject, location, and any notes).

- **Cancel Invite** deletes any invitations in your Outbox that you haven't sent yet. It also sends cancellation messages via email to attendees you've already invited.

Note: You can also choose Event → Send Invitation Now (or press ⌘-Return) to send your invitation; or choose Event → Send Invitation Later (or press Shift-⌘-Return) to add the outgoing email messages to your Outbox without actually sending them. They won't get broadcast until you use the Send All or Send & Receive All command, as described on page 361.

Receiving an invitation

If you're on the receiving end of one of these meeting summonses, but you don't use Entourage (or another *iCalendar-aware* email program) as your email program, you get a note like the one shown in Figure 11-11.

Warning: Even among iCalendar-aware programs, invitations don't always work perfectly. With other people using Entourage or folks using Outlook on the same Exchange server (see the box on page 440), you'll probably have good luck. In other cases, you may just get an attachment with an .ics extension. If you open an .ics file in Entourage, you'll see the event appear in your calendar, but you won't get the Accept and Decline options, and there may even be errors in the time and date. You've been warned.

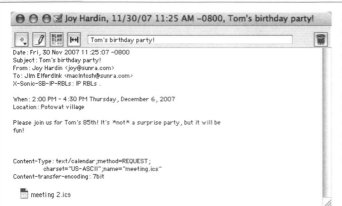

Figure 11-11:
In other email programs like Eudora, invitations sent from Entourage look like ordinary email messages. They contain the relevant time and location information and whatever note the sender created in the body of the message. Attached to the message is the iCalendar data file (meeting 2.ics, in this case). Though Eudora doesn't know what to do with it, double-clicking it inserts the event into iCal, or another iCalendar-aware program.

But if you are using Entourage as your email program, a special thrill awaits: The invitation *inserts itself* into your calendar, complete with times and reminders (Figure 11-12). You even get a yellow banner in the email message window that lets you respond to the invitation by clicking either the Accept, Decline, or Accept Tentatively links at the top of the message. (Buttons with the same functions also appear in the toolbar at the top of the email message.)

Clicking any of these links sends an email message *back* to the sender, whose copy of Entourage now offers even more surprises.

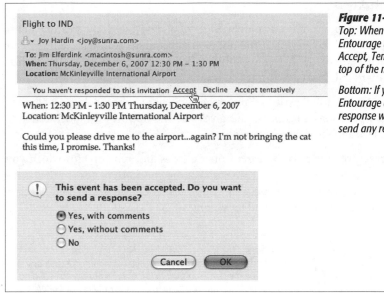

Figure 11-12:
Top: When you receive an invitation in Entourage that's from Entourage, you'll see Accept, Tentative, and Decline buttons at the top of the message.

Bottom: If you click any of the three buttons, Entourage asks whether you want to send a response with or without comments, or not send any response at all.

Receiving RSVPs for your invitation

Now suppose you're the person who sent the original invitation. As your invitees reply to your note, one of two things might happen:

- If you sent the invitation to somebody who doesn't use Entourage, you'll simply receive an uninspired email message that says, for example, "OK, I'll be there."

 After reading this reply, double-click the event on your calendar that represents the get-together. In the event window, you'll see a yellow banner across the top of the message indicating that you've sent invitations. It also contains a "View attendee status" link. When you click the link, a floating window appears that lists all the people you invited, complete with a pop-up menu that lets you track their responses: No Response, Accepted, Tentative, or Declined. Use the pop-up menu to update the list, according to the reply you just received.

- If you sent the invitation to somebody who *does* use Entourage, life is sweet indeed. The program *automatically* updates the Attendee Status window, based on the button that your prospective guest clicked (Accept, Tentative, or Decline) upon receiving the invitation.

Whenever you change the specifics of a calendar appointment about which you've sent invitations (such as its date), Entourage offers to send an updated email message to the guests. The buttons in the upper-left corner of the event dialog box now read Send Update and Send Later (if you've customized the toolbar).

Adding Holidays

Your Entourage calendar doesn't come with any holidays listed. By creating a customizable calendar that can reflect the holidays of different countries, cultures, or religious beliefs, Microsoft didn't presume to know what you celebrate. Fortunately, it's easy to tell Entourage what you want.

To import a set of holidays into Entourage's calendar, choose File → Import. Entourage's Import assistant opens, and gives you the option to import holidays. Choose Holidays and click the right arrow.

Now Entourage presents a list of dozens of countries and religions for which you can import holidays (see Figure 11-13). Turn on the checkboxes next to the countries or religions whose holidays you want to import, and click OK. Those holidays now appear in your Entourage calendar.

Figure 11-13:
To add holidays to your Entourage calendar, click Holidays, turn on the checkbox next to the country or religious holidays you want to import, and then click the right arrow button. Entourage takes care of the rest. You can import, one, some, or all of these holidays, if you like. As a convenience, Entourage labels them with the category called, as you might expect, Holidays.

Note: The holiday data that Entourage imports might contain significant days that aren't technically holidays. For example, if you import United States holidays, "Tax Day" (April 15) winds up on your calendar—an example of a special day that you can observe, but probably don't *celebrate.*

Your Very Own Holidays

In this trick, you set up a file containing any number of occasions—corporate events for the year, a softball league game schedule, full and new moons, the birthdays of your favorite rock stars, and so on—so that your colleagues can import them into their own calendars.

The Holidays file isn't difficult to decipher. If you visit your Applications → Microsoft Office 2008 → Office folder, you'll see a Text file called Holidays. If you open it in a text editor or Word, you'll discover that it's just a simple list of holidays in this format:

> Father's Day,2008/6/15
> Father's Day,2009/6/21
> Father's Day,2010/6/20
> Father's Day,2011/6/19

Each country, region, or religion is preceded by a bracketed title and a number indicating the number of entries for the category. In other words, it's easy enough to create Holiday files of your own.

First, make a copy of the Holidays file in the Finder, and rename it something like "My Holidays." Then open your file in Word 2008; delete the existing text; type the name of each holiday, followed by a comma, no space, then the date (in year/month/day format); press Return and type the next holiday the same way.

When you're finished, type a category name and the total count at the top of the file (use the default Holidays file as an example), and then save it as a text-only file. Finally, choose File → Import, select Holidays, and open your customized Holiday file just as you would any other.

Saving Calendars as Web Pages

One of the calendar module's best features is its capability to save your calendar as a Web page. You can make your calendar available to a select few (perhaps via Mac OS X's built-in Web Sharing), or you can post the result on the Internet for all to see. For example, you might use this feature to post the meeting schedule for your book club, or to make clear the agenda for a series of upcoming Nonviolent Communication workshops that all of your co-workers will need to consult.

Note: There's no way to include only certain categories on a Web-published calendar, so that only your corporate appointments are publicized but not your private ones. You can, of course, maintain a separate calendar under a different Entourage *identity* (see page 495 for this purpose).

Begin by choosing File → Save as Web Page. The Save as Web Page window appears (Figure 11-14). Here, you customize how your saved calendar is going to look and work. For example, you can specify:

- **Start and End dates.** This option prevents you from saving an entire century's calendar in HTML form.

- **Include event details.** Use this option if you want your Web page to include the notes that you've entered in a calendar event's notes area.

- **Use background graphic.** Turn on this box if you want your Web-page calendar superimposed on a picture. Then click the Choose button to the right. You'll then be asked to select a graphics file from your hard drive.

Tip: To avoid the ridicule and wrath of your audience, use the graphics feature with caution. Choose only an extremely light, low-contrast image, so that the text of the calendar is still legible when superimposed over it. If possible, choose a graphic image that's roughly the same size as the calendar, too, so Entourage doesn't stretch it out of shape. Also remember that downloading an enormous background image over a modem is no one's idea of a good time.

- **Web page title.** The text you enter in this box will appear as the Web page's title.

- **Open saved Web page in browser.** If this box is turned on, Entourage will open the newly saved calendar in your Web browser just after saving it, so that you can make sure it wound up the way you intended.

Once you've set your options, click Save.

Next, in the Save dialog box, name the calendar file (suppose it's *SummerWorkshops*—it's a good idea to use no spaces in your title). Select a folder location on your hard drive, and then click Save. Entourage creates two new icons on your hard drive—an HTML file called SummerWorkshops.htm, and a folder called SummerWorkshops. The folder contains a bevy of graphics and HTML files that comprise your calendar.

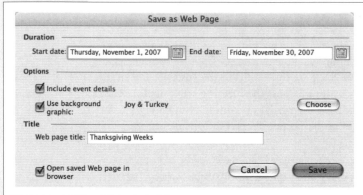

Figure 11-14:
When you save your calendar as a Web page, you can control the range of dates, whether to include event details, and whether or not to use a background graphic. You're welcome to give your Web page a title more imaginative than Calendar.

If you chose "Open saved Web page in browser" (Figure 11-14), your newly saved calendar now appears. Review it for accuracy, and marvel that it has live links; clicking an item brings up details about it in the right-hand frame of the Web page (Figure 11-15).

Tip: The Web pages created by Entourage exploit such up-to-date Web-browser features as frames, style sheets, and JavaScript. In one respect, however, they are mired in the past: if you use the "Open the saved Web page in browser" option, Entourage summons Internet Explorer if you have a copy of it on your computer—even though it's not your default Web browser and you probably haven't used it for years. With any luck, Microsoft will squash this bug by the time Office 2012 arrives, but in the meantime, select the .htm file Entourage created, choose File → Get Info, change the "Open with" pop-up menu to your preferred browser, and click the Change All button. From now on, Internet Explorer remains undisturbed in a far-off corner of your hard drive, while your preferred browser opens these Web calendar previews.

Your Mac as Web Server

If you have a full-time Web connection, such as a cable modem or DSL service, you can use the Mac's own Web Sharing feature to post your calendar for the entire online world to see. A complete discussion of this feature awaits in *Mac OS X: The Missing Manual,* but here's a summary.

Open the Mac OS X System Preferences, click Sharing, and turn on the Web Sharing checkbox (called Personal Web Sharing in Tiger). Make a note of the personal Web site address that appears in the window, something like, *http:// 192.168.2.99/~jim/.*

Next, return to the Finder and open your Home folder (Option-⌘-H). Once there, you'll find a folder called Sites. Drag your calendar file and folder into it.

To view your calendar, open a Web browser and enter a URL in this form:

http://192.168.2.99/~jim/SummerWorkshops.htm

Of course, for 192.168.2.99, substitute the actual address you noted in the Sharing preferences window, replace Jim with your Mac OS X account name (preceded by a ~), and replace SummerWorkshop.htm with the name of the calendar file Entourage created.

If the calendar appears properly in your Web browser, the next step is to send that link to your friends or colleagues who need this timely information.

If you have a home router, you'll need to configure it to *port forward port 80* to your computer, and provide the address of your *router* to your friends or colleagues. (For more information use your favorite Internet search engine to search for "port forwarding.")

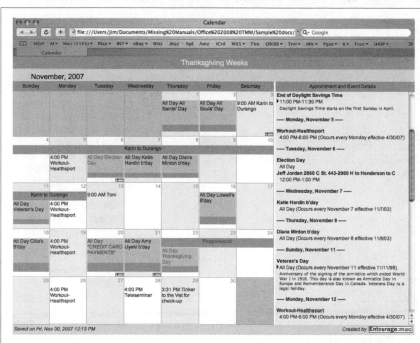

Figure 11-15:
When you save an Entourage calendar as a Web page, it retains most of its pertinent details, such as events, times, and even notes associated with those events. If you've attached a note to an event, you can click the small, flippy triangle next to the event to reveal the note in the list pane on the right. You can save a single day or several months as Web pages; just one more way Entourage can help keep those who need to know in the know.

If the file looks good, the final step is to upload the Web page to a Web server so others can see it. Of course, this step requires that you have a Web site (unless you're hosting it yourself—see the box on page 461). You can contact your Internet service provider to find out how much Web space your account grants you and what steps to take to post new Web pages there. There's also Apple's annual $100 .Mac service, which includes up to 10 GB on the Web, along with email and other perks.

Note: These Web calendars provide a frozen-in-time version of your Entourage calendar. If you make changes to your calendar that you want reflected in the Web version, you'll have to repeat the Save As Web Page process.

Tasks and the To Do List

Entourage lets you create a To Do list of any kind of tasks you can think up, and it does its best to help you accomplish these objectives, goading you with gentle reminders if you so desire. You can also add just about any other kind of Entourage item to your To Do list and benefit from similar reminders.

You can put Entourage into Task view either by clicking the Tasks button at the upper left, choosing View → Go To → Tasks, or pressing ⌘-5. Entourage displays a simple list of tasks, complete with due dates and categories (see Figure 11-16). In the Tasks and To Do List pane on the left you'll discover the two parts of Entourage's To Do system, labeled Tasks and To Do List.

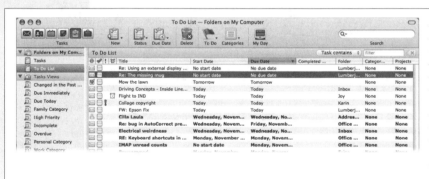

Figure 11-16:
Entourage's Tasks toolbar includes three specifically task-related buttons—New, Status, Due Date, and To Do—as well as a few of the old favorites. Use the Tasks and To Do pane to choose to view the entire To Do List, the Tasks list, or one of the filtered Tasks Views. The Quick Filter bar below the toolbar lets you quickly locate tasks containing certain words or that you've assigned to certain categories or projects.

The To Do chores that you create from scratch Entourage calls Tasks, keeping them in the Tasks list *and also* in the To Do List. If however you create a To Do

---

item by flagging an email message, calendar event, project, or contact, then Entourage adds those items to the To Do List only. Click the icons in the Tasks and To Do List pane to switch between the two lists.

Changing Your Views

When you first enter the Tasks module, Entourage shows you a simple list of all tasks you've entered or imported—a view which you can alter to suit your preferences. To do so, cruise over to the View menu and select one of the following (the menu command changes slightly depending on which list you're viewing, Tasks or To Do List):

- **All Tasks (All To Do Items).** This screen shows all the tasks or To Do items in your busy life; it's the view Entourage shows you unless you choose otherwise. It even displays the tasks you've completed—something that makes most people feel terrific.

- **Incomplete Tasks (Incomplete Items).** Displays everything that you have yet to complete. In most cases this is more useful, and definitely less cluttered, than displaying All Tasks (To Do Items).

- **Completed Tasks (Completed Items).** Displays all the items you've checked off as completed.

- **Due Today.** Focuses on the present; this option shows just what's due today.

- **Due This Week.** Displays everything that's due in the current week. (The current week is defined by the Calendar work week settings you choose in Entourage → Preferences → General Preferences → Calendar.)

You can also filter the tasks with the options displayed in the Tasks Views pane at the left of the window. Click the flippy triangle next to Tasks Views to see them all:

- **Changed in the Past 7 Days.** Shows every task that you've edited in the last seven days.

- **High Priority.** Gives you a list of tasks that you've marked high priority (described on the next page).

- **Due Today.** Shows just today's items.

- **Incomplete.** Displays all the tasks that lie before you.

- **Overdue.** You can view incomplete tasks whose due date has come and gone—helpful for setting a new due date, or perhaps deleting with a smile.

- **Category** and **Project.** You can view tasks by category or project. In this case, you can select only from categories or projects that you have assigned to tasks. For example, if you have no tasks assigned to the Work category (lucky you!), that category doesn't appear as an organizing option.

No matter what view you select, there are five columns to the left of the tasks' subject:

- **Links** (indicated by a tiny chain-link icon) shows if the task is linked to any other item, such as a message or a calendar event (see page 467).

- **Status** (indicated by a tiny checkmark icon) shows a checkbox, which you can turn on when the task is complete (or sooner, as you realize some things just aren't worth your time).

- **Priority** (indicated by a tiny exclamation point) is the same as the priority column found in Mail—Highest, High, Normal, Low, and Lowest. It helps you keep focused on your highest priorities.

- **Recurring** (indicated by a double arrow) shows, at a glance, whether the task is a one-time deal or something you can look forward to on a continuing basis.

- **Reminder** (indicated by a tiny alarm clock) shows a similar alarm clock icon if you've set a reminder for a particular task—in other words, it's a reminder reminder.

- You specify what appears in the rest of the columns—the **Task** subject, **Start Date, Completed Date, Categories**, and **Project**—when you create your To Do items, described next.

Creating Tasks

To create a new Entourage Task, take your pick of the usual array of options:

- Choose File → New → Task.

- If you're already in the Tasks view, press ⌘-N.

- Click the New toolbar button. (If you're not already viewing your To Do list, choose Task from the New pop-up button.)

An Untitled task window appears (Figure 11-17). Conduct your task-recording business like this:

1. **Type a name for the task.**

   This becomes the subject that appears in your Tasks list. Do yourself a favor and make it a good, descriptive one: "Meeting with professional organizer," for example, instead of just "Meeting."

2. **Change its priority, if you like.**

   If you take a moment to categorize your tasks this way, you'll be able to sort your task list by priority. Every creative soul invents more tasks than are doable, so why not focus on the most important ones?

3. **Specify a due date for this item, if you like.**

   Turn on "Due date" and enter a deadline date. Feel free to use any of the same date-setting tricks described on page 448.

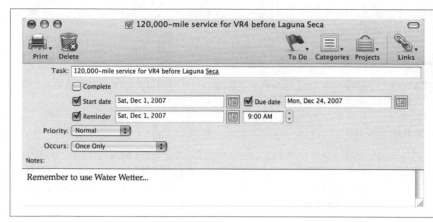

Figure 11-17:
The task window lets you create, edit, print and delete tasks; but more importantly it lets you see the entire task configuration at a glance.

There's only one difference between a dated To Do item and one that doesn't have a due date: When the specified date goes by, an incomplete To Do item shows up in boldface in the Tasks window. If you double-click it, you'll see "Due yesterday," "Overdue by_ days," or Overdue next to an attention-getting alarm clock icon at the top of the task's description window.

4. **If this To Do item reflects a recurring task, such as your weekly bath, use the options in the Occurs pop-up menu.**

   You'll be able to specify a duty that recurs daily, weekly, monthly, or yearly. The Occurs options here work much like those described for events on page 449.

Tip: If you set your task to recur, a new Edit button pops to the right of the Occurs pop-up menu. You can click this button to further refine the recurrence. However, if you turn on the "After task is complete, create a new task due in _", then once you check off the task, the next one resets to one day (or week, month, or year) from when you got it done, not the original recurrence date. This is perfect if you have to submit a report, say, every 30 days, but not on the same day every month.

---

5. **Turn on the Reminder checkbox, and set a date and time for the reminder to poke its nose into your computer reverie—in the form of a pop-up dialog box displayed by the Office Reminders program.**

   See page 469 for more on reminders.

6. **Make notes for more information.**

   Tab to the Notes box to type or paste text that helps describe your task.

7. **Assign it to a project, if you like.**

   If you've created any projects in Entourage's Project Center, they're listed under the Projects button.

8. **When you've tweaked your task configuration to perfection, close the window (press ⌘-W).**

   Entourage closes the window, saves your task, and adds it to the To Do List.

If you need to create more tasks (new opportunities constantly arise), press ⌘-N, and then start over again at Step 1.

Other Task Tricks

Once you've recorded some To Do items, you can manipulate them in ways that should be familiar if you've used the Entourage calendar.

Editing a task

Change a task's name by selecting the task, clicking the task's subject, and then waiting about one second for the editing box to appear. Type a new name and then press Enter or Return. You can change its category or project by clicking in either of those columns; a pop-up menu of your choices appears.

You can change a task's priority, repeat status, and so on, by double-clicking its name in the Tasks list (or by highlighting it and pressing ⌘-O, or choosing File → Open Task). The dialog box shown in Figure 11-17 reappears, allowing you to change any aspect of a task.

Completing a task

After finishing a task, you can celebrate by turning on its checkbox in your list. Once you do so, Entourage puts a line through the task to give you the satisfaction of crossing it off your list. If a task's window is open, you can also turn on the Complete checkbox and then close the window. (When you check off a recurring task, Entourage only marks that specific instance complete. The next recurrence will rise like a phoenix from the ashes when due.)

Deleting a task

To delete a task, click it in the task list and then either press the Delete key, click the Delete button, press ⌘-Delete, or choose Edit → Delete Task. (You'll be asked to confirm the deletion. And that's fortunate, because no Undo command exists, and the deleted task doesn't go into the Deleted Items folder; instead, it's gone forever.)

Tip: You can select multiple tasks (in preparation for deleting them en masse, for example) just as you would email messages: using either the Shift-clicking or ⌘-clicking tricks described in the box on page 376.

Printing tasks

It's easy enough to print out a list of your to-dos. To print only some of them, start by highlighting the ones you want (see the preceding Tip).

Now press ⌘-P or choose File → Print. This triggers the custom Entourage Print window, which lets you choose which tasks to print (all tasks, selected tasks, tasks due today or this week, and so on), what style you want to use for printing them, and whether you want to print those pages on standard paper or special Franklin-Covey, Day-Timer, or Day Runner paper.

When you finally click Print, you're on your way to a hard copy reminder of the errands and objectives that await you.

Linking tasks

Linking tasks to other Entourage items is a great use of the Links function, since it lets you draw connections between the tasks that you're working on and any email messages, calendar events, or contacts that might be related to them. When you have a task's window open, you can create a link with the click of a Links button, which opens the Links window. If you use the Links button's pop-up menu, your choices let you link that task either to an existing Entourage item or to a new one you create on the spot. In the Tasks list, click and hold for a second in the Links column to access the pop-up menu.

My Day

This new Entourage outpost lets you keep an eye on your most urgent project elements—your current schedule and To Do items—without opening or even launching Entourage. You don't have to confront your full calendar, your entire To Do List, or your email, giving you a fighting chance at concentrating on today's tasks without getting sucked into the e-maelstrom.

My Day is a mini application that acts like a Mac OS X Widget emigrated from the Dashboard to the desktop. The small My Day window provides a quick view of your day's schedule and To Do List from Entourage (even if Entourage isn't running).

The top section of the My Day window shows scheduled events; the bottom section shows To Do items and icons showing the type of the item and whether it's past-due (Figure 11-18). Click the date display at the top to open the Go To Date window and jump to a different date. You can also use the left and right arrow buttons to move day by day, or click the button between the arrows to come back to today. Buttons at the bottom of the window let you create a new To Do item, print today's schedule and To Dos, and open the My Day preferences window.

When you install Office 2008, My Day adds itself to your logon items and automatically appears in the upper-right corner of your screen. If you'd rather it not appear unbidden, choose My Day → Preferences → General and turn off "Open after computer logon" (Figure 11-19). While you're in Preferences, you can also choose a keyboard shortcut to summon My Day, choose to keep the My Day window in the forefront, or show My Day as a menulet at the right end of your menu bar.

Clicking a My Day event displays the event's location. Double-clicking an event or To Do item in the My Day window opens Entourage and displays the event or To Do item so you can read all the details or edit it.

Although My Day exists mostly as a quick view into your Entourage schedule, you can *add* a task to your To Do List without opening Entourage. Simply click the New Task button at the bottom of the window and the "Create a task" drawer

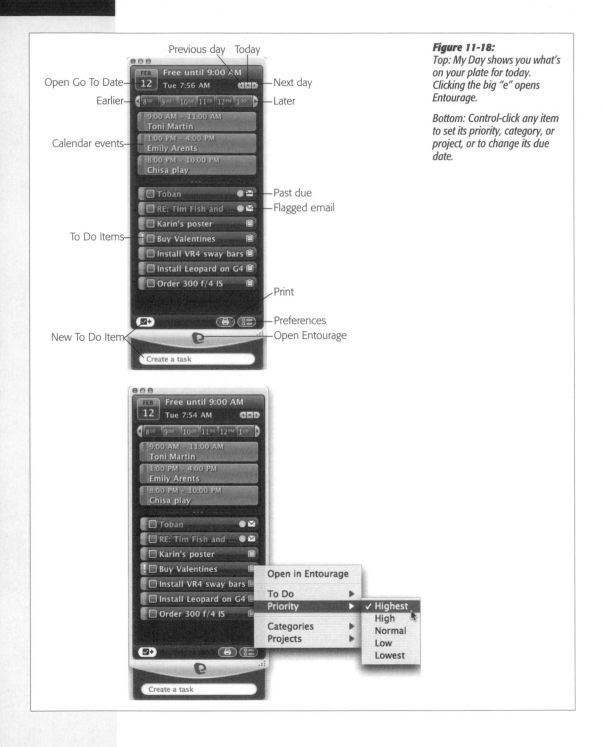

Previous day Today

Open Go To Date

Earlier —————— Later

Calendar events

Past due

Flagged email

To Do Items

Print

Preferences

New To Do Item

Open Entourage

Next day

Figure 11-18:
Top: My Day shows you what's on your plate for today. Clicking the big "e" opens Entourage.

Bottom: Control-click any item to set its priority, category, or project, or to change its due date.

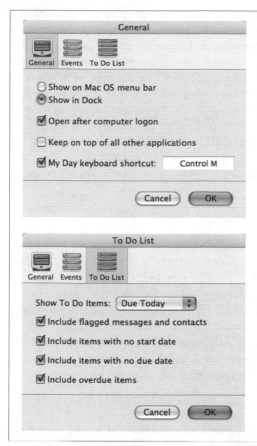

Figure 11-19:
Top: The My Day preferences window gives you control over how and when the program appears and what it displays. If you click the radio button marked "Show on Mac OS menu bar," the My Day application menu disappears and all menu items—including My Day Preferences—appear under the menulet icon in the menu bar.

Bottom: The To Do List preferences window lets you choose which To Do items to display.

slides downward. Type in your new task and press Return to add it to My Day's To Do list—and to Entourage's. Finally, you can celebrate completing a task by clicking its checkbox to remove it from the My Day display and mark it as complete in Entourage's To Do List.

Office Reminders

After you've set up a reminder for an appointment or task in Entourage (or via a Flag as a To Do Item in any Office 2008 program), Office displays handy onscreen alerts when your reminders come due. You can instruct these alerts to go away or to return later, or you can use them for quick access to appropriate appointments, tasks, or messages.

Office 2008 uses a small add-on program called Microsoft Office Reminders to handle these tipoffs. (It's in the Microsoft Office 2008 → Office folder, if you're curious.) When an event or To Do item or comes due, Office Reminders appears as a separate item in the Mac OS X Dock. When you've dealt with any pending items, Office Reminders vanishes, reappearing when it's time for the next reminder or follow-up.

It might sound complicated to deal with yet another program to handle alerts and notifications, but Office Reminders is straightforward. First, you can manage everything about alerts and notifications within Entourage, so you don't really feel like you're using a separate program. Second, using a separate tiny program to handle alerts and notifications means these alerts work *all the time,* even when no Office 2008 programs are running. (Of course, you can turn off Office Reminders at any time, so you won't be interrupted as you demo your Photoshop techniques to a room full of artists who probably don't really care that *The Beverly Hillbillies* is going to start in five minutes on Channel 64. Choose Office Reminders → Turn Off Reminders, or within Entourage choose Entourage → Turn Off Office Reminders—and then slap a Post-it on your screen to remind you to turn Office Reminders back on later.)

The Reminders Window

When a reminder comes due, the Office Reminders window appears in front of any other programs, a sound plays, and the name of the item appears. If more than one item is due, the Office Reminders window lists them all, but you'll have to either scroll or drag the window larger to see them all. Figure 11-20 shows five different kinds of notifications: a Microsoft Word document flagged for follow-up, a contact that's been flagged as a To Do List item, a task set up in Entourage, an email message reminder, and a calendar reminder. The Office Reminders window also displays to important buttons: Snooze, and Dismiss. Snooze and Dismiss also act as pop-up menus; see the next section for details on these options.

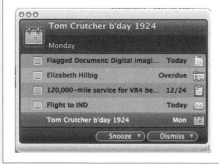

Figure 11-20:
Here Office Reminders shows five items: a Microsoft Word document that's flagged for follow up, a contact that's been added to the To Do List (and is overdue), a task, an email message reminder, and a calendar reminder. The highlighted item appears at the top of the window. Double-click any of them to open the linked item.

Reminders show three basic items:

- **Icon.** A reminder's icon indicates where the alert came from. For example, a reminder about an appointment displays a calendar icon, and a flagged Microsoft Word document appears with a Word document icon (Figure 11-20).

- **Subject.** The reminder's title is the subject of the appointment or task you set up, or it indicates the title of the document or message you flagged.

- **Due date.** Office Reminders also shows the item's due date or, for reminders of pending calendar items, how much time remains until the event. If an item is past due (like the second item in Figure 11-20), Office Reminders shows Overdue followed by the due date.

You can double-click any item in the reminder list to open the associated item immediately. Opening a flagged document or message doesn't dismiss or snooze the alert in Office Reminders (see next section); it just brings the flagged item front and center for you to act on, so you don't first have to hunt around your computer for it.

Tasks and flagged documents also have a checkbox you can use to mark an item as complete. This checkbox actually performs two functions in one easy step: It indicates that you're finished with an item *and* dismisses the alert box.

Acting on Reminders

When a reminder appears, you can process it in one of three ways: by opening it, snoozing it, or dismissing it.

- **Open Item.** Double-clicking an item opens the corresponding document, task, calendar entry, or mail message in Entourage. (If an item is already highlighted, you can also summon it with a single click of the large icon at the top of the reminder window.)

- **Snooze.** Use the Snooze button to make an alert go away—for now. The selected item reappears in five minutes to nag you again. If you want items to snooze for a different amount of time (say, until tomorrow morning), use the Snooze pop-up menu (see Figure 11-21).

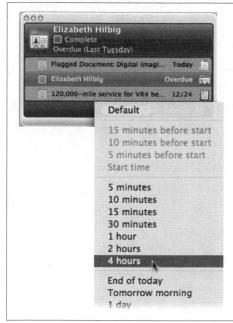

Figure 11-21:
Use the Snooze pop-up menu to specify when you'd like an alert to reappear. Some of the choices are obvious—come back in 10 minutes, 2 hours, 4 days, and so on—but some choices (like "15 minutes before start" and "End of today") are nicely flexible.

- **Dismiss.** Click Dismiss to make a selected alert go away, never to be seen again.

  If you want to dismiss all the items shown by Office Reminders, choose Dismiss All from the Dismiss pop-up button. All the current reminders are dismissed (although no documents or tasks get marked as completed).

Tip: You can select multiple items in the Office Reminders window just by Shift-clicking to select a range of items, or ⌘-clicking to choose nonadjacent items in the list—exactly as in the Finder or in the Entourage email list. At that point, the Snooze and Dismiss buttons affect *all* the corresponding items letting you snooze or dismiss a bunch of related items all at once.

- **Mark as Complete.** Use the Complete checkbox on tasks and flagged items to indicate you're finished with the task or item you flagged. Unlike other elements appearing with individual alert items, turning on the Complete checkbox both marks the task as completed *and* dismisses the alert, so that the item disappears from Office Reminders.

Note: Watch out—the program doesn't allow enough time to *un*check the box if you make a mistake. If you turn on the Complete checkbox on an item that you really *aren't* done with, you have to return to Entourage's Task list, where the item appears with a line through its name. To "uncomplete" an item, turn off the Complete checkbox in the Status column (and set up another reminder, if you like).

Configuring Office Reminders

Office Reminders is a simple program, generally keeping out of sight until the moment when you want to be prompted about something. You can change only two settings: whether the program is turned on or turned off and whether or not an alert sound plays when an item comes due.

Turn Office Reminders on or off

Sometimes you might not want Office Reminders to display alerts onscreen, even if something comes due. For instance, you can be using your Mac to give a demo or presentation to clients—or concentrating on the New York Times Sunday crossword. (We all have our priorities.)

Here are the two ways to turn off Office Reminders:

- In Entourage, choose Entourage → Turn Off Office Reminders.

- If Office Reminders is already on your screen, click its window once to ensure it's the frontmost program, and then choose Microsoft Office Reminders → Turn Off Reminders.

Turning Office Reminders back on again is almost identical:

- In Entourage, choose Entourage → Turn On Office Reminders.

- If Office Reminders is on your screen, click its window once to make it the frontmost program, and then choose Microsoft Office Reminders → Turn On Reminders.

Turn Office Reminders sounds on or off

Office Reminders generally plays a sound when an alert appears. If you don't want to hear these sounds, turn them off by choosing Microsoft Office Reminders → Turn Off Sounds. Alternatively, choose Entourage → Preferences → General Preferences → Notification and turn off the checkbox next to "Reminder sound." To turn the sound back on, just turn the "Reminder sound" checkbox back on.

Categories

Categories are labels you can apply to just about any Entourage item. They're designed to let you apply an organizational scheme to a group of items that don't otherwise have much in common. For example, you can define a category related to a trip that you're taking, or to a certain work project, and apply that category to dissimilar Entourage information bits (calendar, email, and to-do items, for example). Each category can have its own color, making it easy to identify those items at a glance. Categories, in other words, are a yet another convenient, easy-to-use means of helping you organize and keep track of your Entourage information.

Setting Up Categories

Entourage comes with an assortment of prefab categories—Family, Friends, Holiday, Junk, Personal, Recreation, Travel, and Work. If you import holidays into Entourage—see the box on page 459—they show up in a category of their own.

Note: Don't confuse Categories with Entourage's Project Center feature. Although both are methods for organizing disparate bits of information, the Project Center does much more than merely assign an organizational label to an item. For a full discussion of the Project Center, flip to page 475.

You can also create new categories, of course. For example, every organized activist needs categories like Environment, Salmon, Blogging, and Fundraising. To do so, choose Edit Categories from the Categories pop-up button on the toolbar, or choose Edit → Categories → Edit Categories. Either way, you now face the Categories window (Figure 11-22). To create a new category, click New and type the name you want for your new pigeonhole. Entourage assigns a color to your new category, but you can choose any of the 13 colors listed on the pop-up menu, or choose Other to mix your own color.

Anything you can create, you can delete. Expunge a category by clicking its name and then clicking Delete.

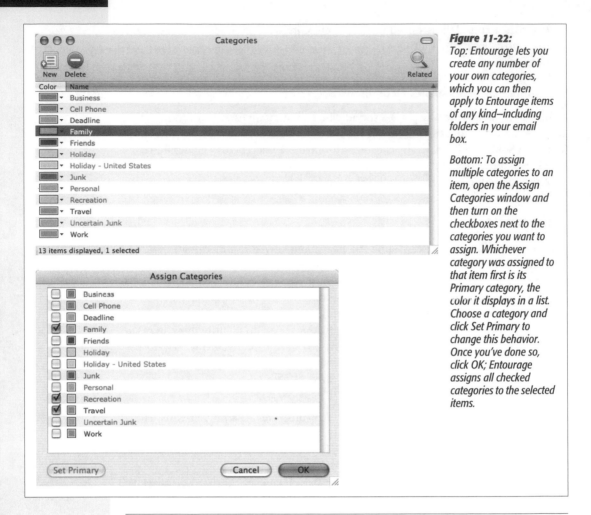

Figure 11-22:
Top: Entourage lets you create any number of your own categories, which you can then apply to Entourage items of any kind—including folders in your email box.

Bottom: To assign multiple categories to an item, open the Assign Categories window and then turn on the checkboxes next to the categories you want to assign. Whichever category was assigned to that item first is its Primary category, the color it displays in a list. Choose a category and click Set Primary to change this behavior. Once you've done so, click OK; Entourage assigns all checked categories to the selected items.

Tip: The Categories window has one other nifty feature: the Related button. Select a category for which you'd like to search for items, and then click this button. Entourage shows you a tidy listing of all the items in your Entourage world—messages, tasks, and so on—to which you've assigned that category.

Assigning a Category

To assign a category to an Entourage item—an email message, calendar event, task, note, news message, contact, or even an item in the email Folder list—simply highlight it. (You can also highlight several at once, if you want to categorize them all the same.) Use the Categories pop-up button in the toolbar or the Edit → Categories submenu to choose a category. Entourage assigns the category to the selected item for you and changes its color accordingly.

Tip: The main window for certain kinds of Entourage information, including email messages, tasks, notes, and the Address Book, includes a column called Categories. One of the easiest ways to apply a category to an item is to click in this column; a pop-up menu of your categories appears.

You may sometimes need to place an individual Entourage item into more than one category. For instance, a note with flight information might pertain to both the Travel and Work categories. To do so, click the Categories button (or choose Edit → Categories → Assign Categories) to bring up the Assign Categories window (Figure 11-22), where you can assign as many categories as you want by turning on the appropriate checkboxes.

Tip: You can assign more than one category to an item. Only the primary (first) category determines the color of the item.

Project Center

When it comes to keeping your life—and your work—on track, Entourage's Project Center is possibly its most powerful tool. That's surprising, given the fact that it's also possibly Entourage's least-utilized feature. Using Project Center, you can organize projects large and small—such as a national training workshop, a remodeling project, a vacation trip, or a fundraiser—and track all the documents, files, people, tasks, and emails associated with the event in one convenient location.

Starting a Project

Before delving into the deep secrets of projects, it helps to have some experience creating your own. There's no doubt that the easiest way to create a project is with the New Project Wizard. Here's how:

1. **From the Entourage toolbar, select New menu button → Project.**

   The New Project Wizard appears. Fill in the blanks as shown in Figure 11-23, and then click the right arrow button.

2. **On the next screen you can set your project's *watch folder* location and import items. In other words, you tell Entourage where to keep the documents you're going to use for this project and which existing items (if any) to keep with this project from now on.**

   If you choose to automatically create a project watch folder, Entourage creates a folder that matches your project's name. But maybe you've already accumulated some files on your Mac. You can manually set the Project Watch Folders: Browse to the location of the folder that you wish to set, and do so yourself. You can also set a folder within Entourage to store the project's email messages. (Something with a name similar to the project is a good idea.)

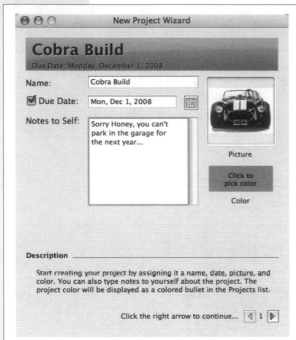

Figure 11-23:
The initial window of the New Project Wizard lets you customize your project. Drag whatever image you have pertaining to the project into the image window. (Perhaps one of a check to symbolize the bonus you'll receive when you complete your project ahead of deadline?) Choosing a color, by clicking in the appropriate box, makes your project window stand out from other project windows and colors the bullet that appears next to Project-related items in your To Do List, calendar, and so on. Set an overall due date and, if you want, type notes to yourself about the project. Use the Properties button to change any of these items later.

Note: If you pick the wrong watch folder during the New Project Wizard setup, you can designate a different one any time by clicking the Properties button in the toolbar at the bottom of the Project Center window. Doing so gives you access to all the properties you set via the Wizard.

If you have an existing Entourage category or Project that you want to become this *new* project, choose it from the From Category or From Project menu. (If you choose a category, Entourage imports *everything* under that category—contacts, tasks, calendar events, and so on.) After you're finished, click the right arrow to continue.

3. **On the third screen, you set the rules for the project, and also decide if you want a project folder alias on the desktop.**

   Here are your options:

   • **Associate e-mail from Project contacts.** Perhaps there are contacts in your address book that are intricately involved in the project. If the project is writing a cookbook with your sisters, for example, you'll want to keep track of all email correspondences from your sisters regarding this project. Once you add your sisters to your Project (see the Tip below), all email from them gets associated with the project, too.

- **Associate e-mail with the following subjects.** By the same token, you'll want to associate any emails with subjects that include the words *Cookbook* or *Recipe* to your cookbook project. Type in the email subjects you choose here.

- **Don't apply other rules to these messages.** It's not a good idea to apply other Entourage rules (see page 396) to project messages. Doing so can lead to some strange and unexpected filings including placing project email in non-project watch folders.

- **Apply Rules to existing messages.** This, on the other hand, is often a good idea. Clicking this box applies the new rules you just created (associating contacts and subjects with your project) to messages that you've already received. It's a nifty way to get your project off to an organized start. However, it has the potential to fill up your email watch folder with all those messages from your sister relating to her endless remodeling and redecorating plans.

- **Add Project Watch Folder alias to the Desktop.** Why not? It makes it easy to find and drag files to. But if you're a neat freak and prefer a spotless desktop, you can accomplish the same thing by manually adding the folder to your Sidebar or Dock.

4. **Read the summary on the final wizard screen and check to make sure that the location of your project watch folder, as listed on this screen, is correct.**

   This final page also has some helpful hints for adding items to your project, and sharing it. Click the right arrow to complete your project's construction.

The Project Center Window

To start working in a project, click the Project Center button, or choose View → Go To → Project Center, or press ⌘-6. The Project Center slides onto the screen, as shown in Figure 11-24.

The Project Center initially displays two panes beneath a familiar set of Entourage toolbar icons. The six view buttons on the left of the Entourage toolbar are the same as those displayed in all other Entourage toolbars, in that they can transport you back to the Mail, Address Book, Calendar, Notes, or Tasks views.

To the right of these icons is the New button, which you can click to begin your new project adventure, or to create a new whatever (email, task, contact, and so on) from its pop-up menu. If you're done with a project—either because you've completed it or someone else has stepped in to take over—delete it with the Delete button. (When you delete a project you're just deleting this organizational index,

Figure 11-24:
The Project Center window provides access to all the vital project functions and lets you switch between projects using the folder list on the left. Click the Overview tab for the big picture: the calendar, Tasks, recent mail, and recent files associated with each project.

not the actual messages, to-do items, appointments, and so on associated with it.) The Spotlight Search field on the right lets you search your computer for whatever you like.

Note: The Project Center toolbar changes to complement your selection. For example, after you open a project, the toolbar provides additional options: an Open button, and Categories and Projects menu buttons.

Project Views

On the left side of the Project Center screen rests the folder list that lets you choose what you view in the larger project viewing pane on the right. The folder list panel displays the Project Center and Custom Views icons. If you have several ongoing projects, the Project icon has a little flippy triangle adjacent to it. Click the triangle to view or hide your projects, and then click the project name to display it in the viewing window.

Click the flippy triangle adjacent to Custom Views to display the custom views options. You can choose to view all the Entourage items Due Today, or material that fits into any category that you've established in Entourage. Note that these views encompass all of Entourage, not just one of your projects. (Unlike the other views that only show one type of material, like Mail or Contacts, these custom views have a mixture of all of the above.) You can hide the folder list—and get more viewing space—by choosing View → Hide Folder List. Repeat the command, which now reads Show Folder List, to bring it back.

The Project Center's right window really displays the meat of the matter. When you first open the Project Center, the window lists your current projects. Double-click any of the listed projects to fill the view window with it and you're ready to get to work.

Getting Around the Project Center

The Project Center truly shoehorns an amazing amount of information into a relatively small space, as shown in Figure 11-25. The main Project Center view window displays the project du jour. You can view different aspects of your project by selecting one of the seven tabs at the top of the window. Their descriptions follow:

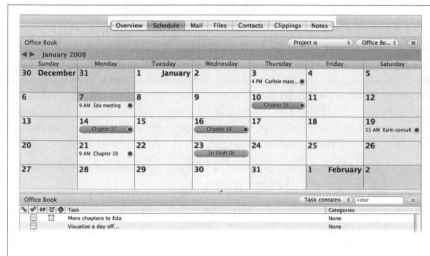

Figure 11-25:
Each of the tabs in the Project Center, like the Schedule tab shown here, gives you a window specially tailored for working on a particular aspect of your project. If you've used Entourage before, parts of the Project Center will look familiar. The Schedule tab, for example, borrows heavily from Entourage's Calendar view. The beauty of the Project Center is the way it combines Entourage's disparate features into compact views. In addition to Calendar events, the Schedule tab lets you access tasks related to the same project.

Overview

The Overview tab provides the overall project information. This is the Project Center window Entourage shows you first, and where you'll want to go to get a general grasp of the status of your project. It's extremely useful, for example, if you've been working on a different project for a while and want to get reacquainted with this one. From the Overview display you can access the disparate elements of your project.

- **Calendar.** A seven-day calendar runs across the top of the Overview display. Click the arrows on either end of it to page through previous or subsequent weeks. The calendar shows events and tasks that you've set for the project. It's a great way to double-check what you really should be working on this week. To add any event, Control-click (or right-click) any day and choose New Calendar Event. Menu surfers can click the New menu button and choose Calendar Event from the pop-up menu.

Tip: Keep the names for your calendar events short, like *Dinner-Hal's.* Doing so lets the entire event header display on the calendar. (Of course, pausing your cursor over long-winded calendar events also displays their entire subject.)

- **Task.** Below the seven-day calendar resides a Task pane. Double-click a task to see more details or edit it. You can organize the tasks by any of the columns by clicking on the column header. More often than not, you'll organize them by date (unless you have a boss who likes you to turn in your assignments in alphabetical order).

  Three columns line up to the left of the task's name: Status, Priority, and Shared. When you complete a task—or are just tired of messing with it—place a check in the box in the Status column. The Shared column denotes a task's shared status (page 487). To the right of the task you'll find columns for Categories, Priority, and Due Date. You can Control-click (or right-click) a task's subject and set its priority in the pop-up menu (page 464). Or, if you prefer, double-click the task to open its window where you can change any of its attributes.

  The Task and Shared columns always appear in this panel; turn the other columns on or off using the View → Columns menu.

- **Recent Items and Files.** Listed below the task list are two columns-worth of stuff that you've recently worked with. What kind of stuff? That's up to you: Click the title bar in either column to choose what you'd like to display. Items include Recent Items, Due this Week, Past Due, New & Recent Mail, Important Contacts, Microsoft Messenger Contacts, Recent Notes, and Recent Files. You can also choose a category to see all the items covered by it.

At the bottom of the Overview window are five buttons that control what you can do with the project.

- **Share.** Organizing an endeavor—like co-authoring that cookbook with your sisters—as a project is a fantastic idea. But an even better one is to share the work with them. You can do that by *sharing* your project, and this button is the key that unlocks the sharing door. Sharing files and projects allows several people to share all the files and project information. Entourage creates a shared folder on a local file server, WebDAV server, or an iDisk, and moves any shared files to that shared folder. Shared files are accessible only when you're connected to the file server.

  When you're working in a shared project, you need permission to access both the shared project file and the location where it's stored. Not all files can be shared, but notes most certainly can. For more details see page 487. You'll find this Share button at the bottom of each view in the Project Center.

- **Backup.** Afraid that lightning might strike or that someone *will* actually invent a virus that wipes your Mac's hard drive? If so, you've probably got a system-wide backup plan already in place. But, an extra copy of an important project never hurts, so this button lets you back up your project and all its pertinent files. Click the Backup button to open a dialog box where you can create an Entourage archive file (see page 422), saving it to, for example, an external hard drive.

- **Properties.** Click the Properties button to access the Project Properties dialog box—looking very much like the Project Center Wizard—as shown in Figure 11-26. Think of this as a mini-overview, one from which you can massage your project, as discussed in the box on page 483.

- **Add.** Click the Add menu button to add anything from a task to an email to the current project. Simply choose what type of Entourage item you wish to add, scroll to it in the list box that appears, and click Add. You'll find this button at the bottom of each view in the Project Center.

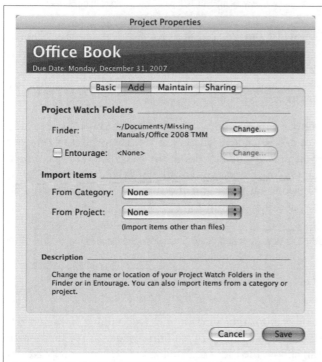

Figure 11-26:
Use the Project Properties window's four tabs to add to or modify any of your project's settings—such as, assigning a different watch folder or importing items from a related project.

Note: When using this method to add tasks, contacts, messages, or notes, you can click a column header in the list box to sort the items you're adding by that column.

- **Remove.** Highlight the item that you wish to remove, and then click the Remove button to do so. You'll find this button at the bottom of each view in the Project Center.

Schedule

The Schedule tab displays just about what you would imagine—a schedule of events and tasks related to your topic. From here you can look at what you need to do, and see how soon it needs to be done. The Schedule tab displays the following bevy of information:

- **Calendar.** The calendar displays Day, Work Week, Week, or Month. You may also jump to any date that you wish—your last day before retirement, for example—by clicking the View Date button and filling in the information.

  Left and Right arrow buttons above the calendar let you scroll back and forth one day, work week, week, or month—depending on your current view.

Note: If the Quick Filter bar is showing (View → Show Quick Filter), you can use it to filter your calendar's contents by, for example, changing the "Project is" menu to a different one of your projects. Be aware, though, that if you change that pop-up menu to "Category is" or "Subject contains," Entourage displays those items for *all* the projects, not just the one you're working with. Not particularly helpful in most cases.

- **Tasks.** The tasks pane provides a list of tasks associated with the project. Double-click any of the tasks to open it. The task will open in the familiar Entourage task window. The task list also has columns indicating special attributes of each task, including Links (a link appears if the Task includes links), Status, Priority, whether the task is recurring, Reminder, and Shared.

  The **Tasks Quick Filter bar** pop-up menu lets you filter the tasks by their allegiance to a project or category. Choose whether to filter by project or category, and then in the adjacent pop-up menu, choose the category or project you're interested in. (You can add or remove any of the status columns to the left of the task title by right-clicking on them and choosing from the pop-up menu, depending on your level of clutter-tolerance.)

Note: At the bottom of the Schedule view are four buttons: Share, New, Add, and Remove. They do the same things as the buttons at the bottom of the Overview tab.

Mail

Clicking the Mail tab displays all of the email messages pertaining to the current project in the folder list. Click the Arrange By column header to see the pop-up menu from which you can choose the order to display the messages; click "Newest on top" to alter the chronological order that the messages are displayed. Most of the choices on the "Arrange That" pop-up menu are familiar, but Show in Groups (see the box on page 375) and Edit Custom Arrangements (see the box on page 390) are unique to Entourage's approach to organizing email.

Working with these messages is much like working with messages in Entourage's email mode: If you double-click a message in the mail list, Entourage opens it in a garden-variety message window; single-click a message, and it appears in the preview pane.

Project Properties at a Glance

A very close relative of the New Project Wizard, the Project Properties box can modify basic project parameters, add folders and items, and much more. Four tabs divide the box: Basic, Add, Maintain, and Sharing.

- **Basic.** The Basic tab lets you rename the project (in case, perhaps, your boss doesn't like the name you chose). You can also select a new due date by either typing it into the window or choosing it from the mini-calendar adjacent to the window. (If your project looks like it will go on forever, you can remove the checkmark beside the due date). The Notes to Self field is the place for quick jottings. (When displaying the Project Palette in other Office programs such as Word, you can type the notes right into the Notes to Self field—a convenient way to type short reminders or fleeting flashes of brilliance.)

- **Add.** In this section, you can choose what folders to associate with the project, if they've changed since you first set up the project. Files in these folders show up in the list of recently used files on the Overview page and under the Files tab in the Project Center. You can change the location of this folder by

clicking on the Change button and browsing to your new folder location. To associate an Entourage email folder (and all the messages that you place in it) with your project, place a checkmark beside Entourage, and then select the folder by clicking Change and browsing to the location. Import items from other categories and projects by choosing them in the Import items section.

- **Maintain.** In addition to associating email messages from a particular folder, you can also associate mail from specific contacts, and with particular subjects. Using the same techniques as when setting up your project (see page 475), tell Entourage which email messages to bring into the project now or edit your original rules.

- **Sharing.** At first it looked like you could whip this baby out all by yourself—but then reality sets in and you need to call in some help. If you didn't share your project when you first created it (page 486), you can do so now from the Project Properties box.

Feel free to adjust the relative size of the panels in this Mail view. To do so, pass your mouse over the center of the splitter bar. When the curser changes to a double-sided arrow, click and drag the bar. Choose View → Columns or Control-click (right-click) anywhere in the column headers to see the full list of available columns.

Tip: You can also right-click any message in the message list, and choose from a myriad of message options, including Reply, Forward, Redirect, and so on.

At the bottom of the Mail tab are four buttons. Share, Add, and Remove are the same buttons as the ones at the bottom of the Overview tab (page 479). The fourth one, New, as you'd expect starts a new email message.

Files

Clicking the Files tab displays a list of files associated with your project. Specifically, these are the files stored in the folder and location you designated when you birthed your project. You can change the location of this folder by returning to the Overview tab, clicking the Properties button at the bottom of the window, and

---

selecting the Add tab in the Project Properties dialog box. Under Project Watch Folders, click Change, and then browse to the folder you wish to include. Highlight the folder and click Open.

Tip: You can see where these files are located without opening the Project Properties box. The secret: Add a Path column to the Files list. Simply right-click any of the column headers and choose Path. The newborn column is undoubtedly too narrow to display the entire path, but place your cursor over one of the column header divider lines, and drag the column header wider until you see the whole thing. The other secret: You can use this trick to customize the columns in any of the Project Center's tabs.

You can open any of the files or folders in the Files window just as you would in any Finder window. Perhaps you want to send one of your project files to a friend. Well, you can do that too, as shown in Figure 11-27.

At the bottom of the Files tab are four buttons, which operate much like the ones on the Overview tab (page 480), but with the following twists:

- **Share.** Click here if you wish to share this project or the highlighted file. Not all files can be shared, but most can; see the Warning below.

Warning: Sharing a file *moves* it from its original location to the project's watch folder. If you're used to accessing it from somewhere else, like your Documents folder, place an alias of the file in the Documents folder (or wherever). (In the Finder, open the project's watch folder, click the file and press ⌘-L. Then drag the alias anywhere you like.) This way, you can share the document as part of your project and still have a convenient way to access it.

- **Send.** Send a file to a friend, as described in Figure 11-27.

- **Add.** If you've previously written a file that you wish to add to the project, you can click the Add button. The Add File window appears. Click the file you wish to add, and then click Open.

- **Remove.** Select a file in the window and click the Remove button to remove it. This doesn't delete the file, just disassociates it from the project.

Contacts

The Contacts tab displays a list of Entourage Address Book items that you've associated with the current project. Highlight a contact in the top pane to display a detailed view of the contact's information in the bottom pane. You can also right-click a contact in the top pane to send the person an email, assign the contact to another project or category, copy or delete the contact, or print the contact information.

If you're looking for one particular contact, you can search the list using the Quick Filter bar at the top of the window. For example, if you know the company a salesperson works for, but can't remember his name, you can narrow the search to "Company contains." Just type in the first three or four letters of the company—say "Micr" for Microsoft—and you're off to the searching races.

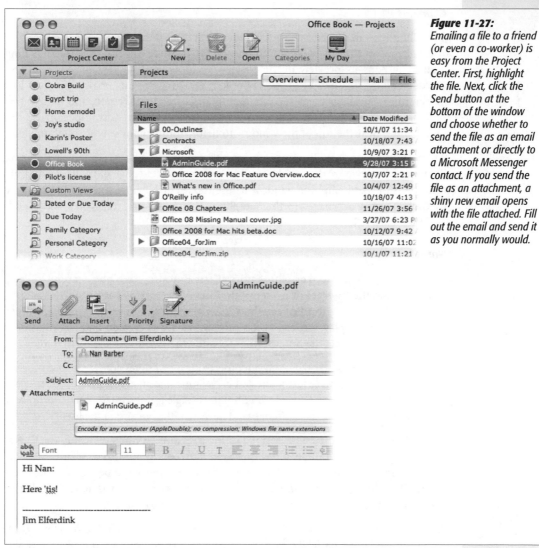

Figure 11-27:
Emailing a file to a friend (or even a co-worker) is easy from the Project Center. First, highlight the file. Next, click the Send button at the bottom of the window and choose whether to send the file as an email attachment or directly to a Microsoft Messenger contact. If you send the file as an attachment, a shiny new email opens with the file attached. Fill out the email and send it as you normally would.

At the bottom of the Contact tab are five buttons. Share, Add, and Remove work much like the ones in the Overview panel (page 480), except that Add takes you straight to a list of everyone in your Entourage Address Book. New opens Entourage's standard untitled contact window, and the Messenger button is a quick way to launch the Microsoft Messenger program that Office 2008 installed on your Mac. From here, you can sign into an existing Windows Live account or start a new one. If any of your project contacts are also on Messenger, you can communicate with them this way.

Clippings

The Clippings tab displays all the *clippings* (that is, chunks of text and graphics that you've saved in the Office Scrapbook) associated with the current project. Clicking a clipping pops its preview in the preview window, and its keywords in the keywords window, just like in the Scrapbook (page 727). If your project involves lots of clippings—perhaps a catalog containing lots of pictures, logos, and paragraphs of boilerplate text—you'll be grateful for those keywords, and you can use the Quick Filter near the top of the window to help winnow your way through the list.

At the bottom of the Clippings tab are three buttons: Share, Add, and Remove. Share and Remove work just like in the Overview panel (page 480). The Add button opens the Add Clipping window listing those clippings you've created recently by dragging text or images to the Scrapbook. Click the one that you wish to add, and then click Add.

Notes

Perhaps you're a note-taker who enjoys using Entourage's Notes feature to copy research from the Internet or jot reminders to yourself. If you assign those notes to a project (by clicking the Projects button in the Notes window), you'll see them listed here. The display lists the note's title, when it was created and last modified, categories and projects the note belongs to, and whether it's linked or shared.

As in other Project Center tabs, you can order your list of notes according to any of the column headings. If you're just interested in the most recent additions to your trove of notes, click the Date Modified column until its triangle points down. Your most recent note is listed first, and all the stuff that's old news is at the bottom of the list.

You can search the notes, as described in the previous sections, by using the Quick Filter bar to narrow your search. Your three narrowing options are Title is, Category is, and Project is. If you select Title is, you have to then type all (or a portion) of the title you're looking for. Choosing Category is or Project is activates a list of categories and projects. Choose the one that you want to sort by.

At the bottom of the Note tab are four now-familiar buttons: Share, New, Add, and Remove. They basically work the same as the buttons in the Overview tab (page 480), except that New now lets you create a new note, and Share lets you share either the entire project or just the selected note.

Sharing

Your mother told you it was good to share, and of course she's right. Sharing projects places the project—or pieces of the project—on a common server that all project members can access. That can be anything from a personal workstation to a corporate file server. Sharing makes collaboration easier than ever. For example, if you're performing an aerodynamic and structural analysis of adding a bathroom to a passenger jet, you might have people providing input from throughout your large design and production plant. Sharing the project lets all the people involved contribute and view files, and browse the schedule—to name but a few of the advantages.

Sharing a project

To share a project, do the following:

1. **Open the Project Center by clicking on its button on the Entourage window. Once there, select the project you want to share from the folder list.**

2. **Click the Share button near the bottom of the window, and then choose Start Sharing Project.**

   Entourage launches the Project Sharing Assistant, which begins with an information screen. After reading this brief introduction to sharing, click the right arrow to move to the next screen.

3. **Pick the name of the project you want to share.**

   The pop-up menu on this screen lists all the projects that aren't shared yet.

   Now it's time to choose a location to store your shared project data. Click the right arrow to move on.

4. **Click Choose, and then browse to a folder to store the shared project.**

   You can choose an Appleshare file server, an HTTP DAV server, or an iDisk. Note that you may also save the data on your own Mac, if you're so inclined and your project buddies have access to it. Click the right arrow when done.

5. **Choose whether to store current project data or begin storing from this point on.**

   More often than not, it's the best idea to store current project data, so that everyone working on the project has the same information. Be aware, however, that if you do decide to share, Entourage immediately *moves* your files to the shared server. You may want to make yourself a backup copy first. Again, click the right arrow when you're finished.

6. **Choose whether to share new items as they're added.**

   If you choose No, you give yourself a chance to decide later whether you want to share a certain new document or note that you add to the project. If you choose Yes, anything you add to the project gets shared immediately.

Note: You can decide to share or stop sharing any project item at any time. Just click the Share button at the bottom of most Project Center panels and choose Share Item or Do Not Share Item.

---

7. **Click the right arrow one last time.**

   Entourage shows you a summary screen, explaining where the project is located, and providing a couple of tips. For instance, you can identify shared items by the yellow diamond icon, and adjust your sharing policies later in Project Properties (page 481). Click Close when you're done reading.

Tip: Some items are unsharable. For example, you can't share Address Book groups, email messages, notes containing multimedia elements, or Scrapbook Clippings.

Sharing the shared project

Of course, what's the point of a shared project that isn't shared? And to share the project, you're going to need to tell folks about it. Well, you could walk across the hall or pick up the phone and tell your fellow workers, but wouldn't an email be better? Here's how to notify potential new members by email.

1. **In the Project Center, select a shared project.**

2. **On the Overview tab, click the Share button at the bottom of the window, and then select "Invite people to join project."**

3. **Click "Create E-Mail Invitation."**

   A minty-fresh email swims onto your monitor, with your invitation written in the body and a link to click in order to join the shared project.

4. **Now just address and send it…and you're done. Now doesn't sharing feel good?**

Tip: If you save your shared project to a shared folder on your computer, you won't be able to send email invitations to others. They'll have to subscribe to the project manually by selecting Subscribe to a Project on the File menu.

Accessing Projects from Other Office Programs

Entourage is the place to set up your projects, but it's not the only Office program that can access and modify projects. You can view your projects from Word, Excel, and PowerPoint as well. Here are the ways:

- **Project Gallery.** You can access projects from the Project Gallery (which opens when you launch Word, Excel, or PowerPoint). Click the Project Center tab, select your project and click Open. You can also double-click any of the project files displayed in the Projects Gallery, or select the file and then click Open. If the Project Gallery isn't visible, choose File → Project Gallery.

- **View menu.** Choosing View → Project Palette in Word, Excel, and PowerPoint opens the Toolbox's Project Palette. Click the arrow next to the currently displayed project to view a pop-up menu with a list of all your projects. Click the project that you wish to display.

- **Toolbox.** Click the Toolbox icon on the Standard Toolbar in Word, Excel, and PowerPoint to open the Toolbox, and then click the briefcase icon to display the Project Palette (Figure 11-28). You can get a quick overview from this panel; or, for full detail, click the Go to Project Center button at the panel's bottom.

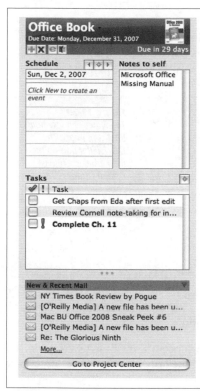

Figure 11-28:
You can also open the Project Center from other programs in Office 2008. To do so just click View → Project Palette, or, if the Toolbox is open, click the briefcase button at its upper right. This panel provides a capsule view of the items in your project that you're most likely to need at your fingertips, like today's schedule, currently due tasks, and recent email messages. (For more detail, see page 729.) The Project Palette shows only one project at a time; choose from the pop-up menu at the top to choose among them. Here, the project is called "Office Book." Clicking the Go to Project Center button at the bottom of the Project Palette opens the main Project Center window shown in Figure 11-24.

Notes

The oft-ignored Notes can store any random thought and odd thing that you want to copy and paste or write down. You can attach a note to any other Entourage element, making it ideal for tasks like these:

- Typing the driving directions to an event you've added to your calendar.

- Adding a record of a follow-up phone call you had with a contact to an email message.

- Adding phone-call details, physical descriptions, or Web site addresses to somebody's card in your Address Book.

- Creating miscellaneous notes you might otherwise write on a piece of paper, for example, a birthday gift idea that pops into your head, a scrap of info you discover while Web browsing, a packing list for taking your presentation on the road, or the name of a new CD you hear on the radio.

Notes View

To put Entourage into Notes view, click the Notes button in the upper left of the Entourage main window, or choose View → Go To → Notes (⌘-4). The right side of the Entourage main window fills with your notes, as shown in Figure 11-29.

Figure 11-29:
The Notes window holds the list of notes. The Quick Filter pop-up menu item labeled "Title is" actually means "Title contains." It helps you filter your thousands of memos down to a more manageable few.

Creating Notes

To create a new note once you're viewing the Notes list, click the New button or press ⌘-N. (If you're not already in Notes view, choose File → New → Note, or choose Note from the New button's pop-up menu.)

An Untitled note window like the one shown in Figure 11-30 appears. Give the note a title, press Tab, and then type the body of the note into the lower, larger box (driving directions, an order number, or whatever).

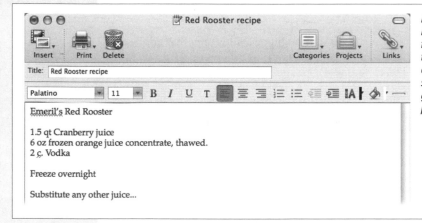

Figure 11-30:
Notes provide a resting place for all of those random facts that should be attached to other Entourage items, or simply miscellaneous goodies that you want to preserve

As you go, don't miss the formatting toolbar that lets you add colors, fonts, and other visual spice to a note. These formatting controls have the same HTML capabilities as email messages, meaning you can paste a formatted note into an email message when you need to share one of your notes. You can also paste—or drag—formatted text from another program (say, a Word document) into a note where the text retains much of its formatting. Notes can also contain URLs, pictures, sounds, movies, background images, and so on—giving Entourage Notes a clear advantage over the kind you scrawl on your scratchpad. Although Notes are mostly intended to help organize small bits of text and information, they can grow quite large, holding hundreds of kilobytes of text if necessary.

Once you've typed your note (or pasted text into it), just close the window. Your note's title now shows up in the Notes list (if you don't see it, make sure you're in the Notes view by clicking the Notes button or pressing ⌘-4). Now that you've got yourself a note, here are some of the cool things you can do with it:

- Link it to another Entourage element like an appointment or contact (page 467).

- Give it a Category (page 473), so you can keep all your family-related notes together, for example. (Control-click [or right-click] the note in the list and choose from the Category submenu.)

- Assign it to a Project. Control-click (or right-click) the note and choose from the Projects submenu. This way, every time you open the Project Center or Project Palette, all your notes taken-on-the-fly that relate to that project will be in one place, along with email and everything else you need for that project.

To delete a note, highlight its name in the list and then press Delete (or click the Delete button in the toolbar, or choose Edit → Delete Note, or press ⌘-delete).

Tip: Notes love to link up with other Entourage elements (calendar appointments, for example). Don't miss the discussion of Links that begins on page 467.

Printing Notes

To print a note, Control-click (or right-click) a note in the list and choose Print from the pop-up menu, choose File → Print, or click the Print button in the toolbar of an open note. Entourage displays Notes' Print window, where you can choose to print all notes or just the selected ones. You can also specify how those notes are laid out (cut lines, page numbers, and so on) and whether any pictures in your notes get printed. Finally, you can select whether the notes should be printed in a format that works with planners like FranklinCovey or Day-Timer, or even add your own form to that list with a click of the Add button.

Synchronization

For those who believe that organization is the key to life—those who believe that if they can just get all those meetings, reports, and schedules into one all-encompassing database that life will suddenly become a bowl of cherries—Entourage offers hope. By synchronizing with your Palm, Blackberry, cell phone, or iPod, you can take part of your Entourage database with you when you're forced to stray from the comfort of your computer. If you actually enjoy being away from computing devices no matter how pocketable, there's always paper, pencils, and that Day-Timer that's been keeping you on track since the 70s. But at least consider the possibilities Entourage offers. One of the most exciting aspects of Entourage is its ability to synchronize the information in its Calendar, Address Book, Notes, and Tasks with your handheld so that you can carry the Mac-based details of your life around in your pocket. Every time you make a change to this information, either on the handheld or Mac, the next synchronization session updates both machines so that they contain the identical information.

In Mac OS X version 10.4.3, Apple debuted *Sync Services*, a centralized synchronization scheme that lets your Entourage calendar and Address Book, Apple Address Book, iCal, as well as your .Mac account (if you have one) and your cell phone, iPod, or Palm all synchronize to a single unified database. This master Sync Services database—which actually bears the somewhat Orwellian official name of *Truth database*—resides on your hard drive (in the Home → Library → Application Support → SyncServices folder, if you must know). The *Sync Engine* handles the exchange of data between this master database and Entourage, iCal, your iPod, and your cell phone, for example.

Anytime you create, remove, or modify an item on any program tethered to Sync Services, those changes get recorded in the Truth database. The next time one of the other programs checks in with the Truth, it makes matching changes to its own database. Since all the programs and devices are utilizing the same master database, compatible data displayed in the Entourage Address Book, your cell phone, and your Palm will always match (assuming you sync your external devices regularly).

In addition, since Sync Services can also synchronize with a .Mac account, you can keep data on multiple computers—and their synced devices—synchronized via .Mac over the Internet.

Note: Not all cell phones can communicate with Sync Services. See *www.apple.com/macosx/features/isync/index.html* for the master list of iSync Supported Devices. Palm Tungsten and Zire families of PDAs work fine, but to sync other Palm OS PDAs, Blackberries, and Pocket PCs, you may need to purchase third-party software such as The Missing Sync from *www.markspace.com*.

Setting Up Entourage Synchronization

The first step in the process is to configure Entourage to share information with Sync Services' Truth Database.

Choose Entourage → Preferences → General Preferences → Sync Services and turn on any or all of the checkboxes for synchronizing contacts, events, and notes (see Figure 11-31, top) if you're connected to a Exchange Server you'll see pop-up menus under the contacts and events items which allow you to choose to use the address book or calendar files on your computer, or the ones on the Exchange server. When you make your choices and click OK, the Synchronization Options window appears (Figure 11-31, bottom) and asks you an extremely important question: "How do you want to synchronize the information that you selected?" In other words, since you're about to synchronize Entourage's database with Sync Services' Truth Database, which data set do you want to keep?

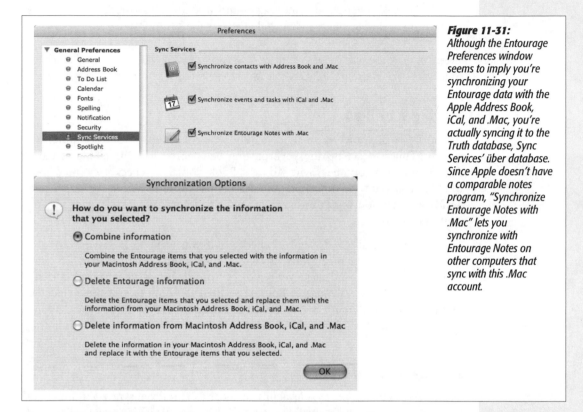

Figure 11-31:
Although the Entourage Preferences window seems to imply you're synchronizing your Entourage data with the Apple Address Book, iCal, and .Mac, you're actually syncing it to the Truth database, Sync Services' über database. Since Apple doesn't have a comparable notes program, "Synchronize Entourage Notes with .Mac" lets you synchronize with Entourage Notes on other computers that sync with this .Mac account.

Entourage gives three scenarios for synchronizing with Sync Services:

- **Combine information.** This safest choice merges your Entourage data with the Sync Services Truth Database and nothing gets deleted. Choosing this option will likely require you to later sort through your data to remove duplicates or unwanted items. (But since you've established synchronization, all those future changes get applied to the Truth database, and therefore to all your synced programs and devices.)

- **Delete Entourage information.** This option deletes everything in Entourage, replacing it with the data from Sync Services' Truth. You'd want to choose this if you haven't used Entourage much and have a more accurate list of contacts on your cell phone or in the Apple Address Book, for example.

- **Delete information from Macintosh Address Book, iCal, and .Mac.** Use this option if your Entourage database contains "the truth," as far as you're concerned. The Sync Services Truth Database gets wiped clean and refilled with your Entourage data. You might choose this option if Entourage's Address Book and Calendar are the only ones you ever consult—and you don't know or care what information may be lurking in your cell phone, iCal, and so on.

Once configured, Sync Services works automatically, updating its Truth Database when you make changes in Entourage—and updating Entourage when another application or device makes a change that affects the Truth Database.

Note: Entourage categories don't transfer to the Apple Address Book or iCal. However, they are recorded in the Sync Services database and do come through when you sync another copy of Entourage via .Mac.

Syncing Your iPod

If your PDA of choice is an iPod or iPhone, connect it to your computer and launch iTunes to set up its synchronizing behavior. Click the Contacts tab in iTunes and turn on the "Sync Address Book contacts" checkbox, and choose whether you want to import all contacts or just those in selected groups. Then decide whether you want to use any of your precious iPod storage space for your contacts' photos.

Turn on the "Sync iCal Calendar" checkbox if you want to keep your appointments in your little music box as well. Either select "All calendars" or click "Selected calendars" and make your choices from its list of calendar categories. If you only keep your calendar in Entourage, then the only one of these calendars that makes any difference is the one labeled Entourage. The other calendars may contain dates from iCal but all your Entourage events end up in iCal's Entourage calendar.

Syncing with .Mac

One of .Mac's best features is its ability to act as a centralized sync point for multiple computers. (Learn about all the rest of its features by visiting *www.mac.com*.) If you have, for example, an office computer, a home computer, and a laptop or two, you can easily set them all up to check in over the Internet with .Mac, keeping your Entourage Calendars, Address Book, and Notes synchronized on any, or all, of those machines. To do so, you need to turn on .Mac syncing on each computer. Open → System Preferences → .Mac, click the Account tab, and enter your .Mac member name and password. If you don't have a subscription, click the Learn More button to sign up for one—with a free 60-day trial.

Click the Sync tab and turn on the checkbox labeled "Synchronize with .Mac" and set its pop-up menu to your desired synchronization frequency—Automatically is a good choice if you have an "always-on" Internet connection (see Figure 11-32). Then turn on the checkboxes for the various items you're interested in synchronizing: Calendars, Contacts, and Entourage Notes—as well as, perhaps, Bookmarks or Keychains.

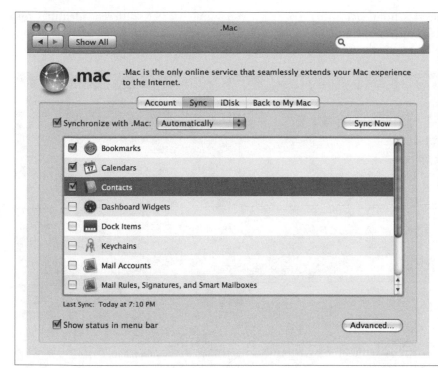

Figure 11-32:
The Sync tab of the .Mac preferences window lets you choose when and what to synchronize with your online .Mac account. Click the Advanced button to view a list of all the computers that are set to synchronize with this .Mac account, and when they last synchronized.

Multiple Identities

If you start singing the praises of multiple identities to your psychotherapist, you'll definitely get her to sit up and take notice—and probably not in a good way. But make the same comments among a group of Microsoft Office power users and, if you get any response at all, it will come in the form of a knowing nod or an agreeing grunt. When Microsoft refers to multiple identities it's talking about an Entourage feature that lets several members of a family, school, or work circle use the same program on the same Mac—but maintain independent calendars, email accounts, mailing list info, rules, messages, preferences, signatures, to do lists, address books, and so on.

You'll find reference to these *identities* throughout the Office 2008 suite. For example, the currently selected Entourage identity is the source of names for the AutoText feature in Word, as described on page 78. (That's also why you can't edit or switch identities while Word, Excel, or PowerPoint are open. They depend on the currently active Entourage identity for some of this information.)

To some extent Mac OS X makes the identities feature obsolete. After all, it's typical now for everyone who shares a Mac OS X machine to sign in with a name and password—and therefore each person's mail, calendar, and other information is *already* separate. Still, there's nothing to stop you from using Identities on Macs configured with but one user account (because it's just you and a spouse, say, with no secrets from each other), or when you want to create different identities for *yourself* (a Work and a Home collection of email, for example). For more detail on handling multiple users and identities, see the box below.

Identities vs. Multiple Users in Mac OS X

Identities are for convenience, not security—that is, they're not guarded by passwords. Anyone sitting in front of your Mac can switch among your Entourage identities at will, read your email, modify or delete your contacts, calendar items, or even delete your identity altogether.

To protect your data with a password, you should set up individual accounts for each person who uses your Mac, instead of using Entourage identities. At its core, Mac OS X is a multiuser operating system, and each account holder has his own desktop, Documents folder, programs, bookmarks, music and picture collections, and more—all of which can be protected from other people who use the same machine. You set up user accounts in the → System Preferences → Accounts panel. See the Mac OS X Help menu for more details.

If you've already set up identities in Entourage before you've created Mac OS X user accounts, more work is involved to move one of those identities into your newly created user account. Each identity that you've created is represented by its own folder in the Home → Documents → Microsoft User Data → Office 2008 Identities folder of whoever first set up Mac OS X.

To straighten out your folder setup, you can move the identities to other Mac OS X users. First, log in as the Mac OS X user who has the Entourage identities you want to move. Find the appropriate identity folders within your Office 2008 Identities folder, and then drag (or copy) them to your Home → Public folder.

Next, log in from your new account. Then navigate to your Public folder and copy the appropriate identity folders to this new account. The next time each of these Mac OS X users opens Entourage, the copied identity will be in place, revealing only that person's email, calendar, and so on.

Creating a New Identity

When you first set up Entourage, you get a single identity. (Of course, you can have multiple email *accounts* within that identity.) To create a *new* identity, proceed like so:

1. **Quit all Microsoft Office programs except Entourage. In Entourage, choose Entourage → Switch Identity (Option-⌘-Q).**

   (Just be careful not to hit *Shift*-⌘-Q, which logs you off your Mac!)

   Entourage asks you if you really want to switch identities.

2. **Click Switch.**

   The identity management window opens (Figure 11-33). In this window, you can create, rename, or delete a selected identity (or quit Entourage). Be careful before you delete an identity. Once an identity's gone, you can't retrieve any of its information.

Tip: If you turn on "Show this list when opening Entourage," Entourage gives you a tidy list of identities each time you start up the program, making it easy to specify which identity to use for that session.

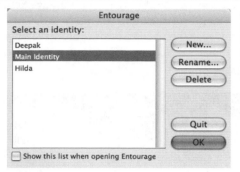

Figure 11-33:
Any identities that you create in Entourage show up in this window. Use the three buttons along the right-hand side to create a new one, change a name, or delete an identity you've outgrown. When you delete an identity you delete all of its Entourage data: messages, calendar, address book, and so on.

3. **Click New.**

   The small New Identity window pops up.

4. **Type a name for your new identity.**

   Choose a descriptive name for the new identity.

5. **Follow the Entourage Setup Assistant.**

   Once you've chosen a name for your new identity, Entourage asks you if you want it to be your default email program. Your reply here actually changes a system-wide setting in Mac OS X, so this choice will apply to *all* your Entourage identities.

POWER USERS' CLINIC

Take Your Entourage on the Road

If it's time for a trip and you have to leave your main computer at home, consider packing your Entourage identity along with you. Locate your identity in your Home → Documents → Microsoft User Data → Office 2008 Identities folder and copy it to the same folder on your laptop, where you can fire up Entourage and experience the comfort of your entire Entourage world—email, calendar, and address book, To Do list—just as you left it at home.

If you're traveling without portfolio—or without laptop—just copy the identity to a USB flash drive. When you reach your destination, transfer it to another Mac running Office 2008 and enjoy your familiar Entourage surroundings no matter how far from home you find yourself. When it's time to head home copy your identity back to the USB drive for the journey.

While you're enjoying this home-away-from-computer-home lifestyle, you'll be able to *receive* all your email without a problem. Depending on your SMTP, or outgoing, email server you may or may not be able to *send* mail without making some adjustments to your account setup. If you use .Mac or Gmail for sending mail, you won't have any problem. And, as all savvy travelers know, there's always Web mail.

When you find yourself safe and sound back home once again, transfer the identity one more time back to your main computer, where it replaces the old version of itself in the Office 2008 Identities folder and continues handling your email, calendar, and contacts without you ever having experienced an anxiety-filled day of separation from your Entourage life.

After you choose Yes or No, Entourage walks you through the Entourage Setup Assistant to create your new identity—a process identical to what you did when you first set up Entourage (see page 354). When you're done, Entourage opens its main window, displaying that familiar "Welcome to Entourage 2008" mail message in your new Inbox.

UP TO SPEED

A Quick Filter Find

Entourage's Search is a simple tool to use, but for even quicker searches use the Quick Filter. Located in the upper right of the Entourage window, this straightforward find function lets you rapidly search, for example, the email folder you're currently working in (see Figure 11-34). If you don't see it, choose View → Show Quick Filter (or Calendar → Show Quick Filter if you're in the calendar view).

To use it, first set your search criteria in the pop-up menu (or menus). Then type what you're looking for in the search box. As you type, Entourage filters the list of items, narrowing it down further the more you type. The email Quick Filter lets you search by Subject, From, To, Category is, or

Project is. Look through messages related to a specific project or category, or ask the second pop-up menu to search for matches that either contain or begin with the letters you've typed. This is a handy tool, especially if you can't remember if the message came from Mr. Brashear or Mr. Shear.

Other Entourage views (Notes, Tasks, Address Book, and Calendar) have a Quick Filter in the same place, with various pop-up menus that let you tailor your search for those kinds of items.

Figure 11-34:
Anytime you want to find something in one of Entourage's list views, resist the temptation to just start scrolling through the list. Instead, type a few letters of what you're looking for in the Quick Filter and let Entourage swiftly sift a few likely suspects from your prodigious stockpile of information.

Finding Messages

In a short time—shorter than you might think—you'll collect a lot of email messages, contacts, and other Entourage items. Trying to find a particular morsel of information just by browsing becomes impractical. ("I remember reading something about a good deal on Mac memory in some mailing-list posting just last week. Now where the heck did I file it?...")

For Office 2008, Entourage has tied into Mac OS X's Spotlight search system, making it easier to find the Entourage information you're looking for—and speeding up the process dramatically. If you find yourself searching for the same or similar thing, over and over, you can save your search and reuse it in the future with a single click.

Searching in Entourage

To conduct a basic search, just type the word or phrase you're searching for the Search field at the right end of the Entourage toolbar. When you stop typing, Entourage starts searching, displays the Search bar, and fills in the list with the items it finds (see Figure 11-35). This search examines not only the sender, recipient, and subject of emails, but also the contents of the message. The same is true for contacts, calendar, notes, and tasks: all text is fair game.

Use the buttons on The Search bar to narrow or expand your search. For example, when searching for email you can search in the current folder, all folders on your computer, all messages, or in everything—which means everything in Entourage.

Figure 11-35:
Use the omnipresent Search field in the Entourage toolbar to search for all the items containing your search term somewhere in their text. The more you type, the more Entourage whittles down your results. The Search bar provides buttons to focus on the current folder or other parts of your Entourage data repository. The Save button preserves this search so you can repeat it easily later (see page 501) while the plus-sign button switches you into the advanced search mode for a more precisely targeted search.

Double-click an item in the list to open it, click column headings to sort the list, or use any of the toolbar buttons to perform the standard Entourage maneuvers.

Refine your search by clicking the plus-sign, "Show advanced search" button near the right end of the Search bar. Two more toolbars appear beneath the Search bar. Use the pop-up menu in the lower bar to choose which field to search in. Depending on the field you choose you can make more choices from pop-up menus or fill text into the search box (see Figure 11-36). To search on more than one criterion, click the "Add search criteria" plus-sign button at the right to summon another search field. Continue adding and filling out search fields until you've specified your search formula with sufficient exactitude. Finally, use the pop-up button just above to determine whether your results match all or any of the search criteria (that's an *AND* or *OR* search for the logicians in the audience).

Figure 11-36:
After performing a basic search, click the plus-sign button at the right end of the Search bar to summon the advanced search controls. You can include multiple criteria in your search by clicking the plus-sign button to the right of each search field then set the pop-up menu at the top to match all of the criteria or any of the criteria. As you manipulate these pop-up menus and fields, Entourage searches showing the results in the list below.

By using multiple search criteria you could find, for example, a message containing the words *global warming*, sent by your friend Erica within the last 90 days. Or all the messages in your folder containing the name *Bootsy*.

Find Related Items

Entourage has another way of searching for related items—the Find Related Items command. It lets you find all email messages to or from an individual person in one fell swoop—a handy technique when there are hundreds or thousands of messages in your message list, and you're trying to find the messages that constituted a particular correspondence.

To use this feature, open your address book. Click the name of a person listed, and then choose Contact → Find Related Items. Entourage searches for any messages sent to or received from that person. The results appear in a Search Results window, which you can save as a custom view, if you like.

Links

The Link command lets you weave your own Web of connections between Entourage items. You might use it to connect, for example, someone in your address book to a specific calendar event *and* to all of the messages sent to and from that

---

POWER USERS' CLINIC

Saved Searches

After you perform a search, the results appear in a search results list. If you click the Save button in the Search bar, you save the search itself, enabling you to repeat the same search over and over without the work setting up your search criteria again.

For example, you could set up a saved search that rounds up only the messages that are less than a week old, from your mentor, with a subject line pertaining to your current project.

To save a search, perform a search, and then click the Save button in the Search bar. A Save Search window appears. Name your search ("Laughter yoga," for example) and click Save. Your search now appears with its own icon in the Mail Views folder at the bottom of the folder list.

Entourage comes with a handful of prefab Saved Search Items—such as messages received today and high priority messages. You can edit or delete saved searches by control-clicking (or right-clicking) them in the folder list and making your choice from the pop-up menu. When you edit a saved search, Entourage reopens the search bars at the top of the list window.

To perform one of your saved searches, just click its name; Entourage automatically shows the matching items on the right side of the main window, temporarily hiding all others.

---

person *regarding* that calendar event, *and* to your notes of topics to discuss with that person face-to-face.

Once you've set up such a link, you can use it to quickly open the event to which it's linked. When you've linked an item, a small link icon appears in the item's listing in Entourage's main window. To open a link, click the link icon and select a linked item from the menu that pops up (see Figure 11-37, top).

You create a link like this:

1. **Select the item that you want to create a link for.**

   For example, click an email message, click an item on your calendar, or highlight the name of one of your To Do items.

2. **Choose from the Tools → "Link to Existing" submenu to create a connection with a piece of information already in Entourage.**

Tip: You can also click in the Links column (if the Links column isn't visible, right-click the column headers and select Links) to display the Links pop-up menu. From the pop-up menu, you can surf over to linked messages or link to new or existing messages, calendar events, tasks, notes, contacts, or groups.

Now, when you choose "Link to Existing", you also have to choose what you want to link to (message, task, or whatever). After doing so, the "Link to" window opens, where you can browse to the Entourage item you want to link to, highlight it, and click the Link button as shown in Figure 11-37, bottom. Voilà! You're linked.

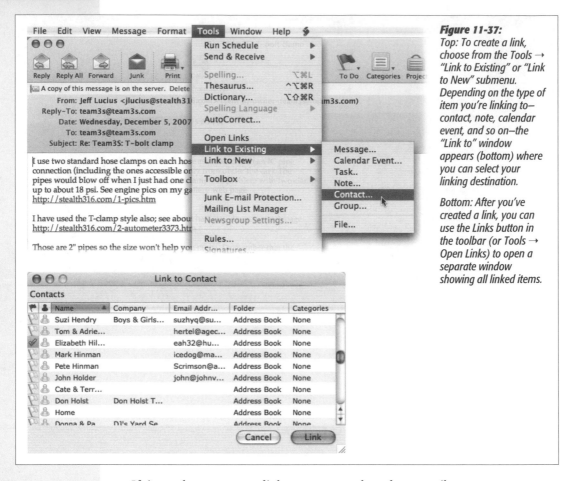

Figure 11-37:
Top: To create a link, choose from the Tools → "Link to Existing" or "Link to New" submenu. Depending on the type of item you're linking to—contact, note, calendar event, and so on—the "Link to" window appears (bottom) where you can select your linking destination.

Bottom: After you've created a link, you can use the Links button in the toolbar (or Tools → Open Links) to open a separate window showing all linked items.

If, instead, you want to link to an empty, brand new mail message, news message, calendar event, task, note, contact, or group, choose from the Tools → "Link to New" submenu. Entourage creates the corresponding tidbit (email message, calendar event, or whatever) right away and lets you fill in the details on the fly. When you save the new item, Entourage automatically forges the link. For example, if you link somebody's email message to a new note, Entourage creates a new note where you can dash off some of your immediate thoughts on the matter.

Using Links

A tiny chain-link icon appears next to linked Entourage items. In Office 2008, you can click the link icon and choose Open Links to open the Links To window. Click a linked item in the Links To window to instantly open that item.

To view the Links To window, use one of these techniques:

• Click the chain-link icon that appears next to a linked item and select Open Links.

- Open an item that displays the chain-link icon, and then use the Links button on the Entourage toolbar.

- Highlight an item showing the chain-link icon and then choose Tools → Open Links.

The "Links to" window lets you go beyond simply opening link items. Its toolbar buttons—Open, Remove, To New, or To Existing—let you open the item to which the link leads, remove a link, or create a link to new or existing items, respectively.

Checking Your Spelling

In parts of Entourage that involve lots of text (such as notes and mail messages), you can ask Entourage to check your spelling for you. If you set Entourage's preferences to check spelling as you type, it marks suspect words with a red squiggly underline. Control-click (or right-click) the underlined word and choose from the pop-up-up menu's list of spelling suggestions.

If you prefer a more traditional spell checker that operates from a window, open the note or message you want to check and choose Tools → Spelling (⌘-Option-L). Work your way through the document using the Spelling window's buttons. The procedure works like it does in Word (see Figure 11-38 and page 62), and in fact relies on the same spelling dictionaries.

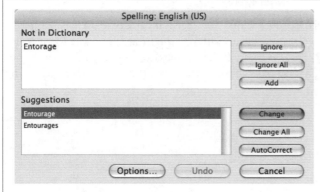

Figure 11-38:
Entourage's Spelling window flags questionable words; you click the buttons on the right to ignore, add, or correct those words. The Options button at the bottom is a direct link to the Entourage's Spelling preferences, where you can control the various spell check options.

The Script Menu

There's no more conspicuous badge indicating that Microsoft has gotten Macintosh religion than its embrace of AppleScript, the Macintosh-only programming language. As a happy result, even advanced-beginner programmers can automate the Office programs with custom features.

Entourage's impressive AppleScript capabilities begin with the Script menu that houses several AppleScript scripts, which add useful features such as the following:

- **Create Event from Message.** When you highlight an email message and choose this command, Entourage creates a new calendar event based on the message. All you have to do is fill in a few details. Even better, the event is automatically linked to the original message.

- **Create Note from Message, Create Task from Message.** These commands create Notes or Tasks linked to your message.

- **Insert Text File.** When you choose this command, Entourage opens the "Choose a File" dialog box, so that you can locate a text file to insert into the body of a message. This feature can be handy when you want to email quick, canned responses from time to time.

- **Save Selection.** Here's a great way to save some critical information that's been emailed to you into its own text file on your desktop. Highlight some text, choose Script → Save Selection, and then provide a file name and location when Entourage asks for it.

The best thing about this menu, however, is that you can add your own scripts to it. (Of course, writing such scripts requires some familiarity with programming AppleScript.) Save such scripts as compiled scripts (not text files or applets), and then drop them into your Home → Documents → Microsoft User Data folder → Entourage Script Menu Items folder. They'll show up in the Entourage Scripts menu the next time you run the program.

If you aren't an AppleScript programmer, you can still capitalize on this feature by downloading scripts other people have written. Longtime Microsoft Most Valuable Professional (MVP) Paul Berkowitz has a massive collection of Entourage scripts at *www.scriptbuilders.net* (search for Berkowitz). (See page 769 for more on scripting.)

Part Three:
Excel

3

Basic Excel

The best ad Microsoft ever ran for Excel went like this: "99% of spreadsheet users use Microsoft Excel. What are we doing wrong?" It was good because it was true; Excel is the biggest thing going when it comes to hardcore business programs. But Microsoft still seems determined to keep finding ways to make it better, stirring the hearts of accountants, statisticians, and list makers the world over.

Like the rest of its Office brethren, Excel 2008 includes a bunch of new, helpful tools: Ledger sheets are an assortment of preformatted worksheets designed to perform common tasks such as balancing a checkbook, tracking an investment portfolio, or creating an expense report. The new Formula Builder walks you through the steps needed to create these sometimes-daunting equations. If you're already an old hand with formulas, Formula AutoComplete assists you whenever you start typing a formula in the Formula Bar. Charts in Excel 2008 have also been vastly improved, with new templates and tools to provide effects like 3-D, transparency, and shadows. The Chart tab of the Elements Gallery provides easy access for previewing and inserting any of the dozens of Excel chart styles. Finally, Microsoft keeps doing its part to fuel sales of large monitors: Mac fans can now create spreadsheets with more than 16,000 columns and one million rows—achieving spreadsheet-cell parity with their PC-using counterparts.

Spreadsheet Basics

You use Excel, of course, to make a *spreadsheet*—an electronic ledger book composed of rectangles, known as *cells,* laid out in a grid (see Figure 12-1). As you type numbers into the rectangular cells, the program can automatically perform any number of calculations on them. And although the spreadsheet's forte is working with numbers, you can use them for text, too; because they're actually a specialized database, you can turn spreadsheets into schedules, calendars, wedding registries, address books, and other simple text databases.

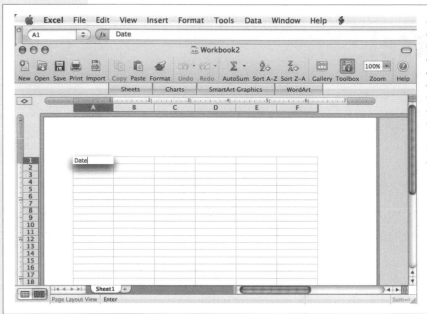

Figure 12-1:
Excel 2008 has all the usual Mac OS X doodads, like close, minimize, and zoom buttons and a status bar. In the status area at the bottom left, Excel tells you what it thinks is happening—in this case, Enter indicates the active cell (A1) is being edited.

Opening a Spreadsheet

A new Excel document, called a *workbook,* is made up of one or more pages called *worksheets.* (You'll find more on the workbook/worksheet distinction in Chapter 14.) Each worksheet is an individual spreadsheet, with lettered columns and numbered rows providing coordinates to refer to the cells in the grid.

You can create a plain-Jane Excel workbook by selecting File → New Workbook (⌘-N), or you can use the Office Project Gallery (File → Project Gallery). If you happen to find a template that fits what you're trying to do, like planning a budget, the Gallery can be a real timesaver. For even more timesavings, check out Excel 2008's new Ledger Sheets category, a collection of preformatted ledger templates for a variety of common list and financial tasks—with formulas already calculated for you. You can choose from address lists, gift lists, check registers, budgets, invoices, expense reports, portfolio trackers, and lots more.

Tip: Once you've added a Ledger Sheet, you can use it as-is or customize any part of it. Even without any spreadsheet skills, you can start filling in these preformatted sheets without having to think about cell formatting, cell references, or formulae—and still take advantage of Excel's data- and number-crunching prowess. (But you'll still find this chapter helpful when it comes time to customize a ledger sheet—or if you're interested in how it's doing what it does.)

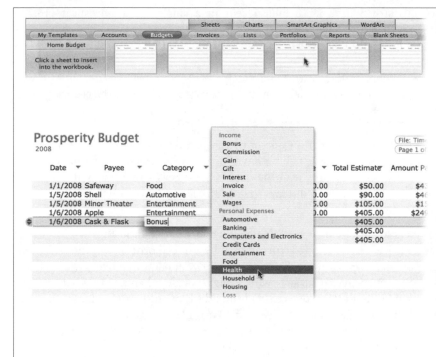

Figure 12-2:
Top: You can quickly add a ledger sheet to an Excel workbook by clicking the Elements Gallery's Sheets tab and clicking one of the Ledger Sheet category buttons. As you move your cursor over the thumbnails, the sheet title appears at the left; click a thumbnail to add the sheet to your workbook. Start typing to enter your data, and use Tab or Return to move to the next column.

Bottom: Some columns (such as Category) feature a gray triangle, click it to choose an entry from a pop-up menu. (Ledger Sheets are actually lists, which are described starting on page 541.)

Whether it stars out plain or preformatted, each worksheet can grow to huge proportions—about 16,000 columns wide (labeled A, B, C… AA, AB, AC… AAA, AAB, AAC, and so on, and on, and on), and one million rows tall (see Figure 12-3). Furthermore, you can get at even more cells by adding more worksheets to the workbook by clicking the plus-sign button next to the worksheet tabs at the bottom left or by choosing Insert → Worksheet. Switch between worksheets by clicking their tabs.

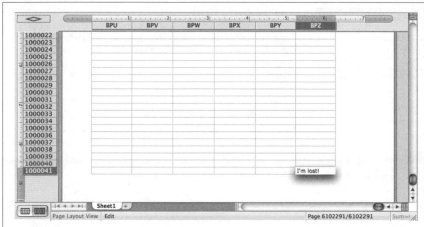

Figure 12-3:
You can't scroll all the way to cell BPZ10000041 in a new spreadsheet (well, you can, but it may take several days), but you can leap to that far-distant cell by typing BPZ10000041 in the Name box on the left side of the Formula bar and pressing Return.

In total, you can have 17.18 billion cells in a single Excel worksheet (16,384 columns × 1,048,576 rows = 17,179,869,184 cells, to be precise). The only company that needs more space than *that* for its accounting is Microsoft itself.

Tip: Newly minted worksheets always bear the name Sheet1, Sheet2, and so on. To rename a worksheet, double-click the sheet's name (it's on the tab on the bottom) and type in a new one. Sheet names can be as long as 31 characters.

Each cell acts as a container for one of two things: data or a formula. *Data* can be text, a number, a date, or just about anything else you can type. A *formula,* on the other hand, does something with the data in *other* cells—such as adding together the numbers in them—and displays the result. (There's more on formulas later in this chapter.)

Excel refers to cells by their coordinates, such as B23 (column B, row 23). A new spreadsheet has cell A1 selected (surrounded by a thick border)—it's the *active* cell. When you start typing, the cell pops up slightly, apparently hovering a quarter-inch above your screen's surface, with a slight shadow behind it. Whatever you type appears in both the active cell *and* the Edit box on the right side of the Formula bar. If you prefer, you can click in the Formula bar and do your typing there. When you finish typing, you can do any of the following to make the active cell's new contents stick:

- Press Return, Tab, Enter, or an arrow key.

- Click another cell.

- Click the Enter button in the Formula bar.

Tip: When you enter information into a cell by pasting, you may see a smart button pop up in the immediate vicinity (Figure 12-4). Clicking the button's arrow reveals a contextual menu with a number of formatting options specific to the information you're pasting and where you're pasting it.

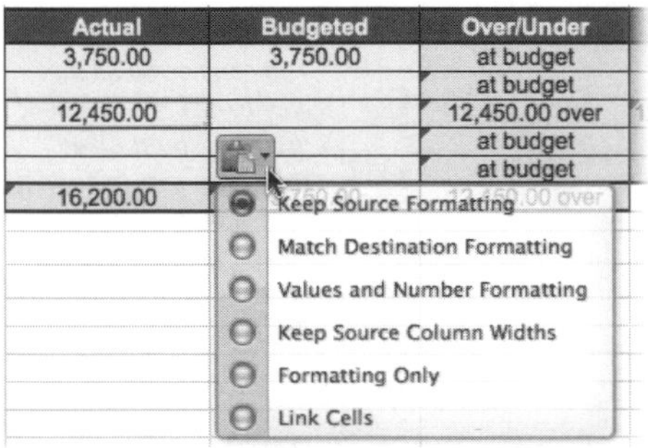

Figure 12-4:
A smart button often appears just after you paste data into a cell. Click its arrow to display a small pop-up menu from which you can choose to retain the source formatting (so that the text will retain the formatting it had in its original location or document) or match the destination formatting (in which Excel automatically adjusts the text to the formatting in the current workbook). Variations include pasting just the values and number formatting, pasting the source column width, pasting just the cell formatting, and creating a link to the source cell (see page 611). Since Excel isn't psychic, the smart button gives you a chance to tell it whether you had the old or new formatting in mind.

A View to Thrill

Page Layout view first appeared in Excel 2004 and its benefit is obvious—you can now see how your printed page will look without looking at a print preview of your work. In fact, some people work in this view from the get-go, so they can design their spreadsheet to fit on whatever size paper they'll eventually print it on. You no longer have to construct a spreadsheet, print it, and then be surprised by the results. Working in Page Layout view provides gloriously instantaneous feedback on how your numerical creation will look when it goes to hard copy. This view is so popular that Microsoft has made it the view you see when you open a new spreadsheet. On the downside, in Page Layout view, you get to see less of your creation onscreen, due to all those blank page margins (but what better excuse to invest in a new 30" monitor?).

If you'd prefer your new Excel documents to open in the traditional Normal view, visit Excel → Preferences → View and choose Normal from the "Preferred view for new sheets" pop-up menu.

To switch views while you're working on a spreadsheet, click the view button in the lower-left corner of the document window (or use the View menu to choose Normal or Page Layout). Whichever view you choose, it affects only your onscreen view—your spreadsheet prints identically.

Data Entry

Working in an Excel sheet is simple, at its heart: You enter data or a formula into a cell, move to the next cell, enter more information, and so on. But before entering data in a cell, you have to first *select* the cell. Clicking is the easiest method; after you click a cell, the cell border thickens and as soon as you start typing, the cell does that popping-up thing.

Tip: When you double-click a cell, it pops up from the spreadsheet and you find yourself again in the editing mode. If, perhaps due to an over-eager mouse-button finger, you keep landing in this "in-cell editing" mode accidentally, choose Excel → Preferences → Edit panel, turn off "Double-click allows editing directly in the cell," and click OK. Now you can only edit cell contents in the Edit box on the Formula Bar.

To select a cell far away from the current active cell, enter the cell's *address* (the column letter followed by the row number) in the Name box on the Formula bar and press Return (see Figure 12-3). Or choose Edit → Go To (or press F5), to summon a dialog box where you can enter the address of the lucky cell in the Reference field.

But the fastest means of getting from cell to cell is to use the keyboard. Excel is loaded with keyboard shortcuts that make it easy to plow through an entire sheet's worth of cells without having to touch the mouse. Here's the cheat sheet:

Keystroke	What Happens
Arrow key	Selects a different cell—the next one above, below, to the left, or to the right of the current one.

Keystroke	**What Happens**
Shift-arrow key	Selects the current cell and the one above, below, to the left, or to the right. Hold the Shift key down and press the arrow key more than once to extend the selection.
Option-left arrow, -right arrow	Makes the previous or next sheet in the workbook active.
Control-arrow key	Moves the active cell to the next non-empty cell in the direction indicated by the arrow key.
Return	Accepts the entry and moves the active cell down one row. (Unless you've changed that behavior in Excel → Preferences → Edit.)
Shift-Return	Accepts the entry and moves the active cell up one row. (Unless you've changed that behavior in Excel → Preferences → Edit.)
Tab	Accepts the entry and moves the active cell right one column (or to the first cell in the next row in a multiple-cell selection).
Shift-Tab	Accepts the entry and moves the active cell left one column.
Control-Option-Return	Starts a new line within the same cell.
Control-Return	Fills each selected cell with the same entry. (First select the cell range, type the data that you want repeated in each cell, and then hit Control-Return to fill all of the cells.)
Esc	Cancels an entry.
Delete	Deletes cell contents.
Control-D	Fills the active cell with the contents of the cell directly above it.
Control-R	Fills the active cell with the contents of the cell directly to the left of it.
Control-'	Fills the active cell with the formula in the cell directly above it, and leaves the cell in Edit mode.
Control-;	Enters the current date.
Control-Shift-:	Enters the current time (to the nearest minute).

Tip: Return doesn't have to select the next cell down; it can select any of the four neighboring cells, or do nothing at all. You change what the Return key does in the Excel → Preferences → Edit panel.

Window Tricks

Because spreadsheets can be wide, sprawling affairs, Excel is filled with window-manipulation tools that let you control how the program uses your precious screen real estate.

For example, when you need to see a few more rows and columns, choose View → Full Screen. Excel hides all of its toolbars, status bars, and other nonessential items. Your precious cells fill your monitor. Choose View → Full Screen again (or click Close Full Screen on the tiny, one-button toolbar) to bring back the bars.

Another example: As shown in Figure 12-5, Excel's scroll bars have vertical and horizontal split boxes, which you can double-click or drag to split a sheet into independently scrolling sections, as shown here. (Note the discontinuity in the lettering and numbering of rows and columns in this illustration; the result of scrolling each pane to a different part of the spreadsheet.) To remove the split, just double-click the split box or the split bar that separates the panes. (Or choose Window → Remove Split.)

You don't have to split the window if all you want to do is keep the row and column names in view while scrolling the rest of the document, however. Excel has a much more streamlined means of locking the column and row labels: Click in the cell just below and to the right of the row/column label intersection, and then choose Window → Freeze Panes. Now scrolling affects only the body of the spreadsheet; the row and column labels remain visible.

If, on the other hand, you wish you could split your spreadsheet into six or more panes in order to work on widely separated bits of data, open additional Windows by choosing Window → New Window. Open as many additional windows as you, your monitor, and your multitasking abilities require. Each window is a separate view of the same spreadsheet; make a change in one window and it affects them all.

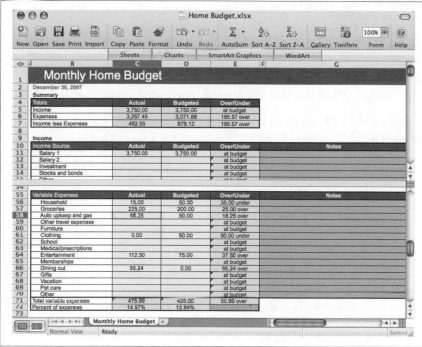

Figure 12-5:
Double-click or drag the horizontal or vertical split boxes to simultaneously view two or four parts of a large spreadsheet in one window. Double-click the bar between panes to remove the split view.

Excel is positively brimming with keyboard shortcuts—the table on page 512 is just the tip of the iceberg. For a complete list, open Excel Help and search for "Excel keyboard shortcuts." (By not including the entire list in this book, we're saving a small forest somewhere in Oregon.)

Kinds of Data

You can enter four kinds of data into an Excel spreadsheet: numbers, text, dates, or times (not including formulas, which are described beginning on page 529). Mostly, entering data is as straightforward as typing, but exceptions lurk.

Numbers

- There are only 21 characters that Excel considers numbers or parts of numbers: 1 2 3 4 5 6 7 8 9 0 . , ( ) + - / $ % e and E. Anything else is treated as text, which is ineligible for performing most calculations. For example, if Excel sees *three* in a cell, it sees a bunch of typed characters with no numerical value; when it sees *3.14,* it sees a number.

- Depending on the formatting of the cell where you're entering numbers, Excel might try to do some work for you. For example, if you've applied *currency formatting* to a cell, Excel turns *3/2* into $1.50. But if you've formatted the same cell as a Date, Time, or General, Excel turns *3/2* into a date—March 2 of the current year.

- When you've formatted a cell to accept General input, and the number you've entered is longer than 11 digits (such as *12345678901112*), Excel converts it to scientific notation (*1.23457E+13*).

- Excel's number precision is 15 significant digits—anything over 15 will be lost.

Text

- Text can be any combination of characters: numbers, letters, or other symbols.

- To make Excel look at a number as if it were a string of text (rather than a number with which it can do all kinds of mathematical wizardry), you have to either precede the number with an apostrophe or *format* the cell as a text-based cell. To format the cell, choose Text from the Format menu in the Formatting Palette's Number pane. Alternatively, select the cell and choose Format → Cells (or right-click the cell and choose Format Cells from the shortcut menu). Click the Number tab and then select Text from the Category list. Click OK.

Dates

- You can perform math on dates, just as though they were numbers. The trick is to type an equal sign (=) into the cell that will contain the answer; then enclose the dates in quotation marks and put the operator (like + or *) between them. For example, if you click a cell, type =*"12/30/2007"-"5/25/1963"*, and then press Enter, Excel fills the cell with 16290, the number of days between the two dates.

Tip: If you're trying to determine someone's age with this calculation, you probably want to write it as *=("12/30/2007" -"5/25/1963")/365* which gives a result in years: 44.63013699.

This math is made possible by the fact that dates in Excel *are* numbers. Behind the scenes, Excel converts any date you type into a special date serial number, which is composed of a number to the left side of a decimal point (the number of days since January 1, 1904) and a number on the right (the fraction of a day).

POWER USERS' CLINIC

The Beginnings of Time

The original Macintosh used a starting date of January 1, 1904—which lingers on to this day. Windows PCs, by contrast, use a starting date of January 1, 1900. Excel workbooks can now support either date system, but you may run into problems when linking or copying dates between workbooks based on different date systems. You can change the date system for a workbook by choosing Excel → Preferences → Calculation and turning off the checkbox for "Use the 1904 date system."

If copying or linking between workbooks gives you results that are 1462 days off from what you expect, you'll need to add a correction formula. Visit *www.support.microsoft. com/kb/214330* to read Microsoft's knowledge-base article that describes the problem in detail and supplies formulas for correcting it.

• When entering dates, you can use either a slash or a hyphen to separate months, days, and years. Usually it's OK to format date and time numbering at any time. However, you'll avoid occasional date recognition problems by applying date or time formatting *before* you enter the data in the cell.

Times

• Excel also treats *times* as numbers—specifically, as the fractional part of a date serial number, which is a number representing the number of days since midnight on January 1, 1904.

• Excel bases times on the 24-hour clock, or military time. To enter a time using the 12-hour clock, follow the number with an *a* or *p.* For example, to Excel, *9:34* always means 9:34 a.m., but *9:34 p* means 9:34 p.m.—and *21:34* also means 9:34 p.m. Whether you type *9:34 p* or *21:34,* Excel displays it in the spreadsheet as 21:34 unless you format the cell to display it in the AM/PM format.

• As with dates, you can perform calculations on times by entering an equal sign and then enclosing the times in quotation marks and typing the separator in the middle. For example, *="9:34"-"2:43"* gives you 0.285416667, the decimal fraction of a day between 2:43 a.m. and 9:34 a.m. If you format the cell with time formatting, as described on page 566, you instead get a more useful 6:51, or six hours and 51 minutes' difference.

WORKAROUND WORKSHOP

When Excel Formats Numbers as Dates

If you enter what looks like a date to Excel (say, May 3, 1999), and then later, in the process of revising your spreadsheet, enter a number containing a decimal (such as 23.25), Excel converts your decimal into a date (23 becomes January 23, 1904).

What's going on?

All cells start out with a generic format. But when you enter what Excel interprets as a date or time, Excel automatically applies date or time formatting. In this example, when Excel interpreted the first entry as a date, it applied date formatting to the cell.

Later, when the first entry was replaced with a decimal number, Excel retained the date formatting—and merrily displayed the number as a date. You don't have to let Excel guess at what format you want, though. Take charge! Select the cells in question and choose Format → Cells (or right-click the cells and choose Format Cell from the shortcut menu). Use the Number tab to select the appropriate format, and your troubles are over.

Similarly, to keep Excel from turning two numbers separated by a forward slash into a date, and keep it as a fraction instead, put a 0 and a space in front of the fraction (enter 0 1/4)—or just format the cell with the *Number* category. Excel now understands that you intended to enter a fraction.

Note: If the times in a calculation span midnight, the calculation will be wrong, since times reset at midnight. Fix it by adding 24 hours to the calculation—or even better by using the MOD function. (See page 531 for more on functions.)

Tedium Savings 1: AutoComplete

Excel 2008 is teeming with features to save you typing. The first, *AutoComplete*, comes into play when you enter repetitive data down a column. Find out more in Figure 12-6.

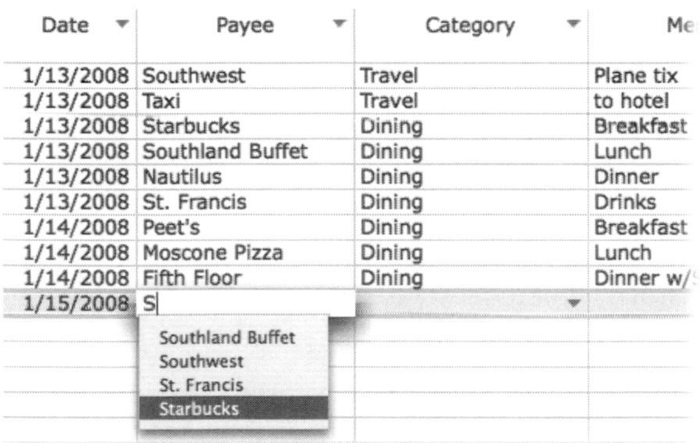

Date ▼	Payee ▼	Category ▼	Me
1/13/2008	Southwest	Travel	Plane tix
1/13/2008	Taxi	Travel	to hotel
1/13/2008	Starbucks	Dining	Breakfast
1/13/2008	Southland Buffet	Dining	Lunch
1/13/2008	Nautilus	Dining	Dinner
1/13/2008	St. Francis	Dining	Drinks
1/14/2008	Peet's	Dining	Breakfast
1/14/2008	Moscone Pizza	Dining	Lunch
1/14/2008	Fifth Floor	Dining	Dinner w/
1/15/2008	S|		

Southland Buffet
Southwest
St. Francis
Starbucks

Figure 12-6:
Excel's AutoComplete function watches as you type in a given cell. If your entry looks as though it might match the contents of another cell in the same column, Excel shows a pop-up menu of those possibilities. To select one, press the down arrow until the entry you want is highlighted, and then press Return. Alternatively, just click the entry in the list. Either way, Excel finishes the typing work for you.

Tedium Savings 2: Formula AutoComplete

Formula AutoComplete is a new feature appearing in Excel 2008, extending the AutoComplete concept to the chore of writing formulas. Instead of having to remember all the elements for a formula, Excel prompts you with valid function names and syntax as you type.

Tedium Savings 3: AutoFill

Excel's AutoFill feature can save you hours of typing and possibly carpel tunnel surgery, thanks to its ingenious ability to fill miles of cells with data automatically. The Edit → Fill submenu is especially useful when you're duplicating data or typing items in a series (such as days of the week, months of the year, or even sequential apartment numbers). It has seven options: Down, Right, Up, Left, Across Sheets, Series, and Justify.

Here's how they work. In each case, you start the process by typing data into a cell and then highlighting a block of cells beginning with that cell (see Figure 12-7). Then, choose any of the following:

- **Down, Up.** Fills the selected block of cells with whatever's in the top or bottom cell of the selected block. You might use one of these commands when setting up a series of formulas in a column that adds a row of cells.

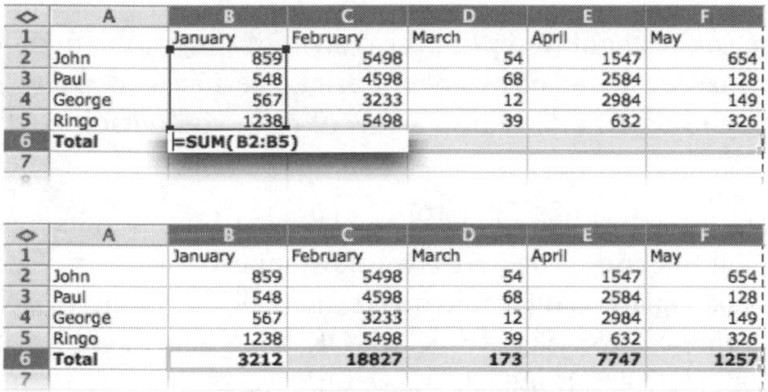

	A	B	C	D	E	F
1		January	February	March	April	May
2	John	859	5498	54	1547	654
3	Paul	548	4598	68	2584	128
4	George	567	3233	12	2984	149
5	Ringo	1238	5498	39	632	326
6	Total	=SUM(B2:B5)				

	A	B	C	D	E	F
1		January	February	March	April	May
2	John	859	5498	54	1547	654
3	Paul	548	4598	68	2584	128
4	George	567	3233	12	2984	149
5	Ringo	1238	5498	39	632	326
6	**Total**	**3212**	**18827**	**173**	**7747**	**1257**

Figure 12-7: *Filling a range of cells with formulas is where AutoFill really shines. You can drag the formula in cell B6 though cells to the right and then choose Edit → Fill → Right (top). Excel fills the cell with totals of the columns above them (bottom).*

- **Right, Left.** Fills the selected range of cells with whatever's in the leftmost or rightmost cell. For example, you'd use this feature when you need to put the same total calculation at the bottom of 23 different columns.

- **Across Worksheets.** Fills the cells in other sheets in the same workbook with the contents of the selected cells. For example, suppose you want to set up worksheets that track inventory and pricing over different months in different locations, and you want to use a different worksheet for each location. You can fill in all of the general column and row headings (such as part numbers and months) across worksheets with this command.

  To make this work, start by selecting the cells whose contents you wish to copy. Then select the sheets you want to fill by Shift-clicking a group of sheet tabs or ⌘-clicking non-contiguous sheet tabs at the bottom of the window. (If you can't see all the tabs easily, drag the slider between the tabs and the horizontal scroll bar. When you drag it to the right, the scroll bar shrinks, leaving more room for the tabs.)

Choose Edit → Fill → Across Sheets. A small dialog box (see Figure 12-8) asks whether you want to copy data, formats, or both across the selected worksheets. Make your choice by clicking one of the radio buttons, and then click OK.

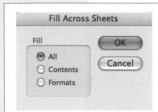

Figure 12-8:
You can copy three ways into other worksheets: All (both the formats and data), Contents (the data or formulae), or Formats (just the formats in the worksheet).

- **Series.** Fills the selected cells with a *series* of increasing or decreasing values based on the contents of the topmost cell (if the selected cells are in a column) or the leftmost cell (if the cells are in a row).

  For example, suppose you're about to type in the daily statistics for the number of dot-com startups that went out of business during the first two weeks of 2008. Instead of having to type 14 dates into a row of cells, you outsource this task to Excel.

  Enter *1/1/2008* in a cell. Then highlight that cell and the next 13 cells to its right. Now choose Edit → Fill → Series. The Series window appears, where you can specify how the fill takes place. You could make the cell labels increase by months, years, every other day, or whatever. Click OK; Excel fills the cells with the date series 1/1/2008, 1/2/2008, 1/3/2008, and so on.

Tip: The above example reflects the way Americans write dates, of course. If you use a different system for writing dates (perhaps you live in Europe or Australia), and you've used the Mac's International preference pane (choose → System Preferences) to specify that you like January 14, 2008 written *14/1/2008*, the next time you launch Excel it automatically formats dates the way you like them.

The other options in this dialog box include Linear (adds the amount in the Step field to each successive cell's number), Growth (*multiplies* by the number in the Step field), and AutoFill (relies on the lists described in the next section).

- **Justify.** Spreads the text in a single cell across several cells. You'd use this function to create a heading that spans the columns beneath it. If the cells are in a row, this command spreads the text in the leftmost cell across the selected row of cells. If the cells are in a column, it breaks up the text so that one word goes into each cell.

Note: At this writing, the Justify command doesn't work in the current version of Excel (version 12.0). Until Microsoft fixes it, you can achieve the same effect by selecting the group of cells, choosing Format → Cells → Alignment, and choosing Center Across Selection from the Horizontal pop-up menu.

Using the Fill handle

You don't have to use the Edit → Fill submenu to harness the power of Excel's AutoFill feature. As a timesaving gesture, Microsoft also gives you the *fill handle* (see Figure 12-9), a small square in the lower right of a selection rectangle. It lets you fill adjacent cells with data, exactly like the Fill commands—but without a trip to a menu and a dialog box.

	January	February	March	April	May
John	859	5498	54	1547	654
Paul	548	4598	68	2584	128
George	567	3233	12	2984	149
Ringo	1238	5498	39	632	326
Total	**3212**				

	January	February	March	April	May
John	859	5498	54	1547	654
Paul	548	4598	68	2584	128
George	567	3233	12	2984	149
Ringo	1238	5498	39	632	326
Total	**3212**	**18827**	**173**	**7747**	**1257**

Figure 12-9:
To use the fill handle, select the cell containing the formula or values you want to replicate and drag the tiny fill handle at the lower-right corner of the selection across the cells you want to fill. When you release your mouse, Excel fills the cells and displays the smart button, giving you the option to fill with or without formatting, or with formatting only.

To use it, select the cells containing the data you want to duplicate or extend, then drag the tiny fill handle across the cells where you want the data to be, as shown in Figure 12-9. Excel then fills the cells, just as though you'd used the Fill Down, Right, Up, or Left command. (To fill a series, Control-click the handle and choose an option from the shortcut menu.)

Tip: Excel can perform some dramatic and complex fill operations for you if you highlight *more than one* cell before dragging the fill handle. Suppose, for example, that you want to create a list of *every third* house number on your street. Enter *201 Elm St.* in the first cell, then *204 Elm St.* in the next one down. Highlight both of them, and then drag the fill handle at the lower-right corner of the second cell downward.

Excel cleverly fills the previously empty cells with *207 Elm St., 210 Elm St., 213 Elm St.,* and so on.

What's more, the fill handle can do *smart filling* that you won't find on the Edit → Fill submenu. For example, if you type *January* into a cell and then drag the fill handle across the next bunch of cells, Excel fills them with February, March, and so on; ditto for days of the week. Drag beyond December or Saturday, and Excel starts at the series over again. In fact, if you type January, March, drag through both cells to select them, and then drag the fill handle across subsequent cells, Excel fills them in with May, July, and so on. How cool is that?

What's more, you can teach Excel about any other sequential lists you regularly use in your line of work (NY Office, Cleveland Office, San Diego Office, and so on). Just choose Excel → Preferences → Custom Lists panel; click Add and then type the series of items in order, each on its own line. Click OK; the AutoFill list is now ready to use.

Tip: You can also type the list in a column of cells, select the cells, and then choose Preferences → Custom Lists → Add.

Selecting Cells (and Cell Ranges)

Selecting a single cell in Excel is easy. Just click the cell to select it. Often, though, you'll want to select more than one cell—in readiness for copying and pasting, making a chart, applying boldface, or using the Fill command, for example. Figure 12-10 depicts all you need to know for your selection needs.

- **Select a single cell.** To select a single cell, click it or enter its address in the Name box (which is shown in Figure 12-1) or press F5.

- **Select a block of cells.** To select a rectangle of cells, just drag diagonally across them. You highlight all of the cells within the boundaries of the imaginary rectangle you're drawing. (Or click the cell in one corner of the block and then Shift-click the cell diagonally opposite.)

- **Select a noncontiguous group of cells.** To select cells that aren't touching, ⌘-click (to add individual independent cells to the selection) or ⌘-drag across cells (to add a block of them to the selection). Repeat as many times as you like; Excel is perfectly happy to highlight random cells, or blocks of cells, in various corners of the spreadsheet simultaneously.

- **Select a row or column.** Click a row or column *heading* (the gray label of the row or column).

- **Select several rows or columns.** To select more than one row or column, *drag through* the gray row numbers or column letters. (You can also click the first one, then Shift-click the last one. Excel highlights everything in between.)

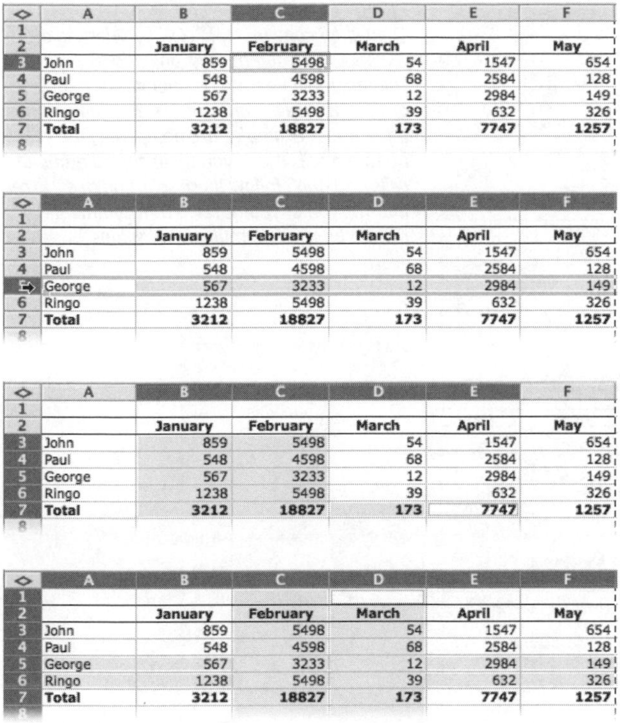

Figure 12-10:
You can highlight spreadsheet cells, rows, and columns in various combinations. You can copy using rectangular-shaped selections, but you can apply cell formatting changes to any group of selected cells.

Top: Click a cell (or arrow-key your way into it) to highlight just one cell.

Second from top: Click a row number or column letter (row 5, in this case) to highlight an entire row or column.

Third from top: Drag to highlight a rectangular block of cells; add individual additional cells to the selection by ⌘-clicking.

Bottom: ⌘-click row headings and column headings to highlight intersecting rows and columns.

- **Select noncontiguous rows or columns.** To select two or more rows or columns that aren't touching, ⌘-click, or ⌘-drag through, the corresponding gray row numbers. You can even combine these techniques—highlight first rows, then columns, and voilà! Intersecting swaths of highlighting.

- **Select all cells.** Press ⌘-A to select every cell on the sheet—or just click the gray, far upper-left rectangle with the diamond in it.

Tip: To select within the *contents* of a cell, double-click the cell and then use the I-beam selection tool to select the text you want.

Moving Things Around

Once you've selected some cells, you can move their contents around in various ways—a handy fact, since few people type everything in exactly the right place the first time. Excel only lets you copy groups of cells that are basically rectangular in shape or that share the same rows and multiple columns or the same columns in multiple rows. Figure 12-11 shows some acceptable and unacceptable selections for copying.

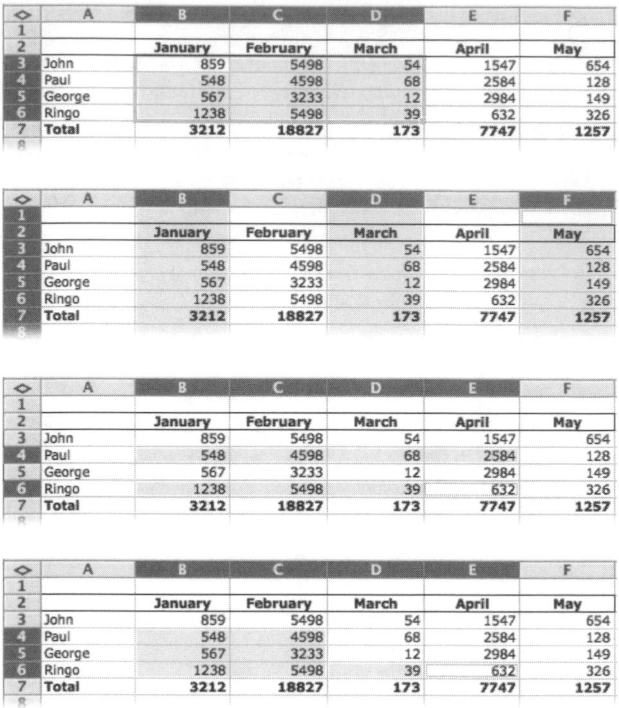

Figure 12-11:
Thou shalt copy multiple cells by selecting a rectangular group of cells, an entire row or column, multiple rows or columns, or matching groups of cells in various rows or columns. The three upper examples are acceptable, the bottom one is not. If you try to copy a group of cells and don't follow these selection rules, Excel informs you of your error: "That command cannot be used on multiple selections."

Cutting, copying, and pasting

Just as in any other Mac program, you can use the Edit menu commands—Cut (⌘-X), Copy (⌘-C), and Paste (⌘-V)—to move cell contents around the spreadsheet—or to a different sheet or workbook altogether. When you paste a group of cells, you can either select the same number of cells at your destination, or select just one cell—which becomes the upper left cell of the pasted group.

But unlike other Mac programs, Excel doesn't appear to cut your selection immediately. Instead, the cut area sprouts a dotted, *moving border,* but otherwise remains unaffected. It isn't until you select a destination cell or cells and select Edit → Paste that the cut takes place (and the shimmering stops).

Tip: Press the Esc key to make the animated dotted lines stop moving, without otherwise affecting your copy or cut operation. One more piece of advice: Check the status bar at the bottom of the window to find out what Excel thinks is happening ("Select destination and press ENTER or choose Paste," for example).

Paste Special

The Edit → Paste Special command summons a dialog box inquiring about *how* and *what* to paste. For example, you might decide to paste the formulas contained in the material you copied so that they continue to do automatic math—or only the *values* (the results of the calculations as they appear in the copied material).

Tip: This dialog box also contains the mighty Transpose checkbox, a tiny option that can save your bacon. It lets you swap rows-for-columns in the act of pasting, so that data you input in columns winds up in rows, and vice versa. This kind of topsy-turvy spreadsheet modification can be a great help if you want to swap the orientation of your entire spreadsheet, or copy a group of cells between spreadsheets which have juxtaposed rows and columns.

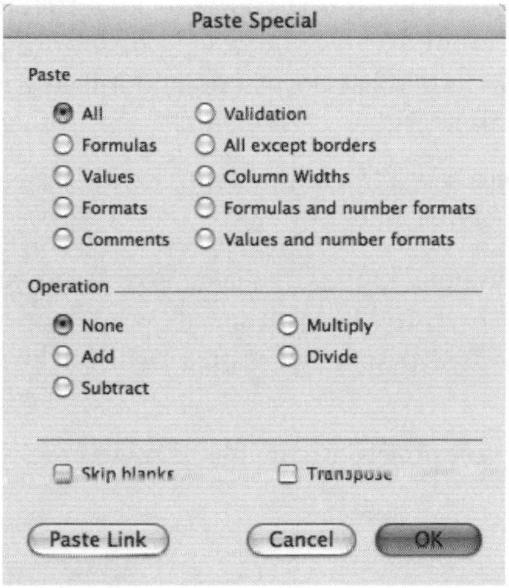

Figure 12-12:
The Paste Special command lets you paste formulas, comments, and formatting independently. The Operations options let you perform a mathematical operation as you paste, such as adding what you've copied to the contents of the cells you're pasting over.

Drag-and-drop

Excel also lets you grab a selected range of cells and drag the contents to a new location. To do this, select the cells you want to move, then point to the thick border on the edge of the selection, so that the cursor changes into a little hand that grabs the cells. You can now drag the selected cells to another spot on the spreadsheet. When you release the mouse button, Excel moves the data to the new location, exactly as though you'd used Cut and Paste.

You can modify how dragging and dropping items and Excel works by holding down these modifier keys:

- **Option.** If you hold down the Option key, Excel *copies* the contents to the new location, leaving the originals in place.

- **Shift.** Normally, if you drag cells into a spreadsheet area that you've already filled in, Excel asks if you're sure you want to wipe out the cell contents already in residence. If you Shift-drag cells, however, Excel creates enough new cells to make room for the dragged contents, shoving aside (or down) the cell contents current occupants in order to make room.

- **Option and Shift.** Holding down both the Option *and* Shift keys as you drag copies the data *and* inserts new cells for it.

- **Control.** Control-dragging yields a menu of 11 options when you drop the cells. This menu lets you choose whether you want to move the cells, copy them, copy just the values or formulas, create a link or hyperlink, or shift cells around. It even lets you cancel the drag.

Inserting and Removing Cells

Suppose you've just completed your spreadsheet cataloging the rainfall patterns of the Pacific Northwest, county by county, and then it hits you: You forgot Humboldt County in California. Besides the question of how you could possibly forget Humboldt County, the larger question remains: What do you do about it in your spreadsheet? Delete the whole thing and start over?

Fortunately, Excel lets you insert blank cells, rows, or columns into existing sheets through the Insert menu. Here's how each works.

- **Cells.** The Insert → Cells command summons the Insert dialog box. It lets you insert new, blank cells into your spreadsheet, and lets you specify what happens to the cells that are already in place—whether they get shifted right or down. See Figure 12-13.

- **Rows.** If you choose Insert → Rows, Excel inserts a new, blank row above the active cell.

Figure 12-13:
When you select cells and then choose Insert → Cells, Excel asks where you want to put the new cells (top). The two buttons at the bottom let you insert entire rows or columns. Excel then inserts the same number of cells as you've selected in the location selected, and moves the previous residents of those cells in the direction that you specify (bottom). In addition, the Format smart button appears, giving you three choices: format your new cells to match those above, those below, or without formatting at all.

Tip: If you select some cells before using the Insert → Cells command, Excel inserts the number of rows equal to the number of rows selected in the range. That's a handy way to control how many rows get added–to add six blank rows, highlight six rows, regardless of what's in them at the moment.

- **Columns.** If you choose Insert → Columns, Excel inserts a new blank column to the left of the active cell. If you've selected a range of cells, Excel inserts the number of columns equal to the number of columns selected in the range.

Warning: If the cells, columns, or rows that you send shifting across the spreadsheet by inserting cells already contain data, you can mangle the entire spreadsheet in short order. For example, data you entered in the debit column can suddenly end up in the credit column. Proceed with extreme caution.

Find and Replace

Exactly as in Word, Excel has both a Find function, which helps you locate a specific spot in a big workbook, and a Replace feature that's ideal for those moments when your company gets incorporated into a larger one, requiring its name to be changed in 34 places throughout a workbook. The routine goes like this:

1. **Highlight the cells you want to search.**

   This step is crucial. By limiting the search range, you ensure that your search-and-rescue operation won't run rampant through your spreadsheet, changing things you'd rather leave as is.

2. **Choose Edit → Find. In the resulting dialog box, specify what you want to search for, and in which direction (see Figure 12-14).**

   You can use a question mark (?) as a stand in for a single character, or an asterisk (*) to represent more than one character. In other words, typing *P?ts* will find cells containing "Pats," "Pots," and "Pits"; while typing *P*ts* will find cells containing "Profits," "Prophets," and "Poltergeists."

   The "Find entire cells only" checkbox means that Excel will consider a cell a match for your search term only if its entire contents match; a cell that says "Annual profits" isn't considered a match for the search term "Profits."

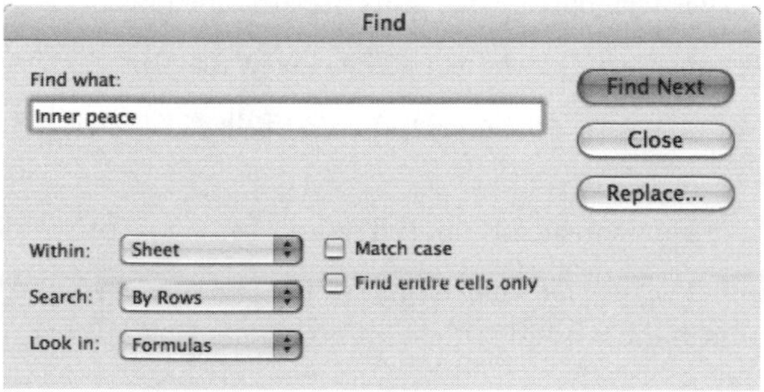

Figure 12-14:
Using the Search pop-up menu, you can specify whether Excel searches the highlighted cells from left to right of each row ("By Rows") or down each column ("By Columns"). Use the "Look in" pop-up menu to specify which cell components are fair game for the search: formulas, values (that is, the results of those formulas, and other data you've typed into the cells), or comments. Turn on "Match case" if you're trying to find "Bill" and not "bill."

3. If you intend to *replace* the cell contents (instead of just finding them), click Replace; type the replacement text into the "Replace with" box. Click Find Next (or press Return).

Each time you click Find Next, Excel highlights the next cell it finds that matches your search phrase. If you click Replace, you replace the text with the "Replace with" text. If you click Replace All, of course, you replace *every* matching occurrence in the selected cells. Use caution.

Erasing Cells

"Erase," as any CIA operative can attest, is a relative term. In Excel, the Edit → Clear submenu lets you strip away various kinds of information without necessarily emptying the cell completely. For example:

• **Edit → Clear → All** truly empties the selected cells, restoring them to their pristine, empty, and, unformatted condition. (Control-B does the same thing.)

• **Edit → Clear → Formats** leaves the contents, but strips away formatting (including both text and number formatting).

• **Edit → Clear → Contents** empties the cell, but leaves the formatting in place. If you then type new numbers into the cell, they take on whatever cell formatting you had applied (bold, blue, Currency, and so on).

• **Edit → Clear → Comments** deletes only electronic yellow sticky notes (see page 635).

None of these is the same as Edit → Delete, which actually chops cells out of your spreadsheet and makes others slide upward or leftward to fill the gap. (Excel asks you which way you want existing cells to slide.)

Tutorial 1: Entering Data

If you've never used a spreadsheet before, the concepts described in the previous pages may not make much sense until you've applied them in practice. This tutorial, which continues with a second lesson on page 536, can help.

Suppose that you, Web marketer extraordinaire, are preparing to write your next bestseller, *The Two-Hour Workweek*, and you'd like to include some facts and figures about your remarkable rise to success. So you cancel your morning hang gliding lesson and crank up Excel to get a handle on your years of part-time toil.

1. **Create a new spreadsheet document by choosing File → New (⌘-N).**

Excel fills your screen with the spreadsheet grid; the first cell, A1, is selected as the active cell, awaiting your keystrokes.

2. **Begin by typing the title of your spreadsheet in cell A1.**

Profit and Loss Statement: Time is Not Money might be a good choice. As you type, the characters appear in the cell and in the Edit box in the Formula bar.

3. **Click outside of cell A1 to get out of the entry mode, click back on cell A1 to highlight it, and then press ⌘-B.**

   Excel inserts your text into cell A1. Since all the cells to the right of A1 are empty, Excel runs the contents of cell A1 right over the top of them. When you press ⌘-B, Excel formats the first cell's text in bold, to make a more impressive title for your spreadsheet.

4. **Press Return three times. And then press ⌘-S.**

   Excel moves the active cell frame down a couple of rows, selecting cell A4. Even if you haven't entered any data yet, save the spreadsheet by pressing ⌘-S (or choosing File → Save), naming it, and then choosing a suitable destination. Now as you continue to work on your spreadsheet, periodically press ⌘-S to save your work as you go along.

5. **Type *January*.**

   You need to track expenses over time: to track the project by calendar year, name the first column *January*. You could now tab to the next cell, enter *February*, and work your way down the spreadsheet—but there's an easier way.

   As noted earlier, Excel can create a series of months automatically for you, saving you the effort of typing *February, March,* and so on—you just have to start it off with the first entry or two.

6. **Click once outside cell A4 to get out of entry mode, and then click cell A4 again to select it. Carefully click the tiny square at the lower-right corner of the high-lighted cell; drag directly downward through 11 more cells.**

   Pop-out yellow screen tips reveal what Excel intends to autofill into the cells you're dragging through. When the screen tip says *December,* stop.

   Excel enters the months and highlights the cells you dragged through. Figure 12-15 shows this step.

   Now it's time to add the year headings across the top.

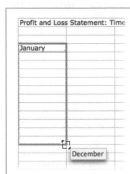

Figure 12-15:
Drag the lower-right corner handle of a cell to autofill a sequence of months, dates, or times. (In this example, if January is in row 4, December will end up in row 15.)

7. **Click cell B3 to select it. Type** *2004.* **Press Tab, type** *2005,* **and then press Enter.**

You'll use the same AutoFill mechanism to type in the names of the next four years. But just dragging the tiny square AutoFill handle on the 2004 cell wouldn't work this time, because Excel wouldn't know whether you want to fill *every* cell with "2004" or to add successive years. So, you've given it the first *two* years as a hint.

8. **Drag through the 2004 and 2005 cells to highlight them. Carefully click the tiny square at the lower-right corner of the 2005 cell; drag directly to the right through three more cells.**

Excel automatically fills in *2006, 2007,* and *2008,* using the data in the first two cells to establish the sequence.

If you like, you can now highlight the year row, the month column, or both, and then press ⌘-B to make them boldface (see Figure 12-16). Chapter 13 has more details on formatting your spreadsheets.

Now that the basic framework of the spreadsheet is in place, you can begin typing in actual numbers.

Profit and Loss Statement: Time is Not Money					
	2004	**2005**	**2006**	**2007**	**2008**
January	-1895	2323	12151	21979	30659
February	-1470	3142	12970	22798	29684
March	-1109	3961	13789	23617	32984
April	-752	4780	14608	27436	31597
May	-321	5599	15427	25255	31449
June	-648	6418	16246	26074	30945
July	-288	7237	17065	26893	34697
August	-305	8056	17884	29712	32458
September	-96	8875	18703	28531	33125
October	59	9694	19522	31350	35698
November	298	10513	20341	30169	34254
December	1697	11332	21160	30988	35412

Figure 12-16:
You can make the headings stand out from the data you'll soon put in the cells by changing the font style and alignment (see Chapter 13). In this example, the row and column headings are bold, and the column headings are centered.

9. **Click cell B4, January 2004. Enter a figure for your January income.**

Your first several months of operation showed a loss since you were investing in lots of "Get Rich Quick on the Internet!" programs. You invested heavily at the beginning, and your losses in January were $1,895. Since this is a loss, enter it as a negative number, and leave off the dollar sign—just type *-1895.*

10. **Press Return (or the down arrow key).**

Excel moves the active cell frame to the next row down.

11. **Type another number to represent your loss for February; press Return. Repeat steps 9 and 10 until you get to the bottom of the 2004 column.**

For this experiment, the exact numbers to type don't matter too much, but Figure 12-16 shows one suggestion. Perhaps, toward the end of that first year, you started making money instead of losing money.

12. Click in the January 2005 column (C4); fill in the numbers for each month, pressing Return after each entry. Repeat with the other years.

Remember, this is a success story, so type ever-increasing numbers in your columns, because once you started making money, it was an ever-upward trend. But then your income kind of leveled off toward the end of 2007 as you cut back your work week to two hours.

When you've successfully filled your spreadsheet with data, save your work one more time. You'll return to it later in this chapter—after you've read about what Excel can *do* with all of these numbers.

Formula Fundamentals

Without *formulas,* Excel would just be glorified graph paper. With them, Excel becomes a number-crunching powerhouse worthy of its own corner office. Excel formulas do everything from basic arithmetic to complex financial analysis. And Excel 2008 makes working with formulas easier than ever. Formula AutoComplete helps you write formulas even if you can't remember all the arcane elements of particular formula. As you type, Excel presents valid functions, names, and named ranges for you to choose from. In addition, the new Formula Builder joins the toolbox, where you can search for, learn about, and build formulas by following simple instructions.

Basic Calculations

A *formula* in a cell can perform calculations on other cells' contents. For example, if cell A1 contains the number of hours in a day, and cell A2 contains the number of days in a year, then you could type *=A1*A2* into cell B3 to find out how many hours there are in a year. (In spreadsheet lingo, you'd say that this formula *returns* the number 8760.)

After typing the formula and pressing Return, you'd see only the mathematical answer in cell B3; the formula itself is hidden, though you can see it in the Formula bar if you click the cell again (Figure 12-17).

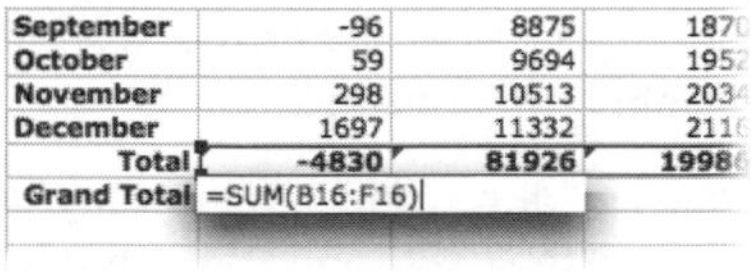

September	-96	8875	1870
October	59	9694	1952
November	298	10513	2034
December	1697	11332	2110
Total	-4830	81926	1998
Grand Total	=SUM(B16:F16)		

Figure 12-17:
The Rangefinder highlights each cell that's included in the formula you're currently typing. Furthermore, the color of the outline around the cells matches the typed cell reference.

Formulas do math on *values.* A value is any number, date, time, text, or cell address that you feed into a formula. The math depends on the *operators* in the formula—symbols like + for addition,–for subtraction, / for division, * for multiplication, and so on.

Tip: Your formulas don't have to remain invisible until clicked. To reveal formulas on a given sheet, press Control-` (the key in the upper-left corner of most keyboards). This command toggles the spreadsheet cells so that they show formulas instead of results. (Excel widens your columns considerably, as necessary, to show the formulas.) To return things to the way they were, press Control-` again.

Consider that keystroke a shortcut for the official way to bring formulas into view: Excel → Preferences → View panel. Under Window options, click Formulas; click OK. Repeat the whole procedure to restore the results-only view. Aren't you glad you've now memorized the Control-` shortcut?

Error checking

If you make a mistake when you're typing in a formula, Excel's error-checking buttons attempt to return you to the straight and narrow. For example, if you type *=suum E3:E6*, Excel displays "#NAME?" in the cell. Click the cell to display the error-checking button, as shown in Figure 12-18. Clicking the tiny arrow on the right of the button displays several options and bits of information, like the following:

- **Error Name.** The name of the error heads the list. Fortunately, it's a descriptive name of the error, like Invalid Name Error.

- **Help on this Error.** Click here to view the Excel Help screen on this particular error. This information may help you understand where you went wrong.

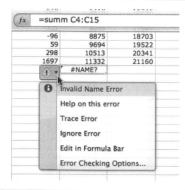

Figure 12-18:
If you choose to edit the formula in the Formula bar, the alleged formula becomes active in the Formula bar. There you can edit it, and with any luck fix the problem. Note that when presented in the Formula bar, the formula's cell references are color coded to indicate which color-coded cell they apply to.

- **Trace Error.** Draws lines to the cells that might be causing the errors. Examine the cells in question to determine what you might have done incorrectly.

- **Ignore Error.** The computing equivalent of saying "never mind." Choosing this item tells Excel to leave the formula as you entered it. (Excel obeys you, but let's hope you know more than Excel does—there's no guarantee that the formula will work.)

- **Edit in Formula Bar.** This option lets you edit the formula in the Formula bar as described in Figure 12-18.

• **Error Checking Options.** Opens the Excel → Preferences → Error Checking tab. Here you can turn error checking on and off, and tell Excel which kinds of errors to look for, like empty or missing cells in formulas.

To enter a simple formula that you know well, just double-click the cell and start typing (or click the Edit box in the Formula bar, shown in Figure 12-18, and typed there). The cursor appears simultaneously in the cell and in the Edit box, signaling that Excel awaits your next move.

Your next move is to type an equal sign (=), since every formula starts that way. Then type the rest of the formula using values and operators. When you want to incorporate a reference to a particular cell in your formula, you don't actually have to type out B12 or whatever—just *click* the cell in question. Similarly, to insert a range of cells, just drag through them.

Tip: If you mess up while entering a formula and want to start fresh, click the Cancel button at the right end of the Formula bar. (It looks like an X.)

To complete a formula press Enter, Return, Tab, or an arrow key—your choice.

Functions

When you tire of typing formulas from scratch (or, let's be honest, when you can't figure out what to type), you can let Excel do the brainwork by using *functions*. Functions are just predefined formulas. For example, the SUM function adds a range of specified values [=SUM(B3:B7)] so you don't have to type the plus sign between each one [=B3+B4+B5+B6+B7]. Excel 2008 adds Formula Auto-Complete and the Formula Builder to help you find and enter functions properly. In addition, Excel Help is a veritable Function University with detailed information and examples for all of its functions.

Function screen tips and AutoComplete

Screen tips (Figure 12-19) for function help are a real boon to spread-sheeting neophytes and dataheads alike. As you start to type a function into a cell, Auto-Complete pops up a list of function names matching what you've typed so far. Click one to add it to the cell. Then a screen tip displays the syntax of the function in a pale yellow box just below where you're typing. Not only does the screen tip show you how to correctly type the function it believes you have in mind, but you can also use the screen tip in other ways. For example, you can drag the screen tip to reposition it (to get a better look at your worksheet), click a piece of the tip to select it, or click the function to open up its Help topic in a separate window.

Tip: If you want to turn off function screen tips, choose Excel → Preferences and select the View tab. Remove the checkmark next to "Show function ScreenTips."

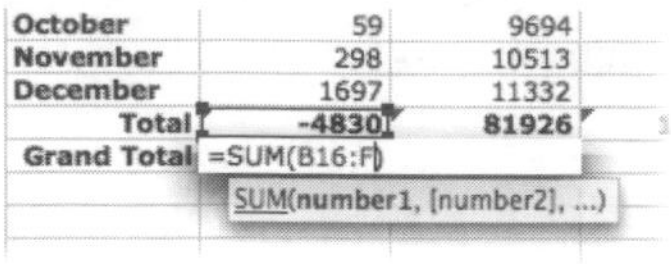

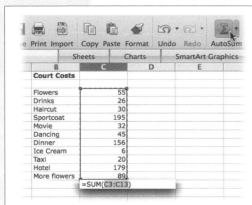

Figure 12-19:
Excel's Function screen tips make an educated guess at what you're trying to do—usually a pretty darn good one—and provide the correct syntax for doing it. Here the SUM screen tip explains how to add a series of numbers.

The AutoSum button

You don't need access to Microsoft's reams of focus-group studies to realize that the most commonly used spreadsheet function is *adding things up*. That's why Excel comes equipped with a toolbar button that does nothing but add up the values in the column directly above, or the row to the left of, the active cell, as Figure 12-20 shows. (The tutorial that resumes on "Tutorial 2: Yearly Totals" also shows why AutoSum is one of the most important buttons in Excel.)

Figure 12-20:
The powerful AutoSum button on the Standard toolbar (upper right) is the key to quickly adding a row or column. A click of the button puts a SUM function in the selected cell, which assumes that you want to add up the cells above it. Note that it doesn't write out C3+C4+C5+C6+C7+C8+C9, and so on; it sets up a range of numbers using the shorthand notation C3:C13. When you press Return, you see only the result, not the formula.

The flippy triangle to the right of the AutoSum button reveals a menu with a few other extremely common options, such as the following:

- **Average.** Calculates the average (the arithmetic mean) of the numbers in the column above the active cell. For example, if the column of numbers represents your Web site revenues for each month then using this function gives you your average monthly income.

- **Count Numbers.** Tells you *how many* cells in a selected cell range contain numbers.

- **Max** and **Min.** Shows the highest or lowest value of any of the numbers referred to in the function.

- **More Functions.** When you choose this command, the Formula Builder appears, described shortly.

Tip: After you click the AutoSum button (or use one of its pop-up menu commands), Excel assumes that you intend to compute using the numbers in the cells just *above* or *to the left of* the highlighted cell. It indicates, with a moving border, which cells it intends to include in its calculation.

But if it guesses wrong, simply grab your mouse and adjust the selection rectangle by one of its corner handles or just drag through the numbers you *do* want computed. Excel redraws its border and updates its formula. Press Enter to complete the formula.

UP TO SPEED

The Anatomy of a Function in a Formula

Like Web-page and email addresses, formulas with functions have a regular form. If you understand that anatomy, you'll find working with formulas much easier.

The first element in a formula is the equal sign (=), which signals to Excel that what follows is a formula, not plain old data. Next comes the function name, like SUM. After the function name comes a left parenthesis, which tells Excel that the function's *arguments* are coming next

Arguments in this case have nothing to do with the validity of the entries in your expense report, and everything to do with telling the function what *values* to process—values being the numbers or text in a cell.

Some functions have one argument, others have more, and a few have none. To use more than one argument, separate them with commas. Finally, finish the function with a closing parenthesis. Each function expects its arguments to be listed in a very specific manner, or *syntax*.

For example, the formula =SUM(B4:B8,20) adds the contents of cells B4, B5, B6, B7, and B8, and then adds 20. *SUM* is the function, *(B4:B8,20)* are the arguments.

Given the many functions and operators Excel provides, you can do more number crunching in an hour with Excel than you probably did in your entire grade-school experience. (Unless, of course, you used spreadsheets in grade school, in which case you're probably not reading this section anyway.)

Looking up functions with the Formula Builder

Whipping up the sum or average of some cells is only the beginning. Excel is also capable of performing the kinds of advanced number crunching that can calculate interest rates, find the cosine of an arc, find the inverse of the one-tailed probability of the chi-squared distribution, and so on. It's safe to say that no one has all of these functions memorized.

Fortunately, you don't have to remember how to write each function; save that brainpower for the Sunday Times crossword. Instead, you can use Excel's new Formula Builder to look up the exact function that you need. To call up the Formula Builder, click the *fx* button on the formula bar, choose View → Formula Builder, or click the Toolbox button on the Standard toolbar and then click the *fx* button.

The new Formula Builder takes the place of Excel 2004's Paste Function dialog box and greatly simplifies finding and inserting functions. The top of the Formula Builder displays a search field (see Figure 12-21) where you can type any bit of information relating to the function you're looking for. You can type *cosine*, for example, and the Formula Builder displays in its main panel the six functions, which somehow relate to cosine. Click any of the functions to read a brief description and the syntax for that function. Double-clicking the function does two things: it inserts the function in the active cell of your spreadsheet and opens the Arguments pane of the Format Builder where it displays the arguments (if any) it's extracted from your spreadsheet, and at the bottom of the window displays the result.

Just like when you use the AutoSum button, if Excel guesses wrong and highlights the wrong cells in your spreadsheet, either readjust the selection rectangle or click the appropriate cells. Press Return to enter the function into your spreadsheet.

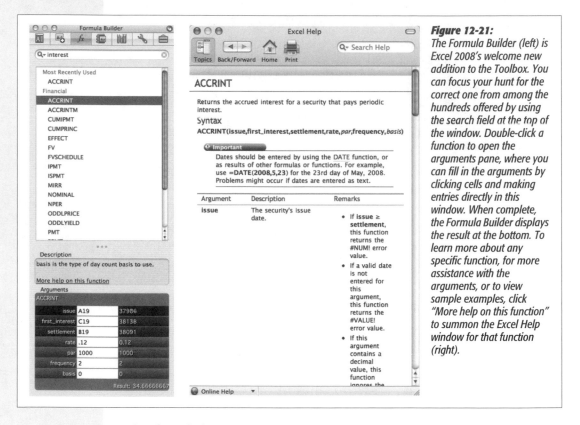

Figure 12-21:
The Formula Builder (left) is Excel 2008's welcome new addition to the Toolbox. You can focus your hunt for the correct one from among the hundreds offered by using the search field at the top of the window. Double-click a function to open the arguments pane, where you can fill in the arguments by clicking cells and making entries directly in this window. When complete, the Formula Builder displays the result at the bottom. To learn more about any specific function, for more assistance with the arguments, or to view sample examples, click "More help on this function" to summon the Excel Help window for that function (right).

Using the Calculator to assemble formulas

What with all the operators, parentheses, cell addresses, functions and such—all of which have to be entered in exactly the correct order—assembling a formula can be a painstaking business. The new formula builder eases much of that pain, but you can choose another approach to formula creation: Excel's built-in calculator.

Choose Tools → Calculator to summon this virtual pocket pal which features a lot of the standard buttons that you might find on a pocket calculator, plus parentheses buttons, an IF button (to insert an IF statement), and a SUM button (to insert a SUM function). As shown in Figure 12-22, the Calculator window also has three fields: a large one up top that displays the current formula (and also lets you type your own formula, if you're so inclined) and two smaller ones below it, which show the answer to the formula and the formula's destination cell.

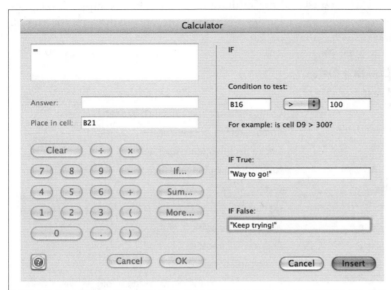

Figure 12-22:
The Calculator lets you build a formula with just a few button clicks—in this case, an IF statement that presents different messages depending on the value of B16. Once you've perfected the formula, click OK to insert it into the active cell.

To create a formula, click the calculator's buttons as you would on a real calculator. If you prefer clacking on your keyboard, you can also enter the numbers that way. As you build your formula with the various calculator buttons, the formula shows up in the top window, and the result of the calculation shows up in the Answer field.

Once you've built your formula, click OK to paste it into the spreadsheet. (And show it off to your friends who use Excel for Windows, as they don't yet have a calculator.)

If you want to access other functions (besides the IF and SUM functions), click More to bid the calculator adieu and return to the more knowledgeable Formula Builder.

Tip: If you need a little help with a balky formula that you've already entered (perhaps you haven't gotten its syntax just right), select the cell and open the Formula Builder. It helpfully displays its Arguments pane for the formula in question, so you can see the error of your ways—or the error of your formula, at least.

Order of Calculation

As you no doubt recall from your basic algebra class, you get different answers to an equation depending on how its elements are ordered. So it's important for *you*, the purveyor of fine Excel formulas, to understand the order in which Excel makes its calculations.

If a formula is spitting out results that don't jibe with what you think ought to be the answer, consult the following table. Excel calculates the operations at the top of the table first, working its way down until it hits bottom. For example, Excel computes cell references before it tackles multiplication, and it does multiplication before it works on a "less than" operation.

Excel's Calculation Order
Computed first

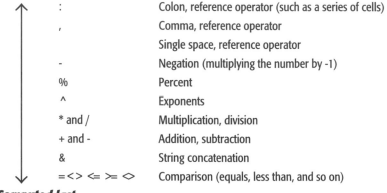

:	Colon, reference operator (such as a series of cells)
,	Comma, reference operator
	Single space, reference operator
-	Negation (multiplying the number by -1)
%	Percent
^	Exponents
* and /	Multiplication, division
+ and -	Addition, subtraction
&	String concatenation
=<> <= >= <>	Comparison (equals, less than, and so on)

Computed last

For example, Excel's answer to =2+3*4 is not 20. It's 14, because Excel performs multiplication and division within the formula *before* doing addition and subtraction.

You can exercise some control over the processing order by using parentheses. Excel calculates expressions within ( ) symbols before bringing the parenthetical items together for calculation. So in the above example, =(2+3)*4 returns 20. Or, the formula =C12*(C3-C6) subtracts the value in C6 from the value in C3 and multiplies the result by the value in C12. Without the parentheses, the formula would read =C12*C3-C6, and Excel would multiply C12 by C3 and *then* subtract C6—a different formula entirely.

Tip: Excel does its best to alert you to mistakes you make when entering formulas manually. For example, if you leave off a closing parenthesis (after using an open parenthesis), Excel pops up a dialog box suggesting a fix—and sometimes just fixes it without asking.

Tutorial 2: Yearly Totals

Suppose you've entered a few numbers into a spreadsheet, as described in the tutorial earlier in this chapter. Finally it's time to put these numbers to work. Open the document shown in Figure 12-16.

Now that it has some data to work with, Excel can do a little work. Start with one of the most common spreadsheet calculations: totaling a column of numbers. First create a row for totals.

1. **Click cell A17 (leaving a blank row beneath the month list). Type** *Total.*

   This row will soon contain totals for each year column.

2. **Click cell B17, in the Total row for 2004. Click the AutoSum button on the Standard toolbar.**

   In cell B17, Excel automatically proposes a *formula* for totaling the column of numbers. (It's =*SUM(B3:B16)*, meaning "add up the cells from B3 through B16.") The moving border shows that Excel is prepared to add up *all* of the numbers in this column—including the year label *2004!* Clearly, that's not what you want, so don't press Enter yet.

3. **Drag through the numbers you** *do* **want added: from cell B4 down to B15. Then press Return.**

   Excel adds up the column.

   Now comes the real magic of spreadsheeting: If one of the numbers in the column *changes,* the total changes automatically. Try it.

4. **Click one of the numbers in column B, type a much bigger number, and then press Return.**

   Excel instantly updates 2004's total to reflect the change.

Tip: The AutoSum feature doesn't have to add up numbers *above* the selected cell; it can also add up a *row* of cells. In fact, you can even click the AutoSum button and then drag through a *block* of cells to make Excel add up all of *those* numbers.

You *could* continue selecting the Total cells for each year and using AutoSum to create your totals. Instead, you can avoid repetition by using the Fill command described earlier in this chapter. You can tell Excel to create a calculation similar to the 2004 total for the rest of the columns in the spreadsheet.

5. **Click the cell containing the 2004 total (B17) and drag the selection's Fill handle (see page 519) to the right, all the way over to the 2008 column (F17).**

   As you drag, Excel highlights the range of cells for column totals, and when you release your mouse, it fills those cells with column totals as shown in Figure 12-23.

   You could've accomplished the same thing by first just selecting the range of cells and then choosing Edit → Fill → Right—but why would you want to?

   Either way, Excel copies the contents of the first cell and pastes it into every other cell in the selection. In this example, the first cell contains a *formula,* not just a total you typed yourself. But, instead of pasting the exact same formula, which would place the 2004 total into each column, Excel understands that you want to total each column, and therefore enters the appropriate formula in each cell of your selection. The result is yearly totals calculated right across the page.

Finally, to make the yearly totals in the tutorial example more meaningful—and see just how much money you actually made—calculate an overall total for the spreadsheet.

Profit and Loss Statement: Time is Not Money

	2004	2005	2006	2007	2008
January	-1895	2323	12151	21979	30659
February	-1470	3142	12970	22798	29684
March	-1109	3961	13789	23617	32984
April	-752	4780	14608	27436	31597
May	-321	5599	15427	25255	31449
June	-648	6418	16246	26074	30945
July	-288	7237	17065	26893	34697
August	-305	8056	17884	29712	32458
September	-96	8875	18703	28531	33125
October	59	9694	19522	31350	35698
November	298	10513	20341	30169	34254
December	1697	11332	21160	30988	35412
Total	-4830				

November	298	10513	20341	30169	34254
December	1697	11332	21160	30988	35412
Total	-4830	81926	199862	324798	392962

Figure 12-23:
Top: To total all of the columns in the spreadsheet quickly, drag the Fill handle from the cell containing the total for the first column (B17) all the way over to the last column.

Bottom: When you release the mouse, Excel creates a total for each of the selected columns.

6. **Click cell A19 and type** *Grand Total* **and then press Tab.**

Excel moves the active cell to B19.

To calculate a lifetime total for the spreadsheet, you need to tell Excel to add together all the yearly totals.

7. **Click the AutoSum button on the Standard toolbar.**

In this case, the cells you want to add aren't lined up with the Grand Total cell, so the AutoSum button doesn't work quite right; it proposes totaling the column of numbers above it.

8. **Drag across the yearly totals (from B17 through F17).**

As you drag across the cells, Excel inserts the cell range within the formula and outlines the range of cells. In this example, the function now reads, =SUM(B17: F17)—in other words, "add up the contents of the cells B17 through F17, and display the result."

9. **Press Return (or Enter).**

Excel performs the calculation and displays the result in cell B19, the grand total for the rags to riches story of an Internet marketer.

Named ranges

Once your spreadsheet grows beyond the confines of your screen, you may find it difficult to find your way back to areas within it that you work on the most frequently. By designating a cell or group of cells as a *named range,* you can quickly jump to a certain spot without having to scroll around for it. You can use named cells as a quick way to navigate a large spreadsheet. Once you've created a named range, click the Name pop-up menu in the Formula bar and choose it from the list. Excel instantly transports you to the correct corner of your spreadsheet, where you'll find the named range selected and waiting for you.

As you create formulas, you may find yourself referring over and over to the same cell or range of cells. For example, in the profit and loss spreadsheet (Figure 12-23), you may need to refer to the 2008 Total in several other formulas. So that you don't have to repeatedly type the cell address or click to select the cell, Excel lets you give a cell, or range of cells, a name. After doing so, you can write a formula in the form of, for example, =*Total2008-Taxes* (instead of =B17-F27). Or, you may find yourself doing the same operation on the same range of cells over and over, for example, totaling or averaging your monthly expenses. By designating a monthly expense totals as a named range, you can create surprisingly readable formulas that look like =*SUM(Expenses)* or =*AVERAGE(Expenses).*

To create a named cell or range, simply select the cell or range, enter a name for it in the Formula bar's Name box, and press Return (or choose Insert → Name → Define) as shown in Figure 12-24.

Note: Named ranges take one-word names only: Excel doesn't accept spaces or hyphens. And, as you'd expect, no two names can be the same on the same worksheet: Excel considers upper- and lowercase characters to be the same, so *profit* is the same as *PROFIT.* Additionally, the first character of a name has to be a letter (or an underscore); names can't contain punctuation marks (except periods) or operators (+, =, and so on); and they can't take the form of a cell reference (such as B5) or a function (such as SUM()).

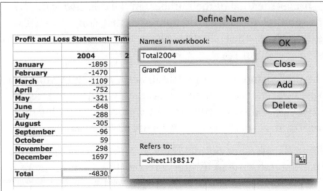

Figure 12-24:
To name a cell or range of cells, select it, enter a name for it in the Formula bar's Name box, and press Return. From now on, you can use the Name box pop-up menu to jump directly to that point in your spreadsheet.

From now on, the cell's or range's name appears in the Formula bar's Name pop-up menu. The next time you want to go to that cell or range or use it in a formula, you need only click that pop-up menu and select it from the list. In addition, Excel displays the name instead of the cell address whenever you create a formula that refers to a named cell or range.

If you need to change or remove a name, choose Insert → Names → Define to display the Define Names dialog box. From there, you'll find it easy to delete, create, or edit names.

References: absolute and relative

When you create a formula by typing the addresses of cells or by clicking a cell, you've created a *cell reference*. However, rather than always meaning *B12*, for example, Excel generally considers cell references in a *relative* way—it thinks of another cell in the spreadsheet as "three rows above and two columns to the left of this cell," for example (see Figure 12-25). In other words, it remembers those cell coordinates by their position relative to the selected cell.

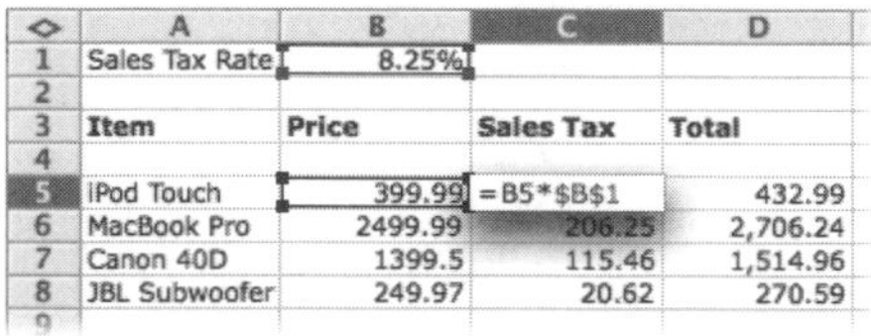

◇	A	B	C	D
1	Sales Tax Rate	8.25%		
2				
3	Item	Price	Sales Tax	Total
4				
5	iPod Touch	399.99	=B5*B1	432.99
6	MacBook Pro	2499.99	206.25	2,706.24
7	Canon 40D	1399.5	115.46	1,514.96
8	JBL Subwoofer	249.97	20.62	270.59

Figure 12-25:
The formula in cell C5 calculates the sales tax for the item priced in B5. The sales tax rate is stored in B1. Thus, the formula in C5 multiplies the price (B5) by an absolute reference to the sales tax rate (expressed B1). When you copy this formula, it always refers to the fixed cell B1.

Relative cell references also make formulas portable: When you paste a formula that adds up the two cells above it into a different spot, the pasted cell adds up the two cells above *it* (in its new location).

The yearly totals in Figure 12-23 show how this works. When you "filled" the Total formula across to the other cells, Excel pasted *relative* cell references into all those cells that say, in effect, "Display the total of the numbers in the cells *above this cell*." This way, each column's subtotal applies to the figures in that column. (If Excel instead pasted absolute references, then all the cells in the subtotal row would show the sum of the first-year column.)

Absolute references, on the other hand, refer to a specific cell, no matter where the formula appears in the spreadsheet. They can be useful when you need to refer to a particular cell in the spreadsheet—the one containing the sales tax rate, for example—for a formula that repeats over several columns. Figure 12-25 gives an example.

You designate an absolute cell reference by including a $ in front of the column and/or row reference. (For the first time in its life, the $ symbol has nothing to do with money.) For example, A7 is an absolute reference for cell A7.

You can also create a *mixed reference* in order to lock the reference to *either* the row or column—for example, G$8, in which the column reference is relative and the row is absolute. You might use this unusual arrangement when, for example, your column A contains discount rates for the customers whose names appear in column B. In writing the formula for a customer's final price (in column D, for example), you'd use a *relative* reference to a row number (different for every customer), but an *absolute* reference to the column (always A).

Tip: There's a handy shortcut that can save you some hand-eye coordination when you want to turn an absolute cell reference into a relative one, or vice versa. First, select the cell that contains the formula. In the Formula bar, highlight only the cell name you'd like to change. Then press ⌘-T. This keystroke makes the highlighted cell name cycle through different *stages* of absoluteness—for example, it changes the cell reference B4 first to B4, then to B$4, then to $B4, and so on.

Excel, the List Maker

After spending years loading up Excel with advanced number-crunchy features like pivot tables, database queries, and nested formulas, in 1999 Microsoft decided to step back and conduct some studies to see how its customers were enjoying their NASA-caliber spreadsheet program.

And what were 65 percent of Excel fans doing with all this power?

Making lists.

That's right—most people use the software that drives uncounted businesses and statistical analyses for nothing more than building lists of phone numbers, CD collections, and so on.

That's why Microsoft, which never met a feature it didn't like, created the Macintosh-only List Manager, which simplifies building and manipulating lists (Figure 12-26). Excel does this by creating something called a *list object,* which is nothing more than a simple database. It's made up of rows (which are the same as database *records*—that is, the individual "Rolodex cards" of an address database) and columns (which are like the *fields* in a database record—that is, the address, city, zip code, and other bits of information). These rows and columns are contained inside a list frame.

The List Manager has a number of features that improve upon using regular spreadsheet cells to store your lists (and upon Excel *databases,* as they were called long ago):

- The list frame, a special border that appears when you click a list object, clearly outlines your data. You don't have to wonder which cells are meant to be part of the list.

Heading row

List Frame (thickens when list object is selected)

AutoFilter (to sort and filter list)

Figure 12-26:
List objects are among Excel's best features. These self-contained mini-databases allow you to create a list in record time. The top row has in-cell buttons for popping up the AutoFilter menu. This menu lets you sort your list and temporarily hide any unwanted data. In the optional Total row at the bottom, you can quickly insert formulas via in-cell buttons that pop up the Function menu.

New record row (for entering new data)

Total row (shows column totals, averages, and so on)

Function menu
(to quickly enter
functions for
Total row)

- Excel keeps the column headings of a list completely separate from the data beneath them. As a result, they won't disappear or get sorted into the rows of the list itself, as might have happened outside a list object.

- You always get an empty record row at the bottom of the list, making it easy to add a new record; just click in the row and type.

- Lists have pop-up AutoFilter menus that make it simple to sort their rows or even *filter* them (so that only certain rows remain visible).

- Unlike Excel databases of old, you can have more than one list per spreadsheet.

The List Manager feature, in other words, is ideal for tasks like these:

- Build a list of all of the DVDs in your vast collection and sort them by genre, rating, number of stars in reviews, whether discs have director's commentaries—the possibilities are endless.

- Create a restaurant list for every city you visit, complete with names, categories, comments, and telephone numbers. When leaving for a trip to Detroit, you can filter that list so that it shows only the names of eateries in Detroit.

- Make an inventory list, with prices, part numbers, and warehouse location; you can later add a column to that list when you remember that you should have included something to indicate availability. Plus, you can format your list with alternating row colors that still alternate properly when you add a new column.

Just try *any* of these tricks with a plain spreadsheet and you'll soon understand exactly why Microsoft gave special attention to the List Manager.

Building Your List with the List Wizard

Excel's List Wizard walks you through building a list. Here's how to build a new list from scratch—in this example, a catalog of your burgeoning DVD collection.

Tip: To build a list object out of an existing list, first select all of the cells that make up your existing list, and then choose select Insert → List. The List Wizard walks you through turning your ersatz list into the real deal.

---

1. **In a new spreadsheet, click where you want the list to be.**

   You can always move it later.

2. **Choose Insert → List.**

   Excel presents the List Wizard (see Figure 12-27). The first screen asks you for the location of the data for your list and where you want the list to appear. Leave the data location radio button set to None (in this example, you'll be typing in the data *after* setting up the list), and leave the list location radio button set to "On existing sheet."

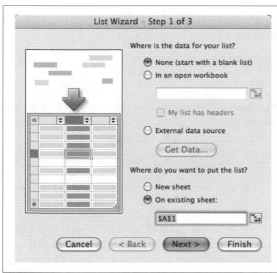

Figure 12-27:
The first step in the List Wizard has three options for data sources for your lists: None (meaning you'll enter the data as you go along), Excel worksheet (use this to convert a selection into a list), and External data source (which lets you access a database via Microsoft Query and ODBC— more on page 614). As for where the list goes, you can specify a location in the worksheet currently open, or you can tell Excel to create a whole new sheet for your list to call home.

3. **Click Next.**

   Now the List Wizard wants you to specify the columns for your list (see Figure 12-28). If you've ever used FileMaker Pro or another database program, you should be familiar with this process—it's very similar to the one used to create fields for a database file.

Figure 12-28:
The second step of the List Wizard looks like a database field definition dialog box, and for good reason—Excel lists are databases, at heart. In this step, you can create as many or as few columns as your list needs, and specify settings for each column.

Your DVD collection list will include six columns: Title, Director, Year, Cost, Rating, and Comments.

4. **Type *Title* into the Column name field.**

The List Wizard lets you classify each column as one of 10 data types, such as numbers, text, or dates. It even lets you set a column to be *another* list or a calculated value, which lets you bring formulas into your lists.

5. **From the "Data type" pop-up menu, choose Text; click Add.**

Excel adds the Name column to its list.

6. **Type *Director*, then click Add; type *Year*.**

The "Data type" pop-up menu remains set to the correct setting—*Text*—for the Director column. For the Year column, choose "Whole number," since you're interested only in the year, not an exact date. Click Add again.

7. **Type *Cost*; change the "Data type" pop-up menu to read Currency. Click Add.**

8. **Type *Rating*; set the Data type to Whole number and click the Settings button.**

The Column Settings dialog box appears. Once you've created a column, you can double-click its name to get back to this dialog box. Here, you can change the settings for the column (including its name and data type). You can also specify a *default* value for it—that is, each time you add a new row to your list, Excel will fill in a canned entry for this row automatically. If most of your DVDs are Blu-ray disks, for example, your DVD-database list might contain a Disk-type column with *Blu-ray* set up to be the automatic value for each new video you add to your list. (For the DVDs of other types, you could always type in something different.)

Column Settings also has a checkbox called "Unique values only." If you use this option, Excel requires that whatever you type into this list column is *unique* (not duplicated in the list)—for example, a serial number.

Suppose you turn this on for the Title field in a DVD list. When somebody tries to enter the name of a DVD that you've already cataloged, Excel beeps, alerting them that this column is supposed to contain unique values, and refuse to budge until the entry is changed.

You can also format cells using two handy buttons. By clicking the Formatting button, you bring up Excel's Format Cells dialog box, where you can set up this column's type and formatting characteristics: number formatting; text alignment, rotation, and indentation; font size, style, and color; cell borders; fill patterns and colors; and whether a cell is locked or hidden. (The first half of Chapter 13 gives you much more on these possibilities.)

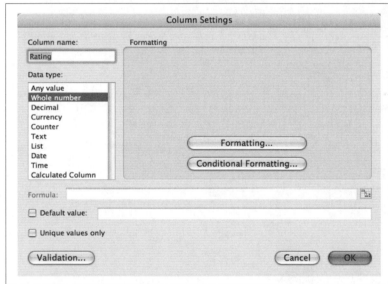

Figure 12-29:
The Column Settings dialog box contains much of the power behind Excel's lists. Here you can set a column's data type, whether the data entered in a column has to be a specific kind of data, and how Excel formats that data. The Conditional Formatting button is the key to some of the graphic power of lists, letting you specify changes in appearance depending on how the data in the column changes.

The Conditional Formatting button, on the other hand, brings up the Conditional Formatting dialog box, where you can set a series of rules to change a cell's formatting *automatically,* depending on what's happening in the cell. This feature can do things like make positive numbers in your Profits column appear in green, and losses in red. (You'll find more on conditional formatting in Chapter 13.)

Finally, Column Settings has a Validation button. It summons a powerful window called Data Validation, where you can specify limits for the text or numbers typed into each cell in this column—and what happens if somebody disregards the limits.

9. **For the DVD rating column, click the Validation button and in the first Settings tab, enter Whole number, Between 1 and 10 (see Figure 12-30, top).**

   Also turn on the "Ignore blank" checkbox so that you can leave this column blank if, for example, you haven't viewed the DVD yet.

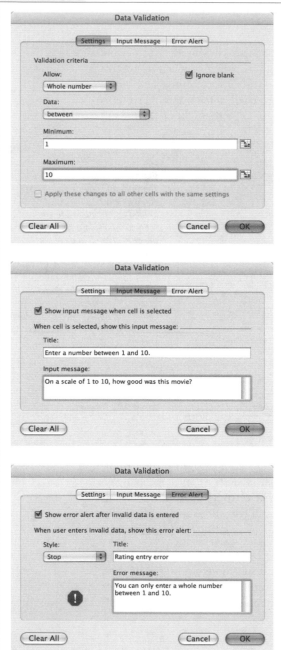

Figure 12-30:
The Data Validation window has three tabs.

Top: Settings lets you set up what kind of data should be entered in a given column, like numbers only or text of a specific length.

Middle: Input Message lets you create an alert message that will appear when a cell in the column is selected.

Bottom: Error Alert lets you tell Excel what kind of remonstrance to display if someone tries to enter data that doesn't fit what you had in mind. You also get to choose which icon is shown in the error alert—a stop sign, a caution sign, or an exclamation point in a speech bubble—and to determine what options for continuing the warning dialog offers.

10. Click **Input Message**, turn on the checkbox, and type a brief title and the input message you'd like to appear when you land on a cell in this column (**Figure 12-30, middle**).

Perhaps, *On a scale of 1 to 10, how good was this movie?*

11. Click **Error Alert**, turn on the checkbox, enter a title and message to appear when you attempt to enter the wrong type of data in this column, and set the Style pop-up menu to **Stop** (**Figure 12-30, bottom**).

The pop-up menu lets you determine what happens when Excel sees an entry error: *Stop* prevents you from continuing until you enter the data properly; *Warning* presents a dialog box where the default button returns you to data entry mode so you can try again; and *Information* presents a dialog box that informs you you've made an error, but lets you press Return to continue on to the next cell.

12. Click **OK to return to the Column Settings dialog box, and click OK again.**

Excel returns you once again to the Wizard.

13. Create a final text column for *Comments*, and click Next to continue.

Finally, step 3 of 3 (at least according to the List Wizard). In this ultimate step, you name the list, choose to show the totals row, and control whether the list's visuals—its display of pop-up menu controls and such, that is—appear.

Of particular interest here is the "Autoformat list after editing" checkbox. If you turn it on and then click AutoFormat, you're given a list of 16 preset formats (color and accent schemes) for the list, as shown in Figure 12-31.

The DVD list requires a total row to keep track of what you've spent on your collection and perhaps discover the average rating for your collection. Turn on the "Show totals row" checkbox.

14. Click **Finish.**

You return to your spreadsheet, where the newborn list appears.

You're done with the List Wizard, but not with the list; it still needs some touching up. By widening the columns, you can make room for column entries that are extra long. (If, by some chance, you need to add a column to your list later, you can click the Insert Column button in the List toolbar.)

Click the cells in the Total row beneath the Cost and Rating columns and use the pop-up menu to choose *SUM* for Cost, and *Average* for Rating (see Figure 12-26).

Congratulations—you've just made a list to help you organize your cinema collection! To start filling it with information, click the upper-left cell and type the first movie's name. Press Tab after you fill in each cell, or Return whenever you want to jump down to the next row. The list frame grows automatically to accommodate your growing stack of rows.

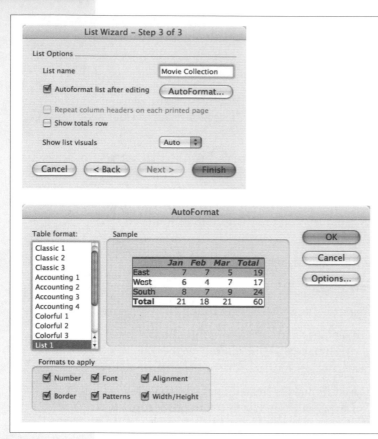

Figure 12-31:
Top: The final step in the List Wizard lets you set some general list options and apply automatic formatting via the AutoFormat button.

Bottom: Each of these prefab design templates is designed to save you time and increase readability. Click the Options button to choose how many aspects of the preset format to include in your list.

As you go, you may note that AutoComplete works in list objects as well as in regular worksheets. In fact, Excel may sprout a pop-up list as you enter information into a cell. The list consists of entries you've added to the column that begin with the same characters you've typed in the cell. If a sprouted list contains an entry you want to reuse, just click the entry (or press the down arrow until you highlight the desired entry and then press Enter); Excel fills in the cell you were editing, saving you some typing.

Note: Excel offers a list of entries you've used in the column *even* if you've turned on the "Unique values only" option for the column. It just goes to show you: Even smart software can be pretty simple-minded.

What to Do with a List

An Excel list is a dynamic, living object that has more in common with a database than it does with a regular pencil-and-paper list. What follows are some basic things that you can do with a list, just to get you on the road to your personal list-making nirvana. For many of these tricks, you'll need the List toolbar. It generally opens when you click a list so that its frame appears; if you don't see it, choose View → Toolbars → List.

Add a row or column

To add a row to a list, select a cell or cells in the row *below* where you want the new row to appear, and then click the Insert Row button on the List toolbar. To insert a column in a list, select a cell or cells *to the right* of where you want the new column to appear, and then click the Insert Column button. The new column appears to the left of the selected cell or cells. You can also get to either of these insert commands by choosing Insert → Row or Insert → Column from the List pop-up button in the List toolbar.

Delete a row or column

To delete a row or column, select a cell or cells in the row or column you want to delete, and then choose Delete → Row or Delete → Column from the List pop-up button in the List toolbar.

When you delete a column or row in a list that you've formatted with an alternating colored-row scheme using AutoFormat, Excel automatically reshades all of the rows and columns so that they're still alternating—something that you'd have to do by hand if you tried this in a spreadsheet without the list feature.

Rearrange a row or column

To move an entire row to a new location, select it by moving the cursor over the list border to the left, and then click to select the row (as shown in Figure 12-32, top). Now move the row by dragging it by one of its borders, as if it were a range of cells (the cursor should look like a hand). Moving an entire column works the same way: Select it by moving the cursor over the list border until it changes to the downward-pointing arrow shape (Figure 12-32, bottom), and then click to select the column. You can now move the column by dragging one of its side or bottom borders.

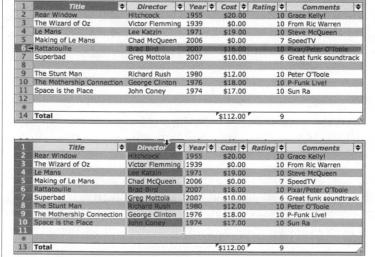

Figure 12-32:

Top: To select a row in a list, click at its left border. (The cursor turns into an arrow when you're in the right spot.)

Bottom: To select a column, use the same technique: Click at the top of the column, but make sure you're arrow cursor has a black bar on top of it—otherwise you'll select the entire spreadsheet column.

Sort and filter the list

You can pop up the AutoFilter menu on the right side of each column heading to *sort* your list (change the order of your records) and *filter* it (choose which records to show and which to conceal). Figure 12-26 shows the menu.

Note: If the in-cell buttons for the AutoFilter menu don't appear in the top row when you click the list, check the List toolbar and turn on Visuals and AutoFilters.

Slicing and dicing your list is easy with the three-part AutoFilter menu. Choose commands from the top part to sort the list in ascending or descending order based on the entries in that column. The middle part lets you filter the list using three different commands: Show All reveals all items in the list, Show Top 10 shows the top or bottom number of items or percent (for numerical items only) that you choose in the dialog box that appears, and Custom Filter lets you build your own filter. The bottom part lists the unique entries in the column; if there are duplicate entries, Excel shows only one of each.

Tip: For more advanced sorting, select Sort from the List pop-up button in the List toolbar. The Sort dialog box lets you choose three criteria by which to sort your list, much as you might do with a database.

By selecting Custom Filter from the pop-up AutoFilter menu, you open up the Custom AutoFilter dialog box, where you can create your own filter (see Figure 12-33). In it, you can set up a rule to filter the data with some simple operations and logical statements.

For example, you can show all data that's greater than a certain value or contains the word "blue." The Custom AutoFilter understands wild card characters, too. That is, you can insert a question mark (?) to mean "any typed character," or an asterisk (*) to represent any number of any characters. Although AutoFilter has only two fields that you can define and only two logical operators (AND, OR), you can use these in combination to build some complex filters indeed. However, you can't save this custom filter—it's a one-shot deal. The next time you choose Custom Filter in the AutoFilter menu you'll discover the Custom AutoFilter dialog box slate is once again blank.

Use the total row

A great feature in Excel's List Manager is the total row—which you can use by turning on the "Show totals row" checkbox in step 3 of 3 in the List Wizard. (You can also hide or show it by clicking the Total Row button in the List toolbar.)

The total row appears at the bottom of the list. If the rightmost column of your list contains number fields, Excel automatically adds up its contents and displays the result in the rightmost total row cell. If not, Excel counts the number of occupied rows appearing in your list and shows that result in the cell instead. (You can change this function using the pop-up Function menu that becomes available when you click the rightmost cell in the total row.)

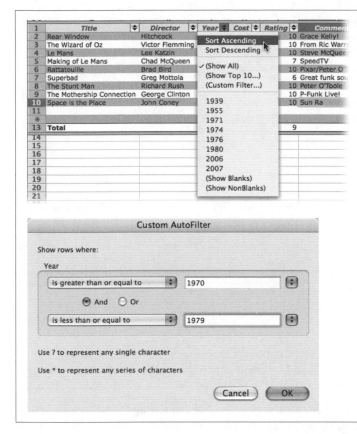

Figure 12-33:
Top: Click the Auto Filter button above any column to quickly sort or filter your list by the contents of that column.

Bottom: Choose Custom Filter to create your own temporary filter using one or two criteria and a logical and/or statement.

But you're not limited to placing a formula beneath the rightmost column. Using the Function pop-up menu in each cell of the total row, you can summon a variety of functions (see Figure 12-34). If you'd rather, you can choose Other and then work in the Formula Builder to concoct your own, even more complex formula. (You can even enter any formula you like using the Formula bar or the Formula Builder, and that formula needn't have *anything* to do with the items in the list.)

Move or delete the whole list object

Before you can move or delete a list object, you first have to select it. To do so, click the list to make its frame appear. Then position the cursor over the frame until the cursor turns into a hand. Now you can:

- Delete the list by choosing Edit → Clear → All.

- Move the list by dragging it to a new location or by choosing Edit → Cut. Then click where you want the upper-left cell of the list to move to, and choose Edit → Paste. Excel moves the list to the new location. You can move the list elsewhere on its worksheet, or switch to a different sheet in the workbook by clicking a tab at the bottom of the window. (If you paste a list into a different Excel workbook, the data appears, but not the list object.)

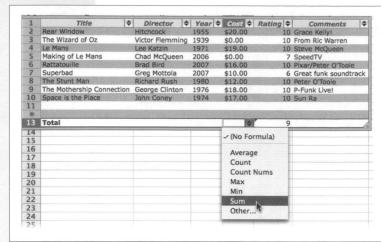

Figure 12-34:
To quickly add a formula to a cell in the total row, click the cell to activate its pop-up menu. Choose a function from the menu, or choose Other to bring back the Formula Builder, putting Excel's entire function collection at your mouse tip.

Note: Microsoft recommends that a list object containing more than 50 rows go on its own *listsheet.* Control-click the Add Sheet (+) button and choose Insert List Sheet.

The List Menu

The List toolbar gives you access to some of Excel's most powerful list-related features (see Figure 12-35). Most of its buttons relate to features you already encountered during your list construction.

But take special note of the List pop-up button, which is rife with useful commands. Some of them (Insert, Delete, Clear Contents) are self-explanatory. A few others could stand clarification:

- **Sort.** Opens the advanced Sort dialog box, where you can sort your list by up to three criteria (by Company, for example, and then alphabetically within each company group).

- **Filter.** AutoFilters are the canned filtering options that appear when you open the pop-up menu atop any column (such as Ascending, Descending, Top 10, and so on). Using this Filter command, however, you can choose AutoFilter to turn *off* the pop-up menu controls, thus removing your option to use those canned filters in case you never use them for that column. (The other commands in this submenu apply to old-style Excel databases, not to list objects.)

- **Form.** Calls up the Data Form, which lets you work with your list in a database-like environment.

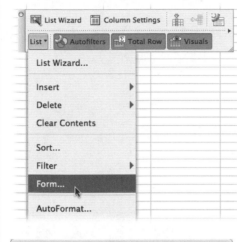

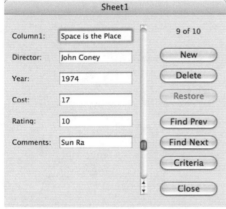

Figure 12-35:
Top: Whenever you create a list object, Excel invokes the List toolbar (if you don't see it, choose View → Toolbars → List). The arrow on the right edge opens a menu with commands for jumping around quickly in a list.

Bottom: The List button on the left gives a trove of helpful commands, including Form, which summons the Data Form, an alternative, database-like window for viewing, entering, and searching your list data.

- **Chart.** Turns your list into a chart, as described in Chapter 13.

- **PivotTable Report.** Opens the PivotTable Wizard to help you turn your list into a PivotTable (see Chapter 14).

- **Remove List Manager.** Converts the list back into a block of ordinary cells.

- **Refresh Data.** Grabs fresh data from the list's external data source, if it has one (see page 615).

Formatting and Charts

When you enter information in an Excel 2008 spreadsheet, your text appears in crisp, 10-point Verdana type. Serviceable, but do spreadsheets *have to look so* drab? Excel comes packed with formatting tools that let you show off your design genius and take spreadsheets from blah to brilliant.

For starters, Excel has a broad selection of fonts, colors, and borders to make your sheets stand out. Excel can also import pictures (either clip art provided by Microsoft or images of your own) and movies. You can even use Excel's drawing tools to create your own works of art.

The only reason many people put up with the chore of creating a spreadsheet in the first place is to produce charts. Whether you call them charts or graphs, they're graphical representations of lots of little bits of data—data that you first have to organize in a spreadsheet. Once those numbers are in place, the stage is set for a modern miracle: from the stultifying columns of numbers springs a gorgeous chart, dramatically revealing the hidden pattern behind the numbers. Not all charts are gorgeous, but they all reveal patterns and trends in the data that can be impossible to see in other ways.

If you've prepared your spreadsheet properly, creating a chart in Excel 2008 is a quick and easy process—and the results can be truly eye-popping thanks to the new OfficeArt graphics engine. The new Elements Gallery makes the process of previewing the dozens of chart styles, and inserting charts far easier. And once you've got a chart to work with, new 3-D effects, fills, and transparency allow for endless customization.

This chapter covers all of these visual aspects of Excel, including the payoff moment of printing out your graphically stunning spreadsheets and trend-clarifying charts.

Formatting Worksheets

When it comes to spreadsheets, the term *formatting* covers a lot of ground. It refers to the size of the cell, how its borders look, what color fills it, as well as how the *contents* of the cell are formatted (with or without dollar signs or decimal points, for example)—anything that affects how the cell looks.

Excel offers two ways to add formatting to your spreadsheet: by using Excel's automatic formatting capabilities or by doing the work yourself. Odds are, you'll be using both methods.

Automatic Formatting

If you're not interested in hand-formatting your spreadsheets—or you just don't have the time—Excel's AutoFormat tool is a quick way to apply formatting to your sheets. It instructs Excel to study the layout and contents of your spreadsheet and then apply colors, shading, font styles, and other formatting attributes to make the sheet look professional.

Note: AutoFormat is best suited for fairly boring layouts: column headings across the top, row labels at the left side, totals at the bottom, and so on. If your spreadsheet uses a more creative layout, AutoFormat may make quirky design choices.

To use the AutoFormat feature, select the cells you want formatted, and then choose Format → AutoFormat. The AutoFormat dialog box appears, complete with a list of formats on the left (see Figure 13-1). By clicking each one in turn, you'll see (in the center of the dialog box) that each one is actually a predesigned formatting scheme for a table-like makeover of the selected cells.

On the right is a button labeled Options, which lets you control the formatting elements that will be applied to the selected cells.

Once you've selected an AutoFormat option (and made any tweaks to the applied formats), click OK. Excel goes to work on the selected cells (see Figure 13-1). If you don't care for the results, you can always undo them with a quick ⌘-Z.

The Format Painter

Another way to quickly apply formatting to a group of cells is the Format Painter. Suppose you've painstakingly applied formatting—colors, cell borders, fonts, text alignment, and the like—to a certain patch of cells. Using the Format Painter, you can copy the formatting to any other cells—in the same or a different spreadsheet.

To start, select the cell(s) that you want to use as an example of good formatting. Then click the Format button (the little paintbrush) on the Standard toolbar.

Profit and Loss Statement: Time is Not Money

	2004	2005	2006	2007	2008
January	-1895	2323	12151	21979	30659
February	-1470	3142	12970	22798	29684
March	-1109	3961	13789	23617	32984
April	-752	4780	14608	27436	31597
May	-321	5599	15427	25255	31449
June	-648	6418	16246	26074	30945
July	-288	7237	17065	26893	34697
August	-305	8056	17884	29712	32458
September	-96	8875	18703	28531	33125
October	59	9694	19522	31350	35698
November	298	10513	20341	30169	34254
December	1697	11332	21160	30988	35412
Total	-4830	81926	199862	324798	392962

Profit and Loss Statement: Time is Not Money

	2004	2005	2006	2007	2008
January	-1895	2323	12151	21979	30659
February	-1470	3142	12970	22798	29684
March	-1109	3961	13789	23617	32984
April	-752	4780	14608	27436	31597
May	-321	5599	15427	25255	31449
June	-648	6418	16246	26074	30945
July	-288	7237	17065	26893	34697
August	-305	8056	17884	29712	32458
September	-96	8875	18703	28531	33125
October	59	9694	19522	31350	35698
November	298	10513	20341	30169	34254
December	1697	11332	21160	30988	35412
Total	-4830	81926	199862	324798	392962

Figure 13-1:
The AutoFormat dialog box is an expeditious way to make your spreadsheets more readable—and more attractive. You can transform the stock Excel appearance (top) to an eye-catching and more comprehensible presentation (bottom) with two quick clicks. Each scheme may include font selections, shadings for table rows, background patterns, and so on.

Now, as you move the cursor over the spreadsheet it changes to look like a + sign and a paintbrush.

Next, drag the cursor over the cells (or click a single cell) you'd like to change to match the first group. Excel applies the formatting—borders, shading, font settings, and the like—to the new cells (Figure 13-2).

Tip: To format discontinuous areas without going back to the paintbrush, double-click the paintbrush button. Now you can apply the format multiple times. To stop, click the paintbrush button again.

Formatting Cells by Hand

If the AutoFormat feature is a bit too canned for your purposes, you can always format the look of your spreadsheet manually. When formatting cells manually, it's helpful to divide the task up into two concepts—formatting the cells themselves (borders and backgrounds), and formatting the *contents* of those cells (what you've typed).

Changing cell size

When you open an Excel worksheet, all the cells are the same size. Specifically, they're 1.04 inches wide (the factory-set width of an Excel column) and 0.18 inches tall (the height of an Excel row). The good news is that there are several ways to set a cell's height and width. Here's a rundown:

Profit and Loss Statement: Time is Not Money					
	2004	**2005**	**2006**	**2007**	**2008**
January	-1895	2323	12151	21979	30659
February	-1470	3142	12970	22798	29684
March	-1109	3961	13789	23617	32984
April	-752	4780	14608	27436	31597
May	-321	5599	15427	25255	31449
June	-648	6418	16246	26074	30945
July	-288	7237	17065	26893	34697
August	-305	8056	17884	29712	32458
September	-96	8875	18703	28531	33125
October	59	9694	19522	31350	35698
November	298	10513	20341	30169	34254
December	1697	11332	21160	30988	35412
Total	-4830	81926	199862	324798	392962

Monthly Income from Day Job

	2004	2005	2006	2007	2008
January	987	1152	876	1289	1894
February	987	1152	876	1289	1894
March	987	1152	876	1289	1894
April	987	1152	876	1289	1894
May	987	1152	876	1289	1894
June	987	1152	876	1289	1894
July	987	1152	876	1894	2015
August	987	1152	1289	1894	2015
September	987	1152	1289	1894	2015
October	987	876	1289	1894	2015
November	987	876	1289	1894	2015
December	987	876	1289	1894	2015
Total	11844	12996	12577	19098	23454

Figure 13-2:
The Format Painter can take everything but the data from the cells on the top, and apply it to the cells on the bottom.

Note: If you use the Metric system, you can change to centimeters or millimeters on the Excel → Preferences → General tab. Choose from the "Measurement units" pop-up menu. Unfortunately, 4.59 millimeters is just as hard to remember as 0.18 inches.

- **Dragging the borders.** Obviously, you can't enlarge a single cell without enlarging its entire row or column; Excel has this funny way of insisting that your cells remain aligned with each other. Therefore, you can't resize a single cell independently—you can only enlarge its entire row or column.

To adjust the width of a column, drag the divider line that separates its *column heading* from the one to its right, as shown in Figure 13-3; to change the height of a row, drag the divider line between its row and the one below it. In either case, the trick is to drag *in the row numbers or column letters.* Your cursor will look like a bar between two arrows if you drag in the right place.

Note: Excel adjusts row heights automatically if you enlarge the font or wrap your text by turning on the Wrap text control in Format → Cells → Alignment (unless you've set the height manually, as described above).

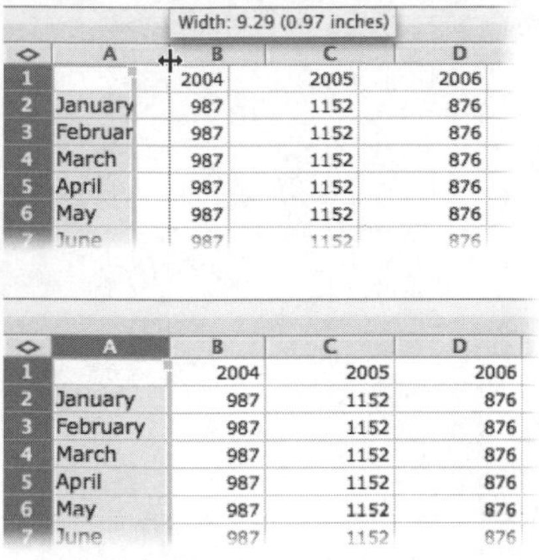

Figure 13-3:
Changing the width (top) of a column or height of a row is as simple as dragging its border in the column letters or row numbers. A small yellow box pops up as you drag, continually updating the exact size of the column or row. When you let go of the mouse, the column or row assumes its new size, and the rest of the spreadsheet moves to accommodate it. If you select multiple columns or rows, dragging a border changes all of the selected columns or rows—a lovely way to keep consistent spacing.

- **Menu commands.** For more exact control over height and width adjustments, choose Format → Row → Height, or Format → Column → Width. Either command pops up a dialog box where you can enter the row height or column width by typing numbers on your keyboard.

- **Autosizing.** For the tidiest spreadsheet possible, highlight some cells and then choose Format → Row → AutoFit, or Format → Column → AutoFit Selection. Excel readjusts the selected columns or rows so they're exactly as wide and tall as necessary to contain their contents, but no larger. That is, each column expands or shrinks just enough to fit its longest entry.

Tip: You don't have to use the AutoFit command to perform this kind of tidy adjustment. You can also, at any time, make an individual row or column precisely as large as necessary by double-clicking the divider line between the row numbers or the column letters. (The column to the *left* of your double-click, or the row *above* your double-click, gets resized.) When using this method, there's no need to highlight anything first.

Hiding and showing rows and columns

There are any number of reasons why you may want to hide or show certain columns or rows in your spreadsheet. Maybe the numbers in a particular column are used in calculations elsewhere in the spreadsheet, but you don't need them taking up screen space. Maybe you want to preserve several previous years' worth of data, but don't want to scroll through them. Or maybe the IRS is coming for a visit.

In any case, it's easy enough to hide certain rows or columns. Start by highlighting the rows or columns in question. (Remember: To highlight an entire row, click its gray row number; to highlight several consecutive rows, drag vertically through the row numbers; to highlight nonadjacent rows, ⌘-click their row numbers. To highlight certain columns, use the gray column letters at the top of the spreadsheet in the same way.)

POWER USERS' CLINIC

Conditional Formatting

Cell formatting doesn't have to be static. With Conditional Formatting, you can turn your cells into veritable chameleons, changing colors or typography on their own, based on their own contents.

A common example is setting up income-related numbers to turn bold and bright red when they go negative, as is common in corporate financial statements. Another common example is using this feature to highlight in bold the sales figures for the highest-earning salesperson listed in a column.

To use conditional formatting, select the cell(s) that you want to change on their own, and then choose Format → Conditional Formatting. In the Conditional Formatting dialog box, set up the conditions that trigger the desired formatting changes.

For example, to set up a column of numbers so they'll turn red when negative, use the first pop-up menu to choose "Cell Value Is" and the second to choose "less than." Finally,

type 0 into the text field, as shown in Figure 13-4. Then click Format to specify the typographical, border, and pattern changes you want to see if a highlighted cell's contents fall below zero. For example, in the Font tab, choose red from the Color pop-up menu and Bold from the Font Style list. Click OK.

By clicking the Add button at this point, you can even add a second set of conditions to your cells. For example, you might want your monthly income spreadsheet to show numbers over $10,000 with yellow cell shading.

You can apply up to three conditions to the same selection, but if more than one condition applies, Excel uses the first one to apply. In other words, if condition one doesn't apply, but conditions two and three do, Excel uses the second condition.

The dialog box previews how your cells will look if a condition is met. If everything looks right, click OK. You return to the spreadsheet, where numbers that meet your conditions now display their special formatting.

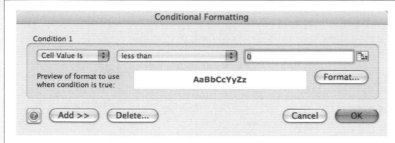

Figure 13-4:
Choose Format → Conditional Formatting to make cells style their contents according to the conditions you set in this dialog box. Let Excel tell you when your finances are "in the red" by formatting any negative numbers with that eye-catching color. Use the pop-up menus in the first line to set the condition and then click the Format button to tell Excel how to format the cell when that condition is met.

Next, choose Format → Row → Hide, or Format → Column → Hide. That's all there is to it: The column or row disappears completely, leaving a gap in the numbering or letter sequence at the left or top edge of the spreadsheet. The row numbers or column letters surrounding the hidden area turn blue.

Making them reappear is a bit trickier, since you can't exactly highlight an invisible row or column. To perform this minor miracle, use the blue-colored row numbers or column headers as clues. Select cells on either side of the hidden row or column. Then choose Format → Row → Unhide, or Format → Column → Unhide.

Alternatively, you can also select a hidden cell (such as B5) by typing its address in the Name box on the Formula bar, and then choosing Format → Row → Unhide, or Format → Column → Unhide.

Cell borders and colors method one: The Format Cells window

The light gray lines that form the graph-paper grid of an Excel spreadsheet are an optical illusion. They exist only to help you understand where one column or row ends and the next begins, but they don't print (unless you want them to; see page 596).

If you'd like to add solid, printable borders to certain rows, columns, or cells, Excel offers three different methods: the old, but most versatile Format Cells dialog box, the "Borders and Shading" section of the Formatting Palette, and the very similar Border Drawing *toolbar*. All techniques let you control how lines are added to the cell's edges, but only the Formatting Palette and the toolbar let you change borders and shading without first opening a dialog box to make the changes.

To add cell borders using the time-honored Format Cells command, highlight some cells and then choose Format → Cells (or press ⌘-1). The Format Cells dialog box appears; now click the Border tab to show the border controls. In this tab, you'll see three sections: Prescts, Border, and Line (see Figure 13-5).

1. **If you don't want to use the default line style and color, choose new ones in the Line section.**

   Excel loads your cursor with your desired style and color.

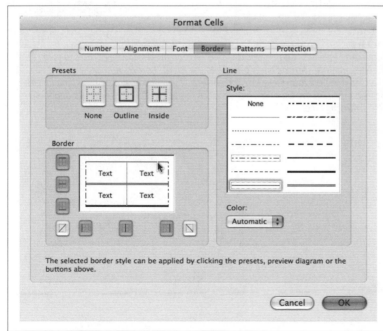

Figure 13-5:
Click directly in the preview area inside the Border section to place borders where you want them. First, select the style and color of line on the right side, and then click in the preview area to place the line. Or if you're feeling more button-oriented, use the eight buttons around the left and bottom edges of the preview area to draw your horizontal and vertical borders, and the oft-overlooked diagonals.

2. **To create a border around the *outside* of your selection, click the Outline preset button; to create borders for the divisions *inside* your selection, click the Inside button; and click both buttons for borders inside and around your selection.**

   As you click the buttons, Excel displays a preview of your work in the Border section. If you change your mind, click None to remove the option.

3. **If the Outline and Inside presets aren't what you have in mind, apply custom borders. Click directly between the guides in the preview pane to add or delete individual borderlines, or use the buttons that surround the preview.**

   To change a line style, reload the cursor with a new style from the Line section and then click the borders in the preview area you wish to change.

   If you mess up, click None in the Presets area and start again.

4. **Once the borders look the way you'd like, click OK.**

   Excel applies the borders to the selection in your spreadsheet.

Cell borders and colors method two: The Formatting Palette

To use Excel's Formatting Palette to draw borders, select the cells to work with, and then open the "Borders and Shading" portion of the palette by clicking the "Borders and Shading" Title Bar.

In this section of the palette, you'll see six controls that help you box in your cells and apply colors and patterns (Figure 13-6).

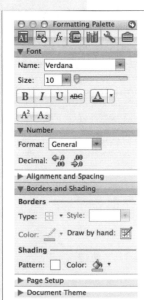

Figure 13-6:
The Formatting Palette's "Borders and Shading" section makes adding borders to your spreadsheet painless. Click the flippy triangle to the left of "Borders and Shading (or anywhere on that bar) to show or hide the controls. If you don't see the Formatting Palette, choose its name from the View menu, or click the Toolbox button in the toolbar and then click its Formatting Palette button.

Here's what each control does:

- **Type.** The button itself indicates the kind of border you've already applied to the selected cells; if you haven't applied a border, the icon on the button is a faint, dotted-line square. In any case, click it to open a pop-out palette of 18 different border styles, covering most conceivable border needs. The first 12 borders are standard fare, mostly outlines and single lines. The last six styles show more variety; some put borders on two sides of a selection or include thicker borders on one side. (If you point to one of these border styles without clicking, a yellow pop-up screen tip gives a plain-English description of its function.)

  This pop-up palette should be your first stop. Some of the other palettes described here aren't even available until you've first selected a border type.

- **Style.** Choose a line style, such as dotted lines or thick lines.

- **Color.** This button lets you choose from one of 40 preset line colors. Note that you can also leave the line color set to Automatic (which usually means black) if you choose.

Tip: If the idea of 40 *preset* colors puts the artist in you into a huff, calm down—you can mix your own presets. Choose Excel → Preferences → Color, choose one of the presets, and click Modify. Blend a new hue and you'll find it available anywhere Excel uses color. Even better, if you've already used that preset color, Excel changes it to reflect your new choice.

- **Pattern.** Instead of changing the style of *line* surrounding the selected cells, this button offers patterns with which to fill the selected cells' *backgrounds*. (The bottom half of this menu specifies the color that Excel will use to draw the black areas of the displayed patterns.) You'll probably find that most of the patterns make your cell contents illegible, unless you also select a very light color for the fill. However, both pattern and fill color can be very useful for headings or areas of your spreadsheet that don't display text. ("Automatic," by the way, means "no pattern.")

- **Fill color.** Clicking this button reveals options for 40 preset fill colors for your cell backgrounds. Here again, use this option with caution; unless you also change the text color to a contrasting color, you should use only very light colors for filling the cell backgrounds. (See the previous Tip to create custom colors.)

- **Draw borders by hand.** Clicking Draw by Hand brings up the Border Drawing toolbar, a Lilliputian toolbar with five unlabeled buttons. (Point to each without clicking to reveal its pop-up yellow label.)

The first one, Draw Border, pops up so you can choose between two modes: Draw Border and Draw Border Grid. The Draw Border tool lets you create a border that encloses an otherwise unaffected block of cells just by dragging diagonally in your spreadsheet; the border takes on the line characteristics you've specified using the other tools in the toolbar. The Draw Border Grid tool works similarly, except that it doesn't draw one master rectangle. Instead, it adds borders to every cell *within* the rectangle that you create by dragging diagonally, "painting" all four walls of every cell inside.

POWER USERS' CLINIC

Protecting the Spreadsheet Cells

Excel's Format Cells dialog box is a real workhorse when it comes to applying a bunch of formatting changes to a sheet. The first five of its tabs—Number, Alignment, Font, Border, and Patterns—let you exercise pinpoint control over how your spreadsheet—both cells and text—looks and feels, as described in this chapter.

The last tab—Protection—is the exception to the formatting rule. The Protection tab has only two options, presented as

checkboxes: Locked and Hidden. These two options let you protect selected cells from changes or hide formulas from view.

But be warned: Neither of these options takes effect unless you also protect the sheet through the Protection feature, which is nestled in the Tools menu.

To erase borders from the spreadsheet, click Erase Border and then drag across any unwanted borders (or those painted in by mistake). Press Esc to cancel the eraser cursor. (The middle button, Merge Cells, is described on page 572.) The active extremity of the eraser cursor is the very bottom—which appears to sparkle.

Tip: You can tear palettes off the Formatting Palette, which makes for easy access if you need to get to their functions frequently. To do so, click the Font Color button, for example, and then click the double-dotted line at the top of the pop-out. The Font Color palette "tears off" and becomes a window unto itself.

Changing How Text Looks

Borders and fills control how cells look whether or not they actually contain anything. Excel also gives you a great deal of control over the appearance of your text—which in spreadsheets is often numbers. The text controls in Excel are divided into three major categories: number formatting, font control, and text alignment.

Adding number formats

Number formats in Excel add symbols, such as dollar signs, decimal points, or zeros, to whatever raw numbers you've typed. For example, if you apply Currency formatting to a cell containing *35.4*, it appears in the spreadsheet as $35.40; if you apply Percentage formatting, it becomes 3540.00%.

What may strike you as odd, especially at first, is that this kind of formatting doesn't actually change a cell's contents. If you double-click the aforementioned cell that says $35.40, the trappings of currency disappear instantly, leaving behind only the 35.4 that you originally entered. All number formatting does is add the niceties to your numbers to make them easier to read.

To apply a number format, select the cells on which you want to work your magic, and then select the formatting that you want to apply. Excel comes prepared to format numbers using eleven broad categories of canned formatting. You get at them in any of three ways:

- The Format pop-up menu in the Number section of the Formatting Palette (better known as "the easy way"), as shown in Figure 13-7.

- The Format Cells dialog box that appears when you choose Format → Cells (or Control-click some cells and choose Format Cells from the shortcut menu).

- The old Formatting toolbar (choose View → Toolbars → Formatting). The new Formatting Palette is light-years more flexible, so if you have the screen space for it, you can safely ignore the Formatting toolbar. (Unless you, as a diehard Excel 98 fan, have a raging antipathy toward change, that is.)

Each method gives the same broad categories of formatting; however, options in the Formatting Palette and toolbar are far fewer. Instead, they apply the most popular choice (for example, $ signs when you choose the currency formatting) without asking your opinion. The Format Cells dialog box, on the other hand, gives you more control over each format, along with a helpful preview of the result.

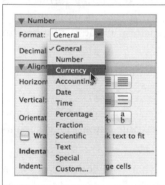

Figure 13-7:
The Number section of the Formatting Palette provides quick access to common number formatting options via the Format pop-up menu. It also lets you increase or decrease the number of decimal places shown by clicking the Increase Decimal or Decrease Decimal buttons.

The following descriptions identify which additional controls are available in the Format Cells dialog box:

- **General.** This option means "no formatting." Whatever you type into cells formatted this way remains exactly as is (see Figure 13-8).

- **Number.** This control formats the contents as a generic number.

  Format Cells dialog box extras: You have the option to specify exactly how you want negative numbers to appear, how many decimal places you want to see, and whether or not a comma should appear in the thousands place.

- **Currency.** A specific kind of number format, the Currency format adds dollar signs, commas, decimal points, and two decimal places to numbers entered in the selected cells.

A Number of Options	
35396.573	General
35396.57	Number
$35,396.57	Currency
$ 35,396.57	Accounting
11/28	Date
13:45	Time
3539657.30%	Percentage
35396 4/7	Fraction
3.54E+04	Scientific
35396.573	Text
35397	Special

Figure 13-8:
Here's how the 11 different number formats make the number 35396.573 look. Some of the differences are subtle, but important. The contents of Text formatted cells are left-justified, for example, and the Number format lets you specify how many decimal places you want to see. Date and Time formats treat any number you specify as date and time serial numbers—more a convenience for Excel than for you.

Format Cells dialog box extras: You can specify how many decimal places you want to see. You also get a Currency Symbol pop-up menu that lists hundreds of international currency symbols, including the euro. You can also set how Excel should display negative numbers.

Tip: The Currency setting in the Formatting Palette applies dollar formatting only if that's the currency you've typed in the Numbers section of the Format tab of the International panel of the Mac's System Preferences program.

- **Accounting.** A specific kind of *currency* format, the Accounting format adds basic currency formatting—a $ sign, commas in the thousands place, and two decimal places. It also left-aligns the $ sign and encloses negative numbers in parentheses.

  Format Cells dialog box extras: You can opt to use a different currency symbol and indicate how many decimal places you'd like to see.

- **Date.** Internally, Excel converts the number in the cell to a date and time *serial number* (see page 515) and then converts it to a readable date format, such as 11/22/2008.

  Format Cells dialog box extras: You can specify what date format you want applied, such as 11/22/08, November-08, or 22-Nov-2008.

- **Time.** Once again, Excel converts the number to a special serial number and then formats it in a readable time format, such as 1:32.

  Format Cells dialog box extras: The dialog box presents a long list of time-formatting options, some of which include both the time and date.

- **Percentage.** This displays two decimal places for numbers and then adds percent symbols. The number 1.2, for example, becomes 120%.

  Format Cells dialog box extras: You can indicate how many decimal places you want to see.

- **Fraction.** This option converts the decimal portion of a number into a fraction. (People who still aren't used to a stock market statistics represented in decimal form will especially appreciate this one.)

  Format Cells dialog box extras: You can choose from one of nine fraction types, some of which round the decimal to the nearest half, quarter, or tenth.

- **Scientific.** The Scientific option converts the number in the cell to scientific notation, such as 3.54E+04 (which means 3.54 times 10 to the fourth power, or 35,400).

  Format Cells dialog box extras: You can specify the number of decimal places.

- **Text.** This control treats the entry in the cell as text, even when the entry is a number. (Excel treats *existing* numbers as numbers, but after you format a cell as Text, numbers are treated as text.) The contents are displayed exactly as you entered them. The most immediate change you'll discover is that the contents of your cells are left-justified, rather than right-aligned as usual. *(No special options are available in the Format Cells dialog box.)*

- **Special.** This option formats the numbers in your selected cells as postal Zip codes. If there are fewer than five digits in the number, Excel adds enough zeros to the beginning of the number. If there's a decimal involved, Excel displays it rounded to the nearest whole number. And if there are more than five digits to the left of the decimal point, Excel leaves the additional numbers alone.

  Format Cells dialog box extras: In addition to Zip code format, you can choose from several other canned number patterns: Zip Code + 4, Phone Number, and Social Security Number. In each case, Excel automatically adds parentheses or hyphens as necessary.

- **Custom.** The Custom option brings up the Format Cells dialog box, where you can create your own number formatting, either starting with one of 39 preset formats or writing a format from scratch using a small set of codes. For example, custom formatting can be written to display every number as a fraction of 1000—something not available in the Fraction formatting.

Add or remove decimal places

To add or remove decimal places, turning *34* and *125* into *34.00* and *125.00,* for example, click the Decimal buttons in the Formatting Palette, as shown in Figure 13-7. Each click on the Increase Decimal button (on the left) adds decimal places; each click on the Decrease Decimal button (on the right) decreases the level of displayed precision by one decimal place.

Changing fonts

Excel lets you control the fonts used in its sheets via the Font portion of the Formatting Palette. As always on the Macintosh, highlight what you want to format, and then apply the formatting—in this case using the Formatting Palette.

Of course, you can highlight the cell(s) you want to format using any of the techniques described on page 520. But when it comes to character formatting, there are additional options; Excel actually lets you apply different fonts and font styles *within* a single cell (but not for formulae). The trick is to double-click the cell and then use the I-beam cursor to select just the characters in the cell that you want to work with—or select the characters in the Edit box of the Formula bar. As a result, any changes you make in the Formatting Palette affect only the selected characters.

Once you've highlighted the cells or text you want to change, open the Fonts section of the Formatting Palette (Figure 13-9) to reveal its four main controls:

- The **Name** pop-up menu lets you apply any active font on your Mac to the highlighted cell(s).

Tip: If your Mac has numerous fonts installed, you may find it faster to specify your desired font by typing its name in the Name field rather than by using the pop-up menu. As you type, Excel's AutoComplete guesses your intention and produces a pop-up menu for you to choose from. As soon as the correct font name appears, click it (or select it using the up- and down-arrow keys), and press Return.

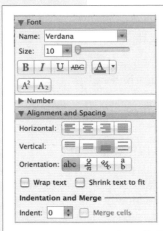

Figure 13-9:
Top: By tweaking the controls in the Font section of the Formatting Palette, you can quickly create your own custom text look.

Bottom: The "Alignment and Spacing" section of the Formatting Palette provides precise control over how text fills a cell; it can even be used to join cells together.

- The **Size** pop-up menu lets you choose from commonly used font sizes (9-point, 18-point, and so on). If the size you want isn't listed, type a number into the Size field and then press Enter or Return. (Excel accommodates only whole- and half-number point sizes. If you type in any other fractional font size, such as 12.2, Excel rounds it to the nearest half-point.)

- The **font style** item has buttons for applying bold, italic, underline, or strikethrough (or any combination thereof).

Tip: As you've no doubt come to expect, you can apply or remove these font styles to selected characters or cells without even visiting the Formatting Palette; just press ⌘-B for bold, ⌘-I for italic, ⌘-U for underline, or Shift-⌘-hyphen for strikethrough. In fact, you can use keyboard shortcuts to apply shadow and outline styles, which don't even appear in the Formatting Palette (probably because they look terrible). Try Shift-⌘-W for shadowed text, and Shift-⌘-D for outlined text.

- The **font color** control lets you choose from one of 40 different text colors for the selected text, cell, or cells.

- Finally, two last buttons allow you to change the selected text to **superscript** or **subscript**—which only works in cells formatted as text.

Changing the standard fonts

Whether you want a funky new font to lighten up your serious number crunching, or you want to switch back to the Geneva 9-point of your childhood, you can make that your standard font choice with a quick trip to the Excel → Preferences → General panel (Figure 13-10). After you change the Standard font and Size (the controls are right in the middle of the General panel) and click OK, Excel displays a warning message, noting that you have to quit and restart Excel before the new formatting takes effect in new worksheets.

Tip: To change fonts in old worksheets, press ⌘-A to select the entire sheet, and then change the formatting in the Format → Cells → Font tab. Or open the Formatting Palette and change it in the Font pane.

If you want to start all your new Excel spreadsheets with more than just a different font, you can create a template containing a variety of fonts, default text (your company name in the header, for example), formulas, and any other kind of custom formatting. Create a template exactly the way you'd like to see every new Excel spreadsheet begin life, choose File → Save As, name it *Workbook,* and turn off the "Append file extension" checkbox. Choose Excel Template (.xltx) from the Format pop-up menu and save the file in the Microsoft Office 2008 → Office → Startup → Excel folder. You can create a similar template for new worksheets by making a one-worksheet template named *Sheet* and saving it in the same location. From now on all new workbooks started by pressing ⌘-N or worksheets added when you choose Insert → Worksheet are based on those files.

If you later decide to change your standard workbook or worksheet template, follow the same procedure and replace the *Workbook* and *Sheet* Templates with new ones. If you'd rather return to the standard, completely blank workbook and worksheet appearance, just delete those two templates.

To make broader changes, that you can use optionally, instead of every time, you can create another template—a generic document that can be used over and over to start some of your new Workbooks. Because a template can hold formatting and text, it's a great base for a Workbook that you redo regularly (such as a monthly report).

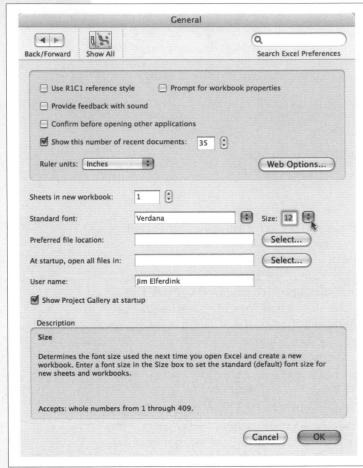

Figure 13-10:
The Excel Preferences → General pane lets you set what you'd like to see every time you start Excel. You can control the number of sheets in a new workbook, the font and font size, your preferred location to save Excel files, and even have an entire folder full of Excel documents open all at once. (Microsoft appears to be betting on the popularity of bigger and bigger monitors—you can choose font sizes up to 409 points!)

To make a template, create a new workbook or a copy of one that already looks the way you like it. You can select the entire sheet or specific sections of it, apply formats (as described in this chapter), and even include text (column headings you'll always need, for example). When you finish formatting the sheet, choose File → Save As. In the Save dialog box, enter a name for the template in the "Save As" field, and then choose Excel Template (.xltx) from the Format menu. Excel gives your file an .xltx extension and switches the Where pop-up menu to "My Templates." Click Save.

Back in Excel, close the template workbook.

Thereafter, whenever you'd like to open a copy of the template, choose File → Project Gallery. Click the My Templates category, and double-click your template.

Aligning text

Ordinarily, Excel automatically slides a number to the right end of its cell, and text to the left end of its cell. That is, it right-justifies numbers, and left-justifies text. (*Number formatting* may override these settings.)

But the Formatting Palette gives you far more control over how the text in a cell is placed. In the Text Alignment section of the palette (Figure 13-9, bottom), you'll find enough controls to make even a hard-core typographer happy:

- **Horizontal** affects the left-to-right positioning of the text within its cell. Click one of the four buttons to specify left alignment, centered text, right alignment, or full justification. You probably won't see any difference between the full justification and left-alignment settings unless there's more than one line of text within the cell. (And speaking of full justification, note that it wraps text within the cell, if necessary, even if you haven't turned on the text-wrapping option.)

- **Indent** controls how far text should be indented from the left edge of its cell. Each time you click the up arrow button, Excel slides the text approximately two character widths to the right. You can also click in the Indent field and type a number, followed by Enter or Return.

  It's especially important to use this control when you're tempted to indent by typing spaces or pressing the Tab key. Those techniques can result in mis-aligned cell contents, or worse.

- **Vertical** aligns text with the top, middle, or bottom of a cell. If the cell contains more than one line of text, you can even specify full vertical *justification,* which means that the lines of text will be spread out vertically enough to fill the entire cell.

- **Orientation** rotates text within its cell. That is, you can make text run "up the wall" (rotated 90 degrees), slant at a 45-degree angle, or form a column of right-side-up letters that flow downward. You might want to use this feature to label a vertical stack of cells, for example.

- **Wrap text** affects text that's too wide to fit in its cell. If you turn it on, the text will wrap onto multiple lines to fit inside the cell. (In that case, the cell grows taller to make room.) When the checkbox is off, the text simply gets chopped off at the right cell border (if there's something in the next cell to the right), or it overflows into the next cell to the right (if the next cell is empty).

- **Shrink to fit** attempts to shrink the text to fit within its cell, no matter how narrow it is. If you've never seen 1-point type before, this may be your opportunity.

- **Merge cells** causes two or more selected cells to be merged into one large cell (described next).

Merging cells

Every now and then, a single cell isn't wide enough to hold the text you want placed inside—the title of a spreadsheet, perhaps, or some other heading. For example, the title may span several columns, but you'd rather not widen a column just to accommodate the title.

The answer is to *merge cells* into a single megacell. This function removes the borders between cells, allowing whatever you put in the cell to luxuriate in the new space. You can merge cells across rows, across columns, or both.

To merge two or more cells, select the cells you want to merge, verify that the Text Alignment portion of the Formatting Palette is open, and then turn on the Merge Cells checkbox, shown in Figure 13-11.

Warning: Merging two or more cells containing data discards *all* of the data except whatever's in the upper-left cell.

To unmerge merged cells, select the cells and turn off the Merge Cells checkbox; the missing cell walls return. Note, however, that although the combined space returns to its original status as independent cells, any data discarded during the merge process doesn't return.

You can also merge and unmerge cells by using the Format Cells dialog box. To do this, select the cells to merge, then press ⌘-1 (or choose Format → Cells or Control-click the cells and choose Format Cells from the contextual menu). In the Format

Profit and Loss Statement: Time is Not Money					
	2004	**2005**	**2006**	**2007**	**2008**
January	-1895	2323	12151	21979	30659
February	-1470	3142	12970	22798	29684
March	-1109	3961	13789	23617	32984
April	-752	4780	14608	27436	31597
May	-321	5599	15427	25255	31449
June	-648	6418	16246	26074	30945

Figure 13-11:
Because Excel treats merged cells as one big cell, you can align the contents of that cell any way you'd like; you don't have to stick to the grid system imposed by a sheet's cells. One typical use for this is centering a title over a series of columns. Without using merged cells, centering doesn't do the job at all. When you merge those cells together and apply center alignment, the title is happily centered over the table.

Cells dialog box, click the Alignment tab, and then turn on (or turn off) the Merge cells item in the Text control section.

Adding Pictures, Movies, and Text Boxes

Although you probably won't want to use Excel as a substitute for Photoshop (and if you do, you have to be seriously creative), you *can* add graphics and even movies to your sheets and charts. Plus, if you're artistically inclined, you can use Excel's drawing tools to create your own art.

When using Excel for your own internal purposes—analyzing family expenditures, listing DVDs, and so on—the value of all this graphics power may not be immediately apparent. But in the business world, you may appreciate the ability to add clip art, fancy legends, or cell coloring (for handouts at meetings, for example). You can even add short videos explaining how to use certain features of your product—or even of the spreadsheet itself.

Although you can add text to cells, and merge cells to create larger text cells, you may often find it helpful to add larger blocks of text to a spreadsheet for explanatory paragraphs, descriptions of your services, or disclaimers reminding your clients that past performance is no guarantee of future results. Enter the Text Box, a mini text document or sidebar that you can place anywhere in a spreadsheet.

Excel gives you two ways of embellishing your spreadsheets with graphic elements of all kinds, the Insert → Picture submenu, and the Object Palette. All these tools work precisely as explained in depth in the Word section of this book.

When you add one of these graphic objects to Excel, it floats on top of the grid rather than inside a cell. You can resize and reposition these objects—and you'll usually want to position them over empty cells. However, Excel lets you cover up any parts of your spreadsheet data with these graphic objects without so much as a warning murmur. Consider yourself forewarned.

Objects in Excel spreadsheets feature a couple of extra options (or properties) you won't see in Word or PowerPoint. Since you're often adding rows and columns to spreadsheets as you work, graphic objects in Excel move along with whatever cells they happen to be sitting on top of. (If they didn't, you'd risk inadvertently covering your data-filled cells with a picture as you add new columns, for example.)

But if you don't like this behavior, you can change it—you can fasten the objects to a place on the page instead of in the cell grid. Here's how: Select the object and choose Format → Picture (or Object, Shape, or Text) and click the Properties tab, and then choose one of the three Object positioning buttons:

- **Move and size with cells.** This option keeps the object tied to the cells beneath it no matter how many columns or rows you add in front of it in the spreadsheet. Additionally, if you resize the columns or rows under this object, it automatically resizes along with them, so it always covers the same number of cells.

- **Move but don't size with cells.** This option keeps the object tied to the cells beneath (it's actually locked to the cell that its upper-left corner touches) it but the object remains the same size no matter how you resize the columns or rows beneath it.

- **Don't move or size with cells.** This option connects the object to a spot on the page, completely ignoring the cell grid. If you add or remove rows or columns the object stays in the same place on the page.

Inserting by the Picture submenu

To insert a picture, use the Insert → Picture submenu, which presents five options. Here's a summary:

- **Clip Art.** This command brings up the Microsoft Clip Gallery, a database containing hundreds of images in 31 categories. You can also search for specific images using the built-in search feature (see page 736).

- **From File.** Using this option, you can import into your sheet any graphic file format that QuickTime understands, including EPS, GIF, JPEG, PICT, TIFF, or Photoshop.

- **Shape.** Choose this command to summon the Object Palette's Shapes pane, from which you can insert many different automatically generated shapes—arrows, boxes, stars and banners, and so on (see page 737).

- **Organization Chart.** When you choose this menu item, Excel launches the Organization Chart application, which lets you create a corporate-style organization chart with ease. (This kind of chart, which resembles a top-down flowchart, is generally used to indicate the hierarchy of employees in an organization. But it's also an effective way to draft the structure of a Web site.)

- **WordArt.** The WordArt menu command opens the WordArt Gallery. You can add text and apply some wild effects, including 3-D effects, gradients, shadows, or any combination.

Inserting by the Object Palette

The Insert menu works splendidly, but it's a little slow and stodgy. In Excel 2008 you can add shapes, clipart, symbols, and photos with a quick click on the Object

Palette. To access them, click the Object Palette button in the Toolbox. The palette is divided into four sections—an objects section and a graphics section. The object section includes:

- **Shapes.** This palette lets you add any of Office's AutoShapes (see page 737).

- **Clip Art.** Click this tab to quickly access Office's collection of clip art and stock photos—although it's not as complete or searchable as the Clip Gallery accessed by choosing Insert → Picture → Clip Art (see page 734).

- **Symbols.** Adds the © (copyright) symbol and scores of other possibilities, saving you a trip to the Insert → Symbol dialog box (see the box on page 223).

- **Photos.** This tab provides a shortcut to your iPhoto collection or any other folder full of photos. (See page 292).

Inserting movies and sounds

Choose Insert → Movie to open the Insert Movie dialog box with which you can locate any QuickTime movie on your Mac to make part of your worksheet. Select it, and then click Choose. The movie appears with its upper-left corner in the selected cell. You can then resize and reposition it, and then double-click the cinematic masterpiece to play it (see page 294). You can insert a sound file in exactly the same way—it lands on your spreadsheet as a loudspeaker icon.

Inserting text boxes

Choose Insert → Text Box; Excel transforms your cursor into a letter A with a crosshair icon. Drag it diagonally anywhere on your spreadsheet to create a text box. When you release the mouse button, the insertion point begins blinking inside, awaiting your text entry. Move your cursor toward any of the text box's edges until it takes on a four-arrow shape—then you can drag and reposition the box. Surprisingly, unlike text boxes in Word, Excel text boxes feature the green rotating handle sprouting from their top. Drag it to rotate the box.

Excel text boxes are ready for text editing with one click. If you want to change the look of the text box itself—its fill color, line, shadow, and so on—you have the entire Formatting Palette at your disposal (see page 91).

If you don't want to take the time to format the appearance of a text box one element at a time, try the Formatting Palette's Quick Styles and Effects pane. Click one of the six effects tabs, and then click one of the style thumbnails to apply it to your text box. You can combine the effects to quickly create various 2-D and 3-D effects using shadows, reflections, glows, and so on (see page 751).

Charts

To paraphrase the old saying, "a graph is worth a thousand numbers." Fortunately, Excel can easily turn a spreadsheet full of data into a beautiful, colorful graphic, revealing patterns and trends in the data that otherwise might be difficult or impossible to see.

In place of the aged Chart Wizard of Excels past, Excel 2008 presents the new Chart Gallery. When you click its button beneath the toolbar, you can quickly scan through and choose a chart type from Excel's abundance of styles—and then make it your own by modifying it.

The keys to making an effective chart are to design your spreadsheet from the beginning of charthood, and then to choose the right chart type for the data (see Figure 13-12).

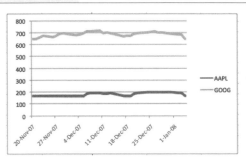

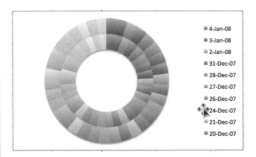

Figure 13-12:
Here's an example of the importance of choosing the right chart type to match your data. Both charts use the same set of data, but the line chart on the top is appropriate for the kind of data presented. Conversely, the doughnut chart below is the wrong way to present this information. All you get is a rainbow of colors that fails to communicate any useful information.

Chart Parts

Most charts share the same set of features to display your spreadsheet information as shown in Figure 13-13.

- **Axes.** An *X axis* (or category axis) and a *Y axis* (or value access) are the horizontal and vertical rulers that provide a scale against which to plot or measure your data. One axis corresponds to the row or column headings—in Figure 13-13 example, the row headings for date intervals. The other axis is the scale determined by the data *series*—in this case, dollars. 3-D charts may include a third Z axis (or series axis), at right angles to the other two, appearing to protrude from the plane of your screen right at you. Excel sometimes calls this the Depth axis.

- **Axis labels.** This term may refer either to the tick mark labels ("January, February, March…") or to the overall title of the horizontal or vertical scale of your chart ("Income, in millions" or "Months since inception," for example).

Tip: The X axis is the horizontal axis; the Y axis is the vertical. (Only the pie charts and doughnut charts don't have axes.) Having trouble remembering? Remember that the letter Y has to stand upright, or vertically. The letter X looks like an X even if it's lying on its side.

- **Series.** Each set of data—the prices of Apple stock, for example—is a *data series*. Each datum (or data point) in the series is plotted against the X and Y axes of the chart (except for pie and doughnut charts that don't have axes). On a line chart, each data point is connected to the next with a line. In a bar chart each data point is represented by a bar. Figure 13-13, column B of the spreadsheet contains the data series for Apple, and column C contains the series for Google. The chart data series can be drawn from either columns or rows of a spreadsheet.

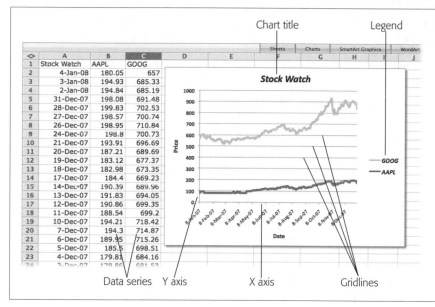

Figure 13-13:
The parts of a chart. The X axis corresponds to the rows in the spreadsheet. The Y axis corresponds to the units represented in the spreadsheet—like dollars. The data series are the columns—this is the information that gets charted. The legend identifies the data series, and tells the viewer how to interpret the chart.

- **Legend.** Just like the legend on a map, this legend shows what the lines or symbols represent. The legend displays the headings of the columns containing the data series and can also display the symbol used for the data points on the chart.

- **Gridlines.** To help readers align your chart data with the scales of one or both of the chart axes, you can choose to display gridlines extending from the axis across the chart. Gridlines come in two flavors: major gridlines line up with each unit displayed on the axis, minor gridlines further break up the scale between the major gridlines.

Understanding Data Series

To master Excel charts, you'll have to first master the concept of a *data series*. Put simply, a data series is a group of numbers or data points that represent a single row or column of numbers from a spreadsheet (such as monthly revenues). In a simple bar or column chart, Excel turns each data series into its own set of bars or columns and assigns a different color to each.

For example, suppose you have a chart with two data series—that is, the numbers begin life as two spreadsheet columns, as shown here with Revenue and Profit columns.

When you create the chart, each month's revenue might show up as a blue bar, and each month's expenses as a green bar. Each set of like-colored bars came from the same data series.

One more tip: When you make a chart from a selection of cells, whichever there is fewer of—rows or columns—becomes the data series. You can always switch this arrangement, swapping the horizontal and vertical axes of your chart, once the chart is born.

Step 1: Select the Data

The first step is to select the data that you want to chartify. You select these cells exactly the way you'd select cells for any other purpose (see page 520).

Although it sounds simple, knowing which cells to select in order to produce a certain charted result can be difficult—almost as difficult as designing the spreadsheet in the first place. Think ahead about what you want to emphasize when you're charting, and then design your spreadsheet to meet that need.

Here are a few tips for designing and selecting spreadsheet cells for charting:

- When you're dragging through your cells, include the labels you've given to your rows and columns. Excel incorporates these labels into the chart.

- Don't select the *total* cells unless you want them as part of your chart.

- Give each part of the vital data its own column or row. For example, if you want to chart regional sales revenue over time, create a row for each region, and a column for each unit of time (month or quarter, for example).

- It's usually easier to put the data series into columns rather than rows, since we tend to see a list of data as a column. Furthermore, the numbers are closer together.

- Keep your data to a minimum. If you're charting more than 12 bars in a bar chart, consider merging some of that data to produce fewer bars. For example, consolidating a year's worth of monthly sales data into quarterly data uses 4 bars instead of 12.

- Keep the number of data series to a minimum. If you're charting more than one set of data (such as gross revenues, expenses, and profits), avoid trying to fit six different data series on the same chart. Use no more than three to avoid hysterical chart confusion. (A pie chart can't have more than *one* data series.)

- Keep related numbers next to each other. For example, when creating an XY (Scatter) chart, use two columns of data, one with the X data and one with the Y data.

- You can create a chart from data in nonadjacent cells. To select the cells, hold down the ⌘ key while clicking or dragging through the cells to highlight them, as described on page 520. When you finally click one of the thumbnails in the Chart Gallery, Excel knows exactly what to do.

Step 2: Choose a Chart Style

When you click the Elements Gallery's Charts tab or choose Insert → Chart, Excel 2008's new Chart Gallery appears, with its row of buttons for choosing different chart types, and thumbnails that you click to insert a chart (see Figure 13-14). You can also access the Chart Gallery by clicking the Gallery button in the Standard toolbar or just clicking the Charts button in the Gallery bar below the toolbar.

Tip: If you've been charting in previous versions of Excel, you may be expecting the appearance of the Chart Wizard. But that Wiz is no more. The new Chart Gallery now does all that wizardry and then some.

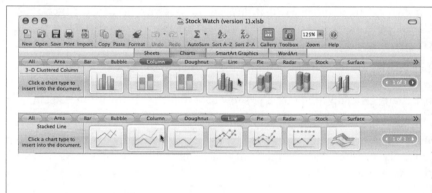

Figure 13-14:
Click the Gallery button in the toolbar to reveal Excel 2008's new Chart Gallery. Choose the various chart types by using the category buttons, and then click one of the thumbnails to insert a chart in your spreadsheet. If it's not exactly what you had in mind, click another thumbnail to recreate the chart in that style.

Your first challenge is to choose the kind of chart that's appropriate for the data at hand. You don't want to use a pie or doughnut chart to show, say, a company's stock price over time (unless it's a bakery). Excel makes it easy to preview how your selected data looks in the various chart types. Click one of the Gallery thumbnails, and Excel inserts that style chart in your spreadsheet. As you click other thumbnails, the chart display changes to the new style. Once you've got the correct chart type, you can resize it and drag it into position, just as you would with a picture. If you later decide you'd like a different style, select the chart and click a different style in the Gallery.

Here are your chart style options, each of which gives several variations:

- **Area** charts are useful for showing both trends over time or across categories *and* how parts contribute to a whole. **3-D area** charts are the way to go when you want to compare *several* data series, especially if you apply a transparent fill to reduce the problem of one series blocking another.

- **Column** charts are ideal for illustrating data that changes over time—each column might represent, for example, sales for a particular month; or for showing comparisons among items. As you'll see in the Chart Gallery, Excel offers 18 variations of this chart type. Some are two-dimensional, some are three-dimensional, some are stacked, and so on.

  Stacked-column charts reveal totals for subcategories each month. That is, the different colors in each column might show the sales for a particular region, while 3-D charts can impart even more information—sales over time plotted against sales region, for example.)

  3-D Column charts let you compare two sets of data. You can apply a transparent fill applied to the front data series to make it easier to see the ones behind it.

  Cone, cylinder, and pyramid charts are simply variations on basic column and bar charts. The difference is that, instead of a rectangular block, either a long, skinny cone, narrow cylinder, or a triangular spike (pyramid) represents each column or bar.

- **Bar** charts, which resemble column charts rotated 90 degrees clockwise, are as good as column charts for showing comparisons among individual items—but bar charts generally aren't used to show data that changes over time. Again, you can choose stacked or 3-D bar chart variations.

- **Bubble** charts are used to compare three values: the first two values form what looks like a scatter chart, and the third value determines the size of the "bubble" that marks each point.

- **Doughnut** charts function like pie charts, in that they reveal the relationships of parts to the whole. The difference is that the various rings of the doughnut can represent different data sets (data from different years, for example).

- **Line** charts help depict trends over time or among categories. The Line sub-type has seven variations; some express the individual points that have been plotted, some show only the line between these points, and so on.

- **Pie** charts are ideal for showing how parts contribute to a whole, especially when there aren't very many of these parts. For example, a pie chart is extremely useful in showing how each dollar of your taxes is spent on various government programs, or how much of your diet is composed of, say, pie. The Pie subtype has six variations, including "exploded" views and 3-D ones.

- **Radar** charts exist for very scientific and technical problems. A radar chart features an axis rotated around the center, polar-coordinates style, in order to connect the values of the same data series.

- **Stock** charts are used primarily for showing the highs and lows of a stock price on each trading day, but it's also useful for indicating other daily ranges (temperature or rainfall, for example).

- **Surface** charts act like complicated versions of the Line chart. It's helpful when you need to spot the ideal combination of different sets of data—the precise spot where time, temperature, and flexibility are at their ideal relationships, for example. Thanks to colors and shading, it's easy to differentiate areas within the same ranges of values.

- **XY (Scatter)** charts are common in the scientific community; they plot clusters of data points, revealing relationships among points from more than one set of data.

Excel creates the chart floating as a graphic object right in your spreadsheet with a handsome, light-blue selection border. Charts remain linked to the data from which they were created, so if you change the data in those cells, the chart updates itself appropriately.

Step 3: Check Your Results

Make sure your chart represents the range of cells you intended. If not, you can go back to Step one and start over again, or click the Edit button in the Chart Data pane of the Formatting Palette (or Control-click the blue chart border and choose Select Data from the pop-up menu). The Select Data Source window appears displaying the current chart data range and the included data series (see Figure 13-15).

If you need to adjust the data range you can edit the contents of the "Data range" fields, where the spreadsheet, starting cell, and ending cell are represented with absolute cell references (see page 540). The easier way to do it is to click the cell-selection icon to the right of the "Data range" field. This icon, wherever it appears in Excel, always means "Collapse this dialog box and get it out of my way, so that I can see my spreadsheet and make a selection."

Now is also your opportunity to swap the horizontal and vertical axes of your chart, if necessary, by clicking the Switch Row/Column button (also available in the Chart Data pane of the Formatting Palette as "Sort by" buttons).

The bottom section of the Select Data Source dialog box displays the data series included in the chart, and it also lets you add or remove a data series. To add another series, click Add. Name the new series by clicking in the Name field, and clicking the spreadsheet cell that labels a series. Then click the Y Values field and indicate the value a range by dragging through the data cells in your spreadsheet (see Figure 13-15).

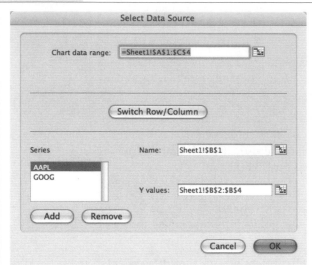

Figure 13-15:
The cell-selection icon just to the right of each of the three fields, appears in dozens of Excel dialog boxes. When you click it, Excel collapses the dialog box, permitting access to your spreadsheet. Now you can select a range by dragging. Clicking the cell-selection icon again returns you to the dialog box, which unfurls and displays, in Excel's particular numeric notation, the range you specified.

Step 4: Design the Chart Content

With the correct style chart in place, representing the correct range of spreadsheet data, you can now turn your attention to fine-tuning the various chart parts. Turn first to the Chart Options and Chart Data panes of the Formatting Palette (see Figure 13-16). Their various controls let you change the look of every conceivable chart element, including the chart and axes titles, how gridlines are displayed, where the legend is placed, how data is labeled, and whether the spreadsheet cells used to make the chart are displayed.

- The **Titles** section lets you enter names for your chart's title, its X axis, its Y axis; and its Z axis and second X and Y axes (if you have them). Select the various items with the pop-up menu and enter your titles in the box below. These names appear as parts of the chart.

- The **Axes** section lets you choose which of your charts and axes appear on the chart. Depending on the type of chart and your data, you can choose to show or hide the Vertical, Horizontal, Depth, Secondary Vertical, and Secondary Horizontal axes.

- Use the **Gridlines** buttons to show the Vertical, Horizontal, or Depth gridlines for the Major units—and the same options for the Minor units (see page 577).

- The **Other options** pop-up menu lets you add **Labels** to your chart data points. You can choose to add labels for either the data Value (the Y-axis value), or the Label (the X-axis value). Use the **Legend** pop-up menu to include a chart legend and determine where to place it in relation to the chart, to the left, right, bottom, and so on. The *legend* is the key that tells you what the chart's elements represent—its lines, pie slices, or dots. It's just like the legend on a map. After Excel places the legend in your chart, you're free to move it to another position.

Figure 13-16:
The Chart Options and Chart Data panes of the Formatting Palette contain most of the controls you need to set up your charts contents. Once the content is in place, you can move along to tweaking its appearance.

- The **Data Table** pop-up menu in the Chart Data pane tab lets you choose whether your chart shows the actual data that was used to build it, along with the chart itself. If you choose Data Table, this data appears in a series of cells below the chart itself. Choose "Data Table with Legend Keys" to make Excel reveal how each data series appears on the chart. You might find this option helpful should you display your chart separately from the spreadsheet—in a linked Word document, for example.

Step 5: Refine the Chart's Appearance

Like so many computer constructions, creating the content is just the beginning. Once your chart appears on screen, it's time to cozy up to your mouse and glee-fully putter with its appearance using Excel's abundance of alluring formatting options.

When modifying your chart, start with the most urgent matters:

- **Move the chart** by dragging it around on a sheet.

- **Resize the chart** by dragging any of its corner or side handles. (If you don't see them, the chart is no longer selected. Click any area inside the chart to select the whole chart, bringing back its blue border.)

- **Delete some element of the chart** if you don't agree with the elements Excel included. For example, for a simple chart you might not need a legend. Get rid of it by clicking it and then pressing the Delete key.

- **Reposition individual elements in the chart** (the text labels or legend, for example) by dragging them.

- **Convert a chart from an object to a chart sheet (or vice versa)** by selecting the chart and then choosing Chart → Move Chart and making the appropriate choice in the resulting dialog box.

- **Rotate a 3-D chart** by double-clicking the blue chart selection border to open the Format Chart Area dialog box. Click the 3-D rotation tab and use the up and down arrow buttons or type new numbers into the X, Y, and perspective fields (see Figure 13-17).

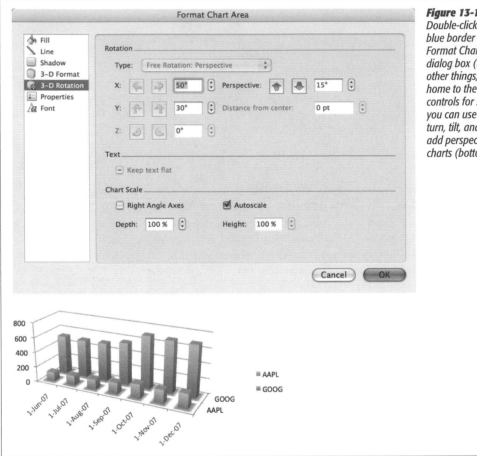

Figure 13-17:
Double-click a chart's blue border to open the Format Chart Area dialog box (top). Among other things, this box is home to the 3-D rotation controls for 3-D charts; you can use them to turn, tilt, and twist, and add perspective to 3-D charts (bottom).

- **Move series in a 3-D chart** to put smaller series in front of larger ones. Start by double-clicking any data series to open the Format Data Series dialog box, and then click the Order tab. Watch the chart as you click Move Up or Move Down.

To quickly change the appearance of a chart, select it and use the Formatting Palette's Chart Style and Quick Styles and Effects panes. For example, you can experiment with different chart color schemes using the Chart Style buttons. If you don't see a color combination you like, head down to the Document Theme palette and choose a different set of theme colors—which re-colors all of the Chart Style options. The Quick Styles and Effects pane lets you apply fill colors to individual chart elements, and add shadows and glows. (Modifying charts with Quick Styles and with the other Formatting Palette panes works the same as with other kinds of objects in Office, as described starting on page 744.)

The most complete chart appearance controls are found in the Format dialog boxes, many of which await your investigation (see Figure 13-18). To open the dialog box, just double-click the pertinent piece of the chart. For example, when working with a bar chart, you have the following options:

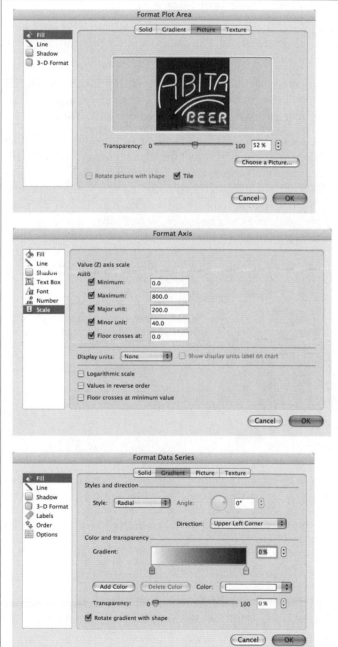

Figure 13-18:
By double-clicking the individual elements in a chart, you open a multitabbed dialog box that lets you change every conceivable aspect of them.

Top: The dialog box that appears when you double-click a chart background.

Middle: The choices that appear when you double-click an axis.

Bottom: Additional choices that appear when you double-click a chart bar.

- **Change the border or interior color** of the chart by double-clicking within the body of the chart.

- **Change the font, color, or position of the legend** by double-clicking it.

- **Change the scale, tick marks, label font, or label rotation of the axes** by double-clicking their edges or slightly outside their edges.

- **Change the border, color, fill effect, bar separation, and data label options of an individual bar** by double-clicking it. You can even make bars partially transparent, revealing hidden series at the rear, as described in the next section.

You'll also notice that when you select a chart, the Formatting Palette has specialized formatting controls relevant to your selection. Using the palette, you can change the chart type, gridline appearance, legend placement, and so on.

And if you still haven't found your preferred method of formatting a finished chart, choose View → Toolbars → Chart to reveal the Chart toolbar (Figure 13-19). It has a pop-up menu listing the various chart components (such as Corners, Floor, Legend, and Series Axis). Use it to select one of those items instead of double-clicking the chart itself. Then you can edit or delete that item as you normally would. This selection method can be much easier to work with if your chart is small, cramped, or contains a lot of data series.

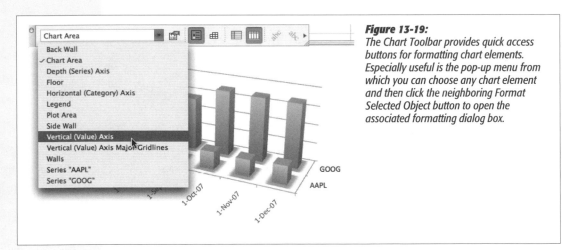

Figure 13-19:
The Chart Toolbar provides quick access buttons for formatting chart elements. Especially useful is the pop-up menu from which you can choose any chart element and then click the neighboring Format Selected Object button to open the associated formatting dialog box.

Tip: You can copy a selected chart into another program either by dragging it or by using the Copy and Paste commands in the Edit menu.

Transparent Bars

Individual bars of a chart can be partially or completely see-through, making it much easier to display 3-D graphs where the frontmost bars would otherwise obscure the back ones.

You can apply transparent fills to most chart types, but their see-through nature makes the most sense in charts with at least two data series, where the front series blocks a good view of the rear (Figure 13-20, top).

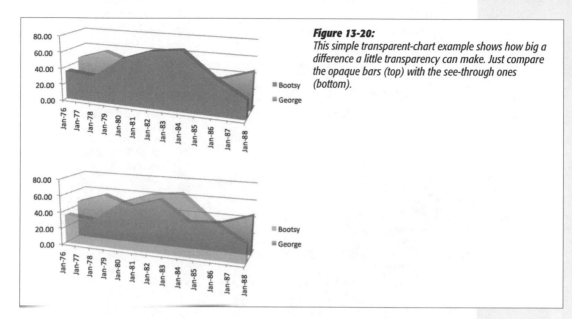

Figure 13-20:
This simple transparent-chart example shows how big a difference a little transparency can make. Just compare the opaque bars (top) with the see-through ones (bottom).

Begin applying a transparent fill to a data series by clicking the series (the bar or column, for example) and opening the Formatting Palette's Colors, Weights, and Fills pane. To make transparency available, you first have to change the color, even if it's to "change" the color to the *current* color by using the eyedropper on the object you're working with. You can then use the Transparency slider to adjust the opacity.

You can do the same thing via the Format Data Series dialog box, which appears when you double-click a series. When you first open this dialog box, the Color pop-up menu is set to Automatic, which prevents you from accessing the transparency option. But as soon as you choose another color from the pop-up menu, the Transparency slider becomes active and you can adjust the transparency of the series.

To format a multi-series 3-D chart for maximum "Wow" factor, you may also wish to rotate it (by double-clicking the blue chart selection border, clicking the 3-D rotation tab and typing new numbers into the X, Y, and perspective fields) or change the series order (double-click a series and work in the Order tab).

Advanced Charting

The Chart Gallery suffices for almost every conceivable kind of standard graph. But every now and then, you may have special charting requirements; fortunately, Excel can meet almost any charting challenge that you put before it—if you know how to ask.

Error bars

On some charts—such as those that graph stocks and opinion polls—it's helpful to graph not only the data, but also the range of movement or margin of error that surrounds the data. And that's where *error bars* come in. Error bars let you specify a range around each data point displayed in the graph, such as a poll's margin of error (Figure 13-21).

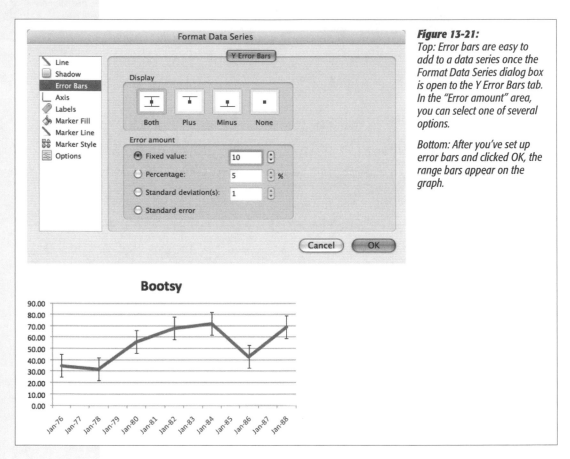

Figure 13-21:
Top: Error bars are easy to add to a data series once the Format Data Series dialog box is open to the Y Error Bars tab. In the "Error amount" area, you can select one of several options.

Bottom: After you've set up error bars and clicked OK, the range bars appear on the graph.

To add error bars to a chart, first select the data series (usually a line or bar in the chart) to which you want to add error bars. Choose Format → Selected Data Series (or double-click the selected line or bar) to bring up the Format Data Series dialog box. To add error bars along the Y axis—the usual arrangement—click the Error Bars tab; then choose display and error amounts for your bars. Click the OK button to add the error bars to your data series. If you want to remove them later, open the Format Data Series dialog box and set the Display to None.

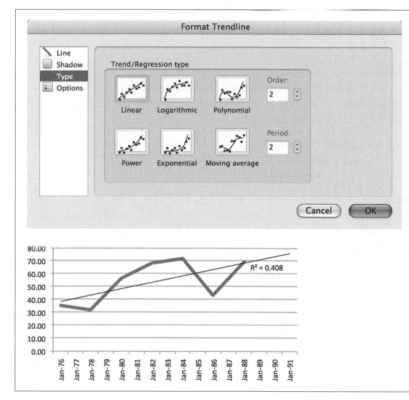

Note: You can add error bars to 2-D area charts, bar charts, bubble charts, column charts, line charts, and scatter charts. In fact, X axis error bars can even be added to scatter charts. (You'll see this additional tab in the Format Data Series dialog box.)

Trend lines

Graphs excel at revealing trends—how data is changing over time, how data probably changed over time before you started tracking it, and how it's likely to change in the future. To help with such predictions, Excel can add *trend lines* to its charts (Figure 13-22). Trend lines use a mathematical model to help accentuate patterns in current data and to help predict future patterns.

Figure 13-22:
Top: The Add Trendline dialog box gives you six trend lines from which to choose. If the trend line allows for it, you can also set the trend line's parameters in the Options tab.

Bottom: Once you've applied a trend line, it appears on top of your chart. You can also predict how the data might change in the future by setting the forecast values in the Options tab. If you set your trend line to display the R-squared value (also under the Options tab), Excel displays this value for you below the line.

Note: You can use trend lines only in unstacked 2-D area charts, bar charts, bubble charts, column charts, line charts, scatter charts, and stock charts.

To add a trend line to your chart, click to select one of the data series in the chart—typically a line or a bar—and then choose Chart → Add Trendline. This opens the Format Trendline dialog box, containing the tabs Line, Shadow, Type, and Options.

The Type tab lets you choose one of these trend-line types:

- **Linear.** This kind of trend line works well with a graph that looks like a line, as you might have guessed. If your data is going up or down at a steady rate, a linear trend line is your best bet, since it closely resembles a simple straight line.

- **Logarithmic.** If the rate of change in your data increases or decreases rapidly and then levels out, a *logarithmic* trend line is probably your best choice. Logarithmic trend lines tend to have a relatively sharp curve at one end and then gradually level out. (Logarithmic trend lines are based on logarithms, a mathematical function.)

- **Polynomial.** A *polynomial* trend line is great when graphed data features hills and valleys, perhaps representing data that rises or falls in a somewhat rhythmic manner. Polynomial trend lines can also have a single curve that looks like a camel's hump (or an upside-down camel's hump, depending on your data). These trend lines are based on polynomial expressions, familiar to you from your high school algebra class.

- **Power.** If the graphed data changes at a steadily increasing or decreasing rate, as in an acceleration curve, a *power* trend line is the way to go. Power trend lines tend to curve smoothly upward.

- **Exponential.** If, on the other hand, the graphed data changes at an ever-increasing or decreasing rate, then you're better off with an *exponential* trend line, which also looks like a smoothly curving line.

- **Moving Average.** A *moving average* trend line attempts to smooth out fluctuations in data, in order to reveal trends that might otherwise be hidden. Moving averages, as the name suggests, can come in all kinds of shapes. No matter what the shape, though, they all help spot cycles in what might otherwise look like random data.

The Options tab, on the other hand, lets you name your trend line, extend it beyond the data set to forecast trends, and even display the R-squared value on the chart. (The R-squared value is a way of calculating how accurately the trend line fits the data; you statisticians know who you are.)

Incidentally, remember that trend lines are just models. As any weather forecaster, stockbroker, or computer-company CEO can tell you, trend lines don't necessarily predict *anything* with accuracy.

Printing Worksheets

Now that you've gone through the trouble of making your sheets look their best with killer formatting and awe-inspiring charts, and you're set to print them out (and show them off).

Print Preview

Viewing a print preview before you send your spreadsheet to the printer can save you frustration and time, and help save an old-growth forest that would otherwise be harvested for the sake of your botched spreadsheet printouts. If you've used previous versions of Excel, you may recall that both Excel and Mac OS X had very similar print-preview functions. For Excel 2008, Microsoft has done away with the program's Print Preview altogether—a shockingly un-Microsoftian feature-reduction if ever there was one—leaving the print-preview function now entirely up to Mac OS X.

Tip: To check out your page-break preview without doing a print preview first, just choose View → Page Layout View or click the Page Layout View button at the bottom-left of the Excel window.

As in any Mac OS X–compatible program, you turn a document into a print-preview file by choosing File → Print and then, in the Print dialog box, clicking the Preview button at the bottom. Your Mac fires up the Preview program, where you see the printout-to-be as a PDF. Use the commands in the Display menu to zoom in, zoom out, scroll, and so on. Each page appears as a separate page image, with thumbnails of all the pages lined up in Preview's drawer at the side of the window.

Tip: To print just a certain portion of your spreadsheet, select the cells that you want to print and then choose File → Print Area → Set Print Area. This command tells Excel to print only the selected cells. To clear a custom print area, select File → Print Area → Clear Print Area. Alternatively, you can set a print selection for just a current print job by selecting the cells you want to print and then clicking the Selection option button in the Print What section of the Print dialog box.

If you've been working on your spreadsheet in Page Layout View, then any print preview may be a bit redundant. Instead, you can quickly flip through the Quick Preview right in the Print dialog box to get a general idea of your spreadsheet's pagination (see Figure 13-23).

Don't miss the best part of the Print dialog box—the PDF button. Choose Save as PDF from its menu to turn your printout into a PDF—or Acrobat—file that you can send to almost anyone with a computer, so they can open, read, search, and print your handiwork. (The software they need is Acrobat Reader, which is free, or Preview, which comes on the Mac.) Other options in this menu let you, among other things, fax a PDF save it into your iPhoto library, or attach it to an email message (but only if you're using Apple Mail—see the box on page 592 for a workaround).

If you're not seeing what you'd like to in the Quick preview window, click the Cancel button to cancel the print job and go back to configuring your document.

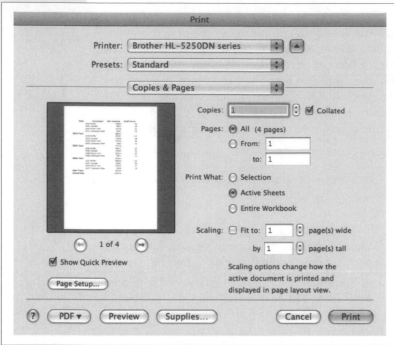

Figure 13-23:
*When you choose File → Print,
the standard print dialog box
appears, subtly enhanced with
Excel-only features. Use the Print
What radio buttons to choose
between entire workbook, just
the active sheets, or only a
selected area. If you need to be
sure to squeeze all the rows or
columns onto a certain number
of pages, click the Scaling
checkbox and enter the number
of pages wide, and tall. This
feature frequently comes in
handy to fit a just-slightly-larger-
than-one-page spreadsheet
onto one page.*

WORKAROUND WORKSHOP

Emailing Without Mail

If you choose Mail PDF from the PDF button in the Print dialog box, the Apple Mail program automatically opens to do the deed. If you don't use Apple Mail—perhaps you use, oh, Entourage—you can change the behavior of your Mac's Mail PDF function. To do so, you have to edit the Automator Workflow that's responsible for the handoff of a PDF to your email program, which isn't as complicated as it sounds.

Open the folder [Hard Drive] → Library → PDF Services and then double-click *Mail PDF.workflow.* The Automator window

appears, with the New Mail Message action showing in the right pane. Delete that action by highlighting it and pressing Delete. Type *Entourage* in the Search field, press Return, and double-click Create New Entourage Mail Message. The Entourage action appears in the right pane. Choose File → Save and then choose Automator → Quit. From now on when you choose Mail PDF from the print dialog box, Entourage handles the task.

Page Setup

Excel's Page Setup dialog box (Figure 13-24) is far more comprehensive than the Page Setup that appears when you choose File → Page Setup in TextEdit, for example. In it, you can control how pages are oriented, how spreadsheets fit on a page, the print quality, the margins, how headers and footers are printed, and the order in which pages are printed. These same controls are also available—and much more accessible— through the Formatting Palette's Page Setup pane.

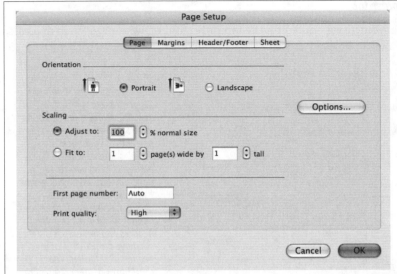

Figure 13-24:
*The Page tab of the Page Setup
dialog box is another place to
start if you want a spreadsheet
to print on one page. A click in
the "Fit to" radio button (in the
Scaling area) automatically
adjusts your spreadsheet's print
size to fit on a sheet of paper. If
you want it to fit on more than
one sheet, adjust the numbers in
the "Fit to" area.*

Page tab

In the Page tab, you can change the orientation for the print job (Portrait for the usual up-and-down style or Landscape for a sideways style—often the preferred spreadsheet format), reduce or enlarge the printout by a certain percent, or—using the "Fit to" radio button—force the spreadsheet to fit onto a certain number of printed pages. (Using this control, of course, affects the printout's type size.) If you don't want the pages of your spreadsheet numbered 1, 2, and so on, then type a different number into the "First page number" field. This is how you force Excel to number the pages beginning with, say, 5 on the first printed sheet.

Note: Setting the starting page number in the Page tab won't make page numbers appear on your sheets; you have to also initiate page numbering in the Header/Footer tab. The easiest technique is to choose a page number option from the Header or Footer pop-up menu.

An Options button on the right brings up the more familiar Page Setup dialog box for your printer, where you can set more of your printer's options (such as paper size).

Margins tab

The Margins tab (Figure 13-25, top) lets you specify the page margins for your printout (and for the header and footer areas). You can also tell Excel to center the printout on the page horizontally, vertically, or both. The Options button, once again, summons the standard Page Setup dialog box for your printer.

Header/Footer tab

If you want something printed on the top or bottom of every page (such as a title, copyright notice, or date), it's time to visit the Header/Footer tab (Figure 13-25, bottom).

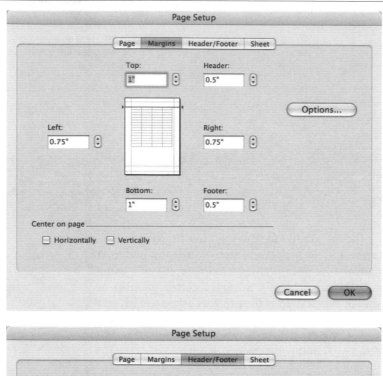

Figure 13-25:

Top: The Margins portion of the Page Setup window gives you power over your sheet's margins when printed, naturally. It lets you set top, left, right, and bottom margins, and it gives you the chance to determine how much top and bottom space is left over for headers and footers—useful if you have particularly large headers and footers. The checkboxes at the bottom of the box let you set how—and whether—your printouts are centered on the page.

Bottom: The Header/Footer part of the Page Setup dialog box is where you can set text to be printed on the top or bottom—or both—of every page.

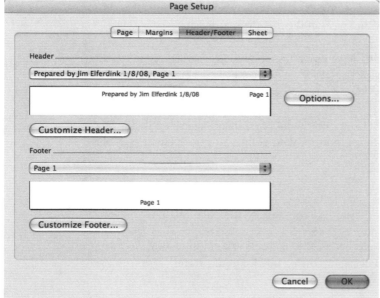

Here, you can use the Header or Footer pop-up menu to choose from a selection of prepared headers and footers—"Page 1 of 7," "Confidential," and so on.

If the header or footer message you want isn't there, click the Custom Header or Custom Footer buttons to bring up a customization dialog box. In it you can enter your own header or footer text; click the Font button to format the text; and use the remaining buttons to insert placeholder codes for the current page number, the total number of pages, the current date, the current time, the file name, and the tab name.

You can combine these codes with text that you type yourself. For example, in the "Center section" box, you could type, *DVD Collection Status as of,* and then click the fourth icon. Excel inserts the code *&[Date].* Now whenever you print this document, you'll find, across the top of every page, "DVD Collection Status as of 9/15/08," or whatever the current date is.

Sheet tab

The last section of the Page Setup dialog box, called Sheet, gives you yet another way to specify which portions of the sheet are to be printed (Figure 13-26). You can type starting and ending Excel coordinates—separated by a colon—into the "Print area" box, or click the cell-selection icon to return to the spreadsheet to select a region of cells you want printed.

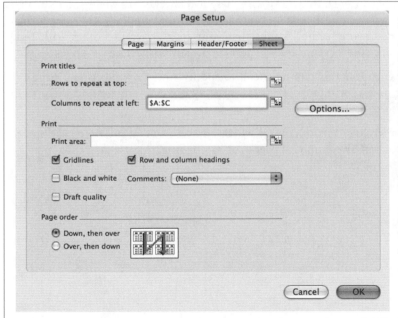

Figure 13-26:
The Sheet portion of the Page Setup window lets you set a print area (if you haven't already done so). If you want to display a certain range of data on every page, you can specify that certain rows repeat at the top of each page and/or columns repeat on the left of each page. It gives you five print options, letting you choose to print gridlines, row and column headings, print in black and white or draft quality, and print comments you may have added to the spreadsheet. Finally, you can choose print order: whether pages are printed down and then over, or over and then down.

You'll also find the following in the Sheet tab:

- **Rows to repeat at top, Columns to repeat at left.** If you've carefully typed the months of the year across the top of your spreadsheet, or product numbers down the left side, you'll have a real mess on your hands if the spreadsheet spills over onto two or more pages. Anyone trying to read the spreadsheet will have to refer all the way back to page 1 just to see the labels for each row or column.

  Excel neatly avoids this problem by offering to reprint the column or row labels at the top or left side of *each* printed page. To indicate which row or column contains these labels, click the appropriate "Print titles" field, and then type the desired row number or column heading directly in the spreadsheet. Or click the cell-selection icon just to the right of each field; this shrinks the dialog box so you can more easily select the repeating cell range.

- **Grid lines, Row and column headings.** For years the answer to one of the world's most frequently asked spreadsheet questions—"How do I get the gridlines to print?"—was buried here in the fourth tab of a buried dialog box. And it still is—but you can more easily access this control via the Formatting Palette's Page Setup pane.

  Excel never prints gridlines or the gray row and column headings unless you turn on their corresponding checkboxes here.

- **Black and white, Draft quality.** Use these two checkboxes when you're in a real hurry. Draft quality speeds up printing by omitting graphics and some formatting. "Black and white" means that your printer won't bother with time-consuming color, even if color appears in the spreadsheet.

- **Comments.** Use this pop-up menu to specify where *comments* (see page 635) appear on the printout—on its last page, or right where you put them in the spreadsheet itself.

- **Page order.** Use this to control whether Excel prints a multiple-page spreadsheet column by column (of pages), or row by row.

Formula and Database Magic

Congratulations, you've mastered enough of Excel to input numbers, perform calculations, create charts and graphs, and log your DVD collection using the List Manager. In fact—you already have far more spreadsheet ability than most people.

If, on the other hand, you're the kind of person who uses Excel for more than a list maker, whose business depends on the flow of numbers, calculations, and projections, there's still more to learn. This chapter covers the eerie realms of power Excel, where several people can work on the same spreadsheet simultaneously over the network, files can connect to databases or even the Web for their information, and you can program Excel to function by itself.

Workbooks and Worksheets

A *workbook* is an individual Excel file that you save on your hard drive. Each workbook is made up of one or more *worksheets,* which let you organize your data in lots of complex and interesting ways. Try thinking of a workbook as a bound ledger with multiple paper worksheets. Although most of the work you do is probably in an individual sheet, it's often useful to store several spreadsheets in a single workbook document—for the convenience of linking multiple Excel worksheets.

Working with Multiple Worksheets

Although it doesn't offer quite the heart-pounding excitement of, say, the Chart Gallery, managing the worksheets in a workbook is an important part of mastering Excel. Here's what you should know to get the most out of your sheets:

Tip: Several of the techniques described here involve selecting more than one worksheet. To do so, ⌘-click the tabs of the individual sheets you want—or click the first in a consecutive series, then Shift-click the last.

- **Adding sheets.** With Excel 2008, Microsoft makes a noble effort to save virtual paper—and in turn preserve a virtual forest. Instead of the three sheets of Excel's past, every Excel workbook now starts out with one sheet, bearing the inspired name Sheet1. (You can set the number of sheets in a new workbook in Excel → Preferences → General panel.)

  To add a new sheet to your workbook, click the plus-sign tab at the bottom of the worksheet or choose Insert → Sheet → Blank Sheet. A new sheet appears on top of your current sheet, with its tab *to the right* of the other tabs; it's named Sheet2 (or Sheet3, Sheet4, and so on).

Tip: To insert multiple sheets in one swift move, select the same number of sheet tabs that you want to insert and *then* click the plus-sign tab or choose Insert → Sheet → Blank Sheet. For example, to insert two new sheets, select Sheet1 and Sheet2 by ⌘-clicking both tabs, and then click the plus-sign tab. Excel then inserts Sheet4 and Sheet5 (to the right of all the other sheets if you click the plus-sign tab, to the right of the selected sheet if you choose Insert → Sheet → Blank Sheet).

- **Deleting sheets.** To delete a sheet, click the doomed sheet's tab (or select several tabs) at the bottom of the window, and then choose Edit → Delete Sheet. (Alternatively, Control-click the sheet tab and choose Delete from the contextual menu.)

Warning: You can't bring back a deleted sheet. The Undo command (Edit → Undo) doesn't work in this context.

- **Hiding and showing sheets.** Instead of deleting a worksheet forever, you may find it helpful to simply hide one (or several), keeping your peripheral vision free of distractions while you focus on the remaining ones. To hide a sheet or sheets, select the corresponding worksheet tabs at the bottom of the window, then choose Format → Sheet → Hide. To show (or *unhide,* as Excel calls it) sheets that have been hidden, choose Format → Sheet → Unhide; this brings up a list of sheets to show. Choose the sheet that you want to reappear, and click OK.

Note: You can unhide only one sheet at a time.

- **Renaming sheets.** The easiest way to rename a sheet is to double-click its tab to highlight its name, and then type the new text (up to 31 characters long). Alternatively, you can select the tab of the sheet you want to rename and then choose Format → Sheet → Rename. You can also Control-click the sheet tab and choose Rename from the contextual menu.

Adding Background Pictures to Sheets

Every now and then, it's easy to feel sorry for Microsoft programmers; after umpteen revisions, what possible features can they add to Excel? They must rack their brains, lying awake at night, trying to figure out what else they can invent.

Surely, the ability to add a graphics file as a background image behind your cell grid is an idea that sprang from just such a late-night idea session.

Start by choosing Format → Sheet → Background. An Open dialog box pops up, where you can choose the graphics file (JPEG, GIF, Photoshop, and so on) that you want to use as a background. Once you've selected it and clicked Insert, the image loads as the spreadsheet's background. If the

image isn't large enough to fill the entire worksheet, Excel automatically tiles it, placing copies side by side until every centimeter of the window is filled.

Clearly, if this feature is ever successful in improving a worksheet, it's when the background image is extremely light in color and low in contrast. Most other images succeed only in rendering your numbers and text illegible.

If, after adding an image to a sheet, you decide that it makes things much, much worse, choose Format → Sheet → Delete Background. Your normal white Excel sheet background returns. By the way, the background doesn't print. It's a screen-only thing.

• **Moving and copying sheets.** To move a sheet (so that, for example, Sheet1 comes after Sheet3), just drag its tab horizontally. A tiny black triangle indicates where the sheet will wind up, relative to the others, when you release the mouse. Using this technique, you can even drag a copy of a worksheet into a different Excel document.

Tip: Pressing Option while you drag produces a copy of the worksheet. (The exception is when you drag a sheet's tab into a different workbook; in that case, Excel copies the sheet regardless of whether the Option key is held down.)

As usual, there are other ways to perform this task. For example, you can also select a sheet's tab and then choose Edit → Move or Copy Sheet, or Control-click the sheet tab and choose Move or Copy from the contextual menu. In either case, the Move or Copy dialog box pops up. In it, you can specify which open workbook the sheet should be moved to, whether you want the sheet copied or moved, and where you want to place the sheet relative to the others.

• **Scrolling through sheet tabs.** If you have more sheet tabs than Excel can display in the bottom portion of the window, you can use the four tab scrolling buttons to scoot between the various sheets (see Figure 14-1). Another method is to Control-click any tab-scrolling button and then choose a sheet's name from the contextual menu.

• **Showing more or fewer sheet tabs.** The area reserved for Sheet tabs has to share space with the horizontal scroll bar. Fortunately, you can change how much area is devoted to showing sheet tabs by dragging the small, gray, vertical tab

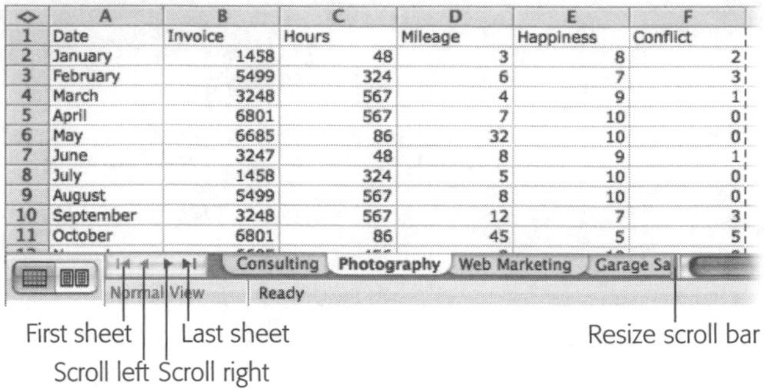

	A	B	C	D	E	F
1	Date	Invoice	Hours	Mileage	Happiness	Conflict
2	January	1458	48	3	8	2
3	February	5499	324	6	7	3
4	March	3248	567	4	9	1
5	April	6801	567	7	10	0
6	May	6685	86	32	10	0
7	June	3247	48	8	9	1
8	July	1458	324	5	10	0
9	August	5499	567	8	10	0
10	September	3248	567	12	7	3
11	October	6801	86	45	5	5

Consulting Photography Web Marketing Garage Sa

Normal View   Ready

First sheet   Last sheet   Resize scroll bar
Scroll left Scroll right

Figure 14-1:
The sheet scrolling buttons become active only when you become so fond of sheets that you can no longer see all their tabs at once. (Or maybe you just have a 12-inch PowerBook.) From left to right, the four sheet scrolling buttons perform the following functions: scroll the tabs to the leftmost tab, scroll the tabs to the left by one tab, scroll the tabs to the right by one tab, and scroll the tabs all the way to the right. Control-click any of the buttons and choose the sheet to go to from the pop-up menu. You can also make room for more tabs beneath your spreadsheet by dragging the left end of the lower scroll bar.

that sits between the tabs and the scroll bar. Drag it to the left to expand the scroll bar area (and hide worksheet tabs if necessary); drag it to the right to reveal more tabs.

Sharing a Workbook

With a little preparation, several Excel fans on the same network can work on a single worksheet at the same time. (If you want to share a workbook, but prevent others from accessing it, read about protection on page 602 first. Bear in mind, some protection commands have to be applied *before* you turn on sharing.) To share a workbook, choose Tools → Share Workbook, which brings up the Share Workbook dialog box. On the Editing tab (Figure 14-2), turn on "Allow changes by more than one user at the same time." Click the Advanced tab for the following options:

- **Track changes.** This section lets you set a time limit on what changes are tracked (see "Tracking Changes" on page 603). If you don't care what was changed months ago, you can limit the tracked changes to 60 days. You can also tell Excel not to keep a change history at all.

- **Update changes.** Here, you specify when your view of the shared workbook gets updated to reflect changes that others have made. You can set it to display the changes that have been made every time you save the file, or you can command it to update at a specified time interval.

  If you choose to have the changes updated automatically after a time interval, you can set the workbook to save automatically (thus sending your changes out to co-workers sharing the workbook) and to display others' changes (thus receiving changes from your co-workers' saves). Or you can set it not to save your changes, and just to show changes that others have made.

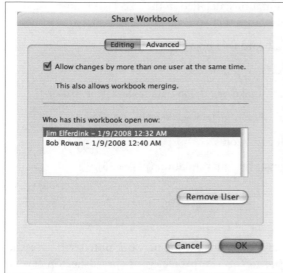

Figure 14-2:
The Share Workbook dialog box reveals exactly who else is using a shared workbook. If you worry that one of your fellow network citizens is about to make ill-advised changes, click his name and then click Remove User. Your comrade is now ejected from the spreadsheet party. If he tries to save changes to the file, he'll get an error message explaining the situation. Please note that there's little security in shared workbooks. As you can see, two people are logged in and able to make changes from two different Macs at the same time. Of course, if you password protect the sheet before sharing it, you'll achieve a basic, keeping-honest-people-honest level of security.

- **Conflicting changes between users.** This section governs whose changes "win" when two or more people make changes to the same workbook cell. You can set it so that you're asked to referee (which can be a *lot* of work), or so that the most recent changes saved are the ones that win (which can be risky). Clearly, neither option is perfect. Since each person can establish settings independently, it's worth working out a unified collaboration policy with your co-workers (see Figure 14-3).

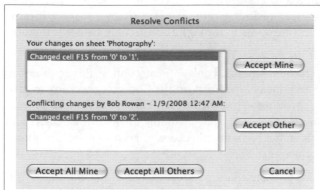

Figure 14-3:
The Result Conflicts dialog box appears when two people try to change the same cell. You're given the option of accepting one change or the other. If Excel lists more than one conflict, you can also choose to accept either all of your changes or all of your co-worker's.

- **Include in personal view.** These two checkboxes—Print settings and Filter settings—let you retain printing and filtering changes that are independent of the workbook. They can be set independently by anyone who opens the workbook.

When you click OK, Excel prompts you to save the workbook—if you haven't already. Save it on a networked disk where others can see it. Now, anyone who opens the workbook from across the network opens it as a shared book.

Shared workbooks have some limitations, detailed in the Excel help topic, "Share a workbook." Here's a summary of things that you *can't* do with a shared workbook:

- Assign, change, or delete a password that protects a worksheet.

- Insert charts, hyperlinks, objects, or pictures.

- Make or change PivotTables, or make or refresh data tables (page 616).

- Merge, insert, or delete blocks of cells; delete worksheets.

- Use automatic subtotals or drawing tools.

- Use or create conditional formats or data validation (page 633).

- View or edit scenarios (page 626).

Protecting the spreadsheet

Fortunately, there's no need to give everyone on the network unfettered access to your carefully designed spreadsheet. You can protect your spreadsheet in several ways, as described here, and your colleagues can't turn off these protections without choosing Tools → Unprotect Sheet (or Unprotect Workbook)—and *that* requires a password (if you've set one up).

- **Protect a workbook from changes.** Choose Tools → Protection → Protect Workbook, which brings up the Protect Workbook dialog box. By turning on Structure and/or Windows, you can protect the workbook's *structure* (which keeps its sheets from being deleted, changed, hidden, or renamed) and its windows (which keeps the workbook's windows from being moved, resized, or hidden). Both of these safeguards are especially important in a spreadsheet you've carefully set up for onscreen reviewing. You can also assign a password to the workbook so that if someone wants to turn *off* its protection, he needs to know the password.

- **Protect a sheet from changes.** Choose Tools → Protection → Protect Sheet to bring up the Protect Sheet dialog box. Turn on the Contents checkbox to protect all *locked* cells in a worksheet (described next). Turn on Objects to prevent changes to graphic objects on a worksheet, including formats of all charts and comments. Finally, turn on the Scenarios checkbox to keep scenario definitions (page 626) from being changed.

  The bottom of the dialog box lets you assign a password to the worksheet; this password will be required from anyone who attempts to turn off the protections you've established.

- **Protect individual cells from changes.** Excel automatically formats all cells in a new worksheet as locked, so if you protect the contents of a sheet you've been working in, all the cells will be rendered unchangeable. If you want *some* cells in a protected sheet to be editable, you have to unlock them while the sheet is unprotected. Unlock selected cells by choosing Format → Cells. In the resulting dialog box, click the Protection tab, turn off the Locked checkbox, and then click OK.

- **Require a password to open a workbook.** Open the workbook you want to protect and choose File → Save As (or, if you've never saved this workbook before, choose File → Save). In the Save dialog box, click Options. In the resulting dialog box (Figure 14-4), enter one password to allow the file to be opened and, if you desire, another to allow file modification.

Tip: Alternatively, choose Excel → Preferences → Security and assign a password to open or to modify the workbook, and use the two buttons to access the Protect Workbook dialog box and the Protect Sheet dialog box.

Figure 14-4:
Entering a password in the top text box prevents others from opening your workbook without the password. If you specify only the second password, people can open the file, but can't make changes without the password.

Warning: Remember these passwords! If you forget them, you've locked yourself out of your own workbook. There's no way to recover them without buying a password cracking program.

- **Hide rows, columns, or sheets.** Once you've hidden some rows, columns, or sheets (page 559), you can prevent people from making them reappear by choosing Tools → Protection → Protect Workbook. Turn on Structure and then click OK.

- Protecting a **shared workbook.** To protect a shared workbook, choose Tools → Protection → Protect Shared Workbook, which brings up the Protect Shared Workbook window. This window presents you with two protection choices. If you turn on "Sharing with track changes" and enter a password, you prevent others from turning off change tracking—a way of looking at who makes what changes to your workbook. Turning on this checkbox *also* shares the workbook, as detailed previously.

Tracking Changes

When people make changes to your spreadsheet over the network, you aren't necessarily condemned to a life of frustration and chaos, even though numbers that you input originally may be changed beyond recognition. Exactly as in Word, Excel has a *change tracking* feature that lets you see exactly which of your co-workers made what changes to your spreadsheet and, on a case-by-case basis, approve or eliminate them. (The changes, not the co-workers.)

To see who's been tiptoeing through your workbook, choose Tools → Track Changes → Highlight Changes, which brings up the Highlight Changes dialog box (Figure 14-5). In it, you can choose how changes are highlighted: by time or by the person making the changes. To limit the revision tracking to a specific area on the worksheet, click the spreadsheet icon at the right of the Where field, select the area, and then click the icon again.

As life goes on with this spreadsheet on your network, Excel highlights changes made by your co-workers with a triangular flag at the upper-left corner of a cell or block of cells (Figure 14-5, middle).

Once you've reviewed the changes, you may decide that the original figures were superior to those in the changed version. At this point, Excel gives you the opportunity to analyze each change. If you think the change was an improvement, you can accept it, making it part of the spreadsheet from now on. If not, you can reject the change, restoring the cell contents to whatever was there before your network comrades asserted themselves.

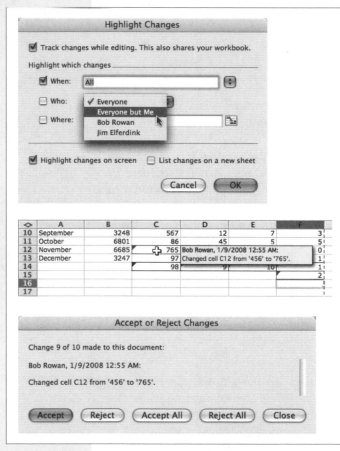

Figure 14-5:
Top: This dialog box lets you turn on change tracking and specify whose changes are highlighted. By turning on Where, clicking the tiny spreadsheet icon next to the box, and dragging in your worksheet, you can also limit the tracking feature to a specific area of the worksheet.

Middle: The shaded triangle in the upper-left corner of a cell indicates that somebody changed its contents. A comment balloon lets you know exactly what the change was.

Bottom: Using this dialog box, you can walk through all the changes in a spreadsheet one at a time, giving each changed cell your approval or restoring it to its original value.

To perform this accept/reject routine, choose Tools → Track Changes → Accept or Reject Changes. In the Select Changes to Accept or Reject dialog box, you can set up the reviewing process by specifying which changes you want to review (according to when they were made, who made them, and where they're located in the worksheet). When you click OK, the reviewing process begins (Figure 14-5, bottom).

Merging Workbooks

In many work situations, you may find it useful to distribute copies of a workbook to several people for their perusal and then incorporate their changes into a single workbook.

Performing this feat, however, requires some preparation—namely, creating a shared workbook (see the previous section), and then configuring the workbook's *change history*. You'll find this option by choosing Tools → Share Workbook and then clicking the Advanced tab (Figure 14-6). The number that you specify in the "Keep change history for" box determines how old changes can be before they become irrelevant. The theory behind this feature contends that you'll stop caring about changes that are older than the number of days that you set. (Tracking changes forever can bloat a file's size, too.)

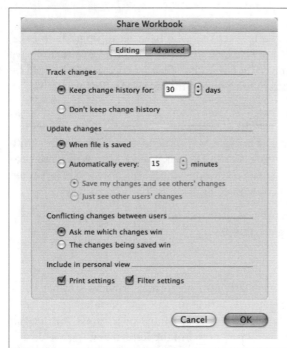

Figure 14-6:
To prep your workbook for later merging, turn on the "Keep change history" option in the Share Workbook dialog box. You also have to complete your merge within the time limit that you set in the "Track changes" area. Once you're ready to bring everything together, choose Tools → Merge Workbooks and select the first workbook that you want to merge into the current workbook.

Once you've prepared your workbook, distribute it via email or network. Ask your colleagues to make comments and changes and then return their spreadsheet copies to you (within the time limit you specified, as described in the previous paragraph). Collect all of the copies into one place. (You may need to rename the workbooks to avoid replacing one with another, since they can't occupy the same folder if they have the same names.)

Now open a copy of the shared workbook and choose Tools → Merge Workbooks, which brings up an Open dialog box. Choose the file you want to merge into the open workbook, and then click OK. This process has to be repeated for every workbook you want to merge.

Exporting Files

Every now and then, you may find it useful to send your Excel data to a different program—a database program, for example, or even AppleWorks (if you're collaborating with somebody who doesn't have Office). Fortunately, Microsoft engineers have built in many different file formats for your Excel conversion pleasure.

To save your Excel file in another file format, choose File → Save As; then select the file format you want from the Format pop-up menu. Here are a few of the most useful options in that pop-up menu.

Note: Apple's Numbers '08 can import files in either .xls or .xlsx format and export in .xls format.

Excel 97-2004 Workbook (.xls)

If you're sharing your document with Excel fans who have yet to upgrade to Excel 2008 for the Mac or Excel 2007 for PC (or if you're uncertain), be sure and save your spreadsheet in this.xls format. The new (.xlsx) file format can *only* be read by Excel 2008 and 2007. (See page xxviii for more on the new XML file formats.)

Comma separated values (.csv)

The *comma-separated* file format is a popular way of getting your Excel sheets into other spreadsheets or databases (AppleWorks, FileMaker, non-Microsoft word processors, and so on). It saves the data as a text file, in which cell contents are separated by commas, and a new row of data is denoted by a "press" of the Return key.

Saving a file as a comma-separated text file saves only the currently active worksheet, and dumps any formatting or graphics.

Tab delimited text (.txt)

Like comma-separated values, the *tab-delimited* file format provides another common way of getting your Excel sheets into other spreadsheets or databases. It saves the data as a text file, in which cell contents are separated by a "press" of the Tab key, and a new row of data is denoted by a "press" of the Return key.

Saving a file as a tab-delimited text file saves only the currently active worksheet, and dumps any formatting or graphics.

Excel template (.xltx)

The Template file format is a special kind of Excel file that works like a stationery document: When you open a template, Excel automatically creates and opens a *copy* of the template, complete with all of the formatting, formulas, and data that were in the original template. If you use the same kind of document over and over, templates are an awesome timesaver. (For more on Excel templates, see page 508.)

To save an Excel workbook as a template, choose File → Save As and then select Template in the pop-up menu of the Save window. Excel proposes storing your new template in the Home → Library → Application Support → Microsoft → Office → User Templates → My Templates folder on your hard drive. Any templates you create this way appear in the My Templates portion of the Project Gallery and in the My Templates portion of the Sheets tab of the Elements Gallery (see page 509).

Tip: When you share templates, play it safe by saving it as an Excel 97-2004 Template (.xlt) unless you're absolutely sure your cohort's Office software is up-to-date.

Web page

Where would a modern software program be without the ability to turn its files into Web pages?

Sure enough, Excel can save workbooks as Web pages, complete with charts, and with all sheets intact. In the process, Excel generates the necessary HTML and XML files and converts your graphics into Web-friendly file formats (such as GIF). All you have to do is upload the saved files to a Web server to make them available to the entire Internet. Once you've posted them on the Internet, others can look through your worksheets with nothing but a Web browser, ideal for posting your numbers for others to review. That's the *only* thing they can do, in fact, since the cells in your worksheet aren't editable.

To save a workbook as a Web page, choose File → Save as Web Page. At this point, the bottom of the Save window gives you some powerful settings that control the Web-page creation process:

- **Workbook, Sheet, Selection.** Using these buttons, specify how much of your workbook should be saved as a Web page—the whole workbook, the currently active sheet, or just the selected cells. (If you choose Workbook, all of the sheets in your workbook will be saved as linked HTML files; there'll be a series of links along the bottom that look just like your sheet tabs in Excel. Here again, though, these features won't work smoothly for everyone, because not all Web browsers understand JavaScript and frames, which these bottom-of-the-window tabs require.)

- **Automate.** This button brings up the Automate window, which lets you turn on a remarkable and powerful feature: Every time you save changes to your Excel document, or according to an exact schedule that you specify, Excel can save

---

changes to the Web-based version automatically. Of course, you'll still be responsible for posting the HTML and graphics files to your Web server.

To set up a schedule, click "According to a set schedule" and then click Set Schedule. In the Recurring Schedule window, set the Web version to be updated daily, weekly, monthly, or yearly. You can also specify the day of the week, as well as a start and end date for automatic updating. Updating happens only when the workbook is opened in Excel.

- **Web Options.** The Web Options dialog box lets you assign appropriate titles and keywords to your Web pages. (The title appears in the title bar of your visitors' browser windows and in search results from search engines like Yahoo and Google; search engines also sometimes reference these keywords.)

  On the Pictures tab, you can also turn on *PNG* (Portable Network Graphics) *graphics,* which makes smaller graphics that download more quickly.

Tip: You can test the workbook-saved-as-Web-page feature by dropping the HTML file on your Web browser's icon. If you prefer, you may also choose File → Web Page Preview to view the Web page.

Spreadsheet properties

Excel gives you the chance to attach additional information to your files through something called *properties.* To call up the Properties dialog box for a worksheet, select File → Properties. In the resulting dialog box, you'll see five tabbed subject areas with all kinds of information about your file:

- **General.** This subject area tells you the document type, its location, size, when it was created and last modified, and whether it's read-only or hidden.

- **Summary.** This feature lets you enter a title, subject, author, manager, company, category, keywords, comments, and a hyperlink base for your document (the path you want to use for all the hyperlinks you create in the document).

- **Statistics.** This tab shows when a document was created, modified, and last printed, as well as who last saved it. It also displays a revision number and the total editing time on the document.

- **Contents.** Here, you'll see the workbook's contents—all of its sheets, even the hidden ones.

- **Custom.** Finally, this tabbed area lets you enter any number of other properties to your workbook by giving the property a name, type, and value. You can enter just about anything here.

Advanced Formula Magic

Chapter 12 covers the fundamentals of formulas—entering them manually, using the Formula Builder, and so on. The following section dives deeper into the heart of Excel's mathematical power—its formulas.

Note: There's a difference between formulas and *functions*. A *formula* is a calculation that uses an arithmetic operator (such as *=A1+A2+A3+A4+A5*), while a *function* is a canned formula that saves you the work of creating a formula yourself (such as *=SUM(A1:A5)*).

Because there's no difference in how you *use* them, this chapter uses the terms interchangeably.

Nested Formulas

A *nested* formula is a formula that's used as an argument (see the box on page 533) to another formula. For example, in the formula *=ABS(SUM(A1:A3))*, the formula *SUM(A1:A3)* is nested within an absolute-value formula. When interpreting this formula, Excel first adds the contents of cells A1 through A3, and then finds the absolute value of that result—that's the number you'll see in the cell.

Nested formulas keep you from having to use other cells as placeholders; they're also essential for writing compact formulas. In some cases (such as with the logical IF function), nesting lets you add real sophistication to your Excel spreadsheets by having Excel make decisions based on formula results.

The Formula Builder

The Formula Builder is a quick way of building powerful mathematical models in your spreadsheets. When activated, the Formula Builder shows every imaginable aspect of a formula: the value of the cells used in it, a description of what the formula does, a description of the arguments used in the formula, and the result of the formula.

To use the Formula Builder, click the Toolbox button in the toolbar and click the Toolbox's *fx* tab. When the Formula Builder pops up (Figure 14-7), it shows one of two things:

- If the currently active cell doesn't contain a function, the bottom of the Formula Builder says "To begin, double-click a function in the list." Use the Search field or scroll through the Formula Builder's long, long list to find your function.

- If the currently active cell contains a function, or if you type a function into your formula, the Formula Builder opens fully and tries to help you with the function.

Once the Formula Builder appears, you can use it to construct your formula. It provides a text box for each function parameter. Typing the parameter in the text box effectively inserts it into its proper place in the formula. You can also click cells or drag through cells in the spreadsheet to insert the cell reference or range in the Formula Builder.

As you fill out the formula in the Formula Builder, the formula's result appears in the bottom of the palette as well as in the active cell. When you're done creating the formula in the Formula Palette, press Return to enter it in the cell.

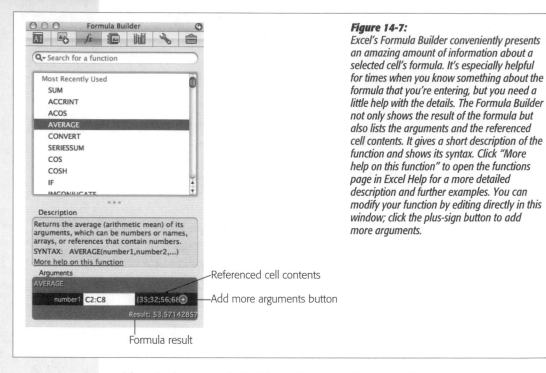

Figure 14-7:
Excel's Formula Builder conveniently presents an amazing amount of information about a selected cell's formula. It's especially helpful for times when you know something about the formula that you're entering, but you need a little help with the details. The Formula Builder not only shows the result of the formula but also lists the arguments and the referenced cell contents. It gives a short description of the function and shows its syntax. Click "More help on this function" to open the functions page in Excel Help for a more detailed description and further examples. You can modify your function by editing directly in this window; click the plus-sign button to add more arguments.

Although the Formula Builder might seem like overkill when it comes to simple formulas (such as a SUM), it's a big help when you're dealing with more complex formulas. It outlines the parameters that the formula is expecting and gives you places to plug in those parameters. The rangefinder feature (page 529) also makes it easier to track your calculations. (The rangefinder highlights each cell cited in the calculation with the same color used to denote the cell in the calculation. It's a sharp way to keep track of what you're doing, and which cells you're doing it with.)

Circular References

If you create a formula that, directly or indirectly, refers to the cell *containing* it, beware of the *circular reference*. This is the spreadsheet version of a Mexican standoff: The formula in each cell depends on the other, so neither formula can make the first move.

Suppose, for example, you type the formula *=SUM(A1:A6)* into cell A1. This formula asks Excel to add cells A1 through A6 and put the result in cell A1—but since A1 is included in the range of cells for Excel to add, things quickly get confusing. To make matters worse, a few specialized formulas actually *require* that you use formulas with circular references. Now, imagine how difficult it can be to disentangle a circular reference that's *inside* a nested formula that *refers* to formulas in other cells—it's enough to make your teeth hurt. Fortunately, Excel can help.

For example, when you enter a formula containing a circular reference, Excel immediately interrupts your work with a dialog box that explains what's happening. You may enter a formula that doesn't itself contain a circular reference, but instead completes a circular reference involving a group of cells. Or the formulas in two different cells might refer to each other in a circular fashion, as shown in Figure 14-8.

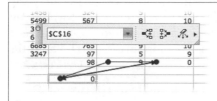

Figure 14-8:
Double-click the tracer arrow to jump to the next cell involved in the circular reference, or click the buttons on the toolbar. With these tools, Excel reveals the various cells involved in the circular reference; eventually, you should be able to untangle the problem.

To leave the formula as is, click Cancel. For help, click OK, which brings up a Microsoft Office Help window loaded with directions and the Circular Reference toolbar. (Excel also overlays circles and tracer arrows on the cells of your spreadsheet.)

Iterations

On the other hand, certain functions (mostly scientific and engineering) *need* circular references to work properly. For example, if you're doing a bit of goal-seeking (page 623), you can use circular references to plug numbers into a formula until the formula is equal to a set value.

In these cases, Excel has to calculate formulas with circular references repeatedly, because it uses the results of a first set of calculations as the basis for a second calculation. Each such cycle is known as an *iteration*. For example, suppose you want to figure out what value, when plugged into a formula, will produce a result of 125. If your first guess of 10 gives you a result of 137 when plugged into the formula, a circular reference can use that result to *adjust* your guess (say, reducing it to 9.5), then make a second pass at evaluating the formula. This second pass is a second iteration. If 9.5 doesn't do the trick, Excel can make a third iteration to get even closer, and so on, until it reaches a level of accuracy that's close enough.

To turn iteration on (and set some of its parameters), choose Excel → Preferences; click Calculation. In the Calculation panel, turn on Limit Iteration, and change the number of iterations and, if you like, a maximum change value. Excel automatically stops after 100 iterations, or when the difference between iterations is smaller than 0.001. If you make the maximum number of iterations larger or the maximum change between iterations smaller, Excel can produce more accurate results. Accordingly, it also needs more time to calculate those results.

Connecting to Other Workbooks

Formulas aren't necessarily confined to data in their own "home" worksheet; you can link them to cells in other worksheets in the same workbook, or even to cells in other Excel documents. That's a handy feature when, for example, you want to run an analysis on a budget worksheet with your own set of Excel tools, but you don't want to re-enter the data in your workbook or alter the original workbook.

To link a formula to another sheet in the same workbook, start typing your formula as you normally would. When you reach the part of the formula where you want to refer to the cells in another worksheet, click the sheet's tab to bring it to the front. Then select the cells that you want to appear in the formula, just as you normally would when building a formula. When you finish clicking or dragging through cells, press Enter and Excel instantly returns you to the sheet where you were building the formula. In the cell, you'll find a special notation that indicates a reference to a cell on another sheet. For example, if a formula on Sheet 3 takes the sum of G1 through G6 on Sheet 1, the formula looks like this: *=SUM(Sheet1!G1:G6)*.

To link a formula in Document A to cells in another workbook (Document B), the process is almost identical. Start typing the formula in Document A. Then, when it's time to specify the cells to be used in the formula, open Document B. Select the cells you want to use by clicking or dragging; when you press Enter, they appear in the formula. Excel returns you to the original document, where you'll see the Document B cells written out in a *path notation* (see Figure 14-9).

Once you've set up such a cell reference, Excel automatically updates Document A each time you open it with Document B already open. And if Document B is closed, Excel asks if you want to update the data. If you say yes, Excel looks into Document B and grabs whatever data it needs. If somebody has changed Document B since the last time Document A was opened, Excel recalculates the worksheet based on the new numbers.

Figure 14-9:
External cell references display the path to the worksheet of the external spreadsheet between single quotation marks in the formula bar. If you move the file or rename any volumes or folders along the path, you'll break the link. You can manually update the external reference in the formula bar, but it's often easier to just double-click the cell, press Return, navigate back to the external document, and let Excel update the reference. (And you won't risk a path-breaking typo.)

Tip: If you want Document A updated automatically whenever you open it (and don't want to be interrupted with Excel's request to do so), choose Excel → Preferences, click Edit, and then *turn off* "Ask to update automatic links." Excel now automatically updates the link with the data from the last saved version of Document B.

Keeping Track of References

The problem with referring to other workbooks in formulas is that things change—and cause confusion. Suppose, for example, that one Excel workbook, Document A, contains a formula in reference to a cell in Document B. But if somebody renames Document B, renames the disk it's on, or moves the file to a different folder, Excel can't find Document B. The link to the external workbook is broken.

When you try to update those references, Excel tells you that it can't find the sheet containing the data it needs and it displays an Open dialog box, asking you to locate the missing data. Now all you need to do is navigate to Document B—even if it has a new name or it's on a new hard drive—and click OK. Excel fixes the reference so that everything works normally.

For the curious (or the coders), there's a manual way to fix such a broken link, too. Click the cell with the external reference; the formula—complete with the external reference—appears in the Formula bar. Inside the formula, there's a series of names with colons and brackets, as shown in Figure 14-9.

Think of this path notation as a street map to the location of the external file on your hard drive. The first phrase after the left parenthesis and single quote is the name of the hard drive (PB12HD, in this illustration). Then come a series of folder names separated by colons; in this illustration, the file is in the jim user directory, in the Documents folder, and then in a folder called Investments. Finally, you'll find the file's name (Stock Watch.xlsx, in this example) inside the brackets.

The phrase to the right of the right bracket identifies one worksheet name inside the file (Sheet1). After that, there's another single quote and an exclamation point, which marks the end of the external reference. Then, finally, there's the name of the cell (expressed as absolute cell references with $ signs, as described on page 540) used in the formula.

Armed with this information, you can repair a broken external cell reference. If you renamed the hard drive, correct the problem by changing the first name in the list to match the new hard drive name. If you've changed the folder location of Document B, you can correct the situation here by typing the proper folder path. If you've renamed Document B, simply enter the new file name in the space between the brackets

Auditing

Every now and then, you'll find a formula whose cell references are amiss. If the formula references another formula, tracing down the source of your problems can be a real pain. Excel's Auditing tools can help you access the root of formula errors by showing you the cells that a given formula references and the formulas that reference a given cell. Brightly colored *tracer arrows* (these won't appear in an Excel workbook saved as an HTML file) appear between cells to indicate how they all relate to each other.

The key to correcting formula errors is the Tools → Auditing menu item, which has five submenu choices:

- **Trace Precedents** draws arrows from the currently selected cell to any cells that provide values for its formula.

- **Trace Dependents** draws arrows from the currently selected cell, showing which *other* formulas refer to it.

- **Trace Error** draws an arrow from an active cell containing a "broken" formula to the cell or cells that caused the error.

- **Remove All Arrows** hides all the auditing arrows.

- **Show Auditing Toolbar** hides or shows the Auditing Toolbar. This toolbar's buttons turn on (and off) the kinds of arrows described in the previous paragraphs, all in an effort to help you trace how formulas and cells relate with each other. It also contains buttons for attaching comments, for circling invalid data, and for removing those circles.

Working with Databases

Excel has much in common with database programs. Both kinds of software keep track of a list of *records* (like cards in a card catalog—or rows of a spreadsheet), and let you browse through those records and even perform some calculations on them. No wonder Excel is so adept at incorporating database files into its spreadsheets; Excel 2008 can access data in Web pages and FileMaker Pro databases, and may be able to use *open database connectivity* to access data from additional databases such as Microsoft SQL Server. Open database connectivity, usually called ODBC (pronounced "oh-dee-bee-see"), is a standard set of rules for transferring information among databases, even if the databases are in different programs from different companies.

POWER USERS' CLINIC

Open Database Connectivity (ODBC)

In order to use ODBC to import data, you need to install a driver for the database you want to query. Microsoft doesn't supply drivers to Office 2008 customers; instead, you have to purchase a driver from another company, such as Actual Technologies (*www.actualtechnologies.com*) or OpenLink Software (*www.openlinksw.com*).

Excel 2008 comes equipped with the necessary smarts to use Microsoft Query—software that puts a graphical user interface on the task of creating database queries. With this program, you can create and modify queries in Excel 2008—if you have the driver installed, that is. Look for it in the Applications → Microsoft Office 2008 → Office folder.

Once you've rounded up and installed all the required ODBC software, you can get started with ODBC by scanning the Microsoft Query Help files, investigating the commands listed on the Data → Get External Data submenu, playing with the External Data toolbar (View → Toolbars → External Data)—and perhaps by speaking to your corporate IT department. However, the full rundown on using ODBC to connect to these industrial-strength databases is beyond the scope of this book. (But if you're an ODBC expert, consider writing *ODBC: The Missing Manual* yourself.)

Fetching FileMaker Pro Data

Excel loves to import data from FileMaker Pro databases directly into its worksheets—no muss, no fuss, no messy translation workarounds.

Here's how to go about it:

Note: Excel can only work with FileMaker databases if you actually *have* FileMaker on your Mac.

Step 1: Import the database

You can import a FileMaker Pro database in either of two ways. First, you can bring the data into Excel once, where you continue to work on it (this is called a *one-time* import). Second, the data can remain connected to FileMaker, and updates itself in Excel when it's updated in FileMaker (this is called an *updating* import).

- **For a one-time import,** which puts data into Excel as a *list sheet* (a sheet containing nothing except a list object, as described on page 541), choose File → Open, then navigate to, and double-click, the FileMaker file's icon in the Open dialog box.

  If you make changes in FileMaker and want the changed data to come into Excel, you have to reimport the entire database.

- **For an updating import,** which places data in an Excel worksheet and lets you control how often cells update (reflecting changes made in FileMaker), choose Data → Get External Data → Import from FileMaker Pro. (You need to have a workbook open in Excel for this menu option to be available.)

In either case, an amazing thing happens: Excel triggers FileMaker Pro to launch, opening the specified database. Then the FileMaker Pro Import Wizard window appears. On the first screen, specify which of the FileMaker file's fields you want to import (Name, Address, Phone, or whatever). You can also specify the end order for them to appear in Excel, as shown in Figure 14-10.

Click Next to continue.

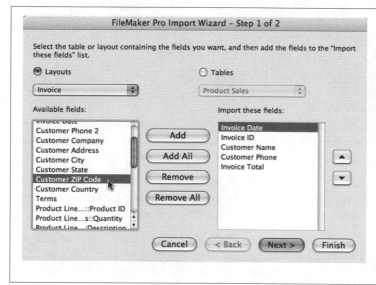

Figure 14-10:
If one of the FileMaker file's layouts contains the fields you want, click the Layouts button and select its name from the pop-up menu. Otherwise, click the Tables button and select the database file name from its pop-up menu (which also displays the names of other linked FileMaker files) to display the list of every field in the database. Next, choose the fields you want by double-clicking each in the "Available fields" pane on the left. (Move all fields at once by clicking the Add All button.) This action adds each selected field to the pane on the right. You can then rearrange the order of the fields in the right-hand list by selecting one and then clicking the up and down arrow buttons on the right.

Step 2: Choose only the data you want

The next screen in the FileMaker Import Wizard offers to *filter* (screen out) the records that you import into your Excel workbook (see Figure 14-11). The wizard lets you specify three criteria to help eliminate unwanted data from the import process. (If you want *all* of the data, skip this step by clicking Finish.)

Click Finish to continue. Excel launches into importing the data from your File-Maker file.

Note: This process may take a long time (depending, in part, on how much data you're importing). Because there's no progress bar, spinning cursor, or any other sign that Excel is working, you might assume that the program has crashed. Go brew a fresh pot of coffee or stick your head out the door for some air, but don't switch out of Excel; the program is communicating with the database and constructing the spreadsheet.

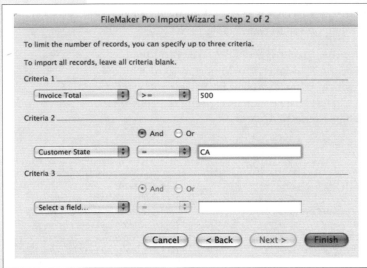

Figure 14-11:
Suppose you want to import only the records for clients who have spent more than $500 and live in California, so that you can thank them and invite them to your annual goal-setting retreat. Set the Criteria 1 pop-up menu to Invoice Total, set the middle pop-up menu to >=, and type 500 into the final field. After filling in Criteria 1, you can set up additional requirements in the Criteria 2 and Criteria 3 rows, such as Customer State = CA.

If you began this process by choosing File → Open, you're all set; Excel produces a new listsheet, a worksheet with the database's contents embedded in it as a list object. Listsheets also display the List toolbar (see page 549).

If, on the other hand, you chose Data → Get External Data → Import from File-Maker Pro, Excel now asks you exactly where you'd like the imported data to be placed. You can specify a cell or opt to create a new worksheet (Figure 14-12).

After telling Excel where and how to place the data, click Finish. Excel imports the data and shows the External Data toolbar. If you turned on the "Use List Manager" checkbox in the properties section of the FileMaker Import Wizard, it also shows the List toolbar. The External Data toolbar lets you quickly change options on incoming database information, set special query criteria, and refresh data from a database.

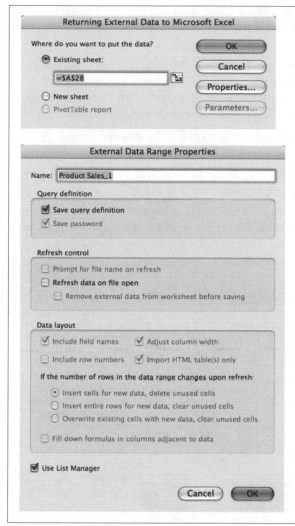

Figure 14-12:
The last step in bringing in FileMaker Pro data is choosing where the data goes (top). With the click of a radio button, it can be delivered into the worksheet currently open or into a new worksheet. Clicking Properties brings up the External Data Range Properties dialog box (bottom), whose options include "Refresh data on file open" (sets whether Excel receives fresh data every time the file opens) and "Use List Manager" (puts data into a list object). The list object offers easy sorting and filtering. But to use the data layout controls in this dialog box, you have to first turn off "Use List Manager" and forgo the extra features it provides. (See page 541 for List Manager info.)

Note: You may encounter an error message when Excel attempts to open a FileMaker database: "Microsoft Office is not able to run FileMaker Pro at this time." Of course, there are many reasons why Office might not be able to run FileMaker—it's not installed, it's compressed, or it's out on a lunch break. You can solve the problem, though, by launching FileMaker on your own—just double-click its icon in the Finder.

Grabbing Data from the Web

If pulling data from a database on your computer or network isn't exciting enough, Excel also has the ability to grab data from certain Web sites (and FTP or intranet sites). Excel comes with three sample Web queries that help show the power of this little-known feature. To see how it works, give the sample queries a try (actually, they can be very useful if you're creating spreadsheets to track your portfolio).

- **MSN MoneyCentral Currencies.** This query grabs the current currency value for about 50 countries on an open exchange. Check it before you head out on an international trip, so you'll know what to expect when you exchange your currency—and help you understand why you only paid €5 for a beer.

- **MSN MoneyCentral Major Indices.** This query grabs data for around 20 stock exchanges, including the Dow, S&P 500, FTSE 100, and NASDAQ.

- **MSN MoneyCentral Stock Quotes.** This query looks up data including last value, close value, volume, and change for a stock symbol you specify (Figure 14-13). (If you're among the thousands of people who use Excel to track your stock market holdings, behold the dawn of a new era—you no longer need to type in the latest stock prices. Your software can do it automatically.)

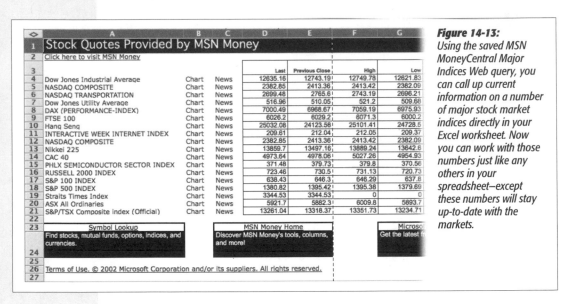

Figure 14-13:
Using the saved MSN MoneyCentral Major Indices Web query, you can call up current information on a number of major stock market indices directly in your Excel worksheet. Now you can work with those numbers just like any others in your spreadsheet—except these numbers will stay up-to-date with the markets.

To use one of these predesigned Web queries, choose Data → Get External Data → Run Saved Query, which brings up an Open dialog box. Double-click one of the queries listed here. (You can find the saved queries in the Microsoft Office 2008 → Office → Queries folder.)

Excel then asks you where in the spreadsheet you want to put the information that it downloads from the Web. (This modest dialog box calls itself Returning External Data to Microsoft Excel.) After you select a location and click OK, Excel connects to the Internet, downloads the information, and inserts it into the spreadsheet.

Importing Data from a Text File

Databases and the World Wide Web both make effective data sources, but sometimes you just want to pull some information out of a text file and into your Excel worksheet. For example, you might have a tab-delimited list of contacts that your marketing guru emailed you, and you'd like to get it into Excel. Here's how to do it:

Choose Data → Get External Data → Import Text File; in the resulting Open dialog box, navigate to, and double-click, the text file that you want to import. Alternatively, choose File → Import, click the Text file button, and click Import. Either way, the Text Import Wizard appears and walks you through a three-step process to choose the delimiter type, choose which columns to import, and set the column data format before Excel sucks the data into the current worksheet

Analyzing and Viewing Your Data

Like a good piece of Swiss Army Software, Excel provides tools that go beyond the basics. Using features like PivotTables, Scenarios, and Goal Seeking, Excel lets you sharpen your powers of visualization as you look at your data in new and interesting ways.

Making a PivotTable

A *PivotTable* is a special spreadsheet entity that helps summarize data into an easy-to-read table. You can exchange the table's rows and columns (thus the name Pivot-Table) to achieve different views on your data. PivotTables let you quickly plug different sets of numbers into a table; Excel does the heavy lifting of arranging the data for you.

PivotTables are useful when you want to see how different-but-related totals compare, such as how a retail store's sales per department, category of product, and salesperson relate. They let you build complicated tables on the fly by dragging various categories of data into a premade template. PivotTables are also useful when you have a large amount of data to wade through, partially because Excel takes care of subtotals and totals for you.

Here's how to create a PivotTable from data in an Excel sheet.

Step 1: Choose the data source

Suppose, for example, that you're the Executive Director for a community non-profit, trying to decide which fundraisers bring in the most donors for the time and money spent. You have a spreadsheet showing four years' worth of data on five different fundraisers (such as each event's revenue, number of new donors, and hours of staff and volunteer time). But you can't yet see the trends that identify which fundraisers bring in the most new donors for the least time investment while achieving the highest revenues. A PivotTable, you realize, would make the answer crystal clear.

Select a cell in the data range from which you want to create a PivotTable. Choose Data → PivotTable Report, which brings up the PivotTable Wizard. This will walk you through the process of creating a PivotTable in three steps.

In the first step, select the data from which you want to create a PivotTable. Your choices include an Excel list, multiple consolidation ranges (which use ranges from one or more worksheets), and another PivotTable. If you've installed the necessary ODBC-related software (see the box on page 614), you can also use data from an external data source.

In this example, you want to create a PivotTable from existing data in an Excel sheet. Choose "Microsoft Excel list or database"; click Next to continue.

Step 2: Choose the cells

This PivotTable Wizard asks for the cell range that you want to use in your Pivot-Table. Excel—bless its digital heart—takes its best guess, based on the active cell when the wizard was invoked. If that range is *not* correct, type the range you want in the Range field or use the cell-selection triangle (see page 520) to select the range yourself. Click Next to continue.

Step 3: Direct the PivotTable

Finally, Excel asks where you want to place your new PivotTable. You can put it either in a new worksheet or in an existing worksheet at a specific location. Because this table is relatively small, place it in the same worksheet as the source data.

This last screen gives you two additional customization buttons:

- The **Layout** button opens the Layout window, where you can exercise some control over how the PivotTable is laid out.

- The **Options** button opens the Options window, where you can choose to include grand totals, to preserve cell formatting, and how you want data sources handled.

To finish your PivotTable, click Finish.

Step 4: Pivot

At this point, Excel has dropped a blank PivotTable into the specified location, but its poor cells are empty. To help you insert data, Excel opens the PivotTable tool-bar, which you can use to add elements to your blank slate.

The bottom of the PivotTable toolbar shows a few names that coincide with the column names in your original data (Figure 14-14); these are called *field names*. To complete your PivotTable, you drop these field names onto the row axis (the column on the left), the column axis (the row across the top), or the data field (the big empty space in the center). A different table will form, depending on which data fields you drop on which axes.

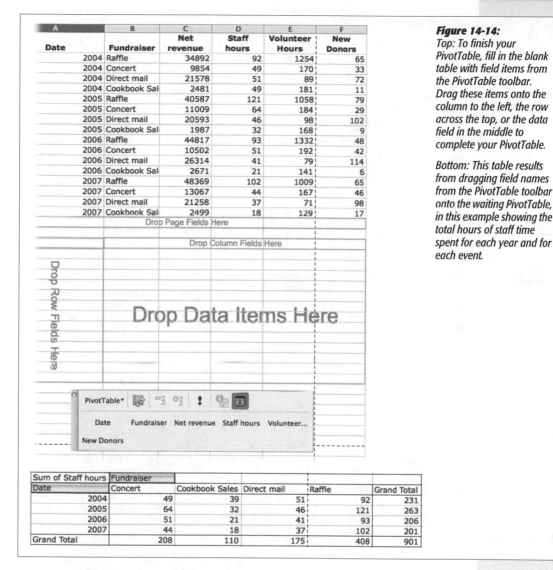

Figure 14-14:
Top: To finish your PivotTable, fill in the blank table with field items from the PivotTable toolbar. Drag these items onto the column to the left, the row across the top, or the data field in the middle to complete your PivotTable.

Bottom: This table results from dragging field names from the PivotTable toolbar onto the waiting PivotTable, in this example showing the total hours of staff time spent for each year and for each event.

Step 5: Build the table

You, the weary executive director, now want to build a table relating how much revenue each fundraiser brought in to the staff time it ate up. Drag the Date field name onto the Row Field area, the Fundraiser field name onto the Column Field area, and the Staff Hours field name onto the data area.

As depicted in Figure 14-14, Excel builds a table that displays how many staff hours each fundraiser required, and adds the totals for each fundraiser (at the bottom) and for each year (at the right).

Step 6: Massage the data

Now that you've created your simple PivotTable, you can quickly rearrange it to glean the juicy results from it by dragging field names to different areas in the Pivot-Table, or you can add a new dimension by dragging yet another field name (in the case of the executive director, the number of new donors) onto the table. If you add a new field to the data area, Excel divides each row into two, showing how the data for each date interrelate. The more field names you drag into the data area, the more complex your table becomes, but the more chance you'll have to spot any trends (Figure 14-15). Field names can also be added to the row and column axes for an entirely different kind of table.

Sum of Staff hours	Fundraiser				
Date	Concert	Cookbook Sales	Direct mail	Raffle	Grand Total
2004	49	39	51	92	231
2005	64	32	46	121	263
2006	51	21	41	93	206
2007	44	18	37	102	201
Grand Total	208	110	175	408	901

Sum of New Donors	Date				
Fundraiser	2004	2005	2006	2007	Grand Total
Concert	33	29	42	46	150
Cookbook Sales	11	9	6	17	43
Direct mail	72	102	114	98	386
Raffle	65	79	48	65	257
Grand Total	181	219	210	226	836

Date	Data	Fundraiser				
		Concert	Cookbook Sales	Direct mail	Raffle	Grand Total
2004	Sum of New Donors	33	11	72	65	181
	Sum of Staff hours	49	39	51	92	231
	Sum of Volunteer Hours	170	181	89	1254	1694
2005	Sum of New Donors	29	9	102	79	219
	Sum of Staff hours	64	32	46	121	263
	Sum of Volunteer Hours	184	168	98	1058	1508
2006	Sum of New Donors	42	6	114	48	210
	Sum of Staff hours	51	21	41	93	206
	Sum of Volunteer Hours	192	141	79	1332	1744
2007	Sum of New Donors	46	17	98	65	226
	Sum of Staff hours	44	18	37	102	201
	Sum of Volunteer Hours	167	129	71	1009	1376
Total Sum of New Donors		150	43	386	257	836
Total Sum of Staff hours		208	110	175	408	901
Total Sum of Volunteer Hours		713	619	337	4653	6322

Figure 14-15:
These three PivotTables were created using the same data source—the only difference is that the fields from the PivotTable toolbar were dragged to different areas on the blank PivotTable. In the case of the complicated PivotTable (bottom), three different fields were dragged to the data field, creating three totals at the bottom of each column and grand totals at the right. Exercise this option with caution, since dragging multiple fields to the same axis can quickly render a PivotTable unreadable. If your table turns to hash, press ⌘-Z repeatedly to undo your steps.

Though PivotTables start out *totaling* rows and columns you needn't stop there. Control-click (or right-click) any of the totals and choose Field Settings. In the PivotTable field dialog box you can choose other functions for your summaries, such as Average, Max, Min, and so on. Click the Options button if you'd like your summaries expressed as percentages or differences.

Analyzing Your Data

PivotTables aren't the only way to analyze your Excel data. In fact, if you're the type who loves to answer those "what if" questions posed by board members or your spouse, then Excel has some great tools for you: *data tables, goal seek,* and *scenarios.*

Data tables

Data tables let you plug several different values into a formula to see how they change its results. They're especially useful, for example, when you want to understand how a few different interest rates might affect the size of a payment over the life of a five-year loan.

Data tables come in two flavors: one-variable tables (where you can change one factor to see how data is affected) and two-variable tables (where you can change two factors). The only hard part about using a data table is setting it up. You'll need to insert the formula, the data to substitute into the formula, and an *input cell* that will serve as a placeholder for data being substituted into the formula.

To create a one-variable table, arrange the data in your cells so that the items you want plugged into your calculation (the interest rate, for example) are in a continuous row or column; then proceed as shown in Figure 14-16. If you choose a row, type the formula you want used in your table in the cell that's *one column to the left* of that range of values, and one row below it. If you choose a column, type the formula in the row above the range of values, and *one row to the right* of it. Think of the values (the interest rates) as row or column heads, and the formula's location (the payment amount) as the heading of an actual row or column in your soon-to-be-formed table. You'll also need to decide on the location of your input cell; it should be outside this table.

For example, to see the effects of different rates of interest on a proposed loan, set up a table similar to the one at the top of Figure 14-16, where column B contains one possible interest rate, the loan term, and the loan amount. Column C contains a list of other possible loan rates, while D3 contains the formula to calculate payments based on the values in column B: *=PMT(B4/12,B5,-B6)*.

If one "what if" is good, two has got to be better—and Excel is happy to oblige by creating a two-variable data table. Using the same example, you can compute payments based on different rates *and* a different number of monthly payments in much the same way as a single-variable data table.

To create a two-variable table, enter a formula in your worksheet that refers to the *two* sets of values plugged into the formula. Now proceed as shown in Figure 14-17.

If you still don't see the information you really need after Excel creates one of these tables, you can simply replace values in the table—for example the loan amount, terms, or interest rates—and Excel updates the results in the table.

Goal seek

When you know the answer that you want a formula to produce but you don't know the values to plug into the formula to *get* that answer, then it's time for Excel's *goal seek* feature.

◇	A	B	C	D
1	One Variable: Rate			
2			Rate	Payment
3	Happy Home Mortgage			1,476.26
4	Interest rate	5.00%	5.00%	
5	Term	360.00	5.25%	
6	Loan Amount	275,000.00	5.50%	
7			5.75%	
8			6.00%	
9			6.25%	
10			6.50%	

◇	A	B	C	D
1	One Variable: Rate			
2			Rate	Payment
3	Happy Home Mortgage			1,476.26
4	Interest rate	5.00%	5.00%	
5	Term	360.00	5.25%	
6	Loan Amount	275,000.00	5.50%	
7			5.75%	
8			6.00%	
9			6.25%	
10		Table	6.50%	
11			6.75%	
12		Column input cell: B4	7.00%	
13				
14		Cancel OK		
15				

Row input cell:

◇	A	B	C	D
1	One Variable: Rate			
2			Rate	Payment
3	Happy Home Mortgage			1476.26
4	Interest rate	5.00%	5.00%	1476.26
5	Term	360.00	5.25%	1518.56
6	Loan Amount	275,000.00	5.50%	1561.42
7			5.75%	1604.83
8			6.00%	1648.76
9			6.25%	1693.22
10			6.50%	1738.19

Figure 14-16:

Top: To create a single-variable What-If data table, start by entering one set of data and a formula to calculate your result. Column B contains the values needed to calculate loan payments. Cell D3 contains the PMT formula to calculate monthly payments. Enter your set of substitute values in a column starting one column to the left and one row below the cell containing the formula. (Or one column to the right and one row above for a row-oriented data table.)

Middle: Select the group of cells containing your substitute values and the formula and choose Data → Table to summon the Table dialog box. Since this is a column-oriented table, click the Column input cell field and then click cell B4—the cell containing the value in the formula to be replaced by the substitute values.

Bottom: When you click OK, Excel builds the table, calculating the payment for each interest rate.

Note: If you've been using Solver—Goal Seek's more capable big brother—in previous versions of office, you'll be disappointed to see that Microsoft removed it from Excel 2008, apparently due to the change to the .XML file format.

To use it, choose Tools → Goal Seek. In the resulting dialog box (Figure 14-18), fill in the following three fields:

- **Set cell.** Specifies which cell to start from—the cell containing the formula you're using to seek your goal. For example, Figure 14-18 shows a mortgage calculation. The Set cell (the upper-right cell), which shows the amount of the monthly payment, is D3. The purpose of this exercise is to find the amount you can mortgage if the most you can pay each month is $1,200.

- **To value.** Specifies the value that you want to see in that cell. In the example of Figure 14-18, the To value is $1,200—that's what you and your spouse agree you can pay each month.

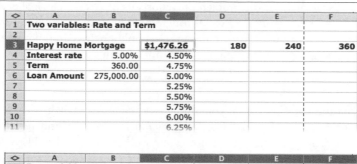

Top table:

	A	B	C	D	E	F
1	Two variables: Rate and Term					
2						
3	Happy Home Mortgage		$1,476.26	180	240	360
4	Interest rate	5.00%	4.50%			
5	Term	360.00	4.75%			
6	Loan Amount	275,000.00	5.00%			
7			5.25%			
8			5.50%			
9			5.75%			
10			6.00%			
11			6.25%			

Middle table:

	A	B	C	D	E	F
1	Two variables: Rate and Term					
2						
3	Happy Home Mortgage		$1,476.26	180	240	360
4	Interest rate	5.00%	4.50%			
5	Term	360.00	4.75%			
6	Loan Amount	275,000.00	5.00%			
7			5.25			
8			5.50			
9			5.75			
10			6.00			
11			6.25			
12			6.50			
13			6.75			
14			7.00			

Table

Row input cell: B5

Column input cell: B4

Cancel | OK

Bottom table:

	A	B	C	D	E	F
1	Two variables: Rate and Term					
2						
3	Happy Home Mortgage		$1,476.26	180	240	360
4	Interest rate	5.00%	4.50%	2103.73	1739.79	1393.38
5	Term	360.00	4.75%	2139.04	1777.11	1434.53
6	Loan Amount	275,000.00	5.00%	2174.68	1814.88	1476.26
7			5.25%	2210.66	1853.07	1518.56
8			5.50%	2246.98	1891.69	1561.42
9			5.75%	2283.63	1930.73	1604.83
10			6.00%	2320.61	1970.19	1648.76
11			6.25%	2357.91	2010.05	1693.22

Figure 14-17:
Top: In a two-variable data table, one set of data serves as one axis, and the second set serves as the second axis (top). The formula sits in the upper-left corner (C3), and it refers to two input cells outside of the table (B4 and B5). Enter one set of values in a column starting just below the formula, and the second set of values in a row starting just to the right of the formula. Select the range of cells containing the formula and all of the input values that you just entered, and choose Data → Table.

Middle: Enter the addresses for the row input cell (B5 for the term) and the column input cell (B4 for the rate) and click OK.

Bottom: Excel creates a beautiful table of payments based on how two variables interact showing you payments for a variety of interest rates for a 15-, 20-, or 30-year term.

Figure 14-18 table:

	A	B	C	D	E
2			Rate	Payment	
3	Happy Home Mortgage			1476.26	
4	Interest rate	5.00%	5.00%	1476.26	
5	Term	360.00			
6	Loan Amount	275,000.00			
7					
8					
9					
10					
11					
12					
13					
14					

Goal Seek

Set cell: D3

To value: 1200

By changing cell: B6

Cancel | OK

Figure 14-18:
By letting Excel determine how much the financed amount will be, you can keep your loan payment to $1,200. Using the same data from the data tables example, Excel informs us that for $1,200 per month we can afford a $223,537.94 loan at 5% for 360 months.

- **By changing cell.** Tells Excel which cell it can tinker with to make that happen. The key cell in Figure 14-18 is B6, the loan amount, since you want to know how much you can spend on a house with a $1,200 mortgage payment.

Click OK to turn Excel loose on the problem. It reports its progress in a Goal Seek Status dialog box, which lets you step Excel through the process of working toward your goal. There are a couple of caveats: You can select only single cells, not ranges, and the cell you're tweaking has to contain a value, not a formula.

Scenarios

Scenarios are like little snapshots, each containing a different set of "what if" data plugged into your formulas. Because Excel can memorize each set and recall it instantly, scenarios help you understand how your worksheet model is likely to turn out given different situations. (You still have to enter the data and formulas into your spreadsheet before you play with scenarios, though.) In a way, scenarios are like saving several different copies of the same spreadsheet, each with variations in the data. Being able to quickly switch between scenarios lets you run through different situations without retyping any numbers.

To create a scenario, choose Tools → Scenarios to bring up the Scenarios Manager, where you can add, delete, edit, and merge different scenarios, as shown in Figure 14-19.

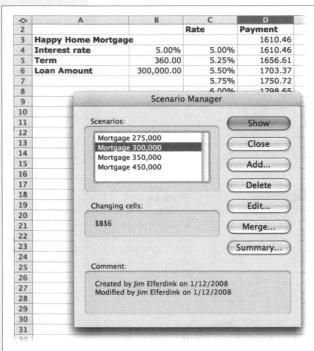

Figure 14-19:
In the Scenario Manager dialog box, you can switch between saved scenarios, add new ones, edit existing ones, merge scenarios from other worksheets into the Scenarios list, and even summarize your scenarios to a standard summary or PivotTable. The Scenarios list displays all of the scenarios that you've created and saved, and by selecting a scenario and clicking Show, Excel plugs the scenario values into the worksheet and shows the results.

The listbox on the left side displays all of the scenarios that you've saved. By selecting a scenario and then clicking a button on the right, you can display your scenarios in your spreadsheet, or even make a summary. Here's what each does:

- **Show.** The Show button lets you switch between scenarios; just select the scenario you want to view, and then click Show. Excel changes the spreadsheet to reflect the selected scenario.

- **Close.** As you expect, this button simply closes the Scenario Manager.

- **Add.** Click this button to design a new scenario, courtesy of the Add Scenario dialog box (Figure 14-20). It lets you name your scenario and specify the cells you want to change (either enter the cell references or select them with the mouse). Excel inserts a comment regarding when the scenario was created. You can edit this comment to say anything you like, making it a terrific place to note exactly what the scenario affects in the spreadsheet.

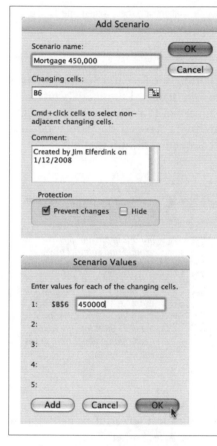

Figure 14-20:
Top: Clicking Add in the Scenario Manager calls up the Add Scenario dialog box, shown here. (It changes to say Edit Scenario when you fill in the "Changing cells" field.) In this box, you name your scenario and tell Excel which cells to change when showing it.

Bottom: Once you click OK, you see the Scenario Values dialog box, where you enter the new values for the cells that you specified in the previous window.

After clicking OK, you're taken to the Scenario Values dialog box, where you enter new values for the cells you specified in the previous window. Once you're done entering your new values, click OK. The new scenario appears in the Scenario Manager.

- **Delete.** This button deletes the currently selected scenario.

- **Edit.** The Edit button opens the Edit Scenario dialog box, which looks just like the Add Scenario box. Use this box to edit a previously saved scenario.

- **Merge.** This command merges scenarios from other worksheets into the Scenario list for the current worksheet. To merge scenarios, open all of the workbooks that contain scenarios that you want to merge, and then switch to the worksheet where you want the merged scenarios to appear. This is your destination worksheet for the merge.

  Open the Scenario Manager (Tools → Scenarios) and click Merge, select the workbook that has the scenarios to merge, and then select the sheet containing the actual scenarios.

Tip: When you're merging scenarios, make sure that your destination worksheet is the same as all of the scenarios. Otherwise, merged data will still appear in the proper cells, but if those cells aren't properly placed or formatted, it'll look strange.

- **Summary.** When you click the Summary button, the Scenario Summary dialog box appears. It has two radio buttons: one for a standard summary (which creates a table) and one for a PivotTable summary (a PivotTable of your changes *really* lets you tweak the numbers). Figure 14-21 shows a standard summary, complete with buttons for expanding and contracting the information.

Scenario Summary				
	Current Values:	Mortgage 275000	Mortgage 300000	Mortgage 350000
Changing Cells:				
B6	350,000.00	275,000.00	300,000.00	350,000.00
Result Cells:				
D4	17500.00	13750.00	15000.00	17500.00
D5	18375.00	14437.50	15750.00	18375.00
D6	19250.00	15125.00	16500.00	19250.00
D7	20125.00	15812.50	17250.00	20125.00
D8	21000.00	16500.00	18000.00	21000.00
D9	21875.00	17187.50	18750.00	21875.00
D10	22750.00	17875.00	19500.00	22750.00
D11	23625.00	18562.50	20250.00	23625.00
D12	24500.00	19250.00	21000.00	24500.00

Notes: Current Values column represents values of changing cells at time Scenario Summary Report was created. Changing cells for each scenario are highlighted in gray.

Figure 14-21:
A summary report shows all of the scenarios in your worksheet. Click the + and – buttons in the margins to expand and contract rows. Once Excel creates a summary, you can edit it, to dress it up or just make it more readable. For example, you could copy and paste the interest rates from the worksheet into the Result Cells column which now shows cell references.

Tapping the Data menu

Granted, PivotTables and databases are some of the most powerful elements found in the Data menu, but they're not the only ones. A few other commands in the Data menu let you perform additional tricks with your data.

- **Sort.** This powerful menu command lets you sort selected data alphabetically or numerically with much greater control than when using the Toolbar's Sort buttons. You can perform several levels of sorting, just as you can when sorting database items—for example, sort by year, then by month *within* each year. As shown in Figure 14-22, the beauty of the Sort command is that it sorts entire *rows*, not just the one column you specified for sorting.

Tip: Clicking "Header row" avoids sorting the top-row column labels into the data–a common problem with other spreadsheet software. Excel leaves the top row where it is, as shown in Figure 14-22.

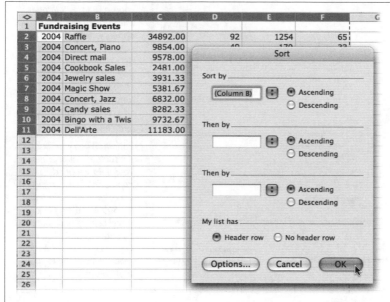

Figure 14-22:
A table sorted alphabetically by event. Highlight the table (including the header row of across the top), and then choose Data → Sort. In the Sort dialog box, specify (using the Sort by pop-up menu) that you want to sort the rows according to the text in column B. turn on the radio button for "Header row" to exclude that row from the sorting. When you click OK, Excel sorts the rows into the proper order.

• **Filter.** When you choose AutoFilter from this submenu, you get pop-up menus at the top of each column in your selection (Figure 14-23). You can use them to hide or show certain rows or columns, exactly like the filters found in list objects (see page 550). AutoFilter pop-up menus can be applied to only one selection at a time in a worksheet. Also on the Filter submenu, Show All displays items that you hid using the AutoFilter pop-up menus, and Advanced Filter lets you build your own filter. (Consult the online help if you want to build an advanced filter.)

Figure 14-23:
You can quickly and easily sort the rows of selected data by choosing Data → Filter → AutoFilter, then choosing from the pop-up menus that appear. For example, this command sorts the rows in ascending order by revenues.

• **Subtotals.** This command automatically puts subtotal formulas in a column (or columns). The columns need to have headings that label them (Figure 14-24 shows an example).

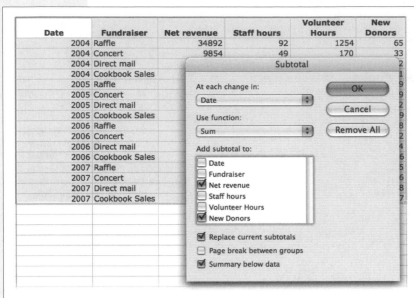

Figure 14-24:

Top: Select a set of data that could stand some subtotals. When you choose Data → Subtotals, the Subtotal dialog box appears. In this box, you can choose the column that determines where subtotals go (in this case, at each change in the date), which function is used, and in which columns the subtotal appears.

Bottom: When you click OK, the subtotals appear in your data, grouped appropriately according to the column you selected in the Subtotal dialog box. (Excel uses its outlining notation, as described on page 633, making it easy to collapse the result to show subtotals only.)

Date		Fundraiser	Net revenue	Staff hours	Volunteer Hours	New Donors
	2004	Raffle	34892	92	1254	65
	2004	Concert	9854	49	170	33
	2004	Direct mail	21578	51	89	72
	2004	Cookbook Sales	2481	39	181	11
2004 Total			68805			181
	2005	Raffle	40587	121	1058	79
	2005	Concert	11009	64	184	29
	2005	Direct mail	20593	46	98	102
	2005	Cookbook Sales	1987	32	168	9
2005 Total			74176			219
	2006	Raffle	44817	93	1332	48
	2006	Concert	10502	51	192	42
	2006	Direct mail	26314	41	79	114
	2006	Cookbook Sales	2671	21	141	6
2006 Total			84304			210
	2007	Raffle	48369	102	1009	65
	2007	Concert	13067	44	167	46
	2007	Direct mail	21258	37	71	98
	2007	Cookbook Sales	2499	18	129	17
2007 Total			85193			226
Grand Total			312478			836

To use this feature, select the relevant columns, including their headings, and then choose Data → Subtotals. In the Subtotal dialog box that pops up, you can tell Excel which function to use (your choices include Sum, Count, StdDev, and Average, among others) and whether to include hidden rows or columns in the subtotal. If you've selected more than one column, you can add the selected function to whichever column or columns you choose.

- **Text to Columns.** Suppose you've pasted a phrase into a single cell, and now you'd like to split each word into a separate column. Or maybe a cell contains several cells worth of text, each separated by a nonstandard delimiter (such as a semicolon) that you'd like to split in a similar fashion. "Text to Columns" is the solution, as shown in Figure 14-25.

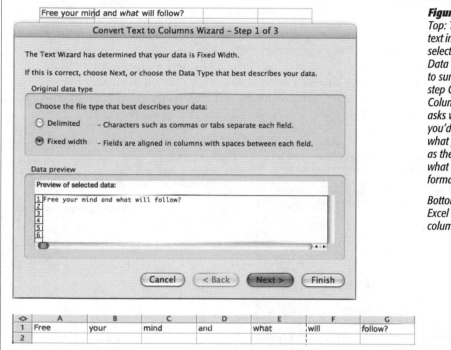

Figure 14-25:
Top: To split delimited text into several columns, select the cell and choose Data → Text to Columns to summon the three-step Convert Text to Columns Wizard. Excel asks what kind of split you'd like to perform, what punctuation serves as the delimiter, and what the data and cell formatting looks like.

Bottom: Click Finish, and Excel splits the data into columns.

- **Consolidate.** The Consolidate command joins data from several different worksheets or workbooks into the same area, turning it into a kind of summary. In older versions of Excel, this command was important; in Excel 2008, Microsoft recommends that you not use it and instead simply type the references and operators that you wish to use directly in the consolidation area of a worksheet. For example, if you track revenues for each region on four different worksheets, you can consolidate that data onto a fifth worksheet. (If you insist on going old-school, learn more by reading the "Consolidate data" entry in Excel's online help.)

Data form

A spreadsheet is certainly a compact and tidy way to view information. But for the novice, it's not exactly self-explanatory. If you plan to turn some data-entry tasks over to an assistant who's not completely at home with the row-and-column scheme, you might consider setting up a *data form* for him—a little dialog box that displays a single spreadsheet row as individual blanks that have to be filled in (see Figure 14-26). Data forms also give you a great way to search for data or delete it one row (that is, one record) at a time.

To set up a data form, start with a series of columns with column headers at the top—a list does nicely. These headers serve as categories for the data form. Then, with the cursor in the list, choose Data → Form, which brings up the data form window for that particular list (Figure 14-26).

When the form appears, the text boxes show the first row of data in the list. You can scroll through the rows (or records) using the scroll bar. On the right, buttons let you perform the following functions: add a new record (or row) of data at the bottom, delete the currently selected row, click Criteria to enter search criteria in the text boxes next to the field names, and then search for that information using Find Prev and Find Next. Finally, the Close button closes the window.

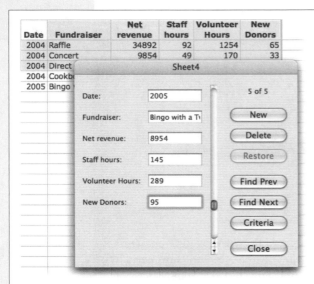

Figure 14-26:
The fields in a data form correspond to the columns in the spreadsheet. Data forms work like miniature databases. With them, you can quickly add and remove whole rows of data in a list, as well as search through a list for all matches.

Viewing Your Data

Excel worksheets can grow very quickly. Fortunately, Excel has some convenient tools to help you look at just the data you want.

Custom views

Excel can memorize everything about a workbook's window: its size and position, any splits or frozen panes, which sheets are active and which cells are selected, and even your printer settings—in a *custom view*. Custom views are snapshots of your view options at the time that the view is saved. Using custom views, you can quickly switch from your certain-columns-hidden view to your everything-exposed view, or from your split-window view to your full-window view.

Validating Data

To ensure that the right kind of data is entered in a cell or cells, use a built-in Excel feature called Data Validation. This feature makes sure that dates, for example, don't end up in cells meant for currency.

To set up data validation for a cell or cells, select them and then choose Data → Validation, which brings up the Data Validation dialog box. This box has three tabs: Settings, Input Message, and Error Alert.

In the Settings tab, you can choose which data types are allowed to be entered (such as whole numbers, decimals, or lists). In the Input Message tab, you can enter a message that will pop up when you (or whoever uses this spreadsheet) select the cell in question. The Error Alert tab, meanwhile, lets you specify which error message Excel should display when someone enters the wrong kind of data.

To create a custom view, choose View → Custom Views, which brings up the Custom Views dialog box. To make Excel memorize your current window arrangement, click Add (and type a name for the current setup); switch between custom views by clicking a view's name in the list and then clicking Show.

Outlining

In Excel, *outlines* help to summarize many rows of data, hiding or showing levels of detail in lists so that only the summaries are visible (see Figure 14-27). Because they let you switch between overview and detail views in a single step, outlines are useful for worksheets that teem with subtotals and details. (If you're unfamiliar with the concept of outlining software for word processing, consult page 191, which describes the very similar feature in Microsoft Word.)

You can create an outline in one of two ways: automatically or manually. The automatic method works only if you've formatted your worksheet in a way Excel's outliner can understand:

- Summary *columns* have to be to the right or left of the data they summarize. In Figure 14-28 at top, the D column is a summary column, located to the right of the data it summarizes.

- Summary *rows* have to be immediately above or below the cells that they summarize. For example, in Figure 14-28 at bottom, each subtotal is directly below the cells that it adds together.

If your spreadsheet meets these conditions, creating an outline is as easy as selecting Data → Group and Outline → Auto Outline.

If your data isn't so neatly organized, you'll have to create an outline manually. Select the rows or columns of data that you want to group together into one level of the outline; choose Data → Group and Outline → Group. A bracket line appears outside the row numbers or column letters, connecting that group. Keep selecting rows or columns and grouping them until you've manually created your outline.

Figure 14-27:
Top: An outlined spreadsheet fully expanded.

Bottom: The same spreadsheet partially collapsed. Clicking a + or – button opens or closes detail areas, while clicking the number buttons in the upper-left corner displays just the first, second, or third levels of detail for the entire outline. This example shows three levels, but Excel allows up to eight levels of detail in outlines.

	Date	Fundraiser	Net revenue	Staff hours	Volunteer Hours	New Donors
1	Date	Fundraiser	Net revenue	Staff hours	Volunteer Hours	New Donors
2	2004	Raffle	34892	92	1254	65
3	2004	Concert	9854	49	170	33
4	2004	Direct mail	21578	51	89	72
5	2004	Cookbook Sales	2481	39	181	11
6	**2004 Total**		68805			181
7	2005	Raffle	40587	121	1058	79
8	2005	Concert	11009	64	184	29
9	2005	Direct mail	20593	46	98	102
10	2005	Cookbook Sales	1987	32	168	9
11	**2005 Total**		74176			219
12	2006	Raffle	44817	93	1332	48
13	2006	Concert	10502	51	192	42
14	2006	Direct mail	26314	41	79	114
15	2006	Cookbook Sales	2671	21	141	6
16	**2006 Total**		84304			210
17	2007	Raffle	48369	102	1009	65
18	2007	Concert	13067	44	167	46
19	2007	Direct mail	21258	37	71	98
20	2007	Cookbook Sales	2499	18	129	17
21	**2007 Total**		85193			226
22	**Grand Total**		312478			836

	Date	Fundraiser	Net revenue	Staff hours	Volunteer Hours	New Donors
1	Date	Fundraiser	Net revenue	Staff hours	Volunteer Hours	New Donors
6	**2004 Total**		68805			181
11	**2005 Total**		74176			219
16	**2006 Total**		84304			210
21	**2007 Total**		85193			226
22	**Grand Total**		312478			836

Figure 14-28:
Top: Because the column of subtotals (column D) is to the right of the data to which it refers, this spreadsheet can be automatically outlined.

Bottom: Each subtotal is beneath the cells it summarizes, making this spreadsheet, too, a fine candidate for automatic outlining.

	A	B	C	D
25		Arcata	Garberville	Subtotal
26	January	3456	4456	7912
27	February	4567	4538	9105
28	March	8343	7643	15986
29	April	6576	4589	11165
30	May	4578	2457	7035
31	June	3787	6783	10570

	Date	Fundraiser	Net revenue
1	Date	Fundraiser	Net revenue
2	2004	Raffle	34892
3	2004	Concert	9854
4	2004	Direct mail	21578
5	2004	Cookbook Sales	2481
6	**2004 Total**		68805
7	2005	Raffle	40587
8	2005	Concert	11009
9	2005	Direct mail	20593
10	2005	Cookbook Sales	1987
11	**2005 Total**		74176
12	2006	Raffle	44817
13	2006	Concert	10502
14	2006	Direct mail	26314
15	2006	Cookbook Sales	2671
16	**2006 Total**		84304
17	2007	Raffle	48369
18	2007	Concert	13067
19	2007	Direct mail	21258
20	2007	Cookbook Sales	2499
21	**2007 Total**		85193
22	**Grand Total**		312478

Outlines can have eight levels of detail, making it easy to go from general to specific very quickly. Thick brackets connect the summary row or column to the set of cells that it summarizes; a + or – button appears at the end of the line by the summary row or column.

To expand or collapse a single "branch" of the outline, click a + or – button; if you see several nested brackets, click the outer + or – buttons to collapse greater chunks of the outline. Also, the tiny, numbered buttons at the upper left hide and show outline levels and correspond to Level 1, Level 2, and so on, much like the Show Heading buttons on the Outlining toolbar in Word (see page 193).

Tip: Although outlines were originally designed to hide or reveal detail, you can use them to hide *any* rows or columns that you like.

Flag for Follow-Up

Sometimes, when you're presenting the contents of a workbook to someone else—or when you're up battling a bout of insomnia by going through your old Excel workbooks—you come across something in a spreadsheet that needs updating, research, explanation, or some other kind of follow-up. Excel's *flag for follow-up* feature lets you attach a reminder to a file, which you can program to appear (as a reminder box on your screen) at a specified time. See page 469 for more on Office Reminders.

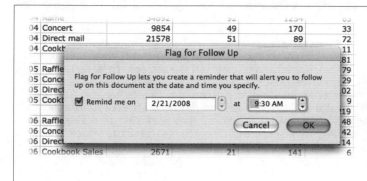

Figure 14-29:
To flag a file for follow up, choose Tools ▸ "Flag for Follow Up", which produces the "Flag for Follow Up" dialog box (inset). In this box, you can set a time and date to be reminded that you need to attend to your worksheet. (Press Tab if you have trouble moving the insertion point around in the dialog box.) Click OK and save the document. Excel creates a task in Entourage; the reminder pops up at the specified time—as long as your computer is on. Otherwise, you'll see the reminder the next time you turn on your Mac.

Adding a Comment

Here's another way to get your own attention (or somebody else's): Add a *comment* to a cell—a great way to annotate a spreadsheet. A note might say, for example, "This figure is amazing!—Congratulations!," or "I had no idea that old cookbook was still selling so well!" See Figure 14-30 for details.

To edit a comment that already exists, select the cell and then choose Insert → Edit Comment. To *delete* a comment, select the cell with the comment and choose Edit → Clear → Comments. You can also reveal all comments on a worksheet at once by choosing View → Comments.

Tip: Like the Stickies program on every Mac, Excel comment boxes lack scroll bars. If you have a lot to say, keep typing past the bottom boundary of the box; Excel expands the note automatically. You can press the up and down arrow keys to walk your insertion point through the text, in the absence of scroll bars. (Alternatively, drag one of the blue handles to make the box bigger.)

POWER USERS' CLINIC

Proofing Tools

A spelling error can ruin the credibility of an otherwise brilliant spreadsheet, especially when you've gone through the trouble of getting it to look just right. Running a spell check on your spreadsheet before you show it to others can prevent just such an embarrassing mishap. Fortunately, Excel is part of the larger Office suite—which includes spelling tools.

To run a spell check on your spreadsheet, choose Tools → Spelling. Excel scans the text in your spreadsheet; if it comes across a suspect word, the Spelling dialog box appears. It

works much like the Word spell checker described on page 64, and, in fact, relies on the same spelling dictionaries. There's probably not much call for a definitions dictionary in spreadsheets these days, but if you run across a term in a spreadsheet that you don't know (taxable, for example), you can access Office's definitions dictionary by selecting the word and opening the Reference Palette in the Toolbox (or choosing Tools → Dictionary) or by typing in the word you'd like defined.

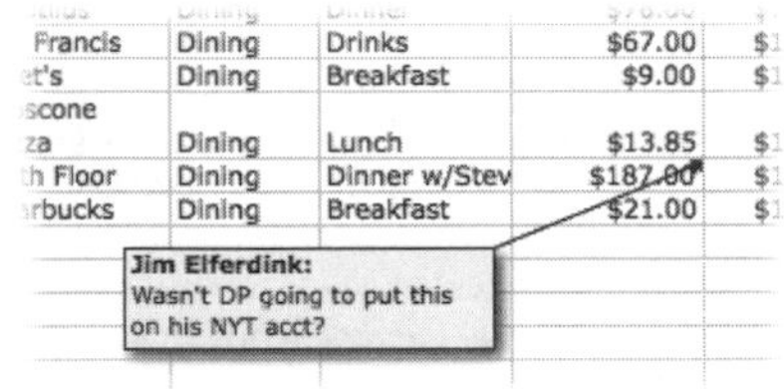

Figure 14-30:
To add a note to a cell, click the cell and then choose Insert → Comment. A nice yellow "sticky note" opens with your user name on the top (as it appears in the Excel → Preferences → General tab). Type your comment in the window. When you click elsewhere, the note disappears, leaving only a small triangle in the upper-right corner of the cell. To make the comment reappear, let the cursor hover over the triangle. (If you prefer to see comments all the time, change that setting in Excel → Preferences → View.)

Part Four: PowerPoint

4

Planning and Creating Great Presentations

Communication takes many forms, from smoke signals to Web pages; from rude gestures to polished oratory; from an order at the drive-through to a speech at the podium. And whether you're a Great Communicator or a first-time speaker, what you're really doing in any of these instances is making a *presentation*: you're delivering information to others to get your point across.

PowerPoint's a great tool to help you make presentations. But it's only a tool. Don't fall into the trap of thinking the computer presentation is the star of the show. *You* are the star of the show. PowerPoint, your handouts, your guest speakers, and your sharp new suit are all playing supporting roles.

Before you even boot up your computer, it's worth spending some time thinking about your presentation's goal (convince Mom and Dad to let you go away to camp, for example) and who your audience is (two people who know you very well). As a wise man once said, "Scratch 'em where they itch." To succeed, your presentation has to resonate with the audience's needs, expectations, and assumptions. The first two parts of this chapter help you plan an effective presentation tailored to your audience. The last section deals with presentation nuts and bolts— picking out laptops, projectors, and so on.

If you're an award-winning member of the dinner-speech circuit and you just bought this book to learn how to use Office and PowerPoint, then by all means skip ahead to the next chapter to learn the ins and outs of the program. But if you have limited or no experience giving knock-'em-dead presentations, this chapter's loaded with advice that can help you plan, prepare for, and deliver your pitch.

Planning the Presentation

It doesn't matter if you're planning on talking one-on-one—teaching your daughter how to operate the lawnmower—or speaking to thousands of Macworld attendees: if you care about the message you're about to deliver, it's worth spending time organizing your thoughts before you begin composing your presentation.

Tip: While you're planning your presentation, don't forget to make a contingency plan too. Identify parts of your presentation you could simplify, gloss over, or cut out completely in case your guest speaker rambles on for ten minutes instead of three; audience questions take much longer than anticipated; or you have to send someone to find the janitor when you turn on your projector and trip a circuit breaker.

The Goals of Your Presentation

Begin by thinking through what you want your presentation to accomplish. There's nothing worse than being on the receiving end of an aimless talk. In other words, what do you want your audience to walk away with? Here are some examples:

- Gain knowledge or skills.
- Understand a new concept.
- Be inspired or moved.
- Change their behavior.
- Change their belief system.
- Take action.
- Buy something.
- Donate to your organization or invest in your company.
- Become involved in a process or a cause.
- Get media coverage for your business or organization.

Know Your Audience

In order to increase the likelihood of achieving your goal, you need to learn as much as you can about the kind of people who'll be in the audience. Put yourself in their shoes and figure out how you can make your presentation interesting and relevant to them. Sometimes you'll know exactly who you're talking to: the members of your project team, the Board of Directors, or your fellow Rotary members. In these cases, you've probably already got a pretty good idea of who these people are, what interests them, what their group culture is like, and what the norms are for typical presentations.

At other times the audience may be much more of an unknown quantity: the attendees at a conference you've never been to before, reporters at a press conference, a brand new client, or the circuit court judge. In this case, make an effort to learn about your audience to give yourself a better chance of really connecting with them.

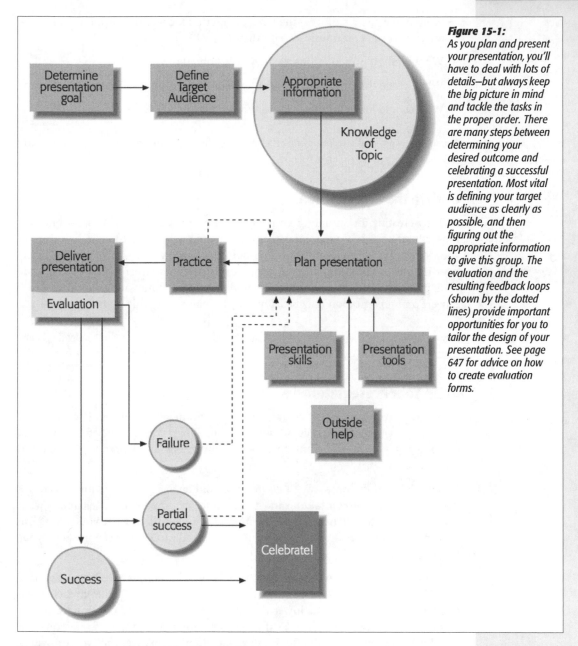

Figure 15-1:
As you plan and present your presentation, you'll have to deal with lots of details—but always keep the big picture in mind and tackle the tasks in the proper order. There are many steps between determining your desired outcome and celebrating a successful presentation. Most vital is defining your target audience as clearly as possible, and then figuring out the appropriate information to give this group. The evaluation and the resulting feedback loops (shown by the dotted lines) provide important opportunities for you to tailor the design of your presentation. See page 647 for advice on how to create evaluation forms.

Tailor the Presentation to the Audience

With your presentation goal and target audience clearly in mind, you can tailor what you're going to say to this particular group.

• What language do they speak?

• Do they use a colloquial language or jargon?

- How might their culture—their regional, ethnic, class, or corporate culture—affect how you communicate with them?

- What kinds of presentations are they accustomed to viewing?

- What would this audience consider appropriate dress for a presenter?

- What would make this topic important to this audience?

Tip: Interview potential audience members or other people who've presented to this group previously and ask for advice on how to make your presentation succeed.

Outline the Presentation

Start by creating an outline of your presentation on paper or in Word—but save PowerPoint's Outline view for later, when it's actually time to start working on your slides. Start rough with the high points of what you want to say and refine your outline as you go. If your presentation is part of a larger event, then outline your part from the time you take the podium to the time you leave the stage. A PowerPoint presentation may be all or only a small part of this outline.

Tip: Using Word's outlining feature (page 19) will save you time later, since you can transfer it right into PowerPoint, as described on page 661.

Build Your Presentation

Work from your outline to create your PowerPoint presentation. The following chapters cover the mechanics of working with PowerPoint. But before you start creating slides, refine your outline so you'll know how and where to make use of those slides.

It's certainly not the only way to do it, but an old favorite structure for speeches is the overview, the presentation, and the review. In other words, tell them what you're going to tell them, then tell them, and then tell them what you told them. That may sound excessively simple, but it's a wonderfully easy way to keep your audience oriented.

You might find it useful to start with a joke, a quip, or humorous anecdote—especially a self-deprecating one—that somehow relates to your topic. If skillfully delivered, this kind of icebreaker helps lower the audience's defenses and can endear you to them. But if you can't tell jokes, or if you're sure you're going to be so nervous you could never pull it off, don't attempt it. You certainly don't want to start off with a poorly-told joke that falls flat.

Remember as you design your presentation—and later as you make it—your job is to communicate your information clearly, simply, and interestingly. Your mission is to engage the audience and keep their attention for the duration. Keep these points in mind when you're sketching out what you want to say:

- Know your subject thoroughly—but don't feel you have to tell everything you know.

- Use as many slides as you need—and no more. Slides are supporting materials—use them where they do the most good. It's possible you could give an hour-long talk and use five slides. Some slides may be up for several minutes each, while others may be on screen for only a few seconds.

- Slides are especially good for tables and charts, pictures, and strong bullet points.

- Don't fill your slides with text. Use a larger font than you think you need.

- If you have several bullet points on a slide, build them in one at a time as you discuss each one. Otherwise, your audience will be reading ahead and not listening.

- Try to approximately balance your use of slides containing bullet points, charts, and pictures.

- Try to make your presentation interactive. For example, present a problem or question to the audience and open it up for discussion. Alternatively, ask them to discuss the question with their neighbor for a few minutes and then gather responses from the room.

- Vary the pace of the presentation—especially if it's a long one—by pulling audience members up for demonstrations, bringing out surprise guests, giving attendees one minute to furiously scribble responses to your question, and so on.

- Use every different communication method at your disposal: auditory, visual, and direct experience. Involve the right brain by using stories, movement, or song.

- Be careful with how much color you use in your slides. You don't want color to distract from the point you're making, and you always want your slides to be legible.

- Don't use slide animations or fancy transitions just because it's easy to do so. These features should serve the presentation, not distract from it.

- Your presentation should keep the audience involved by keeping them thinking or reacting emotionally; by generating questions, new thoughts, and new dreams.

Practice

Practice giving your presentation to a coworker, an indulgent spouse, or an attentive dog, and listen carefully to any feedback—from the humans anyway. Watch yourself in the mirror or shoot a video of yourself as you practice. Pay special attention to your gestures, expressions, and body language. Be yourself, but remember you're essentially "on stage"—even if your audience is composed of only two people. And in order to reach an audience you need to project not only your voice, but your movements and gestures as well.

Have someone else proofread your slides. If you have to proofread them yourself, print out the slides so you can see the words on paper instead of on-screen. Misspelled words or incorrect punctuation that you read over a dozen times on-screen will jump out at you on a printed page. Double- and triple-check the spelling of people's names or product names that appear in your slides.

Tip: At this point, you can use your watch to get an idea of how long it takes to do your presentation, factoring in time for introductory comments and any question-and-answer period. Once you've finalized your script and typed out your slides, you can use PowerPoint's rehearsal mode (page 701) to determine the exact timing.

Delivering the Presentation

If you're responsible for the whole event, it falls on to you to deal with a handful of tasks that seemingly have nothing to do with your presentation. Factors like lighting and furniture can have a huge impact on your audience's experience. Unfortunately, if you're late or equipment fails, your audience may be less receptive to your message.

Try to take care of the following ahead of time so you can solve any problems before the audience arrives.

- Know how to unlock the doors, adjust the lights, and control the temperature. If you have to dim the lights in order to see the screen, make sure there's a light projecting on you whenever you're speaking so your audience can see you.

- If you have control over the way the room is set up, place the podium at center stage and your screen off to the side. The slides are for speaker support—what you're saying is the main attraction.

- Set up and test the equipment, or coordinate with your tech support people who'll be running the lights and the public address system.

- If your audio person needs to manage inputs—say, from your laptop's sound output and your microphone—print a slide list for her (see page 715) with all the audio cues clearly indicated. For example, she might need to fade out the "walk-in" music and turn on your microphone input; or she may need to turn up the sound from your computer's audio during a part of the presentation while turning off your mic.

- Set up tables or set out information packets or programs.

- Make sure there are clear signs prominently posted to help attendees find the room so they know they've come to the right place.

- Figure out the parking situation, handicapped access, and restroom locations.

- Greet people as they come in to make them feel welcome and help them get oriented.

Welcome Your Audience

When it's time to start and your audience is seated, don't launch right into your program. Welcome the audience, introduce yourself, and tell them what presentation they're attending so they know they're in the right room. Make sure everyone has a seat and a program. Tell them how long the session will run, if there will be a break, and where the bathrooms are. Explain how you'd like to handle questions from the audience—whether they should shout them out at any time, save them until the end, line up at a microphone, or whatever. If you've brought printed handouts (page 715) or posted your slides on the Web, let the audience know they don't need to take notes.

Explaining these seemingly simple things to your audience may seem like a waste of time, but it actually serves to increase their comfort level, lower their defenses, and make them feel like they're part of the group—all of which will make them better and more receptive listeners.

Introduce Your Presentation

The time has come to finally talk about your topic. Try to open with a bang—catch people's attention and tell them how this presentation is going to be valuable to them, and what they're going to take away from it.

At this point you may want to query your listeners to see how they relate to your topic—both for your own benefit and theirs. Ask for a show of hands: "How many of you are running Mac OS X Server?" "Who's had, or has a loved one who's had breast cancer?" "How many of you are parents of seventh or eighth graders?"

Choose your questions so all the audience members see themselves as part of one or another of these groups. The responses you get will give you a better idea of the makeup of the audience—and it helps everyone feel like they belong as they identify with others who respond similarly.

Now that your audience has told you something about themselves, tell them something about yourself. For example: why are you qualified to speak on your topic?

Making the Presentation

After all your preparation, planning, and practice, giving your presentation should be a piece of cake. You've got great information, you know it inside out, and you've tailored it to this particular group of people. Relax and enjoy the process of sharing. During your talk keep these points in mind:

- If you don't feel relaxed, fake it. Your audience will never know the difference. Never make apologies for being nervous.

- Speak to the audience—don't just read from a script or recite. Look your listeners in the eye—in all parts of the room.

- Don't stare at your laptop or look behind you at the screen.

- Enthusiasm is contagious—smile! Let the audience see how enthusiastic you are about your topic.

- Vary your cadence when speaking—pauses can be very powerful.

- Don't read your slides (unless there's a compelling need to for the benefit of blind or foreign-language speaking members of the audience).

- If you have a slide full of text it probably doesn't need to be there—that's what should be in your speech. In fact, don't even use complete sentences in your slides—sentences belong in your speech.

Review

Wrap up your presentation with a review. Now's when you "tell them what you told them." Let audience members know what you hope they've gained from this presentation and what you expect them to do with it—buy your product, sign up for a time share, host a foreign-exchange student, or whatever.

Make any other concluding statements, put up a slide with your contact information, and remind them where you'll be after the presentation if they have more questions. Explain how you sincerely want their feedback on this presentation so that you can improve it in the future. Urge them to take a moment to fill out feedback forms, assuming you've chosen to prepare them as described in the next section.

Finally, thank them for coming and for their attention—and take a bow as the audience applauds and cheers.

Evaluating the Presentation

You've completed your presentation. You think you did a pretty good job—the audience applauded, no rotten fruits or vegetables hit the stage, and several people told you, "Nice job." But how can you be sure? Getting feedback is a step that's often overlooked, and while not appropriate for every presentation, it's a vital tool for judging your success using something other than guesswork. Audience feedback can tell you whether you succeeded in getting your message across, how useful the information is to the audience, and how you might improve the presentation—or similar presentations—next time.

The quickest, most direct—and least accurate—feedback method is to simply question your listeners and ask for a show of hands (see the box on page 647). If you go this route design your questions carefully because you can only ask about three or four without annoying most folks.

Feedback Fundamentals

Gathering feedback from your audience shouldn't be an afterthought. It's the only way you'll know how well you're doing and how you can do better in the future. Whether you just ask for a show of hands or provide an evaluation form, the information you receive can be invaluable.

For example, say your presentation is entitled *Controlling Gophers in Your Yard and Garden*. You're presenting to a group of organic gardeners, many of whom you know object to killing animals. Your goal is for the members of the audience to learn about and choose from different methods of gopher control appropriate to their situation and their ethical values.

If you only have time for raised-hands feedback, you might want to ask your audience the following questions—and be sure to write down your estimate of their responses:

- **Question:** Do you now know what approach you want to take to deal with your gopher problem? (Show of hands for yes, show of hands for no.)

- **Question:** For those of you who raised your hand *yes*, do you know enough to feel you can succeed with your chosen method? (Show of hands if you do know enough, show of hands if you don't know enough.)

- **Question:** If you raised your hand *no* to the first question, have you gained useful information that will be helpful in choosing an approach to gopher control in the future? (Show of hands for yes, show of hands for no.)

Tip: Consider using Instant feedback. Throw out some raised-hand feedback questions part way through your presentation. You'll be able to gauge how well you're doing, and be able to modify your presentation to make the best use of your remaining time.

Designing an evaluation form

If you have a lot riding on the outcome of your presentation, consider hiring a professional evaluator to design evaluation forms and help you interpret the results. There are many different approaches to designing these forms. The type of presentation you're giving and the type of outcome you're hoping for will determine the kinds of questions you need to ask.

You can design evaluation questions as review questions (to see if your listeners recall the points you made) or you can ask participants what they got out of the presentation. Questions can be answered with a simple yes or no, with a set of multiple-choice answers, or according to a rating scale. People are likely to skip open-ended, essay-type questions that take too long to complete.

Design your evaluation questions carefully in order to judge your success and target ways to improve your presentation next time. Use a mix of simple yes/no or checkbox questions along with open-ended questions and rating scales. One side of one page is about as much as you can ask of your audience—remember, they're doing you a favor by filling this out.

Tip: There's an excellent example of an evaluation form you can download at *www.missingmanuals.com/cds*.

When you ask your listeners to fill out an evaluation, you're turning the tables on them—asking them to give *you* information. It's not always easy to get your audience to cooperate, so consider using some kind of incentive. For example, you could give a small gift in exchange for completed evaluation forms or use the forms in a drawing for door prizes.

Tip: Whether you ask questions or prepare a questionnaire, make sure to budget time for the evaluation. Evaluations need to be completed immediately after your presentation. Don't expect your participants to turn them in later in the day or mail them to you—it just won't happen.

Presentation Hardware

If you're lucky, you'll have complete control over every aspect of your presentation—including the computer, the projector, and all the other technical bits and pieces that are required.

Often, though, you'll be using others' equipment; plugging your laptop into a video projector at a conference; or just showing up with your presentation on a CD and running it on someone else's computer. When the equipment isn't your own, you have to be more flexible and ready to improvise.

Laptops

You can run PowerPoint 2008 presentations on any of the current crop of Mac-Books and MacBook Pros. Older laptops, especially G4 machines, are apt to have some difficulty presenting some of the more complex animation and transition affects. To get the best performance, use JPEG's for image files, MP3s for audio files, and don't use 3-D or shadow effects. Presentations intended for single viewers—like self-paced lessons—are well-suited to a desktop computer. But for most presentations, the portability of a laptop makes it the computer of choice.

Projectors

Depending on the size of your audience, the type of room you're in—and the size of your budget—you can show your PowerPoint presentations right on your laptop, on an external monitor, or with a video projector.

If you're presenting to a group and you're able to dim the lights, a projector is usually your best bet. The video projector market is booming, fueled by home theater buffs and computerized presenters like you. Prices are falling and new models are emerging weekly—resulting in a bewildering array of projectors to choose from. Prices start at about $500, but plan on at least $800 as a minimum price for a bright, high-resolution projector.

What your audience sees when you're presenting

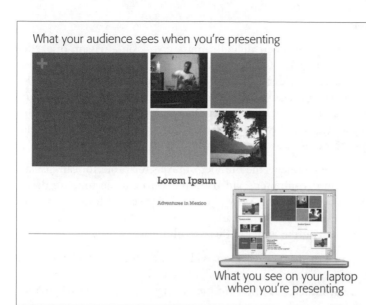

Lorem Ipsum

Adventures in Mexico

What you see on your laptop
when you're presenting

Figure 15-2:
While the audience sees your slides on the big screen, your MacBook can help you keep your place in the presentation—and keep you from looking over your shoulder to see what's on the screen. It can display the current slide and the next slide, your slide notes, and a clock or timer telling you either elapsed time or the remaining time in your presentation. If you need to rush to the finish, or go back to the beginning, the thumbnails on the left let you jump to any slide in the presentation. You'll learn how to display these onscreen features in the next chapter.

Tip: If you're not familiar with video projectors and you're considering dropping $1000 or more to purchase one, you should really find a store where you can compare the models you're interested in under lighting conditions that are similar to the way you'll be using it. Get a head start on your comparison shopping by visiting *www.projectorcentral.com*, where you can read reviews and buyer guides, and post projector-related questions on their forum.

Figure 15-3:
When your audience starts bumping heads as a result of leaning in to look at your laptop screen, it's time to consider a video projector. The variety of sizes and prices available is growing rapidly, and though the prices are coming down, it's still a big investment. Consider renting a projector if you need one infrequently. Then when you're ready to buy, you'll better understand the features you need (and by then you'll get even more for your money).

Choosing a projector

If the thought of shopping for a new digital camera gives you a frisson of excitement, then deciphering the specs of video projectors should be right up your alley. There are three basic types of video projectors: LCD (liquid crystal display), DLP (digital light processing), and LCOS (liquid crystal on silicon). Most of the time the projector type is less important than its key specifications. After you figure out your budget and how large and heavy a projector you're willing to carry around, consider these important criteria:

- **Resolution.** This figure represents the number of pixels the projector can display, and should match your computer's video output. Most projectors are designated SVGA (800×600 pixels) or XGA (1,024×768 pixels). More pixels gives you a sharper screen image and—surprise, surprise—cost more. All Macbooks and MacBook Pros can output either of these resolutions.

- **Brightness.** Like slide or movie projectors, video projectors produce an image on the screen by projecting it with a very bright light. The intensity of that light is measured in ANSI lumens. Methods of measuring lumens vary from manufacturer to manufacturer, so consider these specifications as only ballpark figures. Less than 1000 lumens is fine when projecting on smaller screens or in darkened rooms, but will be too dim on larger screens or under brighter lighting conditions. 1500 lumens is a good minimum for rooms that can't be darkened—but you'll only know for sure by trying out a projector under similar projection conditions.

- **Inputs.** Projectors designed for a home theater system may feature only S-video and composite video inputs. Mac laptops can output in this format—if it's your only option. Projectors designed for computer presentations have either a VGA connector, a DVI connector, or both (and quite possibly S-video and composite video inputs as well). Connect your laptop using the VGA connection or, if available, the DVI connection. Some newer, higher-end projectors have only a DVI connection.

Renting projectors

If you don't find yourself giving PowerPoint presentations at the drop of a hat, you may be better off renting a projector. Look in the Yellow Pages under Audio-Visual Equipment to find a local outlet. And if you don't have a local AV house, you can even rent equipment by mail (or least, by UPS). When you rent, you can take advantage of the newest technology, get a projector that suits the requirements for your particular presentation space, and let somebody else worry about repairs and bulb replacement.

Projection screens

The screen is an often overlooked element of projection quality. A poor screen—or wall—can make the best projector's image look terrible. There are as many different kinds of screens available as there are projectors, starting at about $100 for rollup screens. Any screen will be better than a regular wall, although you can get very good results in a darkened room with a smooth, matte white painted wall.

Projection screens come in a wide variety of surfaces which provide varying amounts of *gain,* enhanced brightness attained by directing the light from the projector back to the audience instead of allowing it to scatter in all directions. High-gain screens have a lower viewing angle. In other words, they reflect more light to viewers closer to the centerline of the screen. A matte white screen—or a flat, white wall—provides the widest viewing angle and the least gain.

Remote Controls

Using a remote control for your PowerPoint presentation gives you the freedom to move away from your laptop—and you'll appear much more professional when you're not reaching for the computer to advance each slide. Even if you like the security of the podium and want to keep an eye on your speaker's notes on your PowerBook's screen, by using a remote control you can advance slides while gesturing or with your hand in your pocket. When you're ready to break free of the podium, the remote lets you stroll the stage or amble through the audience—while still controlling your presentation.

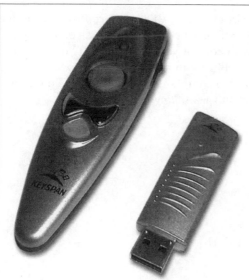

Figure 15-4:
Plug this remote's USB receiver into your computer and you needn't be tied to the lectern to change slides. Whether you're seated at a table or mingling with the audience, a handheld remote lets you spend more time connecting with your audience, and less time connected to your computer.

If you've got a MacBook or MacBook Pro, you've already got the remote control that came with your laptop, intended mostly as a way to control Apple's Front Row feature. The Apple Remote communicates with your computer via infrared (just like a TV remote)—so you do have to point it at your computer and it won't function if it's in your pocket.

Tip: Be sure to *pair* your Apple Remote with your computer so it can be controlled only by that particular remote. Otherwise, a jokester in the audience could control your presentation with *his* Apple Remote. To create this bond of remote-control monogamy, make sure you're logged in as an Admin user. Then, from a few inches away, point the remote at the IR sensor on the front of the computer, and press and hold the Menu and Next/Fast-forward buttons simultaneously for five seconds. (If you ever need to un-pair, choose → System Preferences → Security and click Unpair.)

Most other remote controls use RF (radio frequency) to communicate with a receiver plugged into your laptop's USB port. Because they use radio waves there's no need to point the remote control at your laptop. But when you *do* need to point something out on one of your slides, some remotes have a built-in laser pointer, so you don't have to fumble with more than one handheld device.

Some remotes can also function as a mouse, or control your iTunes and DVD playback. However, when you're in the midst of the presentation you may find that simpler is better—and the only buttons you really need are forward and backward. The winner of the simplicity competition is the Power Presenter RF, sporting only forward and back buttons and a laser pointer (*www.powerremote.com*). The sleek and popular Keyspan Presentation Remote (or its more powerful sibling, the Presentation Remote Pro) adds a mouse controller to the mix (*www.keyspan.com*).

There's also the possibility that you already own a RF remote control—albeit one with *lots* of buttons: your cell phone. Salling Clicker software lets you use certain Bluetooth mobile phones and PDAs to control your computer. If your Mac has built-in Bluetooth—or you've added a Bluetooth adapter—then this $20 piece of software is all you need to turn your phone into a remote control for PowerPoint and many other programs. Learn more at *www.salling.com*.

Building a PowerPoint Presentation

Slideshows derive their power from their simplicity. By displaying a single static image at a time, slide shows can present information simply and clearly—and often with more impact than you could achieve with a moving picture—whether you're teaching geography to a class of third-graders or pitching an ad campaign to a Fortune 500 CEO.

PowerPoint gives you the ability to create very basic, simple slides—for example, just words on a plain background or a single picture—or a complex blend of photographs, animation, movies, and sound, to create dazzling presentations that grab and hold your audience's attention.

Whether you opt for simple or fancy, you start by picking a PowerPoint *theme*—a pre-designed template that gives your slide show a cohesive style or look. You then use *layouts* to create the individual slides and arrange them in the proper order.

PowerPoint 2008 introduces 50 new slide themes—coordinated templates containing fonts, colors, and visual effects designed to give your presentation a unified look. As you build each slide, the new layouts keep your designs consistent from slide to slide, keeping your text and objects aligned from slide to slide. In addition, you can create your own custom layouts with text and image placeholders, backgrounds graphics, and so on. You'll find Slide Themes and Slide Layouts tabs in the Elements Gallery, where you can quickly preview them and apply them to your slideshow.

Finding Your Way Around PowerPoint

When you launch PowerPoint, your first stop is the Project Gallery (unless you've turned off the "Show Project Gallery at startup" checkbox in PowerPoint → Preferences → General). The Project Gallery opens to whichever tab you used last—click New and then double-click PowerPoint Presentation to open a completely blank presentation. Or click Office Themes in the Category list and then choose one of the themes to base your slideshow on.

Tip: No matter what you choose here in the Project Gallery, you can always change to a different theme once PowerPoint opens.

The Three-Pane View

When the PowerPoint window opens, you see the first slide of your chosen theme in the main *slide pane* (see Figure 16-1). PowerPoint's three-pane Normal view lets you concentrate on one slide at a time, yet lets you quickly navigate through your slides or add notes. The largest pane shows you exactly what your audience will see (apart from animations and other special effects). The pane on the left gives you an overview of the entire presentation in thumbnail or outline format. Since this presentation is brand-new, it shows only one slide. As you add more slides to the presentation they appear in the outline pane—where you can reorder them by dragging the thumbnails.

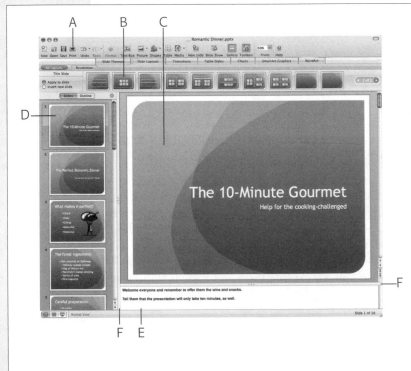

Figure 16-1:
Topped by the toolbar (A), and the Elements Gallery (B), the PowerPoint window displays three panes. The slide you're editing occupies center stage on the slide pane (C). Here you can edit the slide's text; add pictures, charts, and other objects; change backgrounds; and so on. The Outline pane (D) displays thumbnail images of each slide in the presentation (when in Slides view) or an outline of your slides' text when in (Outline view). You can enter random notes to yourself or your presentation script in the Notes pane (E). If you use an external monitor or projector to present your show, PowerPoint can display these notes on your screen and hide them from the audience. Adjust the size of the panes by dragging the divider bars (F).

The third pane, below the slide, is never going to be seen by the audience—it's for your own notes, visible on your computer display during your presentation—while the audience sees only your slide on the room's main screen. The Notes pane is also handy as you're creating your presentation for "notes to self" about the slide you're creating—for example, to remind yourself to double-check a fact or replace a product photo with a new version. Although the slide area is the biggest when you start a new presentation, you can resize the panes by dragging their dividers. In fact, you can hide the outline and notes panes by dragging the dividers all the way to the edges of the window.

At the top of the window you'll find the familiar Standard toolbar and Elements Gallery. Click the toolbar's Gallery button or just click one of the gallery tabs to reveal slide themes, slide layouts, transitions, table styles, and so on (see Figure 16-2).

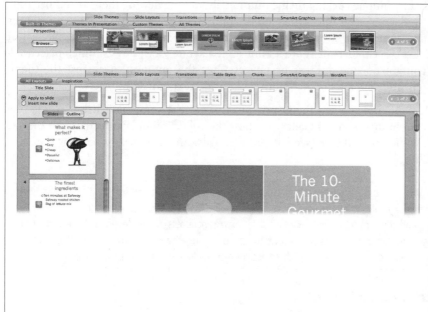

Figure 16-2:
Top: Click the Elements Gallery's Slide Themes tab to view PowerPoint's collection of pre-designed templates. As you click from one thumbnail to another, PowerPoint displays the new design in its slide pane—and converts any slide you've already created to the new theme.

Bottom: Every slide theme contains a set of layouts, available via the Elements Gallery's Slide Layouts tab. Layouts fix the arrangement of text boxes and graphic objects on the slide, allowing consistent positioning from slide to slide.

Step 1: Specify a Theme

Even though your slides may display different kinds of information—text, charts, tables, and pictures, for example—it's usually best if they follow a consistent design that uses the same fonts, background graphics, color scheme, and so on. The design sets the overall tone for the presentation, so your choice of one that suits the topic and audience is critical.

Pre-designed Templates

Thankfully, Microsoft makes life easier for presentation newbies—and for anyone who's not a trained graphic designer—by providing an assortment of prefab themes and layouts. They let you start building your slideshow without having to spend any time on the design elements or layouts. When project deadlines are looming and there are a million things that need to be done (including creating a presentation), you'll welcome these timesaving features.

You can choose a theme in the Project Gallery's Office Themes Category, but you'll probably appreciate PowerPoint 2008's new theme chooser in the Elements Gallery. Click the Slide Themes tab of the Elements Gallery bar to reveal the line up of colorful theme thumbnails, and use the arrow buttons at the right end of the gallery to scroll through the other theme options. If a theme looks like it might work, click it to display it in the slide pane.

You can continue clicking theme thumbnails and previewing them at full size until you find your ideal one. Don't be disappointed, by the way, when your chosen theme doesn't show the same colorful pictures as the thumbnail. Unlike the picture and text placeholders of Word's Publishing Layout View, PowerPoint's placeholders contain no dummy text or images—just the outlines set against the theme background, and the instruction to click to add text or insert objects.

PowerPoint opens a new theme using its first-page slide layout. Click the Slide Layouts tab in the Elements Gallery to show the collection of layouts that you can use with your chosen theme (see Figure 16-2). Click them as well, to see how they look at full size.

Tip: When choosing a theme, consider how you're going to present the final product. All the included designs look terrific when projected from the Mac itself (using a portable projector, for example). On the other hand, if you plan to *print* the various slides (say, as handouts), avoid designs with solid colors in the background. Not only will they take forever to print on an inkjet (and consume a lot of ink or toner), but the blended background on some of these designs may not look as smooth as it did onscreen.

Starting from Scratch

Although themes can save you hours of work, there's a downside to using them, too. Since you'll be choosing from the same repertoire as millions of other PowerPoint fans, your slideshow just may look just like someone else's—maybe even the speaker who came before you. The only surefire way to guarantee a unique look is to design your presentation yourself. Fortunately, it's not as hard as it sounds. To access a blank presentation from the Project Gallery, click the Blank Documents category and then double-click PowerPoint Presentation. Or, if you're already in PowerPoint, click the blank "Office" theme—the leftmost thumbnail in the Themes gallery, or choose File → New Presentation (⌘-N).

Either way, you're now facing a blank white slide in the slide pane. Click the Element Gallery's Slide Layouts tab and choose a layout for your first slide (see page

666). Then you can use PowerPoint's various text and drawing tools to build each slide from scratch. Although designing slides this way involves a lot more work than simply choosing a template, you'll be rewarded with a presentation that doesn't *look* like it came out of a can. Even if all you do is create a different slide background color, pattern, or image, you can have a completely unique look with minimal effort, since you can still use all of PowerPoint's pre-designed layouts.

Adding Slides

Add some of your own the text to your first slide by clicking where it says "Click to add title" and then start typing. Then add a new slide to the presentation in any of the following ways:

- Click the New Slide button in the toolbar.

- Choose Insert → New Slide.

- Press ⌘-Shift-N.

- Control-click (or right-click) in the Outline pane, and from the pop-up menu, choose New Slide.

- Click the "Insert new slide" button at the left end of the Slide Layouts gallery and then click any of the layout thumbnails (which now sport large green plus signs).

PowerPoint creates the new slide, displays it on the slide pane, and adds its thumbnail to the outline pane directly beneath the selected slide.

Note: When PowerPoint creates a second slide in the show, it automatically uses the second slide layouts for the new slide—but any other time you create a new slide, PowerPoint creates it in the same style as the selected slide.

With the new slide selected in the outline pane, click the Slide Layouts tab to display them in the Elements Gallery. Click any of the layouts and the selected slide takes on this new appearance, ready for you to plug in text and images. If you don't like its looks, click another to choose a different design.

Take a moment to create four or five slides from various layouts and add some text so you have some slides with which to experiment.

Changing Designs in Midstream

Unlike, say, home decorating, changing your presentation's color scheme and other elements requires nothing more than a few quick mouse clicks. Just click the Slide Themes tab of the Elements Gallery to return to PowerPoint's trove of themes. Click one to apply it to your presentation. If you don't like the change, choose Edit → Undo Document Theme (⌘-Z) to revert, or just click another theme.

When you change themes, PowerPoint changes all the slides in your presentation to the new theme. If you'd like to change the theme for just part of your presentation, select two or more slides in the outline pane (by Shift-clicking or ⌘-clicking) and then click a new theme in the gallery. PowerPoint changes your selected slides to the new theme. You may find switching from one thing to another helpful to differentiate different segments of the presentation.

Each PowerPoint theme has a set of colors chosen to provide contrast between its various elements while maintaining a uniform color palette. If you don't agree with any of these colors, choose Format → Theme Colors to display the Create Theme Colors window. Double-click any of the color swatches to change that color using the Color Picker (page 747). PowerPoint displays the results of your meddling in the small Preview diagram (see Figure 16-3). Click Apply to All to see your color change reflected throughout the presentation. Your new custom color collection is added to the Colors palette in the Formatting Palette's Document Theme pane. You can also make a wholesale change to the theme colors by selecting a different collection from this pop-up menu. (Be sure to make note of the collection you start with so you can always return if you decide you're making things worse.)

Figure 16-3:
If you want to create your own color collection, choose Format → Theme Colors. In the resulting Create Theme Colors dialog box, you can choose new colors for the slide's background, text, fills, accents, and links.

You can also change the slide background, choosing from a dozen variations for each theme. Open the Slide Background pane of the Formatting Palette and click any of the background thumbnails to apply that background to your theme. Many of the theme designs have background graphics as well—frames or images. Click Hide Background Graphics to remove them from the theme. (See page 670 for more on backgrounds.)

Adding Your Own Templates

In many corporations, PowerPoint slideshows are an every-day occurrence—as are rules and regulations. You may be required to use a PowerPoint template, designed and approved by your company, as the basis for all slideshows you give. (Don't worry if your company is Windows-based—templates for the Windows version of PowerPoint work just fine on Macs.)

If you're given such a required template, it's easy to make it ready for easy access each time you begin to create a slideshow. Just drag the template file into Home → Library → Application Support → Microsoft → Office → User Templates → My Templates folder. It'll show up in the Project Gallery under the My Templates group. In fact, you can transform *any* PowerPoint file into a template by dragging

it into this folder. If you're creating your own template choose File → Save As and choose PowerPoint Template (.potx) from the format pop-up menu. PowerPoint tucks it into the My Templates folder unless you tell it to do otherwise. (Consider saving your templates in the .pot format if you might be sharing them with people who have yet to upgrade to Office 2007 or 2008.)

When you open it, you'll get a blank copy of that file (called "Presentation1," for example), even if it wasn't a Power-Point template to begin with. PowerPoint is smart enough to figure: "If it's in the Templates folder, I'm probably supposed to treat it as a template."

Step 2: Writing the Outline

A picture may be worth a thousand words, but it's the rare presentation that doesn't include at least some text. Deciding how to transform possibly boring facts into compelling word slides is often the most challenging part of creating a presentation, so words are a good place to begin before you get too hung up on design. If you've already worked up an outline in Word, skip ahead to page 661 to import it into PowerPoint.

Otherwise, open PowerPoint's Outline view by clicking the Outline button at top of its pane. When you do so, the pane gets wider to accommodate your text, and the thumbnails are reduced to mere specks.

Each numbered slide icon at the left of the Outline pane represents an individual slide. Whatever you type adjacent to the slide icon becomes that slide's title, whether or not there's a title placeholder in the slide's layout (see Figure 16-4). Indented lines below the title correspond to the slide's subtitle and bullet text. (Bullet text refers to lines of text denoted by special *bullets* markers—see page 101).

To generate more outline text, you can do any of the following:

- **Add a slide.** Press Return after typing a title to start another title—and another slide. Each title corresponds to a slide.

- **Demote text.** Press Tab to *demote* a title into a bullet point under the previous title or bullet point. (Demote is outlining jargon for "make less important," or "move down one level in the outline.") If you continue pressing Tab, you can continue the demotion, down to five levels below the title. PowerPoint indents the line of text farther and farther to the right as you press Tab. Alternatively, you can drag the slide or text to the right.

- **Promote text.** Press Shift-Tab to *promote* a bullet point into a more important bullet point or—at the top level—to a slide title. Or you can drag text to the left to promote it. (Promote, as you might guess, means to "make more important," or "move up one level in the outline.")

Note: When you use the Tab key in the Outline pane, it doesn't matter where in the line of text you place your insertion point—at the end, at the beginning, or somewhere in the middle.

- **Create another bullet point.** Press Return after typing a bullet point to start another bullet point.

- **Add a slide beneath a bullet point.** Press Shift-⌘-N after typing a bullet point to start a title for a new slide.

- **Expand or contract the slide outline text.** Control-click (or right-click) a slide's text and choose Collapse → Collapse to collapse the subtext of the selected slide or slides. Choose Collapse → Collapse All to hide the subtext of the entire outline—leaving only the slide titles visible. Control-click and choose Expand → Expand (or Expand All to again reveal the slides' subtext).

- **Show formatting.** To display the outline in the same fonts used in the slides, Control-click (or right-click) any of the slide text and choose Show Formatting.

- **Delete a slide.** Select one or more slides, and then press Delete; Control-click (or right-click) the slide title and choose Delete Slide; or choose Edit → Delete Slide.

- **Move a slide.** Drag the slide icon up or down the list, and drop it when the blue line is directly above the slide you want to move it above.

- **Duplicate a slide.** Choose Edit → Duplicate slide, press ⌘-D, or Control-click (or right-click) the slide title and choose Duplicate Slide. PowerPoint creates the duplicate slide just below the original.

Note: You can select more than one slide by Shift-clicking or ⌘-clicking additional slides, or by dragging up or down through the slide text, or to the right of it. Then you can apply any of the above techniques to add, delete, move, or duplicate the selected slides.

If you'd rather push buttons than drag slides around directly in the Outline pane, choose View → Toolbars → Outlining to summon the Outlining toolbar (see Figure 16-4). It has buttons for promoting, demoting, moving, expanding and contracting, and showing formatting.

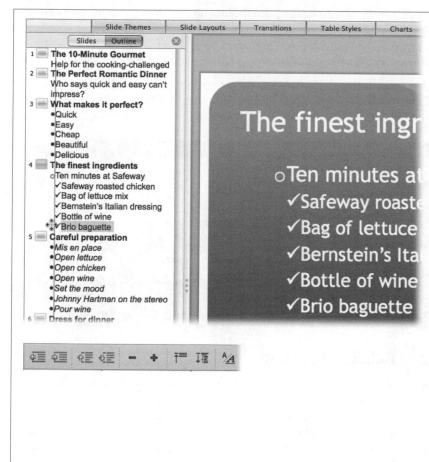

Figure 16-4:
*Top: You can drag topics
or bullet points into a
different order as you
build your outline. The
cursor changes to crossed
arrows when you mouse
over a draggable slide or
bullet icon. A horizontal
line indicates where
PowerPoint thinks you
want to place the item
when you drag up and
down to reorder; a
vertical line indicates the
indent level where
PowerPoint intends to
place the item. As you
work on your outline in
the left-hand Outline
pane, you get to see your
work in the Slide pane.*

*Bottom: Choose View →
Toolbars → Outlining to
call forth the Outlining
toolbar. Its button
collection lets you
promote, demote, or
move items up and down
the outline; collapse or
expand subordinate items
for one slide, or the
whole outline; or hide or
show the font formatting
in the outline view.*

As you're creating slide text, remember that your audience will probably be reading everything for the first time, so it's important not to pack too much text into each frame. Generally, it's best to limit your slides to about seven lines, with no more than seven words on each line. Simpler is always better. As you type your slideshow's outline, you can watch the slide being built in the Slide pane—handy feedback to avoid typing too much text for a bullet. (You can also type directly in the slide, as described on page 672.)

Using a Word Outline

The PowerPoint outliner isn't the only outliner in Office 2008. If, having cuddled up with Chapter 6 for several evenings, you're already proficient with the outliner in Word, you may prefer to write up your slideshow in Word. Fortunately, you can easily transfer your outline into PowerPoint. It's easiest if you began in Word: with the outline open in Word 2008, choose File → Send To → PowerPoint. PowerPoint opens (if it's not already open) and converts the outline into a presentation automatically.

You can also *import* it from the PowerPoint end. To do so, you have to first save your Word outline in .rtf format—the only outline format PowerPoint is prepared to deal with. Then launch PowerPoint and choose Insert → Slides From → Outline File. Navigate to the Word document containing your outline and double-click it.

Whichever method you choose, PowerPoint produces one slide for every level 1 heading in your outline, and creates bullet points for every subheading, quickly creating the basis for a slide show.

Step 3: Building the Show

It's much better to show blank white slides containing an effective message than fancy graphics that don't say anything. That's why it's an excellent idea to begin your presentation planning with the Outline pane. Once the outline's in good shape, it's time to start thinking about the cosmetics—how your slides look. Power-Point's tools make it easy to adapt your design (or Microsoft's design) for all the slides simultaneously.

Warning: Choose File → Page Setup and set the Size options *before* you design your slides. A radical change to these options later in the game may result in cut off graphics or unintended distortions, as though your slides were being projected through a fun-house mirror. PowerPoint's standard setting, On-screen Show (4:3), is the one to use for display with a video projector.

Using Masters

In the same way that slide themes let you alter the look of your presentation in a flash, *slide masters* save time by letting you make changes that apply to the entire theme, or just certain layouts (Figure 16-5). *Background master items* appear on every slide, unless you specify otherwise (see page 671). When you add, delete, move, or replace a background master item, you see the change reflected in all of your slides that use it. For example, if you want to add a company logo to all your slides, just place it on the *slide master;* PowerPoint updates all the slides instantly. Other master items serve as placeholders for the title and bullet text. Changes you make to them on the slide master—the size and color of the font, or the appearance of the bullets, for example—are automatically reflected throughout the presentation.

Once you have a slide master, you can create slide layouts based on it. Layouts act as mini-masters, so you can have a wide collection of related looks for your slides. You can delete master items from layouts and add more text boxes or text and graphic placeholders that don't appear on the master slide.

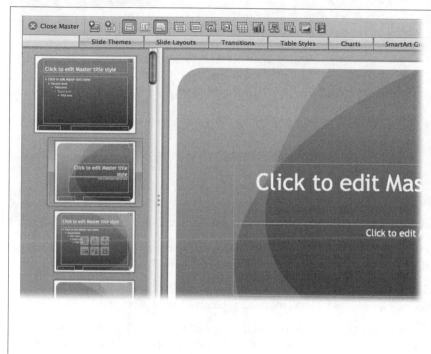

Figure 16-5:
When you choose View → Master → Slide Master, PowerPoint reveals the blueprints hidden behind every one of the theme's slide layouts. PowerPoint shows the slide master at the top of the stack, and each layout displayed beneath. Click the slide master, and any changes you make in the slide pane cascade through all the layouts. Make changes on a layout, and they apply only to that one layout. Whenever you are in Master view, PowerPoint displays the Master toolbar: its buttons let you create new masters, new layouts, and insert every possible kind of content placeholder.

In fact, PowerPoint has four different categories of master items: slides, titles, handouts, and notes. Here's how they work.

Slide master

The *slide master*—or, as most people would call it, the master slide—is a special slide whose background, font size and style, bullet style, and footer (whatever appears at the bottom of every slide) determine the look of these elements on every slide it controls.

Editing the slide master

To look at and change the slide master, choose View → Master → Slide Master. PowerPoint displays the slide master at the top of the Outline pane and—befitting its sovereignty—larger than the layouts below (see Figure 16-6). The slide pane

---

Understanding Templates

When you choose one of PowerPoint's slide themes from the Elements Gallery, you're actually choosing a Power-Point *template*, a collection of pre-designed *layouts* based on a slide *master* using an *Office Theme*. Here's the breakdown of those various elements:

- **Office theme.** The Formatting Palette's Document Themes pane lets you choose various collections of colors and fonts in any office program. Office themes make it easy to apply consistent looks to PowerPoint, Word, and Excel documents. You'll find eight colors in each theme color palette, and two fonts—a heading font and a body font—in each theme font collection.

- **Slide master.** The slide master stores color and font themes, background text and graphics, and layouts. Each master can contain one or more layouts.

- **Layouts.** The positioning and formatting of text and graphic elements on the slide makes up the slide layout. Layouts allow consistent positioning of text and objects from slide to slide (see Figure 16-2).

- **Slide theme.** PowerPoint's collection of slide themes—not to be confused with the Office color and font theme—usually contain one slide master and several layouts, although some contain more than one slide master. If you create and save your own template (see the box on page 659), it could possibly have just one master and one layout.

gives you close a view of this monarch and its component master items, each staking out their area with a pale outline:

- **Title Area.** This area usually contains some dummy text in the large title font, a placeholder for the real text that will appear in your slides.

- **Object Area.** The settings you make in this area determine how the body of your slides—text, charts, pictures, and media clips—will look and where they will sit.

- **Date Area, Footer Area, and Number Area.** These boxes at the bottom of the slide master show where the date and time, slide number, and miscellaneous footer text will appear on each slide. (These same boxes appear in the preview in File → Page Setup → Header/Footer → Slide tab.)

Note: In View → Master → Slide Master mode, the placeholder text (such as "Click to edit Master title style") is irrelevant. Don't bother editing it; doing so has no effect on your actual slides.

By changing the font size, style, color, and placement of these items, you can change how PowerPoint draws those elements on your slides. For example, if you want all of your slides' titles to be in 24-point Gill Sans Ultra Bold, just click once inside the placeholder text to select the box; then use the Formatting Palette to change the font to 24-point Gill Sans Ultra Bold. Now, any existing slides that have titles (and any *new* slides you make) will display the title in 24-point Gill Sans Ultra Bold.

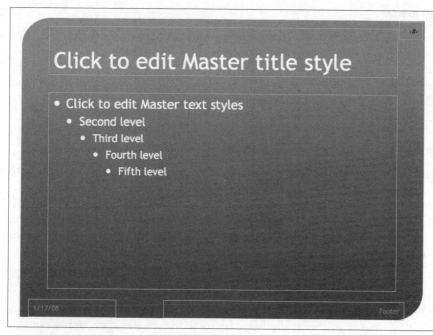

Click to edit Master title style

• Click to edit Master text styles
    • Second level
        • Third level
            • Fourth level
                • Fifth level

1/17/08   Footer

Figure 16-6:
The slide master generates certain elements that will be reflected in every slide in the presentation. The Master forms the basis for every layout in the Slide Theme, each of which can have additional elements such as text, graphic, or media placeholders.

Adding new elements to a slide master

The title, bulleted text items, and various footers revealed on your slide master can appear on every slide; all you have to do is fill them in. But if you need *additional* text to appear on each slide (such as your department or project name), you can create additional default text blocks on your slide master.

To do so, click the Text Box button on the Standard toolbar shown in Figure 16-1. (If it's not there, choose View → Toolbars → Standard.) Click the slide master where you want the new text box to appear, type some dummy placeholder text, and then use the Formatting Palette to set its font, color, and style. (To pre-size the text box, click the slide master and drag to create a text box before you begin to type.)

When you start creating slides, you won't base any new slides directly on the slide master. Instead, you create slides based on slide layouts—which are themselves based on the slide master.

Handout master

A PowerPoint *handout* is a special page design that lets you place several slides on a single sheet for printing and distributing to your audience. Set up the design of your handouts by choosing View → Master → Handout Master, and then adding or editing the elements you want. (You can read more about handouts on page 715.)

Notes master

In PowerPoint terminology, a *note* is another form of handout—one that features a miniature slide at the top half of the page, and typed commentary at the bottom (see page 655). Once again, you can specify the basic design of your notes printouts by choosing View → Master → Notes Master, and then editing the design you find here (such as altering the font, resizing the notes field or slide image, or adding graphics). Predictably, those changes appear on every notes page in the presentation.

Slide layouts

When you're in the Slide Master View, PowerPoint displays slide layouts beneath the master slide in the outline pane. Each slide layout is based on the master slide, though it doesn't necessarily contain all the master objects, and possibly contains other objects or placeholders not found in the master. You can think of the master slide as the blueprint for all the slide layouts, and a slide layout as the blueprint for the slide you create.

When you're in Normal view or Slide Sorter view, you'll find all the slide layouts for the current theme in the Slide Layouts tab of the Elements Gallery. Buttons at the left end of the gallery give you two choices for what happens when you click one of the layout thumbnails: apply that layout to the selected slide, or insert a new slide based on that layout.

Modifying slide layouts

Choose View → Master → Slide Master and click any layout in the outline pane to display it in the slide pane. Here you can add, delete, resize, rotate, or reposition any of the slide elements. Any changes you make affect slides you've already created using that layout in the presentation—as well as those you make from now on. (Working with slide elements is discussed beginning on page 675.)

View Controls

Becoming familiar with PowerPoint's View controls, which are in the lower-left corner of the PowerPoint window (see Figure 16-1), will help you get the most out of the program. These three buttons let you switch among PowerPoint's three main view modes: Normal, Slide Sorter, and Slideshow. The View menu contains two additional view modes: Notes Page and Presenter Tools. Here's a rundown on them all:

- **Normal view** is the standard three-pane view, as shown in Figure 16-1. You control what you see using buttons at the top of the outline pane: Slides displays thumbnails of each of your slides, while Outline displays the outline text of your slides. The Slides mode makes it easy to find your way around your presentation visually, but the text in those slides is too small to read. Outline mode is great for presentations that contain a lot of text. This view shows all the text—the slide titles, subtitles, and each bullet point—but not an image of what the slide looks like. You can edit slide text directly in the outline, making it a great way to create slides and enter text quickly (see page 659).

Tip: In any multipane view, you can drag the boundaries between the panes to make individual panes larger or smaller. (A row of three dots in the center of these lines denotes a draggable boundary—but you don't have to put your cursor on the dots themselves.)

- **Slide Sorter view.** Back in the day, slide show producers had to don white gloves to sort actual 35mm slides by hand and load them into projector trays. This process was impossible without a *light table* to lay the slides on, shuffle them around into different orders, and decide which ones to cut from the show and which ones to send to the lab for duplication. PowerPoint's Slide Sorter View is your virtual light table (Figure 16-7). Here you can reorder, delete, or duplicate your virtual slides; or designate slides for PowerPoint to skip during a presentation. Now you need white gloves only if you want to make a fashion statement.

  To can drag either a single slide or several at once; click the gray margin between slides and drag through several slides or Shift-click the first and last in a range. You can select more than one slide in any noncontiguous group by ⌘-clicking. A vertical "your slide will go here" line appears when you drag slides.

  Slide Sorter View makes a handy navigational aid. Double-clicking a slide in Slide Sorter view opens the slide in the Normal view.

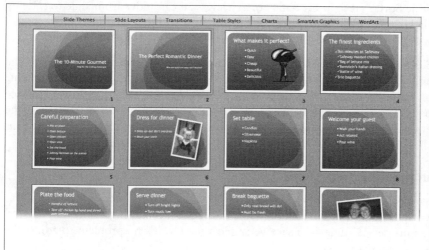

Figure 16-7:
You can rearrange slides in the Slide Sorter view by dragging them, or delete slides by selecting and then pressing Delete (or choosing Edit › Delete Slide). You can also work with transitions (page 685) in Slide Sorter view; a small icon below a slide, shown here on slide 1 and 2, represents a transition. Click the icon to see a high-speed preview of the transition. Use the Standard Toolbar's Zoom control to vary the slide size in this view.

- **Notes Page.** If you find the notes pane at the bottom of Normal view too confining, choose View → Notes Page to see the current slide and a large Notes field displayed on a single page—the very same page you can print as a handout. The Notes page derives its layout from the Notes master.

- **Presenter Tools.** If you choose this view, PowerPoint displays the presenter tools on your screen as it begins your slide show. (Your audience sees just the current slide projected before them.) See page 705 for more on using Presenter Tools.

- **Slideshow.** When you choose this view, PowerPoint actually begins the slideshow. See page 701 for more detail.

Navigation

No matter which view you're using, moving among the slides in your show is easy. For example:

- **Normal view.** The outline is always on the left of the slide; all it takes to move to a slide is a click anywhere within or alongside its outline text. If, for example, you want to go to the fourth slide in the presentation, just click somewhere in the fourth outline text. PowerPoint displays that slide in the slide pane.

  When you're looking at slide thumbnails when the outline pane is in Slides mode, you can use the scroll bar or the up- and down-arrow keys to move through the slides. (In Outline mode, those same keys move through each line of text).

- **Slide Sorter view.** In the Slide Sorter view, you can move from slide to slide by clicking the slide, or by using the arrow keys to move the selection rectangle around. If you double-click a slide, PowerPoint switches to Normal view.

- **Slideshow.** When you're in Slideshow view, each individual slide takes up the entire screen or window—no menus, no scroll bars, no controls. There are lots of key combinations that help you move around while in Slideshow view (see page 703). For example, you can use the right or down arrow key to move to the *next* slide in a slideshow, or the left or up arrow key to move to the *previous* slide. Press the Esc key to exit the show and return to the previous view.

Manipulating Your Slides

As you construct the show, new ideas will inevitably pop into your head. Topics you originally expected to fill only three bullet points on a single slide may expand to require several slides—or vice versa. Fortunately, it's no problem to adjust the slide sequence as you go.

Inserting new slides

Inserting a new slide into the lineup once you've created a few is easy. Just click anyplace in the outline topic or the slide *before* the spot where you want the new slide to appear, and then choose Insert → New Slide (⌘-N). PowerPoint inserts a new slide in the layout of the selected slide. Alternatively, click the "Insert new slide" button at the left end of the Slide Layouts Gallery (or choose Insert → Slides From → Slide Layout) and click any of the layout thumbnails to insert a slide of that type below the selected slide.

Inserting slides from other presentations

You can reduce your work, reuse entire slides, and recycle great layouts from other presentation files simply by choosing Insert → Slides From → Other Presentation. The "Choose a File" dialog box appears; locate and single-click the PowerPoint file whose slides you want to import.

At the bottom of the dialog box, choose "Import all slides" or (if you want to handpick the slides worth importing) "Select slides to insert." Then click Open.

If you chose "Select slides to insert," you now see the Slide Finder dialog box, offering miniatures of the slides. If you want to import slides with their existing design intact, as opposed to letting them inherit the new presentation's theme, turn on "Keep design of original slides." Click a slide or shift-click to select multiple slides, click Insert, and then—after PowerPoint inserts the slides in your presentation behind the dialog box—click Close (or if you need to, continue selecting and inserting slides from the Slide Finder window).

Tip: You can also import slides by opening both presentations and dragging thumbnails from one to the other. This method, however, doesn't give you the choice to "keep design of original slides." The slides you move assume the theme of the presentation you drag them into.

Duplicating a slide

You can duplicate a slide—including its contents—so you can use it in another part of the presentation, or modify it to create a new version of the slide. Select a slide and choose Edit → Duplicate or press ⌘-D. You can also use the pop-up menu by Control-clicking (right-clicking) a slide and choosing Duplicate Slide. PowerPoint creates the duplicate slide just below the original. If you press the Option key while you drag one or more slides, the cursor sprouts the green-ball-with-plus-sign that indicates you're copying the item. Release the mouse button when the cursor is over your intended destination, and PowerPoint duplicates the selected slide or slides, and drops them into that spot.

Deleting a slide

In Normal or Slide Sorter view, click the slide and then press Delete, Control-click (or right-click) a thumbnail and choose Delete Slide from the pop-up menu, or choose Edit → Delete Slide.

Moving slides around

The easiest ways to rearrange your slide sequence are by dragging thumbnails around in Slide Sorter view, dragging the slide thumbnails in the outline pane, or dragging the tiny slide icons up and down in the Outline pane. In addition, you can use the Cut, Copy, and Paste commands to copy, move, or remove slides or groups of slides.

Tip: The pasting trick in Slide Sorter view is to select the slide just *before* the spot where you want the pasted slides to appear.

Hiding slides

PowerPoint can skip slides you want to remove from the presentation without actually deleting them. You can use this trick to try out two different versions of a particular slide you're working on, or to modify presentation for certain audience. You can hide a slide or an entire section of the presentation for one audience and then turn it back on for another. For example, your travelogue on Amsterdam could feature the beautiful flower markets and your canal cruise for one audience—and its famous coffee shops and red-light district for another.

Select a slide or group of slides, Control-click (or right-click) the slide, and choose Hide Slide from the pop-up menu. PowerPoint superimposes a little crossed-out symbol over the slide's number and dims the slide in the outline pane.

During a presentation, hidden slides appear dimmed in the Presenter Tools slide gallery. If you want to show a hidden slide, click it or press H when you're on the preceding slide.

Bring skipped slides back into the show by selecting them, Control-clicking, and choosing Hide Slide again, which removes the checkmark from the menu command.

Tip: If you have to deliver similar presentations to two or more groups repeatedly, save yourself the trouble of remembering to reconfigure the presentation by creating a Custom Show (see page 606) or by just duplicating the entire PowerPoint file. Then either delete or skip slides to tailor the duplicate presentations to the specific audience.

How to Build a Slide

The outliner is an excellent tool for creating the text and the overall flow of your slideshow. But sooner or later, you'll want to work on the slides themselves—to add charts or other graphics, modify text that doesn't fit quite right—and perhaps edit your concluding slide when new data becomes available five minutes before your meeting.

Using Backgrounds

Creating a PowerPoint slide is much like creating a page in a page-layout program. In fact, it's very similar to creating a page in Word 2008's Publishing Layout View.

Starting off, PowerPoint lets you set a background color, gradient, pattern, or graphic for your slide or you can create a backdrop by adding shapes and importing graphics. Then on top of that background you'll add text boxes, pictures, tables, charts, and other graphics—and possibly movies and sounds. PowerPoint shares many of the techniques for creating and manipulating layout objects with Word, as discussed in Chapter 8.

Changing backgrounds

Every slide begins life with a backdrop, courtesy of its slide master. If you'd like to override or enhance that backdrop on a particular slide, however, choose Format → Slide Background, or Control-click (or right-click) the slide and choose Format Background from the pop-up menu, to summon the Format Background dialog box (Figure 16-8). Click the Fill tab on the left and the Solid tab at the top to change the background color. Click the pop-up menu and choose any color variation from the palette of Theme Colors; one of the ten more-intense Standard Colors; or click More Colors to choose any color at all, via the Color Picker (page 747). You can tone down the background by using the Transparency slider.

PowerPoint adjusts the slide as you make your choices. The checkbox marked "Hide background objects" lets you hide any objects, such as background pictures or text, that may be present on the slide master. Click Apply to apply your changes to the background of the selected slide only, or "Apply to All" to change the backgrounds for all the slides in the presentation.

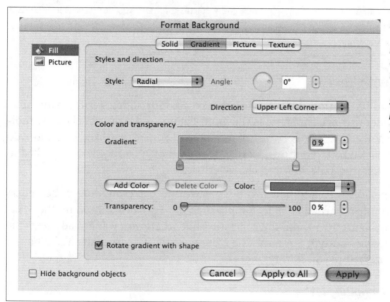

Figure 16-8:
The Format Background dialog box lets you add or change background colors or add gradients, pictures, or textures to the background. Working with the Transparency slider is essential—especially with pictures and textures—to ensure your text is still readable.

Tip: The Background dialog box has two buttons: *Apply* changes only the background of the current slide; *Apply to All* changes every slide in the presentation, even slides with customized backgrounds—use it with caution.

If you want something more elaborate than a solid background color, choose one of the Format Background dialog box's other three tabs: Gradient (a smoothly shifting color blend), Picture (a graphics file from your hard drive), Texture (a realistic image of some natural material, such as wood grain, marble, or burlap). See Chapter 19 for much more on these special tabs.

Shutting Off Two Annoying PowerPoint Features

If, as you add text to a box, you notice that the words and paragraphs are shrinking, don't panic. PowerPoint is just trying to help, trying to make your text fit into the placeholder text box. PowerPoint makes the text spill over onto another line only if shrinking the font size and line spacing fails.

If you find this feature annoying, you can turn it off easily enough: Just choose PowerPoint → Preferences, and, in the dialog box, click the AutoCorrect button. Click the Auto Format As You Type tab, turn off the option called "Autofit body text to placeholder," and then click OK.

Another feature that sometimes annoys: When you select more than one word and end your selection halfway through a word, PowerPoint selects the rest of that word for you. (This feature may sound familiar—the same thing happens in Word.)

This quirk can be frustrating when all you want to do is get rid of an errant suffix. To turn this feature off, choose PowerPoint → Preferences → Edit tab and turn off "When selecting, automatically select entire word." Now you can select as much or as little of a word as you like.

Tip: Be careful with this feature. Photos, textures, and gradients can make your text very difficult to read. Assuming you want your slides to be legible, make judicious use of the Transparency slider to reduce the opacity of these backgrounds.

Working with Text

There are two straightforward ways to add text to your slides. First, if your slide master includes text placeholders, as shown in Figure 16-6, you can click the individual placeholder text items (which typically read something like "Click to Add Text"), and then type in your own words. Because these placeholders are linked to the slide master, they reflect its font characteristics.

The other method is to add new text boxes (with no corresponding placeholders on the master) to a particular slide. Simply click the Text Box button on the Standard toolbar (Figure 16-9), and then click the slide where you want to add text (the text box grows as you type). Alternatively, drag on the slide to create a text box of the desired size before you start typing.

Editing and formatting text

Adjusting the type characteristics of any kind of text box is easy—click the text you want to adjust. You've just activated the text box. Now you can select part or all of the text to change its font, size, or style, using the Formatting Palette or the Format menu.

Note: The outline only shows text inside placeholders (titles, subtitles, and bullet points), so it doesn't display text that you add using the Text Box tool. You can change the formatting of text in the outline, but the changes appear only on the slide—after all, an outline with 72-point bold text would look really odd.

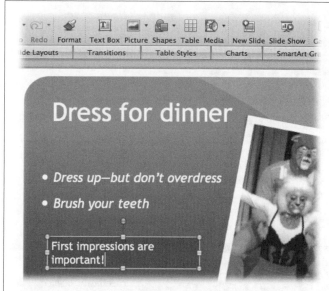

Figure 16-9:
Click the Toolbar's Text Box button and drag to position a text box on your slide. Text boxes begin life only one line tall, but expand as you type more. Drag the box to reposition it, drag one of its handles to resize it, or drag its green stalk to rotate it.

When you select a text box, the Formatting Palette unfurls its entire array of text and object adjustments. You can use Quick Styles; Shadows; Reflections; Colors, Weights, and Fills (for the text box background); and Size, Rotation, and Ordering—in addition to the font and alignment controls. All these object controls function exactly like they do in Word, and are described in detail in Chapter 8.

Formatting bullets

Traditionally, bullet-point lists play a huge role in business presentations. And just as being able to prescribe the silver bullet is an important CEO's skill, learning how to format bullets is a key PowerPoint skill.

To change the bullet style, click to put the insertion point in the text where you want the change to happen. Next, open the "Bullets and Numbering" pane of the Formatting Palette, and choose a bullet style from the Style pop-up menu you find there.

Other characters as bullets

You needn't be content with the mundane dot, box, or checkmark as your bullet symbol. Choose "Bullets and Numbering" from the Style pop-up menu of the "Bullets and Numbering" pane (or choose Format → "Bullets and Numbering") to call up the "Bullets and Numbering" section of the Format Text dialog box. Here you can choose from an assortment of other preset buttons or click the Custom Bullet pop-up menu to see others. Choose Character from that menu to reveal the Character Palette, from which you can choose any character—including all the optional symbols and dingbats—from any font on your Mac (see Figure 16-10).

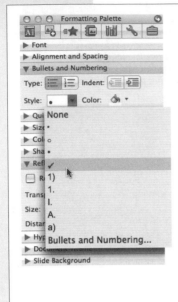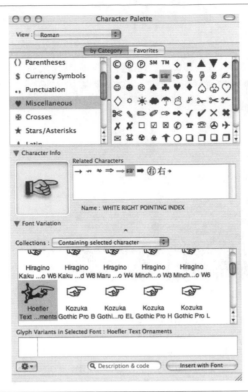

Figure 16-10:
The Formatting Palette's "Bullets and Numbering" pane (left) lets you choose the style, color, and size of your bullets. Choose "Bullets and Numbering" from its Style pop-up menu to open the "Bullets and Numbering" section of the Format Text dialog box. And from its Custom bullet pop-up menu choose Character to reveal the Character palette (right). This window gives you access to every possible character in all of your fonts, including all the optional characters like checkboxes, pointers, hearts, and smiley faces. Choose any one of these for your custom bullet.

Graphics as bullets

You can even use a little graphic as the bullet—a JPEG file showing a flag, a map, or your boss's head, for example.

To specify a graphics file on your hard drive that you want to use as a bullet, proceed like this:

1. **Click the text of the bullet that you want to modify.**

   The insertion point flashes next to the bullet point.

2. **Choose Format → "Bullets and Numbering" → Bullets and select Picture from the "Custom bullet" pop-up menu.**

   The Choose a Picture dialog box appears.

3. **Navigate to and double-click the graphic you want to use as a bullet.**

   PowerPoint replaces the bullet with your chosen picture at the same size as the text. To adjust the bullet size, enter a new percentage in the "Size: _% of text" box or use its up- and down-arrow button.

Adding Graphics, Charts, and Tables

Even if you're delivering the greatest news, a text-only presentation is a surefire way to put your audience to sleep. By inserting graphics, charts, tables, movies, and other objects into your presentations, PowerPoint lets you add visual information to spice up your slideshow. After all, you'll probably be speaking along with your presentation, so the slides need to reinforce your spoken message and display information you can't put into words For example, you may want to insert a video clip of your company president explaining why this year's sales numbers are so much higher than the forecast. Or, you want to include pictures of your products when giving a marketing presentation, along with the all-important tables and graphs. Here's how to go about using these specialized objects.

Graphics

PowerPoint gives you lots of options for bringing graphics into your slides. The Elements Gallery and the Toolbox's Object Palette house most of your choices, while the Insert menu holds the rest. Using these access points, you can insert photos or other pictures, clip art from office's Clip Art collection, charts, tables, AutoShapes, SmartArt graphics, movies, and sounds. For the most part, working with objects in PowerPoint is exactly the same as working with objects in Word's Publishing Layout View; chapter 20 covers object manipulation in depth. The following sections detail what's different about objects in PowerPoint.

Tables

Not surprisingly, building tables in PowerPoint is very similar to making tables in Word. But PowerPoint makes formatting tables much easier thanks to the new Elements Gallery and its Table Styles tab. Click the tab to reveal a whopping array of preformatted table colors and styles, displayed as thumbnails. When you click one of them, PowerPoint displays the pint-sized Insert Table dialog box, which awaits your designation of the number of columns and rows for your table. Click OK, and PowerPoint plops the table of your chosen style onto your slide, sporting a thick blue selection frame and a flashing insertion point in the upper-left cell. (If you choose Insert → Table instead of using the Elements Gallery, after you designate the number of columns and rows, PowerPoint creates a table in the Theme color and style.)

You can begin typing in that cell, or use the tab key to move from cell to cell. If you continue to tab after reaching the lower-right cell, PowerPoint adds another row to the table.

A third method of table creation uses the Table button in the Standard toolbar. Click it and drag through the cells in its pop-up menu to create a table of the desired dimensions (see Figure 16-11). As you drag, the menu grid expands to a maximum of 25×25—in case you need to create a crossword puzzle on your slide. When you release the mouse button, PowerPoint inserts the table—again in the Theme color and style.

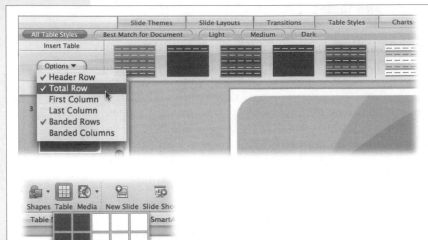

Figure 16-11:
Top: The Table Styles gallery includes dozens of predesigned tables you can insert with a single click. The buttons immediately above the thumbnails let you narrow your choices to see just those tables that PowerPoint thinks are the best match for your document—light ones, medium ones, or dark ones. The Options button pop-up menu at the left end of the Gallery gives you control over how PowerPoint formats the rows and columns, including or excluding a header row, total row, row and column banding, and so on.

Bottom: You can create a table very quickly using the Insert Table pop-up button on the Standard toolbar. Drag downward from this icon to specify how many rows and columns you want. PowerPoint creates it in the theme colors, and drops it into your slide.

You can easily change the appearance of a table once it's in your slide by clicking it once to select it, and then clicking one of the thumbnails in a Table Styles gallery. You can continue clicking your way down the Gallery until you find the ideal table color and style.

Once the table appears, you can adjust its size by dragging the resize handles at each corner, and you can move it or rearrange its interior by dragging the table's borders.

Tip: You can also *draw* a table directly on your slide by calling up the Table toolbar (View → Toolbars → "Tables and Borders") and then using the Draw Table tool. It works just like its Word counterpart, detailed on page 150.

Choose View → Toolbars → "Tables and Borders" to reveal the "Tables and Borders" toolbar. These tools along with those found in the Table and "Borders and Shading" panes of the Formatting Palette cover the basics for making changes like these to your PowerPoint table.

- **Change border lines.** To change a border's style, width, or color, make your selections using the Border Style, Border Width, and Border Color controls in either the toolbar or the Formatting Palette's "Borders and Shading" pane, and then click the borders you want to change using the Draw Table tool.

- **Change text alignment.** To change how text is aligned in a cell, select the cell (or cells); then click the Text Alignment buttons in the Formatting Palette's "Alignment and Spacing" pane, which let you align text at the top, center, or bottom of the cell; as well as left, right, center, justified, or distributed horizontal alignment.

- **Merge or split cells.** By erasing the line between two cells using the Eraser tool, you can tear down the barrier between them, creating one larger cell. (Another method: Select the cells that you want to merge by Shift-clicking them, and then click the Merge Cells button.)

  On the other hand, you can also split a cell in two—PowerPoint's version of cellular mitosis. Click the Draw Table tool and then drag to "draw in" the new border (Figure 16-12). Alternatively, select the cell you want to split and then click the Split Cell button, which vertically divides the cell.

- **Add or remove columns and rows.** The menu commands in the Table pop-up button (see Figure 16-12) let you insert columns and rows as well as delete them. They also let you merge and split cells, set how borders look, and specify how cells are filled.

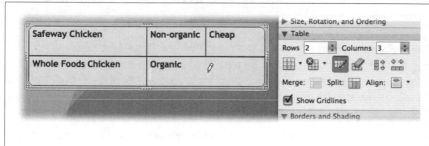

Figure 16-12:
The Formatting Palette's Table pane features commands that let you insert and remove columns and rows as well as split and join cells. You can also draw new cell borders to split cells, or you race cell borders to join cells by using the Draw Table and Table Eraser tools.

Use the Formatting Palette's "Quick Styles and Effects" pane to add preset shadows, glows, reflections, and 3-D effects to a table or individual cells. Select an entire table by clicking its frame—the insertion point disappears. The next formatting change you make applies to the whole table. If the insertion point is blinking in a table cell, the formatting change you make applies only to that cell.

For the last word in Table formatting, select a table, cell, or group of cells and choose Format → Table. This dialog box duplicates commands found in the Formatting Palette, but it also provides the only way to change cell fill colors, gradients, pictures, or textures (see page 745).

Movies and sounds

PowerPoint makes inserting movies and sounds just as easy as inserting still pictures, making it a cinch to insert a short movie of a climactic raffle drawing, a 360° view of your latest prototype, or a morale-building snippet from *Scrubs*. Via the Insert menu, PowerPoint can import movies and sounds in six different formats—from the Clip Gallery, from files, and from CD audio tracks. You can also record your own sounds directly into PowerPoint.

- **Movie from File.** Choose Insert → Movie (or choose Insert Movie from the Toolbar's Media button) to open the Insert Movie dialog box. Navigate to a QuickTime-compatible movie file and click Choose.

  When you insert a movie, PowerPoint asks if you want it to play automatically when the slide comes up during the slideshow. If you click No, the movie won't play until you click it.

  Inserting a movie displays the Formatting Palette's Movie pane, whose checkboxes let you hide the movie, play the movie full-screen, make the movie loop over and over, and rewind the movie after playing. The pop-up menus let you choose to play the movie automatically as soon as you land on the slide, only after you click it, or across slides—which keeps the movie playing even as you move on to other slides. Finally, the Play button lets you play the movie in the slide while you're editing, and the Show or Hide Controller button determines whether or not PowerPoint displays QuickTime's movie controls (see Figure 16-13).

Tip: Be careful when you embed movies in your PowerPoint presentation. These movies are *not* saved inside your PowerPoint presentation. Instead, the presentation maintains a *link* to the movie on your hard drive. If you copy your presentation to, say, your laptop, but forget to copy the movie file as well, you'll be in for a rude surprise when the conference-room lights dim. The slide will appear showing the first frame placeholder of the movie, but nothing happens when you click it.

Avoid this problem by saving your multimedia PowerPoint presentation as a *package*—a single folder that contains the PowerPoint file and every linked file it needs, ready for backing up, burning to CD, copying to your laptop, and so on. Choose File → Save As, and then, in the Format pop-up menu, choose Power-Point Package.

Because these sound clips don't take up much space, PowerPoint generally embeds them directly in the PowerPoint file. This time, you generally *don't* have to worry about bloating your presentation or losing the link to the sound file when you

Figure 16-13:
The small filmstrip icon in the lower-left corner of an embedded movie (top) is actually a switch that, when clicked, reveals the simple QuickTime movie controller (bottom).

move the presentation to a different disk. (If you choose PowerPoint → Preferences → General, you'll see that you can specify the sound-file threshold for automatic embedding. For example, PowerPoint makes sounds smaller than 100 K part of your presentation's file, but it leaves larger ones on the hard drive, like the movies described in the previous tip.)

- **Sound from File.** Click the Toolbar's Media button and choose "Insert Sound and Music" from its pop-up menu (or choose Insert → "Sound and Music" → From File) to call up the Insert Sound dialog box. Navigate to and double-click any sound file. PowerPoint can make use of any sound file format that Quick-Time can understand—AIFF, SND, WAV, MP3, AAC, and lots more. Once again, PowerPoint asks if you want the sound to play automatically when its slide appears during your slideshow. If you click No, you'll have to click the sound icon (a small speaker) to make it play.

You can drag this icon anywhere on the slide.

Note: Planting a *large* sound file on a slide is like planting a movie there: you're actually installing a *link* to the sound file on your hard drive, not the file itself. This feature keeps the size of your presentation much smaller, but it also means that you have to remember to move the sound file when you move the presentation to another machine. Otherwise, you'll find yourself with a soundless presentation.

Once again, the best way to be sure your sounds travel with you is to save your show as a PowerPoint package (see the Tip on the previous page). To do so, choose File → Save As, name your show, and choose PowerPoint Package from the Format pop-up menu.

- **Play CD Audio Track.** You can also grab a track from a music CD to serve as a soundtrack for your slideshow. This vestigial feature is mostly pointless in the age of iTunes—perhaps a tad more useful than a command called "Play 45 rpm recording"—but it still works. When you select Insert → "Sound and Music" → Play CD Audio Track, PowerPoint displays the Play Options dialog box is, where you can set the start and end points for your sound. When this slide appears during the actual presentation, the song begins to play automatically (or when you click it, at your option).

Note: The music won't play unless the actual audio CD is already inserted in your Mac at the time of your presentation. Avoid all the hassle by ripping the track to iTunes and dragging it to your PowerPoint project folder. See the box on page 296 for details of how to export just part of an iTunes song.

- **Record Sound.** The Insert → "Sound and Music" → Record Sound command lets you record your own sounds to insert into the presentation. You'll find this most useful for recording narration—or voice-over as it's called. (See page 698 for more details on recording narration and the importance of using a good microphone.)

Before you record, you have to verify that your microphone or other sound input device is working. Open the Sound System Preferences panel and click the Input tab. Make sure that the correct device is selected, and adjust the input volume if necessary. Quit System Preferences.

Now, in PowerPoint, choose Insert → "Sound and Music" → Record Sound. PowerPoint presents a Record Sound dialog box (see Figure 16-14). Click Record, speak or sing or squawk into your Mac's microphone, and then click Stop. You can play back the sound by clicking Play to make sure it's just what you want. If so, click Save.

You'll find a little speaker icon on your PowerPoint slide; click it during a presentation to hear your recording. (Unlike imported sounds and movies, these sounds *are* part of the PowerPoint file rather than links to separate files on your hard drive. Be aware that sound files can greatly inflate the size of your PowerPoint document.)

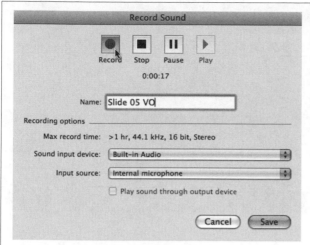

Charts

If your presentation is just crying out for a chart—and what presentation isn't?—click the Element Gallery's Charts tab and choose any of the chart styles by clicking one of the thumbnails. Doing so launches Excel, and opens a spreadsheet containing a small amount of dummy information. Replace it with your own data and close the spreadsheet. Excel doesn't prompt you to save your spreadsheet, because PowerPoint *embeds* your chart and its data into the current slide. (Embedding puts the output of one program into a document belonging to another. In this case, Excel's output is appearing in a PowerPoint document.)

When you return to PowerPoint, you'll see your newly minted chart resting gracefully on your slide. Since it is, in fact, an Excel chart, you can double-click its various elements to change their appearance, size, or remove them all together. You can also change to a different chart type by clicking another thumbnail in the Chart Gallery—exactly as you would in Excel, and exactly as described starting on page 576.

If you need to change your chart's data, Control-click (or right-click) the chart and choose Edit Data from the pop-up menu—again launching the Excel spreadsheet containing your data. (The fact that you can edit it again in its parent program is the gift of an embedded object.)

You can also insert a graph that you've already created in Excel. Open the Excel document containing the chart and simply drag the chart from Excel onto the slide in PowerPoint. Alternatively, you can select the chart in Excel, choose Edit → Copy, switch back to PowerPoint and choose Edit → Paste. Either way, the chart ends up embedded in your current slide. If you later change the data in your Excel spreadsheet PowerPoint reflects the change in its copy of the graph.

MEMORY LANE

A Charting Legacy

Having the full range of Excel's charting capabilities at your fingertips in PowerPoint is one of the great improvements of Office 2008. In earlier versions of PowerPoint, you had to create graphs via a small program called Microsoft Graph—a sort of Excel Lite. Never one to remove an existing feature without a fight, Microsoft has retained the now-redundant and seriously outclassed Microsoft Graph—while moving it far to the sidelines.

If you feel the urge to kick it old-school, choose Insert → Object and choose Microsoft Graph Chart from the Object type list. Click OK to launch Microsoft Graph, which displays a spreadsheet and a sample chart filled with some dummy data. Replace it with your own data, modify the chart or choose a new style using the toolbar commands, and then choose Graph → Quit & Return to [PowerPoint file name]. Microsoft Graph deposits its chart handiwork in your slide and then shuffles back to its assisted living facility.

Other objects

The Insert → Object command is the first step to embedding several other kinds of visuals onto a PowerPoint slide. The objects can come from such other Office programs as Equation Editor, Excel, Microsoft Graph, Organization Chart, or Word.

As shown in Figure 16-15, the resulting dialog box lets you either choose an existing document to install onto your slide, or create a new one. If you plan to insert an existing file into your slide, *first* choose the object type and then click "Create from file." The instant you turn on "Create from file," the standard Mac OS X Open File dialog box appears so that you can select the document you want.

What happens next depends on what you do in the Import Object box:

- **"Create new" with "Display as icon" turned on.** An appropriate icon now appears on the slide. You can click the icon to open the corresponding program and create a new document. If you're inserting a Word or Excel document into the slide, choose File → Close & Return to [Your PowerPoint file's name] when you're done. (The other Office programs—Graph, Equation Editor, and Organization Chart—have different commands for returning to Power-Point, but they're all under the Application or File menu.)

- **"Create new" with "Display as icon" turned off.** The appropriate program opens so that you can create your new object. Choose File → Close & Return to [Your PowerPoint file's name] when you finish. Your new object appears on the slide.

- **"Create from file" with "Display as icon" turned on.** PowerPoint takes you back to your slide, where an icon for your embedded object appears. Double-click the icon should you ever want to edit or display the object.

- **"Create from file" with "Display as icon" turned off.** The chart, equation, or document appears on the slide. (For Word or Excel files, you see only the first page or worksheet.) Double-click to edit or view the object in its parent program.

You may reasonably scratch your head at the prospect of placing an entire Word or Excel document onto a slide, especially if the document is larger than the slide itself.

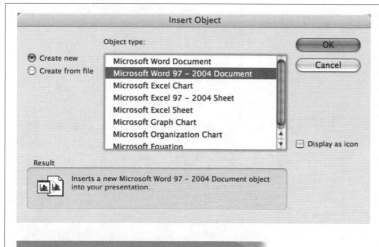

Figure 16-15:
Top: In the Insert Object dialog box, you can choose whether you want to bring in an existing document or create a new one on the spot. (If you click "Create from file," the "Choose a File" dialog box opens immediately, which is a bit disconcerting.)

Bottom: Turning on "Display as icon" plants a document icon on your slide instead of the document itself. Click it to open the document in the program that created it.

After scratching for a few moments, though, you'll probably realize that Microsoft has provided a dandy way to link supporting documents and reference materials to your PowerPoint presentation. When, during your pitch, some shortsighted co-worker objects, "I don't recall the marketing plan we talked about last month being quite so ambitious," you can click the Word document's icon that you've placed on the slide in anticipation of just such a protest—and smugly open the actual Word file, in Word, for all to see.

Note: Unfortunately, the "Display as icon" and, indeed, this whole object-embedding business, relies on a message technology called Object Linking and Embedding (abbreviated OLE and often pronounced "o-LAY"). As noted in the more complete discussion on page 753, Object Linking and Embedding has a reputation for behaving oddly. It works best when linking to very small documents on computers that have lots of memory.

Hyperlink

The Insert → Hyperlink turns the selected text or graphic into a clickable link, capable of opening another PowerPoint file, any other Macintosh file, a specified Web page on the Internet, or a pre-addressed email message. You'll find a complete description of this feature on page 46.

Polishing and Presenting in PowerPoint

Building the outline and creating individual slides in PowerPoint are obviously necessary to produce a great presentation. But PowerPoint's real talent lies in its ability to pull those images together into a running slideshow. Although good taste sometimes suffers as a result, PowerPoint gives you the tools to enrich your slide presentations with transitions, builds, video, music, sound effects, and voice narration. You can then rehearse your PowerPoint shows to work out the split-second timing. You can even turn your masterpieces into printouts or a Web site for the benefit of those who missed the presentation, or save your slideshows as Quick-Time movies, then edit them again later (back in PowerPoint).

This chapter shows you how to harness these potent PowerPoint features.

Adding Movement

After you've created all your slides and put them in the proper order, the content part of your creation is done. Now it's time to add slide *transitions* to supply sophisticated smoothness—or gee-whiz glitz—as you move from slide to slide. You can also add *object builds*—animations within a slide. Besides adding some visual excitement to your slideshow, transitions and builds can help you present your information more clearly, add drama, signal changes in topic, and—if you use them wisely—give your slideshow a much more professional, polished appearance.

Transitions

If you don't add a transition, PowerPoint changes slides instantly—or *cuts*—from one slide to another. Besides the simple cut, PowerPoint has 64 other slide transition styles to choose from. They range from simple *dissolves* (where one slide melts into the next) and *wipes* (where one slide moves across the screen to replace the other) to striking pinwheels, checkerboards, and twirling 3-D cubes. You owe it to yourself to sample all the transitions once just so you know what's available. Even with all this variety, though, it's a good idea to rely on simple transitions and use the pyrotechnics sparingly. You don't want your audience to walk away impressed by your fancy transitions—and unable to remember your message.

Transitions serve two very different purposes in a slideshow: They can either create smooth segues from one slide to another, or they can provide a dramatic punctuation to highlight the break between slides. When you choose transitions, consider carefully whether you're trying to just move smoothly to the next slide, provide a noticeable break between topics, or startle the audience with your visual prowess. Always consider your message and your audience as you choose transitions. If your presentation is a pep booster for the cheerleading team, you almost can't have too much color and action. But if you own a funeral home and your presentation to the bereaved describes the various services you offer, stay away from the goofy pinwheel, checkerboard, or news flash transitions. Transitions are like fonts—you usually need only one or two styles in a single document. If you have any doubt about which transition to use, err on the side of simplicity.

Tip: When you add a transition to a slide, you're creating the transition *into* the current slide *from* the previous slide. You can't create a transition out of the last slide of a presentation. If you want to end with a transition—to fade to black, for example—you need to create a black slide for the ending of the show and transition *from* the last slide *to* the black slide.

Add a transition

Transitions, as the term implies, appear in the spaces between slides in a show. To add a transition in PowerPoint, you first need to specify the location by selecting the slide that *ends* the switcheroo. If, for example, you want to insert a transition between the fourth and fifth slides in a show, select slide five in one of the following ways:

- In Normal view, click in the outline heading or the slide thumbnail.

- In Slide Sorter view, click the slide thumbnail.

After selecting a slide, add a transition by choosing one from the Elements Gallery's Transitions tab (see Figure 17-1, top) which you can reveal in any of the following ways:

- Click the Elements Gallery's Transitions tab and click the transition you want to use.

- Choose Slide Show → Transitions to open the Transitions Gallery, and then click the transition you want to use.

- Control-click (or right-click) a slide in any view, and choose Transitions from the pop-up menu to open the Transitions Gallery. Then click the transition you want to use.

When you add a transition to a slide, PowerPoint highlights the selected transition in the Transitions Gallery with an orange border and indicates its presence by placing a small transition icon beneath the lower-left corner of the slide thumbnail—in Slide Sorter view only (see Figure 17-1, top). You can add transitions in Normal view, but you have to do so with blind faith. When doubts surface, switch to Slide Sorter view for reassurance.

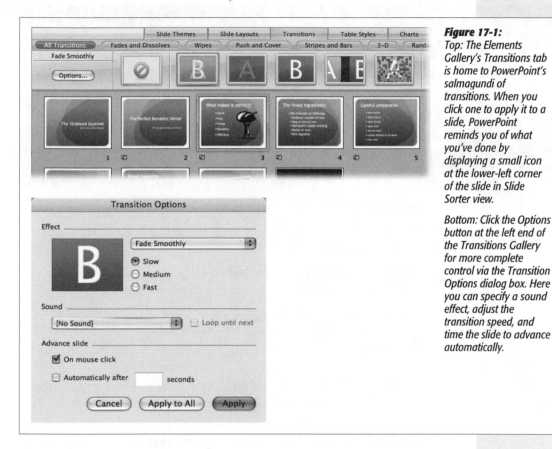

Figure 17-1:
Top: The Elements Gallery's Transitions tab is home to PowerPoint's salmagundi of transitions. When you click one to apply it to a slide, PowerPoint reminds you of what you've done by displaying a small icon at the lower-left corner of the slide in Slide Sorter view.

Bottom: Click the Options button at the left end of the Transitions Gallery for more complete control via the Transition Options dialog box. Here you can specify a sound effect, adjust the transition speed, and time the slide to advance automatically.

You can apply the same transition to several selected slides at once. Press ⌘ as you click an assortment of slides, or Shift-click to select a contiguous group of slides. You can even choose Edit → Select All to select all the slides in your presentation. Now when you click a transition, PowerPoint applies it to all those slides at once.

Choosing transition styles

Although your future audience members are crossing their collective fingers hoping that you'll end up using simple cuts and cross-fades over the course of your slide-show career, PowerPoint dangles before you a mouth-wateringly-long list of special effects. When you click the Elements Gallery's Transitions tab PowerPoint displays transition thumbnails. Hover over one of them with your cursor to display its name at the left end of the gallery. Directly above, category buttons narrow down the bewildering array.

Along with the simple cut (essentially, no transition) and the zany Random (every possible transition in no particular order), PowerPoint gives you a total of 65 transitions, grouped into six basic categories (described here by their visual effects):

UP TO SPEED

Avoiding the Cheese Factor

PowerPoint makes it easy to load up your presentations with funky transitions, sounds, and other cheesy gimmicks. But with power comes responsibility. While you may be tempted to show off all the program's entertaining features in a single presentation, bear in mind that old design adage: Less is more. Please. It's usually best to keep your transitions and sounds simple (or absent) and your designs basic.

If PowerPoint contained only the cut and the cross-fade (Fade Smoothly in PowerPoint parlance) you could live a full and happy presentation life–and so could your audience. With a simple transitions, you won't distract the audience from the important part of the presentation–your message–with a bunch of dazzling effects.

Fades and Dissolves.

- **Fade Smoothly.** The first slide fades away as the second one appears; what most people call a cross-fade or a dissolve.
- **Fade Through Black.** Here, the first slide fades out to black, and then the next one materializes in its place.
- **Cut.** The next slide in the show simply pops in place of the previous one. No frills, no fireworks. This is the most basic, and therefore the most useful, of all the transition types; it's also the "transition" you get if you don't specify *any* transition.
- **Cut through Black.** The first slide disappears, there's a brief period of total black, and the next slide appears. Kind of like blinking your eyes—or having a momentary power outage.
- **Dissolve.** One slide fizzles out and morphs into another in a pixelated, fairy-dust fashion. Think of Captain Kirk beaming up and you've got the idea.

Wipes.

- **Wipe.** The incoming slide squeegees the previous slide off the screen as it comes into view. Like a talented window washer, you can wipe from any direction.
- **Wedge.** Invisible clock hands rotate in opposite directions to wipe away the current slide and reveal the one after it.
- **Uncover.** The existing slide moves offscreen to expose the next image lying behind it. Choose to uncover from any direction.

- **Box.** The incoming slide wipes over the previous image with an expanding or contracting box, opening from either the center or the edges.

- **Wheel.** Similar to Wedge, but rotating wheel spokes erase the current frame and show the next slide.

- **Split.** The first image splits into doors that open either horizontally or vertically to reveal the next slide. Or, doors showing the second image close in over the first image.

- **Strips.** As seen in countless old movies, the incoming image wipes across the screen diagonally from one corner to the opposite corner.

- **Circle.** An expanding circle reveals the next slide.

- **Diamond.** Like the Circle, but in the shape of a diamond.

- **Plus.** Another geometric transition, like Circle, but in the shape of a cross.

- **Newsflash.** The spinning-page effect from old-style newsreels.

Push and Cover.

- **Push.** The second slide pushes the first one away—from whichever direction you choose.

- **Cover.** The new slide scoots in from offscreen to cover the previous image with a framed, three-dimensional effect. The eight variations in this group match the directions from which the incoming slide can enter: top, bottom, left, right, and the four corners. The reverse of Uncover.

Stripes and Bars.

- **Blinds.** The first slide closes like a set of Venetian blinds, either horizontally or vertically. As that image moves out, the next one emerges in its place.

- **Checkerboard.** The first image breaks up into a pattern of adjacent squares, which turns into the next image as it sweeps across or down the screen.

- **Comb.** The second slide comes into view as interlocking strips that approach from opposite sides of the frame.

3-D.

- **Cube.** The slide becomes the face of a 3-D cube, which rotates to reveal the upcoming slide.

- **Flip.** Think of a chalkboard that pivots horizontally or vertically and you'll know what this one does.

Random.

- **Random Bars.** Irregular horizontal or vertical slats appear across the image, quickly disintegrating and giving way to the next slide.

- **Random Transition.** If you just can't make up your mind—or are out to seriously annoy your audience—this transition reaches blindly into PowerPoint's transition grab-bag and pulls out a plum. Suitable only for audiences in the three- to five-year-old age group.

Note: Most of these transitions can come from more than one direction (Wipe Right and Wipe Left, for example). You'll find them all arrayed in the Elements Gallery.

Customizing your transitions

Once you've chosen a transition effect, you can tinker with its settings to add variety or to make them conform to your presentation's overall style. Customizing transitions is also an effective way to set your slideshow apart from the efforts of other PowerPoint fans.

To summon the Transition Options dialog box, select a slide and click the Options button at the left end of the Transitions Gallery. Here you can control all aspects of how transitions behave. Some of the things you can manipulate in this box (see Figure 17-1, bottom) are:

- **Effect.** Use this section to preview transition effects by choosing a new transition from the pop-up menu or selecting a new speed. PowerPoint responds by playing your new effect in the preview box. This is an extremely useful feature, because most transition types have several, sometimes subtle, variations; and the names of some transitions give little clue to their exact function. Also, most effects, especially the more intricate ones, look more impressive at slower speeds.

- **Sound.** In the gratuitous-bells-and-whistles department, nothing beats the Sound section. Using this pop-up menu, you can add a sound effect to your transition: applause, breaking glass, the ever-popular slide projector, or anything else you find in this lengthy pop-up menu. (You can also choose Other Sound to use a sound located elsewhere. PowerPoint recognizes sounds in many common file formats; search for "sound" in the online help to see the full list.)

Tip: You can add new sounds to the pop-up menu by dropping your own WAV (.wav) sound files into the Microsoft Office 2008 → Office → Media → Sounds folder.

The occasional explosion or whoosh can bring comic relief, help you underscore a point, or draw special attention to an image. But for the sanity of those viewing your slideshow, go easy on the noise. Please resist applying sound to every transition, or the next sound you hear will be the silence of an empty auditorium. Avoid turning on the checkbox marked "Loop until next" which keeps the sound-effect snippet playing over, and over, and over, and over until you change the slide. Please.

Note: Don't confuse these sound effects with background music. For background sound, insert a sound object in a given slide using the Insert command, as described on page 679.

- **Advance slide.** Here's where you tell PowerPoint the method you want to use for advancing to the next image in your slideshow. You have two basic choices: advance when you click the mouse (or remote control, or arrow key, or space-bar), or advance automatically after a number of seconds that you specify (the preferred choice if you're designing a presentation to run unattended). You can also turn on both options, thereby instructing the program to change slides after a number of seconds *unless* you click the mouse first.

Multimedia Effects

PowerPoint puts at your disposal a Spielbergian selection of special effects. In addition to the transitions you insert between slides, the program lets you animate particular elements in an image. It also lets you add a soundtrack or voice narration to your slideshow—features that are especially useful if you want to save the presentation as a standalone presentation or movie.

Adding Animations

While slide transitions create animations *between* slides, *animations* (or builds), add animation *within* a slide. You can use animations to do things like make bullet points appear one by one; bring pictures, shapes, or other objects into the slide (singly, or in groups); or display a chart element by element. You can control animations with the mouse or spacebar during a presentation; or you can automate them, bringing in each object or element in a timed sequence.

You can choose from a variety of impressive animation styles that PowerPoint can apply when moving text or objects into a slide, or moving them out. As with transitions, discretion is advised when creating animations. It's nice to have all these options available, but not every slide needs its text to appear as if it's been shot from a machine gun or whirled in a Cuisinart.

Warning: You've been warned: Animations may not show up when you export your PowerPoint presentation as a QuickTime movie (as described on page 706), especially if you've also created transitions between slides.

Since every element of a PowerPoint slide—text boxes, pictures, shapes, and so on—is an *object*, you employ the same techniques to build *pictures* into or out of a slide as you do to build *shapes* into or out of a slide, for example. PowerPoint also gives you further building possibilities for text and charts—all of which are objects made up of many individual elements.

The basic procedure for creating animations on a slide is to select the objects on the slide—text boxes, pictures, shapes, and so on—one at a time, and use the Custom Animation pane in the toolbox to determine how and when each object appears on the slide, whether it does something special while it's on the slide, and then how and when each object disappears from the slide. The *Entrance Effect* (when objects appear on the slide), *Emphasis Effect* (what objects do for special emphasis while they're on the slide), and *Exit Effect* (when objects disappear from the slide) are completely separate operations. You can have any one, two, or all of them.

You can create dramatic animated effects by controlling the Entrance Effect, Emphasis Effect, and Exit Effect order, timing, and direction for various slide elements. Switch to Normal View and click the Custom Animation tab of the toolbox to get started (see Figure 17-2).

Figure 17-2:
The Custom Animation palette in the toolbox is animation headquarters, your personal DreamWorks studio. Its panes and pop-up menus give you access to umpteen animation effects and options. To change the order of animations, select one and use the arrow buttons to move it up or down the list–or the X button to delete it. As you work, click the large Play button to preview the animation.

Note: You can only create animations in the Normal View—the only view that lets you click the various slide elements.

After you choose the text or graphic you want to give life to, click one of the Add Effect button pop-up menus in the Custom Animation palette. Each menu shows the nine effects you've used most recently; choose one to apply it to the current object. If you instead choose More Effects at the bottom of the menu, the Animation Effects window appears, a long scrolling list of effects grouped into four categories—Basic, Subtle, Moderate, and Exciting—that describe how stridently the effect demands attention.

- **Entrance Effect.** Use this tab to select how the element makes its appearance on the slide. If an effect is grayed out, it's not an option for that element.

- **Emphasis Effect.** This option lets you choose an effect that calls attention to an element that already appears on the slide. For example, Change Font Color changes the font to a contrasting color.

- **Exit Effect.** This tab lets you choose an effect to apply when an element disappears from the slide. Other than those options that don't apply to disappearing objects—and a few extra ones that do—the list is identical to the one in the Entrance tab.

Tabs at the top of the Animation Effects window let you switch between entrance, emphasis, and exit effects, just in case you inadvertently clicked the wrong Add Effect button to open this window.

Note: You can apply as many animations to an object as you like, so an element can appear in the Animation Order box more than once.

The Animation Effects window offers dozens of effects, ranging from the wild and wacky to the basic and restrained. A representative few from the restrained end of the spectrum include the following:

- **Appear.** In this, the simplest of all PowerPoint's animations, the selected item just pops into its predetermined spot on the slide.

- **Dissolve.** The selected object gradually materializes before your eyes, in a sparkly, pixelated way.

- **Fly In.** The selected object shoots in and comes to rest at its rightful spot in the layout.

- **Fly Out.** The selected object rockets off the slide.

- **Flash Once.** The selected object simply flashes once in a silent, subliminal kind of way.

When you click one of the animations in the Animation Effects window, Power-Point previews it for you on the slide in the slide pane—assuming the "Show preview" checkbox at the bottom of the window is turned on. Continue clicking effects until you strike the perfect balance between your playful yin and your business-like yang. Click OK to add the animation to the slide and display it in the Animation order window. This list shows not only the animations you've applied, but the order in which they happen. To change the sequence, select an element and click the up or down arrow buttons beneath. You can also delete one or more animations by selecting them and clicking the X button. To change an animation effect, double-click it to bring back the Animation Effects window, click the new effect, and click Replace.

Three pop-up menus beneath the Animation order window control the three basic options for animations:

- **Start** lets you choose when the effect happens. The standard setting is *On Click*: the effect happens when you click your mouse or remote control. *With Previous* causes the effect to begin simultaneously with the effect directly above it in the list. If it's the first effect in the list, the effect happens as soon as the slide appears. *After Previous* triggers the effect automatically after the previous effect is finished.

- **Property** determines the main option for the animation itself, such as which side of the screen does it start from, or how much larger or smaller does it make the item. Many effects don't have an adjustable property.

- **Speed** lets you choose one of five durations for the effect, from Very Fast (.5 seconds) to Very Slow (5 seconds).

Yet more animation options await in the lower panes of the Custom Animation palette.

FREQUENTLY ASKED QUESTION

Bullet by Bullet

I've seen smart, well-dressed, people do presentations where their bullet lists don't show up all at once. Instead, each point whooshes onto the screen on command. I've got my new suit—but how can I make my bullet points do that?

It's easy to animate the arrival of your bullets. Select the text box containing your bullets, and choose the Fly In effect from the Add Entrance Effect pop-up menu in the Custom Animation palette. Choose From Left and Fast from the Property and Speed pop-up menus, respectively. (For a more subtle effect, instead of Fly In, try Fade or Dissolve In.)

Once you click OK, your bullet points fly in one at a time, each time you click the mouse (or press an advance key). If you instead want to automate their entrance, you can specify a certain number of seconds between bullet points in the Timing pane. And, in the Text Animation pane, you can choose the bullet level that you want to fly in together as a group—something that makes sense only if you've created bulleted lists within bulleted lists.

- **More Effect Options.** Use the Sound pop-up menu to choose a sound effect to accompany the animation effect or stop a previous sound playing from a previous effect. Select No Sound to maintain glorious silence.

  The "After animation" pop-up menu lets you turn the selected item a solid color when animation finishes, make it disappear from the slide after the animation (Hide After Animation), or disappear as soon as the next animation begins (Hide on Next Animation). The standard setting, Don't Dim, keeps it onscreen after the animation—in other words, does nothing.

- **Timing.** This section lets you set a Delay of so many seconds before the animation begins, and a Repeat for how many times the animation plays over again. Turning on the "Rewind when done playing" checkbox immediately returns the slide to its appearance just before the animation began playing.

- **Text Animations.** If you selected a text object, you'll see this pane appear in the Custom Animation palette. Use the "Animate text" pop-up menu to choose whether the text appears in the animation all at once, by the word, or by the letter. The "Group text" pop-up menu determines whether your lines of text appear as one object, or one line at a time (according to their level in the outline.) You can also determine whether the lines below a certain level in the outline appear as a group by choosing "2nd level," "3rd level," and so on.

  If the object you're animating is a shape with text inside (see page 739) turn on the "Animate attached shape" checkbox to make the shape and its text remain stuck to one another during the animation. Finally, if the text you're animating contains several lines, you can turn on the "In reverse order" checkbox to make the lines appear on screen from last to first.

- **Chart Animations.** When you animate a chart object, this pane appears in the Custom Animation palette to give you control over how the chart appears on your slide. The "Group graphic" pop-up menu lets you choose whether the chart simply appears all at once (As one object), or by series or category, or by element in series or category. Turn on the checkbox at the bottom of the pane if you'd like the chart animation to begin with the appearance of the empty chart background.

Putting Controls on Slides

If you need to jump to various parts of your slide show during a presentation, or if you're creating self-paced learning modules that students run on their own computers, consider adding navigation buttons to the slides. When you require this kind of control, you can embed a host of useful command buttons—for advancing slides, jumping to the end of the show, and so on—right on the slide when you're preparing the show. You can place buttons on individual slides or many slides at once:

- If you want to add a button to just one slide, switch into Normal view and bring up the slide in question.

• If you want to add a button to the same location in a group of slides—or all of them—place it on the slide master. Start by choosing View → Master → Slide Master. (See page 663 for a refresher on working with the slide master.)

Note: Don't try this shortcut if you'll be saving your presentation as a QuickTime movie. For QuickTime movies, you have to put the buttons on each slide individually.

Once the slide where you want to stick your button is displayed, click the Shapes pop-up menu in the Standard Toolbar (or use the Shapes tab in the Object Palette) and make a selection from the Action Buttons submenu as shown in Figure 17-3 (or do the same thing via the Insert Shapes menu in the Drawing toolbar).

The Action Buttons palette has 12 buttons. The four in the middle help you jump around during the show: Previous Slide, Next Slide, First Slide, and Last Slide.

To put an Action Button on your slide, click the button you want. (Alternatively, choose a button name from the Slide Show → Action Buttons submenu.) Then drag diagonally on the slide. PowerPoint draws the button for you, and then opens up the Action Settings dialog box shown in Figure 17-3.

In this box, you can specify exactly what your newly created button will do. The proposed settings are fine for most purposes, so you can generally just click OK. It's worth noting, however, that you can use these controls to make your button do much fancier tricks, as described in Figure 17-3. (Normally, your action is triggered when you click the corresponding button. But if you click the Mouse Over tab in the Action Settings dialog box, you can also specify that something happens when you just point to it instead.)

Later, when the slideshow is running, press the A key to make the arrow cursor appear, and then click your newly created button to trigger the associated event.

Warning: Planning to save your show as a QuickTime movie? Watch out for action settings that don't work well with movies! For example, Microsoft recommends that you not use mouseovers, since they won't work. Also, don't set a button to run another program or to play a sound.

You can put any of eight other Action Buttons on your slides. Some come with preset icons and some have preset Action Settings that match their individual functions.

• **Custom** lets you customize your own action button (to launch a program, for example).

• **Home** zips back to the first slide in the show.

• **Help** lets you create a link to a help slide that you've designed.

• **Information** creates a link to an information slide that you've added.

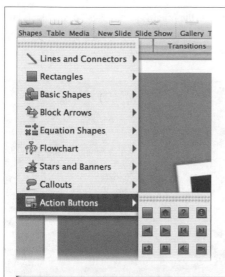

Figure 17-3:

Top: From the Drawing toolbar, choose AutoShapes → Action Buttons and then click an action button to load your cursor with it. Drag to draw the shape of the button on your slide; when you release the mouse, PowerPoint presents you with the Action Settings dialog box.

Bottom: You can use the "Hyperlink to" pop-up menu to specify that a click of your button transports you to another slide, a Web site, or even another Macintosh file. Or you can check "Play sound" to create a button that, when clicked, plays the thunderous applause the occasional heartless audience may not provide.

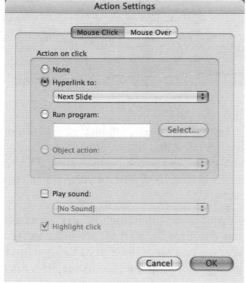

- **Return** takes you back to the last slide you saw (which, if you've been jumping around, isn't necessarily the slide before this one in sequence).

- **Document** launches a Macintosh file or program that you specify.

- **Sound** triggers a sound, and its cousin **Movie** starts rolling a movie that you've set up beforehand.

If you want to change the *appearance* of an Action Button—or any other AutoShape—double-click the button to bring up the Format AutoShape dialog box. To change a button's *action,* control-click (or right-click) it and choose Action Settings from the pop-up menu.

Tip: You don't have to use one of the predrawn shapes on the Action Buttons palette as your visible button—PowerPoint can turn *any* graphic object into a button. Just Control-click it and choose Action Settings from the shortcut menu, and then proceed as described in the preceding paragraphs.

Exit Gracefully

If you've given slideshow presentations with a slide projector, you probably used a solid cardboard "black slide" as the final slide in your tray. This opaque slide prevents a blindingly white screen appearing when you advance the final slide. In PowerPoint, the view of your desktop doesn't sear any retinas, but its appearance is at best unprofessional and at worst embarrassing. (Especially if you forgot to tuck away that *Geeks Gone Wild* folder before the presentation.)

To create a black slide at the end of your PowerPoint presentation, add a slide and choose the blank slide layout. Choose Format → Slide Background; turn on the checkbox at the bottom marked "Hide background objects"; in the

Solid tab, change the Color pop-up menu to black; and then click Apply. Now choose ⌘-D to create a *second* black slide. From now on when you reach the end of your presentation the screen goes black—and stays black even if a nervous presenter gives the remote control an extra click.

The black slide is also the key to creating a fade-out transition at the end of your last slide. Select the black slide, add the Fade Smoothly transition to it, and set the Transition Options to Slow.

While you're at it, you may as well put a black slide at the beginning of your presentation. That way, your audience won't see the first slide until you're really ready.

Adding Narration

If you're worried about laryngitis on the day of your presentation, if you're creating a self-running kiosk show, or if you have an unnatural fear of public *squeaking,* you might want to record voice narration for your slideshow ahead of time. This way, you can sit back and relax while your confident, disembodied voice (or the voice that you hired) plays along with the show.

To get your voice into the Macintosh you'll need a microphone, of course. Some Macs have built-in microphones—but don't be tempted to use them to record narration. The quality is poor and they pick up a lot of noise from the operation of the computer. Some Macs have an analog audio input jack, suitable for a microphone—and some don't. For those that don't, you'll require a USB audio adapter like the iMic from Griffin Technology (*www.griffintechnology.com*).

Tip: Whether you plug directly into your Mac or go through a USB adapter, there's any number of microphones you could use—at any price you can imagine. One good choice in the less-than-$100 range is the Model 33-3013 tie-clip microphone from RadioShack at $25, which delivers surprisingly good voice quality at a very low price.

When you've got your microphone hooked up, visit the Sound panel of System Preferences (click the Input tab) to make sure that you've selected the correct microphone for input. Quit all other sound-recording programs, if any are running. Then:

Recording Narration the Careful Way

Although PowerPoint can record narration for the entire slideshow or a single slide, its recording abilities are pretty primitive—for example, you can't make any adjustments to the EQ, or mix in background music or sound.

You may already have the software you need to get the sound from the microphone onto your hard drive. Garage-Band can handle the task, as can the free, open-source, Audacity (*http://audacity.sourceforge.net*).

When you record, make a separate audio file for *each* slide that requires narration. Experiment with microphone placement and input levels, as well as with your delivery and pacing.

Listen to the playback through headphones or good external speakers—don't try to judge the sound quality using your laptop's built-in speakers. If you're not accustomed to recording narration, try to emulate your favorite radio or TV newscaster.

When you've got a good take, trim off any "dead air" at the beginning and end of the file before saving it—giving it a filename that includes the slide number. Then use the Insert → "Sound and Music" → From File command to insert each narration into its respective slide (see page 700).

1. **Choose Slide Show → Record Narration to bring up the Record Narration dialog box.**

   This box shows the current recording settings, including your maximum recording time based on your free hard-drive space. Since sound files can be huge, the "Link narrations" checkbox lets you save your narration files to any location you like, such as an external hard drive with plenty of free space, rather than embedding them in the presentation file. Click Set to choose where Power-Point saves linked narrations. When you finish recording, that location will contain one AIFF sound file for each slide in your presentation.

   Note: If you link your narrations, moving your presentation to another machine will break the links. The PowerPoint Package format avoids this problem, as discussed in the Tip on page 678.

2. **Click Record.**

   PowerPoint starts running through your presentation. As you advance through the slides, PowerPoint makes a separate, linked AIFF sound file for each slide. Or, if you didn't link the recording, PowerPoint attaches the audio you recorded as a sound object on each slide.

   There's no easy way to re-record just one flubbed slide; for most purposes, it's simplest to start a new take. To start over, end the slideshow using whatever method you normally use (press Esc, for instance). Then, choose Slide Show → Record Narration and begin again. (And if you're *really* having trouble, you can always record individual sound files for each slide, then attach them as described in the box above.)

Note: These voice clips override any other sound effects in the slideshow, so if you're using a recorded narration, any embedded sound effects (including transition sounds) won't play.

---

3. **Record whatever you want to say for each slide, advancing the slides as you normally would (by clicking the mouse, for example).**

   When you reach the end of the slideshow, PowerPoint asks if you want to save the timings (to record the amount of time you spent on each slide) along with your narration. If you click No, PowerPoint saves only the narration. If you click Yes, PowerPoint saves the timings along with the narration, overwriting any existing timings.

   If you choose not to include the timings, each sound will play when you manually advance to a given slide. This way, you can let the narration play, and then discuss each slide, moving on only when you're ready.

Note: Voice recordings can eat up a lot of disk space, so be sure you have enough room on your hard drive to hold the sound. If not, consider saving your voice files to an external hard drive or some other industrial-strength storage area.

Once you're done recording your narration, you've got a self-contained slideshow, suitable for parties or board meetings.

Adding a soundtrack

Instead of adding sound to each slide, you may want to add a soundtrack to an entire slideshow. For example, you may want background music or sound, which doesn't need to be synchronized with the slides, playing through the entire slideshow. On the other hand, you could also use a single soundtrack for an unattended kiosk-type presentation where you've set each slide to advance automatically.

To create a soundtrack, use the Insert → "Sound and Music" → From File command (select the sound file and choose whether you want it to start Automatically or When Clicked) to insert the soundtrack on the first slide or the selected slide. If your soundtrack is shorter than your show, you can loop it so it plays continuously. Click the loudspeaker icon to select the soundtrack, and turn on the checkbox marked Loop Until Stopped in the Formatting Palette's Sound pane.

Then click the Custom Animation palette, select the sound in the "Animation order" list, and click the "After… slides" button in the Media Options pane. Finish by entering the total number of slides in the slideshow—or the number of slides you'd like accompanied by your soundtrack.

When you add a soundtrack in this fashion, it plays right along with any other sounds, narration, or sound effects you've attached to your slides or transitions.

Putting On the Show

Now that you've built your individual slides, folded in your transitions, and sprinkled lightly with animations and sounds, it's time to bake it at 350° for 45 minutes while you run through your final checklist and get dressed.

Setting Up

Before you slick your hair and stride onto the stage, the first preparatory step is to choose Slide Show → Set Up Show. In the dialog box that appears (see Figure 17-4), you can choose the *type* of presentation you want it to be—a typical full-screen slideshow, a small show for an individual reader to browse, or a self-running kiosk-style show that keeps playing until you (or the police) shut it off.

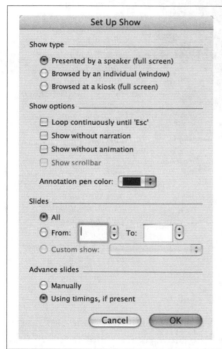

Figure 17-4:
The Set Up Show dialog box lets you select the type of show and show options, and choose which slides to use and how you want them to be advanced: manually, with a mouse click; or automatically, using preset timings.

Rehearsing Your Presentation

As P-Day (Presentation Day) draws near, you can use PowerPoint's *rehearsal mode* to run through the slideshow and work out the timing. It can be very helpful to know how long it takes to show each slide, especially if you have a tight presentation schedule. This handy feature even lets you factor in sufficient time for the laughter to subside after your well-rehearsed "off the cuff" jokes.

To begin the rehearsal, choose Slide Show → Rehearse Timings. The screen fills with the first slide, and PowerPoint shifts into presentation mode. A tiny timer appears in the lower-right corner of the slide, ticking off the number of seconds the slide is spending onscreen. Each time you advance to a new slide, the timer resets itself to zero and begins the count anew for *that* slide.

When you've gone through the whole show, PowerPoint asks if you want it to record those timings for use later in an automated show. If you answer yes, Power-Point logs the timings automatically in the "Advance slide" portion of the Slide Transition dialog box (Figure 17-1). The program then asks if you want it to note those timings in Slide Sorter view, as shown in Figure 17-5. You may as well do this; it's pretty handy to see those time allotments, even if you decide to ignore them and advance the slides manually.

Figure 17-5:
After you've completed your timing run, PowerPoint marks the slide duration beneath each slide in Slide Sorter view. The duration of transitions isn't factored into the timing of each slide, so if you've chosen some of the slower transitions, take their length into account when calculating the timing of your show. If you click the icon beneath the slide, PowerPoint displays the transition in the thumbnail at high speed; click the build icon beneath the slide to watch the build at closer to real time.

Choosing a Navigation Scheme

If you choose PowerPoint → Preferences → View tab, you'll find some useful preference settings that affect the appearance of the show you're about to give. In the Slide Show area, for example, you'll find a pop-up menu with these choices:

- **Pop-up menu button.** Turning on this option means that when you twitch the mouse during your slideshow, PowerPoint will make a subtle toolbar appear in the lower-left corner. Clicking it gives you the same pop-up menu of useful controls (Next, Previous, End Show, and so on) that you usually get only by Control-clicking the screen (Figure 17-6).

- **[No Slide Show Controls].** If you choose this option, your slides remain unsullied by any toolbar, no matter how twitchy your mouse hand is.

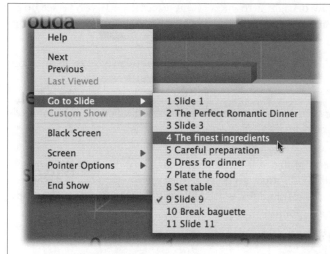

Figure 17-6:
To view the contextual menu in a slideshow, either Control-click a slide or click the pop-up menu button in the lower left corner of the screen (if you've turned it on in the PowerPoint → Preferences → View tab). The resulting menu (shown here) gives you a lot of power. For example, you can choose Pen from the Pointer Options submenu and then scribble circles, arrows, underlines, and other real-time doodles on your slides during the presentation. (You can later erase your additions by choosing Screen → Erase Pen from the contextual menu, or just move to the next slide—PowerPoint doesn't save your scribbles.)

Note: The Preferences → View tab also has an "End with black slide" checkbox—however the black slide it creates isn't completely black. It creates a black slide emblazoned with the words "End of slideshow, click to exit." What part of *black slide* doesn't Microsoft understand? Take the time to create a real black slide as described in the box on page 698.

Presenting Onscreen

Your formal wear is clean and pressed. Now the moment has come—it's time to run your show. Any one of the following options starts the slideshow:

- Click the Slide Show view button in the lower-left corner of the main window. (It looks like an old-time home movie screen—the rightmost button.) The slideshow starts with the selected slide.

- Choose Slide Show → View Slide Show. The slideshow starts with the first slide.

- Choose View → Slide Show. The slideshow starts with the first slide.

- Press ⌘-Return. The slideshow starts with the first slide.

What happens next depends on your computer setup. If you have only one monitor, PowerPoint fills the screen with your first slide (or, if you clicked the Slide Show view button, with the slide that was previously selected). Unless you've chosen to use preset timings, the first slide stays on the screen until you manually switch to the next one (by clicking the mouse or pressing the Space bar, for example).

If you have two screens, the slide only appears on the secondary monitor. The main display—typically your laptop's screen—turns into a command center called Presenter Tools (see page 705).

PowerPoint gives you several ways to move around inside a full-screen show. A simple mouse click or a press of the Space bar moves you to the next slide, as does pressing the down arrow or right arrow key. (One exception: If you've set up an animation on a slide, these advance keys trigger the animation instead of summoning the next slide.)

After you've reached the end of the show, PowerPoint returns you to its previous view.

Note: If you rehearsed your slideshow and chose to save your timings, the show will play automatically to the end, displaying each slide for the predetermined number of seconds.

While your slideshow is running, you can Control-click anywhere on the screen to bring up a contextual menu that gives you such self-explanatory navigation options as Next, Previous, and End Show (see Figure 17-6). It also gives you some less obvious options worth pointing out:

- **Black Screen** blacks out the screen during a discussion.

- **Pointer Options,** as you might imagine, let you pick the kind of onscreen cursor you want to use—Automatic, Hidden, Arrow, or Pen. (Automatic gives PowerPoint the authority to choose a pointer for you; Hidden makes the pointer go away; Arrow is the standard Mac arrow-shaped pointer; and Pen turns the pointer into a writing tool.)

- Finally, the **Screen** submenu's commands let you pause a running slideshow that's otherwise on autopilot, or erase any graffiti that you made with the aforementioned pen tool.

Note: If you're a PowerPoint 2004 veteran and you're looking for Meeting Minder here, you won't find it. Microsoft removed it from PowerPoint 2008. Dust off that flipchart for note-taking.

Controlling the show

Here's the rundown on helpful keystrokes you can use while the slideshow is running:

Table 17-1. Keystrokes for Navigating Slide Shows

What to do	How to do it
Next slide (or start an animation)	Mouse click, Space bar, Return, N, Enter, right arrow, down arrow, Page down
Previous slide or animation	Left arrow, up arrow, Page up, P, Delete
Jump to a certain slide number	Enter the slide number and then press Return
Jump to the first slide/last slide	Home, End
To/from a black screen	B, period
To/from a white screen	W, comma
Erase drawing onscreen	E
Show or hide arrow pointer	A, =

Table 17-1. *Keystrokes for Navigating Slide Shows (continued)*

What to do	How to do it
Change pointer to pen	⌘-P
Change pointer to arrow	⌘-A
Stop/restart a self-running slideshow	S, +
End the slideshow	Esc, ⌘-. (period), - (hyphen)
Go to the next hidden slide	H

Using Presenter Tools

If you've ever had to rush through a presentation because you lost track of time or forgot what was coming up on the next slide, PowerPoint's Presenter Tools is a blessing. While the video projector or other external monitor shows a full-screen presentation, this feature displays the current slide, notes, and upcoming slides in separate panes on your laptop (Figure 17-7). A clock at the top of the screen shows the time or counts the elapsed time since the beginning of the slideshow, so it's easy to pace yourself. Best of all, you don't even have to do anything extra to use Presenter Tools. If your computer supports non-mirrored video and you have a second monitor connected, this feature starts up automatically when you begin the slideshow.

All the shortcuts that work in full-screen mode also work in Presenter Tools. For example, you can advance to the next slide by pressing Return or Space bar. Or if you prefer, you can also navigate by clicking the green arrows at the top of the screen.

Tip: To practice using Presenter Tools on a single monitor, Choose Slide Show → View Presenter Tools.

The Presenter Tools notes pane would be handy even if it only let you read your notes during a slideshow—after all, you can't be expected to remember *everything* when you're at the podium. But Presenter Tools goes a step further by letting you *edit* the notes during your presentation, too. It's the ideal way to keep track of which jokes work and which slides make your audience wince in pain.

Tip: If you move your mouse off the Presenter Tools screen onto the slideshow screen, you can Control-click to bring up the shortcut menu that includes the pen tool and other options.

Recycling Your Presentations

PowerPoint lets you create multiple *custom shows* in a single document. This feature comes in handy if, for example, you want to have both long and abbreviated versions of the same show, or if you want to tailor some material you've used before to a different audience.

Suppose you're going to address two different groups on the topic of deer. You have lots of engaging slides on the topic. But there's a good chance the Bambi Fan

Figure 17-7:
Presenter Tools divides the screen into three panes, much like Normal view. The largest, at the top, shows you exactly what the audience sees, in real time. The pane on the left shows thumbnails of the entire presentation; to go to any slide, click it. The notes pane at the bottom shows your slide notes; the pop-up menu directly above it lets you increase the font size for readability. The Up Next window shows the next animation on the current slide or the next slide in the presentation. In the lower-right corner, you'll find buttons to switch the clock from a clock to a timer, to hide or show the Up Next window, to end the slideshow, or to open the Presenter Tools Help screen with a list of keyboard shortcuts.

Club won't sit through the show you've got planned for Hunters Anonymous. You can solve this moral dilemma by creating a *customized* show for each group, each of whose slides are a subset of the complete deer presentation.

To build such a custom show, choose Slide Show → Custom Shows. The resulting dialog box gives you four choices: New, Edit, Remove, and Copy (Figure 17-8). When you click New, a dialog box pops up that lets you choose the slides you want to include in the custom show. You can also reorder the slides in your custom show and give your custom show a name.

Then, when it's time to give the actual presentation, choose Slide Shows → Custom Shows to bring up a window that lists the custom shows you've built. Click the one you want to present and then click Show; your custom show begins.

Saving Presentations as QuickTime Movies

PowerPoint 2008 retains previous versions' ability to save presentations as Quick-Time movies. This is a nifty idea since anyone with QuickTime installed—Mac or Windows fans—can play these movies even if they don't have PowerPoint. This is a great way for your associates and underlings to give the same kinds of pitches you give without having to spring for a copy of Office—but proceed with caution.

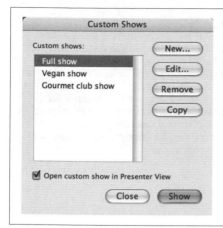

Figure 17-8:
Using the Custom Shows dialog box, you can choose a subset of slides from the current slideshow and reorder those slides any way you want to create a customized presentation. If you turn on the checkbox at the bottom, the show opens in Presenter Tools.

Remember that not every bell and whistle of a PowerPoint slideshow survives the conversion into a QuickTime movie. As noted here and there throughout this chapter, things like action buttons on master slides, many PowerPoint transitions, and certain actions (mouseovers, certain kinds of links, sound, and so on) won't work at all.

To turn an open PowerPoint presentation into a QuickTime movie, choose File → "Save as Movie". This brings up a Save dialog box, which you can use to name your movie file and choose a folder location for it.

Before you save your movie, PowerPoint gives you a chance to fine-tune some of its settings. To begin, click the Movie Options button. PowerPoint responds by opening the Movie Options dialog box shown in Figure 17-9.

The most important settings worth examining here are Movie Dimensions and the Optimization pop-up menu. The latter lets you specify which you value more: compact file size, smooth playback of animations, or picture quality. Depending on the complexity of your file and the screen size you've specified, these virtues may be mutually exclusive. If you want the highest quality animations, for example, the file won't be very small on your hard drive, and the quality of animated photos may suffer.

Tip: After you've saved your slideshow as a QuickTime movie, you may notice your transitions acting flaky. Because the PowerPoint Movie format doesn't actually support PowerPoint transitions, they get translated to a QuickTime equivalent that may be very different from what you intended. For the best results, use simple transitions like Fade Smoothly, or don't use any transitions at all.

The movie Options dialog box also lets you import a sound file to use as a soundtrack. Depending on your presentation, if chosen tastefully, music or some other nondistracting background sound (rainfall or ocean waves, perhaps) can make your movie a more well-rounded presentation. Tread carefully, though, to

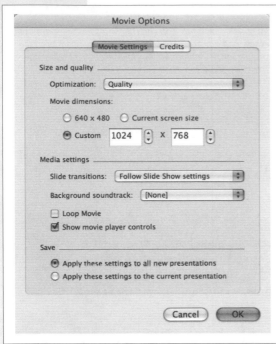

Figure 17-9:
This dialog box lets you specify the size of the QuickTime movie; 640 × 480 creates a tiny window on today's larger screens—1,024 × 768 is a good minimum size. Using the "Background soundtrack" pop-up menu, you can choose an MP3 file or another file to play during the whole slideshow—a handy option in self-running, kiosk situations. Notice the radio buttons in the Save area that let you select whether PowerPoint should use your new settings for just this presentation or use them for future presentations you save as QuickTime movies, as well.

WORKAROUND WORKSHOP

Mac Presentations on Windows PCs

If you're really in demand as a speaker, you'll eventually have to bite the bullet and show a Mac PowerPoint presentation on a Windows computer. Although the QuickTime movie format offers one workaround, it's usually better if you can use the Windows version of PowerPoint 2007 to run your slideshow. When you're preparing your presentation, use fonts that you know will be installed on the Windows PC—Arial and Times New Roman, for example. Import

graphics in cross-platform formats like JPEG and GIF, and convert movies to AVI format using Apple's QuickTime Pro program.

Finally, if you can, do a dry run on a PC (best-case scenario, the actual computer that you'll be using for your presentation) just to outfox any last-minute glitches. Copy your slideshow, along with movies and other linked files, to the PC's desktop and double-click the presentation file.

---

avoid crossing that fine line between "nondistracting" and "sleep-inducing." These background sound files can be in any number of formats, including AIFF, Quick-Time audio, WAV, and MP3.

To add a background soundtrack, choose Select Soundtrack in the Background soundtrack pop-up menu. PowerPoint asks you to locate the sound file that you want to use, which it then attaches to your presentation when you click OK. Power-Point will mix the soundtrack sound with any embedded sounds, including voice narration.

Saving Presentations for the Web

PowerPoint lets you create presentation files that are formatted, coded, and ready to be posted on the Internet. With just a few mouse clicks, you can save your slide-show as a Web page, complete with some nifty JavaScript programming that gives viewers a high level of control over how they watch your show. Just don't set your production-value hopes too high. You'll lose transitions and animations; photos might look terrible; and gradients will suffer from extreme banding. However, if you plan ahead, use simple graphics, Web colors, no transitions or animations, and no gradients, you can get your information up on the Web quickly.

Before you move your presentation onto the Web, you'll first want to see how it looks *after* the conversion. To preview your presentation as a Web page, choose File → Web Page Preview. PowerPoint generates all the necessary graphics, HTML, and JavaScript coding, and then transfers the whole enchilada into your browser. You can then use your browser to click your way through the presentation, which actually looks very much as it would if you were viewing it in PowerPoint's Normal (three-pane) view.

To save your presentation as a Web page (or rather, a set of them), choose File → Save as Web Page. PowerPoint asks where you'd like to save your show. Clicking Web Options opens a dialog box that lets you tell the program such things as what colors to use, where to place navigation buttons, and how to encode images. Once you're satisfied with the options you've chosen, click OK. To actually save the presentation, click Save. PowerPoint automatically renders your presentation as HTML files complete with embedded JavaScript and accompanying Web-ready graphics files. You wind up with a home page and a folder full of HTML files, graphics files, and sound files (see Figure 17-10). You can upload these files to your Web server as you would any other Web page files (see page 344).

TROUBLESHOOTING MOMENT

Funky Fonts

When viewing a presentation that's been converted into a Web page, you may notice that the fonts don't fit quite right—a by-product of the fact that the HTML language of Web pages isn't terrifically brilliant about managing fonts. Although PowerPoint does its best to compensate, sometimes type rendered in HTML is just too large for the allotted space, so chunks of text bump down to the next line.

You can do a couple of things to combat this fat-font problem. Keep your font sizes a shade smaller than you ordinarily would, and try not to squeeze too much copy on a single line. And whenever possible, avoid tables with multiple lines of text; these babies are just waiting to bunch together and run over.

Saving Slides as Graphics

Among its many other gifts, PowerPoint lets you save individual slides—text and all—as graphics files. This can be a handy little feature whenever you want to make sharp-looking, high-resolution images of your presentation to pass along to your friends, your students, or your mom. When PowerPoint saves slides as graphics,

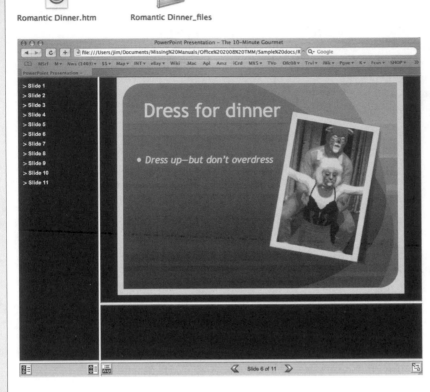

Figure 17-10:
Top: After you've saved your presentation as a Web page, you can find it in the Finder as a single, "home page" file and a folder containing secondary pages and supporting media files. In this example, the presentation is named Romantic Dinner.htm. PowerPoint applies a similar name to the folder.

Bottom: In Safari, buttons at the bottom let you hide (or show) the Outline and Notes panes, switch slides, or see the show at full-screen size. The look of a Web presentation on any individual computer depends on many factors: operating system, fonts installed, screen resolution, browser preferences set by the user, and so on. But you can be sure of one thing: it won't look as nice as it does in PowerPoint.

you'll end up with an individual file for each slide. (As you undoubtedly surmise, transitions, animations, and sounds are all lost in translation.)

Send to iPhoto

The easiest way to save your slides as high-quality graphics is to send them to iPhoto. Once in iPhoto, you can use them in an iPhoto slideshow that you could put on a DVD, add them to an iWeb page, or import them to iMovie. Best of all, if you have a video iPod you can load the slides on it and always have your presentation with you (see the box on page 714).

1. **Choose PowerPoint → Preferences → Save, click the "Dots per inch" button, and set the pop-up menu to 300 dpi for high-quality (6 megapixel) images.**

    Use a higher setting if you're going to be making gigantic prints, or lower settings if you don't care so much about picture quality.

2. **Select the slides you want to export to iPhoto.**

   You can select one or more slides if you want to send just a portion of your slideshow to iPhoto. PowerPoint doesn't care what slides you select if you're going to send the entire slideshow.

3. **Choose File → Send To → iPhoto.**

   The "Send to iPhoto" dialog box appears; iPhoto is about to create a new album for your slides. Give the folder a different name if you don't want it to have the same name as your PowerPoint file.

4. **Click the Format pop-up menu to choose either JPEG or PNG format—your only choices.**

   Both can create visually identical, high-quality images—but JPEG is a more universal format and probably the better choice. This menu controls the format but not the quality—which is why you set that first, back in Step 1.

5. **Choose to send all of the slides or just the selected group.**

   Click All to send the entire slideshow, no matter what slide or slides you've selected.

6. **Click "Send to iPhoto".**

   PowerPoint launches iPhoto, which then creates a new album and imports the slides. When it's done, iPhoto pops to the foreground to show off its newly created album.

Tip: Enable Disk mode on your iPod (in your iPod's Summary tab in iTunes) to make your iPod function like an external hard drive. Then drag your actual PowerPoint file to your iPod to copy it. Now you can plug your iPod into a Mac or Windows PC, launch PowerPoint, choose File → Open, and locate the file on your iPod. This way you can run the full PowerPoint slideshow with all its bells, whistles, animations, transitions, and so on—but without lugging around your own computer. (You can do the same thing, of course, with a USB flash drive. And, the usual considerations with XML file format still apply)

Save as Pictures

If you don't go the iPhoto route, PowerPoint is willing to save its slides in a wider variety of file types. To do so, first select the slide you want to convert, and then follow these few steps:

1. **Choose File → Save as Pictures (or File → Save As—which leads to the same dialog box).**

   A dialog box appears, offering several options.

2. **From the Format pop-up menu, select a graphics file format.**

   JPEG or TIFF are excellent choices for photos. Use GIF or PNG (see the box on page 331) for smaller files, especially if you intend to use the resulting still images on a Web page.

3. **Click Options.**

   At the bottom of the resulting Preferences window, you can choose whether you want PowerPoint to save *all* the slides in the show as graphics or just this one. In addition, you can set up the *file resolution* or *dimensions*. (Choose one or the other—they both adjust the file's pixel dimensions.) If you want high quality graphics for printing or viewing large on screen, try 180 dpi or 1800×1350 pixels—either results in exactly the same size file. Finally, you can specify whether to compress the file (if you need to make it smaller for emailing, for example). The Image Quality pop-up menu's choices run from Least (high compression, small file size, and low quality) to Best (no compression, large file size, and high quality).

Tip: You don't need to set up these options time after time; you can set up your preferred settings only once, on the PowerPoint → Preferences → Save tab. There you'll find the identical graphics-saving options, which affect the proposed values for all your subsequent graphics-saving exploits.

---

4. **Change the settings as desired, click OK; then name the still image and click Save.**

   If you opted to save all of the slides, PowerPoint automatically creates a *folder* bearing your file's name. Inside the folder are the individual graphics files, with names like *Slide1.jpg*, *Slide2.jpg*, and so on.

Printing Your Presentation

Although PowerPoint is primarily meant to display images on a monitor or projected on a screen, you can also print out your slideshow on good old-fashioned paper—which is especially useful, of course, for printing handouts, overheads, and notes. Whatever the format, all printing is done through the same basic procedure: Open the presentation you want to print, make a few adjustments in the Page Setup dialog box and the Print dialog box, then print away.

Page Setup

Before printing your presentation, you should pop open the hood and take a peek at File → Page Setup (see Figure 17-11). After all, this important window is the engine that controls the size of your slides, whether they're for onscreen viewing or printing. Doing so brings you face to face with Microsoft's version of the Page Setup box, which presents you with a pop-up menu offering several preset slide sizes: On-screen show (multiple versions), US Letter, US Ledger, A3, A4, and so on. If you have a custom slide size in mind, you can set its width and height here as well.

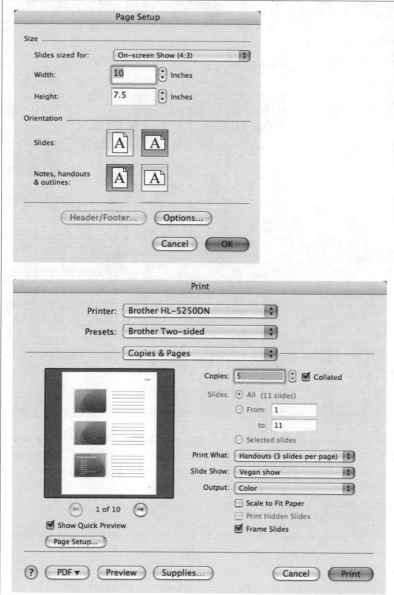

Figure 17-11:
*Top: The basic options in the
Page Setup dialog box let you
size your slides and set a
separate orientation (portrait or
landscape) for slides and other
documents—notes, handouts,
and outlines—that you want to
print.*

*Bottom: In the Print dialog box,
use the Print What pop-up menu
to print an outline, notes, various
styles of Handouts—or full-page
slides. The Output pop-up menu
lets you save your color printer's
ink—and your time—by choosing
Grayscale or Black and White.*

As noted at the beginning of Chapter 16, be sure to make any size adjustments
early in the game; if you fiddle with the knobs in Page Setup *after* the slide has been
made, it'll stretch to fit, possibly giving the image a warped or distorted look, or
knocking certain graphics off the edges altogether. It's worth noting however that
On-screen Show (4:3), Letter Paper (8.5×11 in) and Overhead all use the same
size: 10×7.5 inches.

A Presentation in Your Pocket

If you have an iPod, you have another option for presenting PowerPoint slideshows: you can ask everyone to gather round and watch a slideshow on your iPod screen. Or, more realistically, you can hook your iPod to a TV, monitor, or video projector and run your presentation straight from the iPod—no computer required.

What *is* required is an iPod that can do TV output, and the appropriate video output cable. In early 2008, that means one of the following iPod models:

- iPod Touch
- iPhone
- iPod Nano (3rd generation)
- iPod Classic
- iPod Video (a.k.a. 5th generation)
- iPod with color display (iPod Photo)

Begin by sending your presentation slides to iPhoto as described on page 710, which results in an album in iPhoto containing your slideshow.

Connect your iPod to your computer, triggering iTunes to launch. In the iTunes window, click your iPod's Photos tab and turn on the checkbox marked "Sync photos from iPhoto." Then click the "Selected albums" button and turn on the checkbox for the slide show album in the scrolling list window. Finally, click the Sync button and iTunes sends your slides into the iPod.

Disconnect your iPod from your computer, and you'll find your slideshow in the Photos section. Visit the Slideshow Settings department and adjust such things as time per slide, music, and transitions. Set the TV Out setting to either Ask or On.

Connect your iPod to a TV, monitor, or video projector. If you're using a soundtrack, make sure to connect the iPod's audio output as well as video. Return to the iPod's Photos category and start the show. Use the Next/Fast-forward button to advance to the next slide, or the Previous/Rewind button to return to the previous slide. For further details on using your iPod to play slideshows launch iTunes and choose Help → iPod Help and search for slideshow.

You can use the settings in this dialog box to morph your slideshow into something appropriate for another format—taking it from an overhead projector to a Web banner, for instance. Also, if you want to send your presentation out to be printed at a real print shop, you can adjust the presentation's resolution by clicking the Options button in the PowerPoint → Preferences → Save As panel.

Tip: If you need the options available in the familiar Mac OS X Page Setup dialog box, you can get there quickly by clicking Options in Microsoft's version of the Page Setup dialog box.

Click Header/Footer to make text (such as a slide number, page number, or date) appear on the top or bottom of every slide, or every note and handout. On each tab in the "Header and Footer" dialog box, click the checkboxes and watch the Preview at the lower right to see where the different text elements appear. Once you've turned on a checkbox, select the box's related options and enter text as appropriate.

For example, working in the Slide tab, you can insert a slide number at the lower-right corner of each printed slide (or slide thumbnail on a handout) by turning on "Slide number" and then entering a starting slide number. Turn on "Don't show on title slide" at the bottom of the dialog box if you'd like that number hidden on *title* slides. (Although a title slide is usually the first slide in your presentation, it can theoretically appear anywhere in the show.)

Tip: You can change the locations of the footer boxes on the Slide tab by dragging them on the slide master (see page 663).

Printing Your Slides

When you're ready to commit your presentation to paper, choose File → Print (⌘-P) to bring up the Print dialog box. Here's where you tell PowerPoint exactly what you want to print—slides, handouts, notes, or an outline.

In the Print dialog box, you'll find unique PowerPoint-related print settings (see Figure 17-11, bottom). Here, you can select which chunks of your presentation you want to print (slides, handouts, notes, or the outline). From this spot you can also choose to print a custom show, provided you created one earlier. When you're ready, click Preview to check your choices one last time, or click Print to send your document to the printer.

Tip: You can choose the Layout item in the Copies & Pages pop-up menu to print one, two, four, six, nine, or 16 slides per page. With Layout chosen, use the "Pages per Sheet" pop-up menu to choose the number of slides per page. If you now return to Copies & Pages, the Quick Preview window shows just one slide per page—never fear, however, you'll see the multi-slide layout you chose emerge from the printer.

Notes and Handouts

It didn't take the world long to dispel the myth of the paperless office, and that's evident every time your audience asks you for a hard copy of your presentation. Sure, you can steer some audiences to the Web version of your presentation that you've cleverly posted to the Web in advance (be sure to point this out to your boss as a cost-saving measure you've adopted). But when that approach fails, Power-Point can print out your notes and handouts or convert them to PDF files for electronic distribution.

Every PowerPoint slide can have *notes* attached to it: written tidbits to help you get through your presentation, or to clarify points for your audience. As you build your presentation, the Notes pane in PowerPoint's Normal view provides a place to type notes for each slide. (These notes appear on Web pages if you leave "Include slide notes" turned on in the Appearance tab of the Web Options dialog box when saving your presentation as a Web page.)

Handouts are printouts of your slides, usually featuring multiple slides per sheet of paper. They let your audience take your entire show away with them on paper, to spare them from having to take notes during the meeting. Handouts don't include notes; you'll have to print those out separately.

Note: Both notes and handouts have master pages, which work the same as slide masters; see page 662 for details.

To print your notes and handouts, choose File → Print (⌘-P). This summons a Print dialog box specific to PowerPoint. In the Print What pop-up menu, you can choose to print notes or handouts in layouts that show two, three, four, six, or nine slide miniatures per sheet (see Figure 17-11). Here again, if you click Preview, you'll be shown an onscreen preview of the printout-in-waiting, which you can then save as a PDF file as described above.

Tip: The beauty of the Mac OS X Preview function is that it lets you convert your PowerPoint document— or *any* document—into a PDF file (otherwise known as an Acrobat file). Anyone with almost any kind of computer (Mac, Windows, or Unix) can open the resulting document using the free Acrobat Reader program. (You can create a PDF file immediately by clicking PDF → Save As PDF in the Print dialog box.)

Of course, sending people a PDF file of your presentation isn't quite as exciting as sending them a Quick-Time movie complete with animations and multimedia. But a PDF document is compatible with far more computers. (Plus, it's less detrimental to forests than distributing printouts on paper.)

Part Five:
Office As a Whole

5

Chapter 18: Saving Time with the Project Gallery and Toolbox

Chapter 19: Making the Most of Graphics

Chapter 20: Customizing Office

Saving Time with the Project Gallery and Toolbox

The Project Gallery

No matter which Office program you launch (by clicking its Dock icon, for example), you're greeted by a special document-launching window elegantly named the Project Gallery. The idea is that you don't have to even know the Office program you're going to use for the document—they're all accessible from this central point.

Since Office 2001, the Project Gallery has been the repository for icons that represent the kinds of Word documents and other types of files Office can create for you. (Use the scroll bar to see all of them.) You'll see canned *templates* for résumés, budgets, brochures, fax cover letters, and dozens of others—not to mention Excel, PowerPoint, and Entourage documents like spreadsheets and blank email messages. The idea is that you don't have to launch (or even know) the Office program you're going to use for the document. From anywhere in Office, you can create or open any kind of document. Choose File → Project Gallery in any Office program, or memorize the keystroke Shift-⌘-P.

Tip: If you want to save some of your valuable dock real estate, you can delete those bulky Excel, Word, and PowerPoint icons, and whenever you want to work in Office, just click the Project Gallery icon. Unless you tell it to do otherwise, when you install Office 2008, it plunks the Project Gallery icon. (If not, you can drag it there from Applications → Microsoft Office 2008 → Office Folder.)

The Project Gallery also boasts the nifty ability to access projects you create in Entourage's Project Center. These projects are powerful organizational tools—just the thing you need to keep tabs on everything involved in projects large and small, from planning your honeymoon or writing a screenplay, to crafting a complex health-care proposal or managing your band's Asian tour. Projects track all emails, documents, and files associated with the project and place them in a handy location accessible from Entourage—or any other Office 2008 and program. (See Chapter 11 for more details on projects.)

Tip: If you'd rather not visit the Project Gallery every time you launch Word, choose Word → Preferences → General, and turn off "Show Project Gallery at startup." If you'd rather not see the Project Gallery when you start *any* Office program, click the Project Gallery's Settings tab and turn off "Show Project Gallery at startup."

Opening Documents

Opening any kind of document in the Project Gallery works like this: Click the list items and their flippy triangles in the Category list on the left (see Figure 18-1) until you see the desired template or document type on the right. Then use the scroll bar to see all of the documents of that type, and double-click the icon of your choice to open it.

To see how it works, let's first assume you need to print out some business cards for your new endeavor. Click the flippy triangle next to the Coordinated Forms category (or double-click Coordinated Forms). Then click Business Cards; an assortment of colorful card templates appears in the window. (Icon view is the best way to get an overview of what's available. Click the left-most button just above the category list to switch to icon view.) Double-click a template; a new document opens, all formatted and ready for you to input your own name and other information.

Note: In the icon view, clicking any category adjacent to a flippy triangle displays the generic Project Gallery screen. The screen identifies each of the Project Gallery tabs (see page 2 for details). Click the flippy triangle adjacent to a category, and then a template group under it to see the actual templates.

Choosing Made Easy

Whether you're continuing work on your magnum opus to rival *Harry Potter*, or writing a quick thank-you note to your grandmother, the tabs at the top of the Project Gallery window are a perfect place to start.

New

By now you can guess what the icons on this tab do: open brand-new empty documents, waiting for your own words. Ah, but what kind of document? Several categories of new documents invite your perusal:

- **Blank Documents.** Contrary to the name, not all of these are fresh-linen-flapping-in-the-breeze blank. This category not only includes blank Word documents, PowerPoint presentations, Entourage emails, and Excel Workbooks,

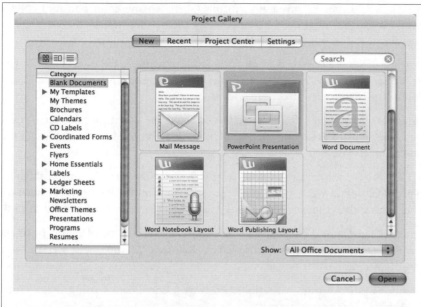

Figure 18-1:
Top: When you launch an Office program, the Project Gallery appears, assuming that you want to open a new, blank document in Word, Excel, Entourage , or, in this case, PowerPoint.

Bottom: If you'd rather not use the Project Gallery's services, click Settings and turn off "Show Project Gallery at startup."

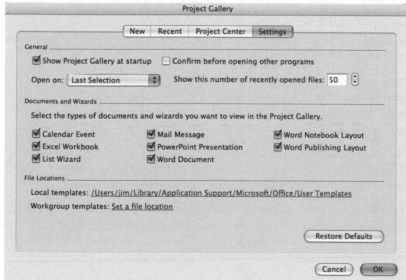

but also a List Wizard for your next get-out-of-town packing list, a shortcut to enter Entourage calendar events, or a spanking-new Word Notebook or Word Publishing Layout.

- **My Templates.** If you've saved any of your own Office documents as templates, Office tucks them away in Home → Library → Application Support → Microsoft → Office → User Templates → My Templates folder, and displays them in this much easier-to-get-to location.

- **My Themes.** If you've saved any custom Office Theme color and font collections, you'll find them here. To find actual theme files, follow the path to My Templates, above, but take a left turn at the My Themes folder.

- **Brochures.** Spread the word about your ocean-view B&B, the benefits of Laughter Yoga, or your videography services by starting with one of these Word Publishing Layout view brochure layouts.

- **Calendars.** Here you'll find a selection of attractive monthly calendar layouts created in Word's Print Layout view. (Unfortunately, you have to change all the date numbers yourself.)

- **CD Labels.** Design and print your own CD or DVD labels starting with these Word Publishing Layout view templates, and then print them on pre-cut, stick-on labels (this such as those available from Avery's CD Stomper; *www.cdstomper.com*).

- **Coordinated Forms.** This category contains an assortment of Word business forms—Agendas, Business Cards, Faxes, Invoices, Memos, and Reports—in coordinated designs.

- **Events.** Create Awards, Invitations, Postcards, and Posters using these Word Publishing Layout view templates.

- **Flyers.** Did your dog run away, or do you need to publicize your next garage sale on the community bulletin board? Choose one of these fine templates—some bulletin-board-ready with tear-off reminder tabs.

- **Home Essentials.** These documents help with the ever-more-complex task of home management. This collection of Excel templates is at the ready to help you get your home in order with loan worksheets, investment calculators, home budgets, meal planners, travel itineraries, and so on.

- **Labels.** Instead of templates this category contains only a single item: the Mailing Label Wizard. When it's time to cast your holiday newsletter to the four winds via snail mail, begin your Word mailing label production here.

- **Ledger Sheets.** A new addition to the Excel template collection for 2008, these preconfigured worksheets are ready for a variety of everyday financial calculations—from tracking your checkbook, to minding an event budget, to filing your expense report.

- **Marketing.** More Word Publishing Layout view templates await here. If your Taco truck needs a new menu, your Buddha shop a new catalog, your city council a new proposal, or your pancake breakfast a new sign; this is the place to start.

- **Newsletters.** If you need a newsletter that's sophisticated, hip, or childlike—or something in-between—these Word Publishing Layout view templates can get you going quickly.

- **Office Themes.** Dozens and dozens of PowerPoint slideshow templates are designed to match your many moods and color preferences.

- **Presentations.** These special PowerPoint templates are complete presentations filled with images and data. Use them as a starting point for your own, or to get a better idea of what PowerPoint can do. Especially recommended: *Introducing PowerPoint 2008*.

- **Programs.** The school play, a recital by a visiting virtuoso, or a family reunion—all are candidates for an informative program. Create one starting with these templates.

- **Resumes.** Whether you're on the job hunt, updating your vitae, or just recording your accomplishments in life, these résumé templates get the job done.

- **Stationery.** These Word templates give you a leg up creating different styles of letters, letterheads, or envelopes. In addition, an Envelope Wizard and a Letter Wizard help you create each of those items via the Wizard interview process.

Keystrokes of the Very Busy

Within the Project Gallery, after you have selected a template type—such as Agendas—you can jump from the category list at left to the templates in the right or middle panel by pressing Tab. Once you've highlighted one of these lists, a blue box surrounds the list, indicating that it's active. Pressing the up and down arrow keys moves you up or down the lists. When the templates are in icon view, you can press any of the four arrow keys to highlight successive icons. (Sorry, Mac OS purists: You can't jump to a particular template by typing the first letters of its name.)

When you've highlighted a category (in the left-side list) marked by a "flippy triangle," press ⌘-right arrow to expand it, or ⌘-left arrow to collapse it again. And when you've finally highlighted the template you want, pressing Return or Enter opens it, of course.

Recent

Clicking this button displays a list of recent documents you've worked on, categorized by relative dates (today, yesterday, last week, and so on). Double-click one of these document icons to open the document. Alternatively, you can select the document and then mouse over to the Open as Copy button if you'd like to preserve your original and make a new version.

You might want to open a copy if, for instance, you're writing a contract for your performance at the Oyster Festival, and you want to base it on the contract you created for the Azalea Festival. Since most of the content will probably remain the same, there's no need to start the document from scratch. (The Open Copy option in the standard Open file dialog box serves the same purpose, but it's nice to have it in the Project Gallery.)

Detrius Jetski

12 Front St. • Carmel, CA 95519
Phone: 707-515-6464 • E-Mail: Dete@jetskya.com

Objective

Donec sollicitudin mi et magna. Proin non est. Vestibulum diam. Quisque in enim. Sed id dui. Nunc nec sapien. Nulla lacus. Quisque in ante vel nunc semper pellentesque. Nam sit amet lacus sit amet ipsum auctor eleifend. Quisque vitae justo eu neque mattis pellentesque. Suspendisse tristique. Nulla facilisi. Pellentesque hendrerit tristique turpis. Pellentesque eget mi. Vestibulum a lacus.

Experience

Ditch Digger   1999 - Present

Etiam cursus suscipit enim. Nulla facilisi. Integer eleifend diam eu diam. Donec dapibus enim sollicitudin nulla. Nam hendrerit. Nunc id nisl. Curabitur sed neque. Pellentesque placerat consequat pede.

Lorem Ipsum dolor   [Insert Dates]

Lorem Ipsum Dolor!
                              Dolor Sit Amet.

Lorem Ipsum Dolor!
                              Dolor Sit Amet.

Quisque libero.

Where?
Nulla consequat accumsan arcu.
Donec feugiat nisl vel dolor.

When?
[Date, Time]

How?
Suspendisse magna felis, eleifend

Quisque libero.

Where?
Nulla consequat accumsan arcu.
Donec feugiat nisl vel dolor.

When?
[Date, Time]

How?
Suspendisse magna felis, eleifend

Figure 18-2:
Top: The Initials Resume template in the Project Gallery's Resumes category provides a clean, modern template to help you land that clean, modern job.

Bottom: One of the many new Publishing Layout View templates, the Informal Invitation in the Events category is formatted for double-sided printing. Just plug in the appropriate information for your next fete and replace the picture with one of your own (unless it is you and your happy friends in this picture).

Conversely, if you're writing the great American novel (or Australian, Armenian, or Azerbaijani), you'll probably want to keep your current chapter in one document, so you'll use the Open button and save over the original document.

Project

Clicking here displays the projects that you've created in the Project Center as shown in Figure 18-3. The Project Center lets you organize complete projects; you can centralize email, Excel files, contacts, documents, and so on in one location. For example, you can place your proposal document for a new restaurant, pictures of possible locations, and all the emails concerning the enterprise in the same project. For more details, see Chapter 11.

Tip: You can also access your projects from the Projects panel of the Toolbox palette. See page 729.

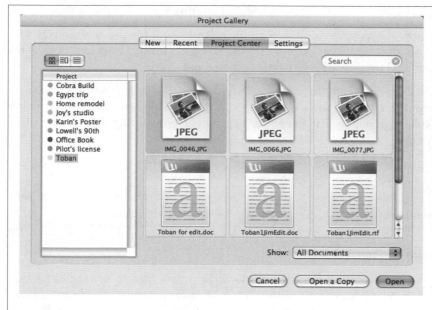

Figure 18-3:
Right here in the Project Gallery, you can see every project you've created in the Entourage Project Center (Chapter 11), complete with all the relevant photos, emails, notes, and documents related to the project. If you have a little trouble getting oriented before your second cup of coffee, this screen is a great place to start your day (although starting in the Project Center in Entourage itself isn't a bad idea either). Use the Project Gallery's Settings tab to open to this screen when you first launch Office for the day.

Settings

Click this tab to access the Project Gallery's preferences. Here you can choose whether you want to show Project Gallery on startup, which types of documents/files you wish it to show, how many recent files to remember, and where to keep your local and workgroup templates. For example, you can have Office remember virtually every document you've used for the past year, or make it show only the templates that your department is supposed to use.

Tip: You can add categories to the Project Gallery's collection by creating new folders in Home → Library → Application Support → Microsoft → Office → User Templates, alongside your My Templates folder. For example, you might want a folder of templates called *Lesson Plans* or *Quizzes*. See page 21 for more about saving templates.

Tweaking the Project Gallery

You can also customize the Project Gallery using the following buttons and menus (see Figure 18-1):

- **View.** These buttons let you choose to view the Project Gallery either in icon view, detail view, or list view. In icon view, each document is represented like a big square, just like the squares on the button. In list view (click the button with the lines on it), the panel of large document icons is replaced by a list of smaller icons. Detail view is a combination: a list view in the center window and at the right, a preview panel where you can see a large preview of what you're about to open, along with file kind, size, and date information

- **Show.** This pop-up menu is like a filter. If you want to view *only* templates for Word documents, for example, choose Word Documents from here. You won't see Excel templates, PowerPoint templates, and so on.

  On the other hand, the setting called All Office Documents has its advantages. From this panel, you can open up any kind of Office document or template without having to first launch the appropriate program by visiting your dock, for one.

- **Open Other.** Click this button to display Office's standard Open dialog box.

Tip: If you tinker with the Project Gallery settings and have a subsequent change of heart, you can always return to the original settings by clicking the all-powerful Restore Defaults button.

Ditching the Project Gallery

To dismiss the Project Gallery, click Cancel or press the Esc key (or ⌘-period). Word, Excel, or PowerPoint automatically opens a new blank document. If you'd rather open an existing document, click Open Other or use one of the methods described below.

Toolbox

Unlike the toolbox in the corner of your garage, Office 2008's Toolbox is easy to get to, puts itself away with the click of a mouse, and is never missing a 9/16" socket. Better still, it can do many things your disorganized, red toolbox could never do. For example, it can store your snippets of inspiration (pictures, text, and so on), provide definitions and other research aids, check your document's compatibility, or provide a window into Office's Project Center. Office 2008 adds the formerly-separate Formatting Palette to the Toolbox, bringing its total number of sections to seven—and making it the one-stop location for tools of all types.

Word, Excel, and PowerPoint share the six standard Toolbox sections: Formatting Palette, Object Palette, Scrapbook, Reference Tools, Compatibility Report, and Project Center. In addition, each program adds one palette of its own. Word has Citations (page 215), Excel has the Formula Builder (page 533), and PowerPoint has the Custom Animation palette (page 693). Those program-specific palettes are discussed in each of the program chapters, and the Formatting Palette and Object Palette are covered in the Word chapters (page 17). Entourage makes use of only three

Toolbox palettes—Scrapbook, Reference Tools, and Object Palette—which you can only access via the Tools → Toolbox menu (or by adding the Toolbox button to the Entourage Standard toolbar).

What follows is a description of the remaining Office-wide Toolbox sections.

Scrapbook

Think of the Scrapbook as, well…a scrapbook. It's a location where you can drag copied snippets from documents or pictures, or Excel spreadsheets.

After opening the Scrapbook, as described in Figure 18-4, copy your text (or whatever) into the Scrapbook window by dragging it or using any of the conventional cut, copy, and paste methods. To reuse the material, click the Paste button (near the middle of the Scrapbook) to paste the material shown in the Scrapbook window into your cursor's current location. There are three pasting options:

- **Paste.** This most common option pastes the material in the exact same format that you copied it.

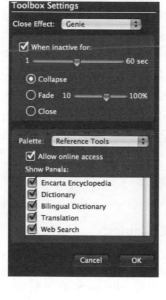

Figure 18-4:

Left: You can open the Scrapbook from any Office 2008 program by selecting Tools → Toolbox → Scrapbook or clicking the Toolbox icon on the Standard toolbar (but not on the Entourage toolbar unless you add the button), and then clicking the Scrapbook icon at the top of the Toolbox. Drag or paste text, pictures, or Excel spreadsheets into the Scrapbook—and there they'll stay until you need them. Copy a clipping from the Scrapbook by dragging it onto your document (or by using any of the usual keyboard shortcuts).

Right: Click the arrow button in the upper right-hand corner to reach the Toolbox Settings, which swivel into view (right). Turn on the "When inactive for" checkbox to cause the toolbox to stash itself away after a certain period of inactivity. The bottom panel determines what you see when you use the various toolbox palettes.

- **Paste as Plain Text.** By golly, they weren't kidding. Use this button if you want to remove all the formatting and paste it as just plain text.

- **Paste as Picture.** This command pastes your snippet as a picture you can format using any of Office's picture tools like color adjustment and shadowing, as described in Chapter 20. You can use this to turn, say, a drawing object into a picture and thus avail yourself of the picture tools.

On the other hand, the Add button takes the selected text, picture, table, or whatever, and transfers it to the Scrapbook. There are four options:

- **Add Selection.** An alternative to the Copy command, this option instantly adds your current selection to the Scrapbook. This is handy if you've highlighted a piece of text—a clever email joke, for example—that you wish to paste into other Office programs.

- **Add File.** Adds the current file to the Scrapbook. It can be any Office document.

- **Add From Clipboard.** Pastes whatever is in your clipboard to the Scrapbook.

- **Always Add Copy.** A good one for the time-challenged or compulsive hoarders among us. After you click this, *anything* you copy or cut is pasted directly into the Scrapbook.

If you have a scrap you no longer need, you can delete it with the delete key or by pressing the Delete button. Three delete options exist on the Delete pop-up menu:

- **Delete.** This choice is the plain, garden-variety delete. It deletes the currently selected clipping.

- **Delete Visible.** Deletes the clipping in the preview window.

- **Delete All.** Deletes all clippings.

Note: When you delete a clipping, it's gone—a part of history. There's no way to get it back. Kind of like your first kiss.

Organizing Clippings

If you have a lot of clippings to keep track of—or you're one of those people who has a Club card at the Container Store—you might want to click the Organize title bar. Doing so lets you place the currently selected clipping into categories and projects (by clicking the appropriate pop-up menu and selecting the desired category or project).

You may also add keywords, which is a great idea when you have tons of clippings. Assigning a Keyword lets you search for the clipping by that word. For example, you might want to add the words, *Thanksgiving, apple,* and *hari,* as keywords for the recipe to Hari's apple pie that he brought to Thanksgiving dinner. To do so, type the words in the box and click Add. Highlighting words and clicking Revert removes them.

Use the pop-up menu at the top of the window to filter your clippings by creation date, project, category, keywords, and so on. Finally, the View pop-up menu lets you view your clippings by List or by Large Preview (if you prefer those over the standard Detail view).

Reference Tools

Like Wikipedia on your iPhone, Word's built-in Reference Tools are handy, easy to use, and out of the way until you need them. Because it's electronic, it also has some unexpected features. Click the Toolbox, and then the Reference Tools tab to open the Reference Tools. Below are the most commonly used dictionary features.

To look up a word in a document, highlight the word, and then choose Tools → Dictionary (or press Shift-Option-⌘-R) or type the word into the window at the top of the Reference Tools. (If no word is highlighted, you can still click to open the dictionary.) You can also control-click (or right-click) the word right in your document and choose Look Up → Definition from the shortcut menu.

Now the word appears in the Dictionary pane with its pronunciation and definitions. Click the language pop-up menu if you'd like to look up the dictionary definition in a different language. Figure 18-5 shows some other ways to use the dictionary.

To go directly to a word, type it in the small box at the top and press Return. The word appears in the dictionary pane. The thesaurus section provides similar words and synonyms. Replace your original word with the selected synonym by clicking Insert. Choosing Look Up provides a definition of the currently selected word.

Searching the Encarta Encyclopedia or MSN provides additional information about the word. This is useful when you want additional information on a word or when the kids are working on a report. Type the word in the upper box and then click Search Encarta Encyclopedia or Search MSN.

You can copy the text of the definition to paste in a Word document, your Scrapbook, email message, and so on. Just drag to select the text in the definition window and then press ⌘-C (or Control-click the definition and choose Copy Article or Copy Selection from the shortcut menu).

Projects Palette

Clicking the Projects Palette button (it looks like a sleek metal briefcase) opens a window into the wonderful world of Projects, a feature extensively covered in Chapter 11. The abbreviated Projects palette available through the Toolbox lets you page through your projects by clicking the tiny triangle next to the current project name, and selecting the project you wish to view from the pop-up menu.

There's also quite a bit more that you can do from this panel, without actually going to the Project Center window. Below the title and picture is a bar that displays when the project is due, along with four buttons:

- **Add Current File.** Adds your current file to the list of files in the project.

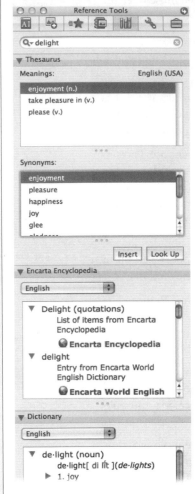

Figure 18-5:
After you type a word into the small box at the top of the Reference Tools, and press Return, you may click the small flippy triangle next to Thesaurus, Encarta Encyclopedia, Dictionary, Bilingual dictionary, Translation, or Web Search, to browse the information. Type a word, such as "delight," for example, and click Thesaurus to find synonyms such as "joy," "glee," and "enchantment." When you click one of the results from Encarta Encyclopedia, Office starts your browser, tools over to Encarta, and shows you the relevant article.

- **Remove Current File.** Removes current file from the list of files in the project.

- **Open Entourage Project Watch Folder.** Opens the project watch folder in Entourage associated with the project.

- **Open Finder Project Watch Folder.** This opens the actual folder where your project watch files are stored.

Below these buttons is the schedule section, which is like a mini day-by-day calendar. It shows the events relating to your currently selected project. Click the blue star to schedule a new event, and the arrows to click through the days.

The "Notes to Self" are just that. You can type directly into this box, or drag high-lighted text into it. Scroll the text using the scroll bar.

Underneath the schedule are the tasks associated with the project. Double-click any of them to open it. In order to celebrate a task's completion you can click to place a checkmark in the box. To set or change the task's priority, right-click the task itself, select Priority, and choose one from the shortcut menu. Any changes you make here are reflected in the Project Center itself.

And finally is a list of email messages associated with the project. Double-click to open and read the message in a separate window.

Although you can do a lot from the Toolbox, sometimes you just need the big picture. Click the big "Go to Project Center" button at the bottom of the Projects palette, and Entourage opens to the Project Center—easy as that.

Compatibility Report

The Compatibility Report checks to see if the document you're emailing to your boss will actually open in his ancient copy of Word 97 (for example). The vagaries of document compatibility—even if they were all created in one version of Microsoft Office or another—can be incredibly complex. Sometimes a feature works fine, other times it doesn't. Sometimes a document just looks and works differently for no apparent reason. The Compatibility Checker makes it simple to figure out what's going on—and even do something about it.

Note: If you open a document that was created in another program or another version of Office, there probably are compatibility issues. The Toolbox icon on the Standard toolbar throbs when Office detects any incompatibility, even something so minor that you may not notice. Click the icon to open the Toolbox and find out what's up.

In addition to checking on the current document, you can also utilize this feature to make a document "backward compatible" to someone with an older version of Office. The Compatibility Report warns you if you're using features that may not work in other versions.

Open the Toolbox, click the wrench icon to open the Compatibility Report panel (or just choose View → Compatibility Report), and proceed as follows:

1. **From the "Check compatibility with" pop-up menu, choose the document type with which you want to compare your open document.**

   Office checks your document for compatibility. In a few seconds, it displays a list of potential problems in the top (Results) window. (Click Check Document if the check doesn't begin immediately.)

2. **Click one of the items in the Results window for more information.**

   A more complete explanation appears in the bottom window.

---

3. **Choose an action.**

   You can click the buttons in the middle of the panel to either Fix or Ignore the error, or "Don't show again." (You can reset those ignored items by choosing Preferences → Compatibility and clicking Reset Ignored Issues.) Sometimes, there is no fix, but Office just wants to explain that some new features may not be available in older documents. If there is something you can do to remedy the problem, such as find the correct document template, the Explanation window often provides a link you can click to go right to work. You can also click the Help button to get more information.

Click the Recheck Document button any time to repeat the checkup as you make your modifications.

Making the Most of Graphics

Office comes with Word for text, Excel for numbers, PowerPoint for slides, and Entourage for email and scheduling. From reading the box, you might conclude that Office is therefore missing one of the cornerstone Macintosh programs: graphics software.

In fact, however, Office comes with a herd of graphics tools, including Office 2008's new SmartArt graphics, the Clip Gallery, AutoShapes, WordArt, and more—built right in and shared among Word, Excel, and PowerPoint.

Inserting a Graphic

You can drag, paste, or insert a picture into a Word, Excel, or PowerPoint document. To insert a graphic, choose Insert → Picture or click the Insert Picture button on the Drawing toolbar (in Entourage choose Message → Insert → Picture) and then select one of the following from the submenu:

- **Clip Art** opens the Office Clip Gallery, as described below.

- **From File** opens a dialog box where you can choose any graphics file on your Mac.

- **Horizontal Line** (Word only) is a quick way to put a horizontal line between paragraphs without opening the "Borders and Shading" dialog box. These lines are actually GIF files. They're more decorative than standard lines and borders, and ideal for use on Web sites (see Chapter 9).

- **AutoShapes** are expanded, elaborate versions of the familiar circles and squares that you create with drawing tools. For instance, AutoShapes include arrows, cubes, banners, and speech balloons.

These two items you choose directly from the Insert menu:

- **WordArt** lets you change the look of text in a number of wacky, attention-getting ways. After typing the text, you can stretch, color, and distort it, using Office's drawing tools (page 737).

- **SmartArt Graphic** lets you insert pre-designed graphics that show things like process flows, hierarchies, relationships, and so on.

The Clip Gallery

Clip art refers to a canned collection of professionally drawn, cartoon-like illustrations designed for use in a wide variety of documents. Designing a birthday card for a child? You can count on finding a soccer ball or kite in any self-respecting clip-art collection. Need a sketch of people at the office for a newsletter article about business travel? Off you go to the clip-art collection.

Fortunately, Office comes with hundreds of pieces of ready-to-use art in a collection called the Clip Gallery. And they're not all cartoonlike graphics either. You'll find 86 stock photographs you can use in your documents without having to worry about securing copyright permissions—everything from flowers, cute animals, and babies to businesspeople, landscapes, and athletes. To review them, choose Insert → Picture → Clip Art. The Clip Gallery opens, as shown in Figure 19-1. (Or click the Clip Art button near the middle of the Drawing toolbar.) The Object Palette gives another portal to your Clip Art collection (see page 726). From there you can simply drag thumbnails to your document, however, it doesn't have the searching or importing features of the Clip Gallery.

Note: In Entourage, you get a "Choose a File" dialog box instead of the Clip Gallery. You have to actually navigate over to the Applications → Microsoft Office 2008 → Office → Media → Clipart folder in order to select your clip art.

Categories

The Categories button in the Clip Gallery window opens a dialog box where you can delete categories from, or add categories to, the Clip Gallery. Neither process deletes or adds any actual pictures; they stay where they always were—in the Applications → Microsoft Office 2008 → Office → Media → Clipart folder. You're just deleting or adding category names into which the pictures can reside.

Figure 19-1:
Click a category in the list at the left to see thumbnails of the available clips. After you've done a keyword search, as shown here, your results appear in the Search Results category. Click a thumbnail and then click Insert (or just double-click the thumbnail) to place the full-size version in your document at the insertion point. (Turn on the Preview box to see the full-size image in a separate window.) When you've finished adding pictures, click Close to make the dialog box vanish.

Online

If you click the Online button, Office launches your Web browser and connects to the Microsoft Office Online Clip Art and Media page, which offers thousands of additional clip art files in a searchable database. You can download them individually or in groups by turning on their checkboxes and clicking the "Download (number of) items" link. After doing so you'll end up with a *.cil* file on your desktop; double-click it to add the images to the Clip Gallery, where they'll appear in the Favorites category.

Adding Your Own Clips

You're not limited to clip art from Microsoft. Not only can you transfer your own images into any Word document with the Insert → Picture → From File command, but you can also make them part of the Clip Gallery. This gives you the opportunity to use the Clip Gallery's search function and organizing features and see thumbnails of your own clip art, too. (iPhoto it ain't, but this feature can be handy.)

To do so, choose Insert → Picture → Clip Art to open the Clip Gallery, and then click Import. Use the Import dialog box to navigate to the graphics file you want to bring into the Clip Gallery. (Make sure the Enable menu shows "Clip Gallery Images"; the kinds of images you can import are JPEG, TIFF, PICT, GIF, PNG, or Photoshop files, as well as clip art from Microsoft.) Use the three buttons at the bottom of the window to copy, move, or create an alias for the image in the clip Gallery; then click Import.

The Properties window appears; you can give the image a new name to display in the Clip Gallery (instead of the file name) and assign categories or keywords. When you click OK, you'll find yourself back at the Clip Gallery, with your newly added image in its window.

Deleting Clips

If you want a clip out of your life forever, click it in the Clip Gallery and choose Edit → Clear. Word asks for confirmation before expunging it.

Search

When you enter a word in the Search box at the top of the Clip Gallery and click Search, Clip Gallery finds all the clips that match (or are related to) that keyword. For instance, if you type in *automobile,* Clip Gallery pulls up all the clips that have "automobile" as a keyword. Cooler yet, it also finds clips with "car" or "vehicle" as keywords—it relies on the Office 2008 Thesaurus to figure out which possible keywords mean the same thing as what you typed!

Working with Clip Art

After placing a piece of clip art into your document, you can click it to produce eight blue handles at its perimeter and one green stalk sprouting from its top. By dragging these handles, you can resize the illustration in a variety of ways:

- **Drag a side handle** to resize the figure in that dimension—drag the top one to make it taller, a side one to make it wider, and so on.

- **Dragging a corner handle** keeps an object in its original proportions as you resize it.

- **Option-drag a side handle to resize** the object from the center outward in the direction you're dragging.

- **Option-drag a corner handle** to resize an object from the center outward *and* maintain its proportions.

- **Drag the green stalk** to rotate the object (see page 744).

- **⌘-dragging** any handle overrides the *drawing grid* (see page 743).

You can also move a graphic around the screen by dragging it freely.

AutoShapes and WordArt

There are two kinds of drawings in Word: those you make yourself using Word's drawing tools (see page 148), and those Word makes for you, via features such as AutoShapes, SmartArt graphics, and WordArt.

AutoShapes

An AutoShape is a ready-made drawing object. As with the simple circle, square, and triangle of times past, you simply drag to size and place them in your document. However, you now have a plethora of new choices, courtesy of Office 2008.

To use an AutoShape in your document, click the AutoShapes button on the Drawing toolbar. (If it's not already open, choose View → Toolbars → Drawing.) Or click the Toolbox button in the Standard toolbar and click the Object Palette's Shapes tab.

As shown in Figure 19-2, each AutoShape menu (or category in the Object Palette's pop-up menu) provides a palette of choices. Click one, then release the mouse; now drag in your document to place the AutoShape—you can always resize or move it later.

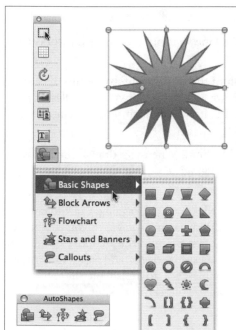

Figure 19-2:

Top Left: The tools on the Drawing toolbar give you (top to bottom): Select Objects, Grid Options, Free Rotate, Insert Picture, Clip Art, Text Box, AutoShapes, Lines, and 3-D.

Bottom Left: You can keep a mini-palette (bottom) of Auto Shapes and Lines open by dragging the palette off the Drawing toolbar.

Right: Called the "adjustment handle," the yellow diamond on some AutoShapes lets you adjust some aspect of the shape—such as the spikiness of a star.

Note: As you drag to create an AutoShape, press Shift to keep the shape in equal length-to-height proportion. For instance, select the rectangle shape and Shift-drag to create a square, or select the oval and Shift-drag to create a perfect circle. As noted earlier, you can also press Shift when dragging to resize such an object without distorting its original proportions.

Lines

Even with the immense variety of AutoShapes and WordArt, some days your own creative juices are flowing. With Office's line tools, you can draw free-form lines and combine them with arrows and AutoShapes to build your own masterpieces.

To get started, summon the Drawing toolbar by choosing View → Toolbars → Drawing, or by right-clicking a toolbar divider line and then selecting Drawing from the Toolbars submenu. Click the Lines toolbar icon, as shown in Figure 19-3. Choose a line type from the Line Style pop-up menu; then drag in your document to place the line you've selected. (As with AutoShapes and WordArt, lines lie *on top of* text in Word—and are invisible in Draft view—unless you wrap them around the text, as described on page 146.)

Figure 19-3:
When a toolbar menu has a strip of dotted lines at the top, you can drag it off the toolbar (left) to create a floating palette (right). The Lines palette contains tools for straight lines, arrows, double arrows, curved lines, free-form shapes, and scribbled lines.

You'll find that each of the options in the Lines pop-up button menu works a bit differently:

- **Line.** Drag for the position and length of the straight line you want; the cursor turns into a tiny cross. To resize the newly drawn line, drag the handles on each side, or reposition it by dragging the line itself (at which time the cursor turns into the four-arrow move cursor).

- **Arrow** and **Double Arrow** work just like lines. When you draw a single arrow, the point appears where you stop dragging; a double arrow automatically springs points on both sides.

- **Curve.** Unlike lines, you draw curves by clicking, not dragging. Click to create a starting point; as you move the mouse, the curve follows. When you click a second time, the line gently curves from the first point to the second. Continue in this same manner. (The curve tool works best for wiggles and waves rather than closed shapes.) When you're done, double-click to finish off the curve. To enclose the shape, click as close as you can to your starting point.

- The **Freeform** tool is a two-in-one special. When you drag with it, the cursor turns into a pencil and works like a pencil—you can draw lines with any bend and direction without the limitations of the Curve tool. The instant you let go of the mouse button, the cursor turns into a cross and becomes a line tool. Clicking the mouse again now draws a straight line, just as with the Line tool. Hold down the mouse button again to go back to freehand drawing.

- The **Scribble** tool is exactly like Freeform without the straight-line feature. You drag it to draw a freehand line; the line ends when you let go of the mouse button.

Editing Lines

To change the color and thickness of lines you've drawn, use the Line formatting tools on the Formatting Palette. Two other line options await only if you Control-click (or right-click) the line and choose them from the shortcut menu:

- **Edit Points.** Don't worry if your line or drawn object doesn't come out perfect on the first try. Just do the best you can, and then Control-click (or right-click) the shape and choose Edit Points from the shortcut menu. You can then drag the little dots to resize and reshape the line. This trick is especially useful for the Curve, Freeform, and Scribble tools.

- **Open Curve.** This unusual command (available on the shortcut menu only) "disconnects" the point where you closed a Curve, Freeform, or Scribble object. Now you can use the edit points to reshape the object. Should you ever want to close the gap again, Control-click the shape again and choose Close Curve.

SmartArt Graphics

Office 2008 introduces a new member to the Office graphics gang: SmartArt graphics. Like collections of AutoShapes choreographed by Busby Berkeley, SmartArt graphics let you visually communicate information in lists, processes, cycles, hierarchies, relationships, and so on. Starting with these graphical templates, you can fill in your text information, refine the formatting, and experiment with different layouts.

Click the SmartArt Graphics tab of the Elements Gallery (or choose Insert → SmartArt Graphic) to display the SmartArt gallery (see Figure 19-4, top). Use the row of style buttons to narrow your choices to List styles, Process styles, Relationship styles, and so on; and then use the scroll buttons at the right end of the Gallery to view all your choices. When you click one of the thumbnails, the graphic appears in your document surrounded by a blue selection frame and accompanied by the dark gray Text Pane (see Figure 19-4, bottom).

You can type directly on the graphic, or in the Text Pane. As you type, you'll see your words appear in the graphic. The Text Pane operates like a little outline. You can make a list of items of equal importance, or you can use the Demote button to move an item down one level of importance, or use the Promote button to elevate an item in importance. As you do, the text in your graphic reflects the new

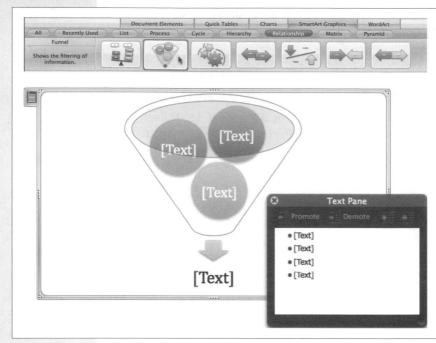

Figure 19-4:
Top: As you hold your cursor over a SmartArt thumbnail in the Elements Gallery, a short description of the diagram appears at the left. Click a thumbnail to insert it in your document.

Bottom: You can enter text either directly in the diagram or in the Text Pane. The button on the upper-left corner of the selection frame hides or reveals the Text Pane.

arrangement, with added or removed bullet points. Two more buttons let you add or remove items from your outline—which you can also accomplish with the Return key and the Delete key.

As you add text to your outline, SmartArt's canniness becomes evident, as it automatically adjusts container size and font size to accommodate your words—always keeping the entire group balanced and in proportion.

When you're working with SmartArt graphics, the SmartArt Graphic Styles pane joins the Formatting Palette. By clicking its various Styles Buttons, you can instantly transform your flat graphic into a variety of 3-D configurations. Similarly, the Colors tab gives a selection of colorization schemes, based on your Document Theme colors.

As you work with a SmartArt graphic, you can click other SmartArt thumbnails in the Elements Gallery to see how your information would look in a different format—and always come back to your original design. For example, you might start out thinking your relationship comparison data would work well in a Balance diagram, but then discover a simple Venn diagram gets your point across much more clearly (see Figure 19-5, bottom).

Although it appears in your document as one unit, a SmartArt graphic is actually collection of regular graphic objects. And like other graphic objects, you can select and modify them just as you would any other graphic—as described later in this chapter and in Chapter 8.

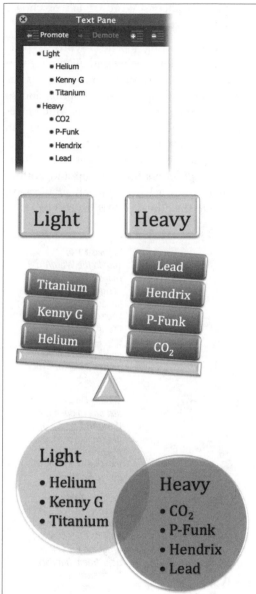

Figure 19-5:
As you enter your data in the SmartArt Text Pane (top), your words appear in the graphic (middle). Click some of the other SmartArt graphics in the Elements Gallery to see the same data displayed in different ways (bottom).

WordArt

Like an AutoShape, a piece of WordArt is a type of ready-made drawing object. In this case, it's used for special text effects—3-D, wavy, slanting, colored, and various other permutations—that would be just right on a movie poster (but should be used sparingly in other situations). Figure 19-6 shows some examples.

To create some WordArt, click the Elements Gallery's WordArt tab or choose Insert → WordArt. Then proceed as shown in Figure 19-6.

When you click a piece of WordArt, the Formatting Palette's WordArt pane appears. This pane contains three basic text tools for spacing and alignment that format the actual text of your WordArt. The Format WordArt button opens the Format dialog box where you can change color, transparency, wrapping, and so on. The most powerful button here is the first one, Format as Shape, which takes the WordArt and makes it conform to one of the 40 different shapes you can choose from the pop-up palette. Stack Text Vertically strings the text downward, so that one letter appears below the other. Equalize Character Height stretches the short letters of the selected WordArt so that all letters line up, top and bottom (except for letters with descenders—g, j, p, q, y—which are strangely unaffected). Double-clicking the WordArt itself takes you to the Edit WordArt dialog box.

Figure 19-6:
Top: In the WordArt Gallery, click a text design that strikes your fancy, and it appears in your document with "Your Text Here" as stand-in text. Click another style in the gallery to replace your first choice.

Middle: Double-click the text box to open the Edit WordArt Text dialog box. Choose a typeface, then type your text banner message; click OK when you're finished.

Bottom: Your new WordArt appears in your document. You can fine-tune its appearance by dragging the yellow adjustment handles, or by stretching or compressing the text box.

Aligning Objects

When you have multiple objects on a page, you may want them to be equally spaced or evenly aligned by their top edges. Instead of working out the measurements and aligning them manually, use Office's built-in alignment features.

To do so, select the objects that you need to line up or arrange (Shift-click each one). Then choose one of the following options from the Align or Distribute menu buttons of the Formatting Palette's Size, Rotation, and Ordering pane. Use the tiny icons on this menu as a visual clue to their functions.

- **Align Left, Align Center, or Align Right.** These commands bring the selected objects into perfect vertical alignment by their left or right edges, or centerlines.

- **Align Top, Align Middle, or Align Bottom.** These commands bring the selected objects into perfect *horizontal* alignment by their top or bottom edges, or centerlines.

- **Distribute Horizontally or Distribute Vertically.** Use these commands to spread your drawing objects across the page or from top to bottom—with an equal amount of space between each one.

You can also use the above commands on a single object, to place it at either side or in the center of a page.

The Drawing grid

Even without using the alignment commands, you might have noticed that it's fairly easy to pull objects into alignment with one another just by dragging. That's because each Word page has an invisible alignment grid that objects "snap to," as if pulled into line by a magnetic force.

To see the grid, click Grid Options on the Drawing toolbar. In the Grid Options dialog box: turn on "Display gridlines on screen;" specify a gridline separation in the "Horizontal every" box (and the "Vertical every" box too, if you like); and then click OK. Now you can see the grid's faint gray lines superimposed on your document.

Note: In Excel, the gridlines are the cell boundaries themselves. You can either snap to these gridlines or snap "To Shape" (see page 577).

Now that you know what the grid looks like, here's how to use the other Grid Options settings:

- To turn the grid off so that you can drag objects around with no spatial restriction whatsoever, turn off the appropriate option under the "Snap objects" section.

Tip: When the grid is turned off, ⌘-drag an object when you *do* want it to snap to the grid. Conversely, when the grid is turned on, ⌘-dragging a graphic moves it exactly where you put it, *without* snapping to the grid.

- You can use the "Snap objects to other objects" box with or without snapping to the grid. When this box is turned on, a dragged object snaps into alignment with the edges of the closest nearby object. If the grid is on, the nearest object overrides the grid.

• Change the default grid spacing (an eighth of an inch) by changing the measurements in the "Grid settings" boxes.

Click OK to apply the grid changes to your document.

Rotating drawing objects

You can rotate drawing objects in either of two ways: freely with the mouse, or in precise 90-degree increments.

• To rotate something, click the object, and then click the Free Rotate button (a curved-around arrow) on the Drawing toolbar. The handles on the object become green dots. Drag any dot to rotate the object on its own axis. The object jumps into its new orientation when you let go of the mouse button. (*Option*-drag to rotate the object on its end instead.)

Tip: Hold down the Shift key while you rotate to pivot in 15-degree increments.

• To rotate in 90-degree increments, click the object, and then in the Formatting Palette's Size, Rotation, and Ordering pane, choose Rotate Left or Rotate Right from the Rotate menu. Repeat the process to continue rotating the object a quarter turn at a time.

• To flip a selected drawing object, click the object, and then in the Formatting Palette's Size, Rotation, and Ordering pane, choose Flip Horizontal or Flip Vertical from the Rotate menu. Flip Horizontal reverses the object from side to side; Flip Vertical turns it head-over-heels.

Note: Pictures and clip art feature a stalk with a green handle sprouting from their top. Drag the green handle to rotate these objects, as described on page 304.

Modifying Objects

Besides arranging an object's size and placement on the page, you can also adjust the way each object looks by adjusting its various properties. Object properties include things like fill color, line color and style, drop shadow, and object opacity. The Formatting Palette, the Format dialog box, and the Color Picker have the commands for making all of these adjustments.

• **The Formatting Palette.** When you click an object, the Formatting Palette provides a plethora of graphics controls (Fill, Line, Size, and so on), the assortment of which varies depending on the type of object at hand. You'll find all of the Formatting Palette's commands duplicated in the Format dialog box—with the exception of the Quick Styles and Effects pane (see Figure 19-7).

• **The Format dialog box.** When you *double-click* an object (other than a text box) or use one of the variations of the Format → Object (Picture, Text Box, and

AutoShape) command, this massive, multitab dialog box appears (see Figure 19-7). Its various panes let you specify every conceivable aspect of the selected object.

Figure 19-7:
The Format Picture dialog box lets you massage the appearance of your inserted pictures in great detail, but using it takes time. Enter the Picture, and Quick Styles and Effects panes of the Formatting Palette. By clicking one of the six buttons across the top, you can enhance your picture with Quick Styles, Shadows, Glows, Reflections, and 3-D Effects. (Perhaps in a future Word version the Text Transforms button will actually do something.) The Picture pane gives an array of controls found in the Formatted Picture dialog box plus the vital Crop button, which lets you crop your pictures visually instead of numerically.

The Format dialog box is Office 2008's way of giving you a sneak peek at the future. Double-click a picture to see what all Format dialog boxes will look like one day (see Figure 19-8). (Apparently Microsoft didn't have time to update everything they'd planned to—and still get the software out in time for Macworld 2008. For now, the Format Picture dialog box features a nonfunctional Text Box tab; the other Format dialog boxes sport a nonfunctional Picture tab.)

Note: The following discussion focuses on the Format dialog box, since it's the most complete. Most of the choices described in this section also appear, however, in the various panes of the Formatting Palette.

Colors and Lines Tab

On this tab of the Format dialog box, you can specify a color, picture, or pattern that will fill in the interior of your picture or drawing.

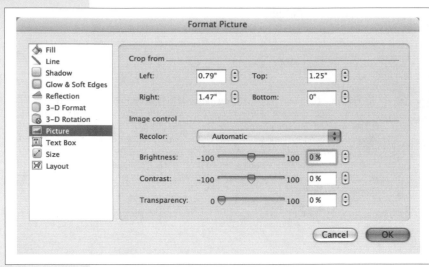

Figure 19-8:
The look of Format dialog boxes to come— available now in a Picture dialog box near you—which feature tabs in a sidebar. The Format dialog boxes for other types of objects still use Word's traditional style with the tabs on top, like the Format Text Box dialog box shown back on page 147.

Note: The "Colors and Lines" tab Fill control is designed to fill in the background of *drawing objects* and *Office clip art.* The corresponding Fills tab in the new Format Picture dialog box has no visible effect on normal pictures, but can provide a background layer that shows through if the picture has transparent areas, or if you've added Transparency in the Fill tab.

Fill Color: Standard palette

Click one of the Color pop-up menus and Word displays its array of Theme Colors— an assortment chosen to coordinate with your template, or a different collection you've chosen in the Formatting Palette's Document Theme pane—and 10 standard colors. This colorful palette appears any time you have the option to change a color in Office. You can also use it to change font color (as shown back in Figure 3-4 on page 97, for example). Click the color you want to apply.

Fill Color: More Colors

If none of the 70 colors meets with your artistic standards, choose More Colors from the Fill Color pop-up menu to open the Mac OS X color picker, which offers five different ways to select almost any color in existence. First of all, you can choose any color that you currently see on the monitor—like a sample from a favorite picture—by clicking the magnifying glass icon and then clicking anywhere on screen, as discussed in Figure 19-9.

The five square buttons at the top of the color picker reveal different panels, each of which provides a unique way to see and even blend colors. Choose the one that best matches how you're used to looking at color. Here are the various color pickers you can try:

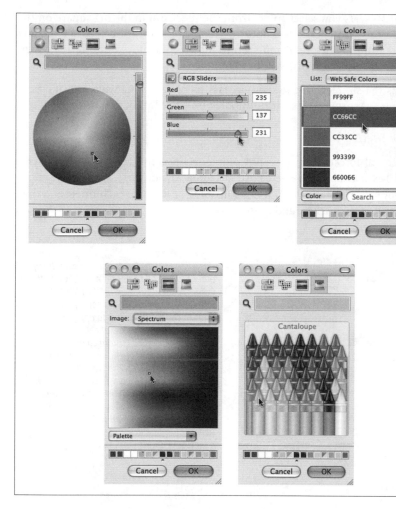

Figure 19-9:
The many faces of the Color Picker, selected from the row of buttons at its top, give you five different ways to choose colors. Click any of the color displays, or use the sliders to pick a color. You can also copy a color from anywhere on your screen in order to do things like match a text box color to that captivating blue of your baby's eyes. Click the magnifying glass and Word turns the arrow cursor into a magnifying glass. Drag it over any color on your screen and click to load that color into the swatch display at the top of the color picker. Save a favorite color by dragging it to one of the row of boxes at the bottom of the color picker—and when you fill up one row, drag the tiny button beneath the row downward to expose more empty squares.

- On the **Color Wheel** panel, you can click anywhere in the circle to choose a color from the spectrum. Use the slide on the right to make the hues brighter or darker.

- The **Color Sliders** panel gives you access to traditional color systems, like CYMK, which lets you blend the ink color used in the printing business—Cyan, Yellow, Magenta, and Black; or RGB, the system computers use to describe colors with Red, Green, and Blue. Choose your favorite color system from the pop-up menu near the top of the panel, and then click the ColorSync pop-up menu (under the magnifying glass) to fine tune your color palette for various devices—scanners, printers, and so on—or paper stocks.

- The **Color Palettes** panel lets you choose, from the pop-up menu, lists of color swatches such as Apple's standard palette or the set of colors that you can use on Web pages. Scroll through the list and click your desired color.

- **Image Palettes** lets you select colors from the spectrum in the big square on the panel. You can also choose to import a graphics file into the square and then pick colors from it—helpful if you want to match colors for your interior design scheme or latest spring sportswear collection.

- **Crayons** is the simplest one to use—as easy as picking a Crayola out of a box. (The names—Asparagus, Spindrift, Bubblegum—are lots of fun, too.)

Fill Color: Fill Effects

If you choose Fill Effects from the Fill Color pop-up menu (or use the Gradient, Picture, and Texture tabs in the new Format Picture dialog box), you get the secret dialog box shown in Figure 19-10. It has four tabs of its own, each offering a dramatic way to fill in the background of the selected object.

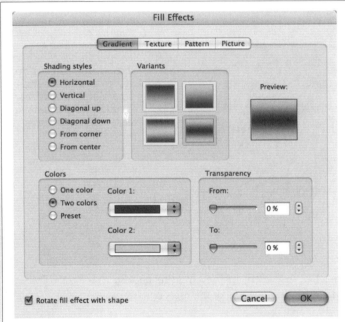

Figure 19-10:
Choosing Fill Effects lets you use something other than a solid color for a fill. Clicking the Colors radio buttons on the Gradient tab lets you use any of Word's color-picking tools to choose the colors to apply to the gradient effects. The Preset choice gives you a list of preinstalled custom color combinations with poetic names such as Late Sunset and Fog. The Transparency sliders add transparency to either end of the gradient effect. And if you turn on "Rotate fill effect with shape" then your gradients maintain their alignment with your object while you rotate it.

- For example, the **Gradient** tab lets you apply smoothly shifting colors within the interior of the drawing object—for rainbowlike, shimmery effects. Use the top controls to specify the colors you want to shift from and to; use the bottom controls to indicate the direction of shifting. Once you set the colors, style, and direction, you can apply transparency to the gradient by using the sliders at the lower right.

- The **Texture** tab is your personal Home Depot for marble, granite, burlap, and other building materials. When you need to dress up, say, a title or heading by mounting it on a stately, plaque-like rectangle, these squares are just the ticket. (Click Other Texture to choose a graphics file on your Mac that you'd like to use instead as a tiled, repeating background pattern.)

- The **Pattern** tab has a variety of two-color patterns. Using the pop-up menus at the bottom of the dialog box, you can specify which is the dark color and which is the light one.

- Finally, when you click the **Picture** tab, you'll find no pictures to choose from—at first. Click Select Picture to choose any picture file on your Mac, including, but not limited to, Office clip art. Click Insert to bring the picture into the Picture tab, where you can see what it will look like. Click OK to use the picture as a fill for your object.

Transparency

This slider, found on the Colors and Lines tab and the Formatting Palette, changes whatever color you've chosen into a transparent version. The text or objects layered above or below it remain visible through the color, courtesy of Mac OS X's Quartz graphics technology.

Line pop-up menus

In the Line section of the Colors and Lines tab, you can choose colors, dash and dot patterns, styles (single, double, and so on), weight or thickness, and transparency. All of it applies to the lines that constitute the selected object, or the frame around a text box or picture.

Pick a Line Color/Pick a Fill Color

Choosing the eyedropper tool on the Line or Fill Color menu buttons in the Formatting Palette's Colors, Weights, and Fills pane (not the Format dialog box) lets you click anywhere on your Mac's screen to pick a color. It can be in any open window, such as a Web page in your browser. When you click a color with the eyedropper, the line or fill takes on that exact color. Word then adds that color to the bottom of all Office color palettes to provide consistent color for your future use.

Arrows (drawing objects only)

If you've drawn a simple line (as opposed to an enclosed shape), you can add an arrowhead to one or both ends, using the Arrow controls here, ideal for callout text boxes or dimension lines.

Size Tab

While you can always resize an object right in your document by dragging its handles, the Size tab has other invaluable features. For example:

- **Height, Width.** These sections let you specify precise measurements for the height and width of your object, in hundredths of an inch.

- **Rotate.** This option lets you rotate an object (not a text box) to any angle.

Note: The size tab of the former Format dialog box features a Reset button which, in the olden days of previous Word versions, lets you quickly recover from sizing mistakes. Alas, the poor Reset button has lost all its powers, and does nothing when you click it. Indeed, the new Format Picture dialog box removes all memory of this useful button.

- **Scale.** These controls let you enlarge or shrink a selected graphic by a specified percentage. (If you turn on **Lock aspect ratio** before adjusting size, the drawing's original height-to-width proportions remain the same. The **Relative to original picture size** box applies only to pictures, not drawings; it lets you use the boxes in the Scale section to change the picture's size by a percentage of the original size. Thus, by changing the percentage to 200, you can double a picture's size without calculating the exact measurements.)

Note: Making bitmapped images (like digital photos) *larger* than they originally appear is a recipe for blotchiness, since you can't have more dots per inch than the image's original resolution. And if you intend to print such graphics, be aware that their standard screen resolution of 72 dots per inch looks good on the screen but isn't fine enough to produce high-quality prints. So if your document is destined for the printer, use digital images of 150 dots per inch or higher.

Picture Tab

The Picture tab and the following special effects tabs appear only in the new Format Picture dialog box, and in the Formatting Palette when you've selected a picture. The tools on the **Picture** tab, as shown in Figure 19-11, provide you precision tools to perfect your image:

- Use the **Crop from** boxes to specify, in hundredths of an inch, how much you'd like to trim off each side of a picture.

- The **Recolor** menu lets you turn your color graphic into grayscale, black and white, or washout. (The washout setting produces an extremely faint image, light enough that you can still read text that flows over it.) In addition, you can choose from a batch of dark and light variations to colorize your picture based on the Document Theme colors (see page 664).

  These choices affect only the image itself, not the fill. You adjust the fill on the Fill tab as described on page 746.

- **Brightness and Contrast** are mainly useful for touching up photographs, but they do affect clip art and other images. Increase contrast for a crisper look; decrease it for a softer effect.

- The **Transparency** control lets you make a picture completely—or just slightly—transparent, so that whatever is behind it shows through. Combining transparency with a fill color is a good way to make a tinted background image.

Figure 19-11:
Use the Formatting Palette's Picture pane to crop a picture within your document. Click the Crop button and drag any of the eight crop handles that appear. When you're satisfied with your cropping, just click outside the picture to finalize it. If you decide later you've made a mistake, select the picture again and click the Reset button to return it to its original, as-imported, state.

If you change your mind about anything you've done to a picture, remember you can undo your changes one by one by choosing the Edit → Undo command, or click the Reset button in the Formatting Palette's Picture pane to take your picture all the way back to square one.

Shadow Tab

Turning on the Shadow checkbox in this tab activates the shadowy world you control to instantly add a third dimension to your page:

- Use the **Style** pop-up menu to choose Outer, the traditional drop shadow style; Inner, to create a shadow that falls within the picture; or Perspective, to make it look like your picture object is illuminated by a Klieg light far above and to your right.

- Twist the **Angle** knob, enter the exact number of degrees, or use the up- and down-arrow button to determine the direction in which the shadow falls.

- Click the **Color** pop-up menu if you'd like your shadow to be something other than black or gray.

- The **Size** slider adjusts the size of the shadow, relative to the picture.

- Adjust the **Blur** control to affect the shadows and softness, mimicking the range from harsh, direct sun to soft window light.

- The **Distance** control determines how far from the picture the shadow falls.

- Adjust the **Transparency** control to affect the darkness of the shadow. If you have black selected as the shadow color, for example, this slider creates shadows from pure black, to gray, all the way to nonexistent.

Glow & Soft Edges

The two effects in this tab both soften the edges of a picture—but do it in very different ways.

- The **Glow** effect adds a soft frame of color around a picture—another technique to make a picture stand out on the page. Use the Color pop-up menu to choose a glow color, the Size slider to determine how wide a glowing frame to create, and the Transparency slider to soften the effect.

- The **Soft Edges** effect creates a soft or feathered edge to the picture, so it blends gradually into the page background. You'll see this technique often used in collages where one picture blends into another. Set the Glow pop-up menu to No Glow and then adjust the Soft Edges slider to see the effect.

Feel free to experiment using the Glow and Soft Edges effects together.

Reflection

Turn on the Reflection checkbox to make your pictures appear to be standing on a highly polished surface, with a reflection extending from the bottom of the picture. A modern look with which are no doubt familiar if you've been hanging around Mac OS X—or especially Steve Jobs' keynote presentations—for very long.

- The **Transparency** control determines the intensity, or density of the reflection.

- Use the **Size** slider to control how much of the picture is reflected below it, from none at zero, to the entire picture at 100%.

- When you slide the **Distance** adjustment to the right, reflection moves away from the bottom of the picture—the same effect you'd see if you were to raise the picture above the reflective surface.

3-D Format

Pixar it isn't, but Word does its best to simulate three dimensionality by giving you the option of adding 3-D effects to your pictures. Using these tools, you can transform a flat picture into what looks like a very thick picture, or a box with the picture wrapped around every side.

- The **Bevel** tab controls what the virtual sides and edges of the 3-D picture look like. Since the picture is turning into a 3-D "box," use the two pop-up menus to determine the kind of edge treatment for the top and bottom of the box. The Width settings control how far that edge intrudes into the picture; while the Height settings control the thickness or depth of the edge treatment.

- The **Depth & Surface** tab's **Depth & Contour** section controls the edge color and "thickness" of your 3-D box. Use the Depth Color pop-up menu to apply a color to the 3-D sides of your picture, and use the Depth setting to determine its thickness.

You can use the Contour Color pop-up menu and Size box to apply a color to all the edges of your box as an additional way to highlight your picture's three-dimensionality.

- The **Surface** section of the Depth & Surface tab lets you choose the material that your virtual 3-D object is built from. Use the pop-up menu to choose from shiny metal, clear glass, a matte surface, and so on. Then use the Lighting pop-up menu to control the virtual illumination for your virtual object. Choose from simple flat lighting, warm sunset light, harsh contrast lighting, and many others; and then choose the direction for your light source using the Angle control.

3-D Rotation

Once you've built a 3-D object from a picture using the 3-D Format tab, make the most of it by using the 3-D Rotation tab to orient it on the page.

- Use the **Rotation** section's Type pop-up menu to choose how your 3-D object appears as you rotate it. Choose Parallel to keep the sides of your object parallel with one another; choose perspective to make it look like the rotated object is receding into space. Then use the Perspective up- and down-arrow buttons to vary the perspective amount.

  The four Oblique settings determine which corner your object rotates around. After choosing the type of rotation, then use the X, Y, or Z buttons to perform the rotation. Click these rotation buttons to rotate 5-degree in the direction indicated on the button, or use the up-and down-arrow button to move in 1-degree increments. Of course, you can also enter a measurement directly in the box.

  You can move the rotation axis away from the plane of the object by the amount you enter in the "Distance from center" box—an effect that's especially visible if you've turned on the shadow or reflection options.

- The **Text** section provides hope that Microsoft has plans for rotating 3-D text boxes in a future version. For now, it remains a tantalizing enigma.

Object Linking and Embedding (OLE)

Linked and *embedded* objects are both chunks of data, like drawings or spreadsheets, nestled within a document in one Office program, but actually created by another.

You edit them in whatever program created them, but behind the scenes, there's a big difference in where their data is stored. A *linked* object's data is stored in a separate file (what Microsoft calls the *source* file). An *embedded* object, on the other hand, is an integral part of the file in which it appears. All its data is stored right there in the document. That's why an embedded object bloats the file size of the document containing it. However, embedding an object means that you'll never have to endure that sickening jolt when you realize you're missing an important speech that you copied to your laptop (as you might if you had only used linking).

The whole process is called Object Linking and Embedding, or OLE for short. You can't get very far on a Microsoft newsgroup or discussion board without seeing that acronym. At user group meetings, the preferred pronunciation is "olé".

Creating Linked Objects

To add a linked object to your Office document, you first have to create that object in a program that offers OLE features. On the Mac, that includes Word, Excel, and Power-Point 2008. For example, you can use linking to incorporate a drawing, spreadsheet, or chart into a Word document; weirdly enough, even another Word document can be incorporated into a Word document.

When you've created the source document, save the file, open the destination Word document, and choose Insert → Object. Besides the usual Office suspects— Excel charts and sheets, and Word documents—the Object window lets you choose from three other object types:

- **Microsoft Equation.** The place to come to create mathematical formulae. You can use its 19 pop-up menus for operators, radicals, Greek letters, and other doodads to create anything from simple fractions to complex equations. When you're done, close the window and the equation appears in your document. Since these typographically impressive equations are graphic objects instead of text, you can resize or manipulate them like any object. If you discover an error in your equation, double-click it to return to the Equation Editor

- **Microsoft Graph Chart.** Office's aged, proto-Excel graphing tool. Very basic, but it does work (see teh box on page 682).

- **Microsoft Organization Chart.** Though it gazes in awe at SmartArt's organization charts, this basic org-chart maker can still help you visualize your career ladder.

In the Object window, highlight the Object type you're after, and click From File to open the Insert as Object dialog box (Figure 19-12), where you can navigate to the source document.

When you've located the source document, select it, turn on Link to File, and click Insert. The entire contents of the source file appear in the destination document inside a resizable border. You can format this object using Word's picture-formatting tools—but to edit the *content* of the linked object, you have to open the actual source file.

Editing Linked Objects

To edit a linked object, simply double-click it. (If you have many linked objects in one document, choose Edit → Links, and then click the link you want to edit in the list box. Links can be identified by the name of the source file.)

If it isn't already running, the source program launches, and the source document opens. Now you can edit the story, rotate the drawing, or revise the numbers in the spreadsheet. When you close the source document, the linked object is automatically updated.

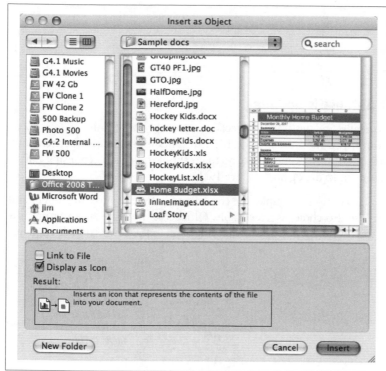

Figure 19-12:
Checking the "Display as icon" box in the Object dialog box creates an icon that links to the source document. Both linked and embedded objects can be displayed as icons.

It's easy to see the limitation of linked objects: Without the source file and the destination file on the same Mac, you can't edit the linked object. If you copy a document containing a linked object to a USB flash drive, email it, or transfer it to your MacBook Air, you'll be able to see, but not edit, the linked object. The bottom line: If you have to edit it on the road, be sure to copy the source file onto the same disk or laptop.

Repairing a broken link

If Office can't find the source file for a linked object—perhaps because you've moved or renamed it—there's a way to remind Office of its location. Choose Edit → Links and select the link in question; click Change Source. An Open dialog box appears where you can choose the source file; this is what tells Office to reconnect it to that link. Navigate to the file and double-click it.

You can use the same technique to change a linked object to a new source file altogether—such as a different graphic or a new fiscal year's ledger. Bear in mind that the new source file has to be in the same program as the original one.

Tip: This is also the technique to use if you want to create a link to only a certain part of a source file—for example, a range of cells in an Excel spreadsheet or an excerpt of a Word document that you've marked with a bookmark. (See page 240 for details on bookmarks.) Type the name of the range or bookmark in the Range/Bookmark box.

Overriding Automatic Updating

Office automatically updates linked objects every time you edit the source document. If, however, you want the linked object to remain unchanged (permanently or temporarily), there are a number of ways to go about it. Begin by choosing Edit → Links to open the Links dialog box (Figure 19-13).

- **Break Link.** This button uncouples the connection between source document and object. (Because this choice is irrevocable, Office asks if you're sure.) From now on, editing the source document does nothing at all to the destination document.

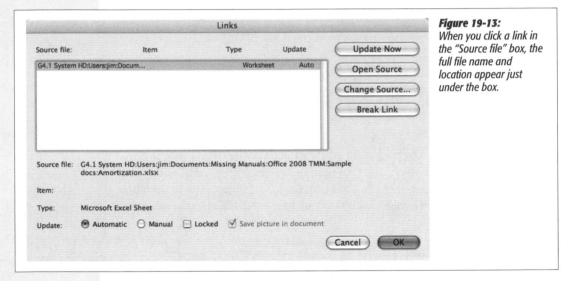

Figure 19-13:
When you click a link in the "Source file" box, the full file name and location appear just under the box.

You can't even repair the link, since the object no longer *is* a link. It becomes a picture, however, and still can be formatted as such (see page 288).

Tip: If you act quickly, you can reinstate a broken link by choosing Edit → Undo Links or pressing ⌘-Z.

- **Locked.** This box prevents changes to the source document from affecting the destination object. You can still double-click the link to open the source document, but any editing you perform there won't have any effect until you turn off the Locked box again *and* click the Update Now button in the Links dialog box.

• **Manual Updating.** Automatic is Office's default way of updating linked documents. When you choose the Manual radio button at the bottom of the Links dialog box, Word updates the linked object only when you click Update Now.

Creating Embedded Objects

Creating an embedded object from an existing file is the same as creating a linked object, except you do *not* turn on "Link to File".

To bring in an external file using this technique, choose Insert → Object. In the dialog box, proceed like this:

• **If the file you want to embed already exists:** Choose the type of file and then click From File. Navigate to and open the source document to embed a copy of it in your Office document.

• **To create a new file (for embedding) on the spot:** In the list box, double-click the kind of object you want to create: Chart, Worksheet, Picture, or whatever. A new window opens, complete with menus and toolbars, where you can begin creating the object. When you're done, close the window; the object appears in your document.

Tip: When creating an embedded picture, you can use any of Word's drawing tools, as described earlier in this chapter. However, when you close the window, the result is a *picture,* not a drawing—you can no longer edit it as you would a drawing.

If, on the other hand, you simply want to insert a drawing object in a Word, Excel, or PowerPoint document, just open the Drawing toolbar (see page 148) and draw away!

Editing Embedded Objects

Like a linked object, an embedded object has a surrounding frame. You can format it using Office's picture tools (see page 148).

To edit it, though, you have to double-click it. (Or click it and choose Edit → Object → Edit. The Edit menu changes to specify the type of object you've selected—Document Object, Worksheet Object, and so on.) The object opens in a separate document window, where you can edit it using the appropriate menus and toolbars.

You can edit an embedded object in any compatible program on your Mac. Just click the object and then choose Edit → Object → Convert. Choose a program in the list that appears, and then click OK. (Most of the time, the Microsoft Office programs will be the only ones available.)

Customizing Office

Microsoft desperately yearns for the approval of its Office customers and relentlessly strives to disprove the adage, "You can't please all of the people all of the time." And just in case Office's designers didn't make the program work the way you think it should, they let you tweak it yourself.

Consequently, very few elements of the way you work in Office are set in stone. Word, Excel, and PowerPoint each let you redesign the toolbars and even rework the menus. In Word and Excel, you can also choose different keyboard equivalents for commands. (Only Entourage is off-the-rack software. You can customize its toolbar, but that's it.)

Even if you're a novice, customization is worth exploring. There will almost certainly come a day when you wish you could choose an easier function keystroke than the one Microsoft chose, or find yourself repeatedly digging deeply for a submenu command. With this chapter as your guide, you can be your own software tailor.

Customizing Your Toolbars

One simple way to customize your toolbars is to drag them around the screen and change their shapes to fit your whims (and your monitor shape). In Office 2008, the Standard toolbars are now permanently docked in the document window—you can turn them on and off via the View menu, but you can't drag them to a different position. To move any other Toolbar, just drag it, using its skinny title bar (next to the close button) as a handle.

You'll soon discover that toolbars are "magnetic." That is, they like to snap against the sides of the monitor, other toolbars, or the Formatting Palette—just about anywhere except an actual document window.

Tip: This snappiness is designed to help you keep your screen tidy, but if you want to stifle your toolbars' law of attraction, press Shift as you drag them.

You can also reshape your toolbar by resizing it as if it were a window: Just drag the diagonally striped area in the lower-right corner, as shown in Figure 20-1.

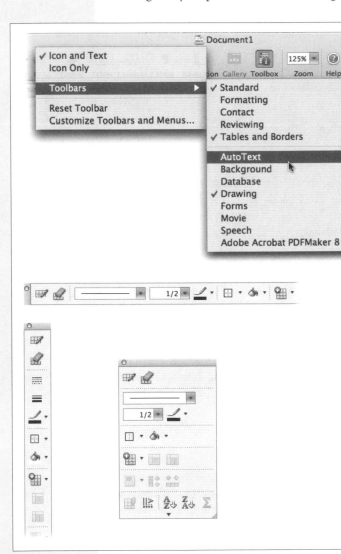

Figure 20-1:

Top: If you Control-click any empty gray space in a toolbar, you get a pop-up menu leading to a submenu listing all toolbars. Checkmarks indicate currently visible toolbars. Choose a toolbar name to make it appear or disappear. The Standard toolbar gives you the additional option of whether or not to display the text label next to your toolbar buttons.

Bottom: The toolbar turns into an outline as you drag its resizing corner. As you drag diagonally, it goes from a vertical toolbar to various incarnations of a rectangle, and finally to a horizontal toolbar—or the other way around.

Showing Other Toolbars

Excel, PowerPoint, and Word each come with a toolbar or two that pop up when the program opens, but that's just the beginning. In fact, Word has 15 toolbars, PowerPoint has 7, and Excel has 15, each dedicated to a certain purpose (such as graphics work, Web design, or reviewing comments). Some toolbars appear automatically when you use a related command or open a corresponding editing area. Others you can summon or dismiss, as needed.

You can open and close toolbars in any of three ways:

- Control-click (or right-click) the More Buttons toolbar icon (usually at the far right or bottom edge of a non-docked toolbar), or Control-click (or right-click) an empty area on any open toolbar or palette. As shown in Figure 20-1, you get a pop-up menu of what Microsoft considers to be the most useful toolbars. Choose the name of the one you'd like to open or close.

- Choose from the View → Toolbars submenu. Here again, you see the same list of toolbars.

- Choose View → "Customize Toolbars and Menus", or Control-click (or right-click) a gray area of a toolbar and choose "Customize Toolbars and Menus" from the pop-up menu. Now you see a list of *all* of the toolbars, even the obscure ones. Turn on a checkbox to make the corresponding toolbar appear or disappear instantly. (Because you don't even have to close the dialog box between experiments, this is the fastest way to have a quick look at all the available toolbars.) Click OK to close the dialog box.

Creating Custom Toolbars

The likelihood of Microsoft *perfectly* predicting which buttons you'd like on which toolbars is about the same as finding the exact wrench you want, the first time you reach into your pile of tools, while laying on your back under the '59 TR3, with oil dribbling on your chin. Fortunately, it's very easy to delete or add buttons on Excel, PowerPoint, or Word toolbars—much easier than crawling out from under that Triumph. In fact, you can, and should, create entirely new toolbars that contain nothing but your own favorite buttons. If you use Word's styles, as described on page 127, for example, it's a no-brainer to create a palette of your favorite styles, so that you can apply them with single click.

To move a button or delete it from a toolbar

To move a button, open the "Customize Toolbars and Menus" dialog box by choosing View → "Customize Toolbars and Menus", and then just drag the button to a new spot on the toolbar—or even to another toolbar. (You can ignore the Customize dialog box itself for the moment. Although it seems counterintuitive, the Customize dialog box needs to be open for this dragging to work.) The button assumes its new place, and the other buttons rearrange themselves to make room.

To get rid of a button on a non-docked toolbar, Control-click the button you wish to remove, and then choose Hide Command from the shortcut menu that appears. For docked toolbars, or if you already have the Customize dialog box open, you can delete a button by dragging it off the toolbar to the desktop or anywhere else in the document window. (Either way, you can get the button back later if you like; read on.)

To add a button to a toolbar

Every now and then, you'll wish you had a one-shot button that triggers some useful command—for inserting the current date into your document, for example.

To add a button to an existing toolbar, choose View → "Customize Toolbars and Menus" and then click the Commands tab. A list of command categories appears, grouped by menu. Click a category in the left box, and a list of associated commands appears on the right, along with an icon for each command, if one exists. It's a staggeringly long list that includes almost every command in the program.

If you click the All Commands category, you'll notice that the names of Office's commands in the All Commands list are a tad user-hostile: No spaces are allowed, and the command's name often runs together with the name of the menu that contains it (such as ToolsSpelling). You'll also notice that each of your Office programs has *hundreds* of commands that don't appear in the regular menus. Furthermore, the names of some commands don't quite correspond to their menu-bar equivalents. For example, the command for Insert → Comment is Insert → Annotation in the All Commands list. So check the menu categories before you resort to the All Commands list.

Tip: Trying to move around quickly in the All Commands category? You can type a letter (or letters) to move to the part of the list beginning with that letter. For instance, type *v* to scroll to commands for viewing or *ins* to jump to commands for inserting.

You can drag *any* of the command icons (and hence the command) in the Customize dialog box onto a toolbar, as shown in Figure 20-2. Some of them, such as Font Color, even take the form of pop-up menus which then become part of your toolbar. In fact, if you drag the command at the bottom of the Categories list called New Menu onto a toolbar, it turns into a pop-up menu that you can fill with any commands you like. You might decide to set up several custom pop-up menus filled with small lists of related styles—one just for headings, for example. The more logical the arrangement, the quicker the access. You can rename your home-made pop-up menu as described in the Tip on the next page.

Weirder yet, look at the top of your screen—there's a *duplicate menu bar* there, floating on its own toolbar! Click one of these phony menus to open it. Now you can drag any menu command *right off the menu* onto your new toolbar, where it will be available for quicker access. Once buttons are on the toolbar, you can drag them around, or even drag them off the toolbar to get rid of them, as long as you don't close the Customize dialog box.

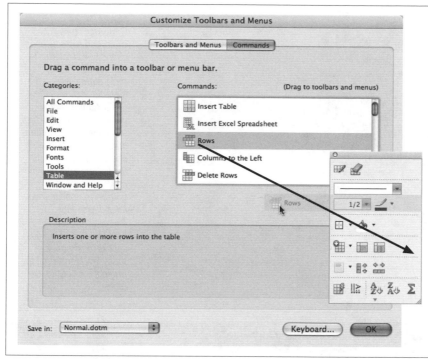

Figure 20-2:
You can easily add commands to a custom toolbar: just drag them one by one from the Commands section of the Customize window to the toolbar. Once you let go, feel free to drag them or their toolbar-mates around into a more pleasing arrangement, or drag the lower-right corner of the toolbar to reshape it.

Tip: If you double-click a toolbar button or pop-up menu while the Customize dialog box is open, you summon the Command Properties dialog box. Here's where you get to specify how you want the command to look in the toolbar: as a little icon, as a plain English word, or both (see the box below). You can also add a separator line before the button (above it or to its left) by turning on "Begin a group."

You can even perform this kind of button editing on non-docked toolbars when the Customize window *isn't* open—in the middle of your everyday work. The trick is to Control-click the button and choose Properties from the shortcut menu.

To design a new toolbar from scratch

Designing a completely new toolbar works much the same way as adding buttons. Choose View → "Customize Toolbars and Menus", select the Toolbars and Menus tab, and then click the New button. You'll be asked to name your new toolbar, which then appears as an empty square floating oddly above the Customize dialog box—and an embryonic toolbar just waiting for you to provide commands. Now click the Commands tab and begin filling your new toolbar with commands and buttons, just as described earlier. Click OK when you're finished.

Attaching Custom Toolbars to Documents

In Word, you can store a toolbar you've created or edited in the Normal template (see page 2), so it will be available for use in any new documents you create if you

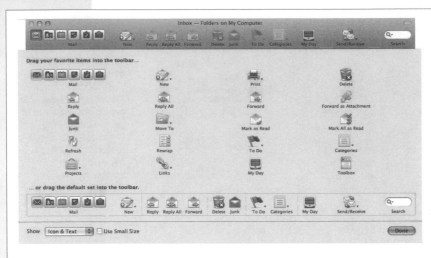

Figure 20-3:
Entourage limits your command customization efforts to its toolbar. Control-click (or right-click) a gray area of the toolbar, or choose View → Customize Toolbar to unfurl this sheet of button possibilities. Drag buttons onto or off of the toolbar, and use the controls at the bottom to determine how you want your buttons to appear. If you later decide that Microsoft's stock arrangement of buttons speaks to you on so many levels, just drag the original set back to the toolbar.

OBSESSIVE USERS' CLINIC

Drawing Your Own Buttons

Not all commands that you drag onto your toolbars come with associated picture buttons (Save As is a good example). Most of the time, all you get is a text button. If you'd prefer an icon, though, you can add one.

The trick is to Control-click the new button on a non-docked toolbar and choose the Properties command. You get the Command Properties dialog box where you see a little blank button icon in the upper-left corner. Click the pop-up menu attached to find 42 alterative button icons vying for

your affection (see Figure 20-4). If one of Microsoft's ready-made buttons will do, choose it from this pop-up menu.

If you don't care for any of Microsoft's microscopic masterpieces, you can design your own button in some other program (Photoshop, for example). Copy it, switch to the Office program you're editing, and then paste the graphic onto a button by choosing Paste Button Image from the menu. Microsoft recommends a 20 × 20 pixel image for maximum good looks. To restore the button's original icon (or lack of icon), choose Reset Button Image at the bottom of the menu.

---

choose "Save in Normal.dotm" in the "Customize Toolbars and Menus" dialog box. But after spending 20 minutes handcrafting the world's most brilliant toolbar, the last thing you want is to confine it forever to your own Mac.

Fortunately, you can share your brilliance with other people just by attaching the custom toolbar to an Excel workbook or Word document (PowerPoint lacks this feature).

- **In Excel.** Choose View → "Customize Toolbars and Menus", and then click the "Toolbars and Menus" tab. Click a toolbar's name in the pane on the left side of the Customize window, and then click Attach.

Figure 20-4:
*Control-click a toolbar button and choose Properties to open
the Command Properties window. The button pop-up menu
lets you choose a different button image from this collection of
icons, circa 1987. Or, copy the cutting-edge icon you designed
in Photoshop and choose Paste Button Image to give the
toolbar your distinct imprint.*

The Attach Toolbars window appears. It works exactly like the Organizer,
described on page 228. Use it to select the destination document and copy the
toolbar into it.

- **In Word.** Choose Tools → "Templates and Add-Ins". Click the Organizer button. Use the Organizer as described on page 228 to copy any toolbar into any
  document *or* template.

Redesigning Your Menus

Not only can you build your own toolbars in Excel, PowerPoint, and Word, you
can also twist and shape the *menus* of these programs to suit your schemes. You
can add and remove items from the various menus, and you can even move the
menus themselves so that they appear in different places on the menu bar.

More than one Excel owner, for example, has found happiness by stripping out the
commands he never used. Conversely, you're missing out in Word if you don't *add*
commands to the menus that you usually need to trigger by burrowing through
nested dialog boxes.

As noted earlier, choosing View → "Customize Toolbars and Menus" doesn't just
open the Customize dialog box. It also opens a strange-looking *duplicate* menu bar
just beneath the real one. If you click a menu name on this Menu Bar "toolbar,"
the menu opens, revealing all of the commands in that menu.

Adding a command

To add a command to a menu, choose, and click the Commands tab. Find the
command that you want to add (by clicking the appropriate category on the left

side first, for example). Then drag the command out of the Commands list and straight onto the *name* of the desired menu (on the *duplicate* menu bar), as shown in Figure 20-5.

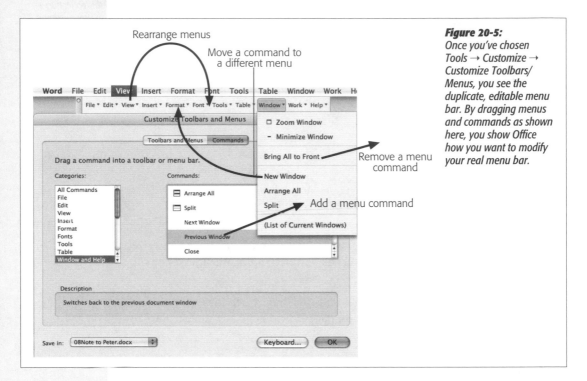

Rearrange menus

Move a command to a different menu

Remove a menu command

Add a menu command

Figure 20-5:
Once you've chosen Tools → Customize → Customize Toolbars/Menus, you see the duplicate, editable menu bar. By dragging menus and commands as shown here, you show Office how you want to modify your real menu bar.

Note: Excel has *two* menu bars—a Worksheet Menu Bar and a Chart Menu Bar. They're listed individually in the Customize dialog box's Toolbars tab. That's because Excel's Data menu changes into a Chart menu when you select a chart. These two menu bars are independent, so if you make changes to the Insert menu item on the Chart Menu Bar toolbar, those changes *won't* be reflected in the Insert menu item on the Worksheet Menu Bar.

As you drag your command over the duplicate menu, the menu opens automatically. As you drag down the menu, a line shows you where the new command will appear when you release the mouse.

Tip: You can even rename your newly installed menu command. Open the duplicate menu bar, then double-click your command to open the Command Properties dialog box. Type the new name and press Return.

Removing a menu command

Suppose that you never use the Dictionary command in Excel's Tools menu; the only word *you* need to know is "Profit."

Getting rid of a menu command—whether *you* put it on the menu or not—is easy. Choose View → "Customize Toolbars and Menus" to summon the strange duplicate menu bar shown in Figure 20-5. Now click the menu title (in the duplicate menu bar) containing the command. Finally, drag the command itself off the menu.

Removing commands from menus doesn't delete them from the program, of course. To restore a command you've removed from a menu, reinstall it as described in the previous section.

Adding a menu

You can do more than just add commands to existing menus. You can also create completely *new* menus, name them whatever you please, and fill them with any commands you like, in any order you like. This feature opens up staggering possibilities of customization: You can create a stripped-down "just the commands you really need" menu for an absolute novice, for example.

To do so, choose View → "Customize Toolbars and Menus", click the Commands tab, scroll to the bottom of the Categories list, and click New Menu. Drag the New Menu command from the Commands list (right side of the window) to the Menu Bar toolbar. Put it anywhere you want—between the File and Edit menus, for example, or to the right of the Help menu.

With the new menu still selected, Control-click your new menu and choose Properties from the shortcut menu. Type a name for your new menu into the Name field. Finally, press Return. (Control-clicking also brings up the Begin Group command, which inserts a separator line into your menu-under-construction.)

Your new menu is installed. Now you can add to it any commands you want, using the same technique described in "Adding a command," on page 765.

Removing a menu

You don't have to stare at the complex Microsoft menus that you rarely use. If you're one of the 99.9% of people who never use the Work menu in Word, for example, by all means ditch it.

Doing so couldn't be easier. Choose View → "Customize Toolbars and Menus" to make the phantom double menu bar appear. Point to the name of the menu you no longer need and drag it directly downward and off the menu bar. Once it's gone, the other menus tighten up and fill its space. (Never fear: You can always bring it back, as described below.)

Moving whole menus, or specific commands

Even the order of menus on the menu bar isn't sacrosanct in Office 2008. If it occurs to you that perhaps the Fonts menu should come *before* the Edit menu, choose View → "Customize Toolbars and Menus". Now you can start dragging around the menu titles themselves (on the duplicate menu bar) until you've created an arrangement that you like.

While you're at it, you can also drag individual commands from menu to menu. As shown in Figure 20-5, start by choosing View → "Customize Toolbars and Menus" from. Then bring the menu command to the screen by opening its current menu in the duplicate menu bar. Now drag the command to the *name* of a new menu, which opens automatically; without releasing the mouse, drag downward until the command is positioned where you want it. Finally, release the mouse button.

Resetting everything back to normal

When you delete a command, it's not gone from Office. You've merely removed it from its menu or toolbar, and it's easy enough to put it back—a handy fact to remember the morning after a late night with some geek buddies that featured a pitcher of Red Bull daiquiris and some overzealous menu modifications.

Open the Customize window (by choosing View → "Customize Toolbars and Menus"). Click the Toolbars tab. In the list at left, click Menu Bar, and then click Reset. You've just restored your menus and commands to their original, factory-fresh condition.

Tip: You can use this technique to restore any of the factory toolbars, too. On the "Customize Toolbars and Menus" Toolbars tab, just turn on the checkbox next to the toolbar you want restored, and then click Reset.

Reassigning Key Combinations

Pressing a staggering number of keyboard shortcuts can trigger an equally staggering number of Office commands. The only problem arises when you discover that Microsoft has chosen something bizarre (like Option-⌘-R for Thesaurus) instead of something more natural (like ⌘-T).

The good news is that you can reassign key combinations for any menu command—in Word and Excel, anyway. (You can't fiddle with the keyboard commands in PowerPoint or Entourage from within the programs. Instead you have to go to System Preferences → Keyboard and Mouse → Keyboard Shortcuts and do it there.)

To begin, choose Tools → Customize Keyboard to conjure up the Customize Keyboard window (see Figure 20-6). It works much like the toolbar-editing dialog box described earlier in this chapter. At left, click a command category; at right, click the name of the command you want to reassign. (After clicking or tabbing into one of these lists, you can jump to a particular category or command by typing the first couple of letters of its name.)

After highlighting the command for which you'd like to change or add a key combination, click in the box beneath the "Press new shortcut key" field. Now press the keys you'd like to use as the new key combo, using any combination of the Shift, ⌘, Option, and Control keys, along with a letter, F-key, or number key.

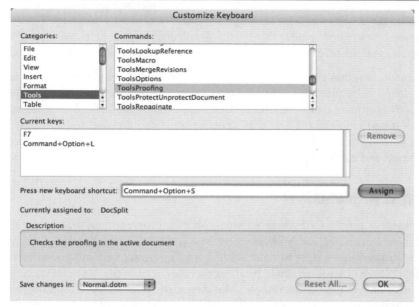

If that keystroke already "belongs" to another command in the Office 2008 program you're using, the Customize dialog box shows you which command has it (Figure 20-6). To reassign that keystroke to the new command and remove it from the original one, click the Assign button. To keep the current setting, press Delete, and then try another keystroke.

Obviously, you can't have two commands linked to a single keystroke. However, you *can* create more than one keyboard shortcut for a single command. For instance, in Word 2008, both ⌘-B and Shift-⌘-B are assigned to Bold.

Tip: If you find yourself frequently triggering a command *accidentally,* you may want to *remove* its assigned keystroke. To do so, click the command name in the list, highlight the keystroke in the "Current keys" list, and then click the Remove button. Click OK to save the changes.

If you don't like the key combinations that you've edited, you can always reset them by clicking the Reset All button in the lower-right portion of the dialog box.

AppleScripting Office

If you're like most people, you probably didn't upgrade to Office 2008 because of its ability to work with AppleScript. But if you're not using AppleScript to streamline your complex or repetitive tasks, you're not tapping Office's true potential for efficiency and speed. And, since Office 2008 does away with VBA—*Visual Basic for Applications*—AppleScript is the main scripting game left. For information on switching from VBA to AppleScript, and AppleScript user guides for Office, visit

Microsoft's Office scripting headquarters at *www.microsoft.com/mac/developers/ default.mspx*. In addition, MacTech Magazine has published a 150-page VBA-to-AppleScript transition guide, filled with detailed examples of converting VBA scripts to AppleScript. You can find it at *www.mactech.com/vba-transition-guide/*.

Fortunately, you don't have to actually be a scripter to reap AppleScript's benefits, since there are hundreds of ready-made scripts you can download and use (turn first to that nexus of all things AppleScript, *http://macscripter.net*). What follows is a quick introduction to the world of AppleScript. If you do want to learn how to write your own AppleScripts, Apple's AppleScript pages (*www.apple.com/ applescript*) and *AppleScript: The Missing Manual* await.

What is AppleScript?

AppleScript is the Mac's built-in *scripting*—that is, programming—language. (It's been around since 1993, with System 7.1.) Even without learning to write your own scripts, you can use scripts to control any program (Apple's or otherwise) whose developers have made it *scriptable*, meaning that they've built the necessary code into their program and provided an AppleScript dictionary. In other words, although the AppleScript language is built into Mac OS X, you can use it to control *programs* like Entourage, Word, iCal, iTunes, Adobe InDesign, and Photoshop.

Why Use AppleScript?

The vast majority of Office fans never dip a toe into AppleScript. But if you use Office to run a business or manage a department, you'll probably find a use for it. The advantage of AppleScript is that you only need to learn one programming language to communicate with *every* scriptable program on your Mac. For example, you can create a workflow that takes data from the Entourage Address Book and puts it into both Excel and FileMaker Pro, then prepares a Mail Merge in Word using the same information to type personalized form letters and envelopes, and then sends an email message from Entourage.

- **Automate.** Perform repetitive tasks automatically in a few seconds, instead of spending minutes or even hours plowing through them yourself. For example, you can run a script in Entourage to set the default address to the Home address, rather than Entourage's default of the Work address. If you have 1,000 contacts, this script will take about a minute to run, as opposed to multiple hours opening and changing each contact manually. Now you can print address labels for your Wear-Your-Bathrobe-to-Work Day cards without skipping the folks whose work addresses you don't know.

- **Customize.** Devise your own routines, sometimes even doing things that are impossible to do yourself onscreen in the first place. The world is your oyster: You can write scripts to duplicate calendar events (Entourage can't do that on its own), add a BCC to your boss on all email messages you send out, add a contact to a particular group without messing about finding or opening the group, remove all single carriage returns pasted into a Word document in one fell swoop without affecting double-returns at ends of paragraphs, and much, much more.

- **Interact.** Control several different programs in one workflow. You can take a letterhead document you've created in Word and have it open as a new letter addressed to a selected Entourage contact, complete with date, address, salutation, and signature already in place. Or you can export full contact information (street, city, state, phone numbers, email addresses, and so on) for every member of a group or category to an Excel worksheet or FileMaker Pro database—or both.

Installing and Running Office Scripts

Whether you choose to write your own scripts or not, you can always run scripts that others have written. Scripts come in two basic forms—*applets* (script programs, also called *droplets*), or as *scripts* (script documents). Developers create their scripts in either of these two forms when they save them.

Installing Applets and Droplets

If the icon is an *applet*, you can store it, and its folder, anywhere at all on your computer. You can move it to your Applications folder, or to a subfolder for scripts within it; or to your Microsoft User Data folder (even though it's not data), or to a subfolder you create within it for Office script applets. You can also drag the applet icon to your Dock, as with any program, so you can launch it from there. If it's a script you'll be using often, dock it.

Run the applet by double-clicking it, like any program, or by clicking it in the Dock (if it's there). Or if it's a droplet (with the down-arrow icon), drag one or more files of the appropriate type—usually a Word, Excel, or PowerPoint document—onto it. You can even store droplets in the Dock and drop files onto it there.

If the icon is a *script document* (it may or may not bear an .scpt extension), then you have to put it in a specific place depending on whether it's a script for Entourage or for one of the other Office programs. Read on.

Installing Script Menu Scripts

When you're in any Office 2008 program, you'll notice a dark, scroll-shaped icon just to the right of the Help menu in the menu bar. That's the Office Script menu, and Entourage's comes preloaded with a few AppleScripts that automate multi-step Entourage processes, like turning the selected email message into an Entourage note. Word, Excel, and PowerPoint don't come with any AppleScripts.

Note: All four Office programs come with a handful of Automator workflows, listed in the Script menu. With Mac OS X Tiger (10.4), Apple introduced Automator, a simple way to automate repetitive tasks with a basic drag-and-drop *workflow* creation. Automator comes with its own library of actions (such as file renaming, folder copying, creating a new mail message, and so on) that you can put together one after the other to create a workflow. You can also add AppleScripts to an Automator workflow, as you would any other action.

To learn more about Automator, check the Mac Help, Sal Soghoian's Automator site (*www.automator.us*), or *Mac OS X Leopard: The Missing Manual.*

Here's how to add to this menu any AppleScripts you've downloaded from the Web or written yourself:

1. **If the script is a script document for Entourage, drag the icon into your Home → Documents → Microsoft User Data → Entourage Script Menu Items folder. (You'll find similar folders for the three other office programs in the Microsoft User Data folder.)**

   You now see a menu item with the name of the script in Entourage's Script menu.

2. **Select the menu item to run the script.**

   You can also set up an Entourage rule to run the script when messages are downloaded or sent (see page 396), or an Entourage schedule to run the script automatically at startup, when you quit, or on a repeating regular schedule (see page 365).

3. **If you wish, you can create a keyboard shortcut for the script if it doesn't already have one. See page 768.**

Running the Scripts

Once you've installed a script, it's ready to run. Here's a quick review of the many ways you can run an AppleScript script:

- To run an applet, just double-click its icon in the Finder or click it once in the Dock

- To run a droplet, drag and drop files onto it.

- To run a Script menu script, just select it in the menu.

- To run an Entourage script automatically, set up a Rule (page 396) or Schedule (page 365) to *Run AppleScript.*

6

Part Six:
Appendixes

Installation and Troubleshooting

Installing Office

If you've installed a recent version of Office, you may have used Microsoft's super-simple drag-and-drop installation—which is no more. Office 2008 now uses Apple's Installer technology.

UP TO SPEED

Office 2008 Hardware and Software Requirements

To use Microsoft Office 2008, your computer has to meet the following requirements:

- A G4 PowerPC (500 MHz or faster), a PowerPC G5, or an Intel processor.

- Mac OS X, version 10.4.9 or later.

- 1.5 GB of available hard disk space for all four Office programs—Entourage, Excel, PowerPoint, and Word. You can save disk space if you don't install all of these programs.

- A color monitor that can show 1,024 × 768 pixels or more.

- 512 MB of RAM. (If you care about speed, more is better, of course.)

- A DVD drive for installation (or access to a network installer).

Using the Installer

The Installer walks you gently through the installation process as it checks to see if your computer is up to snuff, looks for other copies of Office, and asks you if you'd like to install the entire package or just individual programs.

Figuring Out the Formatting

Microsoft recommends that you install Office on a hard drive that's been formatted using Mac OS Extended (HFS +), the default format for Mac OS X. If your Mac came with OS X preinstalled, chances are excellent that your disk is already formatted in this way.

If you inherited this Mac from your cousin and aren't sure how Mac OS X made its way onto your hard disk, check your disk's format by running Apple System Profiler. Choose → About This Mac and click the More Info button to summon the Apple System Profiler. Choose ATA in the Hardware section of the Contents pane on the left, and look for your hard drive on the right. Highlight the hard

drive model name—it may be something like ST3320620A— and look in the bottom pane for the more familiar hard drive name you're used to seeing on your computer. Finally, beneath that, you'll find an indication of the File System—which should say something similar to *Journaled HFS+*.

If it turns out that your disk uses the wrong format, but you're not sure how to proceed, be aware that you are treading firmly on power-user territory. See *Mac OS X: The Missing Manual* for more information about disk formatting—or call in your cousin.

Figure A-1: .
When you open the Office 2008 installation disk, you'll see this simple window with but a single choice. Double-click the Office Installer to begin the installation process.

1. Start by quitting all of your running programs—especially Office programs. The Office installer makes changes to your font collection, which could confuse other running programs.

2. Insert the Microsoft Office 2008 DVD in your computer and double-click the Microsoft Office 2008 disk icon.

3. When the golden, Office: Mac 2008 installer window appears (Figure A-1), double-click the Office Installer icon to get this show on the road.

A small dialog box appears that says, "This package contains a program that determines if the software can be installed. Are you sure you want to continue?" This step checks your processor and operating system to make sure they meet Office's minimum requirements.

4. Click Continue.

When the installer launches, you see a Welcome screen. This screen suggests that you turn off any antivirus software you're using and, more ominously, asks whether you're an administrator. In Mac OS X, only people with Administrator accounts can do important stuff like install new software. If you're not sure, you can check in → System Preferences → Accounts. If you don't have "Admin" listed under your user name, ask someone who does for help. (You can learn more about all this account business in *Mac OS X: The Missing Manual*.)

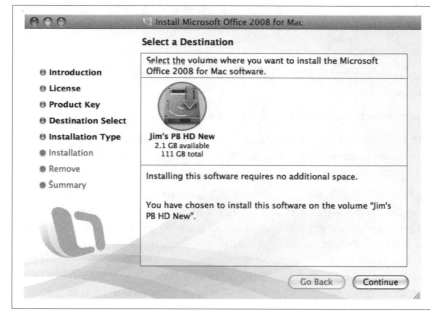

Figure A-2:
If you have more than one hard drive or partition on your Mac, choose the one on which you want to install Office, and click its icon. If you only have one hard drive or partition, there are no decisions to make—but you still have to click the hard drive icon.

5. Click Continue.

The Software License Agreement appears, which you may read in any of 11 languages. Don't worry, you're not signing your life away. (Well, probably not…no one's ever read all the way through to find out.)

6. Click Continue again, and a software license agreement dialog box appears. Click Agree to move on.

---

7. **Fill in your name and (if you like) your email address and other basic information for Office's use. Click Next when you're done.**

   Microsoft uses this as your registration name and address, and puts it in your Entourage Address Book as your "Me" contact, which means that it automatically shows up in all kinds of places in Office (as your return address in envelopes in Word, for example). In other words, entering your information now will save you loads of time later. (You can always change any of this info, even your name, in Office's preferences.)

8. **Type the 25-digit Product Key that came with Office.**

   You'll find this number on the back of the CD case in the Microsoft Office box.

9. **Click Finish when you're done. (If you make a typo, try, try again.)**

   Once you've typed the code correctly, the assistant shows your unique Office 2008 product ID. You'll be asked for it when you register your software with Microsoft for call its help line. Truth is, though, you don't actually need to remember it; you can always retrieve it by choosing the About command from the Word, Excel, PowerPoint, or Entourage menu.

10. **Click Continue.**

    The Standard Install window appears. To install the entire Office package, just click Install.

11. **If you'd like some say about exactly what is about to be installed, click Customize.**

    The Custom Install window appears, bearing checkboxes for the various office components (Figure A-3). Click the Flippy triangle next to Microsoft Office 2008 in order to turn off any individual programs.

    The Standard installation gives you a full installation of all four Office programs described in this book, plus Microsoft Messenger and Proofing Tools. This set of options is what Microsoft thinks most people want, without littering your hard drive with extras...sort of. If you click the flippy triangle next to Proofing Tools, you'll see that you're getting all kinds of foreign language spelling dictionaries. Click the checkboxes to turn off any languages you don't plan on writing. You'll save about a megabyte of hard drive space for each language you eliminate.

    Click the flippy triangles to see everything that's available. If you'll never in a million years create a PowerPoint presentation, for example, you can turn it off now and save a ton of space. You can always pop the DVD in and install it later if you change your mind. If you're stuck on iChat, you may as well turn off Microsoft Messenger.

    If you have a change of heart while you're picking and choosing, click Standard Install to revert to installing the whole shebang. This puts everything you paid for on your Mac—it also eats up one and a half gigabytes of space.

Tip: The Dock Icons checkbox gives you an easy way to remember what you just installed and then launch those programs. Leave it turned on and drag any icons you *don't* want off the dock when the installation is complete.

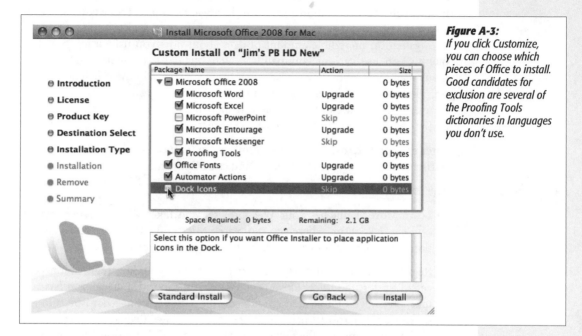

Figure A-3:
If you click Customize, you can choose which pieces of Office to install. Good candidates for exclusion are several of the Proofing Tools dictionaries in languages you don't use.

12. **When you're happy with what you've decided to install, click Install.**

    The installer gets to work. (It may ask you to type your password *again*. Just do it.)

    Soon, the Remove Office window appears, alerting you that it will search for and—at your option—remove earlier versions of Office. If you have room on your hard drive there's no problem keeping earlier versions of Office. (If you have an Office Test Drive, though, you *have to* remove it.)

13. **Click Continue to begin the search.**

    "Search finished" appears when the installer's done poking through all your files, and tells you how many versions of Office it found.

14. **Click Continue, turn on the checkboxes for the versions you wish to remove, and click Continue again.**

    The next message alerts you to how many versions of Office it moved to the Trash.

15. **Click Continue one last time.**

    The "Installation completed successfully" window appears, congratulating you on a successful installation, and advising you that the Office Setup Assistant is about to open to help you complete the setup process.

16. **Click Close to exit the Installer and launch the Office Setup Assistant.**

    The Microsoft Office Setup Assistant appears and first asks if you'd like to participate in Microsoft's Customer Experience Improvement Program. You can read a short description about how the program automatically and anonymously collects information about your hardware setup and how you use Office and other Microsoft services. It doesn't collect any personal information, but it does gather an incredible amount of data about how you use Office: how frequently you use various commands, which keyboard shortcuts you use, how many mail folders you have, how much time you spend in the Calendar, and so on. These juicy tidbits end up in a massive database that helps Microsoft software engineers figure out how people actually use the program. There's a link to a Microsoft Web site that explains it all in great detail.

17. **After reading Microsoft's plea for information, you can click the Yes button to participate, or else leave it set on No and click Continue.**

    The final assistant screen gives you three options:

    - **Learn More.** Launches your Web browser and takes you to *www.microsoft. com/mac/help.mspx*, where you can search Microsoft's Help and How-To sections, or click links for each of the Office programs to learn more about them.

    - **Register.** Opens your Web browser and starts the online registration process. Registering Office, like any software, is a good idea, because it lets you take advantage of a limited amount of free support from Microsoft. On the down side, Microsoft makes you create a Windows Live account (you may already have one; it's the same as an MSN Hotmail, Microsoft Messenger, or Passport account), offers to sign you up for bulk email that you may not want, and asks other nosy questions.

    - **Check for Updates.** Launches Microsoft AutoUpdate (see the box on page xxxi). If there are any updates, you'll want to install them right away, since they fix bugs that always appear when software first hits the shelves.

Click Finish. The Setup Assistant vanishes, and you find yourself staring once again at the Microsoft Office 2008 DVD installer window. Eject the DVD, and head to your Dock or Applications folder and start using Office 2008.

Removing Office

When you install Office, you're actually installing thousands of pieces of software in all kinds of places other than your Applications folder. If you want Office off your Mac and out of your life, you'd never be able to track down and trash them all. Fortunately, you've already installed a program that does just that.

Go to your Applications → Microsoft Office 2008 → Additional Tools → Remove Office folder. Double-click the Remove Office icon. The uninstaller searches for all versions of Office on your Mac and lets you choose which ones you want to remove. You can also choose to remove the programs, or just the preference files (sometimes a handy troubleshooting move). To back out, click Go Back or just quit Remove Office.

Click Remove on the final screen to do the deed. The uninstaller asks for an administrator name and password; when you enter them, it moves all selected versions of Office to the Trash. Emptying the Trash yourself is the final step in removing Office.

Troubleshooting

Once you've installed Office, you're supposed to leave its thousands of software pieces where they lie. If you drag Word out of the Microsoft Office 2008 folder, for example, it won't work; double-clicking it does absolutely nothing.

Nevertheless, it's possible that, while experimenting with your Mac or innocently trying to tidy up your hard drive, you'll end up trashing or moving a file that Office needs to operate. Even when you use Office programs the usual way, your software creates settings and preference files that keep track of how you use and customize the software. Occasionally, a settings file or a bit of software becomes *corrupted,* causing all manner of strange behavior, odd crashes, and chaos. If you're experiencing strange crashes, investigate the possibility that a settings file or a bit of Microsoft software has gone bad.

Check for a Bad Settings or Preference File

To test for a corrupt file, quit all Office programs, and dig into Home → Library → Preferences → Microsoft → Office 2008, then drag onto your desktop Microsoft Office 2008 Settings.plist and any Preference (or Settings) files that relate to your problem program. When you next start the program, it creates fresh, clean copies of these preference files. If your problem goes away, move the old, corrupt files from your desktop to the Trash. (If the corrupt files contain a lot of customization work, you can try further testing to see which specific file causes the problem, or— if you have backups—try restoring a slightly older version of the file.) Here's where you can find these preference and settings files:

- You can find most of them in your Home folder → Library → Preferences → Microsoft → Office 2008.

- Word stores custom style settings in a template called Normal, and this template may be the cause of your woe. You can most likely locate Normal.dotm in your Home → Library → Application Support → Microsoft → Office → User Templates folder.

- Entourage stores custom information (and email) for its main user in Home → Documents → Microsoft User Data → Office 2008 Identities → Main Identity. This folder (and all identity folders) are well worth backing up; if a file in Main Identity (or any identity folder) becomes corrupt, you'll have no recourse but to start again if you don't have backups.

Uninstall and Reinstall Office

With previous versions of the Mac OS, it was fairly easy to remove Microsoft shared libraries and such from the System Folder as a quick test to see if they were corrupted. Under Mac OS X, this picky procedure takes the skills and patience of a brain surgeon, as you're well aware from reading the previous section.

If only, say, Entourage is crashing or behaving badly, it may be worthwhile to isolate and remove only its preferences and support files to see if that solves the problem. But if you have no idea where the problem is coming from, and don't have the patience to figure it out, you may want to take the faster—but more drastic—step of removing *all* of Office's preference files, or removing all Office folders, programs, and their accoutrements from your Mac. You'll have to spend extra time resetting your preferences later, but in return you get the chance to truly start fresh.

Simply run the Remove Office program as described on page 780, and reinstall Office as described at the beginning of this appendix.

Research Your Problem Online

If you want to hunt online for information, you can always try Microsoft's Knowledge Base at *http://support.microsoft.com*. Or, try *www.microsoft.com/mac/help. mspx*, the Mactopia Help Center, with links to top support issues and information for IT professionals. Here you'll find the Office Resource Kit, Microsoft's reference guide aimed at network administrators and consultants.

Your best bet may be turning to your fellow Office 2008 fans and asking them for help. Visit Microsoft's online forum at *www.officeformac.com*. Here you can search for questions similar to yours and see if someone's already answered them. Chances are good someone has, but if not, you can post your question and see if you get an answer. (While you're at it, you might see if you can answer a question or two for someone else.)

Microsoft MVPs—Most Valuable Professionals—maintain several help Web sites where they volunteer their Office expertise for the greater good:

- **The Entourage Help Page.** *http://entourage.mvps.org*

- **The Entourage Help Blog.** *http://blog.entourage.mvps.org*

- **Word:mac.** *http://word.mvps.org/Mac/WordMacHome.html*

- **The PowerPoint FAQ List.** *http://pptfaq.com*

The Office Help System

Given enough time and determination, it's possible that you *could* figure out Microsoft Office 2008 all by yourself. But the fact that you're reading this book indicates you have better things to do with your time. When you need help, there are various resources available, starting with Office's built-in Help system. Of course, the help system can't substitute for a good book, but it can get you out of a jam, show you different—and often faster—ways of doing things, and reveal Office features you never knew existed.

Part of Office 2008's help system is always with you, like a friend tapping your shoulder with the occasional unsolicited hint. Tooltips often pop up to reveal, say, the names of toolbar buttons or AutoText suggestions. The often-ignored Description panels of dialog boxes clarify what you're looking at. (Open Word → Preferences, click any of the preference buttons and watch what happens at the bottom of the box when you pass the cursor over the various options.)

But if you're really having trouble figuring out how to make an Office program do what you want, you can turn to Office's online help screens.

Note: If you used earlier versions of Office for the Mac, you've been amused or annoyed by Max, the Help system's excitable Assistant, in the form of a little Mac Plus with feet and a repertoire of cutesy mannerisms. Always alarmingly out of place in the serious universe of Office, Max has waved his last animated goodbye and shuffled off the screen for good. Office 2008 does away with the Assistant and sends everyone seeking aid to the businesslike Office Help system.

Office Help

The Office for Mac Help window—which is supposed to take the place of a hard-copy manual in Office 2008—appears when you use one of these methods:

- Choose Help → [Program Name] Help (or press ⌘-?).

- Click the Help button on the Standard toolbar or press the Help key.

- Click the "More help on this function" link in Excel's Formula Builder.

The Help window opens, as shown in Figure B-1, titled Word Help, PowerPoint Help, and so on. Each program has its own separate set of help files, meaning you can't look up your Excel questions in the Word Help window. The adornments on this window offer a variety of aids to finding information in the Help system:

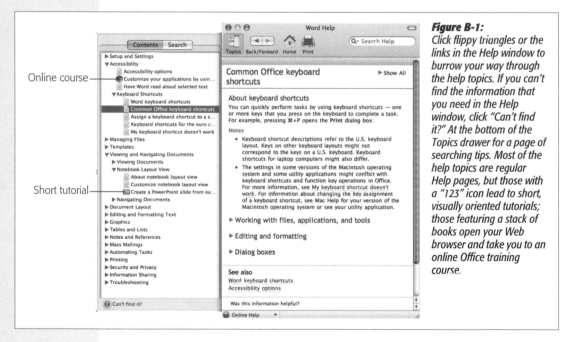

Figure B-1:
Click flippy triangles or the links in the Help window to burrow your way through the help topics. If you can't find the information that you need in the Help window, click "Can't find it?" At the bottom of the Topics drawer for a page of searching tips. Most of the help topics are regular Help pages, but those with a "123" icon lead to short, visually oriented tutorials; those featuring a stack of books open your Web browser and take you to an online Office training course.

- Clicking **Home** (the house button) returns you to the Home window of your current program from wherever you are in the help system. From here you can click one of the Popular topics links that lead to popular Help pages, click the User Community link to head to the Mactopia Product Forums Web pages, or click Contact Microsoft to shuttle over to Office 2008's main Help page on the Web.

- The two **arrows** to the left of the Home button are Back and Forward buttons that work just like the buttons in a Web browser to let you navigate the Help window.

- The **Topics** button hides or reveals the topics drawer, the pane containing your search results list or the Help Contents list. The Topics button always makes sure the drawer won't bump into the edge of your screen, and extends it from the other side of the Help window if that's a possibility. Click Contents if you want to browse through the help topics instead of searching.

- Clicking **Print** prints the contents of the main Help window.

- When you enter a key word or term in the **Search Help** field and press Return, Help displays a list of matching topics in the Topics drawer Search tab. Click one of the topics to display in the main Help window. Click the magnifying-glass icon at the left end of the Search Help field for a list of recent searches.

- The **Contents** tab of the Topics drawer displays the master list of help topics. Click one of these topics (you don't need to click the flippy triangle) for a list of subtopics, as shown in Figure B-1. Each subtopic is a hyperlink that opens the topic's help screen in the main pane.

At the bottom of the Help window, a little pop-up menu lets you choose between Online Help and Offline Help. The preferred position—if you have an always-on Internet connection—is Online Help. Microsoft regularly updates the Help contents, and when this control is set to Online Help, these latest additions are automatically available. When set to Offline Help, you have a much more limited range of help topics to choose from.

Note: Mac OS X 10.5 Leopard features a new search field in the Help menu (see below). This method searches programs on your computer that make use of the Mac Help system—like the operating system and all Apple programs. Searching here will *not* uncover Microsoft Office help topics, because Office uses its own separate Office Help system.

A worthwhile way to get started is to search for "known issues." This search takes you to a Help page titled *Known issues in Office 2008*, which is required reading if you're having any kind of Office trouble or if you're upgrading from an earlier version. Here you'll find a list and descriptions of problems Microsoft knows about. Thanks to Help's online connection, the information you find here is always up-to-date.

Leopard Menu Help

Mac OS X 10.5 (Leopard) features a new search field right in the Help menu. It searches the Mac Help system and only works for Apple programs, as described in the Note above. However, Leopard's amazing new *menu* search capability works great with Office programs. This feature's a lifesaver when you're having one of those menu moments—you know there's a command in a menu somewhere that lets you insert a horizontal line in Word, for example, but you're not sure exactly where. In Word, choose Help (or press ⌘-?) and type *horizontal* into the Search field. Leopard immediately responds with a menu item titled Picture → Horizontal

---

Line listed below the search field. Hold your mouse over that item in the search results, and the Word menu and submenu unfurls before your eyes with a big blue arrow pointing to the command in question (see Figure B-2). Without moving your mouse, click that item, and Word performs the command.

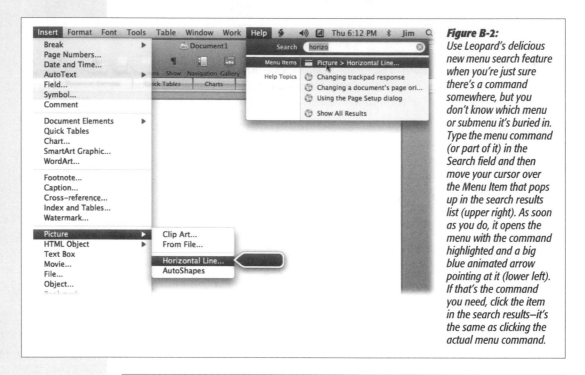

Figure B-2:
Use Leopard's delicious new menu search feature when you're just sure there's a command somewhere, but you don't know which menu or submenu it's buried in. Type the menu command (or part of it) in the Search field and then move your cursor over the Menu Item that pops up in the search results list (upper right). As soon as you do, it opens the menu with the command highlighted and a big blue animated arrow pointing at it (lower left). If that's the command you need, click the item in the search results—it's the same as clicking the actual menu command.

Note: If you're still using Tiger (Mac OS X 10.4), you don't have the menu help feature.

Web-Based Help

Microsoft does a fine job of keeping you updated about what's happening in the world of Office for the Mac. The Microsoft Office for the Mac Web site (called Mactopia) contains online tutorials, instructional articles, software updates and bug fixes, and, when all else fails, a gateway to Microsoft's technical support department.

To go directly to Microsoft's Mac Web site, choose Help → Visit the Product Website. Office launches your Web browser and displays the Office 2008 for Mac product page where all kinds of goodies await, like an online tour and email newsletter sign-up.

The links at the top of the Office 2008 page are the important ones for folks looking to learn more about the program.

- The **Products** link takes you to a page giving an Office 2008 overview with links to the individual programs. It's a great place to start if you're updating from an earlier version of Office.

- **Downloads** is a page listing the newest and most popular Mac downloads for Microsoft products. Come here for Office software updates if you're not using AutoUpdate (see the box on page xxxi). You'll also find a link to find out more about AutoUpdate.

- **Help and How-to** opens a gem of a page that includes how-to articles, top support issues, popular discussions in the forums—and a link to the forums page where you can interact with other Office fans and Office experts. You'll also find links to the IT Professionals pages and, at the bottom, a Get Technical Support link where you can search Microsoft's Office for Mac Knowledge Base and find links to contacting a Microsoft support person by email, online, or phone. (You're free to browse or post to a newsgroup; individual assistance by email or phone can cost you.) This page also has unexpected pleasures like a link to office-related news releases and press coverage, and a link to sign up to participate in a Usability Study (that is, potentially get to test new software and get a "free gift" for your efforts).

- The **Blog** link opens Mac Mojo, the official blog of the Macintosh Business Unit (MacBU) where the engineers who actually created Office hang out and post on various Office issues. You can leave comments on their postings and feel relatively confident that someone in the know is reading—and perhaps responding to them.

Office 2008, Menu by Menu

Because Microsoft Office 2008 is four big programs that work together, there are a lot of menus to cover—one set for each program. While some of these menus overlap, there are some significant differences. These menus also change depending on what's selected in your currently open document.

This appendix takes the menus program by program, so you can look up what you need easily.

Application Menu

Like Mac OS X programs everywhere, each Office program has a menu bearing its name, just to the right of the menu. It contains the Quit command, access to Preferences, and other commands that pertain to the program as a whole. It also has a few Finder commands, potentially saving you a trip to the desktop.

About [Program Name]

Opens a window displaying some legalese and, more importantly, the product ID for your copy of Office. A Microsoft representative may ask you for this number when you call a technical support phone number (which you can find by clicking the Support button).

The Reference Tools button doesn't actually help with looking anything up; it just offers more legalese about any foreign language dictionaries you've installed.

Online Registration

In case you clicked Register Later when you first installed Office (see Appendix A), choose this command when you have the time to go through the registration process.

Application Menu Preferences

This command opens up the Preference window, which contains different panels for various types of settings (these are discussed throughout this book). *Keyboard shortcut:* ⌘-comma (,).

In Entourage, there are two main sections in the Preferences dialog box:

- **General Preferences.** The General Preferences section is divided into 11 categories covering how Entourage works, particularly the Address Book (Chapter 11) and Calendar (Chapter 10).

- **Mail & News Preferences.** The Mail & News Preferences section contains four categories covering how Entourage deals with mail and news messages (see Chapter 9).

Account Settings (Entourage only)

Opens the Tools → Accounts window, as discussed on page 360.

Work Offline (Entourage only)

Disconnects Entourage from the Internet or network, so that you can you write email messages, reply to news messages, or work with tasks, calendar items, or contacts without being interrupted by Entourage's automatic mail-getting schedule (which would otherwise remind you every 10 minutes, "Mail could not be received at this time"). Great for use on planes and in waiting rooms.

Turn Off (or On) Office Reminders (Entourage only)

Tells the Office Reminders program (page 469) to stop reminding you about events, tasks, and documents that you've set for follow-up; or if it's already off, tells it you'd like to see your reminders.

Switch Identity (Entourage only)

Switches your Entourage identity, letting you (or another person using Office) use a different set of accounts (see page 495). *Keyboard shortcut:* Option-⌘-Q.

Services

This is a standard Mac OS X menu, listing useful inter-program commands that mostly do nothing in Office. (That's because Services generally work only in Cocoa programs—programs that were written from scratch for Mac OS X rather than adapted from earlier software, as Office was.) For the full story on Services, see *Mac OS X: The Missing Manual.*

Hide [Program Name]

Hides the current program's windows from view without minimizing the program to the Dock. *Keyboard shortcut:* ⌘-H.

Hide Others

Hides the windows of all other windows, including Finder windows, leaving only windows from the frontmost Office program visible. *Keyboard shortcut:* Option-⌘-H.

Show All

Brings back all hidden windows of the program you're using.

Quit [Program Name]

Quits the frontmost program, but before doing so, gives you a chance to save any changes you've made. *Keyboard shortcut:* ⌘-Q.

Entourage Menus

Entourage's menus, not surprisingly, center on manipulating mail and newsgroup messages, with a whole set of submenus for dealing with tasks, appointments, and contacts thrown in for good measure.

File Menu

Like any other good Macintosh program, Entourage comes equipped with the File menu, which is mainly used for working with files on your hard drive—whether that's creating new files, saving them, or printing them.

Project Gallery

It's the top File menu item in all four Office programs, and it opens the Office Project Gallery window when selected. *Keyboard shortcut:* Shift-⌘-P.

New

Creates a new Entourage file. Since Entourage can create a variety of files, the New command has its own submenu, filled with commands that create a new Entourage document or element.

- **New.** This top item changes, depending on what's selected in Entourage's Folder List window. It might say, for example, New Mail Message, New Newsgroup message, New Task, and so on. *Keyboard shortcut:* ⌘-N.

- **Mail Message.** Creates a blank email message. *Keyboard shortcut:* Option-⌘-N.

- **Calendar Event.** Creates a blank calendar event.

- **Task.** Creates a blank task.

- **Note.** Creates a blank note.

- **Contact.** Creates a blank Address Book entry.

- **Group.** Creates a blank group where you can gather together contacts.

- **News Message.** Creates a blank newsgroup message.

- **Post.** Creates a new post in an Exchange folder.

- **Project.** Opens the New Project Wizard (page 475) so you can start a fresh project.

- **Saved Search.** Creates a new Quick Filter search allowing you to add various criteria and then save it in the Mail Views folder (see the Tip on page 386).

- **Folder.** Creates a new folder in the folder list. (Available in Mail and Custom Views only.) *Keyboard shortcut:* Shift-⌘-N.

- **Subfolder.** Creates a new subfolder in the folder that's selected in the Folder List.

- **Open New Main Window.** Creates a brand-new main Entourage window so you can have, for example, your email and your calendar open at the same time.

Open

Opens the selected item into its own window, whether it's an item in the Folder List (such as a mail folder or the Address Book) or an item inside the browser window (such as a folder or a contact). The command even tells you what you're about to open ("Open Message" for example). *Keyboard shortcut:* ⌘-O.

Open Other User's Folder

Opens another Exchange account's shared mail folder, calendar, or contacts list. (This command is only available if Entourage has an Exchange account configured.)

Close

Closes the frontmost open window, even if it's the Progress window. If Entourage's main window is the only one open, this command closes it. *Keyboard shortcut:* ⌘-W.

Save

Saves any changes made to the frontmost window, whether that window is an email message (which then gets placed in the Drafts folder) or a contact. If the document in the frontmost window hasn't been changed, then the Save command is disabled. *Keyboard shortcut:* ⌘-S.

Save As

Saves the frontmost window as another file. This command essentially makes a copy of the file and closes the original, allowing you to choose a new name and location for the file.

Save As Web Page

(Available in Calendar only.) Lets you save your calendar as a Web page, so that others on the Internet can see what you're up to—if you really want that kind of scrutiny (page 459).

Revert

Throws out any changes you've made to the file in the frontmost window since you last saved it.

Import

Opens Entourage's Import window, which lets you bring in information from various email, personal information manager, and text-based mail and contact files (page 458).

Export

Saves Entourage's contacts as a text file, which you can then use in another program, or exports items to an Entourage archive (page 422).

Share a Project

Initiates the sharing of a project (page 486).

Subscribe to a Project

Lets you subscribe to a shared project that you or another Entourage fan created.

Page Setup

Opens the Page Setup dialog box, where you can control how Microsoft Office prints your pages (on which kind of paper, and so on). The options here depend on the kind of printer you have selected.

Print One Copy

Prints a copy of the frontmost window (or the item selected in the main window) without opening the Print dialog box. Think of it as the fast track to printing. *Keyboard shortcut:* Option-⌘-P.

Print

Opens the Print dialog box, where you can specify the number copies you want printed, among a multitude of other settings. *Keyboard shortcut:* ⌘-P.

Edit Menu

The Edit menu commands focus on editing tools, whether that means moving text around in an email message or memo, looking for a text string inside Entourage's files, managing message threads, or changing an item's category.

Undo

Takes back the last thing that you did, like deleting that vital chunk of text by accident. *Keyboard shortcut:* ⌘-Z.

Redo

Once you've undone something, then the Redo command becomes available, in case you change your mind. *Keyboard shortcut:* ⌘-Y.

Cut

Cuts the selected text or object out of the document and puts it on the Clipboard, ready for pasting into a different window or program. *Keyboard shortcut:* ⌘-X.

Copy

Copies the selected text or object and puts it on the Clipboard, ready for pasting into a different window or program. *Keyboard shortcut:* ⌘-C.

Copy to Scrapbook

Copies to the Scrapbook (page 727). You can store clips on the Scrapbook—and subsequently paste them—from any Office program. *Keyboard shortcut:* Shift-⌘-C.

Paste

Pastes the contents of the Clipboard into a document at the location of the insertion point. *Keyboard shortcut:* ⌘-V.

Paste From Scrapbook

Pastes a clip from the Scrapbook. *Keyboard shortcut:* Shift-⌘-V.

Paste Special

Once you've got something on the clipboard, you can choose how Entourage pastes it from this submenu.

- **Paste As Quotation.** Pastes the text on the clipboard into an open Entourage window as an Internet-style quotation—that is, with > brackets in front of each line, to let your correspondent know you're quoting back something she wrote. *Keyboard shortcut:* Control-⌘-V.

- **Paste As Plain Text.** Removes any formatting, like italics, from the text you're pasting. Useful primarily when you're pasting formatted text from Word into a plain-text email or newsgroup message. *Keyboard shortcut:* Option-⌘-V.

- **Paste As Picture.** Pastes whatever is on the clipboard (such as a Word table, Excel chart, or drawing) as a picture. Useful, and available, only in HTML-formatted email messages, and in Notes.

Clear

Deletes the selected text (or object) from the document without putting it on the clipboard.

Select All

Selects everything (whether that's text or objects) in the frontmost window. *Keyboard shortcut:* ⌘-A.

Duplicate

Duplicates the currently selected item, whether it's a message or a calendar event. This command's wording changes to reflect the kind of object that's selected; it may say Duplicate Message or Duplicate Task, for example. (It can't duplicate items on a remote server, such as an online email account or a news server.) *Keyboard shortcut:* ⌘-D.

Delete

Deletes the selected item (such as a mail message, contact, or folder in the Folder list). Like Duplicate, the Delete command's wording changes to reflect the item being deleted, and it can't be used to delete messages on a news server. *Keyboard shortcut:* ⌘-Delete.

To Do

This menu lets you choose a To Do setting—Today, Tomorrow, Next Week, and so on—or add a Reminder, Mark as Complete, or Clear To Do Flag.

Categories

This menu lists Entourage's categories (a way of labeling your Entourage data, as described on page 473), and it gives you two commands to use with those categories: Assign Categories lets you place the selected item (like a message or a folder) into one or more of your categories; Edit Categories lets you create, change, and delete Entourage's categories.

The prefab categories included in Entourage are: None, Family, Friends, Holiday, Junk, Personal, Recreation, Travel, and Work.

Projects

This menu lists your projects. You may either assign the selected item (email message, note, or whatever) to a project by selecting it or create a new project.

Share Item

Lets you share the item through a shared project.

Do Not Share Item

Select this to stop sharing a previously shared project item.

Get Properties

(Project Center only.) Opens the Project Properties window (see the box on page 483) of the selected project. *Keyboard shortcut:* ⌘-I.

Auto Text Cleanup

Auto Text Cleanup contains six tools to help turn email text into cleaner text, removing some of its gremlins.

- **Straighten Quotation Marks.** Takes fancy curly quotes and turns them into standard straight quotes.

- **Rewrap Paragraphs.** Pulls out the line breaks in the text of a message (see page 380).

- **Increase Quoting.** Increases the level of Internet quoting (with all of the > signs on the left margin of the text) by one.

- **Remove Quoting.** Removes all levels of quoting from of the selected text.

- **To UPPERCASE.** Makes the selected text all capitals.

- **To lowercase.** Makes the selected text all lowercase.

Increase Font Size

Makes the text of an incoming message larger. *Keyboard shortcut:* ⌘- + (Shift-⌘-=).

Decrease Font Size

Makes the text of an incoming message smaller. *Keyboard shortcut:* ⌘- − (hyphen).

Add to (or Remove from) Favorites Bar

Adds the selected folder to or removes it from the Favorites Bar.

Find

Opens Entourage's Find panel, which you can use to search through messages for a text phrase (see page 499). *Keyboard shortcut:* ⌘-F.

Advanced Search

Opens Entourage's Quick Filter view, which lets you search using all kinds of criteria to narrow your search (see the box on page 498). *Keyboard shortcut:* Option-⌘-F.

Find Related Items

Lets you search for messages sent to or received from the currently selected contact.

View Menu

The View menu's commands control how Entourage looks and shows you things. (In Calendar view, this becomes the Calendar menu, but it contains many of the same commands.)

Previous

Moves to the previous item in the currently selected folder. If a message is open, the contents of the open window changes to the previous message. *Keyboard shortcut:* ⌘-[.

Next

Moves to the next item in the currently selected folder. If a message is open, the contents of the open window changes to the next message. *Keyboard shortcut:* ⌘-].

Go To

Choosing one of the items from the submenu does the same thing as clicking the Mail, Address Book, Calendar, Notes, Tasks, and Project Center buttons—it switches to the view of that function.

Hide/Show Toolbar

Hides or shows the toolbar in Entourage's main window (a space-saving gesture).

Customize Toolbar

Opens Entourage's toolbar customization pane so you can add or remove buttons to the Toolbar (page 764).

Hide/Show Quick Filter

Hides or shows the Quick Filter bar at the top of the list pane. *Keyboard shortcut:* ⌘-Shift-L.

Hide/Show Favorites Bar

Hides or shows the folder Favorites Bar directly beneath the Toolbar.

Hide/Show Folder List

Hides or shows the folder list in Entourage's main window. *Keyboard shortcut:* ⌘-B.

Preview Pane

Hides or shows the Preview Pane in Entourage's main window. *Keyboard shortcut, on the right:* ⌘-\, *below the list:* Shift-⌘-\.

Columns

The Columns menu lets you hide or show the various columns in Entourage's main list view. The columns that you can toggle are: To Do Flag Status, Online Status, Message Status, Priority, Attachment, From, Subject, Sent, Received, To, Account, Size, Categories, and Projects.

To save space, hide the ones you rarely consult.

Arrange By

(Mail and Newsgroups only.) Lets you choose how you want to arrange the messages in the folder you're viewing (that is, by subject, sender, and so on). Also lets you turn on Show in Groups, to group similar messages together.

Show Mail Folders Only

Removes any non-Mail folders—like Calendar or Address Book view—from the folders list.

Unread Only

Hides all messages but the ones you haven't yet read. (Choose the command again to bring them back into view.) *Keyboard shortcut:* Shift-⌘-O.

Flagged Only

Makes flagged messages the only thing that you see in list windows. *Keyboard shortcut:* Option-⌘-O.

Expand All

In the folder pane, shows all folders and their subfolders. In the message list, opens up collapsed groups so that you can see all messages.

Collapse All

In the folder list, collapses all subfolders; the equivalent of closing all folders' flippy triangles at once. In the message list, hides all grouped messages so that you can only see the group headers.

Message Menu

The Message Menu provides all manner of commands for dealing with messages, as you may have guessed. (Available in Mail and Newsgroup views only.)

Resend

Resends a selected message in the Sent Items folder. (If a message in the Outbox is selected, this command says Send Message Now instead.)

Send Message Now

(Available when a message you're composing is open in its own window and Entourage is online.) Sends an email or newsgroup message. *Keyboard shortcut:* ⌘-Return.

Send Message Later

(Available when a message you're composing is open in its own window.) Places the email or newsgroup message in the Outbox. *Keyboard shortcut:* Shift-⌘-Return.

Receive Entire Message

If you've selected a partially retrieved message, this command tells Entourage to receive the rest of the story.

Edit Message

Makes a previewed (or opened) message editable, so that you can change its text—even if you didn't create the message (POP accounts only).

Reply

Creates an outgoing reply message for the selected message, with subject and address already filled in. If the message comes from a mailing list, the reply will be addressed to the mailing list. *Keyboard shortcut:* ⌘-R.

Reply to All

Creates a reply to the selected message, preaddressed to every recipient of the original message. *Keyboard shortcut:* Shift-⌘-R.

Reply to Sender

Creates a reply to the selected message, preaddressed to the sender only. *Keyboard shortcut:* Option-⌘-R.

Forward

Forwards the message to a third party, first permitting you to add your own comments to it before you send it along to someone else. *Keyboard shortcut:* ⌘-J.

Forward as Attachment

Forwards the message to a third party as a file attachment, which is useful when you want to preserve the formatting of forwarded HTML messages. *Keyboard shortcut:* Control-⌘-J.

Redirect

Redirects the selected message to someone else, making it appear as though it came from the original sender (see page 383). *Keyboard shortcut:* Option-⌘-J.

Mark as Read

Marks the currently selected message so that it looks like you've already read it (it stops being bold). *Keyboard shortcut:* ⌘-T.

Mark as Unread

Marks the currently selected message as unread (it turns bold)—useful if you've already read it but want to pretend as if you haven't. *Keyboard shortcut:* Shift-⌘-T.

Mark All as Read

Marks all messages in a folder as having been read. *Keyboard shortcut:* Option-⌘-T.

Mark as Junk

Notifies Entourage's junk mail filter that the selected message or messages is junk.

Mark as Not Junk

Tells Entourage's junk mail filter that the selected message (or messages) isn't junk.

Block Sender

Tells Entourage's junk mail filter that messages from the sender of the selected message are always junk.

Check Names

Verifies that email addresses are correctly formatted. *Keyboard shortcut:* Control-⌘-C.

Insert

The submenu commands here let you insert, into an outgoing email or newsgroup message, one of the following items:

- **Picture.** Opens a "Choose a File" window for you to choose a graphics file to attach to a message or, if HTML is turned on, to place in the body of the message.

- **Background Picture.** Opens a "Choose a File" window as above, except that Entourage sizes the picture you use to fill the body of the message. Your typing appears over the picture, provided you choose a contrasting font color.

- **Sound.** Opens a "Choose a File" window for you to choose a sound file, such as a WAV file, to attach to an email message as an attachment.

- **Movie.** Opens a "Choose a File" window, exactly as for a sound. Entourage inserts the movie into an HTML email as in a Web page or attaches it.

Remove Background Picture

Deletes a background picture, if you inserted one using the above command or if you received a message from someone else with a background picture.

Signature

Lets you select the signature for your outgoing message (see page 405).

Priority

Lets you set a priority for your outgoing Entourage message, which will be flagged accordingly in your recipient's email program, if the program understands such priority settings. For messages you've received, this menu lets you set the priority of the selected message from one of five possible choices: Highest, High, Normal, Low, and Lowest.

Security

This submenu, available when you're composing a new message, lets you apply two encryption features that help prevent evildoers from reading your email during its electronic journey. Because you and your recipients need to share each other's digital *certificates* (files that identify you as the sender and decode the encrypted messages), you'll usually use this feature when a corporate administrator has gotten everyone set up for it.

- **Digitally Sign Message.** Adds the file that digitally identifies you as you. Usually your administrator purchases these certificates for everyone using the network.

- **Encrypt Message.** Scrambles the message so that only you and the others with the right certificates can read it.

Add Attachments

Lets you add an attachment to an open message that you're creating (see page 407). *Keyboard shortcut:* ⌘-E.

Save All Attachments

Opens up a Save dialog box where you can save any file attachments to the currently selected message onto your hard drive (see page 391). This command is unavailable, of course, if a message doesn't have any attachments. *Keyboard shortcut:* ⌘-E.

Remove All Attachments

Removes any attachments to the selected message. Great for stripping away annoying VCF files.

Remove Unsafe Attachments

Removes any attachments that Entourage deems to be potentially unsafe (see the box on page 393).

After Sending, Move To

Lets you set a destination folder for your outgoing message. Once you've sent it, Entourage will move the message to the selected folder.

Apply Rule

Applies mail rules (page 396) to the selected message or messages, even if they've already been downloaded to your Mac. The submenu shows two things: your list of individual rules and All Rules, which applies all of your rules to the selected messages.

Move To

This menu command moves the selected message or messages to a folder in the list—a great feature when you're slogging through a mass of messages, trying to clean them up. Its submenu shows a list of folders and a special Choose folder command.

- **Folder list.** This is a list of Entourage folders to which you can move the selected message.

- **Choose folder.** Opens a list of all of Entourage's folders; you can move the selected message to any of them. You can also create a new folder using the controls in this window. *Keyboard shortcut:* Shift-⌘-M.

Add To Address Book

Adds the sender of the selected message to your Entourage Address Book. *Keyboard shortcut:* Option-⌘-C.

Internet Headers

Reveals the Internet headers that show where the message has been on its travels through cyberspace. It works only when a message is open in its own window or selected in a list, not in the Preview pane. *Keyboard shortcut:* Shift-⌘-H.

Source

Opens the selected message's HTML source code—including its headers—so you can take a look at the formatting codes that make it up. *Keyboard shortcut:* Option-⌘-U.

Format Menu

Even though email and news messages both trace their origins to plain text (which doesn't contain much in the way of formatting), the advent of HTML email lets you use a variety of formatting in your missives. Those commands are thoughtfully grouped in the Format menu.

HTML

If HTML is turned on, then all of the Format menu commands listed below are available. Otherwise, most of the commands below are dimmed, and you'll prepare your email messages using good ol' plain, unformatted text only. *Keyboard shortcut:* Shift-⌘-T.

Style

Lets you choose from five different styles for your text, detailed below:

- **Regular Text.** You guessed it—plain vanilla text.
- **Bold.** Makes the selected text bold. *Keyboard shortcut:* ⌘-B.
- **Italic.** Makes the selected text italic. *Keyboard shortcut:* ⌘-I.
- **Underline.** Underlines the selected text (and makes it look like a hyperlink— great for practical jokes). *Keyboard shortcut:* ⌘-U.
- **Fixed Width Font.** Uses a fixed-width font, such as Monaco. A fixed-width font is one in which each character takes up the same amount of horizontal space (for example, an "i" takes up as much space as an "m," making it easier for you to line up text in columns).

Font

Lists all of the fonts installed on your Mac. Choose one to use in your message.

Font Size

Lets you choose a specific point size for your text, just as you would when formatting text in Word (page 93).

Font Color

Lets you choose a color for your HTML-based email fonts. It lists 16 colors: Black, Maroon, Green, Olive, Navy, Purple, Teal, Gray, Silver, Red, Lime, Yellow, Blue, Fuchsia, Aqua, and White—plus Other, which lets you use the color picker to mix your own color (page 747).

Increase Font Size

Increases the size of the selected text. *Keyboard shortcut:* ⌘- +.

Decrease Font Size

Decreases the size of the selected text. *Keyboard shortcut:* ⌘- –.

Character Set

Lets you choose a language character set for your mail: Western European, Central European, Chinese, Cyrillic, Greek, Japanese, Korean, Turkish, or Unicode. This submenu comes factory set to Automatic, meaning that Entourage can detect the languages used in incoming messages. If you get a message loaded with nonsense characters, try choosing the correct language manually.

Alignment

Chooses alignment for the selected paragraphs: Left, Center, or Right.

Numbered List

Turns the selected text into an HTML numbered list.

Bulleted List

Turns the selected text into an HTML bulleted list.

Increase Indent

Indents the selected paragraphs (when creating a quotation, for example). *Keyboard shortcut:* ⌘-].

Decrease Indent

Decreases the indent level. *Keyboard shortcut:* ⌘-[.

Background Color

Lets you choose a shade for the background of your HTML email messages.

Insert Horizontal Line

Inserts a horizontal rule into an HTML formatted outgoing message (page 403).

Tools Menu

Where would a Microsoft program be without a Tools menu? Here you'll find commands that deal with Entourage's general utility operations.

Run Schedule

Here's a look at each item in the submenu (see page 365 for more on schedules):

- **Empty Deleted Items Folder.** Empties the Deleted Items folder of its contents.

- **Send & Receive All.** Sends all queued messages and gets mail from all accounts.

- **Send All.** Sends all waiting messages.

- **Edit Schedules.** Opens the Schedules window, where you can create, edit, and delete schedules.

Send & Receive

This command's submenu lets you send your waiting outgoing mail and download any email waiting for you.

- **Send & Receive All.** Sends all waiting messages and gets mail from all accounts. *Keyboard shortcut:* ⌘-K.

- **Send All.** Sends all waiting messages (but doesn't download incoming mail). *Keyboard shortcut:* Shift-⌘-K.

- **List of accounts.** Every account you have in Entourage is listed here. By selecting the account name, you make Entourage send and receive messages for that one account.

Spelling

Checks the spelling in your message. *Keyboard shortcut:* Option-⌘-L.

Thesaurus

Opens the Reference Tools and looks up the selected word in the Thesaurus. *Keyboard shortcut:* Control-Option-⌘-R.

Dictionary

Opens the Reference Tools and looks up the selected word in the Dictionary. *Keyboard shortcut:* Option-Shift-⌘-R.

Spelling Language

Use the Spelling Language submenu to choose your dictionary language (for spelling and grammar checks) from the following choices: Portuguese (Brazil), Danish, Dutch, English (AUS), English (UK), English (US), Finnish, French, French Canadian, German, Italian, Norwegian Bokmal, Norwegian Nynorsk, Portuguese, Spanish, Swedish, and Swiss German.

AutoCorrect

Opens Entourage's AutoCorrect settings window, where you can set how Entourage automatically attempts to fix your mistakes and add formatting to your messages, exactly as in Microsoft Word (see page 75).

Open Links

Opens a list of links to the selected item or message.

Link to Existing

Lets you link to an existing Message, Calendar Event, Task, Note, Contact, Group, or File, using the Links dialog box (page 388).

Link to New

Lets you link to a Mail Message, News Message, Calendar Event, Task, Note, Contact, or Group that you haven't yet created, and gives you a chance to create it in the process.

Toolbox

The Submenu lets you open the Object Palette, the Reference Tools, or the Scrapbook.

Junk E-Mail Protection

Opens the Junk E-Mail Protection window, where you can set the filter's options (see the box on page 395).

Mailing List Manager

Opens the Mailing List Manager, where you can set options for dealing with mailing lists.

Newsgroup Settings

Lets you set character-set options for the selected newsgroup. Useful if you habituate international newsgroups.

Out of Office

If you have a corporate, educational, or hosted Exchange Server account, then this command lets you set a rule to automatically respond to messages while you're away on vacation or out of the office. Your correspondents will know not to expect an answer from you until you return. This rule runs from the server, which means you don't need to keep Entourage running on your computer.

Rules

Opens the Rules window, where you can create, edit, or delete message rules (see page 396).

Signatures

Opens the Signatures window, where you can create, edit, or delete signatures for your messages.

Schedules

Opens the Schedules window, where you can create, edit, or delete schedules.

Accounts

Opens the Account window, where you can create, edit, or delete mail, news, and directory service accounts (see the box on page 399).

Window Menu

The Window menu corrals all of the window-related Entourage commands in one place.

Minimize Window

Sends the frontmost Entourage window to the Dock. *Keyboard shortcut:* ⌘-M.

Zoom Window

Does the same thing as the green zoom button in the upper-right corner of the window: resizes it to its full size, so that it fills up most of the screen.

Progress

Opens the Progress window, which shows how network operations are progressing. *Keyboard shortcut:* ⌘-7.

Error Log

Open Entourage's Error Log, which tells you about any problems the program had in sending or receiving your messages. *Keyboard shortcut:* ⌘-8.

My Day

Opens the My Day program (page 467). *Keyboard shortcut:* ⌘-9.

Cycle Through Windows

Moves from one open window to the next, one at a time. *Keyboard shortcut:* ⌘-~.

Bring All to Front

Makes all open, nonminimized Entourage windows visible, pulling them out from behind other windows.

Window List

All of the open windows are listed at the bottom of the Window menu. To switch to an open window, select it from this list.

Help Menu

The Help menu gives you access to resources for learning about and troubleshooting Office. Some are stored in the Help system that Office installed on your computer; others are on Microsoft's Web site.

Entourage Help

Opens up Entourage's online help, as described in Appendix B.

Check for Updates

Launches the Microsoft AutoUpdate program (see the box on page xxxi).

Visit the Product Web Site

Opens your Web browser to Microsoft's home page for its Macintosh products.

Send Feedback about Entourage

Opens your Web browser to a Microsoft Web page containing a simple feedback Web form.

Scripts Menu

Entourage works well with AppleScript and Automator—so well that it reserves an entire menu for scripts and workflows. You can use one of the included scripts, and you can add your own scripts to this menu.

About this Menu

Opens a dialog box containing a short description of the Scripts Menu and a button that opens the Word Script Menu Items folder.

Create Event from Message

Attaches the selected message's text to a new Entourage Event (a nifty trick if the message contains, for example, directions to a party). *Keyboard shortcut:* Control-E.

Create Note from Message

Attaches the selected message's text to a new Entourage Note. *Keyboard shortcut:* Control-N.

Create Task from Message

Attaches the selected message's text to a new Task. *Keyboard shortcut:* Control-T.

Insert Text File

Lets you insert a text file. Browse to the file you wish to insert, select it, and its text appears in your message.

Open E-mail Folder

Opens your Microsoft User Data folder in the Finder. This is useful for locating your email files for backup.

Save Selection

Saves your current message to a folder in the Finder.

Sample Automator Workflows

Displays a submenu with a collection of Automator workflows from which to choose.

Excel Menus

These menus are the same no matter what kind of document is open.

File Menu

The commands in the File menu operate on Excel workbooks, whether you're opening them, saving them, or printing them.

Project Gallery

It's the top File menu item in all four Office programs, and it opens the Office Project Gallery window. *Keyboard shortcut:* Shift-⌘-P.

New Workbook

Creates a new Excel workbook. *Keyboard shortcut:* ⌘-N.

Open

Opens Excel's Open dialog box, which you can use to navigate to a file for Excel to open. *Keyboard shortcut:* ⌘-O.

Open Recent

Lets you choose from a list of recently opened Excel documents.

Close

Closes the frontmost Excel workbook window. If the workbook has unsaved changes, Excel will ask you if you want to save those changes. *Keyboard shortcut:* ⌘-W.

Save

Saves any changes to the frontmost window. If the file is a new, unsaved workbook, Excel prompts you to name it and choose a location for it. *Keyboard shortcut:* ⌘-S.

Save As

Saves the frontmost window as another file. This command essentially makes a copy of the file and closes the original file, allowing you to choose a new name and location for the file, if you want.

Save as Web Page

Saves the frontmost Excel workbook as a Web page, converting graphics and graphs to the right kind of graphic formats, and saving all of the data in HTML tables (page 607).

Save Workspace

Memorizes the positions and sizes of any open workbook windows into a separate file. Later, when you open that file, all of the workbooks will be opened to the same size and position.

Web Page Preview

Shows you, in your Web browser, what your workbook will look like as a Web page.

Page Setup

Opens the Page Setup dialog box, where you can set up your Excel printouts. The options depend on the kind of printer you have selected as your default printer.

Print Area

Offers three commands:

- **Set Print Area.** Lets you drag to select the cells you want to print.

- **Clear Print Area.** Undoes the Set Print Area command, so that nothing is selected for printing.

- **Add to Print Area.** Add your selection to the current print area.

Print

Prints the frontmost document on the printer selected in the Chooser. It opens the Print dialog box, where you can specify how many copies you want printed and make other printing-related settings. *Keyboard shortcut:* ⌘-P.

Import

Opens a dialog box where you can choose the kind of file to import, then click the Import button, and locate the file.

Send To

Excel's Send To submenu has only two items: Mail Recipient (as HTML) and Mail Recipient (as Attachment). By selecting one of these options, Excel tells Entourage to send the frontmost file as an HTML email or as an attachment to an email message. It's a great feature, saving you several steps when you're finished working on a spreadsheet and want to email it straight to the interested parties.

Properties

Opens the Workbook Properties window, where you can view and type in keywords and other information about the frontmost workbook, for use later by the Finder's Spotlight search feature (which appears when you choose File → Open).

Edit Menu

The Edit menu gathers together all of Excel's editing tools in one handy place. Many of these commands are similar to, but not identical to, those in other Office programs.

Undo

As in other programs, this command restores the last change you made; in Excel, you can undo (or redo) many steps, taking your spreadsheet all the way back to the way you found it. *Keyboard shortcut: ⌘-Z.*

Repeat/Redo

When you've done something that Excel can do over and over again, you can do so just by selecting the Repeat command. If you've just used the Undo command, the Repeat menu item turns into Redo, which undoes the undo you just did. *Keyboard shortcut: ⌘-Y.*

Cut, Copy, Copy to Scrapbook

Cuts or copies to the clipboard, or copies to the Office Scrapbook, the selected cell, cells, or object. *Keyboard shortcut: ⌘-X, -C, and Shift-⌘-C.*

Paste, Paste from Scrapbook, Paste Special

Pastes what you've just copied to the clipboard or to the Office Scrapbook. Paste Special lets you exercise some control when pasting, by pulling up the Paste Special window, where you can apply formatting. It also lets you link or embed the clipboard contents. *Keyboard shortcut: ⌘-V, Shift-⌘-V.*

Paste as Hyperlink

Pastes the clipboard contents into Excel as a hyperlink, either to a Web site or to a Word document. (Requires that you'd first copied an Internet address or some text out of a Word document.)

Fill

Fills the selected range of cells in the manner you specify in the Fill submenu. There are several different kinds of fills:

- **Down, Right, Up, Left.** Fills the selected range of cells with the contents and formatting the first select cell, in the specified direction (see page 517 for a more patient discussion).

- **Across Sheets.** If you have multiple sheets selected, this copies the selected range of cells across all of the selected worksheets in the same place as the original selection.

- **Series.** Intelligently fills the selected range of cells using the contents of the first cell in the selected row or column as a pattern—useful for filling in a series of dates, for example.

- **Justify.** Spreads the text in the leftmost cell across the selected row of cells.

Clear

The Clear menu empties out a cell or cells; although you might not know it, there are several ways to clear cells. Here are your choices:

- **All.** Clears everything in the cell, including formatting, the cell's contents, and any comments.

- **Formats.** Clears just the cell's formatting, leaving contents and comments alone.

- **Contents.** Clears just the cell's contents, leaving formatting and comments alone.

- **Comments.** Clears any comments, leaving formatting and contents alone.

Delete

Deletes the selected cells or object from the sheet. If you're deleting cells, Excel will ask you whether you want to shift cells up or to the left, or remove entire rows or columns.

Delete Sheet

Deletes the currently active sheet from the workbook. Be sure about it; you can't undo this action.

Move or Copy Sheet

Moves the selected sheet or sheets to a different location in the same workbook or another workbook. It opens the Move or Copy window, in which you can specify where you want to move the sheet and whether or not a copy is made.

Find

Opens the Find panel that you can use to search for a string in formulas, values, or comments. *Keyboard shortcut:* ⌘-F.

Replace

Looks for a string of text and replaces it with another.

Go To

Opens the Go To window, which you can use to go to a specific cell. By clicking the resulting Special button, you can also use it to select a specific type of cells, such as those containing formulas or constants.

Links

Pulls up a window showing information about every link in the currently active document. If the document doesn't have any links to other documents, this option is dimmed.

Object

Lets you edit an embedded object, such as a Microsoft Graph object or a Microsoft Organization Chart object. This menu's name changes to reflect the kind of object that's embedded here, and it lets you either edit an embedded object or convert one OLE object to a different type.

View Menu

The View menu's commands govern what view mode the windows are in, what toolbars are shown, and so on.

Normal

This is the standard Excel spreadsheet view.

Page Layout

Switches to Page Layout view. See the box on page 511.

Toolbox

All the various palettes below are part of the Toolbox—you can't click this menu item directly.

Formatting Palette

Hides or shows the Formatting Palette.

Object Palette

Hides or shows the Object Palette.

Formula Builder

Hides or shows the Formula Builder.

Scrapbook

Hides or shows the Scrapbook.

Reference Tools

Hides or shows the Reference Tools.

Compatibility Report

Hides or shows the Compatibility Report.

Project Palette

Hides or shows the Project Palette.

Elements Gallery

Hides or shows the Elements Gallery.

Toolbars

Using this command's submenu, you can hide or show Excel's toolbars: Standard, Formatting, Border Drawing, Chart, Drawing, External Data, Forms, Formula Auditing, List, Movie, PivotTable, and Reviewing.

Customize Toolbars and Menus

Opens the Customize window, where you can select more toolbars or create your own (see page 759).

Ruler

(Page Layout view only.) Displays a ruler along the top of the Excel page.

Formula Bar

Hides or shows the formula bar. This is one that you should probably leave on, as you'll be using the formula bar quite a bit.

Status Bar

Hides or shows the status bar at the bottom of an open workbook.

Header and Footer

Lets you edit the headers and footers that appear at the top and bottom of every page.

Comments

Shows all comments in the document if they're hidden, and opens the Reviewing toolbar. If comments are already visible, choosing this hides them.

Custom Views

Opens the Custom Views window, which you can use to add, delete, or show custom views that you've saved.

Full Screen

Turns Full Screen mode on and off. In Full Screen mode, your workbook enlarges to take over the entire screen, and Excel hides other elements (such as toolbars and the Formatting Palette).

Zoom

Opens the Zoom window, where you can choose one of seven zoom levels (25, 50, 75, 100, 125, 150, or 200 percent) for magnifying or shrinking the onscreen representation of your spreadsheet, or you can zoom in or out to fit a selection. You can also enter a custom zoom level (from 10 to 400 percent).

Sized with Window

If you have a chart embedded in its own chart sheet, this command ties the size of the chart to the size of the window in which it's embedded. If this command isn't checked, resizing the window has no effect on the size of the chart.

Chart Window

If you have a chart selected, this appears at the bottom of the View menu. It makes Excel open the existing chart in a new chart window.

Insert Menu

If you want to insert something into your Excel documents, then this menu is your best friend. If not, there's no need to go to its parties.

Cells

Inserts a number of blank cells equivalent to the number you've first selected, and opens the Insert window, which lets you set how those cells are placed.

Rows

Inserts a number of blank rows equivalent to the number you've first selected, moving the selected rows down. If you have only one cell selected, Excel inserts only one row.

Columns

Inserts a number of blank columns equivalent to the number you've first selected, moving the selected columns to the right. If you only have one cell selected, Excel inserts only one column.

Chart

Opens the Charts Gallery, which walks you through the creation of a chart, and then it inserts your newly minted chart either into the currently active worksheet or into a whole new sheet reserved for the chart alone.

List

Opens the List Wizard, which walks you through the creation of one of Excel's fancy list objects (see page 541).

Sheet

Lets you choose from its submenu a Blank Sheet, a Chart Sheet, or a List Sheet to insert into your current workbook. Choose Other to pick a worksheet from the Project Gallery or from some other folder.

Page Break

Inserts a page break above the currently selected cell. If the cell is adjacent to a manually placed page break, this command changes to Remove Page Break, which (as you might guess) removes the break.

Function

Opens the Formula Builder, from which you can select one of Excel's functions to insert into the currently active cell.

Name

The Name menu has four submenu choices that let you deal with names in Excel worksheets. Names are plain-English ways of referring to a cell or selection of cells (see page 539).

- **Define.** Opens the Define Name window, where you can add or delete names for a cell or group of cells.

- **Paste.** Opens the Paste Name window, which you can use to paste a named group of cells into a formula. You can also paste a list of your defined names, including the cells to which those names refer.

- **Create.** Opens the Create Names window, which lets you create names based on labels in selected cells.

- **Apply.** Opens the Apply Names window, where you can choose a name range to replace a cell range inside a formula. That cell range has to match an existing named cell ranges; otherwise, the function doesn't work.

Comment

Inserts a comment attached to the selected cell or cells.

Picture

The Insert → Picture submenu lets you grab images from one of six sources. You can read about them in detail in Chapter 20, but here's a summary:

- **Clip Art** opens the Clip Gallery and lets you select a bit of Office clip art to insert.

- **From File** brings up the "Choose a Picture" dialog box, which lets you find and insert your own picture files.

- **Shape** opens the Object Palette; you can start drawing in your worksheet using the AutoShapes tools.

- **Organization Chart** opens Microsoft Organization Chart, which lets you create and insert your own flow charts into the currently active Excel worksheet.

- **WordArt.** Opens the WordArt Gallery, where you can create text art for insertion into the currently active sheet.

Text Box

Lets you draw a text box onto your spreadsheet.

Movie

Brings up the Insert Movie dialog box, where you can select a QuickTime, AVI, or MPEG movie to insert into the currently active sheet.

Object

Opens the Insert Object window, where you can select one of the following Office object types for insertion: an Equation object, a Microsoft Graph Chart object, Microsoft Organization Chart object, or a Word Document object.

Hyperlink

Opens the Insert Hyperlink window, where you can insert a new hyperlink to a Web page, a document, or an email address. If there's already a link in the selected cell, this command opens the link for editing. *Keyboard shortcut:* ⌘-K.

Format Menu

The Format menu gathers together all of the commands that you're likely to use while altering the formatting of your sheets and workbooks.

Cells

Opens the Format Cells window, where you can choose all kinds of formatting options for the selected cells. This menu item changes to reflect the type of object is selected—Picture, Object, WordArt, or AutoShape—and then opens the appropriate Format window. *Keyboard shortcut:* ⌘-1.

Row

This menu has four options that govern the appearance of the selected row or rows:

- **Height.** Opens the Row Height window, where you can set the height of the selected row or rows in pixels. If a worksheet is protected, this option is unavailable.

- **AutoFit.** Makes the selected row precisely as high as it needs to be to accommodate the tallest text in the row. Measured in pixels.

- **Hide.** Hides the selected row or rows from view (it doesn't delete them).

- **Unhide.** Reveals any hidden rows.

Column

Like its sibling menu item, Format → Row, this menu has five options that let you edit the appearance of the selected column or columns:

- **Width.** Opens the column width window, where you can set the width of the selected column or columns (measured in characters).

- **AutoFit Selection.** Makes the selected column precisely as wide as it needs to be to accommodate the longest text in the column. Measured in characters.

- **Hide.** Hides the selected column or columns from view.

- **Unhide.** Reveals any hidden columns.

- **Standard Width.** Resets the selected column or columns to the original setting.

Selected Chart Area

If you have a chart selected, the Select Data Series menu item appears; it lets you format the selected chart's area. This menu item changes to reflect the various items selected in the chart, including data series, plot areas, labels, and legends. All of these open the appropriate Format window.

Sheet

This menu item has four submenus, each of which deals with a formatting aspect for the active worksheet.

- **Rename.** Lets you rename the currently active sheet.

- **Hide.** Hides the selected sheet or sheets.

- **Unhide.** Reveals any hidden sheets in the workbook by presenting you with a list of hidden sheets and letting you choose those you want shown.

- **Background.** Lets you select a graphics file to use as a background for the frontmost sheet.

AutoFormat

Opens the AutoFormat window, where you can select formatting from a range of presets for the selected cells or pivot table.

Conditional Formatting

Opens the Conditional Formatting window, where you can change the selected cells' formatting based on conditions that you define—such as changing a cell's text color to red when its value is negative.

Style

Opens the Style window, where you can add, edit, or remove styles. Styles are a saved set of formatting commands that you can apply to a cell or range of cells with ease.

Tools Menu

Although all menu items are tools, in a sense, most are grouped together because they have some commonality (such as the Insert and Format menus). The Tools menu, on the other hand, is more general in nature. It includes a mix of text tools, sharing tools, and other miscellaneous functions that are powerful but don't necessarily have a common thread.

Spelling

Runs a spell check on the frontmost spreadsheet.

Thesaurus

Opens the Reference Tools and looks up the selected word.

Dictionary

Opens the Reference Tools, and looks up the selected word.

Language

Lets you choose your language for spell checking.

AutoCorrect

Opens the AutoCorrect window, where you can edit what Excel tries to correct while you type, such as changing "abbout" to "about." You can add your own items for Excel to AutoCorrect here.

Error Checking

Checks the sheet for invalid equations and operations. Provides summary.

Share Workbook

Opens the Share Workbook window, where you can change an ordinary workbook into one that can be shared by many Excel fans at once on a network. In this window, you can turn workbook sharing on and off, and you can adjust how changes to the shared workbook are treated.

Track Changes

The Track Changes controls how Excel keeps tabs of changes to worksheets and workbooks made by your collaborators. This menu has two submenu options:

- **Highlight Changes.** Opens the Highlight Changes window, where you can turn change tracking on and control which changes are highlighted.

- **Accept or Reject Changes.** Walks you through the changes that have been made to a workbook, giving you a chance to accept or reject each.

Merge Workbooks

Merges all of the changes from a series of shared workbooks into one single workbook.

Protection

The Protection menu has three submenu choices that let you choose a level of protection for the currently open worksheet or workbook.

- **Protect Sheet.** Protects the frontmost sheet from changes to cells, charts, graphics, or Visual Basic code.

- **Protect Workbook.** Protects a workbook's structure from changes such as deleting, adding, hiding, or showing sheets; also keeps windows from being resized.

- **Protect and Share Workbook.** Protects the workbook's change tracking and sharing status. If the workbook isn't yet shared, Excel will ask you if you want to do so when this item is selected. If it's already shared, this command changes to Unprotect Shared Workbook.

Flag for Follow Up

Opens the "Flag for Follow Up" window, where you can set a reminder attached to the currently open workbook. That reminder will pop up at the time you specify to remind you to do something with the workbook in question.

Goal Seek

Changes the value in a cell until a formula using that cell reaches a value you specify (see page 623).

Scenarios

Opens the Scenarios Manager window, where you can add, edit, merge, and delete a series of scenarios, which are a way of playing "what if" with an Excel worksheet (see page 626).

Auditing

The Auditing menu controls how formulas in a worksheet or workbook interrelate. It has five submenu choices, all of which involve colorful arrows that appear on your spreadsheet, pointing to cells that refer to each other.

- **Trace Precedents.** Makes arrows point to a cell or cells that provide values for the formula in the selected cell. Useful if you're looking for where data comes from.

- **Trace Dependents.** Points to a cell or cells where the value in the selected cell is being used.

- **Trace Error.** If the selected cell contains an error caused by a bad value in a cell that its formula references, an arrow identifies the offending cell.

- **Remove All Arrows.** Removes all of the arrows drawn by auditing commands.

- **Show Auditing Toolbar.** Hides or shows the Auditing toolbar.

Calculator

Opens the Formula Calculator, which you can use to quickly create formulas in a neat touchpad format (see page 534).

Condition Sum

Opens the Conditional Sum Wizard that walks you through writing a formula to take the sum of specific values depending on other values in a list.

Macros

Opens the Macro window, a vestige of VBA macros that Office no longer can use. If you open a document created in an earlier version of Excel that contains macros, you can see them in this window—but not use them.

Add-Ins

Opens the Add-Ins window, where you can turn on or turn off various Add-Ins for Excel. Add-Ins are conceptually similar to Photoshop plug-ins in that they add new functions to Excel.

Customize Keyboard

Opens the Customize Keyboard window, where you can add or modify keyboard commands.

Data Menu

This menu's commands all process the numbers and characters in your worksheet.

Sort

Sorts the selected rows alphabetically, by date, or numerically.

Filter

The Filter menu item lets you hide rows of a list or selection according to criteria that you specify. It has three items in its submenu.

- **AutoFilter.** Turns the AutoFilter pop-up menus at the top of a list object's column. These pop-up menus contain commonly used filters.

- **Show All.** Removes any filtering that's been applied to a list.

- **Advanced Filter.** Opens the Advanced Filter window, which lets you create your own filters for a selected range of cells.

Form

Opens a data form window, which you can use to view, edit, add, and delete data in a list object (see page 553).

Subtotals

Figures out a subtotal and grand total for the selected labeled column; automatically inserts the appropriate cells, moving the selected cells to the right, and puts the spreadsheet in outline mode.

Validation

Opens the Data Validation menu, which lets you control what kind of data is entered in a cell or cell. It also lets you choose a message to display when a cell is selected.

Table

Creates a data table based on a selected row and column input cell. Data tables are useful to show how changing formula values affect a sheet's data (see page 623).

Text to Columns

Opens the "Convert Text to Columns" Wizard, which walks you through the process of converting a chunk of text in a cell (either separated by spaces or by commas) into a series of columns.

Consolidate

Grabs data from one of several sources and consolidates it into a table for easy viewing. This command opens the Consolidate window, where you can choose your consolidation function, and add data sources.

Group and Outline

The commands in this menu let you group data together and create outlines from your groupings. By using grouping and outlining, you can hide and show detailed data, grouping it in ways that help make sense of it (see page 633). For your grouping pleasure, the Group and Outline menu has seven submenu items.

- **Hide Detail.** If you have a summary row or column, this command hides the detail rows or columns. For PivotTables, this command hides detail data in an outer row or column field item.

- **Show Detail.** If you have hidden detail rows or columns, this command shows them. For PivotTables, this command reveals detail data in an outer row or column field item.

- **Group.** Groups data (either cells or items in a PivotTable) together for easy analysis and printing. Grouping cells automatically creates an outline in the frontmost sheet.

- **Ungroup.** Ungroups formerly grouped data, separating group members into individual items.

- **Auto Outline.** Tells Excel to automatically create an outline, which it happily does from the formulas and cell references in the given spreadsheet.

- **Clear Outline.** Removes outlining, of course. If you have selected a set of cells that are in groups, then this command removes the outline in that area. If the selected cells aren't in a group, the outline is removed from the worksheet.

- **Settings.** Opens the Settings window, where you can set some options for outlining and summarizing data in a worksheet.

PivotTable Report

Opens the PivotTable Wizard, which walks you through creating a PivotTable or editing an existing PivotTable (see page 619).

Get External Data

This menu has a collection of commands that link Excel to other data sources (such as databases or Web-based data sources). There are eight commands in this submenu.

- **Run Saved Query.** Pops up the "Choose a Query" dialog box, where you can select a saved data query to run. Excel ships with four pre-saved Web-based queries ready for you to use.

- **New Database Query.** Opens the Query Wizard, where you can create your own database query, you mad scientist, you. (This requires an ODBC driver.)

- **Import Text File.** Imports an entire text file into the currently open worksheet. This command opens the Text Import Wizard, which walks you through how Excel will parse and place the data from the text file.

- **Import from FileMaker Pro.** Pops up the "Choose a Database" dialog box, where you can choose a FileMaker Pro database document to import data from (see page 614).

- **Import from FileMaker Server.** Does the same thing as above, but for File-Maker databases stored on a network.

- **Edit Query.** Edits a query that you created using Microsoft Query to get at data in an external database. If you have used the Import Text File command to bring in a text file, this menu item changes to Edit Text Import, and performs accordingly.

- **Data Range Properties.** Opens the External Data Range Properties window, which lets you change some of the settings for an imported bit of external data (such as whether the query definition is saved, how data is refreshed, and how data is laid out).

- **Parameters.** Lets you set options for a parameter query, a special kind of query that asks you for some information that it will use to retrieve data from the database's tables.

Refresh Data

Refreshes the data in a PivotTable if the table's source data has changed.

Chart Menu

The Chart menu appears only when a chart is selected in Excel; it replaces the Data menu on the menu bar. Many of these options duplicate settings in the chart wizard, giving you a chance to revisit some of those choices.

Chart Type

Opens the Chart Type window, where you can choose a new chart type for the selected chart (see page 575).

Source Data

Opens the Source Data window, where you can choose a different range of cells from which the chart draws its data.

Move Chart

Opens the Chart Location window, where you set where the chart is placed: as a new sheet or as an object in an existing sheet.

Add Data

Opens the Add Data window, which lets you add additional cells to the chart.

Add Trendline

Opens the Add Trendline window, where you can add a trendline to your chart, or change one that's already there (see page 589).

3-D Rotation

Summons the 3-D format window, which lets you manipulate your 3D chart as if it were a real-world, solid item by rotating it, scaling it, or changing its elevation. If the selected chart isn't a 3-D chart, this menu item isn't available.

Window Menu

These commands help you manage your spreadsheet windows.

Minimize Window, Zoom Window, Bring All to Front

These commands behave exactly the same way as they do in Entourage (see page 807).

New Window

Opens a new window on the same file that's currently open—a duplicate view of the same spreadsheet. This arrangement lets you view two (or more) places in the same file at the same time, scrolled to different spots and zoomed independently.

Arrange

Arranges all open windows so that at least a portion of each is visible—which makes switching or dragging data between open files much easier. An Arrange Windows dialog box opens, where you can set how those windows are arranged (Tiled, Horizontal, Vertical, or Cascade).

Hide

Hides the frontmost workbook window without closing it.

Unhide

Displays a list of windows that have been hidden with the Hide command, which you can then Unhide.

Split

Splits the active window horizontally and vertically into four, independently scrolling panes. If the currently active window has been split, this menu command changes to Remove Split.

Freeze Panes

If your sheet has been split into two or four panes, this command freezes the top pane, the left pane, or both. That way, those panes stay in place while you scroll the lower right panes—it keeps column and row titles visible while you scroll through your worksheet. (None of this affects how the sheet prints.) This command changes to Unfreeze Panes if you have already frozen the panes on the sheet.

Window List

The last item on the Window menu is a list of currently open workbook windows. You can switch between them by selecting their names from this menu.

Help Menu

These commands are the same as they are in Entourage, as described earlier in this appendix.

PowerPoint Menus

PowerPoint has many commands in common with the other Office programs. What unique menus it has are dedicated to manipulating slides, text, and images, which is what PowerPoint does so well.

File Menu

PowerPoint's File menu, of course, is for working with files on your hard drive—whether that's creating new files, saving them, or printing them.

Project Gallery, New Presentation, Open, Open Recent, Close, Save, Save As

These commands work exactly as they do in Excel; the only distinction here is the wording of the New command (New Presentation).

Save as Pictures

Saves each slide as a graphics file.

Save as Movie

Creates a QuickTime movie from the frontmost open presentation (see page 706).

Save as Web Page

Saves the frontmost PowerPoint presentation as a series of Web pages, converting graphics and graphs to the proper kinds of graphics files and saving all of the data in HTML files (see page 709).

Web Page Preview

Shows you what your presentation looks like as a Web page. It opens a temporary Web page version of your file in your browser.

Page Setup, Print

These commands work just as they do in Excel.

Send To

PowerPoint's Send To menu lets you send the currently open presentation directly to:

- **Mail Recipient (as Attachment).** Attaches the frontmost presentation as a file attachment to an outgoing Entourage email message, so that you can send it to whomever you like.

- **Microsoft Word.** Sends the frontmost presentation's outline to Word, where you can edit it.

- **iPhoto.** Sends the presentation to iPhoto as a group of JPEG or PNG graphics.

Properties

This command works just as it does in Excel (page 811).

Edit Menu

The Edit Menu gathers together all of PowerPoint's Edit tools into one handy place. Many of these commands are similar to those in other Office programs, but they aren't all the same.

Undo, Repeat/Redo, Cut, Copy, Copy to Scrapbook

These commands work just as they do in Excel.

Paste, Paste from Scrapbook

These commands work just as they do in Excel (page 812).

Paste Special

Opens the Paste Special window, which you can use to paste the contents of the clipboard into the presentation as a linked or embedded file. It also gives you some formatting options when pasting such a file.

Paste as Hyperlink

Pastes the clipboard contents (if you've copied an Internet address or some material from Word) into the frontmost PowerPoint presentation as a hyperlink.

Clear

Clears the selected item from the frontmost presentation document.

Select All

Selects all objects on the screen. If the cursor is currently in an active text object, selects all of the text inside that object. *Keyboard shortcut:* ⌘-A.

Duplicate

Duplicates the selected object, placing the copy slightly below and to the right of the original. Duplicating an item doesn't put it on the clipboard. *Keyboard shortcut:* ⌘-D.

Delete Slide

Deletes the current slide (Normal or Notes view) or the selected slides (in Slide Sorter view).

Find

Opens PowerPoint's Find window, which you can use to search for certain keywords or formatting in Office files on your hard drive. *Keyboard shortcut:* ⌘-F.

Replace

Searches for specific text or formatting and replaces it with other text or formatting that you specify.

Go to Property

Although few living souls have ever tried it, PowerPoint has a unique feature that lets you flag certain blobs of text as having been proofread, approved by the client, and so on. To flag a piece of text in this way, drag through it; choose File → Properties → Custom tab; choose from the list of properties (Disposition, Department, and so on); turn on "Link to content"; click Add; and then click OK.

After having marked up dozens of text swatches in a slide show this way, the Edit → Go To Property command is your ticket to finding those characteristics again. When you choose this command, a tiny dialog box appears, listing all of the flags you'd set up in this way; by double-clicking one, you jump directly to the corresponding blob of text, making it easy to (for example) round up all the text blobs that have yet to be approved before going live with the presentation.

Object

If you've been editing the text inside a text box or table, it's a darned nuisance to have to switch to the arrow tool just to adjust, say, the placement, formatting, or size of that text box or table. This command neatly toggles back and forth between (a) placing the insertion point inside the selected text box or table and (b) selecting the text box or table itself. It saves you a couple of mouse clicks when doing frantic alternation between editing and tweaking.

Special Characters

Opens the Mac OS X Characters Palette, giving you access to every possible special character on your system.

View Menu

The View menu is home to the commands that govern what you see when you're working with PowerPoint: its view mode, whether the presentation is in color or grayscale, and what toolbars and palettes are showing.

Normal, Slide Sorter, Notes Page, Presenter Tools, Slide Show

Switches to the corresponding view; see page 654 for details on these views.

Master

The Master menu takes you to the various master elements in a presentation. It has three submenu choices:

- **Slide Master.** Takes you to the Slide Master for the currently active presentation, where you can add elements, or make formatting changes, that will show up on every slide.

- **Handout Master.** Takes you to the Handout Master, which lets you tweak settings that will appear on every handout page in the presentation.

- **Notes Master.** Takes you to the Notes Master, which lets you change settings for every notes page in the presentation.

Header and Footer

Opens the "Header and Footer" window, where you can create text that repeats on the top or bottom of every slide.

Hide/Show Comments

Shows or hides any comments ("sticky notes") that you or your co-workers have placed in PowerPoint slides.

Grayscale

Takes your presentation into, or out of, Grayscale mode, temporarily removing all color—a useful preview if you plan to print on a standard black-and-white laser printer. If you Control-click your presentation while in Grayscale mode, you get a Grayscale contextual menu that offers various wacky inversions of the black/white/gray color scheme.

Toolbox: Formatting Palette, Object Palette, Custom Animation, Scrapbook, Reference Tools, Compatibility Report, Project Palette

Hides or shows these palettes, which behave the same way in Excel, PowerPoint, and Word—with the exception of the Custom Animation palette which appears only in PowerPoint (page 692).

Elements Gallery

Shows or hides the Elements Gallery.

Toolbars

Shows or hides any of six PowerPoint toolbars: Standard, Formatting, Outlining, Reviewing, "Tables and Borders", and Drawing.

Customize Toolbars and Menus

Opens the "Customize Toolbars and Menus" window, where you can customize your toolbars or create your own (page 759).

Ruler

Hides or shows PowerPoint's rulers (for aligning objects on the page).

Guides

Turns the horizontal and vertical Dynamic and Static Guides on or off (useful T-square-like lines that help you align objects on your slide with each other). Also lets you turn on or off Snap to Grid or Snap to Shape. *Static Guides keyboard shortcut:* ⌘-G.

Zoom

Opens the Zoom window, where you can choose from one of six preset values for magnifying or reducing the onscreen representation of your slides, or enter your own zoom percentage.

Insert Menu

Use the commands in this menu to add things to your PowerPoint presentations or to individual slides.

New Slide

Creates a new slide after the selected slide. *Keyboard shortcut:* Shift-⌘-N.

Duplicate Slide

Duplicates the active slide; places the duplicate after that slide. *Keyboard shortcut:* Shift-⌘-D.

Slides From

- **Slide Layout.** Opens the Elements Gallery's Slide Layouts tab so you can add a new layout to your presentation.

- **Other Presentation.** Lets you pull slides out of another PowerPoint file to insert into the currently active presentation.

- **Outline File.** Imports a Word outline and creates slides (and slide text) from it. Each first-level item is given its own new slide (see page 661).

Slide Number

Adds the slide number to a text box on the active slide (not every slide—you'll have to use a header or footer for that purpose).

Date and Time

Opens the "Header and Footer" window, which you can use to add the current date and time in one of several formats to the current slide. If you want to add the date and time to every slide, again, use a header or footer.

Symbol

Calls up the Object Palette, where you can choose a symbol character from any of the currently installed symbol fonts—or from the symbols contained in a normal font.

Comment

Inserts a comment into the currently active slide, as though it's a "sticky note."

Chart

Opens the Elements Gallery's Charts tab so you can click a chart type to insert in your slide.

SmartArt Graphic

Opens the Elements Gallery's SmartArt Graphics tab so you can click a SmartArt layout to insert in your slide.

WordArt

Opens the Elements Gallery's WordArt tab so you can click a WordArt style to insert in your slide.

Text Box

Inserts an empty text box on the active slide.

Picture

The Insert → Picture submenu lets you grab images from one of seven sources, as described in Chapter 19.

Clip Art

Opens the Clip Gallery, which you can use to add clip art or a stock photo to your presentation.

Shape

Opens the Shapes tab of the Object Palette, by which you can add shapes to your presentation.

Table

Opens the Insert Table window, where you can specify the size of the table that gets inserted when you select this command.

Movie

Pops up an Open dialog box, where you can choose a QuickTime movie file to insert into your presentation.

Sound and Music

Gives you three choices that you can use to get audio into your presentations.

- **From File.** Pops up the Insert Sound dialog box, where you can choose an audio file to insert into your presentation.

- **Play CD Audio Track.** Inserts a track from the currently mounted audio CD so that you can use it as a soundtrack.

- **Record Sound.** Lets you record a sound that can be used in your presentation (see page 698).

Object

Opens the Insert Object window, where you can select one of the following Office object types for insertion: a Word Document object, an Excel Chart object, an Excel Sheet object, a Microsoft Graph Chart object, Microsoft Organization Chart object, or an Equation object.

Hyperlink

Opens the Insert Hyperlink window, where you can insert a new hyperlink to a Web page, a document, or an email address. *Keyboard shortcut:* ⌘-K.

Format Menu

This menu contains all of PowerPoint's formatting commands, which let you manipulate fonts, text alignment and spacing, and colors. When you're working with text, they work exactly the same as text formatting in Word (see Chapter 3).

Font

Opens the Font tab of the Format Text dialog box, where you can set all kinds of font options for the currently selected text: the font, size, style, color, and effects. *Keyboard shortcut:* ⌘-T.

Paragraph

Opens the Paragraph tab of the Format Text dialog box, giving you control over things like indentation, line spacing, and alignment.

Bullets and Numbering

Opens the "Bullets and Numbering" tab of the Format Text dialog box, where you can select a style for your bulleted or numbered items. You can also use this window to insert a picture or character of your own choosing to use as a bullet.

Columns

Opens the Columns tab of the Format Text dialog box, where you can choose the number of columns and the spacing between them.

Alignment

Aligns the selected text in one of five ways: left, center, right, justified, or distributed.

Text Direction

Opens the Text Box tab of the Format Text dialog box, where you can set vertical alignment, text direction, autofit, and internal margins.

Change Case

Opens the Change Case window, where you can change the capitalization of the selected text: sentence case, lowercase, uppercase, title case, and toggle case.

Replace Fonts

Lets you replace one specified font in your presentation with a different font, globally, wherever it may appear—a great tactic when you move your file to a different machine that doesn't have the fonts you used originally.

Slide Layout

Opens the Elements Gallery's Slide Layouts tab, where you can choose from one of the slide layouts to either apply to the current slide, or insert as a new slide.

Slide Theme

Lets you choose a new slide theme for your presentation, either from the Elements Gallery's Slide Themes tab or from a file.

Theme Colors

Pops open the Create Theme Colors window, where you can choose from a set of standard color schemes or create a custom one.

Slide Background

Opens the Format Background window, where you can choose a background fill color for the current slide (or for all of the slides in the presentation).

[Object]

This command's name changes to match whatever you've highlighted on your slide—Picture, AutoShape, or whatever; it opens the corresponding Format window.

Tools Menu

Most of these commands work just as they do in the other Office programs.

Spelling, Thesaurus, Dictionary, Language, AutoCorrect, Flag for Follow Up

These commands work just as they do in Excel.

Review Comments

Shows or hides the Reviewing toolbar, letting you add, edit, delete, or email the "sticky note" comments on your presentation.

Slide Show Menu

This menu contains all of the slide show-related menu commands, used for preparing and running a slideshow.

View Slide Show

Starts the slideshow from the current slide. *Keyboard shortcut:* ⌘-Return.

View Presenter Tools

Starts the slideshow using the Presenter Tools display (page 705)

Custom Shows

Opens the Custom Shows window, where you can add, edit, or remove custom slide show variations on the currently open presentation.

Set Up Show

Opens the Set Up Show window, where you can set options for the currently open presentation.

Rehearse Timings

Runs through your slideshow, keeping track of the amount of time that it takes to show each slide. Those times can be saved with the presentation so that it runs just as long as it did during rehearsal.

Record Narration

Runs through your slide show while recording your voice, making a complete presentation out of what you record. The audio plays back as a series of audio clips to the timings that you set while recording your narration.

Action Buttons

Lets you add action buttons to your slides. You can choose the kind of action button (mostly used for navigating, playing media clips, or opening files) from the submenu: custom, home, help, information, previous slide, next slide, first slide, last slide, last slide viewed, document, sound, and movie.

Action Settings

If you have an Action Button selected, this command opens the Action Settings window, where you can decide what the selected Action Button does.

Custom Animation

Opens the Custom Animation palette in the Toolbox (page 692).

Transitions

Opens the opens the Elements Gallery's Transitions tab, where you can select a transition for the current slide (page 685).

Hide Slide

Hides the current slide so that it's not displayed during a slideshow.

Window Menu

The Window menu commands let you shuffle and manipulate multiple Power-Point windows.

Minimize Window, Zoom Window, New Window, Arrange All, Bring All to Front

These commands work exactly the same as in Excel (page 826).

Cascade

Resizes and rearranges all open windows so that one is on top of the next, and you can see the title bar and a small portion of each window.

Next Pane

Rotates clockwise to the next window pane, making it active.

Window List

The last item on the Window menu is a list of currently open PowerPoint windows. You can switch between them by selecting their names from this menu.

Help Menu

See "Help Menu" on page 808.

Word Menus

Word's menus, once again, have many functions described earlier in this appendix, but there are significant differences.

File Menu

Word comes equipped with a File menu (like almost all other Mac programs), which is mainly used for working with files on your hard drive—whether that's creating new files, saving them, or printing them.

Project Gallery, New Blank Document, Open, Open Recent, Close, Save, Save As

These commands work just as they do in Excel.

Save as Web Page

Converts the frontmost Word document into a Web page, converting graphics into the appropriate graphic formats (see Chapter 9).

Web Page Preview

Shows you what your document would look like as a Web page. It opens a temporary Web page conversion of your file in your browser of choice.

Page Setup, Print

These commands work just as they do in Excel.

Print Preview

Opens up the Print Preview window to show you how a Word document will look when you print it; lets you adjust margins (see page 30).

Send To

Word's Send To submenu has three items: Mail Recipient (as HTML), Mail Recipient (as Attachment), and PowerPoint. They're fully explained on page 38.

Properties

Opens the document Properties window.

Edit Menu

The Edit menu gathers together all of Word's Edit tools into one handy place. Many of these commands are similar to those in other Office programs.

Undo, Repeat/Redo, Cut, Copy, Copy to Scrapbook

These commands work just as they do in Excel.

Paste, Paste from Scrapbook, Paste Special

Again, these commands do the same things as in Excel (page 812)…but in Word.

Paste as Hyperlink

Pastes the clipboard contents into the frontmost Word document as a hyperlink.

Clear

Word's Clear command has a submenu giving you a choice of how much to clear away:

- **Clear Formatting.** Like the Clear Formatting option on the Formatting Palette's Style menu, this option removes formatting while leaving text intact.

- **Contents.** This is the new name of the true Clear command, which deletes selected text without copying it to the Clipboard.

Select All

Selects all text and objects in the document, ready for (for example) copying or deleting. *Keyboard shortcut:* ⌘-A.

Find

Opens Word's Find window, which you can use to search the open document for text or formatting. *Keyboard shortcut:* ⌘-F.

Replace

Searches for specific text or formatting and replaces it with other text or formatting that you specify. *Keyboard shortcut:* Shift-⌘-H.

Go To

Opens the Go To portion of the "Find and Replace" window, where you can enter a place in the frontmost Word document to go to, such as a specific page, section, line number, footnote, or endnote. *Keyboard shortcut:* ⌘-G.

Links

Pulls up a window showing information about every link in the currently active document (see page 46). If the document doesn't have any links to other documents, this option is dimmed.

Object

Lets you edit an embedded object, such as a Microsoft Graph object or a Microsoft Organization Chart object.

View Menu

This menu's commands govern what view mode the windows are in, what toolbars are shown, and so on.

Draft, Web Layout, Outline, Print Layout, Notebook Layout, Publishing Layout

Switches among Word's various document views; see page 18 for descriptions.

Toolbox: Formatting Palette, Object Palette, Citations, Scrapbook, Reference Tools, Compatibility Report, Project Palette

Hides or shows these palettes, which work the same in Excel, PowerPoint, and Word—except for the Citations palette (page 216) which is found only in Word.

Elements Gallery

Hides or shows the Elements Gallery in Print Layout or Publishing Layout View.

Toolbars

Shows a submenu of 13 Word toolbars that you can hide or show by selecting them here.

Customize Toolbars and Menus

Opens the "Customize Toolbars and Menus" window, where you can turn on or off even more Word toolbars or create your own (see page 759).

Navigation Pane

Opens and closes the Navigation Pane (page 198).

Ruler

Hides or shows the ruler in the currently active document (see page 10).

Header and Footer

Switches the currently active Word document to "Header and Footer" mode (and shows the "Header and Footer" toolbar), where you can enter headers or footers that will show up at the top or bottom of every page (see page 209).

Footnotes

Shows footnotes, which also makes them available for editing (see page 221).

Markup

Shows or hides comments or additions and deletions if Track Changes is turned on.

Reveal Formatting

Hides or shows the Reveal Formatting mode, which pops up a balloon with all kinds of details about the formatting where you click.

Full Screen

Turns Full Screen mode on or off. In this mode, almost all of Word's extraneous elements (the status bar, the toolbar, and the like) disappear, leaving the entire screen for the enjoyment of your creative work.

Zoom

Lets you magnify or reduce the onscreen display of your document.

Insert Menu

This collection of Word commands lets you insert specialized text, entire documents or other pictures and objects into your Word documents.

Break

Inserts one of six kinds of breaks into the Word document that interrupt your text at the insertion point: page breaks, section breaks, column breaks, and so on (see page 134).

Page Numbers

Opens the Page Numbers window, which lets you choose a place for page numbers that update automatically.

Date and Time

Opens the "Date and Time" window, from which you can insert the current date and time in a variety of formats. The date and time appear at the insertion point, and it can be made to update automatically to the current date and time whenever the document is printed.

AutoText

The AutoText menu (see page 78) contains 12 commands that let you automatically enter canned bits of text (such as letter salutations) at the insertion point. The Auto-Text menu items are actually categories, with these submenus:

- **AutoText.** Opens the AutoCorrect window to the AutoText tab, where you can enter your own text entries.

- **New.** Creates an AutoText entry from the selected text.

- **Attention Line.** Inserts either Attention: or ATTN: into your document

- **Closing.** Offers 13 ways to close a letter.

- **Header/Footer.** Lists 10 entries appropriate for headers and footers, such as page numbers, the file name, and a "Confidential" stamp.

- **Mailing Instructions.** Offers eight mail-related entries.

- **Reference Initials.** Inserts your initials.

- **Reference Line.** Inserts reply-style entries.

- **Salutation.** Lists four correspondence-starters.

- **Signature.** Inserts your name (or whatever signature you like).

- **Signature Company.** Inserts your company name.

- **Subject Line.** Inserts Subject: into your document.

Field

Opens the Field window, where you can insert a Word field (self-updating text code) at the insertion point (see page 235).

Symbol

Calls up the Symbol window so that you can insert a special character, like ™ or € (see the box on page 223).

Comment

Inserts a comment into the currently active document (see page 167).

Document Elements

Opens the Elements Gallery's Document Elements tab to one of its five categories: Cover Page, Table of Contents, Headers, Footers, or Bibliography.

Quick Tables

Opens the Elements Gallery's Quick Tables tab.

Chart

Opens the Elements Gallery's Charts tab.

SmartArt Graphic

Opens the Elements Gallery's SmartArt Graphics tab.

WordArt

Opens the Elements Gallery's WordArt tab.

Footnote

Opens the Footnote and Endnote window, where you can enter footnote and end-note information (see page 220).

Caption

Opens the Caption window, which you can use to insert a picture caption at the insertion point (see page 242).

Cross-reference

Opens the Cross-reference window, which lets you insert cross references to items in the document (see page 246).

Index and Tables

Opens the "Index and Tables" window, where you can create various indexes, table of contents entries, and authority citations (see page 255).

Watermark

Lets you choose an image or text to place as a watermark (faint background) on each page of your document.

Picture

The Insert → Picture submenu lets you grab images from the Clip Gallery or from a file; additionally, you can insert a Horizontal Line, or an AutoShape.

HTML Object

This menu is meant to help build Web pages, a secondary Word skill described at length in Chapter 8. It has nine submenus:

- **Background Sound.** Inserts a sound of your choice that will be played back when the page is viewed in a browser.

- **Scrolling Text.** Adds text that scrolls annoyingly when your page is viewed in a Web browser.

- **Checkbox.** Inserts an HTML checkbox (complete with name and value) at the insertion point.

- **Option Button.** Inserts an HTML option button (or radio button) at the insertion point.

- **List Box.** Inserts an HTML list box at the insertion point.

- **Textbox.** Inserts an HTML text box at the insertion point.

- **Submit.** Inserts an HTML button (automatically titled Submit) at the insertion point.

- **Reset.** Inserts an HTML Reset button at the insertion point (for resetting a form).

- **Hidden.** Inserts a hidden HTML field at the insertion point.

Text Box

Lets you draw a floating text box (see page 141).

Movie

Brings up the Insert Movie dialog box, where you can select a QuickTime, AVI, or MPEG movie to insert into the document.

File

Lets you insert one Word file into another—at the insertion point—just as though you'd copied and pasted it.

Object

Opens the Object window, where you can select one of several Office object types for insertion (see page 682).

Bookmark

Inserts a bookmark in the currently open document. The bookmark can be used to mark text, pictures or tables (see page 240).

Hyperlink

Opens the Insert Hyperlink window, where you can insert a new hyperlink to a Web page, a document, or an email address (see page 46). *Keyboard shortcut:* ⌘-K.

Format Menu

This menu contains all of Word's formatting commands, which let you work with text controls, alignment, and spacing.

Font

Opens the Font window, where you can make all kinds of marvelous tweaks to the type choices of the selected (or about-to-be-typed) text. *Keyboard shortcut:* ⌘-D.

Paragraph

Opens the Paragraph window, where you can change paragraph-level formatting options (such as line spacing and indents). *Keyboard shortcut:* Option-⌘-M.

Document

Opens the Document window, where you can change document-level formatting options (such as margins and how sections begin).

Bullets and Numbering

Opens the "Bullets and Numbering" window, where you can control how bulleted and numbered lists look (see page 101).

Borders and Shading

Opens the "Borders and Shading" window, where you can add and change borders and shaded areas in your Word document (see page 114).

Columns

Opens the Columns window, where you can set the number of columns used in the current document (see page 136). You can also control the column width and spacing in this window.

Tabs

Opens the Tabs window, where you can add, edit, and remove tab stops in the currently open Word document (see page 111).

Drop Cap

Lets you add a drop cap to the currently open Word document (see the box on page 101). You can choose from one of three styles in the window that pops up.

Text Direction

Lets you choose from three text direction orientations: left to right, top to bottom, or bottom to top. For use primarily in table cells (see page 143).

Change Case

Opens the Change Case window, where you can change the capitalization of the selected text: sentence case, lowercase, uppercase, title case, and toggle case.

AutoFormat

Automatically adds formatting according to the AutoFormat rules that you set to the currently open Word document (see page 84).

Style

Lets you add, edit, and remove styles in the currently open Word document (see page 127).

Background

Hides or shows the Background toolbar, which you can use to add a little color to your Word document (see page 144).

[Object]

This menu's wording reflects whatever's selected in the document window (Picture, AutoShape, and so on). It opens the corresponding Format window.

Font Menu

This menu lists every font you have installed. To select a font, choose its name. Word renders the font names in the actual font, so that you can see what you're selecting (see page 92).

Tools Menu

The Tools menu includes a mix of text tools, sharing tools, and other miscellaneous functions.

Spelling and Grammar

Checks the document for spelling and grammar errors; if Word finds any questionable items, pops open the "Spelling and Grammar" window to give you the opportunity to correct them. *Keyboard shortcut:* Option-⌘-L.

Thesaurus

Opens the Reference Tools palette, which lets you find synonyms or antonyms for the selected word.

Hyphenation

Hyphenates the currently active Word document, which gives better spacing between words in individual lines (see page 140).

Dictionary

Opens the Reference Tools palette, where you can view the selected word's definition (see page 792).

Language

Flags selected text as being in a given language. The advantage of doing this is that Word will thereafter apply the appropriate language dictionary for spelling checks and AutoCorrect entries.

Word Count

Counts up the statistics for the currently open Word document: the number of words, lines, characters, and paragraphs.

AutoSummarize

Tries to summarize the currently open Word document down to its salient points, as described on page 232.

AutoCorrect

Opens the AutoCorrect window, where you can determine what Word tries to automatically correct when it thinks it sees an error in your typing (see page 75). It also lets you enter AutoText items that will fill in automatically as you type, and it lets you set the automatic formatting that's applied to your Word documents both as you type and if you select the AutoFormat command.

Track Changes

The Track Changes menu controls how word keeps tabs of changes to documents. This menu has three submenu options: Highlight Changes and Accept or Reject Changes.

- **Highlight Changes.** Opens the Highlight Changes window, where you can turn change tracking on, plus you can control which changes are highlighted.

- **Accept or Reject Changes.** Walks you through the changes that have been made to a workbook, and accept or reject each.

- **Compare Documents.** Compares the open document with the original saved version of that same document, and shows any changes that you've made.

Merge Documents

Merges changes that have been tracked in the currently open Word document into another document of your choice.

Protect Document

Keeps people from making the kinds of changes that you specify to a document. You can optionally enter a password to protect the currently open document from those changes.

Flag for Follow Up

Opens the "Flag for Follow Up" window, where you can set a reminder attached to the currently open Word document. That reminder will pop up at the time you specify to remind you to do something with that document.

Mail Merge Manager

Opens the Mail Merge Manager palette, which you can use to take control over your mail merge operations (such as mail merges for mass mailings).

Envelopes

Helps you create an envelope, including things such as the delivery address and return address. It also has an option to do a data merge, so that you can draw addresses for your envelopes from a data file.

Labels

Lets you use Word to create mailing labels of all kinds. This command takes advantage of Word's plethora of mailing label templates, and it lets you format those labels for either dot-matrix or laser printing.

Letter Wizard

Opens the Letter Wizard, which walks you through the process of creating a letter suitable for mailing to businesses, friends, or even writing crank letters to the government.

Address Book

Opens the Office Address Book window (which looks suspiciously like the Entourage Address Book), where you can quickly look up contact information.

Macros

This menu used to open a window of VBA macros, which Office 2008 doesn't use. Instead, in the misleadingly named Macros window, you'll find a long list of what are actually Word's *commands*—the commands that are triggered by menu commands or keyboard commands, or by selecting one from this list and clicking Run.

Templates and Add-Ins

Opens the "Templates and Add-ins" window, where you can attach a different template to the currently open Word document, plus, you can use this window to turn on or turn off various Add-Ins for Word. Add-Ins are conceptually similar to Photoshop plug-ins.

Customize Keyboard

Opens the Customize Keyboard window, where you can create and modify Keyboard combinations (see Chapter 20).

Table Menu

Word's Table menu contains a variety of commands to help you draw the perfect table to hold your precious data.

Draw Table

Opens the "Tables and Borders" toolbar, which you can use to draw tables in your Word documents.

Insert

This menu has several options that let you take a little more conservative approach to table creation. It has six options:

- **Table.** Opens the Insert Table window, where you can specify the size and characteristics of your new table.

- **Columns to the Left.** Adds a column to the left of the insertion point in the currently active table. If you have more than one column selected, this command will insert the same number of columns to the left of the insertion point.

- **Columns to the Right.** Adds a column to the right of the insertion point in the currently active table. If you have more than one column selected, this command will insert the same number of columns to the right of the insertion point.

- **Rows Above.** Inserts a row above the insertion point in the currently active table. If you have more than one row selected, this command will insert the same number of rows above the insertion point.

- **Rows Below.** Inserts a row below the insertion point in the currently active table. If you have more than one row selected, this command will insert the same number of rows below the insertion point.

- **Cells.** Inserts the number of cells that you have selected into the currently active table. It also opens the Insert Cells window, where you can specify how things move around to make room for those cells.

Delete

Sometimes you want to remove a table from a document, and this menu (with its four submenu choices) has you covered.

- **Table.** Deletes the currently selected table.

- **Columns.** Deletes the currently selected columns.

- **Rows.** Deletes the currently selected rows.

- **Cells.** Deletes the currently selected cells, and it gives you the option of how you want to shift the remaining cells to take up the room left vacant by the now missing cells.

Select

That's right—there's a special Select menu item for use with tables, and it has four submenu options to help you select just the portions of the table with which you want to work.

- **Table.** Selects the entire table. If the insertion point isn't in a table, this option is left blank.

- **Column.** Selects the column in which the insertion point is located.

- **Row.** Selects the row in which the insertion point is located.

- **Cell.** Selects the cell in which the insertion point is located.

Merge Cells

Merges two or more adjacent selected cells (including the data contained in those cells) into one large cell.

Split Cells

Splits a cell into the number of rows and columns that you set.

Split Table

Plays King Solomon and splits a table at the insertion point, placing a paragraph mark between the two new tables.

Table AutoFormat

Automatically formats the currently selected table using one of a number of color schemes, line thicknesses, and column widths. You get to select an AutoFormat scheme when you select this item.

AutoFit and Distribute

The AutoFit menu item lets you automatically resize a table to fit a variety of factors. This menu item has five submenu selections.

- **AutoFit to Contents.** Makes the table's columns resize themselves to fit the text or numbers that you type in.

- **AutoFit to Window.** Makes the table resize itself to fit a Web browser window. Useful for creating tables meant for the Web.

- **Fixed Column Width.** Makes the width of the selected columns a fixed value. That way, they won't vary in size.

- **Distribute Rows Evenly.** Makes the selected rows the same height.

- **Distribute Columns Evenly.** Makes the selected columns the same width.

Heading Rows Repeat

Makes the selected row a heading row, which means that it will repeat at the top of every page if the table that it's in spans more than one page.

Convert

The two commands in the Convert submenu let you move text into tables and back out again.

- **Convert Text to Table.** Converts the selected text into a table, placing the text in one or more of the table's cells.

- **Convert Table to Text.** Converts the selected table cells into regular text.

Sort

Opens the Sort Text window, where you can sort your table's contents alphabetically, numerically, and so on.

Formula

Sort of a mini-Excel. This command lets you insert a formula into the currently active cell to do basic calculations.

Gridlines

Hides or shows the table's dotted gridlines. These gridlines help you see what you're doing in your current table.

Table Properties

Opens the Table Properties window, where you can set all kinds of options for the currently selected table.

Window Menu

The Window menu provides a home for all menu commands that are window related.

Zoom Window, Minimize Window, Bring All to Front

These commands work exactly as they do in Excel.

New Window

Opens a new window on the same file that's currently open. That way, you can view two (or more) places in the same file at the same time.

Arrange All

Arranges all open windows so that you can see each one. They're stacked vertically. This makes it easy to drag items between them.

Split

Splits the currently active Word window into two independently scrolling panes. If the window is already split, this menu command changes to say Remove Split, which removes the split screen effect.

Window List

The last item on the Window menu is a list of currently open Word documents. You can switch between them by selecting names from this menu.

Work Menu

The Work menu is meant to be your customizable menu, to which you can add various documents that you want to be just a menu selection away.

Add to Work Menu

Adds the frontmost Word document's name to the Work menu. To remove it from the Work menu, see page 7.

Help Menu

Contains the same commands for Office's Help system, as described on page 808.

Index

C

D

data

analyzing with data tables (Excel), 623

analyzing with PivotTables (Excel), 619–622

Data menu (Excel), 823–825

Data Validation feature (Excel), 633

entry (spreadsheets), 511–516, 526–529

forms (Excel), 631–632

selecting for charts (Excel), 578–579

series (Excel charts), 577–578

text files, importing to Excel, 619

data sources (mail merge)

creating new, 263–266

preparing, 262–263

using existing, 266

data tables (Excel), 623

databases

Database Utility (Entourage), 378

importing FileMaker Pro to Excel, 614–617

maintaining (Entourage), 378

ODBC and Excel, 614

dates (Excel)

entering in spreadsheets, 514–515

formats in cells, 566

formatting numbers as, 516

decimal places (Excel), 567

decimal tabs (Word), 113

definitions dictionary (Office), 636

deleting

bookmarks, 240

captions (Word), 244

cells (Word tables), 157

clip art, 736

comments (Excel), 636

comments (Word), 170

cross-references (Word), 248

email contacts, 419

email messages, 375–377

events (Calendar), 454

hyperlinks, 341

indexes in Word, 261

junk mail, 367

list objects (Excel), 551–552

parts of tables (Word), 157

rows/columns (Word tables), 157

slides, 669

styles (Word), 134

subdocuments (Word), 205

tasks/To Do lists, 466

text box in a chain, 145

TOCs, 253

worksheets (Excel), 598

desktop, drag-and-drop to (Word), 49–50

dictionaries, custom (Word), 70–73

digests, mailing list, 411

Directory Services (Entourage), 399

dissolves (PowerPoint), 685, 688

distributing objects (Word), 303

DLP video projectors, 650

Document Map (Word)

customizing, 200

defined, 198

viewing and navigating, 198–199

documents

attaching custom toolbars to, 763–765

Compare Documents feature (Word), 178

converting Web pages to Word, 344

converting Word to PDF, 27

creating Word, 1–2

document proxy icon, 9

Document Theme pane (Word), 324

finding with Open dialog box, 5

formats (Word), 21–22

Master Document (Word), 207

navigating in Word, 50–51

opening in Project Gallery, 720

pasting between (Word), 46

previewing/formatting mail merge, 269

protecting, 10

recent (Project Gallery), 723–724

returning to (Word), 6–7

saving and Finder, 23

saving in Word, 21

scripts to download, 771

templates, attaching (Word), 227–228

templates, creating (Word), 225–226

views (Word), 18–20

dotx extension, 226

Draft view (Word), 19

drag-and-drop text (Word), 47–50

drawing

drawings, defined (Office), 734

shapes (notebooks), 184

tables (Word), 152–154

toolbar buttons, 764

drawing objects

in Word, 149, 184

rotating, 744

drivers, ODBC, 614

drop caps, 101

droplets and applets

installing, 771

running, 772

E

Edit menus

Entourage, 794–797

Excel, 811–814

PowerPoint, 828–830

Word, 838–839

OFFICE 2008 FOR MACINTOSH: THE MISSING MANUAL

Colophon

The author wrote most of this book using Dragon NaturallySpeaking voice-dictation software (*www.nuance.com*) on a Windows laptop, then rushed the Microsoft Word files over the network to a trusty old Power Mac G4 (hot-rodded with twin pipes and a Columbia butt). The author captured the book's illustrations using Ambrosia Software's Snapz Pro X (*www.ambrosiasw.com*) and Adobe Photoshop CS 3 (*www.adobe.com*) to touch them up.

Sumita Mukherji and Loranah Dimant provided quality control for *Office 2008 for Macintosh: The Missing Manual*. Ron Strauss wrote the index.

The cover of this book is based on a series design originally created by David Freedman and modifed by Mike Kohnke, Karen Montgomery, and Fitch (*www.fitch.com*). Back cover design, dog illustration, and color selection by Fitch.

David Futato designed the interior layout, based on a series design by Phil Simpson. This book was converted by Keith Fahlgren to FrameMaker 5.5.6. The text font is Adobe Minion; the heading font is Adobe Formata Condensed; and the code font is LucasFont's TheSans Mono Condensed. The illustrations that appear in the book were produced by Robert Romano and Jessamyn Read using Macromedia FreeHand MX and Adobe Photoshop CS.

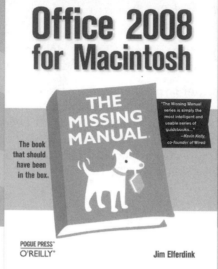